An official publication of

THE AMERICAN SOCIOLOGICAL ASSOCIATION

WILLIAM V. D'ANTONIO, *Executive Officer*

SOCIOLOGICAL METHODOLOGY

1988

VOLUME 18

EDITOR   Clifford C. Clogg

ADVISORY EDITORS   Gerhard Arminger

Ronald L. Breiger

Aaron Cicourel

Jan Hoem

Margaret M. Marini

Ronald Schoenberg

Michael E. Sobel

SOCIOLOGICAL METHODOLOGY 1988
by Clifford C. Clogg

Library of Congress Catalog Card Information

Sociological Methodology. 1969–85
San Francisco, Jossey-Bass.

15 v. illus. 24 cm. annual. (Jossey-Bass behavioral science series)

Editor:	1969, 1970	E. F. Borgatta
	1971, 1972, 1973–74	H. L. Costner
	1975, 1976, 1977	D. R. Heise
	1978, 1979, 1980	K. F. Schuessler
	1981, 1982, 1983–84	S. Leinhardt
	1985	N. B. Tuma

Sociological Methodology. 1986–88
Washington, DC, American Sociological Association

1 vol. illus. 24 cm annual.

| Editor: | 1986 | N. B. Tuma |
| | 1987, 1988 | C. C. Clogg |

"An official publication of the American Sociological Association."

1. Sociology—Methodology—Year books. I. American Sociological
Association. II. Borgatta, Edgar F., 1924– ed.

| HM24.S55 | 301'.01'8 | 68–54940 |

| | rev. | |
| Library of Congress | [r71h2] | |

International Standard Book Number ISBN 0-912764-25-2

International Standard Serial Number ISSN 0081-1750

Manufactured in the United States of America

CONSULTANTS

Paul Allison
Gerhard Arminger
Jogesh Babu
William Bielby
Kenneth Bollen
Phillip Bonacich
Robert Boruch
Henry Braun
Ronald Breiger
Glenn Carroll
Aaron Cicourel
Otis Duncan
Scott Eliason
Robert Fay
John Fox
Zvi Gilula
Michael Greenwood
Wendy Griswold
Charles Halaby
Robert Hauser
Jan Hoem
Graham Kalton
Daniel Kasprzyk
Ronald Kessler
Eric Leifer
Daniel Lichter
J. Scott Long

Margaret Marini
Peter Marsden
Michael Massagli
John McDonald
Ann Miller
Robert Mislevy
Carl Morris
Francois Nielsen
Trond Petersen
Mark Reiser
Willard Rodgers
A. Kimball Romney
Paul Rosenbaum
Donald Rubin
Ronald Schoenberg
James Shockey
Herbert Smith
Michael Sobel
Philip Stone
Ann Swidler
D. Garth Taylor
Stanley Wasserman
Lynn Weidman
Roy Welsch
Michael White
Christopher Winship
Lawrence Wu

CONTENTS

CONTRIBUTORS

Duane Alwin, Institute for Social Research, University of Michigan.

Nazli Baydar, School of Public Health, Columbia University.

William T. Bielby, Department of Sociology, University of California, Santa Barbara.

Donald Camburn, Institute for Social Research, University of Michigan.

Man-tsun Cheng, Department of Sociology, University of California, Los Angeles.

Otis Dudley Duncan, Department of Sociology, University of California, Santa Barbara.

Deborah Freedman, Institute for Social Research, University of Michigan.

Clark Glymour, Department of Philosophy, Carnegie Mellon University.

Mark Granovetter, Department of Sociology, State University of New York at Stony Brook.

Shelby J. Haberman, Department of Statistics, Northwestern University.

Paul W. Holland, Educational Testing Service, Princeton, New Jersey.

Edward E. Leamer, Department of Economics, University of California, Los Angeles.

Margaret M. Marini, Department of Sociology, University of Minnesota.

Trond Petersen, Department of Sociology, Harvard University.

J. N. K. Rao, Department of Statistics, Carleton University.

Nora Cate Schaeffer, Department of Sociology, University of Wisconsin, Madison.

Richard Scheines, Center for the Development of Educational Computing, Carnegie Mellon University.

Burton Singer, Department of Epidemiology and Public Health, Yale University.

Michael E. Sobel, Department of Sociology, University of Arizona.

Roland Soong, Arbitron Ratings Company, New York.

Peter Spirtes, Department of Philosophy, Carnegie Mellon University.

Magnus Stenbeck, Department of Sociology, University of California, Santa Barbara.

D. Roland Thomas, Department of Statistics, Carleton University.

Arland Thornton, Institute for Social Research, University of Michigan.

Donald J. Treiman, Department of Sociology, University of California, Los Angeles.

Michael White, The Urban Institute, Washington, DC.

Linda Young-DeMarco, Institute for Social Research, University of Michigan.

PREFACE

It is a pleasure to endorse the 14 chapters of *Sociological Methodology 1988* and to recommend them to the community of social researchers. Though most of these articles arrived in my office according to some random mechanism, a common theme emerges when they are considered as a whole: Data collection, study design, and statistical or mathematical modelling must be intimately linked to each other in a mature social science. It is no longer acceptable, for example, to design survey questionnaires without reference to the models that will be used to analyze them. It is likewise unacceptable to formulate "general-purpose" models that do not account for special characteristics of the data. The reader will find that nearly all the contributions in the present volume address this general theme, usually in an explicit fashion.

Several of the chapters were actually solicited because of their relevance for contemporary research. (I hasten to point out that all chapters were reviewed thoroughly and underwent substantial revision.) Chapter 8, by Rao and Thomas, deals with analysis of log-linear models from complex samples that include clustering. The failure to take account of sample design is one of the most important problems in current modelling efforts. It is clear that we can solve many inferential issues associated with complex samples using the Rao-Scott adjustments summarized in this chapter. Chapters 11–13 present three contrasting views of how causal inferences can be drawn from data that have not been collected by randomly assigning "treatments" to randomly chosen subjects. That is, these three chapters deal with causal analysis of so-called observational data. I believe that these chapters, as well as Edward Leamer's pointed discussion of them (chapter 14), at least raise the right questions even if they do not answer them to everyone's satisfaction. They indicate that we have come a long way since the time when many social researchers thought we could obtain automatic causal inferences from partial correlations. We owe a debt of thanks to the authors of these chapters for their thorough appraisals of perhaps the most fundamental issue in methodology for social research.

The first chapter, by Otis Dudley Duncan and Magnus Stenbeck, raises general questions about a variety of topics, including the use of panels, the role of cohorts, and the utility of special Rasch-type models in the analysis of panel-cohort data. The substantive problem they address is voter turnout, but the issues they pose extend immediately to the general topic of analysis of change. It is a distinct pleasure to include their contribution and to indeed feature it as the leading chapter. As many readers already know, Duncan officially retired from the business of social research in the fall of 1987, so this chapter will perhaps be his last contribution to the field. I hereby dedicate this volume to Otis Dudley Duncan as a small token of appreciation for the many contributions that he has made to empirical social research and sociological methodology since 1950.

I owe a special debt of thanks to the advisory editors and consultants, who assisted me in reviewing submissions this past year. I also express my gratitude to Ann Kremers for discharging her responsibilities as managing editor and copy editor in such a highly professional and competent manner.

Clifford C. Clogg
Pennsylvania State University
1988

SOCIOLOGICAL METHODOLOGY
❧1988❧

Panels and Cohorts: Design and Model in the Study of Voting Turnout

Otis Dudley Duncan and Magnus Stenbeck*

In submitting this preliminary and tentative analysis of age patterns of participation of the white population in recent presidential elections, we hope to make three kinds of methodological contributions. First, we call attention to the unique design features of a substantial body of archival data that seems to have been insufficiently analyzed, and we begin the exploration of the error structure of these data. Second, we consider how the statistical model for cohort analysis suggested in recent literature (e.g., Mason et al. 1973; Pullum 1980) needs to be modified to take account of the pseudo-panel design of census surveys of voting and illustrate some kinds of inference that may be appropriate for the modified model. The intention here, in part, is to improve upon an earlier ·attempt (Duncan 1981) to formulate the issues raised by substituting a panel design for the conventional analysis of a series of independent cross-section samples. Third, we raise the question of whether an explicit and consistent theoretical basis for the statistical model can be developed using ideas drawn from recent work on latent-trait models (e.g., Duncan 1985, 1986). Corresponding to

This research was supported by NSF grant SES 84-11359. We are grateful to the U.S. Bureau of the Census, Norval Glenn, Barbara A. Anderson, and Brian D. Silver for providing unpublished data, but the full responsibility for the uses made of the data is ours.
*University of California, Santa Barbara

these three concerns are the main sections of the article: "Description and Evaluation of Data," "Exploring Statistical Models," and "Toward a Scientific Model." Our foremost contentions are restated in what we hope is a crisp, if somewhat contentious, fashion in the "General Conclusions," to which the impatient reader may turn at any time.

The preceding paragraph accurately describes the general outline of what turns out to be an essay on method (rather than a research report), but the reader is fairly warned that the ulterior purpose of the exposition is disclosed only by degrees. Whereas we follow disciplinary convention in using a large part of our space to discuss statistical issues, the thesis we wish most to emphasize is that the application of statistical models and methods should be strictly subordinate to the central scientific task. That task we take to be the formulation of cogent theories explaining the processes under study and the invention of research designs suited to the testing of such theories. Our rhetorical strategy is to engender skepticism about statistical models by showing that the best we can do by way of a statistical model for turnout data falls far short as a scientific model of the process by which persons acquire and exercise their tendencies to vote. Others, we hope, will do better.

1. DESCRIPTION AND EVALUATION OF DATA

We use unpublished tabulations, provided by the U.S. Bureau of the Census, of data from the 1984, 1980, 1976, and 1972 November Voting Supplements to the Current Population Survey (CPS). Our main analysis concerns the cross-classification of reported voting in year t (which we call the retrospective report) by reported voting in year $t + 4$ (the current report, i.e., the one pertaining to the election held in the year of the survey), for $t = 1972, 1976, 1980$, using the surveys taken in mid-November of 1976, 1980, and 1984. We use the 1972 current reports to evaluate the retrospective reports obtained in 1976. Our tabulations are consistent with those published in *Current Population Reports*, series P-20; see no. 405 (Table 15) for the 1984 survey (with retrospective data for 1980), no. 370 (Table 15) for 1980, no. 322 (Table 19) for 1976, and no. 253 (Table 28) for 1972.

Questions like the following elicited the responses we analyze: "In any election, some people are not able to vote because they are sick or busy or have some other reason, and others do not want to vote. Did you vote in the election on November 6th [1984]?" This was followed, a few questions later, by "Thinking back to 1980, did you vote in the Presidential election in that year?" These questions were asked of all persons of voting age in the sample household, but could be answered by one respondent (a proxy) on behalf of another. Percentages of respondents answering for themselves varied from 52 percent in 1976 and 53 percent in 1980 to 58 percent in 1984. Proxy respondents are the primary source of "don't know" (DK) answers, which, together with "not reported" (NR), account for 5.4 percent, 4.9 percent, and 5.0 percent of responses to the question on the current election in 1976, 1980, and 1984, respectively.

There is an extensive literature on the overreporting of current turnout in household surveys, which has been regularly noted in CPS as well as in the election studies of the Survey Research Center (SRC); see, for example, *Current Population Reports*, P-20, no. 405, pp. 9–11; Clausen (1969); and Silver, Anderson, and Abramson (1986). We do not review all the kinds of evidence and lines of argument relevant to the estimation and explanation of overreporting, but only consider some specific external and internal comparisons that bear most directly on the data we want to analyze.

We first compare current turnout computed from CPS tabulations with turnout estimated in the SRC vote-validation studies of 1976, 1980, and 1984, making use of unpublished tables kindly provided by Anderson and Silver. An earlier comparison of this kind in regard to the 1964 election is given by Clausen (1969). The SRC studies involve checking the official records of voter registration and turnout; these determinations of electoral participation on a name-by-name basis are not, of course, free of error in themselves, since matching of names and addresses is itself a problematic operation. In view of the goals of our analysis, it is especially relevant to compare CPS and SRC-validation turnout for various age groups. For each of the three years 1976, 1980, and 1984, we have respondents in each of six age intervals (18–30, 31–40, 41–50, 51–60, 61–70, 71 and over), classified in the SRC validation study as voters and nonvoters (missing data excluded) and also CPS respondents classified as "reported voted" or "reported that they did not vote" (including in the latter category DK and NR). Taken together, all these data form a $2 \times 6 \times 3 \times 2$ (turnout by age by year by survey organization) contingency table, which we analyze by means of logit regression models. The dependent variable is the (natural) logarithm of the ratio of number of voters to number of nonvoters. Independent variables include 18 dummy variables allowing for unrestricted interactions of age and year. In addition, we define a dummy variable for survey organization, an interaction of organization with age, treating the latter as an interval scale with values $0,1,2,3,4,5$ corresponding to the age groups, an interaction with the square of this scale, and two dummy variables for the interaction of year and organization. The model is concerned with the variation across $6 \times 3 \times 2 = 36$ logits; accordingly, there are $36 - 18 - 5 = 13$ df when all these interactions are included in the model. We fit the model by means of weighted least squares (minimum logit chi-square regression) after each sample count is increased by 0.5. The CPS counts were derived from the published Table 1 in the report for each year, which shows population estimates in 1,000s, by dividing each 1984 estimate by 3.223 and each 1980 and 1976 estimate by 2.518, in accordance with formulas given in *Current Population Reports*, P-20, no. 405, appendix C. Thus, the CPS "counts" we analyze are not actual sample counts but hypothetical sample frequencies scaled down to allow for sample design effects. Our SRC counts, however, are not so adjusted, so that our chi-square statistics may be somewhat inflated.

The complete model describes the data quite well. The logit chi-square (residual sum of squares) is 4.74 ($df = 13$). When we delete the four interactions involving survey organization but retain the overall contrast between organizations, the logit chi-square statistic, 7.50 ($df = 17$), is still acceptably small, and we see that the coefficient for that variable is smaller in absolute value than its estimated standard error. Hence, the statistics seem consistent with the supposition that there is no difference between organizations in age-specific turnout rates; the logit chi-square for this hypothesis is 8.34 ($df = 18$).

In these analyses, we are working with total "counts" of 5,064 from the SRC studies and 166,780 from the CPS. Hence, failure to detect a difference between organizations cannot easily be explained as a consequence of inadequate sample size. Nevertheless, we might hesitate to draw the apparently obvious conclusion that CPS current turnout reports are unbiased relative to official records of turnout. Indeed, the main reason for supposing that CPS and other surveys overestimate turnout is that they imply a larger number of persons voting than the aggregate of all voters in these records. Our results could be fortuitous, an outcome of compensating biases. Whereas the CPS procedure counts DK and NR as nonvoters, the SRC tabulations used here exclude them as missing data, which amount to 18 percent of the 1976 sample, 20 percent of the 1980 sample, and 15 percent of the 1984 sample—a much higher rate than the 5 percent in the CPS. Hence, reasonable allocations of missing data could produce a gap between the two series that is not evident in the tables we analyzed. We do not firmly conclude, therefore, that the CPS reports are unbiased relative to official turnout, but only emphasize that we find no evidence of a differential bias by age. Making the assumption that there is none will simplify our subsequent analysis, as well as the evaluation of retrospective reports, to which we turn next.

The proportion of missing data is higher for the retrospective question than for current turnout. Together, DK and NR account for 11.4 percent of the retrospective responses in the 1976 survey and 9.1 percent in both the 1980 and 1984 surveys. We conjecture that the higher rate in 1976 concerns the DK category primarily and that the responsible factor is a unique design feature of the 1976 questionnaire. Between the questions concerning the current November 2nd (1976) election and the presidential election in 1972, there were three other retrospective questions, asking whether the person ever voted, when she or he last voted, and whether he or she voted in a primary election earlier in 1976. Thus, there were three opportunities to respond DK before coming to the direct inquiry on 1972 turnout.

But the discontinuity just described may be relatively unimportant by comparison with an undocumented change in tabulation specifications. In the cross-classification of 1972 by 1976 turnout in P-20, no. 322, Table 19, the category "reported that they did not vote in 1976" includes DK and NR on voting in that year. But in the 1976-by-1980 cross-classification (P-20, no. 370, Table 15) and the 1980-by-1984 cross-classification (P-20, no. 405, Table 15), this is not the case, and the footnotes to those tables, therefore, are in error. We conjecture that "did not vote in 1980" (in the 1980 survey) and "did not vote in 1984" (in the 1984 survey) include the DK responses on current turnout but exclude the NR responses. It is hard to account for discrepancies between the cited tables and Table 1 in these two reports on any other assumption. Since our special tabulations were intended to be consistent with Table 19 of the 1976 report and Table 15 of the 1980 and 1984 reports, the same discontinuity affects them. Hence, in the exploration of error structures that follows, the biases we report may reflect both response errors in the strict sense of the term and discrepancies in the classifications.

Whereas the preceding analysis employed aggregated data for persons of both sexes in all racial classifications, our subsequent work concerns white persons only, and we maintain a cross-classification by sex. The restriction to whites is dictated by our decision to work with tables showing turnout by single years of age. Even the large CPS samples generate many sparsely populated cells for the black and "other" populations when the age classification is this detailed. We compare the retrospectively reported turnout four years before the current survey for persons aged 26–81 at the time of the current election with current turnout reported for persons aged 22–77 in the survey four years earlier. Cohort matching by age at last birthday as of election day is all but perfect, inasmuch as elections are always held between the 2nd and 8th of November. We number cohorts with successive integers in such a way that $c = 5$ for persons 77 years old at the time of the 1972 election and $c = 72$ for persons 22 years old at the time of the 1984 election. Thus, retrospective (reported in 1984) and current turnout in the 1980 election are compared for cohorts 13 to 68; comparisons pertaining to the 1976 election involve cohorts 9 to 64; and those pertaining to the 1972 election involve cohorts 5 to 60. For each election, therefore, we have 56 logits for retrospectively reported turnout and another 56 for currently reported turnout. Our model incorporates 56 dummy variables for cohort effects (or a constant and 55 dummy variables for deviations from it), a coefficient for the overall contrast of retrospective and current reports, a linear interaction of cohort by retrospective versus current, and a quadratic interaction term. Models are fitted separately for men and women, so there are six separate problems.

We find only one significant difference by sex in regard to the retrospective versus current contrast and interactions of it with age. In none of the three years is the quadratic interaction significant for either men or women. In the 1976 analysis (1980 retrospective reports), the linear interaction is significant for both. For men, the contrast between retrospective and current turnouts is estimated as $0.405 + 0.00956(\text{age in } 1976 - 49)$, and the interaction has an estimated standard error of 0.00153. The corresponding equation for women is $0.390 + 0.00538(\text{age} - 49)$, with $\text{SE} = 0.00133$. The logit chi-square value for the fit of the equation is 31.73 for men, 26.30 for women, each with

$df = 54$. In the analysis of 1980 turnout (1984 retrospective reports), neither the linear nor the quadratic interaction is significant for either sex. We estimate 0.186 (0.0235) and 0.199 (0.0224) as the overall bias of retrospective reports for men and women respectively. The models including only this term have logit chi-square values of 44.23 and 40.24, each with $df = 55$. Finally, there is no detectable bias in the 1976 reports of turnout in 1972. The model with no contrast between retrospective and current reports yields logit chi-square values of 36.71 for men and 49.60 for women, each with $df = 56$. All these calculations are restricted to persons who were citizens as of the respective survey dates, and we had to make some rough allocations to adjust the 1972 current reports, for which citizenship was given only by broad age groups (P-20, no. 253, Table 23).

The pattern and degree of bias in retrospective reports are, in sum, year-specific, but we hesitate to suggest influences affecting the response process (other than the change in questionnaire design already mentioned) on the basis of these results, which are presumably contaminated by the classification discontinuity described above. Regardless of the sources of the biases, we can hardly ignore them when we take up the problem of specifying a statistical model for the variations in turnout by age.

Because our analyses concern both retrospective and current reports, the data are confined to persons old enough to have voted in both elections. It is perhaps just as well that we ignore the responses for

TABLE 1

Percentage of White Respondents Reporting for Themselves, by Age and Sex, from the 1976 Current Population Survey

Age	Men	Women
18–20	18	36
21–24	34	60
25–29	37	74
30–34	30	78
35–44	29	74
45–54	30	71
55–64	36	71
65–74	45	74
75 and over	48	67

Source. U.S. Bureau of the Census 1978, Table 27.

persons 18–21 years old, since so few of them report for themselves, as we see in Table 1. This may reflect a design feature of the CPS, which regards college students living away from home as members of their parents' households. We also note in Table 1 that at most ages, the proportion of self-reports for males is, very roughly, about half as large as it is for females. Thus, for two of the substantive factors of greatest interest in the study of voting turnout—age and sex—the prevalence of proxy reporting by parents and wives is great enough to warrant concern about unknown biases. Published tabulations concerning self- versus proxy reporting are not sufficiently detailed to permit inferences about such biases.

2. EXPLORING STATISTICAL MODELS

To introduce our analysis of the CPS data, we first consider how these data may extend the results of the first substantial investigation of the relationship of age to voter turnout by means of cohort analysis, i.e., the study of Glenn and Grimes (1968). They prepared tabulations of turnout by age, for white men and women, using Gallup Polls conducted in the presidential election years 1944–64. In their analysis, they controlled for sex and for education, using the categories 0–8, 9–11, 12, and more than 12 years of school completed. Their stan- dardization for education used a rectangular distribution over these categories. In our study of these data, kindly supplied by Professor Glenn, we have taken the education distributions, by sex, reported in the 1960 census for whites aged 25–34, 35–44, 45–54, 55–64, 65–74, and 75 and over as the education distributions for cohorts 6, 5, 4, 3, 2, and 1 (as defined in Table 2) in each election year. Our reweighting of the data is, therefore, tantamount to a poststratification of the Gallup samples, a matter of some importance in view of Glenn's (1977, p. 35) demonstration of strong sampling biases in the earlier polls. (Our procedure does, of course, obscure any differential attrition within cohorts due to educational differentials in mortality.) Applying the census distributions to Glenn's education-specific turnout percentages, we obtain new estimates of turnout for men and women in each ten-year birth cohort. The data shown in Table 2 are the unweighted averages of the male and female percentages.

For four of the cohorts defined by Glenn and Grimes, we can use CPS data to estimate turnout by sex in the elections of 1968–76;

TABLE 2
Mean of Turnout Percentages for White Men and Women in Specified Birth Cohorts, 1944–1984

Cohort Number	Age in 1964	1944[a]	1948	1952	1956	1960	1964	1968[b]	1972[c]	1976[d]	1980[d]	1984[d]
8	10–19	—	—	—	—	—	—	—	—	55	62	66
7	20–29	—	—	—	—	—	—	64	63	66	72	72
6	30–39	—	—	—	—	72	73	72	69	70	75	77
5	40–49	49	71	78	82	80	81	76	72	72	77	78
4	50–59	74	80	83	85	83	80	76	72	70	75	75
3	60–69	81	81	82	83	83	81	74	69	65	—	—
2	70–79	84	79	82	85	83	80	—	—	—	—	—
1	80–89	78	79	76	76	—	—	—	—	—	—	—

Source. 1944–64: Gallup Polls, unpublished tabulations by Norval D. Glenn; 1968–84: U.S. Bureau of the Census 1969, and unpublished special tabulations for 1972–84.

[a] Data for persons 21–29 in cohort 5.

[b] Data for persons 25–34, 35–44, etc., rather than 24–33, 34–43, etc. Denominator includes noncitizens.

[c] Denominator includes noncitizens. Percentages for citizens would be 1 to 3 points higher.

[d] Denominator excludes noncitizens.

and for three of them, the record extends to 1984. Again, the entry in the table is the simple average of the male and female percentages. Published CPS data for 1964 (not shown) are given for age intervals different from those needed to make comparisons with the Gallup series. But a rough calculation involving interpolations suggests that the 1964 Gallup turnout estimates were on average about 5 points higher than the CPS estimates. Hence, there is a major discontinuity in the series between 1964 and 1968. One lesser discontinuity is mentioned in the notes to the table. No doubt there are other discontinuities affecting the comparisons that we are not aware of or have no means of quantifying.

The reweighted Gallup data show some evidence of declining electoral participation at advanced ages; such declines are seen in each of cohorts 1–5, although the changes are so small that in the light of the modest sample sizes of the Gallup Polls, they might well be explained by sampling variations. In the much larger CPS samples, changes of 2 or 3 percentage points are statistically significant except, perhaps, at the very highest ages. Hence, the intracohort decreases for all cohorts between 1968 and 1972 must be taken seriously, as must the intracohort increases between 1976 and 1980. Both changes undoubtedly reflect a mixture of effects due to aging and to the specific elections or the times in which they took place. The same kind of qualification would have to be stipulated for any use of the cross-section age comparisons that can be made in Table 1, most of which show some decline at the advanced ages relative to the somewhat younger ages. Cross-sectional age differences could, of course, reflect cohort-differentiating factors, such as education. Our procedure does not attempt to standardize intercohort comparisons for education or any other factor except sex.

The work of Glenn and Grimes was an important step toward the design we use. Although they noted (1968, p. 568) that "different presidential elections evoke differing degrees of interest and participation," they discounted period effects as an explanation of their main finding, that turnout increases from young adulthood to middle age but is virtually constant thereafter, rather than decreasing, as had been suggested by studies making age comparisons in cross-section data. In subsequent writing, however, Glenn (1977, p. 20) explicitly noted that "cohort studies are not in all respects superior to cross-sectional studies for the purpose of detecting effects of aging." Of special interest to us are his remarks (pp. 20–21) pointing out the potential utility of panel and retrospective studies.

Although data aggregated over cohorts in the fashion of Table 2 may be useful in detecting major trends, we believe there is a strong case (implicit in the procedures and results reported below) for maintaining distinctions among annual cohorts. In all our subsequent discussion, the age index x pertains to single years of age. We analyze the 2×2 cross-classification $\{f_{ijxt}\}$ of turnout in the first election (reported retrospectively) by turnout in the second election four years later (reported in the current survey), where $i = 1$ for a voter and $i = 2$ for a nonvoter in the first election and $j = 1$ for a voter and $j = 2$ for a nonvoter in the second election. Each analysis pertains to data for one of the four phalanxes. Phalanx 18 comprises the 15 age groups, $x = 18, 22, \dots, 74$ as of the first election; and we have cross-classifications of first election by second election for three successive two-wave panels identified by initial election years $t = 72, 76, 80$. Cohorts are identified by numbers $c = t - x + 10$. Phalanx 19 consists of age groups $x = 19, 23, \dots, 75$; and phalanxes 20 and 21 consist of age groups $x = 20, 24, \dots, 76$ and $x = 21, 25, \dots, 77$ respectively. Inasmuch as the four phalanxes so defined have no ages or cohorts in common, it is convenient to specify the model for each phalanx separately.

We consider a model with multiplicative parameters pertaining to age, year, and cohort, and also some additional parameters required to take account of the (pseudo-) panel design and the reporting biases noted earlier. The parameters generate expected frequencies $\{F_{ijxt}\}$ in accordance with these formulas:

$$F_{11xt} = K_{xt} A_x A_{x+4} B_t B_{t+4} C_c^2 R_{xt} H_{xt}, \tag{1}$$

$$F_{12xt} = K_{xt} A_x B_t C_c H_{xt}, \tag{2}$$

$$F_{21xt} = K_{xt} A_{x+4} B_{t+4} C_c, \tag{3}$$

$$F_{22xt} = K_{xt} R_{xt} E_{xt}. \tag{4}$$

The age parameters A_x and A_{x+4} pertain to the contrasts between voters and nonvoters of the designated ages; B_t and B_{t+4} concern that contrast in the designated election years; and C_c pertains to the contrast between voters and nonvoters identified as belonging to cohort c. The nuisance parameter K_{xt} has no substantive meaning but is included to insure that

$$\sum_{i,j} F_{ijxt} = \sum_{i,j} f_{ijxt}.$$

The association parameters R_{xt}, unlike the parameters defined so far, have no counterpart in the conventional exposition of age-period-cohort models for a collection of successive independent cross-sections. The pseudo-panel design explicitly recognizes that within each cohort, there is an association of turnout at $t + 4$ and at t. (The same would hold for a true panel design.) This association can only be observed by virtue of the design. But it is present whether or not it is observed. Thus, the usual model for a collection of cross-sections could seriously distort the process under study, as we shall try to show in more detail later. Finally, error parameters H_{xt} and E_{xt} are included to represent the overreporting of certain sequences ij, which is a special source of vulnerability in the pseudo-panel design. (The true panel design is vulnerable in a different way if, as some analysts have concluded, participation in a panel study tends to stimulate subsequent actual or reported turnout.) The subscripts x and t attached to the error parameters incorporate the possibility that the extent of overreporting varies by age and year. The distinction between E and H is intended to take account of the possibility that the use of proxy respondents and the coding of DK and NR as nonvoting makes it especially likely that the sequence $i = 2$, $j = 2$ will be overreported. It is not implausible that there are other reasons for artifactual response consistency, tending to make $E > 1$, although we have no direct evidence of this, inasmuch as the retrospective question follows the current report and response to it could be affected by response to the earlier question.

The model specified by $(1), \ldots, (4)$ is overparameterized. But before considering modified parameterizations, with statistical analysis in mind, it is useful to investigate some properties of this one. To facilitate exposition, we define symbols V, W, Y, Z as follows:

$$V_{xt} = F_{11xt} F_{22xt} / F_{12xt} F_{21xt}, \tag{5}$$

$$W_{xt} = F_{21xt} / F_{12xt}, \tag{6}$$

$$Y_{xt} = F_{11xt} / F_{22xt}, \tag{7}$$

$$Z_{xt} = F_{12xt} F_{21xt} F_{22xt} / F_{11xt}. \tag{8}$$

If the model parameters in $(1), \ldots, (4)$ are substituted for the F's in

(5),...,(8), we find that

$$V_{xt} = R_{xt}^2 E_{xt},\tag{9}$$

$$Z_{xt} = K_{xt}^2 E_{xt}.\tag{10}$$

Therefore, if it were not for the possibility of a spurious response consistency induced by the pseudo-panel design and a coding convention (reflected in parameter E), estimation of associations and nuisance parameters would be straightforward. We find, after slightly more extensive algebra, that

$$\frac{W_{x+4,t}}{W_{xt}} = \frac{A_x A_{x+8} H_{xt}}{A_{x+4}^2 H_{x+4,t}},\tag{11}$$

$$\frac{W_{x,t+4}}{W_{xt}} = \frac{B_t B_{t+8} H_{xt}}{B_{t+4}^2 H_{x,t+4}},\tag{12}$$

and

$$\frac{Y_{x,t+4} Y_{x+4,t}}{Y_{xt} Y_{x+4,t+4}} = \frac{C_{c-4}^2 C_{c+4}^2 E_{xt} E_{x+4,t+4} H_{x,t+4} H_{x+4,t}}{C_c^4 E_{x,t+4} E_{x+4,t} H_{xt} H_{x+4,t+4}}.\tag{13}$$

We see from (11), (12), and (13) that even in the absence of reporting errors, we cannot estimate the individual parameters pertaining to age, year, and cohort. From the discussion of Pullum (1980, pp. 242–43), however, we surmise that the combinations of age, year, and cohort parameters in these expressions—if the symbols pertaining to errors are deleted—are invariant with respect to alternative linear restrictions placed on some of the parameters to render the remaining ones identified. With respect to the errors, we note some special conditions other than the simple absence of reporting biases that will allow these "second differences" (Pullum 1980, p. 238) to be estimated. If $H_{xt} = H_t$ is the same at all ages (although possibly different in different years), the ratio $A_x A_{x+8}/A_{x+4}^2$ pertaining to age parameters is estimated without bias. If $H_{xt} = H_x$, so that reporting biases are constant over years, the ratio $B_t B_{t+8}/B_{t=4}^2$ pertaining to year parameters can be estimated. Note that only H_{xt} and not E_{xt} is at stake in the two expressions (11) and (12) containing these ratios. Hence, if only "response consistency" errors (parameter E) are involved and not any general tendency to over- or underreport retrospective turnout (parameter H), the age and year ratios (though not the cohort ratios) are not biased. It is interesting that the cohort ratios $C_{c-4}^2 C_{c+4}^2 / C_c^4$ are not disturbed if both error parameters (H and E) are either constant over time or constant over ages; note the cancellations that occur in (13) when either of these conditions holds.

Unfortunately, the evidence considered in the preceding section does not lend support to the assumptions mentioned so far. Indeed, we have no direct evidence at all concerning error E but only conjecture that such an error may result from the conventions used for DK and NR and from the close proximity of the current and retrospective questions in the interview. In the analyses selectively reported below, we have made no serious attempt to estimate E_{xt} but have included such specifications concerning these errors as are needed to obtain a satisfactory fit for our models. In regard to H_{xt}, our specifications are intended to represent the biases detected in the work reported earlier. For $t = 72$, we set $H_{xt} = 1.0$ for all x, in view of the finding that the 1976 retrospective reports of turnout do not differ systematically from the 1972 current reports. For $t = 76$ we specify a log-linear function

$$H_{x,76} = H_0 H_1^{(x-18)/4}$$

for, e.g., phalanx 18, in accordance with the evidence of an age-dependent bias in the 1980 retrospective reports. And for $t = 80$ we let $H_{x,80} = H_3$, a constant that does not depend on age, inasmuch as the bias in 1984 retrospective reports seemed not to vary systematically by age.

Apart from the errors, certain restrictions are needed to obtain a set of identifiable (though not uniquely defined) age, year, and cohort parameters. For convenience, we set $A_{18} = B_{72} = C_8 = C_{64} = 1.0$, bearing in mind that the invariances noted in connection with (11), (12), and (13) do not depend on which parameters are designated to be constrained in this way (Pullum 1980).

We provide few details about the statistics computed in fitting several versions of our general model, equations (1),...,(4). One reason is that we are not here concerned with systematic description of patterns of electoral participation but only wish to illustrate some of the possibilities for enhancing such a description that are opened up by the CPS pseudo-panel design. Moreover, we have not settled on any unique specialization of the model as preferable to other special cases of it, and we are not at all sure that we have detected all the systematic features of the data, even when the fitting of a model yields a nonsignificant goodness-of-fit statistic. The main points of the succeeding discussion are as follows: (a) the "cohort effects" of the conventional age-period-cohort model may be superfluous when the panel design permits a better specification of the actual process that generated the data, (b) "age effects" and "year effects" estimated with the aid of panel data will not, in general, be the same as those estimated from the conventional model applied to a sequence of cross-sections, and (c) a major contribution of the panel design is to permit the detection of association between turnout in each election and the immediately preceding or following election.

Although equations $(1), \ldots, (4)$ include a set of cohort parameters that could detect "effects" of the kind anticipated from the conventional model, we find that these parameters, as a set, do not contribute significantly to the fit of the entire model. When all of them are deleted, the model for one of the phalanxes of men or women has 15 df more than the full model. In none of our eight analyses (4 phalanxes $\times$ 2 sexes) do we find that the resulting increase in the likelihood ratio chi-square statistic (L^2) is significant at the 0.05 level. For the aggregate of the eight analyses, the increase in L^2 amounts to 139.1 ($df = 120$, $P = 0.11$). This contrasts with the result we obtain in carrying out a conventional age-period-cohort analysis of logit turnout rates, using the independent cross-section samples for 1972, 1976, 1980, and 1984, computed from current reports of persons 22–81 years old (disregarding current reports for persons 18–21 years old because of the high incidence of proxy responding). In six of the eight analyses, we find that the increment to L^2 resulting from deletion of all cohort parameters is significant at the 0.05 level. Adding the L^2 values over the eight analyses, we find that the increment comes to 283.1 ($df = 128$, $P < 0.001$).

The comparison of the two sets of results suggests that "cohort effects"—as that term has been understood by investigators adopting the paradigm for cohort analysis provided by Mason et al. (1973)—may be an artifact of a defective design. A set of independent cross-section samples is inadequate for investigating social processes related to aging because it fails to describe accurately the continuity in the life course of specific individuals. Such continuity is handled in the panel design or pseudo-panel design by permitting each individual's behavior on one occasion to be compared with that same individual's behavior on another occasion. The conventional model, to be sure, does acknowledge temporal continuity in a way, but it makes the excessively strong claim that every individual in a cohort shares a common parameter value (the "cohort effect" parameter), which distinguishes it from all individuals in any other cohort, and that the effect of this contrast is exactly the same on all relevant occasions (such as, for example, the 15 presidential elections in which an individual might have the opportunity to vote while passing from age 22 to age 81). A weaker, but perhaps more realistic, assumption suffices for the models considered here, equations $(1), \ldots, (4)$ with parameters C_c deleted: There is an unspecified association between turnout in any election and turnout in the next election such that an individual who votes in one is more likely than a nonvoter to vote (or to have voted) in the other. The two-wave panel design, of course, will not detect associations between nonadjacent elections, and we have no information on how serious this defect may be.

Despite our general negative conclusion about the relevance of cohort-effect parameters for a design appropriate to studies of aging, we carried out two further analyses that might shed further light on this matter. In the first, we identified in our data the specific cohorts that did and did not have the opportunity to vote at ages 18 to 20, which was conferred by the Civil Rights Act of 1970 and the Twenty-sixth Amendment. In phalanx 18, cohorts 68 and 64, but no earlier cohorts, were actually eligible to vote at age 18. If this opportunity affected their later behavior in a uniform fashion, we should expect to see an elevated turnout for cohort 68 in 1980 and 1984 and for cohort 64 in 1976, 1980, 1984, in comparing them with earlier cohorts at the same ages. The same prediction holds for cohorts 67 and 63 in phalanx 19 and for cohorts 66 and 62 in phalanx 20. But cohorts in phalanx 21 would not be expected to show such an effect, since the age at which they were first eligible was not affected by the amendment. Accordingly, we define an "eligibility effect" parameter for the relevant cohorts in each phalanx and predict a positive value for it in phalanxes 18, 19, and 20 but a value of nil in phalanx 21. The result, in brief, is that the estimate of this parameter is not significant in any of the eight calculations. The largest estimate is only 1.43 times as great as its estimated standard error. We cannot, of course, rule out the possibility of a "sleeper effect," one that will be observed only as the cohort ages and turns out for elections after 1984. But this would not be a conventional "cohort effect," which is assumed to be constant over the entire career of the cohort.

Our second attempt to specify cohort effects more precisely relates to the sex differences in age parameters that we noted in results obtained when men and women were regarded as separate populations. Roughly speaking, the estimates for the two sexes are fairly similar below age 45 or 50, but at higher ages there is a progressive divergence producing higher turnout rates for men. This pattern invites explanation in terms of changing sex differences in political socialization. Only our very earliest cohorts could have been directly affected by the Nineteenth Amendment. Cohort 9 was age 21 in 1920, the first year in which all women in the nation were enfranchised. The few earlier cohorts represented in our data are, therefore, the only ones whose first opportunities to vote came after 1920. Cohorts 6, 7, and 8 were not yet 21 in that year, but cohorts 1–5, having turned 21 in 1916 or earlier, had their entry into the electorate postponed, as it were. Women in cohorts 9 to, say, 24 attended school during a period in which women in only a few states were voting in national elections. Varying proportions of women in a wide range of cohorts, up to at least cohort 45 or 50, were born to mothers who reached voting age before 1920 and could, therefore, have had less exposure than their male counterparts to same-sex politically active role models. The complex demography of generational and cohort replacement (see, e.g., the discussion, "Cohorts versus Generations," by Blau and Duncan, 1967, pp. 82–84) suggests that the intercohort transition from disenfranchisement to full political participation would have been a gradual process. Demographic considerations also suggest that the socialization process could have produced differences within as well as between cohorts. Mothers of women in a given cohort are themselves drawn from a wide range of earlier cohorts, and their experiences, accordingly, would have been diverse. This observation serves as a caveat for the interpretation of the results we are about to report.

We seek to detect (rather than to model veridically) a specific feature of this process by fitting a model in which the age parameters for men and women are constrained to be the same but in which a "cohort effect" is defined, for women only, as a quadratic function of cohort number. We easily obtain a satisfactory fit, by the usual criterion of a chi-square statistic too small to be significant at the 0.05 level, for the overall model estimated for phalanxes 19, 20, and 21. But for phalanx 18, we include three ad hoc adjustments of age parameters for women in 1980 and 1984 to meet the criterion. (We omit comment on the possible substantive implications of these adjustments.) Results

FIGURE 1. Estimates of age parameters (log $\hat{A}_x$) for men and women, including ad hoc and cohort adjustments for women, 1976, 1980, and 1984.

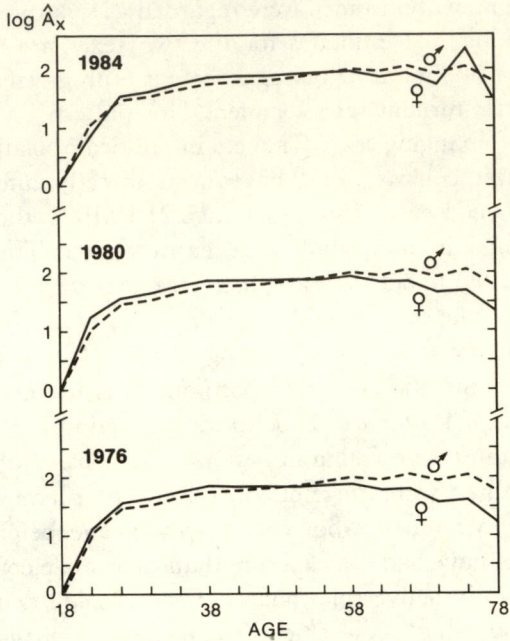

TABLE 3

Estimates of Shifts in Age Parameters for Cohorts of Women, by Phalanx, Derived from Data in 1976, 1980, and 1984 Current Population Surveys

Phalanx	Intercept (SE)	Linear Term (SE)	Quadratic Term (SE)
18	0.015 (0.020)	0.0367 (0.0036)	−0.0038 (0.0008)
19	0.016 (0.021)	0.0325 (0.0037)	−0.0029 (0.0008)
20	0.004 (0.021)	0.0333 (0.0038)	−0.0035 (0.0008)
21	−0.009 (0.021)	0.0329 (0.0040)	−0.0024 (0.0008)

Note. The argument of the function is $(c - p - 40)/4$, where c = cohort number and p = phalanx number.

for phalanx 18 are shown graphically in Figure 1. Table 3 shows the equations used to calculate "cohort effects" for all four phalanxes. In interpreting these results, one should bear in mind the inflexibility of the quadratic functional form. The positive differences between the female and male parameters at the younger ages may, in a sense, be forced by the larger negative differences at the higher ages. But our present limited curiosity is satisfied by the discovery that the coefficient for the quadratic term is significantly negative in every phalanx, although we do not rule out the possibility that recent cohorts of women may be overtaking men.

What we have been calling cohort effects in this analysis of sex differences may more appropriately (as in the title of Table 3) be called shifts in age parameters. Our quadratic function, although its argument is cohort number (minus phalanx number), can be neutrally described as an age-by-sex-by-year interaction rather than as a "cohort effect." To be comfortable with this revision of nomenclature, one need only admit the possibility that age parameters may change in the course of history and that from period to period some populations may undergo "more history" than others. The notion of fixed cohort and age effects, at least in regard to a subject like voting turnout, seems too rigid to capture what is at stake in real historical change; the content of "aging" from x to $x + 4$ must surely change from time to time and vary between socially differentiated populations. In a longer time perspective, the stability of the male age parameters depicted in Figure 1 will no doubt be seen as a temporary lull in "history." (Our restriction of the analysis to the turnout of white men and women in recent elections was well calculated to provide the opportunity to observe such a lull.) Our earlier conclusion that "cohort effects" are superfluous for an analysis exploiting an appropriate design is, therefore, not vitiated by the outcome of the sex comparison. Instead of describing our quadratic function as a parameterization of the pattern of "cohort effects," we should call it a description of sex differences in age patterns and the time trend of these differences.

We turn to our second general point, which highlights the difference between the design we have taken advantage of and the conventional design involving a series of independent cross-sections. The point is simply that the models pertaining to these two designs are not the same, notwithstanding the possibility of specifying "age effects," "period effects," and "cohort effects" within either of them. We could illustrate the large and systematic differences in the numerical estimates of all these kinds of parameters incident to the modification of the design, but it seems preferable to use our space to show succinctly why such differences are all but inevitable. It will facilitate exposition of the essentials if we assume that equations (1),...,(4), with all cohort parameters and the error parameters deleted, comprise a "true" model for the 2×2 table $\{ f_{ijxt} \}$. Now, apart from failures of cohort closure owing to international migration and mortality, the conventional design may be described as one concerned with the column marginals of the modelled table $\{ F_{ijxt} \}$ and the similar table $\{ F_{ij,x-4,t-4} \}$. The marginals of $\{ F_{ijxt} \}$ are produced by

$$F_{.1xt} = A_{x+4}B_{t+4}(A_xB_tR_{xt} + 1)K_{xt}, \tag{14}$$

$$F_{.2xt} = (A_xB_t + R_{xt})K_{xt}, \tag{15}$$

and the marginals of $F_{ij,x-4,t-4}$ may be computed in a similar manner. From (14) and (15) we see that the turnout rate (expressed as the odds on voting) for persons of age $x + 4$ in year $t + 4$ is given by

$$\frac{F_{.1xt}}{F_{.2xt}} = \frac{A_{x+4}B_{t+4}(A_xB_tR_{xt} + 1)}{A_xB_t + R_{xt}}. \tag{16}$$

We also find that the turnout odds for persons of age x in year t, obtained from the column marginals of $F_{ij,x-4,t-4}$, are given by

$$\frac{F_{.1,x-4,t-4}}{F_{.2,x-4,t-4}} = \frac{A_xB_t(A_{x-4}B_{t-4}R_{x-4,t-4} + 1)}{A_{x-4}B_{t-4} + R_{x-4,t-4}}. \tag{17}$$

It is these turnout rates that are analyzed in the conventional model, whose objective is to separate the A and B parameters by means of comparisons between age groups and years. That such comparisons are required for the identification of parameters is implied not only by the occurrence of products of A's and B's in the expressions for turnout odds but also by the occurrence of both subscripts x and $x + 4$ or $x - 4$ and both t and $t + 4$ or $t - 4$ in the fractions (16) and (17).

Under the panel design, we see that the elimination of nuisance parameters follows from dividing (3) by (2):

$$F_{21xt}/F_{12xt} = A_{x+4}B_{t+4}/A_xB_t. \tag{18}$$

(We recall that the error parameter is assumed to be absent and note with interest that the cohort parameter, even if it were present in the original model, would drop out of this ratio.) Comparison of age groups and years can be used to effect the separation of parameters in (18). We note that the ratio (18) can be obtained by dividing (16) by (17) under either of two special conditions, first, that $F_{21, x-4, t-4}/F_{12, x-4, t-4} = A_x B_t / A_{x-4} B_{t-4} = 1.0$, which will hold if the 2×2 table $F_{ij, x-4, t-4}$ is symmetrical, and $R_{xt} = R_{x-4, t-4}$; or, second, that $R_{xt} = R_{x-4, t-4} = 1.0$ (that is, there is no association across individuals between turnout in one election and turnout in the preceding election). Otherwise, it will only be by happenstance that analysis of the ratios (18) and analysis of the ratios (16) and (17) will yield the same parameter estimates. More specifically, the latter pair of ratios cannot be used to estimate A_x and B_t but will estimate some parameters (perhaps inappropriately labeled A and B) that are actually opaque mixtures of A's and B's as well as R's; and their analysis may invite recognition of a set of artifactual "cohort effects" that emerge because of the design's failure to provide a means for recognizing the role of the associations R_{xt}.

In sum, if (1),...,(4), as modified to suit the present discussion, is regarded as a structural model, an age-period model or age-period-cohort model for the turnout ratios can only be characterized as a "statistical model" with parameters that are hopelessly ambiguous from a structural standpoint. It would be exaggerating the utility of such a statistical model to describe it as a "reduced form" of the structural model, as that term is used in econometric theory.

Our third major point about the advantage of the (pseudo-) panel design concerns its ability to provide information on the inter-year association of turnout. For simplicity we ignore the possibility that this association is biased by the parameter E_{xt}, a possible artifact arising from the use of retrospective recall as a surrogate for the genuine panel design. We doubt that all the association can be accounted for by such an artifact. Here, again, we do not attempt to obtain a veridical model of the associations but only to illustrate an interesting aspect of their variation across age groups. Accordingly, we use a merely expedient parameterization, albeit one that seems broadly consistent with the data. We find that the association increases with age, but at a decreasing rate, until a maximum is reached, after which there may be some decline. Table 4 shows estimates of the quadratic function of age that describes the log-odds ratio pertaining to voting in 1972 and 1976. Although the illustrative data are for a single pair of

TABLE 4

Estimates of Equations for the Association (Log Cross-Product Ratio) between Voting in 1972 and Voting in 1976, as a Function of Age and Sex, by Phalanx

Phalanx	Intercept	Linear Term (SE)	Quadratic Term (SE)	Age at Maximum
Males				
18	3.40	0.104 (0.013)	-0.0181 (0.0030)	58
19	3.42	0.098 (0.014)	-0.0185 (0.0031)	59
20	3.30	0.085 (0.014)	-0.0145 (0.0031)	60
21	3.30	0.063 (0.014)	-0.0175 (0.0032)	57
Females				
18	3.51	0.113 (0.011)	-0.0187 (0.0027)	58
19	3.43	0.102 (0.011)	-0.0184 (0.0027)	59
20	3.58	0.084 (0.011)	-0.0195 (0.0027)	56
21	3.36	0.075 (0.012)	-0.0177 (0.0028)	57

Note. The argument of the function is $(x - p - 28)/4$, where p = phalanx number and x = age in years as of the 1972 election.

years, we actually find no evidence of any systematic difference between years in the magnitude of the association at a specified age. In all phalanxes, we obtain a significant positive estimate for the linear term and a significant negative estimate for the quadratic term of the function. The eight equations are in general agreement that the maximum association occurs around age 56–60, that is, about 36 to 40 years after the first age at which members of the phalanx are eligible to vote. The estimates for men and women are quite similar, a result that is somewhat surprising in view of our earlier demonstration of ostensible "cohort effects" that differentiate the age parameters of the two populations.

3. TOWARD A SCIENTIFIC MODEL

Our experience with these data, selectively reported above, suggests that it is fairly easy to specify an acceptable statistical model for either a collection of 2×2 panel tables or a set of cross-sectional turnout rates, if by *acceptable* one means a relatively parsimonious model that yields a nonsignificant goodness-of-fit statistic. One caveat should perhaps be made explicit: Data for a longer series of elections might well show patterns not so easily captured by as small a set of parameters as we find are needed in either our panel analysis or the age-period-cohort analysis of turnout rates for a sequence of only four elections. But regardless of parsimony, all the models so far discussed (not excluding the ones for the panel tables) must be regarded as mere *statistical* models; they have little credibility as *scientific* models. We borrow this distinction from an important article by David Rogosa (1987) and wish to support his emphasis on the distinction with all the rhetorical force we can muster. See also Coleman (1981, pp. 5–6.)

A statistical model may serve very well as a basis for inferences about multivariate population distributions. Unfortunately, the intellectual attractiveness of the problems of statistical inference that arise in working with complex cross-classifications makes it easy to mistake their solution for a contribution to scientific method. We feel it is time to re-establish the correct priorities. The *design* of investigations is the essential ingredient of scientific method, indeed, of empirical science itself. Data analysis by suitable statistical methods is a mere auxiliary to the central scientific task. It was the determination of what observations to make, under what conditions, that required the genius of a Tycho Brahe, a Galileo, a Mendel, or a Pasteur, all of whom could have made good use of statistical methods, had they been available, but none of whose discoveries could have been made by a platoon of statisticians.

Our concluding discussion regards the statistical results reported earlier as mere clues—certainly ambiguous and possibly misleading clues—to what a proper scientific model ought to be trying to explain about how and why electoral participation varies with age. None of the parameters we estimated, least of all the "cohort effects," can be claimed to represent how the processes that generate the data actually work.

One might hope that a re-expression or modification of the statistical model could help in formulating a model with a stronger claim to scientific credibility. The most impressive move in this direction (as far as we know) is reported in an article by Hout and Knoke (1975), which anticipated part of our discussion in remarking, "The obvious preferred data for studying the effects of aging on political activity are longitudinal—panels of individuals from entry into the electorate through maturity and into old age. But no such data exist or are likely to appear" (p. 53). The authors were so eager to get on with their alternative design that they did not stop to notice the potential of mere two-wave (rather than lifetime) panels in combination with repeated observations on identical birth cohorts. Their alternative is suggestive. They look at a sequence of six cross-sections, but before inferring "effects of aging and cohort membership on voting turnout," they undertake to control "the most important social correlates of voting" by means of regressions of turnout on education, occupation, social-class identification, religion, and region, as well as sex and "race." Our interest is not in the list of regressors, the length of which could easily be doubled, and more, by including other factors with statistically demonstrated relationships to turnout. Even a complete list of such factors reported in the research literature would hardly be accepted by knowledgeable investigators as an exhaustive enumeration of sources of variation in turnout rates. Hence, the provocative contribution of the Hout-Knoke project is their more general point that before inferences about aging and cohort parameters can be accepted as providing information about the structure of the process of aging it is essential to take account of *heterogeneity* (Hout, Duncan, and Sobel 1987). But until we have a model formulated in such a way that all heterogeneity is taken into account completely, we will be permanently caught in the predicament of Hout and Knoke at the conclusion of their research: There is still a need for "future researchers...to elaborate our basic social and demographic model to incorporate...other variables" (p. 68).

Heterogeneity, therefore, is one of the foundation stones for any serious gesture toward a scientific model. The other is the postulate that voting is a probabilistic response to whatever events, states, or conditions are conceived as causal influences on turnout. By this we mean that every individual, if (hypothetically) confronted by exactly the same circumstances on two or more occasions, would sometimes vote, sometimes not, in accordance with some, generally unknown, probability that might itself be either constant for that individual (but different for other individuals) or changing. (We do not rule out probabilities that approach zero or unity as closely as might be wished, but only the absolute certainty that any individual will or will not vote.) The elaboration of this postulate will be found in other discussions (Duncan 1986; forthcoming), and we do not duplicate them here. The main point to emphasize here is that the postulate of probabilistic response must be clearly distinguished in both concept and research design from the stochastic variation of data that arises from random sampling of a heterogeneous population. The distinction is completely blurred in our conventional statistical training and practice of data analysis, wherein the stochastic aspects of the statistical model are most easily justified by the idea of sampling from a population distribution. We seldom stop to wonder if sampling is the only reason for making the model stochastic. The perverse consequence of doing good statistics is, therefore, to suppress curiosity about the actual processes that generate the data. These are of at least two distinct kinds: (a) the behavioral processes that give rise to voting by individuals in a population, and (b) the observational processes of data collection, which typically involves random sampling of the population and the use of instruments for observing the relevant behavior. Both sampling and observation are vulnerable to systematic (as documented earlier herein) and random error. We know quite a bit about these matters in regard to (b) and seemingly have mistaken progress in learning about them for the acquisition of knowledge about (a).

Heterogeneity and probabilistic response are brought together in so-called latent-structure models, including models formulated in terms of discrete latent variables or latent classes and models that assume, instead, heterogeneity defined on continuous latent variables or latent traits. (For discussion of the differences between the two types of latent-variable model, see Duncan, Stenbeck, and Brody, forthcoming.) It may be that some elaboration or development of one of these kinds of model could begin to offer something more than the ultimately uninformative fitting of more and more complex but still ad hoc statistical models. We sketch below our sense of how a test of this suggestion might begin, but with no implication that success is imminent or a foregone conclusion. As in all scientific endeavor, the breakthrough will ultimately come (if it does) in the form of an inspired speculation of some individual whose discovery, in the nature of things, cannot be anticipated or, for that matter, assured by indoctrination in philosophy of science, methodology, or statistical inference.

Let π_{ht} be the probability that individual h votes at time t. We postulate a strictly positive latent trait Ω whose value in the case of individual h is ω_h, and we assume a parameter α_{xt} depending on her or his age x and the particular election held at t. Together, ω_h and α_{xt} determine π_{ht} according to the simple logistic model of Rasch ([1960] 1980):

$$\pi_{ht} = \frac{\alpha_{xt}\omega_h}{1 + \alpha_{xt}\omega_h}, \tag{19}$$

choosing the particular α in light of the individual's age. At the next election, the probability will be different, even if we assume no change in ω_h:

$$\pi_{h,t+4} = \frac{\alpha_{x+4,t+4}\omega_h}{1 + \alpha_{x+4,t+4}\omega_h}. \tag{20}$$

Postponing the reckoning with the inevitable complications, we complete the stochastic specification by stating the axiom of local independence, which holds that, conditional on ω_h, voting at $t+4$ is independent of voting at t. As for heterogeneity, it is taken for granted that no two individuals need be located at exactly the same place on the continuum $\Omega > 0$.

We may now calculate the joint probabilities, for individual h, pertaining to the sequence ij, where $i = 1$ if h votes at t, $i = 2$ if not, and $j = 1$ if h votes at $t+4$, $j = 2$ if not. These probabilities π_{hij} are obtained by multiplying (19) by (20):

$$\begin{aligned}
\pi_{h11} &= \alpha_{xt}\alpha_{x+4,t+4}\omega_h^2/D_h, \\
\pi_{h12} &= \alpha_{xt}\omega_h/D_h, \\
\pi_{h21} &= \alpha_{x+4,t+4}\omega_h/D_h, \\
\pi_{h22} &= 1/D_h,
\end{aligned} \tag{21}$$

where $D_h = (1 + \alpha_{xt}\omega_h)(1 + \alpha_{x+4,t+4}\omega_h)$ is the sum of the four numerators of the probabilities (which, accordingly, must sum to unity).

For any individual, the most we can hope to observe (ignoring errors of observation or report) is one of the four response sequences enumerated in (21). But for a sample of individuals, we can observe the frequencies $\{f_{ij}\}$, the very ones we subjected to statistical analysis earlier. Therefore, we must ask what (21), assumed as a model for the way any individual sequence is generated, implies for the frequencies of the sequences in the population to which h belongs, about which we hope to learn something by sampling. With some simplification of the mathematical details, we may pursue this interest by thinking of (21) as providing the expected "frequencies" of the four sequences in a sample of size 1. To obtain expected frequencies $\{F_{ij}\}$ for a sample of size n, we sum over h,

$$F_{ij} = \sum_h \pi_{hij},$$

to obtain

$$F_{11} = \alpha_{xt}\alpha_{x+4,\,t+4}S_2,$$

$$F_{12} = \alpha_{xt}S_1,$$

$$F_{21} = \alpha_{x+4,\,t+4}S_1, \tag{22}$$

$$F_{22} = S_0,$$

where $S_s = \sum_h(\omega_h^s/D_h)$ serves to abbreviate the formulas. The terms S_s are a complex mixture of heterogeneous values of Ω and the α parameters. But we see immediately in (22) the possibility of separating out the latter simply by taking the quotient

$$F_{21}/F_{12} = \alpha_{x+4,\,t+4}/\alpha_{xt}. \tag{23}$$

Now, if it should happen that the α's can be decomposed without remainder into products of the form $\alpha_{xt} = A_x B_t$ and $\alpha_{x+4,\,t+4} = A_{x+4}B_{t+4}$, we could convert (23) into (18), itself derived from (1),...,(4), after simplification of the latter.

The purpose of this exposition is not to offer some piece of mathematical legerdemain to suggest that, after all, the "data analyst" may proceed serenely to exploit the statistical model along lines illustrated earlier. On the contrary, we want to use (19),...,(23) as a lever for raising questions that were only incoherently adumbrated in our earlier remarks on the statistical model.

We comment first on the sense in which statistical inferences concerning log-linear models like those discussed earlier constitute "tests" of the Rasch model. A successful fit involving only age and year parameters (apart from parameters pertaining to reporting errors) can, at most, be claimed to support the decomposition $\alpha_{xt} = A_x B_t$. On the other hand, a finding of significant "cohort effects" would mean that the decomposition breaks down, although (19) would not thereby be fatally compromised. If, as we suggested, the "cohort effects" manifested in sex differences are best understood as patterns of change in age parameters, model (19) will have to be specified for men and women separately. A longer period of observation, with more opportunity for "history" to do its work, could well throw up patterns in the data requiring a multiplicity of specifications of (19)—that is, alternative sets of α_{xt} for different cohorts and subpopulations within them. Such differentiation would constitute the raw material for a bona fide sociology of aging, a field that must surely be impatient with the assumption that there is some fixed content for the experience of aging or fixed effect of growing older. Thus, we doubt that the parameters B_t alone provide enough room for "history."

Even if alternative specifications of α_{xt} are allowed, (19) makes the nontrivial assertion that the individual differences relevant to π_{ht} are permanent, and all individuals in the particular population to which the model applies are subjected alike to the effects represented by α_{xt}. There are, in other words, no interactions of personal and social factors in the determination of the propensity to vote at various stages of the life cycle. Our earlier statistical analysis really sheds no light on the tenability of this claim. Some statistical tests that, in principle, can detect violations of the no-interaction condition are available for three-wave panel data, as described by Duncan (1985). In unpublished exploratory work with multiwave pseudo-panel data obtained with retrospective questions in surveys, we have generally found evidence calling the hypothesis of no interaction into question. It is not clear, however, whether these analyses are fatally compromised by correlated errors in the recall of progressively more remote events.

But we have yet to consider the relevance of our findings about associations in the 2 × 2 tables { f_{ijxt} }. It will be seen that (23) involves no association parameter; and the postulate of local independence specifically excludes such an association as a parameter of the process generating the sequence of acts of voting or not voting. The Rasch model, nevertheless, implies that association will be observed in { f_{ijxt} }, as one can see by computing the cross-product ratio $F_{11}F_{22}/F_{12}F_{21}$ from the parameters in (22), to wit, $S_0 S_2 / S_1^2$. Although the α's shown explicitly in (22) cancel out of this quotient, they nevertheless are involved in the association, as is seen from the formula defining S_s. The S terms also involve all the ω_h in the population of heterogeneous persons (or the sample of it), so that there will be an association even if $\alpha_{xt} = \alpha_{x+4, t+4} = 1$. Roughly speaking, the magnitude of the association will reflect the population variance of Ω: The greater the heterogeneity, the greater the association. Association, we conclude, could be entirely a property of the population, not of the process that produces response. The easiest explanation of an increasing magnitude of association with advancing age (up to a point), therefore, is that the population is becoming more heterogeneous—the variance of Ω is increasing. But if we have gone to the trouble of keeping cohorts separate, the implication of a systematically changing distribution of Ω within a cohort is that our assumption of the constancy of ω_h is false, unless we attribute the entirety of any such change to differential attrition of the cohort. We doubt that differential mortality can explain the increase in association over the first four decades or so of the voter's career, although it is possibly a source of the declining association thereafter if it may be assumed that habitual nonvoters are disproportionately recruited from socioeconomic classes subjected to higher risks of mortality, an assumption consistent with evidence in the demographic literature, which we shall not pause to cite.

If we are thus forced by this line of argument to question the assumption of unchanging ω_h in the simple Rasch model (19), the straightforward interpretation of parameters A_x and B_t as a decomposition of α_{xt} is no longer tenable, and we must wonder if, after all, any such set of parameters can qualify as "structural." The challenge to theory, then, is to come up with an alternative rationalization of the statistical model, by exchanging (19) for a more nearly veridical model of the aging process. Without implying that we have accomplished the redemption of the erstwhile "structural" parameters, we briefly report our gesture toward a more adequate conceptualization of the process linking age and voter turnout. This report can only be regarded as a suggestion for a point of departure for some future investigator with skills in theory construction and mathematics surpassing those we can mobilize at this time.

A certain amount of work has been addressed to the possibility of a dynamic Rasch model that would permit the basic response process to be made more complex by incorporating a learning mechanism or "transfer effect" such that probabilities of later responses are systematically shifted by the earlier responses. Thus, a constrained form of local nonindependence replaces the strong axiom of local independence. The model was suggested by W. F. Kempf and discussed by Kempf and Hampapa (1977) and Duncan (1983).

We define $\eta_{xt} = 1/\alpha_{xt}$ and let $\pi_{xt} = \pi_{ht}(x)$ be the probability that h votes at age x; then (19) can be rewritten

$$\pi_{xt} = \frac{\omega_h}{\omega_h + \eta_{xt}}. \tag{24}$$

No change of substance is involved in this maneuver as such; but now it is easy to modify the model by incorporating the transfer parameter $\kappa_r \geq 0$ to obtain

$$\pi_{xt} = \frac{\omega_h + \kappa_r}{\omega_h + \eta_{xt}}. \tag{25}$$

The value of κ_r depends on r, where $r = 0, 1, \ldots$ is the number of previous occasions on which the response of individual h was "positive," that is, the number of previous presidential elections in which h voted. It need not be monotonically related to r, except for the convention that $\kappa_0 = 0$ and κ_r is (weakly) positive for $r \geq 1$. Conceivably, "fatigue effects" could come into play at higher values of r, although it is not immediately obvious why the mere act of voting 10 or 12 times should lessen the tendency to vote again.

From (25) we obtain

$$1 - \pi_{xt} = \frac{\eta_{xt} - \kappa_r}{\omega_h + \eta_{xt}}. \tag{26}$$

Hence, using (25) and (26) recursively, we may compute the probability of any specific sequence of the actions of voting and not voting. For example, we find that for a person (h) 18 years old in 1972, the probability of the sequence vote, not vote, vote, not vote in the 1972, 1976, 1980, and 1984 elections is

$$\pi_{18,72}\left(1 - \pi_{22,76}\right)\pi_{26,80}\left(1 - \pi_{30,84}\right)$$

$$= \frac{\omega_h\left(\eta_{22,76} - \kappa_1\right)\left(\omega_h + \kappa_1\right)\left(\eta_{30,84} - \kappa_2\right)}{\left(\omega_h + \eta_{18,72}\right)\left(\omega_h + \eta_{22,76}\right)\left(\omega_h + \eta_{26,80}\right)\left(\omega_h + \eta_{30,84}\right)}. \tag{27}$$

See Duncan (1983) for a display of such probabilities computed for all the 16 possible sequences of four binary responses. The occurrence of differences like $(\eta_{22,76} - \kappa_1)$ in the numerator of (27) requires us to place restrictions on the κ_r such that none of these differences can be negative.

We refer the reader to the sources cited for further details on the dynamic model and do not offer a formal assessment of its applicability to the present subject matter. The only result we have to report is the general conclusion that model (25), with appropriate choice of parameter values, is capable of generating an intracohort sequence of 2×2 tables with increasing associations like those we observe in the CPS data. We base this conclusion on numerical simulations with hypothetical values of κ_r, η_{xt}, and $f(\Omega)$, the frequency distribution of Ω in the population. Indeed, it appears that this effect can be produced even if we introduce the constraint $\eta_{xt} = \eta_t$, so that there are no "age effects" but only "year effects" in the model. Thus, (25) might be revised to serve strictly as a model for "learning to vote" (a phrase we once contemplated as a title for this article). In such a model, the parameters κ_r might somehow reflect the social influences on changes in political participation that occur with aging, although we suspect that a rather more complicated model than (25) may be required to simulate such features of the data as the pattern of sex differences reported earlier.

Concluding our remarks on this model, we note a fundamental difference between the rationale of (25) and the one implicit in the conventional age-period-cohort model. Consider the hypothetical "eligibility effect" investigated earlier. It was appropriately described as being "uniform," that is, the same for all members of a cohort. But under model (25), the change in voting age would mean an earlier opportunity for *within*-cohort differentiation to set in. Those taking advantage of the opportunity to vote at 18 would set a course toward higher rates of participation in the future, and those failing to do so would tend to have lower turnout rates in later elections. We feel that a model generating both inter- and intracohort differences is more faithful to Norman Ryder's classic exposition (1965) of the cohort concept than are the later attempts to express the concept in a rigid statistical model.

4. GENERAL CONCLUSIONS

We have chosen the exploration of a specific body of empirical data as the vehicle for an essay, the ulterior intention of which is to advance some general theses about sociological methodology. In our view, the time has come to rectify an imbalance between the application of statistical methods in data analysis and the exploitation of statistical models for data reduction, on the one hand, and, on the other, the development of genuinely explanatory or "structural" models. The central task of methodology should be the critique of research designs—not the exposition of techniques of statistical inference—just as the central task of the research scientist is to contrive the designs that will force "nature" to reveal something about how processes actually work. Our own critique of methods hitherto used for studying the process of aging was undertaken with a specific subject matter, voting turnout, in mind because we (like Glenn 1977) consider it a methodological absurdity to propose all-purpose models for "dependent variables" as diverse as tuberculosis mortality, human fertility, educational attainment, and electoral participation. (For examples, see Hastings and Berry 1979; Mason and Fienberg 1985.) In regard to voting, the investigator obtains considerable leverage if it happens that the institutional setting (as in the United States) makes it natural to assume discrete time with uniform time intervals. Other subjects may offer other kinds of "levers": You can die only once, so that cohort attrition, perhaps cause-specific, is the appropriate and central concern of mortality studies. Educational attainment, we usually assume, is irreversible: One can get more schooling, but not less, while living longer. The kind of probabilistic models suggested here would not, therefore, make sense for these topics. But competent social scientists need not be reminded that the first task in developing explanations is to get clear about what has to be explained.

The reader who is willing to take the preceding paragraph seriously will have no difficulty in formulating a severe indictment of the work we report. Let us anticipate only two devastating observations about it. First, it seems a little odd that a whole inquiry into a quintessentially political act should be carried out with virtually no reference to the content of electoral politics. In particular, a model incorporating "transfer effects" cannot be taken too seriously until there is some consideration of the possibility that the amount of transfer depends on whether one voted for the winner or for the loser or, if the former, whether one has come to regret that vote. Indeed, the "fatigue effect" mentioned above might become plausible if for each voter it were possible to estimate the balance of positive and negative reinforcement pertaining to the life history of political participation. We suspect that by the age of maximum interyear association (as calculated earlier), it is easy enough to become disillusioned with the typical outcome of American presidential politics, even for the habitual voter. (But we have only the introspection of one experienced participant observer of the aging process to support this hypothesis.)

Second, let us note that in addition to the pseudo-panel feature, the CPS design offers another lever not commonly available in surveys of the electorate. This is the practice of treating all adults in each sample household as respondents (even if all but one are allowed to respond via proxy). This means, among other things, that it is possible to compare individuals in a household. An interesting cross-classification is given, for example, in Table 17 of *Current Population Reports*, P-20, no. 405. It shows husband's turnout by wife's turnout for all married couples reporting both (that is, with DK and NR responses deleted). For the whole population of couples, we estimate the log-odds ratio measuring the association of husband's and wife's turnout in 1984 as 3.26, a magnitude quite comparable to the largest associations we observed in studying current versus retrospective turnout of the same individuals. It is quite possible that 3.26 is an overestimate, in view of the lack of independence in the reports created by the use of proxy respondents. But there is every reason to suppose that the true association is substantial. If so, then the tacit assumption of all statistical models of turnout we know of—that turnout is determined for each individual independently of every other individual—is simply wrong. This is not just a complaint that standard errors may be downwardly biased—a mere statistical issue. The point is that the sociology of the situation is all wrong. But surely sociologists, of all scientists, hardly need to be reminded that human behavior is generated by social processes, including (though not restricted to) interaction among members of primary groups.

Another paragraph could be written on the failure of the CPS or anyone else to exploit the comparative advantage of area cluster sampling—not as a sampling design per se, but as a potential resource of data relevant to studies of the impact of local political organization on turnout.

But there is no dearth of such challenges that must be invented and parried by thoughtful investigators who are willing to envision the possibility of moving a discipline immersed in data analysis—abetted, as it is, by a continuous revolution in computational technique and rapid evolution of methods of statistical inference—into the mainstream of scientific inquiry.

REFERENCES

Blau, Peter M., and Otis Dudley Duncan. 1967. *The American Occupational Structure*. New York: Wiley.

Clausen, Aage R. 1969. "Response Validity: Vote Report." *Public Opinion Quarterly* 32:588–606.

Coleman, James S. 1981. *Longitudinal Data Analysis*. New York: Basic Books.

Duncan, Otis Dudley. 1981. "Two Faces of Panel Analysis: Parallels with Comparative Cross-Sectional Analysis and Time-Lagged Association." Pp. 281–318 in *Sociological Methodology 1981*, edited by Samuel Leinhardt. San Francisco: Jossey-Bass.

————. 1983. "On a Dynamic Response Model of W. F. Kempf." *Social Science Research* 12:393–400.

————. 1985. "Some Models of Response Uncertainty for Panel Analysis." *Social Science Research* 14:126–41.

————. 1986. "Probability, Disposition, and the Inconsistency of Attitudes and Behavior." *Synthese* 68:65–98.

————. Forthcoming. "Some Ancient Anticipations of Probability." *Chance*.

Duncan, Otis Dudley, Magnus Stenbeck, and Charles J. Brody. Forthcoming. "Discovering Heterogeneity: Continuous Versus Discrete Latent Variables." *American Journal of Sociology*.

Glenn, Norval D. 1977. *Cohort Analysis*. Beverly Hills: Sage.

Glenn, Norval D., and Michael Grimes. 1968. "Aging, Voting, and Political Interest." *American Sociological Review* 33:563–75.

Hastings, Donald W., and Linda G. Berry, eds. 1979. *Cohort Analysis: A Collection of Interdisciplinary Readings*. Oxford, OH: Scripps Foundation.

Hout, Michael, Otis Dudley Duncan, and Michael E. Sobel. 1987. "Association and Heterogeneity: Structural Models of Similarities and Differences." Pp. 145–84 in *Sociological Methodology 1987*, edited by Clifford C. Clogg. Washington, DC: American Sociological Association.

Hout, Michael, and David Knoke. 1975. "Change in Voting Turnout, 1952–1972." *Public Opinion Quarterly* 39:52–68.

Kempf, W. F., and P. Hampapa. 1977. "Conditional Inference for the Dynamic Test Model." Pp. 81–100 in *Mathematical Models for Social Psychology*, edited by W. F. Kempf and B. H. Repp. New York: Wiley.

Mason, Karen Oppenheim, H. H. Winsborough, William H. Mason, and W. Kenneth Poole. 1973. "Some Methodological Issues in Cohort Analysis of Archival Data." *American Sociological Review* 38:242–58.

Mason, William M., and Stephen E. Fienberg, eds. 1985. *Cohort Analysis in Social Research*. New York: Springer-Verlag.

Pullum, Thomas W. 1980. "Separating Age, Period, and Cohort Effects in White U.S. Fertility, 1920–1970." *Social Science Research* 9:225–44.

Rasch, Georg. [1960] 1980. *Probabilistic Models for Some Intelligence and Attainment Tests*. Exp. ed. Chicago: University of Chicago Press.

Rogosa, David. 1987. "Causal Models Do Not Support Scientific Conclusions: A Comment in Support of Freedman." *Journal of Educational Statistics* 12:185–95.

Ryder, Norman B. 1965. "The Cohort as a Concept in the Study of Social Change." *American Sociological Review* 30:843–61.

Silver, Brian D., Barbara A. Anderson, and Paul R. Abramson. 1986. "Who Overreports Voting?" *American Political Science Review* 80:613–24.

U.S. Bureau of the Census. 1969. "Voting and Registration in the Election of 1968." *Current Population Reports*, ser. P-20, no. 192. Washington, DC: U.S. Government Printing Office.

——————————. 1973. "Voting and Registration in the Election of November 1972." *Current Population Reports*, ser. P-20, no. 253. Washington, DC: U.S. Government Printing Office.

——————————. 1978. "Voting and Registration in the Election of November 1976." *Current Population Reports*, ser. P-20, no. 322. Washington, DC: U.S. Government Printing Office.

——————————. 1982. "Voting and Registration in the Election of November 1980." *Current Population Reports*, ser. P-20, no. 370. Washington, DC: U.S. Government Printing Office.

——————————. 1986. "Voting and Registration in the Election of November 1984." *Current Population Reports*, ser. P-20, no. 405. Washington, DC: U.S. Government Printing Office.

2

The Life History Calendar:
A Technique for Collecting
Retrospective Data

*Deborah Freedman, Arland Thornton,
Donald Camburn, Duane Alwin
and Linda Young-DeMarco**

*This paper details the authors' selection, design, and use of a life history
calendar (LHC) to collect retrospective life course data. A sample of nine
hundred 23-year-olds, originally interviewed in 1980, were asked about the
incidence and timing of various life events in the nine years since their 15th*

This research was supported by NICHD grant R01-HD19342. A substantial part of this paper was written while Deborah Freedman was a fellow at the East-West Center Population Institute. The use of the facilities of the Population Institute are gratefully acknowledged. We benefitted from consultations with Frank Furstenberg of the University of Pennsylvania and Dick Udry of the Carolina Population Center during the planning stage of the study. Helpful comments were received from Joan Scheffler and Bruce Medbery of the Coding Section of the University of Michigan Survey Research Center and from Ronald Freedman, Karen Mason, and Barbara Anderson of the University of Michigan Population Studies Center. The following members of the field staff of the Survey Research Center provided invaluable assistance, particularly with pretesting and revising our survey instruments: Jeanne Keresztesi, Jackie Thorsby, Helen Flanagan, Marian Rowland, Helene Urbach, Elsie Bremen, Mary Jane Stacy, and Virginia Whittington. We greatly appreciate the dedicated and talented interviewers and coders of the Survey Research Center; they made the data collection a success. Keya Tucker prepared the charts and made valuable comments on the manuscript, and Marge Dalian, Donna Krips, and Judy Baughn assisted in manuscript preparation.
*The University of Michigan

birthday. The accuracy of the LHC retrospective data can be tested by comparing the 1980 reports about current activities with the 1985 LHC retrospective reports about those same activities during the 1980 interview month. The following aspects of the LHC are described: (a) the concept, uses, and advantages of the LHC, (b) the time units and domains used, (c) the mode of recording the responses and the decisions and problems involved, (d) interviewer training, and (e) coding. The following results attest to the accuracy of the LHC retrospective data: (a) only four of the calendars had missing data in any month; (b) the data obtained in 1980 about current work, school attendance, marriage, and children showed a remarkable correspondence to the retrospective 1985 LHC reports of these events; (c) the interviewers were positive about the LHC's ability to increase respondent recall.

Social scientists have become increasingly interested in the processes that underlie patterns of development, growth, and change in individuals' lives. Investigations of the dynamics of human behavior are greatly facilitated by explicitly incorporating the timing and sequencing of life course events into the research design and analysis (Marini 1984; Modell, Furstenberg, and Hershberg 1976; Modell, Furstenberg, and Strong 1978; Winsborough 1978). Of course, the life course is not a unidimensional series of events unfolding and evolving over time but a simultaneous unfolding of many dimensions, all interwoven temporally and causally in complex ways (Felmlee 1984; Goldscheider and DaVanzo 1985; Waite and Spitze 1981; Lauro 1979). The development of new and sophisticated statistical methods has facilitated and stimulated empirical estimations of dynamic causal interrelationships among various aspects of the life course (Allison 1984; Tuma and Hannan 1984).

These theoretical and statistical developments have generated a need for high-quality information about many of the activities and events that occur over significant and lengthy periods of the life course. Unfortunately, meeting these data requirements can be difficult, time consuming, and expensive.

One technique for obtaining appropriate timing data uses a continuous registration system in which all relevant activities and events are constantly reported to a statistical agency and assembled for the researcher's use. Another measurement approach utilizes the panel study, which follows and interviews the same individuals over time. However, both of these techniques are expensive and must extend over a considerable time period. In addition, unless the details of events and activities between interviews are collected retrospectively at each interview, the traditional panel study provides only multiple snapshots of individual lives.

A less expensive approach utilizes the standard cross-sectional survey to obtain retrospective information for substantial periods of the life course. This approach is limited by the well-known difficulties of obtaining reliable information retrospectively, but researchers have experimented with ways to improve the quality of retrospective data. The life history calendar (LHC) is one such tool. This paper describes the efforts of one study to utilize and refine this approach to data collection. One important advantage of this study is that it is embedded within a panel study. Thus, we can evaluate the extent to which the retrospective reports about particular events obtained with the LHC differ from the reports obtained when those events actually occurred.

In 1985, we used an LHC in the seventh wave of a panel study to obtain information from a group of young adults, each 23 years old, about the incidence and timing of various life events in the nine years since their 15th birthday. The panel study, of which the 1985 interview is the most recent phase, was begun in 1962 with interviews of the mothers of these young adults shortly after their birth. The young adults themselves were first interviewed in 1980, when they were 18.

The principal reason for using an LHC is the belief that it can improve recall by increasing the respondents' ability to place different activities within the same time frame. On a questionnaire mailed after the fieldwork, almost all the study interviewers stated that they thought the LHC improved respondent recall. A comparison of the 1985 LHC retrospective reports of specific activities and events that occurred in the 1980 interview month with the 1980 reports of those activities attests to the relative accuracy of the data collected with such a calendar. However, the use of this technique is not completely straightforward and has some potential pitfalls. Our purpose in describing our experience is to help prospective users in applying this technique and in deciding when its use is appropriate.

First, we define the LHC, note examples of its use by others, and detail its advantages. Then, we describe our experience with an LHC, beginning with our deliberations about its suitability for our purpose and continuing through the processes of calendar design, interviewer training, fieldwork, and data coding. Finally, we present some findings on the accuracy of the data collected with our LHC.

1. COLLECTING TIME-LINKED RETROSPECTIVE DATA

Information about activities across time has been collected in a number of different ways. For example, time-use studies frequently use a diary approach to record activities in a particular time period. Either the interviewer or the respondent records sequentially the time spent on each activity over the period in question (Juster and Stafford 1985).

Many studies, using a more conventional interview format, have incorporated a chart at an appropriate place within the corpus of the questionnaire to record the details of birth, marriage, work, or migration history. This is a convenient way to record a sequence of events, and the data are easier to code than data recorded in the usual question-response format.

An LHC is usually a separate document that, in essence, amalgamates the charts for a number of different event histories. An important advantage of the LHC is that it enables the researcher to relate and cross-check the timing of events across several different domains. The calendar format is usually a large grid. One dimension of the matrix details the behavioral patterns being investigated; the other dimension is divided into the time units for which these behavior patterns are to be recorded. The interviewer fills in the cells of the matrix with information provided by the respondent.

The earliest example we found of the use of an LHC was in a study done in Monterrey, Mexico, in 1967 (Balan et al. 1969). A full-scale national sample study in the U.S. in 1969 also used this technique (Blum, Karweit, and Sørensen 1969). The LHC has been used more frequently in recent years because of increased research interest in the analysis of life course events and the development of more sophisticated methods for analyzing life course data (Tuma and Hannan 1984).

Various kinds of data have been collected with an LHC. The 1969 national study cited above used an LHC to record the timing of education, employment, and family events and other information about these activities for a study of racial differences. One current study (Mason 1986) uses an LHC to obtain time-specific data on child care, mothers' work and schooling, and the presence of other adults in the household. A 1983 survey in Baltimore (Furstenberg, Brooks-Gunn, and Morgan 1987) used a calendar to record the timing of marriage, cohabitation, pregnancies, schooling, employment, and receipt of welfare over an 18-year period. Another recent survey (Kessler 1985) used an LHC to record the timing of spells of depression and the timing of other events that might trigger or exacerbate such spells. A recent study of Soviet emigres (Anderson and Silver 1986) examined the timing of work and migration in the life course.

2. ADVANTAGES OF AN LHC

A life history calendar can have two main advantages for collecting retrospective survey data. First, it can improve the quality of the retrospective data by helping the respondent to relate, both visually and mentally, the timing of several kinds of events. Events more readily remembered, such as marriages, births, and changes in geographical residence, provide important reference points for recalling less salient events, such as details of employment and living arrangements. The calendar display calls to the attention of both respondents and interviewers any inconsistencies in the timing of events between different domains. The respondents can then utilize the full pattern of their recorded life events to recall the timing of past events more accurately.

Second, very detailed sequences of events are easier to record with an LHC than with a conventional questionnaire. For example, recording monthly sequences over a period of years of the many forms of living arrangements for respondents who frequently change these arrangements would be quite complicated with a conventional questionnaire. It would require ascertaining and recording the beginning and ending dates of many short time intervals spent in each of the forms of living arrangements for which information was needed. With a calendar, the recording can be done graphically with much less difficulty, using symbols to mark the beginning and ending months and connecting them with lines to indicate continued activity.

Of course, the paramount issue in deciding whether to use an LHC is how accurately it will elicit information from the respondent. However, other considerations in adopting an LHC are also important: i.e., special coding problems, the detection and resolution of data inconsistencies, the construction of variables for analysis from detailed data, and possible additional costs. As with any complex data collection process, the advantages of the LHC are best realized if the overall plan includes careful prior consideration of how the data will be processed and used in analysis.

3. DESIGNING AND USING AN LHC

Our experience with an LHC, in the seventh wave of a panel study, involved a sample of approximately 900 young adults, each 23 years old at the time of the interview. This study began in 1962 with personal interviews with a sample of mothers living in the Detroit metropolitan area, each of whom had borne a child in July 1961 (Freedman, Thornton, and Camburn 1980; Thornton, Freedman, and Camburn 1982). The sample was divided equally between mothers for whom this birth was the first, second, or fourth. These mothers have now been interviewed six additional times by telephone. Initially, the primary focus of the study was fertility behavior, but a large body of data about many other aspects of the family was also collected, both in the initial interview and in subsequent interviews.

In 1980, the study was expanded to include personal interviews with the children whose birth made the mothers eligible for the original study (Thornton et al. 1982). Each of these children was then 18 years old. This young adult sample was interviewed again in 1985.

Over the 23 years of the study, we have retained most of our respondents. In the initial wave of the study in 1962, we completed interviews with 92 percent of the target sample of mothers. In the 1985 study, we still had 86 percent of the initial sample of mothers and 85 percent of the children born in 1961. Analysis of the small number of cases lost shows that respondent loss produced no important biases.

In the 1985 interview, an LHC was used to obtain information on various aspects of the lives of the 23-year-olds in the period since they turned 15. Our main interest was the process by which adolescents mature into adults, specifically the sequence and timing of schooling, leaving the parental home, entering the job market, and forming families. We obtained information on each of these life aspects for every month of the nine-year period between ages 15 and 23.

A truncated and reduced version of our LHC is shown in Figure 1. The vertical axis of the calendar displays the various life domains

FIGURE 1. Life History Calendar.

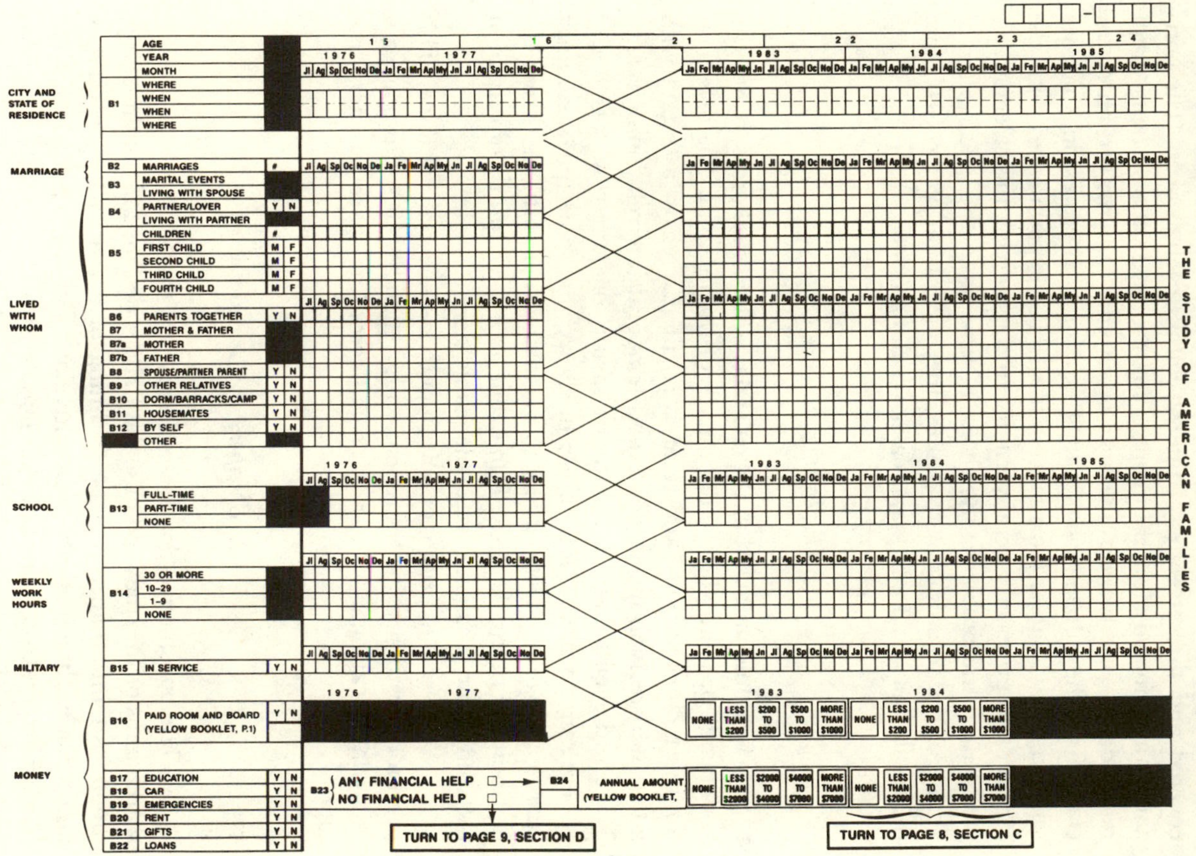

covered and the categories of interest within each domain. The horizontal axis includes all the months for the years these young adult respondents were between the ages of 15 and 23. This version of the calendar is the culmination of a long experimental process in which we selected the variables recorded on the LHC, experimented with the format, and pretested several versions. In constructing this calendar, we resolved several problems: the choice of time units, the specification of domains, the recording of responses, the integration of the LHC into the total interview format, and calendar design.

3.1. *Choosing the Time Units*

The time unit used in the calendar—day, week, month, or year —depends primarily on the data needs of the research. The investigator must choose a time unit that is small enough to ascertain with adequate precision the sequence and temporal interrelation of events. To record events that occur fairly frequently or quite close together, it is necessary to divide time rather finely. At the same time, one must consider the respondents' ability to make fine time distinctions and the feasibility of fitting the desired time unit over the required time span of the study onto a calendar of manageable size.

We used a period of one month as the unit of time. This precluded distinguishing transitions within months but still produced a fairly large calendar with only a small recording space for each time unit.

3.2. *Specifying the Domains*

The substantive domains selected for the LHC reflect the research aims of the study. Because the LHC is designed to obtain a large amount of information about the timing of activities and transitions across many time units, the substantive areas of study must be limited in number and precisely defined. The constraints of respondent time and rapport also mandate the inclusion of only the most salient aspects of each life domain. Our calendar focused on geographical residence, marital and cohabitation statuses and transitions, fertility, living arrangements, school enrollment, employment, military service, and financial interchanges between respondents and their parents.

Variables with different levels of measurement—categorical, ordinal, and interval—can be handled in an LHC. However, the level of measurement significantly influences the design of the calendar and the type of information recorded. For example, on the calendar in Figure 1, B1 (geographical residence) is a categorical variable that can include a multitude of possible locations. For marriage and cohabitation (B3 and B4), categorical variables were entered to record the events that precipitate or alter these states. In each case a separate line was provided to record, in a simple dichotomy, whether or not the respondent was living with a spouse or partner. Each childbirth (B5) and that child's residence pattern with the respondent were entered on a separate line. A series of dichotomous variables (B7–B12) records whether or not the respondent was living in various other arrangements. Most of the living arrangements (B3–B12) are not mutually exclusive, since respondents could live with several different types of people at the same time.

Interval-level variables are used to record school enrollment, employment, and financial interchanges with relatives; categories are grouped for ease of response. The categories for both school enrollment (B13) and employment (B14) are meant to be mutually exclusive as well as exhaustive. For financial interchanges (B16 and B24), only annual information was deemed feasible, so the year serves as the referent unit.

3.3. Recording the Responses

To study life course events, the researcher must ascertain the "state" of each activity in each time unit, mark the transitions between states, and identify successive "spells" of each activity. For some activities, it can be useful to document the specific type of event that produced the transition from one state to another. For example, one can identify the marital event that precipitated the move from living with a spouse to not living with a spouse: separation for marital discord, separation for other reasons, divorce, or death of spouse.

The mode of recording reflects the type of variable or domain being considered. To record time spent in an activity, we entered an X in the month the activity began, drew a line extending through the period in which the activity continued, and entered another X in the

FIGURE 2.   Recording timing of activities.

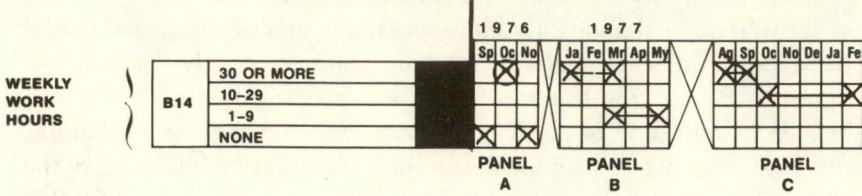

month the activity ended, as illustrated in Figure 2.[1] An activity had to continue for at least one month to be recorded in the calendar. An activity that filled an entire month but did not extend into another month was indicated by a circled X in the month of the activity (panel A). When a respondent made a transition from one category to another within a month, the ending of the first spell and the beginning of the next spell were marked in the same month (panel B). However, when the transition occurred at the juncture of two months, the ending of the first spell and the beginning of the second spell were marked in adjacent months (panel C). Thus, the calendar indicates whether specific activities began, continued, ended, or did not occur in each time unit.[2] Figure 3 illustrates the recording mode for detailing the respondent's living arrangements. The categories are not mutually exclusive, since a respondent could have lived with several persons, related to the respondent in different ways, at the same time. This example illustrates the recording of overlapping residence for a respondent who spent some periods living with varying combinations of parents, spouse, and children.

Figure 4 shows how we recorded information about a categorical variable when the universe of possible categories was so numerous that they could not possibly be precoded. The first and fourth rows of the set were used to write in the actual names of cities and states, and the second and third rows were used to define the periods the respondent was living in the specified locations. The multiple-row structure was chosen to allow ample room for interviewers to clearly write in the

---

[1] Figures 2–6 illustrate the mode of recording. Persons desiring more detailed information about the recording procedures can write the authors for a copy of the LHC instructions.

[2] Other versions of LHCs provide a single box for each year rather than demarcating the months. They attempt to provide enough space in the box to record the date that each transition occurred.

FIGURE 3.   Recording living with several kinds of persons.

					1983												1984							
				Ja	Fe	Mr	Ap	My	Jn	Jl	Ag	Sp	Oc	No	De	Ja	Fe	Mr	Ap	My	Jn	Jl	Ag	Sp	Oc	No	De

(table structure for Figure 3:)

B2	MARRIAGES	# 1
B3	MARITAL EVENTS	
	LIVING WITH SPOUSE	
B5	CHILDREN	# 1
	FIRST CHILD	M
	SECOND CHILD	M F
	THIRD CHILD	M F
	FOURTH CHILD	M F
B6	PARENTS TOGETHER	X N
B7	MOTHER & FATHER	

locations associated with each time period. One could use a similar structure to describe occupations or industries with categories too numerous to precode or to record the precise magnitude of such interval-level variables as earnings, housing costs, and number of hours worked.

Although it is possible and sometimes advantageous to record detailed information about various activities on an LHC, it can also be disadvantageous. The limited space allotted for each time unit on most calendars makes it difficult to record the information in readable form. But a greater limitation is that recording such information on the LHC can make it more difficult to quickly check the consistency of timing data across domains. As Figures 2–5 show, the mode of recording timing data with X's and lines provides a clear picture of time spent in each activity. Recording detailed information between those lines could limit the value of the calendar as a visual device for recalling information and detecting inconsistencies. Calendar entries on the timing of life course events are useful for detecting inconsistencies only if the respondent and interviewer can read them quickly and easily.

FIGURE 4.   Recording places of residence.

There are ways to enter detailed information about particular activities on an LHC without decreasing the usefulness of the calendar format for detecting inconsistencies. For example, one could record occupation and industry data for each segment of the employment history on the last lines of the calendar, preferably right below the employment line, and not impede the interviewer's ability to check for inconsistencies within the body of the calendar. When the calendar space is inadequate for recording the detail needed for occupation and industry, each job segment could be numbered on the calendar and the interviewer could record the needed information about each segment in the main body of the questionnaire.

Our LHC provides an example of how one can record detailed descriptions on an LHC without impairing the calendar's usefulness for detecting inconsistencies. The geographic lines at the top of the calendar require detailed descriptions, but their placement outside the main body of the timing lines preserves the usefulness of the calendar for resolving inconsistencies.

The marriage lines were used to record information about marital states (Figure 5). The initiation and resumption of each marriage were recorded on the marital events row, and a number was used to identify the spouse as the first, second, etc. Each spouse retained his or her own specific identifying number for any reconciliation or remarriage to the same person. Interruptions in a marriage were identified as separations due to estrangement (S) or absences for other reasons (A); divorces were coded with a D and widowhood with a W. These codes were inserted in the marital events line of B3. On the following line, labeled "living with spouse," X's and lines were used to denote periods of marital cohabitation.

A similar set of codes and procedures was used to record cohabitation without marriage (B4). The first row, "partner/lover," identified transitions into and out of cohabiting unions using the marital coding scheme. Marital and nonmarital cohabiting partners

FIGURE 5.   Recording marriage and cohabitation.

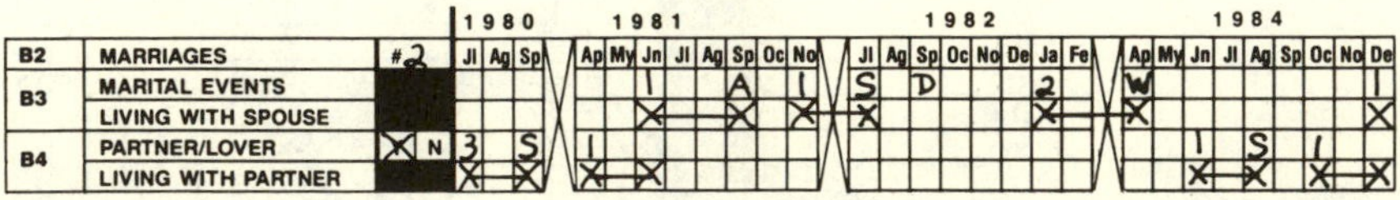

were linked by assigning the appropriate spousal number to a cohabiting partner whom the respondent later married. Cohabiting partners whom the respondent did not marry were assigned numbers following those used for spouses. For never-married respondents, all cohabiting sequences were entered in order and the partners were numbered accordingly.

Figure 5 illustrates the entries made in the marriage and cohabitation lines for a respondent who married in June 1981, lived apart from her husband from September to November 1981 when he had a job elsewhere, became estranged in July 1982, and divorced in September. She married a different person in January 1983, was widowed in April 1984, and remarried her first husband in December 1984. The events are recorded in the first line of B3, and the periods in which she actually lived with her spouse are recorded in the next row. Line B4 shows that she began cohabiting with her first husband in April 1981 and continued so until she married him in June 1981. In June 1984, she moved in with her first husband again, left because of a quarrel in August 1984, joined him again in October, and then cohabited with him until their remarriage in December 1984. She had cohabited with another man, whom she never married, from July 1980 until September 1980, when they separated.

For school enrollment and employment, only timing data were entered, using the system of X's and lines. The categories in these two domains were designed to be mutually exclusive and exhaustive. However, a person who switched between categories in one month would have entries in two different categories for that month.

The categories for financial interchanges were precoded so that the interviewer could check the appropriate calendar box, exactly as in a standard interview format.

3.4. *Integrating the LHC into the Total Interview Format*

There are a number of different ways to integrate an LHC into the total interview format. The LHC could comprise the first part of the interview, and the more usual questionnaire format could be used to obtain the desired additional information. Alternatively, a researcher might choose to alternate the LHC questions about timing in each domain with a set of questions in the usual questionnaire format to obtain additional information about the activities in that domain. We know of no empirical studies of the optimal way to integrate an LHC into a conventional interview format.

Interposing noncalendar questions from the other part of the questionnaire between portions of the calendar interview has some advantages. First, questions in the questionnaire can build on the timing sequences obtained in a particular calendar domain. The placement of these questions right after the calendar questions on that subject could make for greater consistency and avoid the repetition of some timing questions. Second, asking a set of related questions may clarify for the respondent the definition and inclusiveness of the concepts in the calendar.

The combination of formats also has disadvantages. Alternating between the LHC and other types of questions could confuse the respondent and decrease rapport. Moreover, interrupting the flow of the LHC could decrease its effectiveness as an aid to the respondent in recalling the timing of activities and in detecting inconsistencies between entries in the various domains.

In our survey, which separated the LHC completely from the other sections of the questionnaire, we had excellent rapport and believe we obtained good data. We do not know whether rapport or data quality would have suffered from an alternate strategy. Other studies have almost fully integrated the calendar into the other part of the questionnaire, shifting continuously between the two interviewing modes (Furstenberg et al. 1987).

3.5. *Designing the LHC*

Several elements of calendar design and format can facilitate the recording and checking of entries in the LHC.

1. The various domains and the categories within domains should be separated with prominent lines or spaces to keep the categories distinct across the span of the calendar. Our calendar, in addition to leaving blank spaces between the domains, printed the name of the item to be recorded several times along the line in a very faint underlay of blue letters to help the interviewer identify the correct line for entering a particular data item.

2. The organization of the domains in the LHC, indicated in the vertical stub of our calendar, can provide a framework for the interviewing process. Interviewers were told to inquire about all life events

of one kind before proceeding to the next domain. This gave a uniformity to the interviewing process and minimized the likelihood of omitted items. The stub also contained screening devices to simplify the interviewing. For life aspects not universally experienced, a screening question first ascertained whether or not an event occurred in the life of each respondent, and this was recorded in the small boxes provided in the stub. For example, our interviewers asked if the respondent had been married (and how often), had children (number and sex), and had experienced various kinds of living arrangements. The screening responses routed the interview around nonapplicable questions and showed the coders whether the absence of contingent entries stemmed from interviewer oversight.

3. Time intervals should be well demarcated. Following a category within a domain across the time span and entering the events in the correct months can be difficult, so we repeated the labels for the years and months at several intervals down the length of the calendar to help the interviewer and the coder clearly identify the space reserved for each time period. Alternating the background color of the columns for adjacent years helped the interviewer and respondent identify the correct year.

Since all our LHC respondents were born in the same month and year, we could easily print the correct calendar and respondent age labels on the appropriate calendar columns. This provided helpful temporal orientation for our respondents, enabling them to easily identify a particular year and their age status in that year. For varied age samples, the calendar would have to be adapted at the time of the interview by inserting the appropriate age and calendar year labels for each respondent.

Our pretest provided some experience with handling a group of respondents of varying ages. If we obtained the respondent's birth date when the interview was scheduled, we prepared a personalized calendar for that respondent by writing in the correct age and calendar year labels. If this was not possible, we used the first few minutes of the interview time to write in the identifying age and date labels. Another solution would be to provide a sticky tape printed with the calendar years; this could be attached at the time of the interview to identify the calendar years corresponding to the ages of the respondent.

4. The interviewers should be able to easily correct entries as they or the respondents identify inconsistencies across domains. The

calendar should be printed on paper that can withstand frequent erasures, and the writing instrument should produce legible but easily erasable entries.[3]

5. Finally, an attractive professional-appearing calendar can improve respondent rapport and foster greater interest among the interviewers.

4. THE STRUCTURE OF THE LHC INTERVIEW

The potential of the LHC for improving recall can be affected by both the format of the interview and the structure of the questions. There has been considerable variation across studies using LHCs in the degree of structure in both interview format and question style. In one relatively unstructured three-country migration study (Hawley 1984; McDevitt et al. 1986), the interviewers were given an LHC grid containing the domains and time periods and were instructed to fill in the wanted events in the grid. The order and nature of the questions asked were left up to the interviewer.

Another study used a somewhat more structured format: The interviewer was instructed to use one area of the LHC as a focus and to record the changes over time in that area; then, they were to relate those changes to changes in the other areas (Smith and Karim 1980; Fricke, Syed, and Smith 1986). The choice of the initial focus depended on the respondent's particular history and life cycle stage. The interviewer was directed to shift to a different focus when the timing of those events became more central. Examples of the kinds of questions to be used in the interview were provided in the instruction booklet, but no specific question sets were mandated.

A study done in 1983 by Furstenberg used a completely structured interview with specified questions (see Furstenberg et al. 1987). All the LHC questions were incorporated into the main questionnaire document, and the answers for certain sets of those questions were recorded on the LHC.

Our LHC used a fairly structured format with an initial mandated question (or two) for each domain. The interviewer introduced the LHC by saying, "Now I would like to ask you about some of

---

[3] We used an erasable pen, which provided the legibility of an inked line but enabled interviewers to erase during the interview and even several hours later.

the important things you have been doing since you were 15. To help record this information, I am going to use this calendar." Then the interviewer explained the LHC to the respondents so they could understand its layout and use it as an aid in reporting information. The instruction manual suggested the following explanation as a guide: "As you can see, we have the years going across the top; they begin in July 1976, on your birthday, and extend to the present. For those years, I will be asking you about the things listed along the side here—where you lived and whom you lived with, any marriages, any children you may have had, schools you may have attended, and when you were employed."

The interviewer was instructed to begin with questions about the first activity line (the respondent's geographic residence), follow that over the total time period, and then ask in turn the needed questions for each set of activities listed in the stub of the calendar. The initial questions for each activity were incorporated in the questionnaire and were asked precisely as they were written. For example, the interviewer started with B1 and asked, "Let's begin by talking about where you lived during those years. In what city and state were you living when you turned 15." When that was recorded she asked, "Until what month and year did you live there?" If the respondent's residence had changed, the interviewer asked, "Where did you live next?" These two questions were asked until geographic residence was established for the entire period.

The interviewer then asked about marital events, beginning with the question, "Have you ever been married?" and then using the probing questions to obtain all the needed information about any marriages. Each activity line was completely finished before the next line was started, and the entire calendar was completed in the order shown in the vertical stub.

A series of probes was mandated for each activity, but these were not incorporated in the questionnaire. Instead, the interviewers were asked to memorize the probes needed to follow up the introductory questions for each activity. (The probes were also printed on 5×8 cards for reference during the interview, if necessary.) This procedure had some costs, since it required substantial memorization ability and since there was some danger of changes in the language of the probes over time. However, including the probes in the formal questionnaire would also have had substantial costs, since it would have required a fairly complicated and lengthy series of skip patterns to sort out those probing questions relevant for each respondent's particular life pattern in each activity.

The probes for cohabitation illustrate this dilemma. The opening question about cohabitation, the one printed on the questionnaire, is, "Have you *ever* lived together as a partner in an intimate relationship with a (man/woman) without being married to (him/her)?" For all ever-married respondents, the probes are as follows:

1. Did you live together with your (first, etc.) (husband/wife) before you married (him/her)?
2. When did you and your (first, etc.) (husband/wife) start living together?
3. Did you and your (first, etc.) (husband/wife) live together continuously until you were married, or did you live apart for a month or more because you were not getting along or for some other reason?
4. Was this because of difficulty in your relationship or for some other reason?
5. When did this happen?
6. Did you and your (first, etc.) (husband/wife) live together again before you married (him/her)?
7. Was there any other (man/woman) you lived together with as a partner in an intimate relationship without being married to (him/her)?
8. In what month and year was the (first/next) other time you lived with a (man/woman) without being married?
9. When did you and your partner stop living together for any reason after that?
10. Was there any other (man/woman) you lived together with as a partner in an intimate relationship without being married to (him/her)?

A similar series of probes was provided for respondents who never married.

The length and complexity of this set of probes demonstrates the conflict between maintaining the precise language of the probes and preserving the ease of the interviewing process. Incorporating in the questionnaire all the probes needed to determine those cohabitation periods involving a spouse and the extent and nature of all possible breaks and resumptions in each cohabitation spell would require a lengthy and complicated questionnaire that could impede the interviewing process, a cost that must be weighed against the possible gain in probing accuracy.

5. INTERVIEWER TRAINING

Our LHC instrument necessitated more intensive interviewer training than was needed for the previous waves of this study, which did not use an LHC. We used only experienced interviewers, each of whom had participated in previous field studies and had received the initial week of training given all newly recruited interviewers at Michigan's Survey Research Center. Still, the training for our specific study required six days in all, an initial five-day session and one review session after the interviewing began. This is triple the training time used for experienced interviewers in the previous waves of our study.

The training began with an explanation of the layout and structure of the calendar. Next, a script of a life story and a filled-in calendar recording the life events in the story were used to explain how to record those events. Then, the research director conducted a detailed mock-up interview, filling in the appropriate entries for the responses on a projection screen on transparencies that replicated the calendar pages. The interviewers next practiced interviewing with prepared life scripts, taking turns at being the respondent. The trainers observed and corrected their technique and reviewed the accuracy of their completed calendars.

Training the interviewers to use the probes effectively was particularly difficult. The trainers had to demonstrate proper probing techniques frequently and had to show how departures from the proscribed probing method could result in errors and faulty data. Another problem was that interviewers sometimes did not adequately simulate respondents in practice sessions. They tended to provide the correct information to their partner even when the probing was inadequate, thus impeding the mastery of the probes.

One week after the interviewing began, the research staff held an additional day of training to detect and resolve problems. The staff personally edited the interview schedules, and individual conferences were scheduled with interviewers as problems surfaced.

6. FIELDWORK

There are special logistical problems in conducting an interview with an LHC. First, there is one more document to manage. Second, the desired facilities for an LHC interview, a table and chairs enabling the respondent and interviewer to sit side by side and *view* the total calendar, were sometimes lacking. Each interviewer was given a clip board of calendar size to serve as an alternative writing surface and to facilitate sharing the calendar with the respondent. Unfortunately, the clip board for our large calendar ($12'' \times 25''$) was awkward for the interviewers to carry. A smaller calendar would have fit more easily into a briefcase, but it would have been less useful for recording.

When possible, the LHCs were administered in personal interviews. However, respondents who lived outside of our travel range were interviewed by phone; local interviewers were not recruited. Given the complexity of the LHC, we felt that data obtained over the phone by our well-trained interviewers would be better than data obtained in a personal interview by someone who had not participated in our training sessions. Telephone interviews do lack the visual advantage that the LHC provides for the respondent in a personal interview. However, the interviewer can still utilize the calendar to detect discrepancies and provide feedback to the respondent about possible inconsistencies. The respondent, once aware of these errors, can usually reconstruct the proper sequences of events. In this way, the interviewer can use the full spectrum of the calendar to help the respondent relate past events more accurately.

A calendar as long and complex as the one used in our study would not be a feasible instrument for a mail questionnaire. However, a study using a simpler LHC might well use the mails for respondents who cannot be reached otherwise.

7. EDITING THE LHC

A large part of the editing process took place during the interview. The interviewers were trained to check the finished calendar to detect various kinds of inconsistencies and to resolve them with the respondent. An interviewer would typically say, "I seem to have recorded something wrong. Can you help me straighten it out?" Some examples of such inconsistencies are as follows:

1. The status of the respondent in each activity had to be recorded in every month of the LHC. Any months in which there were no entries for these items had to be identified and resolved with the respondent.
2. The "lived with whom" category required careful editing. Although a respondent could be living with several different types of individuals (parent, other relatives, and spouse) at the same time, some combinations were not possible. A respondent could not live with both mother and father (B7) and at the same time with just mother or just father (B7a, B7b). A respondent could not live alone and be simultaneously living with anyone else. Residence with a spouse required a marital event.
3. All filter questions in the calendar stub had to be answered, and the responses had to match the recorded experiences.
4. A respondent could not simultaneously be recorded in more than one category of schooling or work, although a transition between categories was correctly recorded with an X in each month of the transition.

The next stage in the editing process was done by the coders, who edited each calendar before the actual coding. A significant minority of the interviews were also check edited by the research director. The coders were given a list of editing instructions noting possible discrepancies and distinguishing between those discrepancies that the coders could resolve and those that had to be resolved by the research director.

Some examples of ambiguities that the coders could resolve include the following:

1. When a transition between two categories of an activity had been recorded properly with X's but one line had not been drawn, coders could draw the missing activity line.
2. When the number of marriages was left blank but the marriages were all recorded properly on the line, the number box could be filled in accordingly.

3. All entries on the residual "other" line in the "living with whom" category were reviewed for possible reclassification. Some reclassifications, such as changing stepmother to the "other relative" line or changing friend to the "housemate" line, could be handled by the coder. Any doubtful cases were to be referred to the research director.

We did not record the number of calendars with ambiguous information requiring resolution by the research director, but our perception is that there were few. A number of ambiguities involved the "living with whom" domain: The residual category "other" was initially used for kibbutz or commune living, living with a family as a personal aid, and living with a boy friend's relatives or the parents of an ex-fiancee. The individuals in these situations were all changed to "housemates."

The small number of substantive editing problems and the relatively minor problems detected in the editing process indicate the high quality of the data obtained with the LHC. The entire editing process, of course, was confined solely to the 1985 data; we did not use any of the 1980 data.

8. CODING THE DATA

An LHC is more difficult and expensive to code than a conventional questionnaire because it usually involves fairly detailed entries. The large number of data points needed to code the various activities makes the coding process both lengthy and difficult. For example, our calendar generated about 3,100 variables (114 data points for each of 27 different activities). The desirability of 100 percent check coding to ensure accuracy also adds to the expense. Because many of the various life course activities are interrelated, coding errors in one activity line can create a discrepancy within a related activity.

The timing data could have been coded in several ways. We chose to code the "state" of each activity in each month—i.e., whether or not that activity was engaged in during that time period. Alternatively, we could have coded only beginning and ending months, which would define a spell of activity, and the intervening states could have been filled in later on the data tape.

FIGURE 6. Recording different sequences of living with parents and spouse.

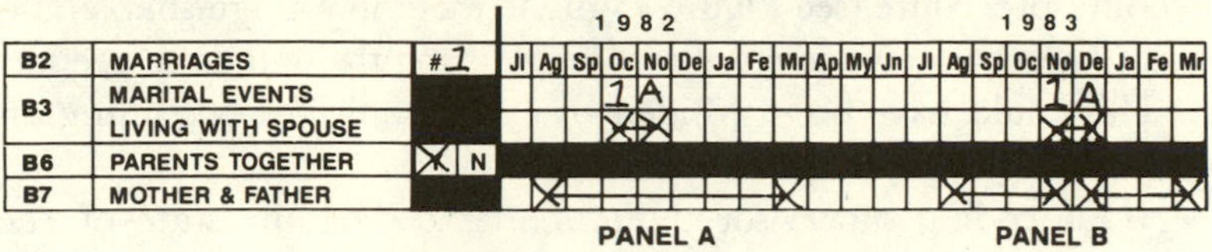

PANEL A   PANEL B

FIGURE 7. Coding of data as recorded in Figure 6.

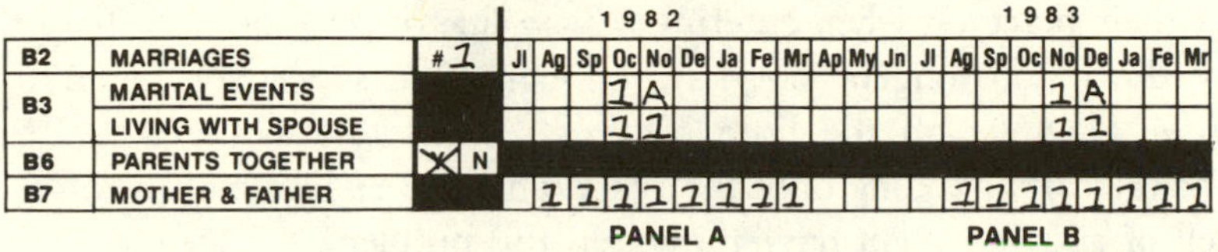

PANEL A   PANEL B

To code our study, we entered the calendar data directly onto the computer using a direct data entry program. A single line of the calendar, complete with labels for months and years, was displayed on the computer screen. The line was broken into three segments, because the width of the computer screen could not accommodate the entire line. For each item, the coders entered a 1 in each month to indicate participation or a 0 to indicate nonparticipation.[4] This produced a coded line with a format very much like the actual filled-in calendar line. We thought this would foster coding accuracy.

In retrospect, this coding scheme created some problems. In domains in which categories were not mutually exclusive, it failed to identify unique beginnings and endings of all spells. Figure 6 illustrates the recording of two situations: In panel A, a spouse joined the respondent in the parental household one month and moved out the next; in panel B, the respondent moved from the parental home into a spousal household one month and then moved back the next. The

---

[4] Each activity line was coded separately. Therefore, if two similar events took place in the same month, such as living with both mother and spouse, each event was coded in that month on its own line. The categories of schooling and work are mutually exclusive. Therefore, only in a month of transition between categories in those domains could there be an entry in the same month in two of the lines, denoting the end of one level of an activity and the beginning of a different level.

recording mode clearly distinguishes these two different situations, but the coding procedure (see Figure 7) made them indistinguishable. This difficulty necessitated a lengthy recoding during the data tape preparation. This could have been avoided by coding only the beginning and ending months of each spell.

Our coding supervisor thought that coding the state of each activity in every month compounded the usual problems of boredom and inaccuracy associated with coding routines. Although the years and months were printed above each segment, the coders sometimes lost their place or, when entering a long line of zeros or ones, held the key down too long or not long enough. The supervisor noted that "after a while, all the little squares seemed to run together." She concluded that coding only the beginning and ending months of each spell of activity might have mitigated this problem.

9. MANAGING THE DATA

A life history calendar can produce a rich set of variables for the analysis of life course events, but managing the data set can be costly. The costs stem primarily from the nature of the data set and the uses for which it is designed. The extensive set of timing variables that can be constructed from the data collected in an LHC expands the research possibilities but can also increase the data management costs. The incidence and timing of each activity is different for each individual; therefore, to construct variables for the inception, span, termination, and interrelationship of the various activities, the researcher must search through the LHC events on the data tape for each individual to locate the relevant items. This is a time-consuming and costly procedure. Constructing the timing variables for studying life course events can be quite complicated, and few ready-made programs are available for this task. Each new variable will probably require a fairly large input of programming time, and a number of programs will probably need to be revised and tested before they can accomplish the desired task.

10. THE RELIABILITY OF THE LHC DATA

The data obtained with our LHC appear to be quite reliable. Although we have no tests of the validity or accuracy of the data, we have some evidence, detailed below, of their reliability.

1. Among the approximately 900 LHCs collected and processed in the study, there are only four in the final data set that have months with no data.
2. The data collected retrospectively with the LHC in 1985 concerning events in the 1980 interview month correspond highly with the data collected at the time of the event in 1980.[5] Such comparisons between 1980 and 1985 data are available for the following items: whether the respondent had ever been married at the time of the 1980 interview, and the month and year of such marriages; the incidence and dates of births up to the 1980 interview; and work and school attendance in the 1980 interview month.
3. The match between the 1985 and 1980 data is not affected by the 1985 interview mode. There is no discernable difference between the data collected by telephone in 1985 and the data collected by personal interview.

10.1. *Marital and Birth Events*

The incidence and timing of the births and marriages reported in 1980 correspond highly with the retrospective reports of these events in 1985. In the 1980 interviews, 28 respondents reported that they had been married; in the 1985 interviews, 26 of these individuals reported the same marriage dates they reported in 1980. The reports of the other two differed by one and three months respectively. In 1980, 855 respondents reported that they had never been married. In the 1985 calendar, 852 of these respondents again reported that they had not been married by 1980. Of the remaining three cases, two reported that they married in the 1980 interview month (and thus did not necessarily give discrepant reports), and one reported that she/he married in the month before the 1980 interview.

[5] To facilitate comparison, we tried to duplicate the phrasing of the 1980 questions in the 1985 questions. However, the technical differences between the LHC and the standard questionnaire created some small differences in the questions for schooling and work. In 1980, respondents were asked about current work and schooling, but they were not asked to specify how long activities had lasted. In the 1985 interview, schooling or work activity in the 1980 interview month was recorded only if it had occurred during that month (though it did not have to fill the entire month) and only if it had lasted at least one month. Copies of the exact questions used in the two surveys for the compared items can be obtained from the authors.

Only ten of the ever-married respondents reported a birth in 1980. For nine of these respondents, the 1980 and 1985 month and year reports matched exactly; the discrepant report erred by only one month.

10.2. *School Attendance*

Table 1 shows the respondents' reports of their 1980 school attendance in the 1980 interview and in the 1985 LHC. This table shows the aggregate distributions of students who attended part time, full time, and not at all during the 1980 interview month, as measured in 1980 and 1985. The responses are remarkably consistent between the two interviews.

The cross-tabulations of the 1980 and 1985 responses reported in Table 2 again show a considerable degree of consistency between the interviews; 87 percent of the respondents (694 out of 797) gave identical answers about school attendance in both interviews. (In each schooling category column, the number of respondents who gave identical answers is circled.) When we restrict our comparison to those who attended school and those who did not, we find that 91 percent of the respondents gave the same answers in 1980 and 1985.

There appears to be no directional bias towards reporting school attendance: Those who attended full time in 1980 were just as likely (about 7 percent) to report in 1985 that they did not attend full time as

TABLE 1

Distribution of School Attendance in 1980, as Measured in 1980 and 1985

	1980		1985	
	N	%	N	%
Full-time attendance	385	48	394	49
Part-time attendance	67	9	48	6
No attendance	345	43	355	45
Total	797	100	797	100

Note. This analysis excludes the 85 respondents who said in 1980 that they were in high school, since these respondents were not asked whether they attended full or part time. In 1985, 75 of these respondents (88 percent) said that they were attending school in the month of the 1980 interview.

TABLE 2

Cross-Tabulation of 1980 and 1985 Responses about School Attendance

	1980 Response							
	Full-time Attendance		Part-time Attendance		No Attendance		Total	
1985 Response	N	%	N	%	N	%	N	%
Full-time attendance	(358)	93	22	33	14	4	394	49
Part-time attendance	13	3	(20)	30	14	4	48	6
No attendance	14	4	25	37	(316)	92	355	45
Total	385	100	67	100	345	100	797	100

Note: The number of respondents who gave identical answers in both interviews is circled. This analysis excludes the 85 respondents who said in 1980 that they were in high school, since these respondents were not asked whether they attended full or part time. In 1985, 75 of these respondents (88 percent) said that they were attending school in the month of the 1980 interview.

those who were out of school in 1980 were to change their response from no attendance to some schooling in 1985. Part-time school attendance was remembered less well than either full-time attendance or no attendance. Of the 67 respondents who indicated in 1980 that they attended school part time, one third said in 1985 that they had attended part time, one third said that they had attended full time, and one third said that they had not attended at all during that month.

10.3. *Employment Status*

Table 3 displays the respondents' 1980 and 1985 reports of their paid employment during the 1980 interview month, subdivided into three categories: no work, part-time work (1–29 hours), and full-time work (30 plus hours).[6] The 1980 and 1985 responses about work are somewhat less consistent than the responses about schooling. The data

[6] The questionnaire included two categories for part-time work: 1–9 hours and 10–29 hours. However, because only 38 respondents indicated at each interview that they had worked 1–9 hours, the two categories were merged.

TABLE 3

Distribution of Employment Status in 1980, as Measured in 1980 and 1985

	1980		1985	
	N	%	N	%
Full-time employment[a]	300	35	367	42
Part-time employment[b]	236	27	240	28
No employment	332	38	261	30
Total	868	100	868	100

Note. This analysis excludes the 10 respondents who said in 1980 that they were in the military.

[a] Full-time employment is 30 or more hours per week.

[b] Part-time employment is less than 30 hours per week.

show an aggregate shift in reports of work status; 8 percent fewer of the respondents reported no work in 1985 than in 1980.

Table 4 shows the cross-tabulations of the 1980 and 1985 responses about employment. Again, the responses show that there is more divergence in reports of work activity between 1980 and 1985 than in reports of schooling. Still, if we dichotomize the variable,

TABLE 4

Cross-Tabulation of 1980 and 1985 Responses about Employment

	Full-time Employment		Part-time Employment		No Employment		Total	
1985 Response	N	%	N	%	N	%	N	%
Full-time employment[a]	(249)	83	63	27	55	17	367	42
Part-time employment[b]	31	10	(153)	65	56	17	240	28
No employment	20	7	20	8	(221)	66	261	30
Total	300	100	236	100	332	100	868	100

Note: The number of respondents who gave identical answers in both interviews is circled. This analysis excludes the 10 respondents who said in 1980 that they were in the military.

[a] Full-time employment is 30 or more hours per week.

[b] Part-time employment is less than 30 hours per week.

restricting the categories to some work and no work, we find that 83 percent of the respondents in 1985 confirmed their 1980 report. Even when we match the responses over the full spectrum of work hours, we find that 72 percent of the respondents gave identical answers in 1980 and 1985.

It is not surprising that the reports about schooling are more consistent over time than the reports about work. School attendance at age 18 represents a long-term commitment, while gainful employment changes more frequently. Thus, recollection of the incidence of work in a particular month might be less reliable than the recollection of school attendance. Respondents in 1985 appear to have noticeable bias towards reporting that they had worked in 1980 when they had indicated otherwise in the 1980 interview. Of the respondents who said in 1980 that they were not working, one third said in 1985 that they had done some work in the 1980 interview month. But of the respondents who reported in 1980 that they were working, either full or part time, only 7 or 8 percent reported in 1985 that they had not worked.

10.4. *Interviewing Mode Differences*

Approximately 55 percent of the 1985 respondents were interviewed in person, and approximately 45 percent were interviewed by telephone. This enabled us to compare the consistency between the 1980 and 1985 responses in each interview mode. We found that the two modes produced almost the same degree of consistency between the 1980 and 1985 reports of schooling and work.

10.5. *The Interviewers' Appraisal of the Accuracy and Convenience of the LHC*

Twenty-two of the 23 interviewers in our study responded to a mail questionnaire about their experience with the LHC. Twenty-one of the interviewers reported that the respondents found the LHC interesting, and 17 of these said that the respondents expressed more than a little interest. Nineteen out of 22 said that it would have been harder to obtain the detailed LHC information with a conventional questionnaire, and 3 said that it would have been "about the same." Eighteen of the 22 interviewers believed that the LHC obtained higher-quality data than would have been obtained with a standard questionnaire, 13 believed that the LHC data were much better, and none of the interviewers believed that the LHC data were worse.

The interviewers gave several reasons for considering the LHC an easier and more accurate technique for collecting these life course data, such as "the LHC was a visual aid for the respondent," "it jogged their memories," "respondents found it enjoyable," respondents found it "less tedious," "it made them more cooperative, less placid," "respondents saw the gaps and inconsistencies instantly," and "it helped them detect and correct recall errors."

11. DISCUSSION

The LHC used in this study seems to have yielded high-quality retrospective data. The very small number of nonresponse items on the LHC, the close correspondence between the 1980 and 1985 responses, and the interviewers' reports about the usefulness of the LHC for aiding respondent recall suggest that an LHC can be an important vehicle for improving the quality of retrospective data.

One important issue in obtaining retrospective data appears to be the degree of volatility of the activity patterns, since respondents find it more difficult to recall widely fluctuating event patterns. The greater accuracy of our schooling data, as compared with our employment data, probably reflects the greater volatility of work patterns. Thus, in selecting variables for a retrospective study, the researcher should be aware that highly variable events will probably be measured less accurately than other events. Still, the LHC enables the researcher to link volatile events to less varying activity patterns and thus improves the accuracy of the data.

The volatility of life events and thus the reliability of recall may also vary with the age of the respondents. However, we have no way of knowing whether the activity patterns of older respondents are more or less volatile than those of our respondents. Most of our respondents had left high school eight to ten months before their 1980 interview. Many were making tentative decisions about school, work, and living arrangements, which for some involved frequent changes. It is possible that a similar study of 30-year-olds might show larger discrepancies between current and retrospective measures, but we have no way of knowing whether the accuracy of the data would be different in an older sample.

Although an LHC has great potential for improving data quality, it can only reach this potential if it is designed and implemented carefully. Unfortunately, because of the relative newness of this technique, researchers can draw on only a limited body of prior experience. What we have tried to do here is share our experience with such a calendar, noting the problems we encountered, the mistakes we made, and the techniques that proved useful, with the hope that other researchers can benefit from our experience.

REFERENCES

Allison, Paul D. 1984. *Event History Analysis*. Beverly Hills: Sage.

Anderson, Barbara, and Brian Silver. 1986. "The Validity of Survey Responses: Interviews of Multiple Respondents in a Household from a Survey of Soviet Emigrants." Research Report No. 86-89. Ann Arbor: University of Michigan, Population Studies Center.

Balan, Jorge, Harley L. Browning, Elizabeth Jelin, and Lee Litzler. 1969. "A Computerized Approach to the Processing and Analysis of Life Histories Obtained in Sample Surveys." *Behavioral Science* 14:105–20.

Blum, Zahava, Nancy Karweit, and Aage Sørensen. 1969. "A Method for the Collection and Analysis of Retrospective Life Histories." Report No. 48. Baltimore: Johns Hopkins University, Center for the Social Organization of Schools.

Felmlee, Diane H. 1984. "A Dynamic Analysis of Women's Employment Exits." *Demography* 21:171–84.

Freedman, Deborah, Arland Thornton, and Donald Camburn. 1980. "Maintaining Response Rates in Longitudinal Studies." *Sociological Methods and Research* 9:87–98.

Fricke, Thomas E., Sabiha H. Syed, and Peter C. Smith. 1986. "Rural Punjabi Social Organization and Marriage Timing Strategies in Pakistan." *Demography* 23:489–508.

Furstenberg, Frank, J. Brooks-Gunn, and S. Philip Morgan. 1987. *Adolescent Mothers in Later Life*. New York: Cambridge University Press.

Goldscheider, Frances Kobrin, and Julie DaVanzo. 1985. "Living Arrangements and the Transition to Adulthood." *Demography* 22:545–63.

Hawley, Amos. 1984. "Economic and Social Facets of Migration in Thailand, Egypt, and Colombia." Final Report to the National Institute of Child Health and Human Development for Grant HD-14943. Chapel Hill: University of North Carolina, Carolina Population Center.

Juster, F. Thomas, and Frank P. Stafford. 1985. *Time, Goods, and Well-Being*. Ann Arbor: University of Michigan, Institute for Social Research.

Kessler, Ronald. 1985. "A Study of Life Events in Everyday Experience." Unpublished manuscript. Ann Arbor: University of Michigan, Institute for Social Research.

Lauro, Donald. 1979. "Life History Matrix Analysis: A Progress Report." Pp. 134–54 in *Residence History Analysis*, edited by Robin Pryor. Canberra: Australian National University Press.

Marini, Margaret Mooney. 1984. "Age and Sequencing Norms in the Transition to Adulthood." *Social Forces* 63:229–44.

Mason, Karen. 1986. "Detroit Child Care Study." Unpublished manuscript. Ann Arbor: University of Michigan, Population Studies Center.

McDevitt, Thomas, Amos Hawley, J. Richard Udry, Saad Gadalla, Boonlert Leoprapai, and Ramiro Cardona. 1986. "Migration Plans of the Rural Populations of Third World Countries: A Probit Analysis of Micro-Level Data from Asia, Africa, and Latin America." *Journal of Developing Areas* 20:473–90.

Modell, John, Frank Furstenberg, and Theodore Hershberg. 1976. "Social Change and Transitions to Adulthood in Historical Perspective." *Journal of Family History* 1:7–33.

Modell, John, Frank Furstenberg, and Douglas Strong. 1978. "The Timing of Marriage in the Transition to Adulthood: Continuity and Change, 1960–1975." Pp. 120–50 in *Turning Points: Historical and Sociological Essays on the Family*, vol. 84, edited by John Demos and Sarane Spence Boocock. Chicago: University of Chicago Press.

Smith, Peter C., and Mentab Karim. 1980. "Urbanization, Education, and Marriage Patterns: Four Cases from Asia." Research Paper No. 70. Honolulu: East-West Population Institute.

Thornton, Arland, Deborah Freedman, and Donald Camburn. 1982. "Obtaining Respondent Cooperation in Family Panel Studies." *Sociological Methods and Research* 11:33–51.

Tuma, Nancy Brandon, and Michael T. Hannan. 1984. *Social Dynamics: Models and Methods*. New York: Academic Press.

Waite, Linda J., and Glenna D. Spitze. 1981. "Young Women's Transition to Marriage." *Demography* 18:681–94.

Winsborough, Halliman H. 1978. "Statistical Histories of the Life Cycle of Birth Cohorts: The Transition from Schoolboy to Adult Male." Pp. 231–60 in *Social Demography*, edited by Karl E. Taeuber, Larry L. Bumpass, and James A. Sweet. New York: Academic Press.

3

Threshold Models of Diversity: Chinese Restaurants, Residential Segregation, and the Spiral of Silence

Mark Granovetter* and Roland Soong†

In many binary decisions, a person's choice depends in part on the composition of the group that has already made one or the other choice. In deciding whether to live in a neighborhood, a person may consider the ethnic composition of the neighborhood. In deciding whether to speak out on a public issue, a person may consider the proportion of previously expressed opinions that are the same as his. Substantial literatures have grown up around these two examples, which go under the rubrics of residential tipping and pluralistic ignorance. We develop a mathematical model that applies to all such binary situations and illustrate it especially by the examples of residential segregation and public opinion. The model builds on and generalizes previous work on these subjects, and it is related to but distinct from the authors' earlier work on threshold models of collective behavior. We conclude with a report on preliminary attempts at empirical measurement.

The authors are listed alphabetically. Early drafts of the paper were prepared by the first author in sabbatical facilities provided by the Harvard University Department of Sociology, and a final revision has benefitted from facilities and services provided by the Stanford University Graduate School of Business during the first author's visiting appointment. Helpful comments from D. Garth Taylor, Steve Rytina, Thomas Schelling, and Harrison White have improved the paper. Partial support of the work was provided by a John Simon Guggenheim Memorial Foundation Fellowship and by NSF grant SPI 81-65055 to the first author.

*State University of New York at Stony Brook
†Arbitron Ratings Company

1. INTRODUCTION

How you choose between two alternatives may depend in part on how others have chosen before you. This dependence may involve the proportion or number (in some reference group) who have previously made one or the other decision. Whether you join a riot or buy a product may hinge on the *proportion* of others who have already done so; then, how many have *not* rioted or bought is as important as how many have. In some situations, absolute numbers seem more important. Whether you turn on your headlights at some given level of daylight probably depends on the *number* of other drivers you have seen do so; those who have not may be ignored. This dependence on either proportions or numbers can be modeled with what we have called threshold models of collective behavior (Granovetter 1978; Granovetter and Soong 1983, 1986).

There are situations typical of socially differentiated populations that require a different model. As with absolute numbers, the focus may only be on that part of the reference group that has made a particular decision, but there may be a special concern with the *group composition* of that part. Few would notice what kind of person turns on his headlights, but many might avoid a riot involving whites and blacks until their own group exceeded a certain proportion of the rioters. Would-be customers of an ethnic restaurant may be very attentive to the proportion of the restaurant's clientele that is from the relevant ethnic group. Here, one attends only to the composition of those who are eating, partly because the set of those who chose not to eat in the restaurant is not easily visible, though it may be well defined. Or consider a club whose members are drawn from some definite, ethnically heterogeneous, eligible population. Individuals may be willing to join only when the proportion of current members who are from their *own* group exceeds some minimum; they pay no attention to those eligible but outside the club.

These situations arise when the social composition of those making a decision—to enter a riot, restaurant, or club—is considered important, for whatever reasons. In clubs, pure social snobbery may be rationalized by a belief that only members of one's own group are congenial companions. This belief is usually grounded in real or imagined barriers of language, culture, or behavior. In an ethnic restaurant, the proportion of diners from the relevant ethnic group may be taken as a signal (Spence 1974) of the quality and authenticity of the cuisine. In deciding whether to engage in some task, individuals may be influenced by a belief that technical competence is available in only one of the groups, or that one can best function cooperatively, keep secrets, and act unselfishly in dangerous situations with co-ethnics. Thus, units of spies and soldiers have often been ethnically homogeneous. However, purely instrumental calculations can also lead to preferring that a group other than one's own be dominant, as when minority parents attempt to enroll their children in a school with a large proportion of the majority group, suspecting that it will be favorably endowed with resources.[1]

2. RESIDENTIAL TIPPING AND THE SPIRAL OF SILENCE

Our interest here is not in explaining such preferences but in constructing a formal model that illuminates their consequences. As we do so, we will refer repeatedly to two illustrations, each with a substantial associated literature. They are substantively quite different from one another and have not previously been discussed together. The differences will be useful in indicating the range of phenomena that can be subsumed under this model and in suggesting some of the modifications needed for particular applications.

The first illustration is residential segregation. Thomas Schelling's seminal papers (1971, 1973, 1978) develop a model for bounded neighborhoods. Each individual resides in the neighborhood "unless the percentage of residents of opposite color exceeds some limit. Each person, black or white, has his own limit. ...If a person's limit is exceeded in this area he will go somewhere else—a place, presumably where his own color predominates or where color does not matter" (1971, p. 167). We use Schelling's account to help generate our formal

---

[1] When interest centers on the proportion from one particular group, it is irrelevant whether that group is one's own, since the population can then be divided into two categories: the particular group and all the others. Joining the riot only when r percent of the rioters belong to one's own group is exactly equivalent to joining only when $(1 - r)$ percent are from the other group(s). For simpler exposition, we will usually speak of two groups; we will show that generalization to n groups is conceptually (if not computationally) straightforward.

model, which subsumes his results and permits important generalizations.

The second illustration comes from the literature on public opinion. Discussions of "pluralistic ignorance" have observed that individuals may fail to speak out on important issues because they falsely perceive their own opinion to be in the minority. Thus, "moral principles with relatively little popular support may exert considerable influence because they are mistakenly thought to represent the views of the majority, while normative imperatives actually favored by the majority may carry less weight because they are erroneously attributed to a minority" (O'Gorman and Garry 1976, p. 450). Noelle-Neumann (1974, 1977, 1984) has introduced some dynamics to this literature with the theory of a "spiral of silence." Her model was inspired by a situation in West Germany in the late 1960s, when followers of the Christian Democratic Party didn't express themselves publicly but Socialist supporters did. This "encouraged people either to proclaim their views or to swallow them and keep quiet until, in a spiraling process, the one view dominated the public scene and the other disappeared from public awareness as its adherents became mute" (1984, p. 5). Taylor suggests that "one's perception of the distribution of public opinion motivates one's willingness to express political opinions. The act of self-expression, however, changes the global environment of opinion, altering the perceptions of other persons and, ultimately, affecting their willingness to express their own opinions" (Taylor 1982, p. 311, 1986).

Noelle-Neumann's extensive public opinion research in Germany has confirmed in many different ways that individuals have definite views on what others believe and that their assessments of those beliefs affect their own willingness to speak out (1984, chap. 2). Similarly, in an analysis of survey data on conflict in Boston over court-ordered busing to achieve school desegregation, Taylor (1986) notes that the extent to which people opposed to busing expressed this opposition—in ways ranging from discussing it with their friends and neighbors to supporting illegal protest actions and boycotts—depended strongly on the extent of opposition to busing that they *perceived* among their neighbors. For example, 56 percent of those who thought none of their neighbors agreed with the court decision discussed their (negative) opinions on busing frequently or very frequently with them, 41 percent of those who thought 10 percent or so of their neighbors agreed with it did so, and 28 percent of those who thought 25 percent or more of their neighbors agreed with it did so.

Our formal model incorporates many of these insights but drops the assumption—prominent especially in Noelle-Neumann's work—that concern about being in the majority or minority has a special status. Instead, we offer a more general argument that each individual has some sensitivity to the predominance of his own opinion among those previously expressed but that these sensitivities may vary continuously. As in previous work on threshold models, small changes in the distribution of sensitivity will have large impacts on equilibrium outcomes. This may help explain why "the intensity of anti-busing protest varies even though the level of opposition to busing is relatively constant in American cities" (Taylor 1983, p. 21).

Both cases illustrate the situation of interest to us. In the first, people are sensitive to the racial proportions in a neighborhood and reside there if those proportions are suitable. In the second, people express their opinion if it agrees with that of some proportion of those who have previously expressed themselves. The racial makeup of those interested in the neighborhood but not living in it and the opinions of those who are silent do not count, partly because they cannot easily be determined. A formal model should predict the exact composition of the neighborhood, or of expressed public opinion, and whether that composition settles down to some equilibrium. In all the examples we have given, the size, homogeneity, and diversity of the final outcome are of special interest. Therefore, for simplicity, we refer to our models as models of diversity.

3. THRESHOLD MODELS OF DIVERSITY

Suppose that each individual belongs to one of two groups and is characterized by a threshold, i.e., the proportion he would have to see of all those choosing one side of a binary decision who are in his own group before he would also make that same choice. For example, a black man is said to have a threshold of 35 percent if he is unwilling to live in a neighborhood unless it is at least 35 percent black. An opponent of nuclear power who would not speak up until 60 percent of expressed public opinion agreed with his view has a threshold of 60 percent. (Note that *threshold*, as it is used here, differs from its use in Granovetter [1978] and in subsequent work on threshold models, because those making one side of the binary decision are ignored. Strictly speaking, we should use some qualifier like *diversity-type thresholds*, but we hope the difference will be clear from context.)

Whites and blacks cannot change their color, but individuals can change their opinions. The model we develop here abstracts from such change and is thus best suited to the study of cases in which expressions of opinion may change but the actual opinions do not. Such stability of opinions may be common. In his book on the Boston school busing controversy, Taylor (1986) notes that the proportion opposed to busing was quite stable over 22 months and five waves of surveys, beginning at 86 percent in wave 1 and varying from 89 to 91 percent from waves 2 to 5. The rancorous conflict of the period did not much affect opinions. Moreover, though individuals cannot change their color, the population racial composition does change, and this may have a similar impact on the workings of the model.

Our notation and discussion will stress the segregation interpretation, since it would be awkward and redundant to develop two separate stories for each equation and analysis. The reader with special interest in public opinion should be able to supply the relevant story in each case, and we will draw on this interpretation for contrast and generality. Assume (as Schelling does) that there is a fixed number of whites, N_w, and blacks, N_b, available to live in the neighborhood and that any number may live there in a given time period. Then, neighborhood population may fluctuate drastically over several periods and may at times be reduced to zero. This fluctuation is one reason that the neighborhood interpretation is not entirely natural, though we will introduce capacity constraints later to make it more plausible. Such fluctuations are easier to imagine for the public opinion interpretation, in which the transaction costs of entering or leaving the set of those expressing their opinions are low.

Outcomes are determined by the exact distributions of thresholds. We will refer especially to the cumulative distribution functions (cdf's) for black and white thresholds. Thus, $F_w(p_w)$ gives the proportion of whites whose threshold is less than or equal to the proportion of whites in the neighborhood, given by p_w. For example, if $F_w(0.25) = 0.65$, 65 percent of the whites have thresholds less than or equal to 25 percent. Then, if the neighborhood is at some time exactly 25 percent white, 65 percent of the white population (including those currently nonresident) will be willing to live in it. If this is more than the number of whites already in the neighborhood, there will be an influx of whites; if less, there will be an outflux. For blacks, the corresponding cdf is $F_b(p_b)$.

We set up the dynamics in discrete time: At the beginning of each period, each individual, black or white, in or out of the neighborhood, observes the racial makeup of the neighborhood in the previous period. If his threshold is met or exceeded (i.e., if the proportion of his own group in the neighborhood is equal to or higher than his minimum proportion), he will reside in the neighborhood that period; otherwise, he will not.[2] This leads us to a pair of coupled first-order difference equations. Let $n_w(t)$ be the number of whites in the neighborhood at time t, and let $n_b(t)$ be the number of blacks. The proportion of whites at t is then $p_w(t) = n_w(t)/[n_w(t) + n_b(t)]$. Suppose the neighborhood is 25 percent white at time t. What proportion of the neighborhood will be white at $t+1$? Those whites resident at $t+1$ will be exactly those whose thresholds are less than or equal to 0.25. If $F_w(0.25)$ were 0.65, and if N_w were the total population of whites available to live in the neighborhood, then at $t+1$ we would have $0.65N_w$ whites in residence. This is the same as saying that

$$n_w(t+1) = N_w F_w[p_w(t)]. \tag{1a}$$

By the same reasoning, we have for blacks

$$n_b(t+1) = N_b F_b[p_b(t)]. \tag{1b}$$

In general, we expect the cdf's to be nonlinear, and exact solution of the system for explicit time paths will rarely be possible, though system equilibria may nevertheless be found explicitly. By forward recursion we can always trace out any desired segment of the time path. Equilibrium requires that $n_w(t+1) = n_w(t)$ and that $n_b(t+1) = n_b(t)$. Call these equilibrium numbers of whites and blacks w and b. Substituting into equations (1a) and (1b) gives us as conditions for equi-

---

[2] Those who shift in or out of the neighborhood during this period do so in no particular order. We do not make Schelling's "somewhat plausible assumption that, as between two whites dissatisfied with the ratio of white to black, the more dissatisfied leaves first—the one with lesser tolerance" (1971, p. 168). Schelling asserts that this assumption is needed for his results, but our model will reproduce them in detail without it. A weaker version of the assumption follows from our setup: If in two successive periods there is a net outflow of whites, all those leaving in the first period are more tolerant (i.e., have a lower threshold) than all those leaving in the second.

librium

$$w = N_w F_w [w/(w + b)], \qquad (2a)$$
$$b = N_b F_b [b/(w + b)]. \qquad (2b)$$

Any admissible pairs (w, b) that satisfy these equations are equilibria. These can always be approximated by simultaneously graphing the two equations and noting all intersections.

Whether a particular equilibrium actually occurs depends on its stability. An equilibrium is asymptotically stable if the system moves back toward it after a slight displacement; it is unstable if the system moves further away. Thus, stable equilibria attract and unstable equilibria repel all nearby trajectories. We expect, in practice, to see only stable equilibria. We may assess the stability of an equilibrium by linearization, i.e., by taking the system as linear near the equilibrium point and approximating its behavior by a Taylor expansion that omits terms of order 2 or higher. This yields the following test for stability (see, e.g., Luenberger 1979, pp. 324–28). Consider the matrix of first partial derivatives of the system, evaluated at an equilibrium. That equilibrium is stable if and only if all eigenvalues of the matrix are strictly less than unity and unstable if any is greater. The test fails (is uninformative) if none exceeds unity but one or more are equal to it. Define w_0 as $n_w(t)$, w_1 as $n_w(t+1)$, b_0 as $n_b(t)$, and b_1 as $n_b(t+1)$. Then, the relevant matrix of partials is

$$\begin{bmatrix} \partial w_1/\partial w_0 & \partial w_1/\partial b_0 \\ \partial b_1/\partial w_0 & \partial b_1/\partial b_0 \end{bmatrix}.$$

Recall that w and b denote the equilibrium numbers of blacks and whites, and let f_w be the probability density of thresholds for whites and f_b the probability density for blacks. (These are just the usual first derivatives of the cdf's F_w and F_b.) Computing the partial derivatives above and evaluating them at some equilibrium point (w, b) then yields

$$\begin{bmatrix} N_w f_w [w/(w+b)] [b/(w+b)^2] & -N_w f_w [w/(w+b)] [w/(w+b)^2] \\ -N_b f_b [b/(w+b)] [b/(w+b)^2] & N_b f_b [b/(w+b)] [w/(w+b)^2] \end{bmatrix}.$$

One eigenvalue of this matrix is zero; stability then depends on whether the nonzero eigenvalue is less than unity. This eigenvalue is

$$N_w f_w [w/(w+b)] [b/(w+b)^2] + N_b f_b [b/(w+b)] [w/(w+b)^2]. \qquad (3)$$

It is qualitatively clear from this expression that the smaller the absolute sizes of the two groups and the larger the numbers of individuals in the neighborhood at equilibrium, the greater the likelihood of stability. For the public opinion interpretation, this implies that the smaller the number holding an opinion and the larger the number expressing one, the greater the likelihood of a stable distribution of expressed opinion. It follows that, other things equal, an issue on which large numbers have an opinion but few express it will engender volatile distributions of public expression. More stability will occur in a small population in which many express their views.

4. USING THE MODEL: STRAIGHT-LINE TOLERANCE DISTRIBUTIONS

We first apply the model to the straight-line tolerance distributions that are Schelling's main illustrations (1971, pp. 167–75; 1978, pp. 155–64), since these have received wide attention. Our more formal account clarifies the interplay between model parameters and neighborhood outcomes, allowing assessment of the parameter ranges over which one can expect Schelling's counterintuitive results. Our Figure 1 is comparable to the first part of Schelling's Figure 18 (1971, p. 169; or see Schelling 1978, fig. 9, p. 158), except that the y intercept

FIGURE 1. $Q(r)$ = proportion of whites with tolerance ratios greater than or equal to r.

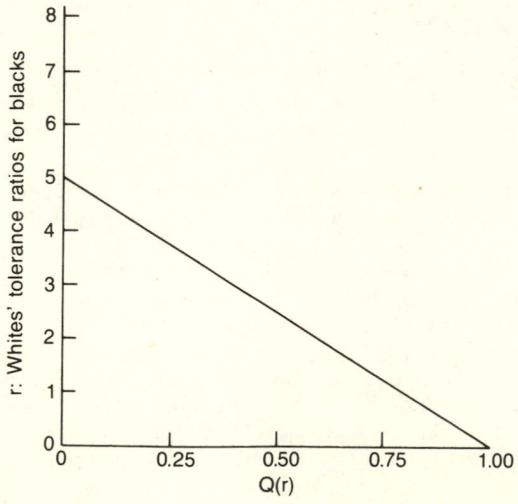

is at 5 rather than 2 (see Schelling 1971, p. 171, or 1978, p. 161). On our y axis are what Schelling calls the tolerance ratios of whites for blacks, i.e., the maximum ratio of blacks to whites that whites can accept and still live in the area. Like Schelling, we assume that an identical distribution governs blacks' tolerance ratios for whites. On the x axis is the proportion of whites with ratios greater than or equal to that given by the y coordinate. Thus, the point (0.25, 3.75) indicates that 25 percent of whites have a black-to-white tolerance ratio of 3.75 to 1, or greater.[3] Denote the proportion of individuals with tolerance ratios greater than or equal to some given ratio r by $Q(r)$. Generalizing the straight-line distribution of Figure 1, suppose the line intersects the y axis at some value, R. By definition, the line must intersect the x axis at unity, so its slope is just $-R$. The equation for the line is then $r = (-R)Q(r) + R$, so $Q(r) = 1 - (r/R)$.

A white who would live in the area as long as the proportion of blacks was less than or equal to one in four has a tolerance ratio of $1/3$; but this is, in our terms, a threshold of 0.75. If some proportion of the population have tolerance ratios greater than or equal to a given r, then this proportion have thresholds less than or equal to the corresponding s. For example, those with tolerance ratios greater than or equal to $1/3$ have thresholds less than or equal to 0.75. They will not live in a neighborhood unless three out of four of its residents are their own color. Denote the cdf of thresholds by F, the thresholds themselves by s, and the tolerance ratios by r. Then, $r = (1/s) - 1$.[4] It follows that in general, $F(s) = Q(r) = Q[(1/s) - 1]$. Substituting in our equation for the straight-line tolerance distribution, we have $F(s) = 1 - \{[(1/s) - 1]/R\} = (1/R)(1 + R - (1/s))$ as the cdf of thresholds for a straight-line tolerance distribution that intersects the y axis at R. Note, however, that for $r > R$, $Q(r) = 0$: By hypothesis, no one has a

---

[3] Schelling refers to this curve as a cumulative distribution of tolerances, but this is confusing, since cumulative distributions usually indicate proportions less than or equal to the value of the random variable. It may also confuse readers that the axes are reversed from the usual depiction of cdf's, perhaps a carryover of the axis reversal practiced by economists in supply-and-demand schedules, in which price, the independent variable, is on the y axis.

[4] We prefer thresholds to tolerance ratios because ratios make it awkward to discuss those willing to live in a neighborhood or express an opinion before other members of their group have done so; i.e., the ratio requires division by zero. In our terms, such individuals simply have a threshold of zero. Thresholds are identical to what Schelling (1973) called individual tipping points.

tolerance ratio greater than R. Correspondingly, for $s < (1/(1 + R))$, we have $F(s) = 0$.

Thus, F is defined piecewise over the argument s, and though straight-line tolerance distributions appear simple at first, the piecewise property implies that the pair of difference equations operating will vary depending on the exact values of the variables at a given time. For example, from equation (1a), we have the relation $n_w(t + 1) = N_w F_w(p_w(t))$. But to evaluate this relation here, we must note that when the argument of F is less than $(1/(1 + R))$, $F = 0$. In this case, $p_w(t) < (1/(1 + R))$, which occurs if and only if $[n_b(t)/n_w(t)] > R$. When F_w is zero, the difference equation for whites reduces to $n_w(t + 1) = 0$. As the distribution of tolerances implies, when the current ratio of blacks to whites exceeds R, no white will want to live in the neighborhood. When the argument of F is greater than or equal to $(1/(1 + R))$, we have $F_w(p_w(t)) = (1/R)[1 + R - (1/p_w(t))] = 1 - [n_b(t)/Rn_w(t)]$ and a corresponding equation of $n_w(t + 1) = N_w\{1 - [n_b(t)/Rn_w(t)]\}$. The analysis is exactly symmetrical for blacks. It follows that there are four different ways to define the system of difference equations:

1. If $n_b(t)/n_w(t) > R$, $n_w(t)/n_b(t) \leq R$, then

$$n_w(t + 1) = 0, \tag{4a}$$

$$n_b(t + 1) = N_b\{1 - [n_w(t)/(Rn_b(t))]\}. \tag{4b}$$

2. If $n_b(t)/n_w(t) \leq R$, $n_w(t)/n_b(t) > R$, then

$$n_w(t + 1) = N_w\{1 - [(n_b(t)/Rn_w(t))]\}, \tag{4c}$$

$$n_b(t + 1) = 0. \tag{4d}$$

3. If $n_b(t)/n_w(t) > R$, $n_w(t)/n_b(t) > R$, then

$$n_w(t + 1) = 0, \tag{4e}$$

$$n_b(t + 1) = 0. \tag{4f}$$

4. If $n_b(t)/n_w(t) \leq R$, $n_w(t)/n_b(t) \leq R$, then

$$n_w(t + 1) = N_w\{1 - [n_b(t)/(Rn_w(t))]\}, \tag{4g}$$

$$n_b(t + 1) = N_b(1 - \{n_w(t)/[(Rn_b(t))]\}. \tag{4h}$$

For each situation, note that at equilibrium, $n_w(t + 1) = n_w(t) = w$ and $n_b(t + 1) = n_b(t) = b$. In situation 1, w must $= 0$; substituting into (4b) gives $b = N_b$. It is easily verified that $(0, N_b)$ satisfies (4a) and (4b). The eigenvalue from equation (3) is then $F_w(w/(w + b)) = F_w(0) = 0$, so $f_w(0)$ also $= 0$. This zero eigenvalue indicates stability.

Situation 2 is exactly symmetrical to situation 1, so we have a second stable equilibrium $(N_w, 0)$. In situation 3, each group finds too many of the other, and everyone leaves the neighborhood. The equilibrium $(0,0)$ satisfies the two equations, but derivatives of any order are equal to zero, and linearization fails in this degenerate case: No Taylor approximation provides any information unless the relevant matrices of derivatives are nonzero. But we can see by inspection the stability characteristics of this equilibrium. If a perturbation results in numbers of whites and blacks within the parameters of situation 3, the equilibrium is stable, because the system then returns to $(0,0)$. If a perturbation results in a situation other than 3, the system moves away from that equilibrium.[5] But stable equilibria in other situations must also be defined in this way: Any perturbation that takes the system out of the parameter region within which an equilibrium was defined leads the system to a stable equilibrium within the new region. Therefore, we can simply say that the equilibrium of region 3 is stable.

In situation 4, the system is governed by a pair of nontrivial equations. Substituting the equilibrium conditions into (4g) and (4h) gives

$$w^2 = (N_w/R)(Rw - b), \tag{4i}$$

$$b^2 = (N_b/R)(Rb - w). \tag{4j}$$

We can solve (4i) for b, yielding $(Rw) - (R/N_w)w^2$, and substitute this

---

[5] But the system will not enter situation 3 unless $R < 1$. This can be shown as follows: Suppose at time t we have $n_w(t)$ whites and $n_b(t)$ blacks. If $n_w(t) = n_b(t)$, then situation 3 can occur only if $R < 1$. If $n_w(t)$ does not $= n_b(t)$, suppose that $n_w(t) > n_b(t)$. Then, $n_w(t)/n_b(t) > 1$ and $n_b(t)/n_w(t) < 1$; thus, they can both be greater than R only if $R < 1$. It follows immediately that if R is less than 1, both ratios cannot be less than 1, so that in this circumstance, region 4 cannot be entered. Thus, for any given value of R, the system may enter either regions 1, 2, and 3 $(R < 1)$ or regions 1, 2, and 4 $(R \geq 1)$. If we plot $n_b(t)$ on the vertical axis and $n_w(t)$ on the horizontal when $R < 1$, the region of stability for the equilibrium in region 3 $(0,0)$ is bounded by the two rays from the origins given by $n_b(t) = n_w(t)/R$ on the left and by $n_b(t) = Rn_w(t)$ on the right. To the left of the first ray, we are in region 1; to the right of the second ray, we are in region 2. As R approaches 0, the middle, stable region for the equilibrium of $(0,0)$ increases, and the size of the other two regions approaches zero asymptotically. This is intuitively reasonable, since a very small value of R implies that each group finds the other nearly intolerable and everyone leaves in droves, emptying the neighborhood.

into (4j). This produces a fourth-degree equation for w:

$$0 = w\left\{\left(R^2/N_w^2\right)w^3 - \left(2R^2/N_w\right)w^2\right.$$
$$\left. + \left[R^2 + (N_b/N_w)R\right]w + \left[(N_b/R) - N_b R\right]\right\}. \qquad (4k)$$

Since the situation for blacks is symmetrical, the same equation (with interchanged subscripts) applies to b. Each of these equations has four roots. For a corresponding pair (w, b) to be an admissible equilibrium, it must fall within the scope of situation 4, w and b must both be real and positive, and we must have $w < N_w$ and $b < N_b$. One root $(0,0)$ is outside the boundaries of situation 4, so we have a maximum of three equilibria here.

Some formidable algebra would yield a general expression for the three equilibria, but it is simpler to use approximations for specified parameters. One can either plot equation (4k) and note the approximate location of zeroes or go back to equations (4i) and (4j) and plot them together, noting the intersections.[6] In the special case in which $R = 5$ and $N_w = N_b = 100$ (as in Schelling 1971, p. 171, fig. 19; 1978, pp. 161–62, fig. 10), the three solutions are found to be approximately $(25.36, 94.64)$, $(80, 80)$, and $(94.64, 25.36)$. All are valid equilibria and can be seen to work by substitution back into the original difference equations. The eigenvalue test shows that the first and third are asymptotically unstable and the middle is stable. For this set of parameters, then, we have three stable equilibria (one each from situations 1, 2, and 4) and two unstable equilibria (from situation 4). The $(0,0)$ equilibrium of region 3 is irrelevant here, because when $R > 1$, this region cannot be entered.

5. A GRAPHICAL METHOD

Some of these results can be seen graphically by generalizing a method suggested by Schelling (1971, p. 169). He draws curves that depict the maximum number of the other group that any fixed number of a group can tolerate. To determine the maximum number of whites

---

[6] This is, in effect, what Schelling has done in Figures 18–29 (1971) and Figures 9–12 (1978, pp. 158–64), though he does not interpret his procedure as simultaneous graphing of equilibrium equations and does not note those intersections that correspond to unstable equilibria. See our further discussion in the next section on graphical methods.

that a given number of blacks could tolerate (i.e., would be willing to live in a neighborhood with), find the black with the *highest* threshold, since that individual has the least tolerance for whites. (We assume that the b blacks in question consist of the black with the lowest threshold, the black with the next lowest, and so on, up to the bth from the bottom of the distribution. This follows from the definition of the task, which is to determine the maximum number of whites that exactly b blacks could live with.) For the public opinion interpretation, the curves indicate the largest number of those with opposite opinions that some fixed number could tolerate and still express their opinion.

By definition of $F(s)$, the cdf of thresholds, the highest threshold s, represented among k percent of the population, is the s that satisfies the equation $F(s) = k$. Here, we have $k = b/N_b$ and $s = [b/(w + b)]$. But when b, N_b, and F are already given, solving this equation yields not only the highest threshold among blacks, but also w, precisely the maximum number of whites the b blacks could tolerate. Suppose, for example, that we wanted to know how many whites the most tolerant 70 in a population of 100 blacks could live with and that the cdf indicated that $F_b(0.40) = 0.70$, i.e., that 70 percent of the black population is willing to live in a neighborhood that is 40 percent or less black or, similarly, that the highest threshold represented within that part of the black population is 40 percent. (This example is drawn from a straight-line tolerance distribution, with $R = 5$. See the cdf in Figure 2.) Thus, all these 70 blacks will be satisfied as long as $[70/(70 + w)] \geq 0.40$, i.e., when $w \leq 105$. The graphical procedure for constructing the curve is as follows. For a given number b, find the proportion (b/N_b) on the vertical axis of the cdf, draw a horizontal line to the cdf, and drop a line to the x axis to find the argument of F that corresponds to that proportion. Once that argument is found, the maximum number of whites can be computed. For each b, then, there is some number w, a function of b that we will call $e(b)$. Here, $105 = e(70)$.

For the 70 blacks and 105 whites in this example, blacks are just 40 percent of the neighborhood, so all blacks are satisfied. But no more blacks will enter the neighborhood, since the next black will, by definition of cdf, have a threshold higher than 40 percent. For blacks, then, the points on $e(b)$ represent an equilibrium situation—thus the notation "e." Therefore, it is not surprising that the equation $b/N_b = F[b/(w + b)]$, from which we derived points for $e(b)$, is exactly the

FIGURE 2. $F(s) = (1/R)[1 + R - (1/s)]$, where $R = 5$: The cdf of a straight-line tolerance distribution.

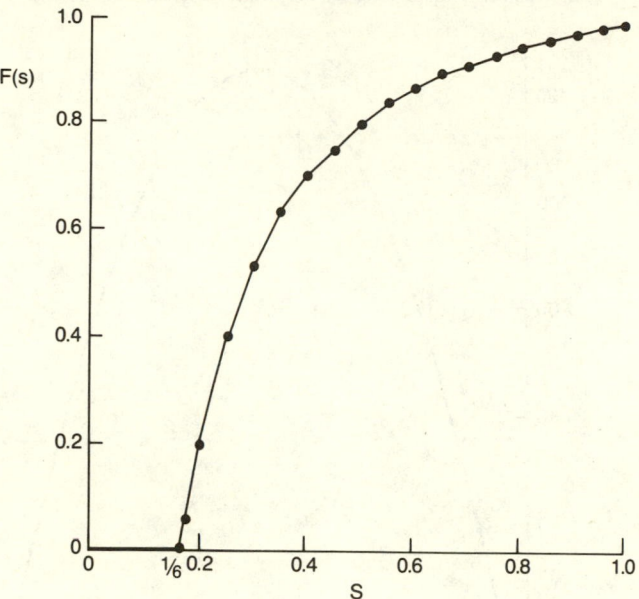

equilibrium equation (2b) for blacks. The situation is symmetrical for whites, and $e(w)$ also corresponds to equation (2a) above.[7]

Figure 2 gives the cdf for a straight-line tolerance distribution. The general equation is $F(s) = (1/R)[1 + R - (1/s)]$, where s (thresholds) is greater than $[1/(1 + R)]$, and $F(s) = 0$ otherwise; here, we let $R = 5$. Though system equations are piecewise (falling into four

[7] Our definition of these curves is broader than Schelling's. He finds the maximum number of whites that a given number of blacks could live with. But we define $e(b)$ to be all those numbers of whites for which some given number of blacks would remain unchanged in the next time period. The two definitions are identical except when the cdf has a horizontal segment, but in the discrete distributions we would find empirically, this is common. Then the procedure of finding b/N_b on the vertical axis of the cdf (drawing a horizontal line to the cdf and dropping a line to the x axis to find the argument of F that corresponds to that proportion) no longer yields a unique solution. In such cases, $e(b)$ is not a single-valued function, because there is a range of numbers of whites for whom there would still be just b blacks in the next time period. When we later introduce preferences for integration, we will find that the definition given by the task of finding the maximum tolerable number of the other group is no longer apt in developing a graphical method but that our more general definition continues to apply.

FIGURE 3. $e(w) = b = R[1 - (w/N_w)]w$, where $R = 5$, $N_w = 100$: The equilibrium curve for whites in a straight-line tolerance distribution. Arrows indicate increases or decreases in the number of whites for given neighborhood racial compositions.

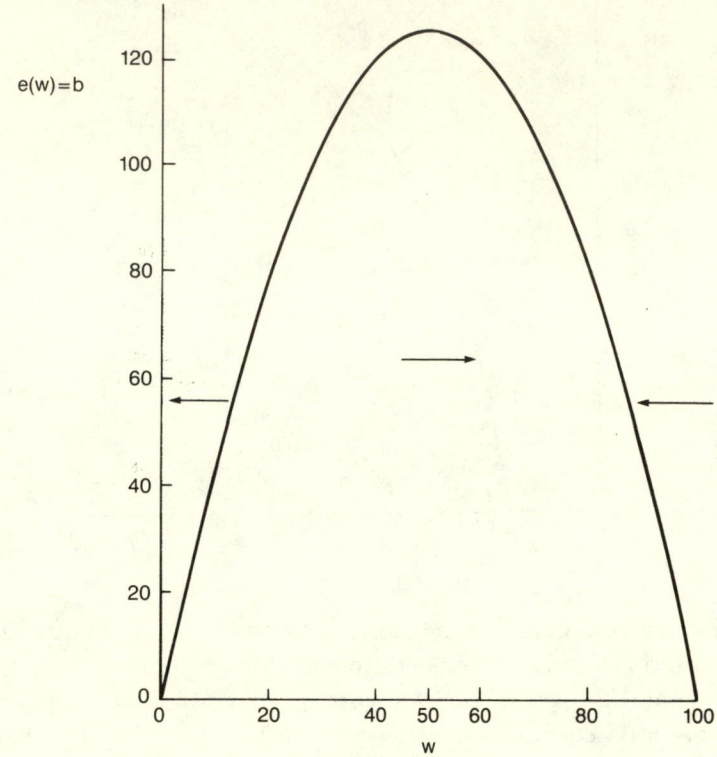

regions, as described above), $e(w)$ and $e(b)$ are continuous, since every value of w/N_w or b/N_b has a unique intersection with F. Because we can find the curve $e(w)$ explicitly by solving $w/N_w = F_w[w/(w + b)]$ for b, we substitute in the assumed equation for F to find that $e(w) = b = R[1 - (w/N_w)]w$, a parabola depicted in Figure 3 for $R = 5$, which is identical to that displayed by Schelling (1971, p. 171, fig. 19). For values of w and b within $e(w)$, more whites will enter, since the number of blacks in the neighborhood is less than the maximum that that number of whites can accept. Outside the curve, whites will leave; on the curve, no change will occur—hence, the arrows in Figure 3. The comparable parabola for blacks, with similar arrows drawn, is super-imposed on the white curve in Figure 4. Within each region we indicate the resultant of the two arrows (as does Schelling 1971, p. 171). The

FIGURE 4. $e(w)$ and $e(b)$ for $R = 5$, $N_w = N_b = 100$: Equilibrium curves for whites and blacks with identical straight-line tolerance distributions. Horizontal arrows indicate direction of change in numbers of whites, vertical arrows the direction for blacks, and diagonal (resultant) arrows the direction of overall change. Stable equilibria are circled, unstable ones are enclosed in triangles.

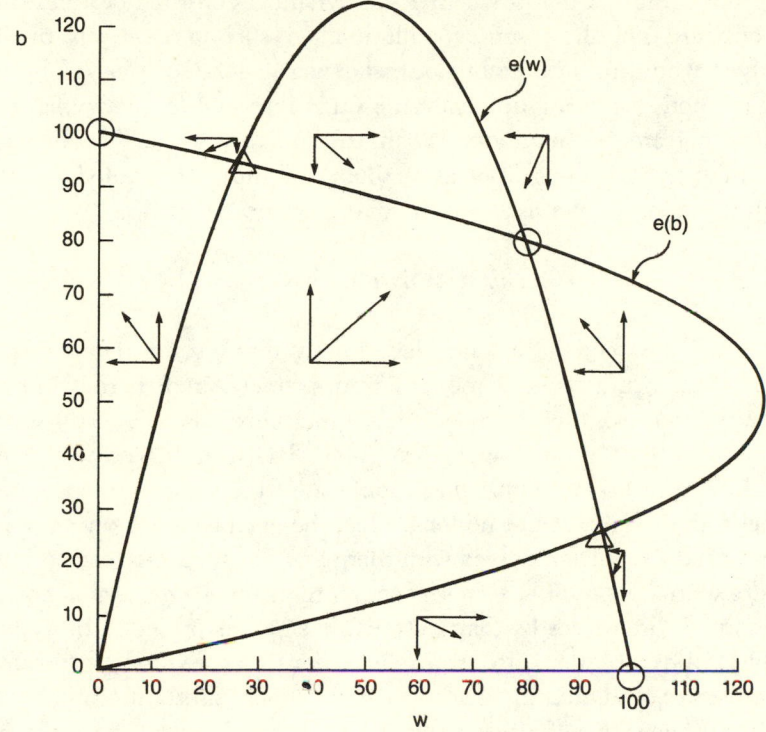

arrows indicate that (80, 80) is a stable equilibrium, as are (0, 100) and (100, 0), and that the equilibria (25.36, 94.64) and (94.64, 25.36) are unstable, because any nearby trajectory will move away from them.

To summarize, we have graphed together the two equilibrium equations; the intersections are thus equilibria and the arrows in the phase diagram give a quick reading on stability. This method shows the dynamics clearly, which may be especially useful if the underlying equations are analytically intractable or result from empirical estimation of thresholds, as we will illustrate later. But compared to a method that works directly with the system of equations on which the graphs are based, it has two important limitations: (1) it cannot be used to indicate the details of the path to equilibrium, and (2) if there is ambiguity about the nature of stability at a particular equilibrium point, it cannot resolve it. In Figure 4, all equilibria are unequivocally stable or unstable; linearization gives eigenvalues of zero or greater than unity. But if the arrows cycled round an equilibrium point, the diagram could not tell us whether the dynamics consisted of an inward or outward spiral or some oscillation. In such a case, eigenvalue analysis would also be ambiguous, showing a value of unity. That is, this method displays graphically the same information available algebraically from linearization. When the linearization is insufficiently informative, so is the graphical method, and only by detailed analysis of the system of equations can the dynamics be clarified.

6. DECISION REVERSALS

In the model thus far, individuals make some decision only when their own group is some minimum proportion of those who have already done so. But later, if their group exceeds some still *higher* proportion, they may change their mind. Individuals who would not speak out until some minimum proportion of those expressing opinions were in their camp might no longer feel the need to speak once a more substantial proportion agreed with them and the situation seemed more securely in hand. This seems even more likely when the action in question is more costly than just expressing an opinion. In typical public-goods situations, for example, actions may require time, effort, or resources, and an individual may have a more substantial impact on the outcome as one of a few actors than as part of a large majority. For example, you may vote for your candidate only if her election is uncertain, not if she has no chance to win or if she is a shoo-in. As perceptions of your candidate's support change, your intention to vote may fluctuate accordingly.

For residential segregation, decision reversals can be interpreted as a preference for integration. Schelling's term *tolerance ratio* nicely captures the sense that there is no positive aspect to participation of the other group; they are merely tolerated up to some maximum, after which one declines to live in the neighborhood. But sometimes variety is the spice of life, and there is, up to a point, a positive preference for the presence of the other group.

We propose a simple formal argument for decision reversals: Each individual is characterized not only by a threshold for the minimum proportion making some decision who are members of his own group but also by a threshold for the maximum proportion. An individual will join in only if the proportion of his own group among those who have already done so falls between these lower and upper thresholds.[8]

A difference-equation model then follows from an argument similar to that used when only lower (segregationist) thresholds are present. Suppose that 75 percent of a neighborhood is white at time t. What proportion of the neighborhood will be white at time $t + 1$? A white who would reside in such a neighborhood would have a lower threshold less than or equal to 0.75. The proportion so willing is $F_{Lw}(0.75)$, where F_{Lw} is the cdf of lower thresholds. But some of these whites may have upper thresholds below 0.75; i.e., they may be unwilling to live in a neighborhood that is as much as 75 percent white. The proportion of such whites is $F_{Uw}(0.75)$, where F_{Uw} is the cdf of upper thresholds for whites. Thus, the proportion willing to live there at $t + 1$ are those for whom 75 percent white is neither too few nor too many—namely, the difference $F_{Lw}(0.75) - F_{Uw}(0.75)$, which we shall call $G_w(0.75)$. Note that G, the difference of two cdf's, is itself no longer a cdf. The system can then be described by the coupled difference equations[9]

$$n_w(t + 1) = N_w G_w(p_w(t)), \tag{5a}$$

$$n_b(t + 1) = N_b G_b(p_b(t)), \tag{5b}$$

where p_w and p_b again refer to the proportions of whites and blacks in the neighborhood.

Since the form of this system is exactly that of equations (1a) and (1b), stability analysis is identical, except that the f_w and f_b of equation (3) are replaced by g_w and g_b, where g is the first derivative of

[8] Schelling asserts that his bounded neighborhood model can be interpreted, without change, to reflect integrationist preferences. But he also notes that it does not accommodate a "lower limit to the acceptable proportion of opposite color, i.e., an upper limit to the proportion of like color in the neighborhood" (1971, p. 180, or 1978, p. 165). As Taylor points out, however, "[to] accurately model a preference for integration...there must be some account taken of the lower limit. A preference for integration means precisely that people will try to live in neighborhoods that are neither too white nor too black" (1984, p. 151n).

[9] A similar argument is presented for threshold models of collective behavior in Granovetter and Soong (1983) and is applied to the analysis of consumer demand in Granovetter and Soong (1986).

the difference function G. Thus, we have asymptotic stability iff

$$N_w g_w [w/(w+b)] [b/(w+b)^2] + N_b g_b [b/(w+b)] [w/(w+b)^2]$$

(6)

has absolute value less than unity.

We offer one example of dynamics with preferences for integration. With both segregation (lower) and integration (upper) thresholds to consider, we have a bivariate density. By definition, one's lower threshold must be lower than or equal to one's upper threshold. Thus, the density is distributed not over the entire unit square but over the upper left triangle, where lower thresholds are on the x axis and upper thresholds are on the y axis. Figure 5 displays one simple bivariate density: The distribution is uniform over a rectangular section of the triangle and zero elsewhere. Then, everyone's lower threshold is less than or equal to some parameter a, and everyone's upper threshold is greater than or equal to a. This is plausible, though it is not required by the assumption of integration preferences. It has the advantage of allowing representation of the density by one parameter. We simplify further by assigning this distribution to both groups, but with possibly different a's, indexed as a_w and a_b.

The bivariate density for whites corresponding to Figure 5 must be just that height above the rectangle that, multiplied by its area, yields the unit volume required for a density. Thus,

$$f_w(s_L, s_U) = 1/[a_w(1 - a_w)] \quad \text{within the rectangle and}$$
$$= 0 \quad \text{elsewhere.}$$

(7)

Then, the marginal densities for lower thresholds are

$$f_{Lw}(s_L) = 1/a_w, \quad \text{where } 0 \le s_L \le a_w, \text{ and}$$
$$= 0 \quad \text{elsewhere,}$$

(8)

and the marginal densities for upper thresholds are

$$f_{Uw}(s_U) = 1/(1 - a_w), \quad \text{where } a_w \le s_U \le 1, \text{ and}$$
$$= 0 \quad \text{elsewhere.}$$

(9)

Corresponding marginal cdf's for lower thresholds are

$$F_{Lw}(s_L) = s_L/a_w, \quad \text{where } 0 \le s_L \le a_w, \text{ and}$$
$$= 1 \quad \text{elsewhere,}$$

(10)

FIGURE 5. Bivariate density of upper (s_U) and lower (s_L) thresholds, uniform over shaded rectangle and zero elsewhere.

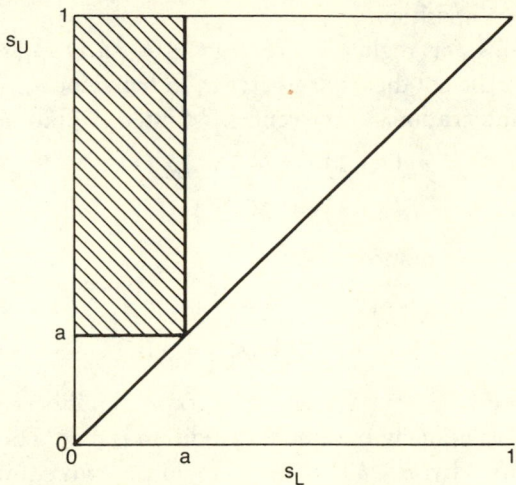

and for upper thresholds are

$$F_{Uw}(s_U) = (s_U - a_w)/(1 - a_w), \qquad \text{where } a_w \leq s_U \leq 1, \text{ and}$$
$$= 0 \qquad \qquad \text{elsewhere.}$$

(11)

The difference, G_w, is then $F_{Lw} - F_{Uw}$, and it is given by

$$G_w(s) = s/a_w, \qquad \qquad \text{where } 0 \leq s \leq a_w, \text{ and}$$
$$= (1 - s)/(1 - a_w), \qquad \text{where } a_w < s \leq 1.$$

(12)

All these equations, with different subscripts, apply to blacks.

From (5a) and (5b) we see that for the preferences in Figure 5, system equations for whites are

$$n_w(t + 1) = (N_w/a_w)p_w(t), \qquad \text{where } 0 \leq p_w(t) \leq a_w, \text{ and}$$
$$= [N_w/(1 - a_w)]\, p_b(t), \quad \text{where } a_w \leq p_w(t) \leq 1,$$

(13)

and for blacks are

$$n_b(t + 1) = (N_b/a_b)p_b(t), \qquad \text{where } 0 \leq p_b(t) \leq a_b, \text{ and}$$
$$= [N_b/(1 - a_b)]\, p_w(t), \quad \text{where } a_b \leq p_b(t) \leq 1.$$

That is, system equations are defined in piecewise fashion. For each group, the first equation applies if the group's current proportion of the neighborhood is less than or equal to its parameter a. Otherwise, the second equation applies.

Because two equations are possible for each group, there are four sets of possibilities, or parameter regions, depending on current neighborhood composition.

Conditions for region 1 are $p_w(t) \leq a_w$ and $p_b(t) \leq a_b$. Both groups are at or below their parameter a, so behavior in neither group is affected by integrationist preferences.[10] System equations are

$$n_w(t+1) = (N_w/a_w)p_w(t),$$
$$n_b(t+1) = (N_b/a_b)p_b(t). \tag{14}$$

In equilibrium these reduce to

$$w = (N_w/a_w)[w/(w+b)],$$
$$b = (N_b/a_b)[b/(w+b)], \tag{15}$$

whence we have $w + b = (N_w/a_w) = (N_b/a_b)$. Equilibria thus exist in this region iff this unlikely parameter condition is met. Then, any point on the line defined by $w + b$ that lies in region 1 is an equilibrium. The stability of these equilibria is assessed by using equations (6), (12), and (15) to compute the relevant eigenvalue, which then turns out to be exactly unity, which is uninformative on stability.

But inspection of the equations (14) shows that when equilibria exist, dynamics consist merely of preserving the initial proportions of whites to blacks but scaling the initial numbers up or down so they add to the constant amount $(N_w/a_w) = (N_b/a_b)$. Thus, if $N_w = 200$, $a_w = 0.8$, $N_b = 100$, and $a_b = 0.4$, then this constant amount is 250, and an initial condition of 100 whites and 50 blacks is scaled up to an equilibrium of 166.67 whites and 83.33 blacks, still in the proportion of 2 to 1. A perturbation of this equilibrium will return the system to the same equilibrium only if it preserves this proportion; otherwise, the system will move to a different equilibrium on the line $w + b = 250$, determined by the new proportions.

Conditions for region 2 are $a_w < p_w(t) \leq 1$ and $0 \leq p_b(t) \leq a_b$. In this region, some whites but no blacks are affected by preferences for integration. We then have

$$n_w(t+1) = [N_w/(1 - a_w)]\, p_b(t),$$
$$n_b(t+1) = (N_b/a_b)p_b(t). \tag{16}$$

---

[10] In region 1, we must have $(a_w + a_b) \geq 1$, since if the sum were less than 1 and if each current proportion were less than its respective a, the sum of current proportions would not equal 1, as it must.

In equilibrium, $w = [N_w/(1 - a_w)][b/(w + b)]$ and $b = (N_b/a_b)[b/(w + b)]$. Solving for w and b in terms only of the system parameters, we get

$$w = [N_w/(1 - a_w)]/\{1 + [N_w a_b/((1 - a_w)N_b)]\},$$
$$b = (N_b/a_b)/\{1 + [N_w a_b/((1 - a_w)N_b)]\}. \tag{17}$$

We may gauge stability of equilibrium by substitution into (6), using (12) and (17), yielding an eigenvalue of zero; thus, the equilibrium of equations (17) is asymptotically stable.

Conditions for region 3 are $0 \leq p_w(t) \leq a_w$ and $a_b < p_b(t) \leq 1$. This region is exactly symmetric to region 2, interchanging the two groups. System equations and equilibria are thus identical, changing b for w, and the variable eigenvalue is again zero, indicating stable equilibria.

Conditions for region 4 are $a_w < p_w(t) \leq 1$ and $a_b < p_b(t) \leq 1$.[11] Here, some whites and some blacks will feel that there are too many of their own color in the neighborhood. System equations are

$$n_w(t + 1) = [N_w/(1 - a_w)] p_b(t),$$
$$n_b(t + 1) = [N_b/(1 - a_b)] p_w(t). \tag{18}$$

Some algebra shows that the equilibria are

$$w = [N_w/(1 - a_w)]^{1/2}/\{[(1 - a_w)N_w]^{1/2} + [(1 - a_b)/N_b]^{1/2}\},$$
$$b = [N_b/(1 - a_b)]^{1/2}/\{[(1 - a_w)/N_w]^{1/2} + [(1 - a_b)/N_b]^{1/2}\}. \tag{19}$$

From (6), (12), and (19) we find that the second eigenvalue here is -1, indeterminate for stability. But if we trace out equations (18) on a calculator, we see that for any set of parameters, every set of initial conditions $n_w(t)$ and $n_b(t)$ leads immediately to an oscillation of period two. The equilibrium point given by the parameters is within the range of the oscillation but is itself never reached. Further, each set of initial conditions leads to its own particular oscillation, unique except that every pair in the same ratio leads to the same oscillation. Finally, the initial white/black ratio reappears every second period. These characteristics could be derived analytically by computing general expres-

---

[11] In region 4, we must have $(a_w + a_b) \leq 1$, since both groups exceed their a parameter. This could not be the case if the sum of the two parameters exceeded 1.

sions for $n_w(t + 2)$ and $n_b(t + 2)$, but it is more illuminating to give a numerical example.

Suppose that a neighborhood has 200 whites and 100 blacks and that $a_w = 0.3$, $a_b = 0.1$, $N_w = 300$, and $N_b = 300$. Each group contains some individuals who believe that there are too many of their own group present. From (19) we see that an equilibrium exists at $w = 200.84$, $b = 177.12$. But from (18) we can compute that at time $(t + 1)$, the numbers of whites and blacks are $(142.86, 222.22)$; at $t + 2$ we have $(260.87, 130.43)$, which reproduces the original 2-to-1 ratio; at $t + 3$ we return to $(142.86, 222.22)$, and so on. The equilibria in region 4 do not attract nearby trajectories. If we were at the equilibrium $(200.84, 177.12)$ and were slightly pushed away to, for example, $(201, 177)$, the system would not return to the equilibrium but would not move very far. Rather, it would settle into the cycle $(200.68, 177.25)$, $(201, 177)$. Similarly, any cycle in progress, if slightly perturbed, would settle into a close-by cycle. Thus, the initial conditions under which the system first enters region 4 determine the amplitude of oscillation.

While the system is entirely deterministic, it is, in two of the four regions, enormously sensitive to initial conditions and may fluctuate in apparently odd ways even without perturbations. Such fluctuations are characteristic of systems of deterministic nonlinear difference equations, and May (1976) has shown that under certain conditions, they may be essentially indistinguishable from random noise. In the general case, numerical methods are required to determine outcomes, but some analytical approximations to observed distributions are usually possible, and these can be related to the techniques used here, to give a reasonable picture of system dynamics.

7. THE GRAPHICAL METHOD WITH DECISION REVERSALS

The graphical method described earlier can also be applied when decisions are reversible. In the segregation example, we again ask, Given a certain number of blacks in a neighborhood, for what number of whites in the neighborhood will that number of blacks not change? When integration preferences are present, there may be more than one such number of whites, even if there are no horizontal segments in the cdf, because there may now be not only too many whites for the fixed number of blacks but also too few.

Suppose we ask, For what numbers of whites will a neighborhood that currently has 30 of a population of 60 blacks continue to have just 30 blacks? The basic difference equation (5b) may be written $n_b(t+1)/N_b = G_b(p_b(t))$, where p_b is the proportion of the neighborhood that is black; i.e., $b(t)/(w(t)+b(t))$. Since the 30 blacks are just 50 percent of the black population, if the neighborhood is to continue to have 30 blacks at $t+1$, the 30 must be a proportion of the neighborhood equal to p_b such that p_b satisfies the relation $0.50 = F_{Lb}(p_b) - F_{Ub}(p_b) = G_b(p_b)$. This is the equilibrium condition for the equation. But since G need not be monotonic, more than one value of p_b may satisfy this relation; i.e., there may be more than one proportion of whites in the neighborhood such that 50 percent of the black population will continue to live in the neighborhood. Any p_b for which the difference in height between lower and upper threshold cdf's is exactly 50 percent will suffice.

Suppose our cdf's were such that $G_b(0.60) = G_b(0.20) = 0.50$. Then, 30 blacks could coexist with exactly 20 whites and with exactly 120 whites. (Note that the 30 blacks in the first and second cases might not be the same.) Since the cdf's whose difference is being taken are monotonically increasing, numbers of whites below 20 would be too few, and some blacks would depart. At 20 whites, 30 blacks would be present next period. Between 20 and 120 whites would be neither too few nor too many, so the 30 blacks would remain and more would enter. At 120 whites, exactly 30 blacks would remain in any subsequent period, but more than 120 whites would be too many and the number of blacks would again fall below 30. If more than two arguments of G yielded the result of 50 percent, these alternations would occur once again.

Figures 6a and 6b show the cdf's and the difference function G discussed above. Our procedure for constructing the curve $e(b)$ is analogous to that outlined earlier, when preferences were only for segregation. We convert the number of individuals in the group in question—here, 30 blacks—to a proportion of the group's population —here, 50 percent—and locate this proportion on the vertical axis of the G curve. Then, we move across the curve horizontally, finding all intersections with G, and take as $e(b)$ the arguments of G corresponding to those intersections, as shown in Figure 3c. Here $e(b)$ is a vector-valued function of b.

In equations, $e(b)$ is found by solving $b/N_b = G_b(b/(w+b))$, the equilibrium equation for blacks, for w. We find $e(w)$ in the same

FIGURE 6.   *A* and *B*, upper and lower threshold cdf's for blacks (F_{Ub} and F_{Lb}) such that $G_b(0.20) = G_b(0.60) = 0.50$. *C*, $e(b)$, the equilibrium curve for blacks implied by the curves in *A* and *B*. Arrows indicate direction of change in numbers of blacks.

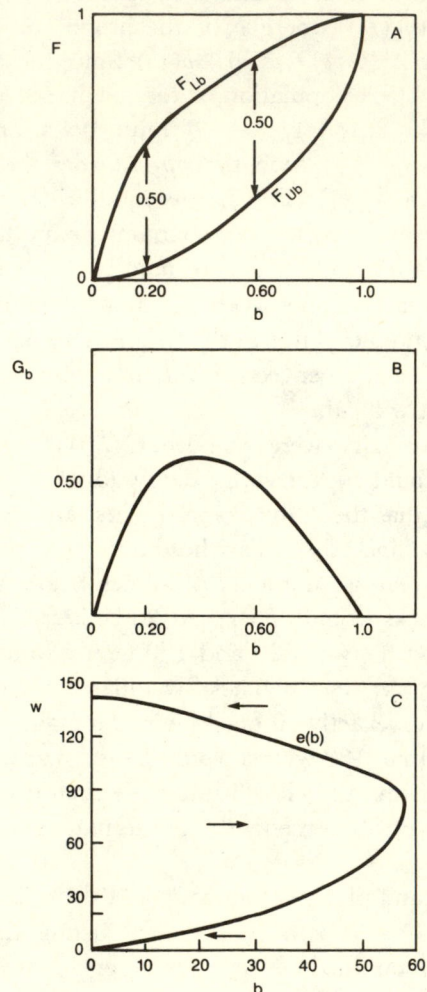

way. The arrows in Figure 6c indicate the changes to be expected in numbers of blacks at each point in the next period. If we superimpose the curves $e(w)$ and $e(b)$, system equilibria will be at the intersections; we can then draw resultants of black and white arrows to produce a phase diagram that gives some insight into the stability of equilibria. The observations made earlier on the values and limitations of such diagrams apply here; they would not, for example, elucidate the dynamics in regions 1 and 4 of the rectangular density discussed above.

8. GENERALIZATION BEYOND TWO GROUPS

Binary decisions may involve more than two groups. For example, there may be more than two candidates to support in an election. Likewise, residential segregation may involve three or more ethnic groups. We analyze exactly three groups and obtain the essentials for generalization to any larger number. Continuing the segregation notation, we retain the subscripts w and b for whites and blacks and add a subscript h to represent Hispanics. We include integration preferences, since their absence is then merely a special case in which no individuals have upper thresholds, i.e., $F_{Uw} = 0$ so that $G_w = F_{Lw}$, etc. The natural generalization of equations (5a) and (5b) is

$$n_w(t+1) = N_w G_w(p_w(t)), \qquad (20a)$$

$$n_b(t+1) = N_b G_b(p_b(t)), \qquad (20b)$$

$$n_h(t+1) = N_h G_h(p_h(t)), \qquad (20c)$$

where $p_i(t) = n_i(t)/[n_w(t) + n_b(t) + n_h(t)]$, the proportion of the neighborhood made up of group i at time t. Generalization to k groups is then straightforward. Analysis of the matrix of first-order partial derivatives shows that at least one eigenvalue is zero. In general, for k groups, stability will depend on $k-1$ eigenvalues, and stability requires that the absolute value of all $k-1$ must be less than unity. Stability analysis is thus much more complex for three or more groups than for two.

Equations (20) assume that each group is sensitive only to the proportion of its *own* members in the population, that it makes no distinctions among other groups and simply lumps them together in the denominator. More complex intergroup preferences could be incorporated by assuming a matrix of weights to be inserted in the denominator of the right side of the equations. Each group has one row in the matrix indicating how it weights each other group. The main diagonal can be standardized to unity. Thus, for example, the row for blacks (bw, bb, bh) might be $(3, 1, 1/2)$. This implies that for blacks, whites in the neighborhood loom larger than life, that seeing one white is three times more salient than seeing one black. For segregation thresholds (lower thresholds), this means that the tolerance of blacks for whites is lower than it would be if the weights were equal. The weight of $1/2$ for Hispanics, less than unity, indicates that blacks believe Hispanics are even easier to live with than other blacks and thus, in this restricted sense, are six times more desirable than whites. For segregation thresholds, this means that when Hispanics live in the neighborhood, blacks are comfortable with fewer other blacks than they would be if all weights were equal. For upper or integration thresholds, the effect is opposite: Because whites are more salient than blacks, it takes more blacks in the neighborhood to trigger blacks' upper threshold than it would if all weights were equal; therefore, blacks stay longer. Correspondingly, since Hispanics are less salient than blacks, their presence causes blacks to reach their upper threshold sooner.[12]

9. CAPACITY CONSTRAINTS

The problem with the segregation interpretation of our models is that there is, at least in the short run, a fixed number of housing units, which may be less than the number of people who want to live in the neighborhood. In neoclassical economic equilibrium, housing prices would adjust to equate supply with demand; but housing markets are often out of equilibrium, so it is useful to indicate how our model is affected.

Consider the neighborhood in Figure 7: Demand comes from 100 whites and 100 blacks, and stable equilibria are $(80, 80)$, $(100, 0)$, and $(0, 100)$. Suppose there are just 50 homes. This capacity constraint can be indicated by drawing in the line $b = 50 - w$, as indicated (see Taylor [1984, p. 146] for a similar diagram). Suppose thresholds and dynamics are as given by equations (4) and that we begin with 10

---

[12] Weights could also be assigned in the analysis of two groups, but these would then simply alter the unweighted thresholds. For example, if whites weighted blacks three times more than whites, a white who had an unweighted threshold of 0.5 would live in the neighborhood if $n_w/(3n_b + n_w) > 0.5$, i.e., if $n_w/n_b > 3$, which is the same as a threshold of 0.75. More generally, if weight w is assigned to the other group and unity is assigned to one's own, an individual with a stated threshold of t will have a normalized or adjusted threshold of $wt/[t(w - 1) + 1]$. Thus, for two groups, the weights may simply be determinants of thresholds that have already been normalized for weighting considerations. However, this method fails when there are more than two groups, because no unique normalized threshold can be obtained from an initial stated threshold and a set of weights.

FIGURE 7. The curves of Figure 4, with added capacity constraints of maximum neighborhood size = 50, indicated by the line $b = 50 - w$.

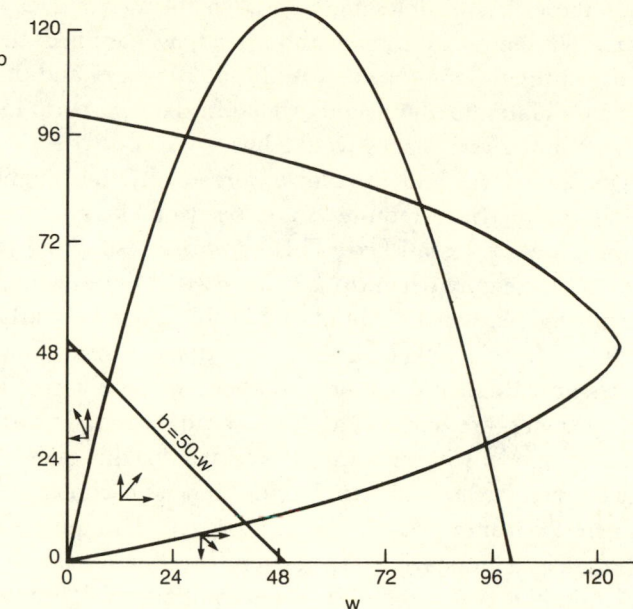

whites and 20 blacks in the neighborhood. This places us in region 4, so equations (4g) and (4h) indicate what will occur. Recalling that $R = 5$, we see from these equations that at time $t + 1$, 60 whites and 90 blacks will want to live in the neighborhood. Since this exceeds the stated capacity of 50, some rationing rule is required. One, but not the only, plausible rule is to fill the houses with whites and blacks according to their proportions among the candidates. Then, we would have 20 whites and 30 blacks in the next period. What will happen next? Applying equations (4g) and (4h) again shows that at $t + 1$, 70 whites and 86.7 blacks will want to live in the neighborhood. If we again take 50 whites and blacks according to their proportions among those who want to live in the neighborhood, we have 22.33 whites and 27.67 blacks. Continuing this process leads us closer and closer to a limiting value of 25 whites and 25 blacks, because the equilibrium, given a capacity constraint and the rationing rule adopted here, is simply the unconstrained equilibrium $(80, 80)$ scaled down linearly to meet the constraint. The stability characteristics of unconstrained equilibria are identical to those of the constrained equilibria.[13]

But there is a troublesome aspect to these dynamics. With 20 whites and 30 blacks in the neighborhood, we applied the system equations and the rationing rule to find that 70 whites and 86.7 blacks would be candidates for the neighborhood in the next period, and thus 22.33 whites and 27.66 blacks would live there. But the 70 and 86.7 include the 20 whites and 30 blacks already in the neighborhood; therefore, our procedure requires some resident blacks to leave even though they are *not* dissatisfied. This complete reshuffling each time period makes sense only when transaction costs of entering or leaving a state are negligible, which is implausible for real neighborhoods. An additional stipulation, which modifies the dynamics of equations (4), seems necessary: Residents in a neighborhood will not vacate if existing racial proportions are such that they would like to live there next period. In the model without capacity constraints, this question cannot arise, since anyone who wants to live in the neighborhood can.

Then, 20 whites and 30 blacks represents an equilibrium, since no one is motivated to leave. In fact, every point on the line $b = 50 - w$ that is within the two parabolas is an equilibrium. These equilibria have only limited stability, however. Any perturbation that leaves whites and blacks in the ratio of 2/3 will restore the 20/30 outcome. But any other change will result in a new equilibrium, along the line. In particular, if a perturbation results in a ratio of x whites to y blacks, the new equilibrium point will be that which scales x and y up to the line, i.e., to that point (w, b) at which $w/b = x/y$ and $w + b = 50$. As the arrows in Figure 7 suggest, points on the line $b = 50 - w$ that are not within both curves lead to either $w = 50$ or $b = 50$, which are stable against perturbations that remain outside one of the curves.

Thus, even with capacity constraints, the basic model works when demand for places does not exceed supply—market equilibrium being included as the special case of equality—or when transaction costs of entering or leaving are negligible. When neither condition is met, system outcomes will be affected in important ways that must be taken into account. In the public opinion interpretation, capacity constraints are likely to be irrelevant, since there is no obvious upper

---

[13] These assertions seem intuitively reasonable to us, so we omit the proofs. However, they are available on request.

limit to the number of individuals who can express their views. Club membership usually involves a capacity constraint, but the transaction costs of entering and leaving may be minimal. Sensing the volatility this implies, many clubs thus impose nonrefundable initiation fees.

10. EMPIRICAL APPLICATIONS

Empirical applications require measurement of the postulated thresholds. We see two ways to proceed. One way is to adapt the economists' concept of revealed preference, attributing thresholds to individuals by observing the distribution of others' decisions before they make their own. This has the advantage of resting on observed facts, but for any given individual, observation is uninformative unless he actually does something. A black who remains in his neighborhood as it changes from 100 percent black to 60 percent is known to have a threshold of 60 percent or less, but this right-censored observation is crude. When we take upper thresholds (integration preferences) into account, it becomes clear that good measurement requires observation over a rather wide range of neighborhood conditions. We must also assume that behavior exactly reflects thresholds and that there is no significant lag between the passing of one's threshold and behavior. If there are lags, and worse, if these vary by individual, then the composition of the neighborhood or of expressed opinion just before movement or the expression of one's views may not accurately reflect the actor's threshold.

The other way to measure thresholds is to ask respondents directly. This method is suspect to the extent that there is no independent check on the validity of respondent reports. However, because it is direct, it does not suffer from the censoring and lag problems of revealed preference measures, and it appears empirically that respondents have no difficulty answering questions of this kind. Noelle-Neumann has shown that peoples' willingness to express their opinions depends on whether they think they are in the majority. She has also explored other determinants of this willingness (1984, chap. 2). She asks respondents, for example, whether, faced with a five-hour train ride with a stranger who has one of two definite views on some subject, they think it would be worth their while to discuss the subject with that person (1984, p. 18). We could extend this question and ask respondents how interested they would be in expressing their opinion in some public setting in which the group was split in various proportions on some question.

For the interpretation of residential segregation, Taylor (1984) reports successful use of a question like this in a telephone survey of 300 black and 300 white residents of Omaha in 1978 on the importance of racial preference in housing choice. Neighborhoods were described as having certain numbers of blacks and whites, and respondents were asked whether they would try to move out of their neighborhood if its racial proportions changed to those given in the question (Taylor 1984, p. 244, n. 1). Each respondent was asked about seven possible mixtures: all white, 1 black/9 white, 3 black/7 white, 5 black/5 white, 7 black/3 white, 9 black/1 white, and all black. Though Taylor drops that part of the data reflecting preferences for integration (1984, p. 151), the question, since it captures for each respondent the acceptable range of neighborhood compositions, does index both segregation and integration preferences and thus permits us to estimate both lower and upper threshold distributions. For example, a white respondent who accepts black/white ratios of 9/1, 7/3, 5/5, and 3/7 but who rejects ratios of 10/0 and 1/9 has a lower threshold of 10 percent and an upper threshold of 90 percent. He is willing to live in a neighborhood that is between 10 percent and 90 percent white. In Table 1 we give Taylor's empirical results, and in Figures 8a and 8b we estimate the corresponding functions $G_w(s)$ and $G_b(s)$ by connecting the measured points with straight lines. (Other assumptions

TABLE 1
Tolerance Schedules Estimated from Omaha Survey Data

Racial Mix	Percentage Who Would Tolerate Mix	
	White	Black
All white	100	95
1 black, 9 white	97	98
3 black, 7 white	87	100
5 black, 5 white	69	100
7 black, 3 white	54	98
9 black, 1 white	36	97
All black	28	95

Source: Taylor 1984, p. 150.

FIGURE 8. *A*, $G_w(s)$: The white difference curve interpolated from the data points of Table 1. *B*, $G_b(s)$: The black difference curve interpolated from the data points of Table 1. *C*, $e(w)$ and $e(b)$ for $N_w = N_b = 100$: Equilibrium curves for whites and blacks implied by the curves in *A* and *B*.

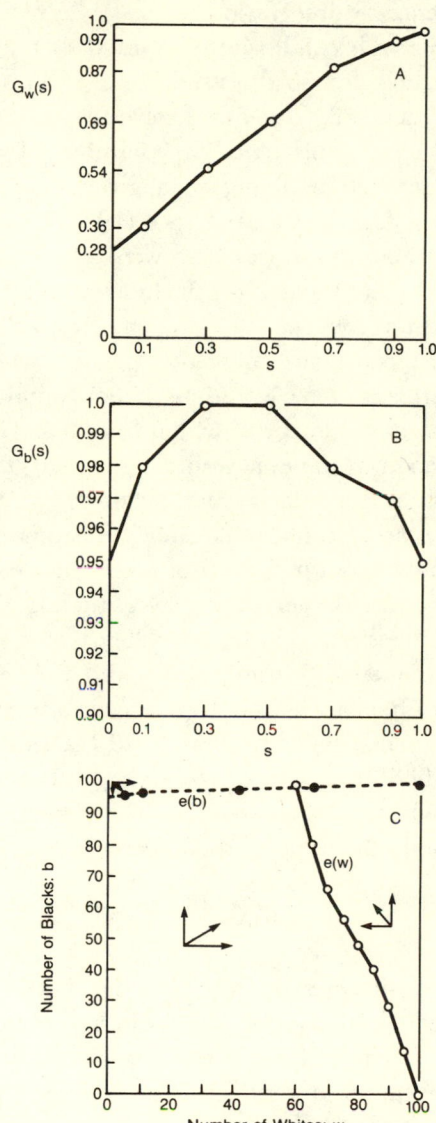

for interpolating intermediate points are possible, but this seemed the most straightforward.) The function $G_w(s)$ is identical to a cdf, $F_w(s)$, of lower (segregation) thresholds, since no whites in this survey indicated any preference for integration.

To construct the equilibrium curves $e(w)$ and $e(b)$, we apply the graphical method described above. For a given number of blacks, for example, we set $b = N_b G(p_b)$ and solve to find w, the point(s) on the curve $e(b)$. We need only specify the numbers of whites and blacks (N_w and N_b) interested in living in a given neighborhood. Taylor draws these curves for 100 of each race (1984, p. 153) but excludes preferences for integration, since these were not treated by Schelling. Our Figure 8c gives $e(b)$ and $e(w)$, including integration preferences. A stable equilibrium point occurs at about 99 blacks and 60 whites, which is 62.3 percent black and 37.7 percent white. Without the integration preferences, $e(b)$ would be a horizontal line at $b = 100$, indicating that for any number of whites from 0 to 100, all 100 blacks in the neighborhood at time t would remain at $t + 1$. The curves would then cross at 100 blacks and about 59 whites. In this case, integration preferences do not make much difference, since no whites have them and only about 5 percent of blacks do. Notice the direction of the small difference: One black leaves, finding the neighborhood "too black," and he is replaced by one white.

Different numerical assumptions would yield very different results. Noting that Omaha was about 12 percent black at the time of the survey, suppose we had 880 whites and 120 blacks interested in some neighborhood. The intersection of $e(w)$ and $e(b)$ occurs at about 118 blacks and 844 whites; whites are then 87.7 percent of the neighborhood, almost exactly the same as their proportion in the population.

11. CONCLUSIONS

Our models fit cases in which one's behavior depends on the previous behavior of others and in which the group composition of those making a certain decision is the crucial element of that dependence. One application is residential segregation. We showed that Thomas Schelling's models can be expressed in terms of our system of two coupled difference equations, permitting an exact mathematical account of his results and such important generalizations as the incorporation of preferences for integration and the extension to more than two groups. The model applies also to a class of public-opinion problems, usually discussed under the rubric of pluralistic ignorance. Another natural linkage is to free-rider problems and the provision of public goods. The techniques of Noelle-Neumann (1984) and Taylor (1984, 1986) suggest that thresholds can be measured with relatively straightforward techniques of survey analysis.

These models have three distinct advantages over most current models: (1) their treatment of dynamics is explicit and central (i.e., they do not deal in comparative statics), (2) they make no assumptions of linear relations among variables, and (3) they are driven not by correlations but by well-defined causal mechanisms. We see models of this kind as part of a broader movement in sociology toward explicit, concrete, dynamic analysis and away from the general linear model, which, assuming that the size of causes must determine the size of consequences, prepares us poorly for the many surprises that social life has in store.

REFERENCES

Granovetter, Mark. 1978. "Threshold Models of Collective Behavior." *American Journal of Sociology* 83:1420–43.

Granovetter, Mark, and Roland Soong. 1983. "Threshold Models of Diffusion and Collective Behavior." *Journal of Mathematical Sociology* 9:165–79.

——————. 1986. "Threshold Models of Interpersonal Effects in Consumer Demand." *Journal of Economic Behavior and Organization* 7:83–99.

Luenberger, David. 1979. *Introduction to Dynamic Systems*. New York: Wiley.

May, Robert. 1976. "Simple Mathematical Models with Very Complicated Dynamics." *Nature* 261:459–67.

Noelle-Nuemann, Elisabeth. 1974. "The Spiral of Silence: A Theory of Public Opinion." *Journal of Communication* 24:43–51.

——————. 1977. "Turbulences in the Climate of Opinion: Methodological Applications of the Spiral of Silence Theory." *Public Opinion Quarterly* 41:143–58.

——————. 1984. *The Spiral of Silence*. Chicago: University of Chicago Press.

O'Gorman, Hubert, and Stephen Garry. 1976. "Pluralistic Ignorance: A Replication and Extension." *Public Opinion Quarterly* 40:449–58.

Schelling, Thomas. 1971. "Dynamic Models of Segregation." *Journal of Mathematical Sociology* 1:143–86.

——————. 1973. "A Process of Residential Segregation: Neighborhood Tipping." Pp. 157–84 in *Racial Discrimination in Economic Life*, edited by Anthony Pascal. Lexington, MA: D. C. Heath.

_____. 1978. *Micromotives and Macrobehavior*. New York: W. W. Norton.

Spence, Michael. 1974. *Market Signaling*. Cambridge, MA: Harvard University Press.

Taylor, D. Garth. 1982. "Pluralistic Ignorance and the Spiral of Silence: A Formal Analysis." *Public Opinion Quarterly* 46:311–35.

_____. 1983. "Public Opinion and Community Conflict: Threshold Models, The Spiral of Silence and Anti-Busing Protest." Mimeo.

_____. 1984. "A Revised Theory of Racial Tipping." Pp. 142–66 in *Paths of Neighborhood Change: Race and Crime in Urban America*, edited by Richard Taub, D. Garth Taylor, and Jan Dunham. Chicago: University of Chicago Press.

_____. 1986. *Public Opinion, Collective Action and Anti-Busing Protest: The Boston School Desegregation Conflict*. Chicago: University of Chicago Press.

4

A Method for Analyzing Backward Recurrence Time Data On Residential Mobility

Nazli Baydar* and Michael White[†]

Social surveys often collect data on duration of current residence. Under certain assumptions, these data can be used to estimate models of duration-dependent residential mobility rates. We use the theory of backward recurrence times in renewal processes to infer the hazard rate of residential mobility from the density of the duration of current residence. We demonstrate that the inferences made using the asymptotic solution of the density of the backward recurrence times will be severely biased if the renewal process has not reached stability. We present an unbiased finite time solution and estimate univariate and multivariate models of residential mobility rates using 1980 U.S. census data on duration of current residence. These models include mover-stayer models represented by mixture densities. The multivariate analysis shows that the most important covariates of residential mobility are age, homeownership, race, and presence of school-aged children.

1. INTRODUCTION

Data on duration of current residence are collected regularly by the decennial censuses and by other large-scale social surveys (e.g., the

We thank Mark Montgomery, Burton Singer, and three anonymous reviewers for their comments. In the early stages of this research, we benefitted from numerous discussions with Erhan Cinlar. Our research has been partially funded by NICHD grants HD19473-01 and HD18739-01.

*Columbia University
[†] Urban Institute

105

Survey of Income and Program Participation [SIPP]) whose main concern is not geographical mobility. Since it is almost impossible to collect complete residential mobility histories, most geographical mobility surveys ask only about intercounty or interstate migration. Therefore, data on duration of current residence are the most common sources of information on residential mobility in the U.S.

We present a method to estimate univariate and multivariate models of duration-dependent residential mobility rates. Our approach is based on the renewal theory and, more specifically, on the theory of backward recurrence times in renewal processes.

The analysis of duration data has been investigated by a few researchers. Sheps et al. (1970) and Menken and Sheps (1970) present an exponential model for open-ended birth-interval data. Sørensen (1977) gives a theoretical discussion of the bias in the mean length of the open-ended intervals used as an estimator of the mean length of the completed intervals. Ginsberg (1978, 1979a, 1979b, 1983) estimates models for duration-of-current-residence data, but he relies on additional data to estimate the parameters of his models. Heckman and Singer (1984) present the general methodological issues involved in modelling data on duration in current status.

Allison (1985) estimates a set of models of time-dependent, age-dependent, and duration-dependent residential mobility rates. His duration-dependence models are very similar to ours, except that he uses the asymptotic results of the theory of backward recurrence times. This approach assumes that the survey measuring the duration of current residence is distant in time from the start of the residential mobility process, i.e., that each individual has been exposed to the risk of residential mobility with his current characteristics long enough that the history of the process has become irrelevant. This is a strong assumption and may have serious effects on the estimates (see Appendix A).

We present a set of models of duration-dependent hazard rates of residential mobility that can be estimated using data on duration of current residence. To estimate these models, we do not have to assume that each individual has been exposed to the risk of residential mobility long enough to have experienced multiple residential moves. We show that it is possible to estimate duration-dependence models controlling for age dependence and dependence on other sociodemographic covariates using a multivariate extension of the renewal model. Our application uses 1980 U.S. census data on duration of current residence.

2. U.S. CENSUS DATA ON RESIDENTIAL MOBILITY

The data that we use come from the public-use microdata sample (PUMS) of the 1980 census of population and housing. Because of the large size of the PUMS, we analyzed only 5 percent of the original sample of households. Residential mobility information comes from responses to the question, "When did [the householder] move into this house or apartment?" To our knowledge, relatively little use has been made of this information. Analyses of census data on geographical mobility often use information on the place of residence five years ago, which has been regularly used to analyze intercounty or interstate migration. Data on duration of current residence from the census and from such surveys as SIPP are the most commonly available sources of information on residential mobility.

The information about the time of move into the current residence is available only in categorical form. We assume that the move occurred at the midpoint of the time bracket.[1] The original data are tabulated in Table 1. The variables we use represent the basic

---

[1] Under this assumption, the likelihood equations can be written in continuous time, and therefore the computations can be substantially simplified. We performed a Monte Carlo simulation exercise to show the impact of this assumption on the estimated model parameters. We simulated a renewal process of residential moves generated by a mixture of a gamma and an exponential density. A series of backward recurrence times was obtained, and the duration dependence of the residential moves was modelled following the methods described in the next section. The backward recurrence times were then grouped into intervals, and the modelling exercise was repeated for each of the following assumptions: (a) the moves occurred at the midpoints of the intervals, (b) the moves occurred at the endpoints of the intervals, (c) the moves occurred at the two-thirds points of the intervals. This exercise was repeated for 100 samples of size 1,000. The first assumption reproduced the true values of the underlying process very closely. The mean value of the parameters were at most 2 percent off, and the 95 percent confidence intervals straddled the true values. The standard deviations of the estimated parameters under this assumption were slightly lower than those estimated using the exact backward recurrence time. The second assumption yielded severely biased parameter estimates. The mean waiting time implied by these assumptions was almost twice its true value. The third assumption also yielded severely biased parameter estimates; however, the implied mean waiting time was only 9 percent upwardly biased. We conclude that the midpoint assumption is plausible for our purposes.

TABLE 1

Data on Duration of Current Residence, by Age of Householder, from the 1980
Census, 5 Percent Sample of the PUMS

	Year Moved into Current Residence					
Age at Census	1979– March 1980	1975– 1978	1970– 1974	1960– 1969	1950– 1959	1949 or earlier
19	68	9	1	—	—	—
20–29	371	263	41	5	7	—
30–39	234	349	188	62	5	8
40–49	94	163	137	177	26	7
50–59	82	121	123	201	141	39
60–69	51	98	87	136	110	87
70 +	40	99	68	99	90	150

TABLE 2

Descriptive Statistics of the Sample of 4,037 Households

Variable	
Proportion of householders who are female	27.2
Proportion of householders who are black	9.4
Proportion of households with married couples or families	62.1
Proportion of households with school-aged children	28.5
Mean age of householders	47.0
Mean number of years spent in current residence	12.0
Mean household income	$20,095.0
Proportion of householders in professional occupations[a]	38.7
Proportion of householders in production occupations[b]	34.5

[a] Includes executives, administrators, managers, professionals in specialty occupations, scientists, health professionals, teachers, writers, artists, and social and religious workers (census three-digit codes 003-199).

[b] Includes farmers, foresters, and fishermen; workers in precision, production, craft, and repair; operators, fabricators, and laborers (census three-digit codes 473-859).

characteristics of the household and the householder. Table 2 provides some descriptive statistics of the sample of 4,037 households. Married-couple and family households constitute only 62 percent of this sample. The remaining 38 percent consists of nonfamily and single-parent households. The householders are predominantly white males, have a mean age of 47, and are evenly distributed over the three major occupational categories (production-related, sales and service, and professional and managerial). Most households occupy a residence owned by one of the members.

3. A METHOD FOR ANALYZING DATA ON DURATION OF CURRENT RESIDENCE

Backward recurrence time data on residential mobility are reported as either times of arrival at (t_a) or durations of (u) current residence. The two forms of data are equivalent if the time of the survey (τ) is known $(u = \tau - t_a)$. Both τ and t_a are measured relative to the time origin (t_o). If an individual has never moved, the duration of current residence (u) is equal to the time of the survey (τ).

The time origin of the process is context-specific and, therefore, should be determined on substantive grounds. It can be the time of birth, the time of marriage, the time of retirement, or any other event that marks the start of the mobility process of interest. We assume that t_o is also observed. Our purpose is to estimate the duration-specific hazard rate of mobility.

Let the density of the duration of current residence (i.e., the backward recurrence time) be $f^*(u)$ and the hazard rate of residential mobility be $h(t)$. We can estimate $f^*(u)$ empirically from the observed frequency distribution of backward recurrence times. Our aim is to represent $f^*(u)$ in terms of $h(t)$ so that the parameters of $h(t)$ can be estimated from the information on backward recurrence times.

The simplest model of residential mobility has a hazard rate that is constant over time (i.e., an exponential or Poisson model). The backward recurrence time density of this process is simple to derive if we assume that residential mobility can be represented by a renewal process (Cox 1962, p. 31; Feller 1966, pp. 11–13):

$$f^*(u) = a \exp(-au), \tag{1}$$

where a is the hazard rate. This was presented to the sociological audience by Sørensen (1977). It is well known that under the exponential model, the density of the length of the left-censored spells in the population is equal to the density of the length of the completed spells (for a graphical proof, see Menken and Sheps 1970). This is known as the waiting-time paradox or length-biased sampling.

Given the expression in (1), we can easily write the likelihood (ℓ) for an exponential model of residential mobility. For a single observation

$$\ell = a^d \exp(-au),\tag{2}$$

where ℓ is the likelihood and

$$d = \begin{cases} 1 & u < \tau - t_o \\ 0 & \text{otherwise.} \end{cases}$$

In general, the hazard rate is duration-dependent. A renewal process with a duration-dependent hazard retains memory; i.e., the unconditional probability that an event occurs at a given time, $m(t)$, depends on the entire history of the process. We define $m(t)$ as

$$m(t)\, dt = dM(t),\tag{3}$$

where $M(t)$ is the renewal function giving the expected number of renewals at time t:

$$M(t) = 1 + \int_0^t M(t-x) f(x)\, dx.\tag{4}$$

Because of the history dependency, the expression for the backward recurrence time density is somewhat more complex when the hazard is duration-dependent.

Cox (1962, pp. 63–66) and Karlin and Taylor (1975, pp. 192–95) give the limiting solution to the backward recurrence time density, and Allison (1985) applies it to backward recurrence time data on intercounty migration. The limiting density is

$$\lim_{\tau - t_o \to \infty} f^*(u) = \mu^{-1} \left[1 - F(u)\right],\tag{5}$$

where μ is the expected length of a spell and $F(t)$ is the distribution function of the completed spells.

Expression (5) closely approximates the finite-time density only if the distance between the time origin and the time of the interview is sufficiently large compared to μ. In other words, if the probability of experiencing no moves between t_o and the survey is almost zero, and if every individual experiences a sufficiently large number of moves, equation (5) can be used to estimate the parameters of the process. These assumptions are very likely to be violated unless the data are collected from individuals who have been exposed to the residential mobility risk for a long enough time relative to the expected length of a spell between two moves. In most cases the limiting solution is a very crude approximation and one needs a finite-time solution to the density of the backward recurrence times. Cox (1962, pp. 62–63) showed that under a renewal model, the probability that the backward recurrence time is greater than u is equal to

$$\Pr\{U > u\} = [1 - F(\tau)] + \int_0^{\tau - u} [1 - F(\tau - x)] \, dM(x). \qquad (6)$$

The second term in (6) represents the probability conditional on at least one event between t_o and τ. The first term accounts for the possibility of no events before τ. It follows from (6) that the density of the backward recurrence time is

$$f^*(u) = [1 - F(u)] m(\tau - u). \qquad (7)$$

The density of the open-ended interval is easily obtained when $m(t)$ is expressed in terms of $h(t)$ and related probability functions of the process. This approach is different from that of Ginsberg (1978, 1979a, 1983), who estimates the renewal density empirically. Ginsberg's approach requires the use of some additional data to estimate the unconditional probability of an event at time t_a. Although the empirical estimation of the renewal density is an attractive and simple solution, it cannot be followed when the only available data are backward recurrence time data, as is the case in the U.S. The questions on most national-level mobility surveys (e.g., the Panel Study of Income Dynamics, the National Longitudinal Survey of Youth) are restricted to intercounty migration, and the surveys of residential mobility (e.g., the Rhode Island study) do not have a national coverage. We cannot, therefore, rely on empirical estimates of the renewal density. Analytical expressions for the renewal density are potentially valuable for the study of residential mobility in developing countries, where multiple sources of data are seldom available.

The renewal density can be derived by taking the Laplace transform of the underlying distribution function. In principle, this

TABLE 3

Some Parametric Hazard Specifications and their Corresponding
Renewal Densities

Function	Density	Renewal Density	
		Finite t	$t \to \infty$
Gamma ($\nu = 2$)[a]	$a^2 t \exp(-at)$	$a/2\{1 - \exp(-2at)\}$	$a/2$
Mixture of two exponentials[b]	$\delta_1 a \exp(-at)$ $+ \delta_2 b \exp(-bt)$	$1/\mu + (\theta - 1/\mu)$ $\exp\{-(\delta_2 a + \delta_1 b)t\}$	$ab/[\delta_1 b + \delta_2 a]$
Mixture of gamma ($\nu = 2$) and exponential[c]	$\delta_1 a^2 t \exp(-at)$ $+ \delta_2 b \exp(-bt)$	$1/\mu + \gamma_1 \exp(-r_1 t)$ $- \gamma_2 \exp(-r_2 t)$	$ab/[2\delta_1 b + \delta_2 a]$

[a] ν is the shape parameter of the gamma density: $[a(at)^{\nu - 1} \exp(-at)]/\Gamma(\nu)$.

[b] $\delta_1 + \delta_2 = 1$; μ is the weighted average of the mean waiting times: $\mu = \delta_1/a + \delta_2/b$; and θ is the weighted average of the two hazards: $\theta = \delta_1 a + \delta_2 b$.

[c] $\delta_1 + \delta_2 = 1$;

$\gamma_1 = \{r_1[\delta_1 a^2 + \delta_2 b(2a - r_1)] - a^2 b\}/\{r_1(r_1 - r_2)\}$;

$\gamma_2 = \{r_2[\delta_1 a^2 + \delta_2 b(2a - r_2)] - a^2 b\}/\{r_2(r_1 - r_2)\}$;

r_1 and r_2 are the roots of $\lambda^2 + (2a - \delta_1 b)\lambda + (2ab\delta_1 + \delta_2 a^2) = 0$, where λ is the Laplace transform parameter (see Appendix A).

lengthy procedure results in an analytical expression for the renewal density if the parametric form of the underlying hazard function is known.[2] However, for many commonly used parametric hazard forms, the corresponding renewal density is very difficult to derive.

Table 3 presents a few parametric hazard specifications and the corresponding finite-time and limiting renewal densities. All the functions considered in this table are from the gamma family. The primary reason for this limitation is the difficulty of obtaining analytical solutions for the renewal densities of other forms. Although the numerical evaluation of the renewal density is possible for any parametric form, it renders the analysis of large social science data sets computationally impractical.

The gamma family models given in Table 3 provide a limited but tractable selection of hazard functions for our purposes. These

---

[2] See Appendix A for a complete description of the mathematics of this derivation.

functions can be used to estimate the parameters of an underlying renewal process using only backward recurrence time data and without making the assumption that the asymptotic behavior of the process is a close enough approximation. The functions presented in Table 3 represent three forms of duration dependence in addition to the constant hazard model. The mixture of two exponentials implies an aggregate hazard function that declines by duration, although the two components of the mixture are constant over time. The gamma model with a shape parameter of 2 implies a hazard function that rises by duration, and the mixture of a gamma and an exponential implies an aggregate hazard function that has a single, left-skewed peak.

The two mixture models presented in Table 3 can be interpreted as simple models of unobserved heterogeneity in residential mobility, or mover-stayer models (Blumen, Kogan, and McCarthy 1955). These models represent two subgroups of a population with distinct migration rates. Rationale for these models has been provided by empirical analyses (Morrison 1971; Spilerman 1972; Sandefur 1985), which have shown that heterogeneity in propensities for geographical mobility persists when other sociodemographic covariates are controlled.

The model with the mixture of two exponentials represents the hypothesis that residential mobility rates are constant over time for each subgroup of the population. The proportions in the high-mobility and low-mobility groups are given by the two weight factors δ_1 and δ_2. The resulting aggregate mobility rate for the population declines by duration, because the population at risk consists of progressively higher proportions in the low-mobility group.

The second mixture model (i.e., the mixture of a gamma and an exponential) assumes that the two subgroups of the population have two distinct patterns of mobility. In the high-mobility group, mobility rates increase by duration to an asymptotic value. The low-mobility group experiences a constant risk of residential mobility. The δ_1 and δ_2 are the proportions of high- and low-mobility individuals, respectively. This model is somewhat more realistic. One expects individuals who are dissatisfied with their residence to have increasing rates of mobility for the first few years as their chances of finding an alternative increase. DaVanzo and Morrison (1981) state that the corrective moves at short durations account for the increasing rates of moves during this period. It is plausible that only the moves of a certain proportion of the population are followed by corrective moves and that the remaining moves are well contemplated, well planned, and result in longer durations of stay.

Given the method described here, we can analyze residential mobility differences among subgroups of the population by estimating the underlying hazard rate for each subgroup with a specific observed characteristic. This is a univariate approach and suffers from all the limitations of univariate analyses of sociodemographic phenomena. Some limited multivariate extensions are possible, and they are presented below.

The univariate approach allows one to analyze the effects of very few covariates at a time, since the sample size limits the number of subgroups that can be formed. One has to determine whether the assumption of a renewal process is valid for the moves of a subgroup of the population with a certain characteristic, because the characteristics of the individuals are measured only at the time of the survey. A

FIGURE 1.   Residential mobility of the whole sample, U.S. 1980.

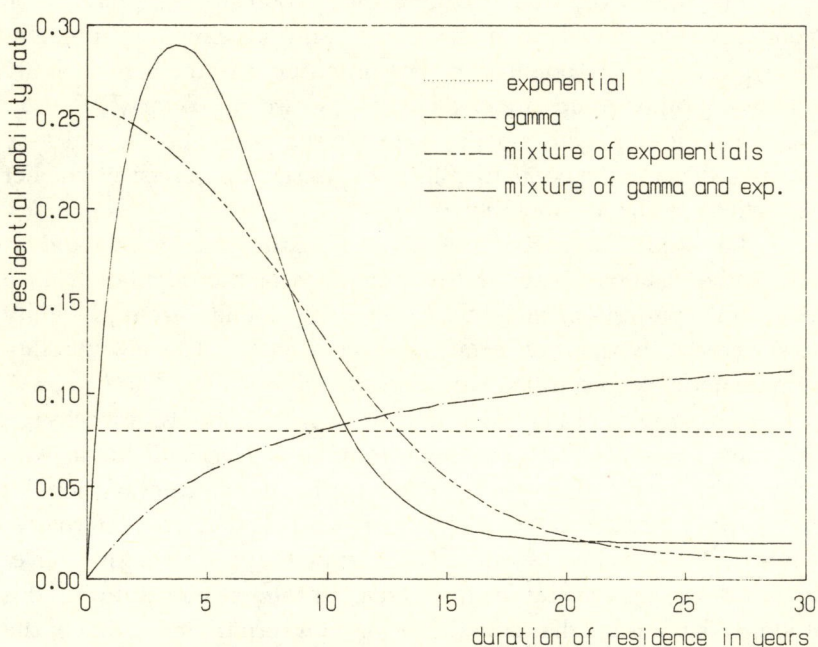

univariate analysis of a covariate is possible if that covariate is likely to have stayed constant over a reasonably long period of time and if the date of last change in the covariate is known. This is almost always equivalent to judging whether the time origin of the process is identifiable in reference to the particular covariate that is being analyzed.

For example, if we are interested in the effects of marriage on an individual's risk of residential mobility (disregarding marital dissolution), the time origin of the mobility process should be specified as the date of first marriage. Individuals who are married at the time of the survey (τ) have been at risk of moving as married persons since the

TABLE 4

Results of the Aggregate Analysis of Data on the Duration of Current Residence, from the 1980 Census, 5 Percent Sample of the PUMS

Model	N	Parameter		
		a	b	δ_1
Whole sample				
Exponential (baseline)	4,035	0.08*	—	—
Gamma	4,035	0.14*	—	—
Mixture of exponentials ($\chi^2 = 1,389.3$, $df = 2$, $p < 0.01$)	4,035	0.28*	0.01	0.92*
Mixture of gamma and exponential ($\chi^2 = 1,543.0$, $df = 2$, $p < 0.01$)	4,035	0.56*	0.02*	0.88*
Age group[a]				
20–29 ($\chi^2 = 32.2$, $df = 2$, $p < 0.01$)	796	2.30*	0.30*	0.49*
30–39 ($\chi^2 = 15.2$, $df = 2$, $p < 0.01$)	808	0.81*	0.08*	0.48*
40–49 ($\chi^2 = 14.4$, $df = 2$, $p < 0.01$)	607	0.56*	0.03*	0.41*
50–59 ($\chi^2 = 21.2$, $df = 2$, $p < 0.01$)	699	0.29*	0.05*	0.16*
60–69 ($\chi^2 = 8.2$, $df = 2$, $p < 0.02$)	557	0.29*	0.03*	0.30*
Cohort				
1944–1961[b] ($\chi^2 = 30.2$, $df = 2$, $p < 0.01$)	1,294	2.30*	0.26*	0.53*
1943–1919[c]	1,692	0.09*	—	—
–1918[c]	1,049	0.04*	—	—

Note: The reported chi squares are relative to the baseline model.

[a] All models of age-group-specific residential mobility are mixtures of gamma and exponential densities.

[b] The model is a mixture of gamma and exponential densities.

[c] The exponential model cannot be rejected.

* Significant at the 0.05 level.

date of their first marriage. The covariates that change continuously over time, such as age or marital duration, cannot be analyzed unless one is willing to form five- or ten-year age or duration brackets.

Identifying the origin of the process requires careful consideration even for the fixed covariates. Our interest is usually in the determinants of the decisions to move made by individuals who can act on their decisions. We identify a time point for each individual after which he/she can act upon his/her decision to move. This time origin has many cultural and individual determinants. In our analysis, we assume that the time origin of the process can be no earlier than age 18. This choice is rather arbitrary, and various other specifications (e.g., the date the parental home was left, the date education was completed, or age 21) are equally plausible alternative specifications.

4. RESULTS OF THE UNIVARIATE ANALYSIS

We tested all three models of duration dependence presented in Table 3 using the residential mobility data from the 1980 census. We

FIGURE 2.   Residential mobility by age groups, U.S. 1980.

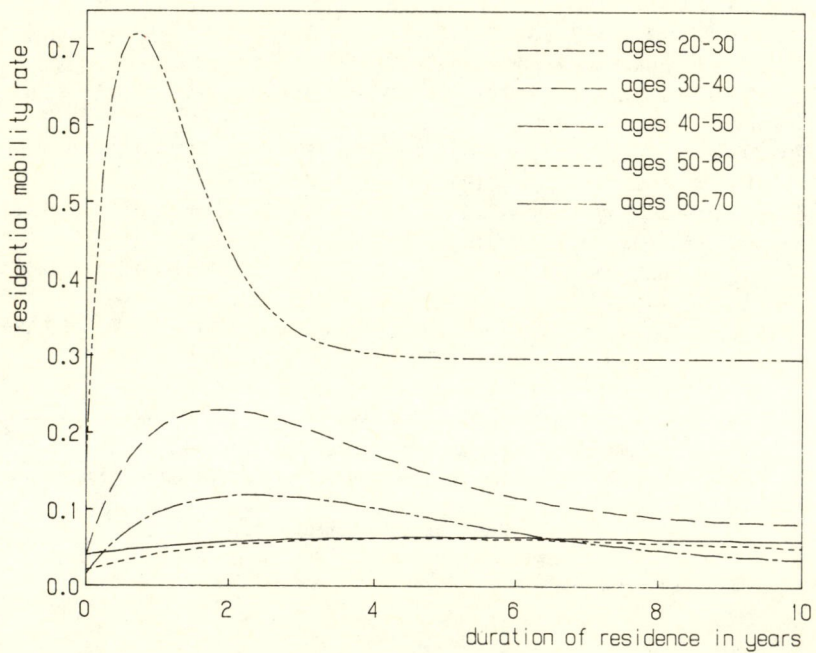

present the exponential model as a baseline model. All models were estimated by the maximum likelihood technique (see Appendix B). Figure 1 displays the estimated hazards of residential mobility for the whole sample.

The likelihood ratio statistic shows that the mixture of the gamma and exponential densities that yields a nonmonotonic hazard rate gives the best fit to the data (Table 4). According to this model, 88 percent of the households belong to the high-mobility group. This group has a mean duration of residence of 3.6 years. For the remaining 12 percent of the households, the estimated hazard rate is very low but different from zero. The low- and high-mobility groups have substantially different rates. The aggregate hazard rate reaches a peak around 4 years of duration and then declines rapidly.

We analyzed residential mobility by age groups by forming subsamples by age at the census and redefining the time origin. For example, the model for the age bracket 20–29 was estimated for the individuals aged 20–29 at the time of the census, and the time origin

FIGURE 3. Residential mobility by cohort, U.S. 1980.

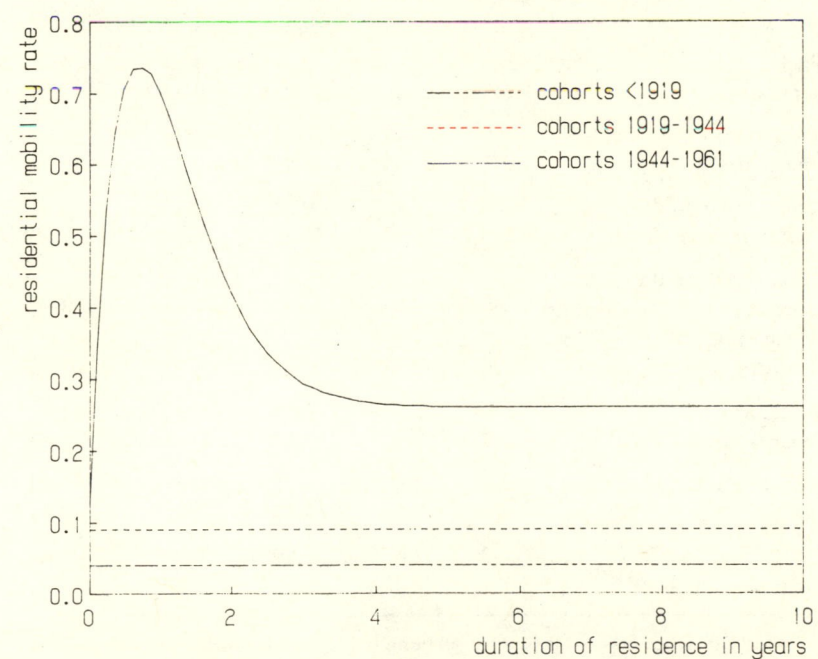

was redefined as the 20th birthday. This analysis (Table 4 and Figure 2) shows substantial differences in residential mobility by age. The rates are highest in the 20–29 bracket, then they decrease uniformly to the 50–59 bracket. The residential mobility rates are slightly higher in the last age bracket (60–69) in early durations than in the previous age bracket, probably because of retirement moves. The mean duration of residence increases steadily from the youngest age bracket to the oldest age bracket, from approximately 2 years to 25 years.

Cohort analysis of residential mobility rates (Table 4 and Figure 3) shows that the youngest cohort, which consists of the householders born after 1944, has the highest mobility rates—an average waiting time of 2.3 years. The estimated proportion of movers is 53 percent,

TABLE 5

Results of the Univariate Analysis of Data on the Duration of Current Residence, for the 1944–1961 Cohorts

Subsample	N	a	b	δ_1	Mean Duration
Female	303	2.20	0.23*	0.61*	2.24
Male	991	2.36	0.27*	0.50*	2.28
Black	149	2.16	0.21*	0.45*	3.01
Nonblack	1,145	2.35	0.27*	0.53*	2.18
Never-married	320	2.46	0.27*	0.72*	1.65
Ever-married	975	2.36	0.21*	0.46*	2.94
Family household	766	2.48	0.21*	0.46*	2.98
Nonfamily household	529	2.33	0.24*	0.69*	1.92
School-aged children present	368	2.18	0.20*	0.03*	4.91
No school-aged children present	926	2.36	0.30*	0.59*	1.90
Homeowners	531	1.67*	0.15*	0.35*	4.82
Tenants	697	2.39*	0.29*	0.68*	1.66
Production workers	524	2.32	0.22*	0.62*	2.30
Others	770	2.32	0.30*	0.45*	2.24
Professionals	342	2.01*	0.29*	0.34*	2.64
Nonprofessionals	927	2.32*	0.24*	0.59*	2.21

* Difference between the paired subsamples is significant at the 0.05 level.

and their average waiting time is less than one year. The two older cohorts have much lower rates of residential mobility. The pattern of duration dependence of residential mobility for these older cohorts is not significantly different from a constant hazard. The estimated mean waiting times for the middle cohort (born 1919–1943) and the oldest cohort (born before 1919) are 11 and 33 years, respectively. One must be cautious in interpreting the age and cohort differentials presented here. The cohort analysis does not control for age differences in residential mobility, and the analysis by age groups does not control for confounding cohort effects. This is a common problem in making longitudinal inferences from cross-sectional data. For example, if the confounding age effects were controlled for, the intercohort variation might be less substantial.

We restrict the analysis of sociodemographic differentials in residential mobility to the cohort of householders born after 1944, i.e., to those under 36 at the time of the census. Our strategy is to estimate the gamma-exponential mixture model for different subgroups of this cohort. The subgroups are defined by a set of dichotomous covariates of residential mobility.

We identified the approximate time origin of the process for each subgroup separately. For the ever-married group and for married-couple family households, the time origin was the date of first marriage. For the group of householders with school-aged children, the time origin was the date the oldest child reached age 6. We had to make assumptions about the time origins for the homeowners and professionals because we had no relevant data. We assumed that age 25 was the time origin for the homeowners and that age 22 was the time origin for the professionals.[3] For all other subgroups, the time origin was set at age 18.

Table 5 and Figure 4 present the results of the analysis of sociodemographic differentials in residential mobility. The analysis

---

[3] We do not expect the bias introduced by these rather arbitrary assumptions to be large. The location of the time origin affects only the total exposure time (τ) that determines the renewal density at time $\tau - u$:

$$m(\tau - u) = (1/\mu) + \gamma_1\exp\{-r_1(\tau - u)\} + \gamma_2\exp\{-r_2(\tau - u)\}.$$

The μ, γ_1, and γ_2 above are constants (see Table 3) with respect to τ and u. Since r_1 and r_2 are small, a few years difference in τ is not likely to change $m(\tau - u)$ a lot. However, large errors in τ for a high proportion of the individuals are bound to introduce serious biases into the estimation of the parameters of the process.

FIGURE 4. Sociodemographic differences in residential mobility, U.S. 1980, cohorts born after 1944.

a. Residential mobility by sex.

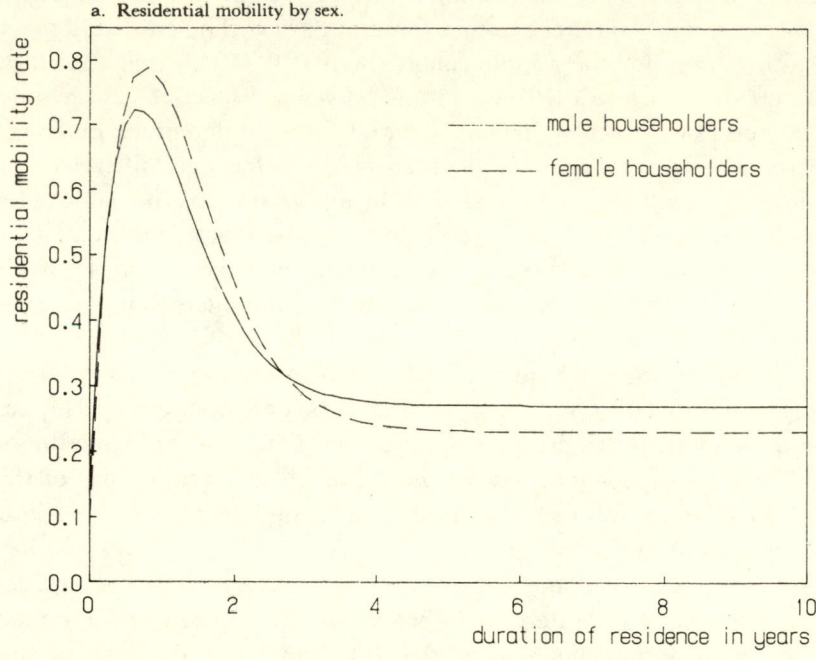

b. Residential mobility by race.

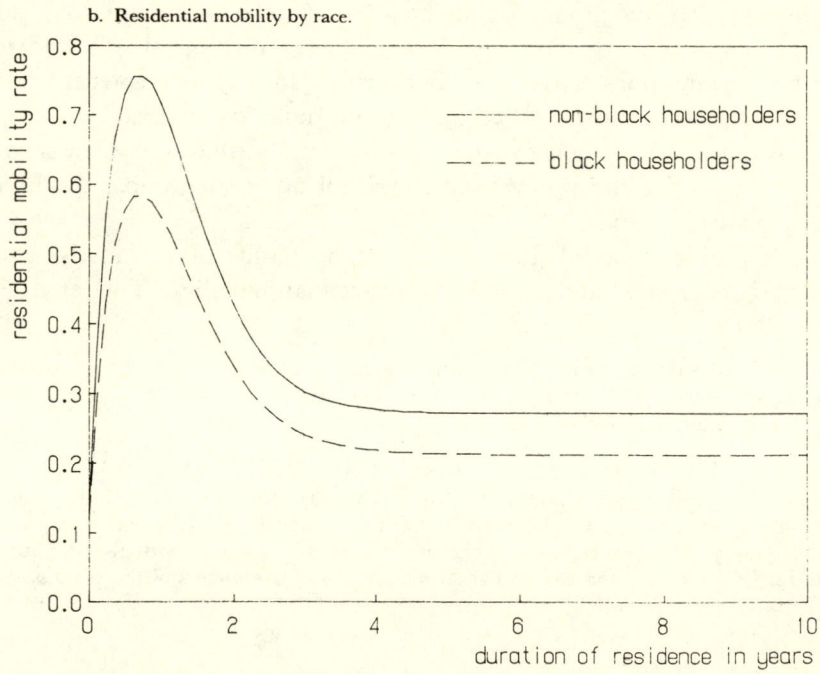

FIGURE 4. *Continued.*

c. Residential mobility by marital status.

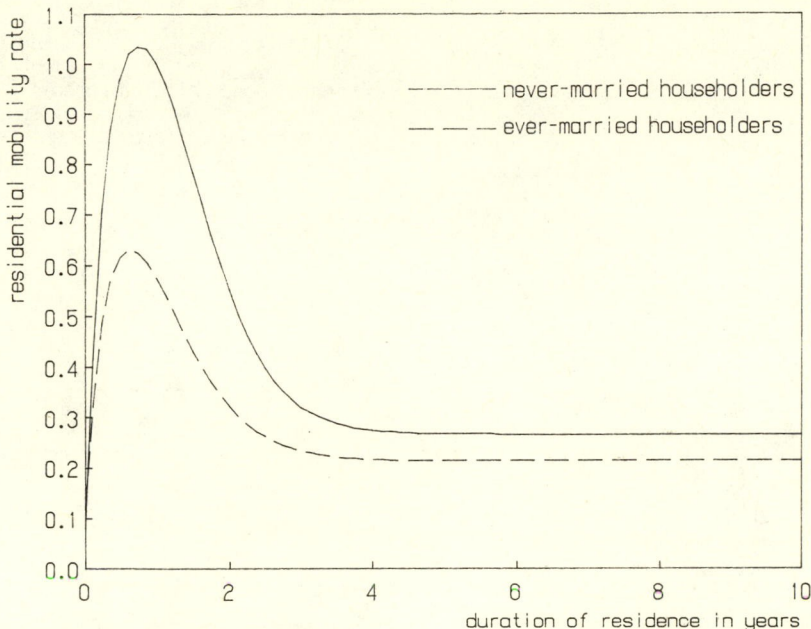

d. Residential mobility by household type.

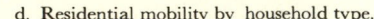
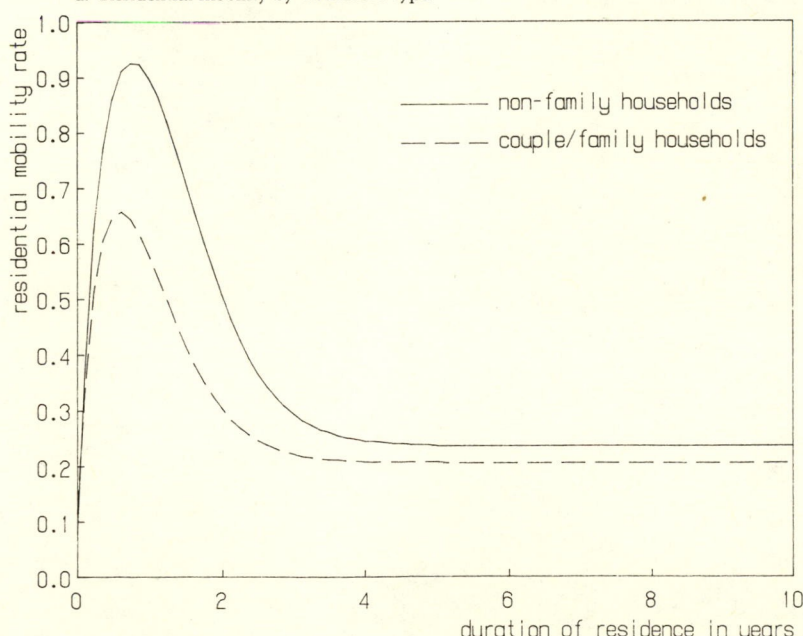

FIGURE 4. *Continued.*

e. Residential mobility by presence of school-aged children.

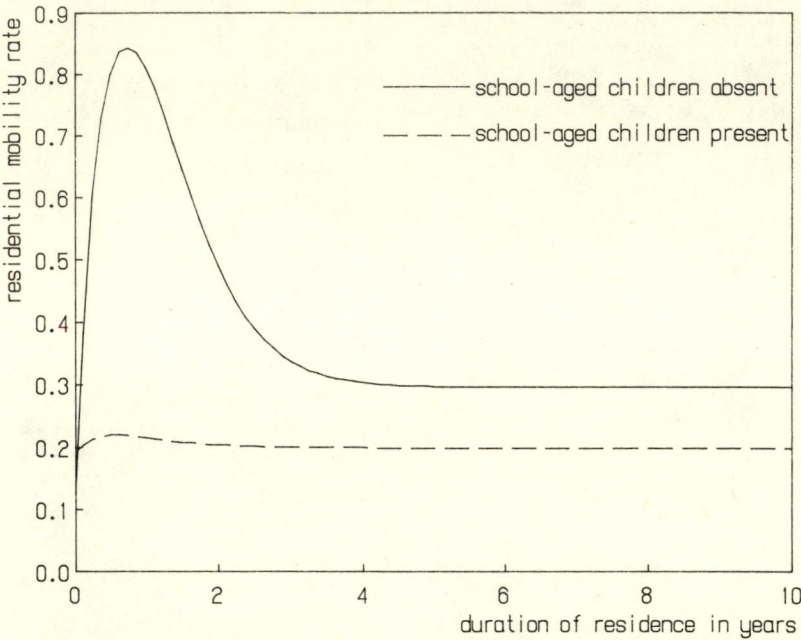

f. Residential mobility by homeownership.

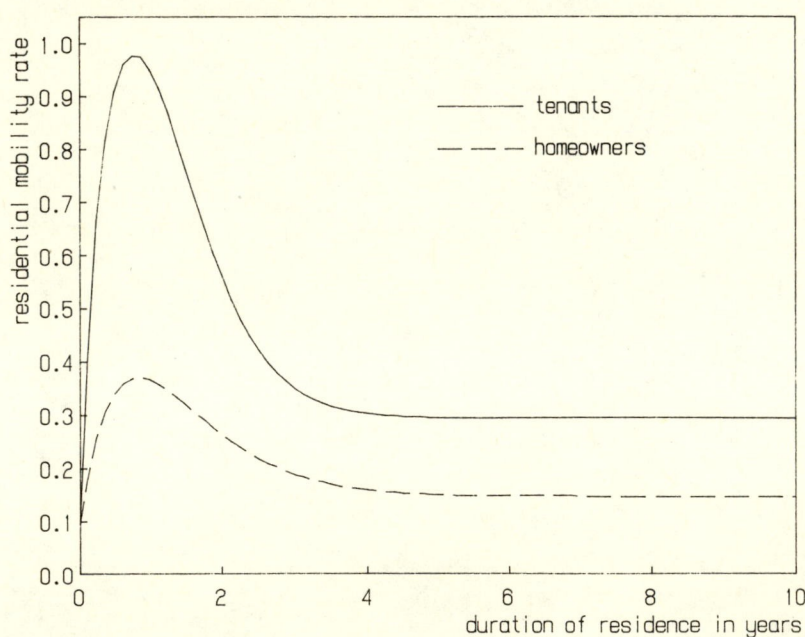

FIGURE 4. *Continued.*

g. Residential mobility by occupation (production vs. nonproduction).

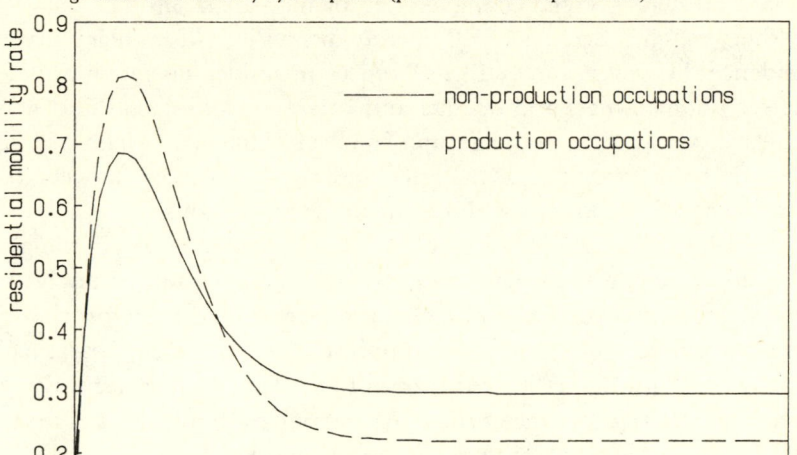

h. Residential mobility by occupation (professional vs. nonprofessional).

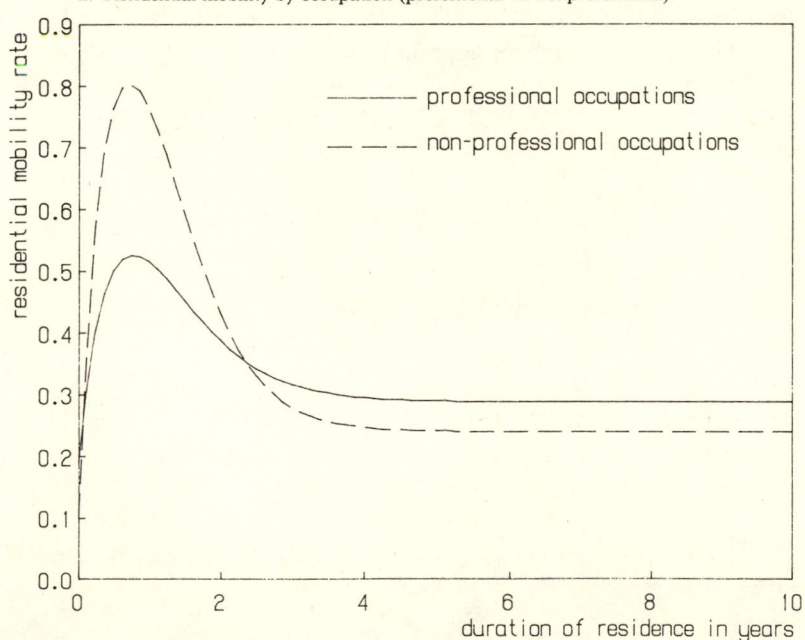

reveals that the mean waiting times for the high-mobility individuals vary little across the sociodemographically defined subgroups. The social and demographic characteristics of individuals are not relevant to their moving decisions if they are dissatisfied with their current residence. However, there are differences in residential mobility rates between homeowners and tenants and between professionals and non-professionals who are in the group of movers. The homeowners are less likely to be movers than the tenants, and of those who are movers, the homeowners have lower mobility rates than the tenants.

Most of the sociodemographic variables considered in our analysis result in significant differences in the residential mobility rates of the low-mobility groups. These differences are more modest across the sex and household-type (family/nonfamily) categories. The parameter that represents the estimated proportion of movers is sensitive to sociodemographic characteristics. All variables result in significant differences in the estimated proportion of movers.

Homeownership and the presence of school-aged children result in the largest residential mobility differences. The mean duration of residence for homeowners in this cohort is approximately 5 years, compared with just over 1.5 years for tenants. The proportion of movers among the householders with school-aged children is only 2 percent, lowest among all subsamples. This subgroup has an expected duration of residence of almost 5 years, compared with 2 years for the householders with no school-aged children.

5. A MULTIVARIATE EXTENSION OF THE RENEWAL MODEL

Most multivariate models of hazard rates have the proportional form

$$h(t) = h_o(t)\exp(\mathbf{X}\beta), \tag{8}$$

where $h_o(t)$ is the baseline hazard,[4] β is the column vector of coefficients, and $\mathbf{X}$ is the row vector of covariates. This specification is attractive because the β parameters, when exponentiated, yield factors that proportionally raise or decrease the hazard rate at a given duration for a unit change in the covariates ($\mathbf{X}$).

[4] The baseline hazard can be parametrically specified or left completely unspecified, as in Cox's proportional hazards model.

Once an expression for the hazard rate is given, it is possible, in principle, to evaluate the backward recurrence time density, $f^*(u)$, given in equation (7). However, an analytical solution is not always possible. When a proportional hazards form is adopted, $m(\tau - u)$ cannot be evaluated analytically. We could not use numerical procedures for the evaluation of the renewal density because they were too costly and too imprecise.

The alternative multivariate model that we present here relates the individual parameters of the process to a set of covariates. Let a and b be the parameters describing the gamma and the exponential components of the mixture model, respectively. We specify

$$a = a_o \exp(\mathbf{X}_a \boldsymbol{\beta}_a),$$
$$b = b_o \exp(\mathbf{X}_b \boldsymbol{\beta}_b). \tag{9}$$

The parameters a_o and b_o are the baseline parameters that describe the residential mobility pattern of the individuals whose covariates are all zero. Thus, a hazard function with parameters a_o and b_o can be interpreted as the baseline hazard.

This formulation is more conveniently interpreted in terms of the mean durations of stay. Let the mean durations of residence of the high- and low-mobility groups with the covariate set $\mathbf{X}$ be μ_a and μ_b, respectively, where

$$\mu_a = 2/a,$$
$$\mu_b = 1/b.$$

Note that the ratio of the mean durations of stay of two individuals with the covariate sets $\mathbf{Y}$ and $\mathbf{Z}$ depends only on the covariate values and the $\boldsymbol{\beta}$ coefficients:

$$_y\mu_a/_z\mu_a = \exp(-\mathbf{Y}\boldsymbol{\beta}_a)/\exp(-\mathbf{Z}\boldsymbol{\beta}_a). \tag{10}$$

In a special case of (9), $\mathbf{X}_a\boldsymbol{\beta}_a$ is equal to $\mathbf{X}_b\boldsymbol{\beta}_b$. This model implies that the ratio of the mean waiting times of the high- and low-mobility groups is independent of the covariate set, i.e.,

$$_y\mu_a/_y\mu_b = 2b_o/a_o, \tag{11}$$

and that the ratios of the mean durations of stay within the high- and the low-mobility groups are equal, i.e.,

$$_y\mu_a/_z\mu_a = _y\mu_b/_z\mu_b = \exp(-\mathbf{Y}\boldsymbol{\beta})/\exp(-\mathbf{Z}\boldsymbol{\beta}). \tag{12}$$

TABLE 6
Results of the Multivariate Model of Residential Mobility Rates

Parameter	Baseline Model	Model 1[a]	Model 2[b]	Model 3[c]
a_0	1.60	1.89*	2.53*	3.92*
b_0	0.12	0.59*	0.56*	0.42*
δ_1	0.30	0.07*	0.15*	0.39*
Female		−0.212*	−0.214*	−0.255*
Black		−0.547*	−0.565*	−0.552*
Hispanic		0.141	0.128	0.287
30–39 age group		−0.460*	−0.480*	−0.541*
40–49 age group		−1.041*	−1.101*	−1.153*
Ever-married		0.145	0.165	0.238
Couple-family household		−0.187	−0.208	−0.275*
School-aged children present		−0.344*	−0.409*	−0.394*
Homeowner (effect on a)			−1.048*	
Homeowner (effect on b)		−0.959*	−0.982*	−1.028*
Professionals		−0.088	−0.082	0.112
Production workers		−0.066	−0.069	−0.089
Completed at least high school		0.053	0.066	0.065

[a] The covariates determine the mean duration of stay of the low-mobility group only. χ^2 (relative to the baseline model) = 474.6, $df = 12$, $p < 0.01$.

[b] The mean duration of stay of the high-mobility group is determined only by the homeownership status of the members of the household. χ^2 (relative to model 1) = 7.6, $df = 1$, $p < 0.01$.

[c] The covariate effects are constrained to be equal for both parameters of the mixture model $(\mathbf{X}_a\boldsymbol{\beta}_a = \mathbf{X}_b\boldsymbol{\beta}_b)$. This model yields a better fit than models 1 and 2, as measured by the maximum likelihood statistic.

* Significant at the 0.05 level.

As in the univariate analysis, the time origin of the process must be identified for each individual before the multivariate analysis is done. However, individuals have different time origins according to different characteristics. We chose the time origin associated with the characteristic that changed most recently.[5] After that date, the individual was assumed to be exposed to residential mobility risks that depend

[5] Let t_{oi} be the time origin associated with the ith characteristic X_i, $i = 1, \ldots, n$. The time origin identified for the purposes of the multivariate analysis is t_o^*, such that

$$t_o^* = \max(t_{oi} | X_i, i = 1, \ldots, n).$$

only on the duration of stay given his/her set of relevant characteristics.

6. RESULTS OF THE MULTIVARIATE ANALYSIS

We tested three multivariate models using a sample of 1,776 householders aged 20 to 49 at the time of the census. The covariates included in the model are sex, ethnicity, age, homeownership, occupation, education, and household composition. The results of the multivariate analysis are summarized in Table 6. The multivariate models that we estimated differ from each other not in the number or type of covariates they include but in the specification of the structure of the relationship between the covariates and the mean durations of stay of the high- and low-mobility groups. Table 6 shows that the covariate coefficients are quite robust to different specifications. The sign, magnitude, and significance of the coefficients remain consistent across the columns of the table.

Following our findings from the univariate analysis that mean duration of residence of the high-mobility group is not sensitive to sociodemographic characteristics, we first estimate a model in which the covariates affect the mean duration of residence of the low-mobility group only.[6] In this model (model 1), the mean duration of residence of the movers is fixed and is independent of the covariates.

Model 1 has a significantly better overall goodness of fit than our baseline model with no covariates. This model indicates that female and black householders have lower rates of mobility. Householders aged 20 to 29 constitute the highest mobility group, followed by those aged 30 to 39 and those aged 40 to 49. Homeownership and the presence of school-aged children have negative effects on the rate of residential moves. The significant differences suggested by the univariate analysis between the ever-married and never-married householders and between occupational categories are not confirmed by the multivariate models that control for the confounding effects of the correlated covariates.

[6] The model can be written
$$a = a_o ,$$
$$b = b_o \exp(\mathbf{X}\boldsymbol{\beta}) .$$
Note that this is a special case of model (9).

Next, we test a model in which the parameter of the mixture model that represents the high-mobility individuals' rate of moving depends on homeownership only (model 2). This addition to the previous model significantly improves the overall fit; however, the effects of the homeownership variable on the residential mobility rates of the movers and stayers are not very different. The remaining coefficients of this model are similar to those of model 1 in sign, significance, and magnitude.

The third model that we estimate (model 3) allows the rates of residential moves of both the low- and the high-mobility householders to depend on the covariates and constrains the proportional effects on the mean durations of stay for both groups to be equal, as in equation (12). This constraint simplifies the model structure and adds some flexibility without increasing the number of parameters to be estimated. It results in a significant improvement in the overall goodness of fit.

Model 3, like models 1 and 2, does not detect significant residential mobility differences between Hispanic and white house-

FIGURE 5.   Results of the multivariate analysis.

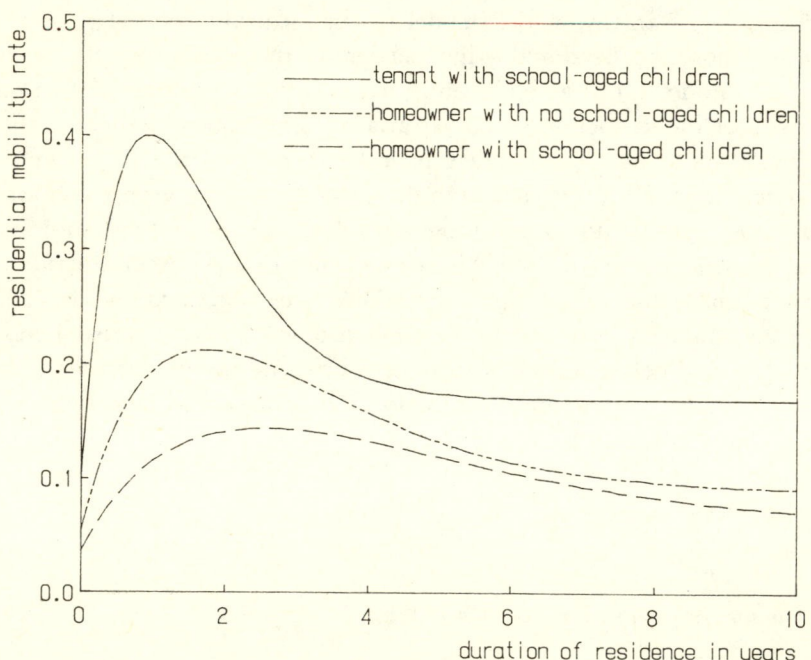

holders, between ever-married and never-married householders (net of current household type), between householders in the three occupational categories, and between householders with more than 12 years of education and those with less. Black and female householders are expected to have longer durations of stay. Family households and households with school-aged children appear to move less often, and homeownership appears again to strongly deter residential mobility.

Figure 5 graphically presents a few results of model 3. The homeowner-tenant differences remain as strong as indicated in the univariate analysis. Homeowners' expected duration of stay is 2.8 times longer than tenants' expected duration of stay.[7] The differences between the householders with school-aged children and those with no school-aged children are smaller when other covariates are controlled. The expected duration of stay for the householders with school-aged children is only 1.5 times longer than the expected duration for the householders without children. In the univariate analysis, this factor was 3.0.

7. CONCLUSIONS

We presented a method to analyze data on duration of current residence to obtain some information about patterns of duration dependence and covariate dependence of residential mobility rates. This method relies heavily on the assumption that residential mobility can be represented by a renewal process. The renewal theory provides a framework to relate backward recurrence times to the underlying density of the process. However, to use this approach, one must evaluate the renewal function, which can be difficult.

Researchers in this area have proposed several ways to circumvent this difficulty. One way of avoiding evaluation of the renewal function is to assume that the residential mobility rates are constant, that they do not depend on duration of residence. This assumption is unrealistic for most applications. Another alternative is to estimate the renewal function empirically using other sources of data (Ginsberg 1978, 1979a, 1979b). Unfortunately, other sources of data are often unavailable, and the researcher has to rely on data on the duration of current residence. Still another alternative is to assume that the

---

[7] This value is obtained directly from the coefficient of the homeowner variable (Table 6, col. 4): $2.8 = 1/\exp(-1.028)$.

asymptotic behavior of the renewal process is a close enough approximation (Allison 1985). The validity of this assumption depends on the mean duration of residence of the underlying process and the total exposure time of the members of the sample. Unless the asymptotic and finite-time estimates are compared, the validity of this approach cannot be judged.

The method presented here uses the finite-time estimates of the renewal function. This approach improves upon previous attempts to model data on the duration of current residence. However, it relies on the availability of an analytical form for the renewal function. This is possible if the underlying density belongs to the gamma family. Although this distributional assumption is somewhat restrictive, the gamma densities and their mixtures can incorporate a fair variety of hypotheses on the patterns of duration dependence.

The multivariate extension of our method makes it possible to estimate the effects of covariates on the duration-specific residential mobility rates. Although the structure of our multivariate model is different from the standard proportional hazards specifications, the coefficients of the covariates can be directly related to multiplicative effects on expected durations of residence and are therefore easily interpreted.

Our analysis of 1980 census data on the duration of current residence shows the wealth of information that can be obtained from backward recurrence time data. The pattern of duration dependence of residential mobility rates is nonmonotonic. The level of residential mobility depends strongly on the demographic characteristics of the householder, the household structure, and homeownership, although the differences in residential mobility between educational and occupational groups are small.

APPENDIX A. DERIVATION OF THE RENEWAL DENSITY

Let $F(t)$ be the distribution function of a renewal process. The renewal function $M(t)$ is related to the distribution function $F(t)$ by

$$M(t) = 1 + \int_0^t M(t-x)\, dF(x) \tag{A-1}$$

or

$$M(t) = \sum_{k=1}^{\infty} F_k(t), \tag{A-2}$$

where $F_k(t)$ is the distribution function of the kth renewal. An analytical expression for $M(t)$ can be derived using an expression for $F(t)$, since the Laplace transforms of the two functions are related by a simple expression (Cox 1962, pp. 53–55). Let M_λ and F_λ be the Laplace transforms of $M(t)$ and $F(t)$, respectively, defined as

$$M_\lambda = \int_0^\infty \exp(-\lambda t)\, dM(t), \qquad (A-3)$$

$$F_\lambda = \int_0^\infty \exp(-\lambda t)\, dF(t), \qquad (A-4)$$

where λ is the Laplace transform parameter. M_λ is related to F_λ as follows:

$$M_\lambda = F_\lambda / (1 - F_\lambda). \qquad (A-5)$$

The Laplace transforms of the distribution functions of the gamma family have a particularly simple form. A gamma function of order n with parameter a has the Laplace transform

$$F_\lambda = [a/(\lambda + a)]^n. \qquad (A-6)$$

As an example, we show the derivation of the renewal model for a mixture of two exponential densities. Equations (A-8) and (A-9) are based on the results given above:

$$f(t) = \delta_1 a \exp(-at) + \delta_2 b \exp(-bt), \qquad (A-7)$$
$$F_\lambda = \delta_1 [a/(\lambda + a)] + \delta_2 [b/(\lambda + b)]. \qquad (A-8)$$

From equation (A-5) and from the tables of Laplace transforms, we obtain the result given in Table 3:

$$m(t) = 1/\mu + (\theta - 1/\mu)\exp[-(\delta_2 a + \delta_1 b)t], \qquad (A-9)$$

where μ is the expected duration of residence and θ is the weighted average of two hazard rates a and b:

$$\theta = \delta_1 a + \delta_2 b. \qquad (A-10)$$

Note that as t gets larger, the second term gets smaller, and in the limit, $m(t)$ converges to $1/\mu$. The effect of the second term on the backward recurrence time density is large when the time since the origin of the process is small compared with the backward recurrence time. For the mixture model discussed here, this is easily seen by combining equations (7) and (A-9). Let u be the backward recurrence time and let τ be the time elapsed since the origin t_o. The backward

FIGURE A-1. Comparison of finite-time and limiting estimates for ever-married householders.

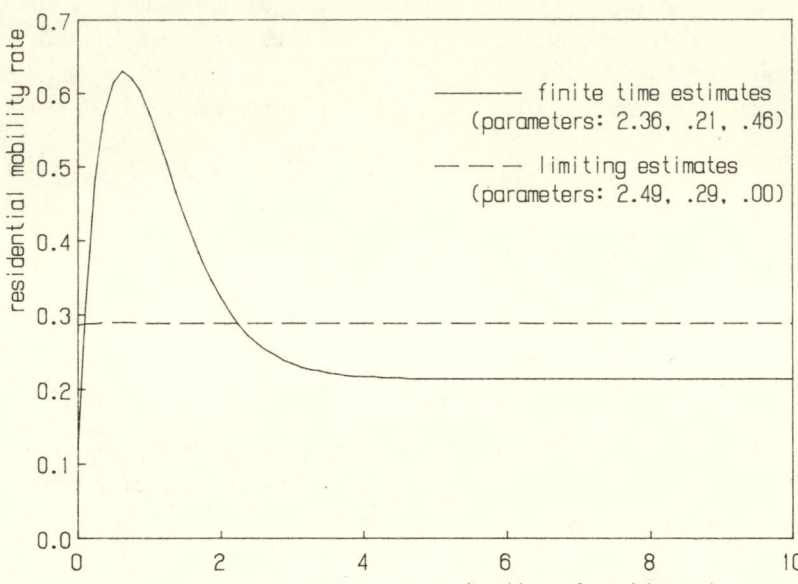

recurrence time density for the mixture of exponential densities is

$$f^*(u) = \left[\delta_1 \exp(-au) + \delta_2 \exp(-bu)\right]$$
$$\times \left[1/\mu + (\theta - 1/\mu)\exp\{-(\delta_2 a + \delta_1 b)(\tau - u)\}\right]. \quad (A\text{-}11)$$

The first term depends only on the backward recurrence time, but the second term depends on the length of the time since t_o relative to the backward recurrence time. When $\tau - u$ is small, this second term becomes important in determining the backward recurrence time density. This is why the determination of the time origin is important in the estimation of renewal models with backward recurrence time data. When the second term is large, the limiting approximation[8] to the renewal density becomes very crude. The estimated parameters of the renewal process under this approximation will be strongly biased. The exact magnitude of the bias will depend on the sample distributions of τ and u. Figure A-1 compares the finite-time estimates of the gamma-exponential mixture model presented here with estimates obtained by

[8] Allison (1985) uses this approximation in an application of renewal models to duration data from the 1968 Panel Study of Income Dynamics.

the limiting "approximation" for the ever-married householders of the 1944–1981 cohorts. The limiting estimates predict that almost all ever-married householders are stayers, and the gamma-exponential mixture practically converges to a single exponential density. These estimates are quite different from the finite-time estimates. If the limiting assumption were appropriate, the finite-time and limiting estimates would be much closer.

APPENDIX B. COMPUTATIONAL METHODS

The methods of estimating the mixture models are not standard. The literature suggests that maximum likelihood performs better than the method of moments, minimum chi square, or Bayes methods in general, but not for every problem (a review is given by Redner and Walker 1984). However, maximum likelihood is the most widely used method for estimating mixture models.

The methods of maximizing the likelihood have also been controversial. While some researchers prefer the EM algorithm, others favor Newton-type algorithms (a comparison of both approaches is given by Redner and Walker 1984). The advantages of the EM algorithm are its global convergence properties and its ability to generate a sequence of iterations with monotonically increasing values of the log likelihood. Its major disadvantage is that it can be intolerably slow (Redner and Walker 1984, p. 197; Trussell and Richards 1985, p. 252).

The maximum likelihood estimates presented in this paper were obtained by the DFP variable metric algorithm (Powell 1971). The DFP algorithm is a quasi-Newton algorithm that updates the Hessian at each stage, using an approximation. In this approach, the Hessian does not have to be reevaluated at each step; therefore the computation costs are low. However, at each additional iteration, the estimate of the Hessian deteriorates. For this reason, we used the DFP algorithm to obtain the estimates of the parameters presented in this paper, but not their standard errors. We estimated the standard errors at a second stage from the numerical estimates of the second-order partial derivatives around the maximum of the likelihood. Monte Carlo simulation exercises showed that our standard error estimates were very close to the empirical standard deviations of the parameter estimates obtained from repeated independent samples.

To make sure that our estimates were not the values at a local maximum, we started the iterations at several (presumably) reasonable starting values. All the starting values we tried were chosen such that the mean waiting time they implied was approximately equal to the mean waiting time that would have been obtained from an exponential model. We found that different starting values did not result in different estimates for this problem.

In the model that represents the mobility process as a mixture of a gamma and an exponential density, the mean waiting time given by the gamma density is constrained to be smaller than the mean waiting time given by the exponential density. This constraint reflects our hypothesis that the gamma density represents the mobility behavior of the movers and that the exponential density represents the mobility behavior of the stayers. It allows us to avoid the so-called label-switching problem in the estimation of mixture models.

REFERENCES

Allison, P. D. 1985. "Survival Analysis of Backward Recurrence Times." *Journal of the American Statistical Association* 80:315–22.

Blumen, I., M. Kogan, and P. J. McCarthy. 1955. "The Industrial Mobility of Labor as a Probability Process." Cornell Studies in Industrial and Labor Relations No. 6. Ithaca: Cornell University.

Cox, D. R. 1962. *Renewal Theory*. London: Methuen.

DaVanzo, J., and P. Morrison. 1981. "Return and Other Sequences of Migration in the United States." *Demography* 18:85–102.

Feller, W. 1966. *An Introduction to Probability Theory and its Applications*. Vol. 2. New York: Wiley.

Ginsberg, R. B. 1978. "The Relationship between Timing of Moves and Choice Destinations in Stochastic Models of Migration." *Environment and Planning*, ser. A, 10:667–79.

——————. 1979a. "Timing and Duration Effects in Residence Histories and Other Longitudinal Data, Part 1: Stochastic and Statistical Models." *Regional Science and Urban Economics* 9:311–31.

——————. 1979b. "Timing and Duration Effects in Residence Histories and Other Longitudinal Data, Part 2: Studies of Duration Effects in Norway, 1965–1971." *Regional Science and Urban Economics* 9:369–92.

——————. 1983. "Moving in a Given Year: A Study in Research Design and Data Analysis." *Tijdschrift voor Economische en Sociale Geografie* 74:253–66.

Heckman, J., and B. Singer. 1984. "Econometric Duration Analysis." *Journal of Econometrics* 24:63–112.

Karlin, S., and H. M. Taylor. 1975. *A First Course in Stochastic Processes*. New York: Academic Press.

Menken, J. A., and M. C. Sheps. 1970. "On the Relationship Between Longitudinal Characteristics and Cross-Sectional Data." *American Journal of Public Health* 60:1506–11.

Morrison, P. 1971. "Chronic Movers and the Future Redistribution of Population: A Longitudinal Analysis." *Demography* 8:171–84.

Powell, M. J. D. 1971. "Recent Advances in Unconstrained Optimization." *Mathematical Programming* 1:26–57.

Redner, R. A., and H. F. Walker. 1984. "Mixture Densities, Maximum Likelihood, and the EM Algorithm." *SIAM Review* 26:195–239.

Sandefur, G. 1985. "Variations in Interstate Migration of Men Across the Early Stage of the Life Cycle." *Demography* 22:353–66.

Sheps, M. C., J. A. Menken, J. C. Ridley, and J. W. Ligner. 1970. "Truncation Effect in Closed and Open Birth Interval Data." *Journal of the American Statistical Association* 65:678–93.

Sørensen, A. B. 1977. "Estimating Rates from Retrospective Questions." Pp. 209–23 in *Sociological Methodology 1977*, edited by D. R. Heise. San Fransicso: Jossey-Bass.

Spilerman, S. 1972. "Extensions of the Mover–Stayer Model." *American Journal of Sociology* 78:599–627.

Trussell, J., and T. Richards. 1985. "Correcting for Unmeasured Heterogeneity in Hazard Models Using the Heckman-Singer Procedure." Pp. 242–76 in *Sociological Methodology 1985*, edited by N. B. Tuma. San Francisco: Jossey-Bass.

5

Analyzing Change over Time in a Continuous Dependent Variable: Specification and Estimation of Continuous State Space Hazard Rate Models

*Trond Petersen**

This paper considers one type of stochastic process, examples of which include such microlevel processes as socioeconomic status and earnings histories. The dependent variable (for example, socioeconomic status) is continuous. Over time it evolves as follows. For finite periods of time—that is, from one calendar date to another—it stays constant at a given value. At a later date, which is a random variable, the dependent variable jumps to a new value, and this jump can be of any size and in any direction. In this type of process, which I call a continuous state space failure time process, the amount of time

This paper was commissioned by David L. Featherman and John R. Nesselroade on behalf of the National Institute on Aging. I gratefully acknowledge financial support from NIA grant AG04367. For detailed written comments and discussions I thank Knut Aase, Gerhard Arminger, Kenneth Bollen, Ørnulf Borgan, Glenn Carroll, Clifford Clogg, Aage Sørensen, Seymour Spilerman, Christopher Winship, Lawrence Wu, and three anonymous reviewers. I also thank Aaron Han, Tormod Lunde, Rachel Rosenfeld, Arthur Stinchcombe, and Mary Waters for discussions and helpful suggestions. Mary Visher commented on the entire paper and kindly permitted me to reproduce results from her dissertation. Materials from the paper were presented at the 1987 annual meetings of the American Sociological Association, Chicago, and at the Demography Workshop at the Harvard University Population Center. I benefitted from discussions at those presentations. The opinions expressed herein are those of the author.
*Harvard University

that elapses between changes in the continuous dependent variable is random,
and the dependent variable, after the change, can take any value. In the
method I propose for analyzing this process, the central step is the definition
of the destination-specific transition rate of the process. This step allows us to
answer two questions: What determines the amount of time that elapses
between changes in the dependent variable, and what determines the new
value of the dependent variable, given that a change has occurred? The
answer to the first question follows from an ordinary hazard rate analysis,
and the answer to the second question follows from a probability model for the
analysis of continuous dependent variables, given that a change occurred. I
develop a special case to distinguish upward from downward changes in the
dependent variable. To illustrate the method, I use data from the Norwegian
Life History Study for Men and analyze the rate of upward shifts in
socioeconomic status and the new value of socioeconomic status, given that an
upward shift occurred.

1. INTRODUCTION

I will consider one type of stochastic process, examples of which are such microlevel social processes as socioeconomic status and earnings histories. The dependent variable is continuous. Over time it evolves as follows. For finite periods of time—that is, from one calendar date to another—it stays constant at a given value. At a later date, which is a random variable, the dependent variable jumps to a new value, and this jump can be of any size and in any direction. The process evolves in this manner from the calendar date when one change occurs to a later date when another change occurs. Between the dates of changes, the dependent variable stays constant.

Two central features characterize this process. First, the amount of time that elapses between changes in the continuous dependent variable is random. Second, the dependent variable can take any value after the change. In brief, we have what I call a continuous state space failure time process. Primary examples of such processes are individual-level status and earnings histories (see, e.g., Sørensen and Tuma 1981; Carroll and Mayer 1986). But such collective phenomena as the scope or intensity of riots, conceptualized as a continuous variable, and the amount of time that elapses between riots can also fall within this class of process (see, e.g., Spilerman 1970, 1971).

In this paper I propose a method for analyzing these processes. I specify a model for the probability of observing a given sequence of the dependent variable over time. The model, which specifies the transition rate for a continuous state space failure time process, answers two questions:

1. What determines the amount of time that elapses between changes in the dependent continuous variable?
2. Given that a change has occurred, what determines the new value of the dependent variable?

The answer to the first question derives from ordinary hazard rate analysis, as used in analysis of duration data. The answer to the second question derives from a probability model for the outcomes of continuous dependent variables, given that a change has occurred. It may take the form of a linear or nonlinear regression model. The two answers together yield a complete model for a failure time process with a continuous state space. The model and the two answers it gives replicate a well-known property of discrete state space failure time analysis: The rate of transition to a specific state equals the overall rate of transition times the probability that the specific state was entered, given that a transition occurred. But, in contrast to discrete state space processes, the state space discussed in this paper is continuous, and the probability of specific destination is replaced with the probability density of a specific destination, given that a transition occurred.

To clarify when the current approach applies, I will provide a brief classification of continuous time processes, ignoring those occurring in discrete time. The first distinction to be drawn is between processes in continuous state space and processes in discrete state space. For the latter, which are failure time processes in discrete state space, methods for analysis of duration or event-history data apply, on which the literature is voluminous (see, e.g., Tuma and Hannan 1984, pt. 2). For continuous state space processes, a further distinction must be drawn between diffusion and failure time processes. In diffusion processes, the dependent variable is in constant motion; that is, it changes all the time and in small time intervals only in small amounts (see, e.g., Lamperti 1977, pp. 125–26). The sample paths of diffusion processes are therefore continuous functions of time. In continuous state space failure time processes, in contrast, the dependent variable remains unchanged for finite periods of time, but at the time of a change, it jumps to a new value, and the jump can be of any size and in any direction. The sample paths are hence discontinuous functions of time, but they have a finite number of points of discontinuity, each occurring when the dependent variable changes. Failure time processes, both in discrete and continuous state space, are often referred to as jump processes because of the discontinuities in the sample paths.[1] The current approach applies to continuous state space failure time processes but not to diffusion processes.

Although many microlevel social processes can aptly be described as continuous state space failure time processes, they have traditionally not been analyzed as such. I will discuss and criticize the main alternative strategies used in the literature.

The first alternative approach assumes that the dependent variable is in constant motion, that is, changing all the time. It is implemented in two ways. The first implementation, developed by Coleman (1968), proposes so-called deterministic linear differential equation models to study change over time in continuous dependent variables, an approach that led to a series of important substantive applications (see, e.g., Sørensen 1979; Nielsen 1980; Rosenfeld 1980; see also the critiques in Nielsen and Rosenfeld 1981). The second implementation, a natural extension of the first, models the change in the dependent variable as a diffusion process, thereby treating the error term in the differential equation more systematically (for extensive treatments, see Tuma and Hannan 1984, chaps. 12 and 15; Karlin and Taylor 1981, chap. 15). It has received few applications in sociology (one exception is the methodological paper by Arminger 1986). Both implementations are conceptually valid when applied to processes in which change occurs all the time, as in some macrosocial and aggregate phenomena (see Freeman and Hannan 1975; Nielsen 1980; Carroll 1981). But when applied to continuous state space failure time processes (as, e.g., in Rosenfeld 1980), both implementations incorrectly assume that the process is in constant motion, thereby essentially ignoring the failure time information, although correctly treating the dependent variable as continuous and correctly capturing the average intraindividual change per unit time.

---

[1] In the probabilistic literature, there are discussions of discrete state space processes that are not failure time processes and of continuous state space processes that are neither failure time nor diffusion processes (see Karlin and Taylor 1981, p. 147; Feller 1971, p. 330). These processes are rare or even nonexistent in social life.

A second approach was proposed by Sørensen (1974), who used difference equations to model the earnings and prestige outcomes of job shifts. This approach correctly assumes that change does not occur all the time, but it ignores the amount of time that elapses between changes. Unlike the first approach, it does not describe the average amount of change per unit time.

The third and final approach was introduced by Sørensen and Tuma (1981), who used hazard rate models to study the amount of time that elapses between upward and downward changes in socioeconomic status (an approach that Rosenfeld [1983] later implemented in the framework of a discrete time logit model). Its strength, in contrast to the other approaches, is that, when applied to continuous state space failure time processes, it focuses on the timing between changes in a given direction; its weakness is that it ignores the size of the changes.

The current approach combines the strengths of each of the alternative approaches while avoiding their respective weaknesses. It focuses on the amount of time that elapses between changes in the dependent variable and on its value (i.e., the destination state) once the change has occurred. Compared with the first approach, it is both more realistic and far simpler to estimate.

The main result of this paper is that the specification of the process can be split into two easy steps. This simplicity may appear surprising if not suspicious: How can a seemingly complicated process be correctly specified by two such simple steps? Other than the mathematical derivations in section 2.2, which prove the two-step procedure, I know of no rigorous response to this concern. At a more intuitive level, I stress, however, that the model is a straightforward extension of models for discrete state space failure time processes. The central idea in the derivation of the model relies on a well-known albeit seldomly used property of the discrete state space framework (utilized, however, by Heckman and Singer 1984, pp. 119–21): The destination-specific rate of transition equals the overall rate of transition times the probability of the destination state, given that a transition occurred. The mathematical implications of this rarely used property are the same as those of the standard approach, in which one focuses directly on the destination-specific rate.

The remainder of the paper is organized in four parts. In section 2, I discuss specification and estimation of the parameters of the continuous state space failure time process and provide comparisons with discrete state space and diffusion processes. In section 3, I elaborate the results of section 2 first by extending the model to distinguish between upward and downward changes in the dependent variable and second by discussing in more detail a model that arises naturally in studies of intragenerational mobility. Finally, in section 4, I present an empirical analysis of the timing and sizes of upward changes in socioeconomic status.

2. SPECIFICATION AND ESTIMATION OF THE PROCESS

This section is divided into six parts: notation, the probability model, estimation, comparison with discrete state space and diffusion processes, comparison with a paper by Kolmogorov (1931), and finally some remarks on the conceptual implications of the main result of the paper.

2.1. *Notation*

Consider an individual for whom the process starts at calendar time Υ_0, which may or may not be a random variable. The realization of Υ_0 is denoted τ_0. The dependent and absolutely continuous random variable is Y, or more precisely $Y(\tau)$ at calendar time τ, where Y need not extend over the entire real line. The realization of Y is denoted y, which at any calendar time τ is $y(\tau)$ and at τ_0 is y_0. The process evolves as follows: Y stays constant at y_0 from τ_0 until a change occurs at some later and random time Υ_1, when it jumps to Y_1. The realization of Υ_1 is denoted τ_1, and the new realization of Y at τ_1 (that is, of Y_1) is denoted y_1. The process proceeds in this manner from one change at calendar time τ_{j-1}, with realization y_{j-1}, to another at τ_j, with realization y_j.

The current approach focuses on the amount of time that elapses between changes, $T_j \equiv \Upsilon_j - \Upsilon_{j-1}$ with realization $t_j \equiv \tau_j - \tau_{j-1}$, and the value of Y after the change, that is, Y_j with realization y_j. The initial condition y_0, τ_0 will be taken as exogenous and will not be modelled here.

The sequence of observed dependent variables to be explained is therefore (suppressing subscripts to individual observations)

$$\left\{ t_j, y_j \right\}_{j=1}^k \equiv \left\{ [t_1, y_1], \ldots, [t_k, y_k] \right\}, \tag{1}$$

FIGURE 1. Hypothetical example of a realization of the continuous state space failure time process. (See section 2.1 for an explanation of the symbols.)

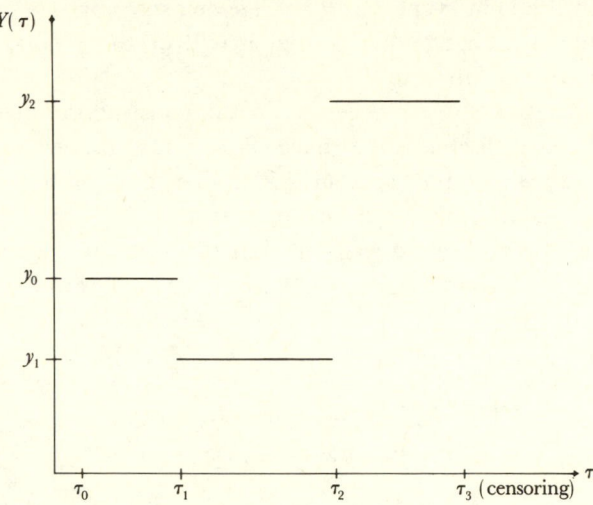

which corresponds to the data on an individual who experienced either k or $k-1$ changes in Y, depending on whether $y_k \neq y_{k-1}$ or $y_k = y_{k-1}$. If no change occurred when the individual was last observed at τ_k, then $y_k = y_{k-1}$ and $T_k > \tau_k - \tau_{k-1}$. An interval from τ_{k-1} to τ_k for which $y_k = y_{k-1}$ is called censored. By construction, censoring may occur only at the last interval from τ_{k-1} to τ_k.

The following notation will be useful in the sequel:

$$H_{j-1} \equiv \{t_i, y_i\}_{i=0}^{j-1} \quad \text{with } t_0 = \tau_0 \text{ and } t_i = \tau_i - \tau_{i-1} \text{ for } i > 0, \quad (2)$$

which summarizes the entire history of the process from τ_0 to τ_{j-1}. A hypothetical individual realization of the process, in which $k = 3$ and Y changed twice, is illustrated in Figure 1.

2.2. *Specification of the Probability Model for the Process*

The likelihood (or probability density) of the entire sequence of the data on an individual can be written

$$P\left[\{t_j, y_j\}_{j=1}^{k} | H_0\right] = \prod_{j=1}^{k} P\left[t_j, y_j | H_{j-1}\right]. \quad (3)$$

The right-hand side of (3) decomposes the likelihood into the products of the likelihoods for each segment of calendar time τ_{j-1} to τ_j, given what has happened up until τ_{j-1}. The term for each segment gives the likelihood of the joint event that a change or censoring will occur after $\tau_j - \tau_{j-1}$ and, if a change occurs, that it will be to y_j, conditional on what has happened up until τ_{j-1}.

To specify (3), we proceed as in the construction of the likelihood in ordinary discrete state space hazard rate models (as, e.g., in Heckman and Singer 1984, pp. 119–21). The probability that Y in a small time interval τ to $\tau + \Delta\tau$ changes from being equal to y_{j-1} to lying between y and $y + \Delta y$, given that the last change occurred at τ_{j-1} (i.e., given no change for an amount of time equal to $t = \tau - \tau_{j-1}$), is

$$
\begin{aligned}
P\big[t \leq T_j < t + \Delta t, \, y \leq Y_j < y + \Delta y \,|\, T_j \geq t, H_{j-1}\big] \\
= P\big[t \leq T_j < t + \Delta t \,|\, T_j \geq t, H_{j-1}\big] \qquad (4) \\
\times P\big[y \leq Y_j < y + \Delta y \,|\, t \leq T_j < t + \Delta t, H_{j-1}\big].
\end{aligned}
$$

The first term on the right-hand side of (4) gives the probability of any change in Y in the time interval τ to $\tau + \Delta t$, regardless of its direction and size, given that the last change occurred at τ_{j-1}. The second term gives the probability that the new value of Y lies between y and $y + \Delta y$, given that a change occurred and given no other change since τ_{j-1}.

It is useful to compute the limit of (4) with respect to Δt and Δy, which yields (after dividing by Δt and Δy)

$$
\begin{aligned}
f\big[t, \, & y \,|\, T_j \geq t, H_{j-1}\big] \\
& \equiv \lim_{\substack{\Delta t \downarrow 0 \\ \Delta y \downarrow 0}} P\big[t \leq T_j < t + \Delta t, \, y \leq Y_j < y + \Delta y \,|\, T_j \geq t, H_{j-1}\big] / \Delta t \Delta y \\
& = \lim_{\Delta t \downarrow 0} P\big[t \leq T_j < t + \Delta t \,|\, T_j \geq t, H_{j-1}\big] / \Delta t \qquad (5) \\
& \quad \times \lim_{\substack{\Delta t \downarrow 0 \\ \Delta y \downarrow 0}} P\big[y \leq Y_j < y + \Delta y \,|\, t \leq T_j < t + \Delta t, H_{j-1}\big] / \Delta y \\
& \equiv \lambda\big(t \,|\, H_{j-1}\big) \times g\big[y \,|\, T_j = t, H_{j-1}\big].
\end{aligned}
$$

Equation (5) is the *instantaneous transition rate* at duration $t = \tau - \tau_{j-1}$ to state y, given no change since τ_{j-1} and given the history of the process up until τ_{j-1}. The first term on the right-hand side is the instantaneous rate of change in Y, regardless of the direction and size of the change. The second term is the density function for the new value of Y, given that a change occurred at $t = \tau - \tau_{j-1}$ and given H_{j-1}.

In an identical manner, we can derive the probability of no change in Y in the time interval τ to $\tau + \Delta t$, given no change since τ_{j-1}, as

$$P\left[T_j \geq t + \Delta t \mid T_j \geq t, H_{j-1}\right]$$
$$= 1 - \lambda\left(t \mid H_{j-1}\right) \Delta t$$
$$= 1 - \int_{y \neq y_{j-1}} \lambda\left(t \mid H_{j-1}\right) \Delta t \times g\left[y \mid T_j = t, H_{j-1}\right] dy, \tag{6}$$

since

$$\int_{y \neq y_{j-1}} g\left[y \mid T_j = t, H_{j-1}\right] dy = 1, \tag{7}$$

because $g[\cdot]$ is a density function for the new value of Y, given that a change occurred.

Using the concepts in equations (5)–(6), we can derive expressions for the likelihood in (3). Let $C_k = 1$ denote that a change occurred at τ_k and let $C_k = 0$ denote that no change occurred. By construction, $C_j = 1$ for all $j < k$. Each term on the right-hand side of (3) pertains to an interval τ_{j-1} to τ_j. Using (5)–(6), we can write each term as

$$P\left[t_j, y_j \mid H_{j-1}\right] = P\left[T_j \geq t_j \mid H_{j-1}\right]$$
$$\times \left\{\lambda\left(t_j \mid H_{j-1}\right) \times g\left[y_j \mid T_j = t_j, H_{j-1}\right]\right\}^{C_j}$$
$$= \exp\left[-\int_0^{t_j} \lambda\left(t \mid H_{j-1}\right) dt\right] \tag{8}$$
$$\times \left\{\lambda\left(t_j \mid H_{j-1}\right) \times g\left[y_j \mid T_j = t_j, H_{j-1}\right]\right\}^{C_j},$$

where, as before, $t_j = \tau_j - \tau_{j-1}$.

The first two expressions on the right-hand side of (8) are identical to those obtained in ordinary event-history or duration analysis. The most natural way to derive the expressions would be by means of a product integral representation, as explained in Kalbfleisch and Prentice (1980, p. 121) and in Cox and Oakes (1984, p. 15), a procedure that is trivial and hence deleted.[2] The last term equals the density of the new value of Y, given that a change occurred. The entire

---

[2] An alternative derivation of the duration part of the likelihood would proceed as in the counting process framework frequently used by statisticians (see the review in Andersen and Borgan 1985). Instead of focusing on the failure time and the value of Y at the time of failure, one focuses directly on Y, specifying the probabilities of $Y(\tau + \Delta t) \neq Y(\tau)$ and $Y(\tau + \Delta t) = Y(\tau)$, given $Y(\tau)$ and the history of the process up until τ.

likelihood for an individual obtains by inserting (8) into each term in (3).

The main result of this paper can now be stated: The likelihood for a continuous state space failure time process can be written in two steps. First, we specify the hazard rate, that is, the instantaneous probability of a change in Y, regardless of the direction and size of the change. Thereafter, we specify the density for the new value of Y, given that a change occurred. For the first term, models for analysis of duration data apply. For the second term, models for the outcomes of continuous dependent variables apply, given that a change occurred. To the latter end, we can specify the distribution of Y after the change as normal, lognormal, exponential, Pareto, or whatever is most appropriate to the task at hand. We can condition on the value of Y before the change and on the amount of time that has elapsed since the last change or, in general, on the entire past history of the process.

Introducing covariates into both the hazard rate and the density for the new value of Y is straightforward. Procedures for introducing covariates into the hazard rate are well known, thanks to the efforts of Tuma and Hannan (see, e.g., Tuma and Hannan 1984; see also Allison 1984). The covariates may also depend on time, so that they change as the process evolves (see, e.g., Petersen 1986a, 1986b). Introducing covariates into the density for the new value of Y is equally straightforward. In the simplest case, we can do it as in a linear or nonlinear regression model.

2.3. *Estimation*

I will discuss estimation of the parameters under two assumptions to be stated below. Let the hazard rate depend on a parameter vector ψ_1 and on an unobservable η_1 with a distribution with parameter vector ϕ_1. Let the density for the new value of Y, conditional on a change, depend on a parameter vector ψ_2 and on an unobservable η_2 with a distribution with parameter vector ϕ_2. The two assumptions are as follows:

1. If there are unobserved heterogeneity terms η_1 and η_2 in both the hazard rate and the density for the new value of Y, given that a change occurred, these are independently distributed across the hazard rate and the density. That is, η_1 and η_2 are independently distributed.

2. The parameters ψ_1 and ϕ_1 pertaining to the hazard rate and to the distribution of the heterogeneity term η_1 in the hazard rate are not functionally related to the parameters ψ_2 and ϕ_2 pertaining to the density for the new value of Y and to the distribution of the heterogeneity term in that density. That is, there are no functional restrictions between the two sets of parameters, ψ_1, ϕ_1 on the one hand and ψ_2, ϕ_2 on the other hand.

Under these two assumptions, maximum likelihood (ML) estimates are obtained first by estimating the hazard rate from the data on the durations between changes, ignoring the direction and size of the changes, and thereafter by estimating the density for the new value of Y, given that a change occurred, using the data on the new value of Y and on the history of the process up until the change in Y. (For an identical result in discrete state space failure time processes, see Heckman and Singer [1984, pp. 120–21].) The two pieces of the likelihood, one pertaining to the durations, the other to the new values of Y, can be maximized separately. This follows from standard ML theory (see, e.g., Engle, Hendry, and Richard 1983, pp. 282–83). If one or both conditions are violated, efficient estimation requires joint maximization of the two pieces of the likelihood. However, if only assumption 2 is violated, separate maximization of the two pieces still yields consistent albeit inefficient estimates (see, e.g., Heckman and Singer 1984, p. 121).

2.4. Comparison with Diffusion and Discrete State Space Processes

Two major conditions characterize the continuous state space failure time process of this paper (see, e.g., Karlin and Taylor 1981, pp. 146–47):

$$\lim_{\Delta t \downarrow 0} P\big[|Y(\tau + \Delta t) - Y(\tau)| > \varepsilon\big]/\Delta t > 0 \quad \text{for all } \varepsilon > 0 \text{ such that}$$

$Y(\tau) + \varepsilon$ and/or $Y(\tau) - \varepsilon$ lie within the state space of Y,

$$(9)$$

$$\lim_{\Delta t \downarrow 0} P\big[Y(\tau + \Delta t) \neq Y(\tau)|T_j \geq t, H_{j-1}\big]/\Delta t = \lambda(t|H_{j-1}) < \infty. \quad (10)$$

The first condition allows for discontinuities (i.e., jumps) of the sample path of Y over time, and the second condition says that the rate of change is finite, thereby ensuring that the process is not in constant motion. (For additional details on [10] see Doob [1953, pp. 255–73, esp. Theorem 2.4, p. 266].)

A diffusion process, a process in constant motion, differs from a continuous state space failure time process primarily in that discontinuities of the sample paths are ruled out. Instead of (9), the central condition characterizing the process is

$$\lim_{\Delta t \downarrow 0} P\big[|Y(\tau + \Delta t) - Y(\tau)| > \varepsilon\big]/\Delta t = 0 \quad \text{for all } \varepsilon > 0, \quad (11)$$

which says that in a small time interval τ to $\tau + \Delta t$, only small changes in Y are likely to occur, implying that Y is a continuous function of τ (see Feller 1971, p. 333). A diffusion process can be obtained as the limit of the process in this paper when (a) the size of each change in Y becomes infinitesimally small and (b) the amount of time that elapses between changes in Y goes to zero, as discussed in Feller (1968, p. 354).

Failure time processes in discrete state space satisfy both conditions (9) and (10). In fact, they can be derived as a special case of the current approach when the state space becomes finite and a positive probability can be attached to each outcome.

Equations (5)–(7) have clear discrete state space counterparts. Y then takes on a countable number of states. The equation that corresponds to (5) is

$$\lim_{\Delta t \downarrow 0} P\big[t \le T_j < t + \Delta t, Y_j = y | T_j \ge t, H_{j-1}\big]/\Delta t$$

$$= \lim_{\Delta t \downarrow 0} P\big[t \le T_j < t + \Delta t | T_j \ge t, H_{j-1}\big]/\Delta t$$

$$\times P\big[Y_j = y | t \le T_j < t + \Delta t, H_{j-1}\big] \quad (12)$$

$$= \lambda\big(t | H_{j-1}\big) \times P\big[y | T_j = t, H_{j-1}\big]$$

$$\equiv \lambda_y\big(t | H_{j-1}\big),$$

which is the rate of transition to state y, given as the overall rate of transition times the probability that state y was entered, given that a transition occurred (see, e.g., Tuma and Hannan 1984, p. 72).

The equation that corresponds to (6) is

$$P\left[T_j \geq t + \Delta t \,|\, T_j \geq t, H_{j-1}\right]$$

$$= 1 - \lambda\left(t|H_{j-1}\right)\Delta t \tag{13}$$

$$= 1 - \sum_{y \neq y_{j-1}} \lambda\left(t|H_{j-1}\right)\Delta t \times P\left[y|T_j = t, H_{j-1}\right],$$

and the equation that corresponds to (7) is

$$\sum_{y \neq y_{j-1}} P\left[y|T_j = t, H_{j-1}\right] = 1. \tag{14}$$

Equations (13) and (14) are standard expressions in multistate hazard rate analysis (for [14], see Cox and Oakes 1984, p. 143; Tuma and Hannan 1984, p. 66).

2.5. Comparison with Kolmogorov

As is often the case, not everything in a new approach is new. In a celebrated paper, Kolmogorov (1931, pp. 456–57) discussed a specification of a continuous state space failure time process similar to the one in this paper, but he did not discuss estimation of the parameters.[3] He focused on the overall rate of transition, $\lambda(t|H_{j-1})$, and on the destination-specific rate of transition, $f[t, y|T_j \geq t, H_{j-1}]$, as defined in the first equality in equation (5). However, he did not carry out the decomposition of the destination-specific rate, as was done in the last equality of (5).

If we specify directly the overall rate and the destination-specific rate, we must take account of the following restriction, from equations (7) and (5), which connects the two:

$$\int_{y \neq y_{j-1}} f\left[t, y|T_j \geq t, H_{j-1}\right] dy = \lambda\left(t|H_{j-1}\right), \tag{15}$$

which says that the overall rate of transition equals the integral over all

[3] See also the related discussion of marked processes in Cox and Oakes (1984, pp. 151–53) and the discussion of the compound Poisson process in Karlin and Taylor (1981, pp. 426–40) and Feller (1971, pp. 326–32).

the destination-specific rates (see Kolmogorov 1931, eq. [177], p. 457). Equation (15) has an analogue in discrete state space analysis, in which the overall rate of transition equals the sum over all the destination-specific rates, as can be seen from equations (12) and (13).

Hence, we should not estimate $\lambda(t|H_{j-1})$ and $f[t, y|T_j \geq t, H_{j-1}]$ without taking (15) into account. Following Kolmogorov's approach, the valid strategy would be to estimate $f[t, y|T_j \geq t, H_{j-1}]$ directly and then obtain $\lambda(t|H_{j-1})$ by integration, using (15).

The procedure outlined in this paper seems preferable. The focus is not on the destination-specific rate but instead on its decomposition in the overall rate times the density of the destination state, given that a transition occurred. It is probably easier to come up with plausible functional forms for the overall rate of transition and the density of the destination state, given that a transition occurred, than to specify the destination-specific rate directly and then obtain the overall rate through integration using (15).

2.6. *Remarks*

The main result of the paper, that the destination-specific rate of transition can be decomposed into the overall rate of transition times the probability density of the destination state given a transition, may prove useful in empirical research. I will therefore provide some remarks that may help in the interpretation of the result.

First, the result does not imply that the probability of a transition is independent of the distribution of the possible destination states. Suppose that a change occurs in the distribution of the possible destination states. In many situations, we would then expect the overall rate of transition also to change (see the discussion in Hachen 1988), as will be discussed further in the next remark and in section 3.2. Nothing in the model specification in section 2.2 precludes this. However, the result of section 2.3, on estimation of the parameters, may no longer hold, in so far as assumption 2 is likely to be violated.

Second, I will discuss how the rate of transition may depend on the distribution of the possible destination states. I do this by embedding the rather context-free statistical model of section 2.2 in a richer model of individual decisions. Consider the case of job mobility. First, we could specify the overall rate at which job offers *arrive* and then the distribution of the offers, given an arrival. If all moves are voluntary, persons will move only when they are offered a job better than their current job; that is, they use a simple decision rule: Accept the first offer for which $y_j > y_{j-1}$, otherwise reject. The overall rate of transition then equals the product of the arrival rate of job offers and the probability that the offer is acceptable, a product that depends on the distribution of job offers. It is clear therefore that even if the rate at which offers arrive remains unchanged, a change in the distribution of job offers will affect the rate at which transitions occur. The researcher may be interested in recovering both the overall rate at which *opportunities for movement arrive* and the likelihoods of the possible outcomes (better or worse) of a movement, given an opportunity to move. Both are characteristics of the social system the employee faces, and focusing only on the rate of movement and the distribution of accepted offers may conceal interesting features of this system. The example will be developed further in section 3.2.

Third, I turn to an issue that sometimes arises in the interpretation of competing risks models (see Allison 1984, pp. 42–44): The decomposition of the destination-specific rate into its two components may tempt researchers to view the model as implying that transitions occur according to a sequential decision-making process or according to two separate causal processes. The actor first chooses to move and thereafter, in an existential moment after he or she has moved into nowhere, chooses the state to enter. This interpretation is implied neither by the current nor by the corresponding discrete state space model. The researcher may of course choose to impose such an interpretation, but few social processes can aptly be described by this particular type of sequential decision-making procedure.[4] Specifically, in the job mobility example given above, transitions occur according to a one-step procedure: Individuals move when an offer for a better job arrives.

---

[4] This interpretation seems occasionally to derive from some conceptual confusion about the difference between the process that determines whether a person belongs to the set of those likely to experience an event and the process that determines the timing and type of the event. For example, one process underlies whether a person is at risk for buying a car (i.e., whether he or she decides to search for a car), and another process underlies when and which type of car is bought.

3. SPECIAL CASES

3.1. *Special Case* 1: *Upward and Downward Shifts*

It is sometimes useful to distinguish upward from downward changes in Y, as has been done in research on intragenerational mobility (Sørensen and Tuma 1981; Carroll and Mayer 1986; Tuma 1986). I first demonstrate how this can be done and then discuss when it would make sense to do so.

To accomplish this, I introduce the new variable

$$D_j = 1 \quad \text{if } Y_j > Y_{j-1},$$
$$D_j = 2 \quad \text{if } Y_j < Y_{j-1}, \tag{16}$$

where D_j equals 1 if change j is upward and 2 if it is downward. We could also allow for lateral shifts—that is, for changes in, say, jobs not leading to any changes in Y—by a direct extension of the current approach.

Upward shifts can be distinguished from downward shifts by straightforward probability calculations on equation (5):

$$f\left[t, y \mid T_j \geq t, H_{j-1}\right]$$

$$= \lim_{\Delta t \downarrow 0} P\left[t \leq T_j < t + \Delta t, D_j = d \mid T_j \geq t, H_{j-1}\right]/\Delta t$$

$$\times \lim_{\substack{\Delta t \downarrow 0 \\ \Delta y \downarrow 0}} P\left[y \leq Y_j < y + \Delta y \mid t \leq T_j < t + \Delta t, H_{j-1}, D_j = d\right]/\Delta y$$

$$\equiv \lambda_d\left(t \mid H_{j-1}\right) \times g\left[y \mid T_j = t, H_{j-1}, D_j = d\right] \quad \text{for } d = 1, 2. \tag{17}$$

The first term on the right-hand side of (17), $\lambda_d(t \mid H_{j-1})$, gives the rate at which shifts in direction d occur. The second term gives the density for the destination state, given that a shift in direction d occurred. I will refer to the first term as λ_d and to the second as g_d. Equation (17) is just another way to decompose the destination-specific transition rate, making explicit whether the change was upward or downward.

One may further decompose the rate of transition in direction d as

$$\lambda_d\left(t \mid H_{j-1}\right) = \lambda\left(t \mid H_{j-1}\right) \times P\left[D_j = d \mid T_j = t, H_{j-1}\right] \quad \text{for } d = 1, 2, \tag{18}$$

where the first term on the right-hand side of (18) is the overall rate of transition and the second term is the probability that the shift occurred in direction d, given that a shift occurred.

To make explicit the direction of the shift, we can therefore write the destination-specific rate of transition as either (a) the product of the rate of transition in direction d and the density of the new value of Y, given a transition in direction d, as in (17), or (b) the product of the overall rate of transition, the probability that the transition was in direction d given a transition, and the density of the new value of Y, given a transition in direction d. I will focus on the former specification.

We can now discuss when it makes sense to estimate separately the rates for upward and downward changes in Y. To do so appears most sensible when λ_1, g_1 depend on a set of parameters, say, ψ_{11}, ψ_{21}, that differ from the parameters, say, ψ_{12}, ψ_{22}, on which λ_2, g_2 depend. This means that the mechanisms or processes that govern the rate of transition in a specific direction and the new value of Y given a transition in a specific direction differ for upward and downward shifts. If so, estimation of the parameters is straightforward, provided assumptions 1 and 2 of section 2.3 are satisfied. First, we use a hazard rate routine to estimate λ_1, λ_2. Thereafter, we use the subsample of shifts in direction d to estimate the density for the new value of Y, given a shift in direction d.

A specific example may help clarify some of the issues. Suppose the new value of Y, given a shift in direction d, can be described by a simple linear regression function, one for each d, as follows:

$$E\left[y_j | z_j, y_{j-1}, D_j = d \right] = \theta_d z_j + \delta_d y_{j-1} \quad \text{for } d = 1, 2, \qquad (19)$$

where z_j is a vector of explanatory variables, θ_d, δ_d are the parameters pertaining to shifts in direction d, and E is the expectations operator. The error term ε implied by (19) has expectations zero, conditional on z_j, y_{j-1} and $D_j = d$.

Under the scenario of (19), the procedure outlined above would be correct. We can consistently estimate θ_d, δ_d by applying least squares to the subsample of new values of Y for shifts that occurred in direction d. No sample-selection bias or truncation accrue from this procedure. Moreover, equation (19) imposes no restrictions on the two rates of shifts. The rates can therefore be estimated without taking (19) into account.

Suppose instead that the new value of Y, given a transition, is given by the linear regression function

$$E\left[y_j | z_j, y_{j-1} \right] = \theta z_j + \delta y_{j-1}, \tag{20}$$

where the parameters θ, δ describe the shifts in both directions.

Under the scenario of (20), using the shifts in direction d alone to estimate θ, δ will require correction for the truncation; otherwise, the estimates will be biased. Specifically, for upward shifts the regression function becomes

$$E\left[y_j | y_{j-1}, z_j, \varepsilon > \varepsilon^* \right] = \theta z_j + \delta y_{j-1} + E\left[\varepsilon | y_{j-1}, z_j, \varepsilon > \varepsilon^* \right], \tag{21}$$

where $\varepsilon^* = -[\theta z_j + (\delta - 1) y_{j-1}]$, ε is the error term implied by (20), and the last term on the right-hand side of (21) differs from zero. Consistent estimation of (20) on the basis of the subsample of upward shifts alone would then necessitate the use of a Tobit-type estimator (see, e.g., Maddala 1983, chap. 6). The obvious procedure in this case is to pool upward and downward shifts and estimate (20) directly.

Moreover, in the case depicted by (20), in contrast to (19), there will be restrictions between equation (20) and the two hazard rates; namely,

$$P\left[\varepsilon > \varepsilon^* | y_{j-1}, z_j \right] = \lambda_1 / (\lambda_1 + \lambda_2), \tag{22a}$$

$$P\left[\varepsilon < \varepsilon^* | y_{j-1}, z_j \right] = \lambda_2 / (\lambda_1 + \lambda_2), \tag{22b}$$

where the left-hand sides are derived from (20) and the right-hand sides from the hazard rates, both giving the probability that a transition was in a specific direction, given that a transition occurred.

In the case of (20), the sensible procedure would therefore be to estimate first the overall rate of transition and then (20), pooling upward and downward shifts. From these estimates, we can derive the rates of transition in each direction and the probability of a shift in each direction, given a shift.

The procedure for distinguishing between upward and downward shifts outlined in this section, as exemplified in equation (19), can be quite powerful for descriptive purposes, as I hope to demonstrate in the empirical analysis in section 4. The variables entering the various equations may also be given strong theoretical justifications. Whether the procedure can be derived from an underlying structural model governing mobility remains an open issue.

3.2. *Special Case 2: Intragenerational Mobility*

The following example, which was discussed informally in section 2.6, arises naturally in the study of intragenerational mobility (see, e.g., Sørensen 1979) and has a clear counterpart in econometric studies of unemployment durations (see Lancaster 1979; Flinn and Heckman 1982). A working person with socioeconomic status or earnings y_{j-1} receives opportunities to move to other states, better or worse, at a rate $\lambda(t|H_{j-1})$. The states or positions offered are sampled from a distribution $g[y|T_j = t, H_{j-1}]$. If the economy or the relevant labor market is strong, all job separations may be voluntary. Assuming that actors maximize status or earnings, shifts will occur only when the offered position is better than the current position, that is, when $D_j = 1$. The researcher will have access to a *sample of upward shifts only*.

The question then is, On the basis of these data, what can be estimated? It is clear that we can estimate the rate of upward shifts,

$$\lambda_1(t|H_{j-1}) = \lambda(t|H_{j-1}) \times P[D_j = 1|T_j = t, H_{j-1}], \qquad (23)$$

provided that the arrival rate of better offers is independent of the history of worse offers (since the latter is typically not observed).

We can also estimate the truncated distribution of job offers, that is, the distribution of offers for positions better than the current position: $g[y|T_j = t, H_{j-1}, D_j = 1]$. Whether we can recover the untruncated distribution (that is, $g[y|T_j = t, H_{j-1}]$) from the truncated distribution depends on the form of g. For example, if g is normal, we can recover the untruncated distribution; but this is not true for all distributions.[5]

If we can recover the untruncated distribution, we can further estimate

$$P[D_j = 1|T_j = t, H_{j-1}] = \int_{y_{j-1}}^{\infty} g[y|T_j = t, H_{j-1}]\, dy, \qquad (24)$$

and then from (23), we can estimate the overall rate $\lambda(t|H_{j-1})$, because both the left-hand side and the second term on the right-hand side of (23) are known.

---

[5] A similar case arises in the analysis of unemployment duration data. For completed spells of unemployment, the observed distribution of accepted wage offers is truncated, because workers accept only those jobs offering a wage above their reservation wage (for a detailed discussion, see Flinn and Heckman 1982, pp. 121–25).

One could argue that analysis should focus only on the rate of upward shifts, $\lambda_1(t|H_{j-1})$, and on the truncated distribution of job offers, because they fully characterize the observed data. This argument may be valid in some substantive situations, but not in general. The overall rate at which offers arrive describes the opportunities for movement within a social system, regardless of the type of movement, a quantity that may be of interest. In a situation in which layoffs are likely, it is useful to know the rate at which offers arrive, since this will tell us the likelihood that a person will obtain any position if laid off. Similarly, if actors no longer move only when better opportunities arise —that is, if they maximize proximity to family or some other non-job-related characteristic instead of status or earnings—knowing the rate at which offers arrive would be useful. For the same reasons, we might be more interested in the untruncated distribution of job offers, because it characterizes the likelihood of all offers, than in the truncated distribution, which only describes the likelihood of outcomes conditional on a better offer.

A specific implementation of equations (23)–(24) may help clarify the ideas. Assume that job offers arrive according to a Poisson process with rate μ ($\mu > 0$). Given the arrival of an offer, assume that it is drawn from an exponential distribution with parameter ξ ($\xi > 0$), a specification that corresponds to a structure of inequality with a pyramidal shape. Both μ and ξ may depend on explanatory variables (time-constant and time-dependent), and ξ may also depend on the time since the last shift.

The overall rate of transition, that is (23), now becomes

$$\lambda_1(t|H_{j-1}) = \mu \times \exp(-\xi y_{j-1}), \tag{25}$$

which is the product of the rate at which offers arrive and the probability that the offer is better than y_{j-1}.

The density for the new value of y, given a shift to a better job, is

$$g[y|T_j = t, H_{j-1}, D_j = 1] = \xi \times \exp[-\xi(y - y_{j-1})]. \tag{26}$$

The likelihood piece pertaining to the duration t_j of job j becomes

$$L_1 = [\mu \times \exp(-\xi y_{j-1})]^{C_j} \times \exp[-t_j \mu \times \exp(-\xi y_{j-1})], \tag{27a}$$

and the piece pertaining to the new value y_j of the job entered,

$$L_2 = \left\{ \xi \times \exp\left[-\xi(y_j - y_{j-1})\right]\right\}^{C_j}, \qquad (27b)$$

where C_j, as in (8), equals 1 if a transition occurred and 0 otherwise. The full likelihood for job j is the product of (27a) and (27b).

From (27b) it is evident that we can consistently estimate ξ from the data on the new values of Y, using the subsample of observed transitions and conditioning on y_{j-1}. We can also recover the untruncated distribution of job offers from the truncated, since the former depends only on ξ. From (27a) it is also clear that we can consistently estimate both μ and ξ from the data on durations, conditioning on y_{j-1}.[6]

However, considering both (27a) and (27b) reveals that assumption 2 of section 2.3 is violated: ξ enters both the overall rate of transition and the density for the new value of Y, given a transition. Efficient estimation therefore requires joint maximization of L_1 and L_2, which is computationally straightforward but requires a special-purpose routine for this particular likelihood.

Finally, suppose that a change occurs in the distribution of possible destination states, that is, in ξ, as discussed in the first remark in section 2.6. From (25) we then see that the overall rate of transition will also change. Specifically, a decrease in ξ will increase the probability of obtaining a better offer and hence increase the overall rate of transition, which is seen from $\partial \lambda_1(t|H_{j-1})/\partial\xi = -\mu y_{j-1} \exp(-\xi y_{j-1}) < 0$.

4. EMPIRICAL ANALYSIS

I present a brief example of the method proposed here using an empirical study by Visher (1984). The data were taken from the Norwegian Life History Study for Men, which was directed by Natalie Rogoff Ramsøy and Kari Skrede at the Institute of Applied Social Research in Oslo and is described in detail in Rogoff Ramsøy (1977, pp. 43–60); see also Visher (1981). The Norwegian Central Bureau of

---

[6] The hazard rate in (25) can be written as $\lambda_1(t|H_{j-1}) = \exp[\mu_0 + \xi_1 y_{j-1}]$, where $\mu_0 = \ln \mu$, $\xi_1 = -\xi$, and ln denotes the natural logarithm. We can therefore use a hazard rate routine for the exponential model to estimate μ_0 and ξ_1. Thereafter, we can derive the estimates of μ and ξ from the equalities above.

Statistics collected and organized the data. The bureau interviewed a representative sample of 3,470 Norwegian men born in 1921, 1931, and 1941 and collected their life histories from age 14 up to the date of interview in 1971. Detailed month-by-month employment histories as well as histories on other life spheres were collected.

The analysis focuses on the rate of upward shifts in socioeconomic status and on the value of socioeconomic status after an upward shift ocurred. An upward shift is defined as a job change that results in an increase in socioeconomic status over the highest level previously attained. Almost all changes in socioeconomic status in this data set are upward. Jobshifts leading to either no change or a downward change in socioeconomic status are treated as if no change occurred, since theories of intragenerational status attainment are primarily about gains in attainment and have little to say about downward and lateral changes in socioeconomic status (see Sørensen 1984, pp. 91–93, 97). If a person holds more than one job before improving his attainment over the previous highest level, the duration before the upward shift is the sum of the durations in the jobs held since the previous highest level of attainment was reached. The measure of socioeconomic status (see Skrede 1971) runs from a low of 3 to a high of 52 and can for all practical purposes be considered continuous.

The rate at which upward shifts occur depends on the sector in which the person works (private or public), on the highest level of socioeconomic status previously attained (i.e., y_{j-1}), on educational attainment (junior high school or less, or high school or more),[7] on occupational position (manager, professional, craftsman, or manual worker), on labor force experience, and on duration since the last upward shift. Other than y_{j-1}, all variables are treated as time-dependent, including labor force experience. The latter is allowed to vary continuously with time since the last upward shift (as detailed in Petersen 1986a, pp. 231–32). Visher (1984, p. 123) specifies the rate of upward shifts as (suppressing subscripts to individual observations)

$$\lambda_1\big(t|H_{j-1}, x(\tau), L_{j-1}\big) = \exp\big[\beta x(\tau) + \rho y_{j-1} + \alpha\big(L_{j-1} + t\big) + \gamma t\big],$$

$$(28)$$

[7] The construction of the variable for educational attainment is explained in Statistisk Sentralbyrå (1973, p. 18). Those coded junior high school or less have junior high school, or its equivalent (in years), or less. Those coded high school or more, have high school, or its equivalent (in years), or more.

where β is a vector of parameters giving the effects of the covariates in x, which includes a constant 1, education, sector, and occupation, measured as of the job held immediately prior to duration t; L_{j-1} is the employee's labor force experience (measured in months) at the date the last upward shift occurred (i.e., at τ_{j-1}); $L_{j-1} + t$ is the labor force experience at duration t after the last shift occurred (i.e., at $t = \tau - \tau_{j-1}$), with effect α; y_{j-1} is the highest socioeconomic status previously reached and ρ its effect; and γ is the effect of duration since the last shift.

The specification for the new value of socioeconomic status, given that an upward shift occurred, is

$$y_j = \theta_1 z_j + \delta_1 y_{j-1} + \varepsilon, \tag{29}$$

where θ_1 is a vector of parameters giving the effects of the covariates in z_j, which includes a constant 1, education, sector, and occupation; sector and occupation are measured as of the job held immediately prior to the change in Y (if that job differs from the job held when status y_{j-1} was entered); δ_1 gives the effect of the highest level of socioeconomic status previously attained; and ε is a stochastic error term (see Visher 1984, p. 158). It is assumed that the parameters pertaining to the new value of Y, given a shift in direction d, differ for upward and downward shifts. Hence, we can correctly estimate (29) on the basis of upward shifts alone, with no correction for truncation, because there is no truncation problem, as discussed in conjunction with equation (19).

In Visher's specification, therefore, the instantaneous rate of an upward change in Y depends on its highest value previously reached, on the time since that value was obtained, and on the exogenous variables, as seen from (28). The density of the new value of Y, given that an upward shift occurred, depends on the highest value of Y prior to the change and on the exogenous variables, but not on time since y_{j-1} was reached, as seen from (29). There is, however, nothing in the general model specification of section 2.2 that prevents us from entering the time elapsed since status y_{j-1} was achieved as a predictor on the right-hand side of (29), as can be seen from (8), a specification that for substantive reasons ought to be pursued in future research.

Assuming that there is no autocorrelation in the ε's and that the expectation of ε, conditional on an upward shift (i.e., on $D_j = 1$) and on the right-hand-side variables in (29), is zero, the parameters of (29) can be consistently estimated by linear least squares. No distribution needs to be imposed on the error term. If the latter is normal, least squares and ML coincide, and if not, least squares still yields consistent estimates, under the usual assumptions. The parameters of the hazard rate were estimated by ML (see, e.g., Tuma and Hannan 1984, chap. 5).

Table 1 gives the estimates of equations (28) and (29) (taken from Visher 1984, table 5.2, col. 1, and table D, panel B, col. 1). I will not comment on every number in the table. Instead, I will focus on the

TABLE 1

Estimates of the Effects on the Rate of Upward Shifts in Socioeconomic Status and of the Density of the New Socioeconomic Status Given that an Upward Shift Occurred (Standard Errors in Parentheses)

Variables	Equation (28)[a]		Equation (29)[b]	
Constant	-3.6420	(0.0416)	10.7800	(0.2052)
Duration (in months), γ	0.0005*	(0.0004)		
Labor force experience				
(in months), α	-0.0050	(0.0004)		
Socioeconomic status before shift	-0.0780	(0.0033)	0.6353	(0.0181)
Education (1 = high school or more)[c]	0.6630	(0.0399)	5.0980	(0.2272)
Sector (1 = public, 0 = private)	0.0960*	(0.0520)	-0.2470*	(0.2893)
Occupation[d]				
Manager	-0.7970	(0.2564)	5.356	(1.370)
Professional	-0.3608	(0.1342)	-0.8122*	(0.7165)
Craftsman	-0.1081	(0.0463)	1.177	(0.2630)
Log likelihood[e]	$-22,727.4$			
N	6,523		3,730	

Note: The data were taken from the Norwegian Life History Study for Men (see Rogoff Ramsøy 1977, pp. 43–60; Visher 1981). For exact definitions of the sample and variables, see Visher (1984, chaps. 5–6).

[a] These are estimates of the rate of upward shifts in socioeconomic status (from Visher 1984, table 5.2, col. 1). The ML estimates were obtained by the so-called BHHH algorithm (after Berndt et al. 1974), as were the standard errors.

[b] These are estimates of θ_1 and δ_1 in the density for the new value of socioeconomic status, given that an upward shift occurred (from Visher 1984, table D, panel B, col. 1). The estimates were obtained by least squares.

[c] The reference category is educational attainment equal to junior high school, its equivalent (in years) or less.

[d] The reference category is manual workers.

[e] Using a likelihood ratio test, we can reject the constant rate model, $\lambda(t)$, against the model in (28) at any reasonable level of significance.

* Not significantly different from zero at the 0.05 level, two-tailed tests.

conclusions from this analysis that one could not obtain solely from analyses of the rate of upward shifts or of the size of shifts. In the first column we see that managers have a lower rate of upward shifts than the other occupational groups. That is, on the average they wait longer before experiencing an upward shift (net of the other variables). From the analysis of upward shifts alone, as in Sørensen and Tuma (1981), one would conclude that managers are the most constrained in their opportunities for increasing rewards, a conclusion that seems plausible in light of their already high rewards and the ceiling effects that may set in. In the second column, we see that managers on the average make the largest jumps, given that an upward shift occurred. From the analysis of the size of the gain alone, as in Sørensen's (1974) difference equation model approach, one would conclude that managers are the least constrained in their opportunities to get ahead. Considering equations (28) and (29) simultaneously yields a more nuanced picture. The process of intragenerational mobility appears to differ between managers and the reference group, manual workers, in the following way. The former wait longer before they experience upward shifts, but once they shift, they also jump further. Managers climb in few, but long, steps, whereas manual workers climb in many, but correspondingly shorter, steps. The approach taken here to the study of continuous state space failure time processes allows us to characterize the difference in the processes in this way.

5. SUMMARY

This paper has presented a method for analyzing continuous state space failure time processes. The dependent variable is continuous, but in contrast to diffusion processes, it stays constant for finite periods of time. Unlike discrete state space failure time processes, the dependent variable, at the time of a change, can jump to any value.

The method developed can be seen as an extension of methods for analysis of discrete state space failure time processes, often known as duration or event-history analysis. It answers two questions. First, what determines the amount of time that elapses between changes in the dependent variable? The answer follows from an ordinary hazard rate analysis. Second, what determines the new value of the dependent variable, given that a change occurred? The answer follows from a probability model for the analysis of continuous dependent variables, given that a change occurred. A special case distinguishing upward from downward changes in the dependent variable was developed. It was illustrated in an empirical analysis of rates of upward shifts in socioeconomic status and the new value of socioeconomic status, given that an upward shift occurred.

The method may prove useful in analyzing a variety of micro-level processes currently studied by sociologists, foremost among which are individual-level socioeconomic status and earnings histories. Migration and welfare histories can also be cast in the current framework. In migration histories, the focus would be on the time before migration and the distance migrated. In welfare histories, the focus would be on the time before entering welfare and the proportion of income that comes from welfare, once welfare is entered.[8] Some macrosocial processes, such as the amount of time that elapses between riots and their scope and intensity once they occur, may also fall within the class of processes considered here.

REFERENCES

Allison, Paul D. 1984. *Event History Analysis. Regression for Longitudinal Event Data*. Beverly Hills: Sage.

Andersen, Per Kragh, and Ørnulf Borgan. 1985. "Counting Process Models for Life History Data: A Review" (with discussion). *Scandinavian Journal of Statistics* 12:97–158.

Arminger, Gerhard. 1986. "Linear Stochastic Differential Equation Models for Panel Data with Unobserved Variables." Pp. 187–212 in *Sociological Methodology 1986*, edited by Nancy B. Tuma. Washington, DC: American Sociological Association.

Berndt, E. R., B. H. Hall, R. E. Hall, and J. A. Hausman. 1974. "Estimation and Inference in Nonlinear Structural Models." *Annals of Social and Economic Measurement* 3:653–65.

Carroll, Glenn R. 1981. "Dynamics of Organizational Expansion in National Systems of Education." *American Sociological Review* 46:585–99.

Carroll, Glenn R., and Karl Ulrich Mayer. 1986. "Job-Shift Patterns in Germany." *American Sociological Review* 51:323–41.

Coleman, James S. 1968. "The Mathematical Study of Change." Pp. 428–78 in *Methodology in Social Research*, edited by H. M. Blalock and A. Blalock. New York: McGraw-Hill.

[8] Stinchcombe (1974, p. 189) outlines a similar approach for analyzing time budgets. He first determines whether a person engages in a certain activity and then, if he or she does, the proportion of his or her time that is devoted to that activity.

Cox, D. R., and D. Oakes. 1984. *Analysis of Survival Data*. London: Chapman and Hall.

Doob, J. L. 1953. *Stochastic Processes*. New York: Wiley.

Engle, Robert F., David F. Hendry, and Jean-Francois Richard. 1983. "Exogeneity." *Econometrica* 51:277–304.

Feller, William. 1968. *An Introduction to Probability Theory and its Applications*. Vol. 1. 3d ed. New York: Wiley.

——————. 1971. *An Introduction to Probability Theory and Its Applications*. Vol. 2. 2d ed. New York: Wiley.

Flinn, Christopher J., and James J. Heckman. 1982. "New Methods of Analyzing Structural Models of Labor Force Dynamics." *Journal of Econometrics* 18:115–68.

Freeman, John, and Michael T. Hannan. 1975. "Growth and Decline Processes in Organizations." *American Sociological Review* 40:215–28.

Hachen, David S. 1988. "The Competing Risks Model." *Sociological Methods and Research* 16 (in press).

Heckman, James J., and Burton Singer. 1984. "Econometric Duration Analysis." *Journal of Econometrics* 24:63–132.

Kalbfleisch, J. D., and R. L. Prentice. 1980. *The Statistical Analysis of Failure Time Data*. New York: Wiley.

Karlin, Samuel, and Howard M. Taylor. 1981. *A Second Course in Stochastic Processes*. New York: Academic Press.

Kolmogorov, A. 1931. "Über die analytischen Methoden in der Warscheinlichkeitsrechnung." *Mathematische Annalen* 104:415–58.

Lamperti, John. 1977. *Stochastic Processes. A Survey of the Mathematical Theory*. New York: Springer-Verlag.

Lancaster, Tony. 1979. "Econometric Methods for the Duration of Unemployment." *Econometrica* 47:939–56.

Maddala, G. S. 1983. *Limited-Dependent and Qualitative Variables in Econometrics*. New York: Cambridge University Press.

Nielsen, François. 1980. "The Flemish Movement in Belgium after World War II: A Dynamic Analysis." *American Sociological Review* 45:76–84.

Nielsen, François, and Rachel A. Rosenfeld. 1981. "Substantive Interpretations of Differential Equation Models." *American Sociological Review* 46:159–74.

Petersen, Trond. 1986a. "Estimating Fully Parametric Hazard Rate Models with Time-Dependent Covariates. Use of Maximum Likelihood." *Sociological Methods and Research* 14:219–46.

——————. 1986b. "Fitting Parametric Survival Models with Time-Dependent Covariates." *Journal of the Royal Statistical Society*, ser. C, 35:281–88.

Rogoff Ramsøy, Natalie. 1977. *Sosial Mobilitet i Norge* (Social mobility in Norway). Oslo: Tiden Norsk Forlag.

Rosenfeld, Rachel A. 1980. "Race and Sex Differences in Career Dynamics." *American Sociological Review* 45:583–609.

_____. 1983. "Sex Segregation and Sectors: An Analysis of Gender Differences in Returns from Employer Changes." *American Sociological Review* 48:637–55.

Skrede, Kari. 1971. *Sosioøkonomisk Klassifisering av Yrker i Norge, 1960* (Socioeconomic classification of occupations in Norway, 1960). Report 71-1. Oslo: Institute of Applied Social Research.

Sørensen, Aage B. 1974. "A Model for Occupational Careers." *American Journal of Sociology* 80:44–57.

_____. 1979. "A Model and a Metric for the Analysis of the Intragenerational Status Attainment Process." *American Journal of Sociology* 85:361–84.

_____. 1984. "Interpreting Time Dependency in Career Processes." Pp. 89–122 in *Stochastic Modelling of Social Processes*, edited by Andreas Diekman and Peter Mitter. New York: Academic Press.

Sørensen, Aage B., and Nancy B. Tuma. 1981. "Labor Market Structures and Job Mobility." In *Research in Social Stratification and Mobility*, vol. 1, edited by Donald Treiman and Robert V. Robinson. Greenwich, CT: JAI.

Spilerman, Seymour. 1970. "The Causes of Racial Disturbances: A Comparison of Alternative Explanations." *American Sociological Review* 35:627–49.

_____. 1971. "The Causes of Racial Disturbances: Tests of an Explanation." *American Sociological Review* 36:427–42.

Statistisk Sentralbyrå. 1973. *Standard for Utdanningsgruppering* (Norwegian standard classification of education). Oslo: Statistisk Sentralbyrå (Central Bureau of Statistics).

Stinchcombe, Arthur L. 1974. *Creating Efficient Industrial Administrations*. New York: Academic Press.

Tuma, Nancy B. 1986. "Effects of Labor Market Structure on Job Shift Patterns." Pp. 327–63 in *Longitudinal Analysis of Labor Market Data*, edited by James J. Heckman and Burton Singer. New York: Cambridge University Press.

Tuma, Nancy B., and Michael T. Hannan. 1984. *Social Dynamics. Models and Methods*. Orlando: Academic Press.

Visher, Mary G. 1981. *Data Documentation for the Norwegian Life History Study* (translated from Norwegian). Madison: University of Wisconsin, Department of Sociology.

_____. 1984. "The Workers of the State and the State of State Workers: A Comparison of Public and Private Employment in Norway." Ph.D. diss., Department of Sociology, University of Wisconsin, Madison.

6

Some Models for the Multiway Contingency Table with a One-to-One Correspondence among Categories

Michael E. Sobel*

Goodman (1985) discusses a class of models for the $R \times R$ contingency table with a one-to-one correspondence between the row and column variables. The most restrictive model in this class combines the features of symmetry and independence, and the least restrictive is the model of quasi symmetry or symmetric association. In this paper, I extend the class of models discussed by Goodman to the $R \times R \times K$ ($K \geq 2$) contingency table and to the $R \times R \times R$ contingency table. Several of the models I discuss have been proposed by previous investigators, but many have not been previously considered. I show how to parameterize these models in new and informative ways, and I develop the relationship between the model parameters and various measures of dependence that are especially useful in tables of the type considered here. To illustrate the types of inferences and interpretations yielded by these models, I present two empirical examples.

For helpful comments on an earlier draft of this paper, I am indebted to Dudley Duncan, Michael Hout, and James Shockey. This material was also presented at the August 1986 meetings of the American Sociological Association in New York. Computations were performed by Rick Axelson, whose assistance is appreciated.

*University of Arizona

1. INTRODUCTION

Multiway contingency tables with a one-to-one correspondence between the categories of some or all of the discrete variables cross-classified arise in a variety of ways. For example, each of the following situations yields an $R^m \times K$ contingency table, where $m = 2, 3, \ldots, M$, and $K = 1, 2, \ldots, K^*$:

1. Two or more judges rate a sample of subjects with respect to a discrete variable.
2. Two or more alternate forms of a discrete item are compared.
3. A sample of respondents is classified by a discrete variable at several time points, as in studies of intergenerational occupational mobility.
4. Matched pairs or triplets, etc., are cross-classified by a common discrete variable.

For other situations, see the examples in this paper.

Various types of specialized models have been considered for the case in which $m = 2$ and $K = 1$ (Caussinus 1965; Duncan 1979; Goodman 1972, 1979, 1981, 1985; Haberman 1974; Hope 1982; McCullagh 1978, 1982). For this case, Goodman (1985) considers various relationships between the models of quasi symmetry (QS), quasi independence (QI), independence (I), symmetry (S), and two models that combine independence assumptions with symmetry. The first of these combines symmetry with quasi independence; this model is called symmetry + quasi independence (SQI). The second combines symmetry with independence; it is called symmetry + independence (SI). For additional material on SI, see Hope (1982) and Sobel (1983).

In this paper, I extend the models considered by Goodman (1985) to the $R^m \times K$ contingency table and develop a variety of new models. Then, I describe measures of the dependence between variables that are particularly well suited for the $R^m \times K$ table (when the models discussed here hold). Finally, I show how to parameterize these models in new and informative ways and develop the relationship between various model parameters and the measures of dependence described here.

For expository purposes, I explicitly consider only two cases: (a) the case in which $m = 2$, $K \geq 2$, and (b) the case in which $m = 3$, $K = 1$. For both cases, the models, measures of dependence, and

TABLE 1
Wife's Education by Husband's Education and Sex of Respondent

Husband's Education and Sex of Respondent	Wife's Education			
	0–11 Years	12 Years	13–15 Years	16 or More Years
Male				
0–11 years	89	34	11	3
12 years	19	94	15	8
13–15 years	4	34	16	7
16 or more years	2	19	22	44
Female				
0–11 years	96	35	5	1
12 years	27	106	22	9
13–15 years	7	33	27	13
16 or more years	1	18	23	36

Source: 1980 General Social Survey (Davis 1980).

parameterizations that are described can be generalized in a straight-forward way to the case in which $m > 3$ (or $m \geq 3$ for case (a)).

To illustrate the types of inferences that are obtained with the models and model parameterizations discussed in this paper, I present an example of each case.

In the first example, I apply the models in section 3.1 to the data in Table 1. These data are from the 1980 General Social Survey, conducted by the National Opinion Research Center (Davis 1980). Respondents were asked to report the number of years of education they completed and, if married, the number of years their spouse completed. Table 1 reports the cross-classification of husband's education by wife's education, by sex of respondent. Haberman (1978, pp. 226–30) analyzed similar items from the 1974 General Social Survey.

In the second example, I apply the models in section 4.1 to the data in Table 2. These data are also from the 1980 General Social Survey. Respondents were asked to indicate their degree of satisfaction with various aspects of life. Satisfaction with friendships, residence, and hobbies are cross-classified. The analysis shows how to exploit the fact that the variables are ordinal. For related material on ordered models for the three-way table, see Agresti and Kezouh (1983), Clogg (1982a),

TABLE 2
Satisfaction with Hobbies by Satisfaction with Residence and Satisfaction with Friendships

Satisfaction with Residence and Friendships	Satisfaction with Hobbies			
	Not or Somewhat Satisfied	Fairly Satisfied	Greatly Satisfied	Very Greatly Satisfied
Not or somewhat satisfied with friendships				
Not or somewhat satisfied with residence	16	1	6	1
Fairly satisfied with residence	5	3	3	3
Greatly satisfied with residence	7	2	4	3
Very greatly satisfied with residence	2	0	1	3
Fairly satisfied with friendships				
Not or somewhat satisfied with residence	7	4	8	4
Fairly satisfied with residence	8	9	15	2
Greatly satisfied with residence	7	15	12	4
Very greatly satisfied with residence	2	1	10	2
Greatly satisfied with friendships				
Not or somewhat satisfied with residence	24	14	33	13
Fairly satisfied with residence	21	24	100	12
Greatly satisfied with residence	2	41	289	70
Very greatly satisfied with residence	10	13	60	36
Very greatly satisfied with friendships				
Not or somewhat satisfied with residence	8	5	14	14
Fairly satisfied with residence	11	7	23	20
Greatly satisfied with residence	7	13	99	74
Very greatly satisfied with residence	11	7	51	136

Source: 1980 General Social Survey (Davis 1980).

Note: The "not or somewhat satisfied" category includes respondents whose answers to the relevant item were "some," "a little," or "none." The "fairly satisfied" category includes respondents who answered "a fair amount." The "greatly satisfied" category includes those who answered "a great deal" and "quite a bit." The "very greatly satisfied" category includes those who answered "a very great deal."

and Goodman (1986). Clogg (1982a) analyzed similar items from the 1977 General Social Survey.

2. SOME PRELIMINARIES: THE $R \times R$ TABLE

In tables with a one-to-one correspondence between the row and column categories, researchers often want to know (a) whether the row and column distributions are identical, and (b) whether there is a tendency for the counts to cluster on or, in the case of ordered data, near the diagonal of the table. When the homogeneity of the marginal distributions is the primary question, various types of marginal homogeneity tests can be used (Agresti 1983; Bishop, Fienberg, and Holland 1975; Bhapkar 1966; Ireland, Ku, and Kullback 1969; Madansky 1963; Stuart 1955). When the tendency for the counts to cluster is the concern, various indices of agreement can be used (Bergan 1980; Cohen 1960, 1968; Clogg 1979). Alternatively, as in this paper, the structure of association in the table might be examined (Hauser and Massagli 1983; Tanner and Young 1985). It should be noted that most researchers who proceed in this fashion do not describe the association in a manner that bears directly on the relative tendency for the counts to cluster on the diagonal, nor do they address both questions simultaneously. For exceptions, see Darroch and McCloud (1986), Sobel, Hout, and Duncan (1985), and Hout, Duncan, and Sobel (1987).

In this section, I describe a set of odds ratios that bears on question (b) when QS holds. Next, I show how the models discussed in section 1 can be parameterized to bear directly on both questions. I describe various properties of this parameterization, including the relationship between the parameters and the set of odds ratios described here.

When QS holds, the structure of association in the $R \times R$ table can be characterized by any set of $R(R-1)/2$ nonredundant odds ratios. Let F_{ij} denote the expected frequency in the (ij)th cell of the table, $i = 1, \ldots, R$, $j = 1, \ldots, R$. Let Γ be the set of odds ratios for all 2×2 tables obtained from rows i and j and columns i and j:

$$\Gamma = \left\{ \gamma_{ij} : \gamma_{ij} = F_{ii}F_{jj}/F_{ij}F_{ji}, \ i < j \right\}. \tag{1}$$

When QS holds, the γ_{ij}, which measure the association in the table with respect to the diagonal cells, suffice to characterize the association in the table, and any other set of odds ratios can be computed from these.

When the cross-classified variables are ordinal, it is often useful to consider the set of local odds ratios:

$$\theta = \left\{ \theta_{ij}: \theta_{ij} = F_{ij}F_{i+1,\,j+1}/F_{i,\,j+1}F_{i+1,\,j},\right.$$
$$\left. i = 1,\ldots, R-1,\ j = 1,\ldots, R-1 \right\}. \tag{2}$$

Goodman (1981) shows that when $\theta_{ij} \geq 1$ for all such ratios, the distribution within the (i')th row is stochastically higher than the distribution within the (i)th row, $i' > i$. Similar remarks apply to the distribution within the (j')th column and the (j)th column, $j' > j$. For further details and discussion of the relationship between isotropy and other concepts, see Agresti (1984), Anderson (1984), and Goodman (1981).

The foregoing suggests that the relationship between the diagonal odds ratios (Γ) and the local odds ratios (θ) will be of interest. It is easy to verify that

$$\gamma_{ij} = \prod_{p=1}^{j-1} \prod_{q=1}^{j-1} \theta_{pq}, \qquad i < j, \tag{3}$$

and, under QS, that

$$\theta_{ij} = \begin{cases} \gamma_{i,\,j+1} & \text{if } i = j, \\ \left(\gamma_{i,\,j+1}/\gamma_{ij}\gamma_{i+1,\,j+1}\right)^{1/2} & \text{if } j = i+1, \\ \left(\gamma_{i,\,j+1}\gamma_{i+1,\,j}/\gamma_{ij}\gamma_{i+1,\,j+1}\right)^{1/2} & \text{otherwise.} \end{cases} \tag{4}$$

From (3), we see that $\gamma_{ij} \geq 1$ if $\theta_{pq} \geq 1$, $p = 1,\ldots, R-1$, $q = 1,\ldots, R-1$. Thus, if $\gamma_{ij} < 1$ for some pair (ij), one or more of the local odds ratios are less than unity. Therefore, if the rows and the columns cannot be reordered so that $\gamma_{ij} \geq 1$ for all (ij) pairs, the joint distribution is anisotropic. Of course, if the rows and the columns cannot be reordered so that $\theta_{ij} \geq 1$, the joint distribution is anisotropic. But note that the result on the γ_{ij} does not depend upon the validity of QS, and note that while there are $R(R-1)/2$ γ_{ij} for any given ordering, in the general case there are $(R-1)^2$ nonredundant local odds ratios. However, from (4), which is valid when QS holds, we see that the condition $\gamma_{ij} \geq 1$ for all pairs does not imply that $\theta_{ij} \geq 1$, $i = 1,\ldots, R-1$, $j = 1,\ldots, R-1$.

Consider now the model QS, written as

$$F_{ij} = \beta_i \beta_j \alpha_{1(i)} \alpha_{2(j)} \delta_{ij},$$ (5)

where $\delta_{ij} = \delta_{ji}$ if $i \neq j$ (as before), 1 otherwise, and where there are $R + 1$ additional restrictions on the α parameters. Note that all the other models in section 1 can be obtained by imposing suitable restrictions on the parameters of (5). For examples of these types of restrictions, see section 3.1.

Several properties of this particular parameterization are of interest. First,

$$\delta_{ij} = (\gamma_{ij})^{-1/2};$$ (6)

i.e., the δ_{ij} parameters directly measure the association in the table with respect to the diagonal cells, albeit inversely to the odds ratios γ_{ij}. From (6) and the remarks following (4), it follows that when the rows and the columns of the table cannot be reordered so that $\delta_{ij} \leq 1$, the joint distribution is anisotropic. This is true whether or not QS holds. When QS holds, (6) is a consequence of (5), and when QS does not hold, (6) can be used to define δ_{ij}. Under QS, it follows from (4) and (6) that

$$\theta_{ij} = \delta_{ij}\delta_{i+1,j+1}/\delta_{i+1,j}\delta_{i,j+1},$$
$$i = 1, \ldots, R-1, \qquad j = 1, \ldots, R-1.$$ (7)

Thus, the distribution is isotropic (under QS) if and only if, under some ordering of the rows and the columns, the local cross-product ratios of the δ_{ij} are at least unity. Clearly, the condition $\delta_{ij} \leq 1$ for all (ij) pairs does not imply that $\theta_{ij} \geq 1$, $i = 1, \ldots, R-1$, $j = 1, \ldots, R-1$.

Second, if and only if QS holds, the α parameters are directly interpretable as marginal shift parameters, and these account for any and all asymmetries of the form $F_{ij} \neq F_{ji}$ (and, hence, for any and all marginal heterogeneity). To see this, note that QS holds if and only if $F_{ij}/F_{ji} = \alpha_{1(i)}\alpha_{2(j)}/\alpha_{1(j)}\alpha_{2(i)}$ for all i and j, and note that $F_{ij}/F_{ji} = 1$ for all i and j if and only if $\alpha_{1(i)} = \alpha_{2(i)}$, $i = 1, \ldots, R$, i.e., if and only if symmetry holds. Thus, ratios of the α parameters, which are invariant with respect to the manner in which the α parameters are subsequently identified, quantify the impact of any and all marginal heterogeneity on asymmetry, and any and all asymmetries are due solely to marginal heterogeneity, as reflected in the ratios $\alpha_{1(i)}\alpha_{2(j)}/\alpha_{1(j)}\alpha_{2(i)}$.

Finally, when the variables can be treated as ordinal, the researcher might wish to entertain one or more log-linear or log-bilinear models with equal row and column scores (Goodman 1981, 1985, 1986), subject to restrictions on the marginal distributions and/or additional restrictions on the structure of association. Such models, which imply QS, describe the local association in the contingency table, and the log-bilinear models can also suggest an appropriate ordering of the rows and columns when this ordering is unknown (Goodman 1981; Clogg 1982b). For any such model, the δ_{ij} can be obtained by using the formulae for the expected frequencies under the model, in conjunction with (1) and (6). For further details, see Sobel et al. (1985).

3. SOME "CONDITIONAL" MULTIPLICATIVE MODELS

3.1. *The Models*

In this section, I consider an $R \times R$ table observed for each of $K(K > 1)$ groups. In this case, interest centers on the structure of association and the marginal distributions, both within and between groups. The models considered are appropriate when K (possibly) different multinomial distributions are sampled, but the models may also be applied when a single multinomial is sampled.

Let F_{ijk}, $i = 1, \ldots, R$, $j = 1, \ldots, R$, $k = 1, \ldots, K$, denote the expected frequency in the (ijk)th cell of the three-way table. The model of conditional quasi symmetry (Bishop et al. 1975, pp. 299–300) states that QS holds in each group. This is the most general model considered in this section. The model, hereafter denoted CQS, may be written as

$$F_{ijk} = \mu_k \beta_{ik} \beta_{jk} \alpha_{13(ik)} \alpha_{23(jk)} \delta_{ijk}, \tag{8}$$

where $\delta_{ijk} = \delta_{jik}$, $k = 1, \ldots, K$, $\delta_{ijk} = 1$ if $i = j$, and the other parameters are subject to additional restrictions that are considered in section 3.2.

From (8), it is clear that for fixed k, $k = 1, \ldots, K$, ratios of the form F_{ijk}/F_{jik} may be interpreted as in section 2. Similarly,

$$\delta_{ijk} = \left(F_{ijk} F_{jik} / F_{iik} F_{jjk} \right)^{1/2}, \tag{9}$$

and thus, for fixed k, the δ parameters may be interpreted as in section 2.

The other models discussed in section 1 are easily extended to the situation considered in this section, and each of these extensions can be obtained in a straightforward manner by imposing further restrictions on the parameters of (8). Thus, the following models are obtained:

$$F_{ijk} = \mu_k \beta_{ik} \beta_{jk} \alpha_{13(ik)} \alpha_{23(jk)} \delta_{ik} \delta_{jk}, \qquad i \neq j, \qquad (10a)$$

$$F_{ijk} = \mu_k \beta_{ik} \beta_{jk} \alpha_{13(ik)} \alpha_{23(jk)}, \qquad i = j; \qquad (10b)$$

$$F_{ijk} = \mu_k \beta_{ik} \beta_{jk} \alpha_{13(ik)} \alpha_{23(jk)}; \qquad (11)$$

$$F_{ijk} = \mu_k \beta_{ik} \beta_{jk} \delta_{ijk}; \qquad (12)$$

$$F_{ijk} = \mu_k \beta_{ik} \beta_{jk} \delta_{ik} \delta_{jk}, \qquad i \neq j, \qquad (13a)$$

$$F_{ijk} = \mu_k \beta_{ik} \beta_{jk}, \qquad i = j; \qquad (13b)$$

$$F_{ijk} = \mu_k \beta_{ik} \beta_{jk}. \qquad (14)$$

Equations (10a) and (10b) state that quasi independence holds for each group; this model is called the conditional quasi-independence model (CQI). Equation (11) states that independence holds in each group; this is the familiar model of conditional independence (CI). Equation (12) represents the model of conditional symmetry (CS) discussed by Bishop et al. (1975, pp. 299–300), and equations (13) and (14) state, respectively, that symmetry + quasi independence (CSQI) and symmetry + independence (CSI) hold in each group. Degrees of freedom for these models are reported in Table 3. It is assumed that $R \geq 4$. In addition, Table 3 describes each model in this section as a pair of hypotheses: The first hypothesis refers to the types of restrictions placed on the α and β parameters, and the second refers to the structure of association between the row and column variables. Subsequently, I will use this description to characterize, in a simple way, the relationships between the various models in this section.

By imposing equality constraints on the α, β, and δ parameters, we can generate analogous models for various types of between-group homogeneity. For example, when CQS holds and when the δ_{ijk} are homogeneous across groups, the following partial association model is obtained:

$$F_{ijk} = \mu_k \beta_{ik} \beta_{jk} \alpha_{13(ik)} \alpha_{23(jk)} \delta_{ij}, \qquad \delta_{ij} = \delta_{ji}. \qquad (15)$$

TABLE 3
Descriptions and Degrees of Freedom for the Models in Section 3.1

Model	Description	df
CQS	$(\mathrm{NH}_{\alpha\beta}, \mathrm{S})$	$K(R-1)(R-2)/2$
CQI	$(\mathrm{NH}_{\alpha\beta}, \mathrm{QI})$	$K(R^2 - 3R + 1)$
CI	$(\mathrm{NH}_{\alpha\beta}, \mathrm{CI})$	$K(R-1)^2$
CS	$(\mathrm{H}_{\alpha s}, \mathrm{S})$	$KR(R-1)/2$
CSQI	$(\mathrm{H}_{\alpha s}, \mathrm{QI})$	$KR(R-2)$
CSI	$(\mathrm{H}_{\alpha s}, \mathrm{CI})$	$KR(R-1)$
CQS + H_δ	$(\mathrm{NH}_{\alpha\beta}, \mathrm{H}_\delta)$	$K(R-1)(R-2)/2 + (K-1)R(R-1)/2$
CQI + H_δ	$(\mathrm{NH}_{\alpha\beta}, \mathrm{H}_\delta + \mathrm{QI})$	$K(R^2 - 3R + 1) + (K-1)R$
CS + H_δ	$(\mathrm{H}_{\alpha s}, \mathrm{H}_\delta)$	$KR(R-1)/2 + (K-1)R(R-1)/2$
CSQI + H_δ	$(\mathrm{H}_{\alpha s}, \mathrm{H}_\delta + \mathrm{QI})$	$KR(R-2) + (K-1)R$
CQS + H_α	$(\mathrm{H}_\alpha, \mathrm{S})$	$K(R-1)(R-2)/2 + (K-1)(R-1)$
CQI + H_α	$(\mathrm{H}_\alpha, \mathrm{QI})$	$K(R^2 - 3R + 1) + (K-1)(R-1)$
CI + H_α	$(\mathrm{H}_\alpha, \mathrm{CI})$	$K(R-1)^2 + (K-1)(R-1)$
CQS + $\mathrm{H}_{\alpha\beta}$	$(\mathrm{H}_{\alpha\beta}, \mathrm{S})$	$K(R-1)(R-2)/2 + 2(K-1)(R-1)$
CQI + $\mathrm{H}_{\alpha\beta}$	$(\mathrm{H}_{\alpha\beta}, \mathrm{QI})$	$K(R^2 - 3R + 1) + 2(K-1)(R-1)$
CI + $\mathrm{H}_{\alpha\beta}$	$(\mathrm{H}_{\alpha\beta}, \mathrm{CI})$	$K(R-1)^2 + 2(K-1)(R-1)$
CS + $\mathrm{H}_{\alpha\beta}$	$(\mathrm{H}_{\alpha\beta s}, \mathrm{S})$	$KR(R-1)/2 + (K-1)(R-1)$
CSQI + $\mathrm{H}_{\alpha\beta}$	$(\mathrm{H}_{\alpha\beta s}, \mathrm{QI})$	$KR(R-2) + (K-1)(R-1)$
CSI + $\mathrm{H}_{\alpha\beta}$	$(\mathrm{H}_{\alpha\beta s}, \mathrm{CI})$	$KR(R-1) + (K-1)(R-1)$
CQS + $\mathrm{H}_{\alpha\beta}$	$(\mathrm{H}_\alpha, \mathrm{H}_\delta)$	$K(R-1)(R-2)/2 + (K-1)(R-1)$ $+ (K-1)R(R-1)/2$
CQI + $\mathrm{H}_{\alpha\delta}$	$(\mathrm{H}_\alpha, \mathrm{H}_\delta + \mathrm{QI})$	$K(R^2 - 3R + 1) + (K-1)(R-1) + (K-1)R$
CQS + $\mathrm{H}_{\alpha\beta\delta}$	$(\mathrm{H}_{\alpha\beta}, \mathrm{H}_\delta)$	$K(R-1)(R-2)/2 + 2(K-1)(R-1)$ $+ (K-1)R(R-1)/2$
CQI + $\mathrm{H}_{\alpha\beta\delta}$	$(\mathrm{H}_{\alpha\beta}, \mathrm{H}_\delta + \mathrm{QI})$	$K(R^2 - 3R + 1) + 2(K-1)(R-1) + (K-1)R$
CS + $\mathrm{H}_{\alpha\beta s}$	$(\mathrm{H}_{\alpha\beta s}, \mathrm{H}_\delta)$	$KR(R-1)/2 + (K-1)(R-1)$ $+ (K-1)R(R-1)/2$
CSQI + $\mathrm{H}_{\alpha\beta s}$	$(\mathrm{H}_{\alpha\beta s}, \mathrm{H}_\delta + \mathrm{QI})$	$KR(R-2) + (K-1)(R-1) + (K-1)R$

Note: $\mathrm{NH}_{\alpha\beta}$ imposes no homogeneity restrictions on the α and β parameters. H_α imposes homogeneity restrictions on the α parameters, and $\mathrm{H}_{\alpha\beta}$ imposes homogeneity restrictions on the α and β parameters. $\mathrm{H}_{\alpha s}$ is H_α with symmetry imposed, and $\mathrm{H}_{\alpha\beta s}$ is $\mathrm{H}_{\alpha\beta}$ with symmetry imposed. S is the hypothesis that the association between the row and column variables is symmetric in each group. QI is the quasi-independence hypothesis, H_δ is the hypothesis that the symmetric association is homogeneous across groups, $\mathrm{H}_\delta + \mathrm{QI}$ is the homogeneous quasi-independence hypothesis, and CI is the hypothesis that the row and column variables are conditionally independent.

Equation (15) states that CQS holds and that the association in each two-way table is homogeneous; thus, the model corresponding to (15) is called $CQS + H_\delta$. Similarly, by modifying equations (10) and (11), respectively, we obtain models $CQI + H_\delta$ and $CI + H_\delta$. Degrees of freedom for these models are reported in Table 3. For related material, see Clogg (1982a). Various types of models with homogeneous marginal parameters can also be considered. When the α parameters are homogeneous across groups, equation (8) reduces to

$$F_{ijk} = \mu_k \beta_{ik} \beta_{jk} \alpha_{1(i)} \alpha_{2(j)} \delta_{ijk}, \tag{16}$$

a model labeled $CQS + H_\alpha$. Models $CQI + H_\alpha$ and $CI + H_\alpha$ are then obtained by modifying equations (10) and (11), respectively. For each of these models, the F_{ijk} satisfy the constraint $F_{ijk}/F_{jik} = \alpha_{1(i)}\alpha_{2(j)}/\alpha_{1(j)}\alpha_{2(i)}$; i.e., ratios of asymmetries are the same in all groups. Degrees of freedom for these models are reported in Table 3.

Additional models can be generated by restricting the β parameters or the α parameters, or both, to be homogeneous across groups as well. For example, equation (8), with homogeneous α and β parameters, reduces to

$$F_{ijk} = \mu_k \beta_i \beta_j \alpha_{1(i)} \alpha_{2(j)} \delta_{ijk}, \tag{17}$$

a model called $CQS + H_{\alpha\beta}$. Similarly, by modifying equations (10), (11), (12), (13), and (14), respectively, we obtain models denoted $CQI + H_{\alpha\beta}$, $CI + H_{\alpha\beta}$, $CS + H_{\alpha\beta}$, $CSQI + H_{\alpha\beta}$, and $CSI + H_{\alpha\beta}$. Note that of these models, only $CI + H_{\alpha\beta}$ (the model of mutual independence) and $CSI + H_{\alpha\beta}$ are hierarchical. Note also that given the parametric structure in (12), $CS + H_{\alpha\beta}$ could just as well be denoted $CS + H_\beta$. Similar remarks apply to $CSQI + H_{\alpha\beta}$ and $CSI + H_{\alpha\beta}$. Degrees of freedom for the models are reported in Table 3.

Finally, the homogeneous association models can be combined with the models with homogeneous marginal parameters in an obvious manner, obtaining models $CQS + H_{\alpha\delta}$, $CQI + H_{\alpha\delta}$, $CQS + H_{\alpha\beta\delta}$, $CQI + H_{\alpha\beta\delta}$, $CS + H_{\alpha\beta\delta}$, and $CSQI + H_{\alpha\beta\delta}$. Note that for the last four of these models, the grouping variable is "completely" independent of the row and column variables (Bishop et al. 1975, p. 37). Note also that for these models, if the distribution of the level variable is not fixed by the sampling design, models in which the μ parameters are homogeneous across levels can be considered. Thus, analogous equiprobability models could be generated. However, such models are

FIGURE 1. Implication graphs for the models in section 3.1. ($NH_{\alpha\beta}$ imposes no homogeneity restrictions on the α and β parameters. H_α imposes homogeneity restrictions on the α parameters, and $H_{\alpha\beta}$ imposes homogeneity restrictions on both the α and β parameters. $H_{\alpha S}$ is H_α with symmetry imposed, and $H_{\alpha\beta S}$ is $H_{\alpha\beta}$ with symmetry imposed. S is the hypothesis that the association between rows and columns is symmetric in each group. QI is the quasi-independence hypothesis, H_δ is the hypothesis that the symmetric association is homogeneous across groups, H_δ + QI is the homogeneous quasi-independence hypothesis, and CI is the hypothesis that the row and column variables are conditionally independent.)

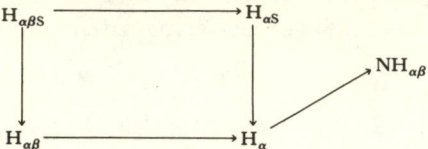

(a) Implications among hypotheses describing the α and β parameters.

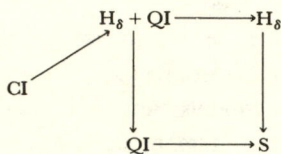

(b) Implications among hypotheses describing the association between the row and column variables.

not appropriate when the sample is taken from K ($K \geq 1$) multinomials; therefore, they are not considered further. Degrees of freedom for the models above are reported in Table 3.

To obtain the logical relationships between any subset of the models in this section (except the equiprobability models), it is useful to consider the alternative descriptions in Table 3. These characterize each model in terms of joint restrictions on the marginal parameters and the association parameters. By combining this characterization with the implication graphs in Figure 1, we readily obtain the logical relationships between any subset of the models in this section. For example, since H_α implies $NH_{\alpha\beta}$ and since H_δ + QI implies H_δ, if the model (H_α, H_δ + QI) holds, the model ($NH_{\alpha\beta}, H_\delta$) holds.

Finally, it is important to note that the models in this section can be applied when the row and column variables are ordered or unordered. When the row and column variables are ordered, and when CQS holds, more parsimonious models appropriate for ordinal data may hold (Agresti and Kezouh 1983; Clogg 1982a; Goodman 1986). In this case, ratios of the α parameters are still invariant under the appropriate ordinal model, and by using the formulae for the expected

TABLE 4

Analysis of Table 1 Using the Models in Section 3.1

Model	df	L^2	χ^2
CQS	6	6.21	6.10
CQI	10	68.32	69.51
CI	18	519.42	554.15
CS	12	37.69	36.66
CSQI	16	100.65	107.42
CSI	24	537.27	563.17
CQS + H_δ	12	10.32	10.55
CQI + H_δ	14	69.76	70.88
CS + H_δ	18	41.18	40.75
CSQI + H_δ	20	101.84	108.79
CQS + H_α	9	9.63	9.39
CQI + H_α	13	71.73	72.95
CI + H_α	21	520.90	554.43
CQS + $H_{\alpha\beta}$	12	13.31	13.04
CQI + $H_{\alpha\beta}$	16	71.97	72.68
CI + $H_{\alpha\beta}$	24	524.60	564.17
CS + $H_{\alpha\beta}$	15	41.37	40.31
CSQI + $H_{\alpha\beta}$	19	101.89	107.27
CSI + $H_{\alpha\beta}$	27	540.95	572.52
CQS + $H_{\alpha\delta}$	15	13.12	13.63
CQI + $H_{\alpha\delta}$	17	72.92	73.96
CQS + $H_{\alpha\beta\delta}$	18	16.09	16.33
CQI + $H_{\alpha\beta\delta}$	20	75.65	76.33
CS + $H_{\alpha\beta\delta}$	21	44.15	43.06
CSQI + $H_{\alpha\beta\delta}$	23	104.57	110.93

frequencies under the ordinal model, in conjunction with (9), we obtain the δ_{ijk} parameters.

3.2. *Analysis of Table* 1

Using GLIM (Baker and Nelder 1978), I fit the models in section 3.1 to the data in Table 1 by maximum likelihood. Table 4 gives degrees of freedom, the likelihood ratio chi square (L^2), and the goodness-of-fit chi square (χ^2) for each model.

Inspection of Table 4 reveals that six models (CQS, CQS + H_δ, CQS + H_α, CQS + $H_{\alpha\beta}$, CQS + $H_{\alpha\delta}$, CQS + $H_{\alpha\beta\delta}$) fit the data ade-

FIGURE 2. Relationships among selected models for the Table 1 data. (Numbers appearing beneath the model name report the L^2 value and the degrees of freedom for that model, respectively. Numbers appearing on lines report the L^2 value and the degrees of freedom for the likelihood ratio test between the models connected by the line.)

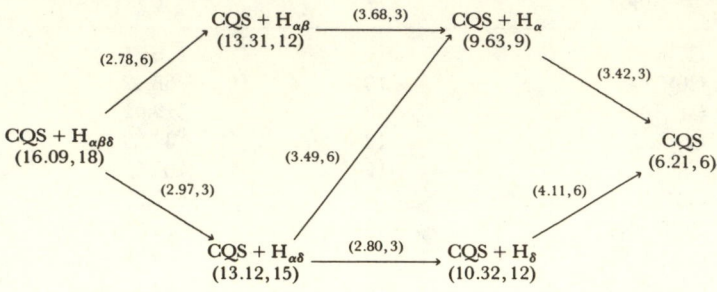

quately, at the 0.05 level of significance. Figure 2 depicts the relationships between these models and reports the differences in L^2 for nested models. Note that CQS + H$_{\alpha\beta\delta}$ implies each of the other models, and note also that none of the other five models fits the data better, at the 0.05 level of significance. Thus, CQS + H$_{\alpha\beta\delta}$ may be preferred for these data. Under this model, husband's education and wife's education are completely independent of the sex of respondent. However, if husband's education and wife's education were not completely independent of the sex of respondent, as Haberman (1978, pp. 226–30) found in his analysis of similar items from the 1974 General Social Survey, we would conclude that men and women differ in their responses to the educational items, and we would doubt the objective value of the data.

The additive form of CQS + H$_{\alpha\beta\delta}$ is

$$F_{ijk}^* = \mu_k^* + \beta_i^* + \beta_j^* + \alpha_{1(i)}^* + \alpha_{2(j)}^* + \delta_{ij}^*,$$

where $F_{ijk}^* = \ln(F_{ijk})$, $\mu_k^* = \ln(\mu_k)$, etc. Table 5 presents estimates for the parameters of the model under the following identifying restrictions: $\mu_1^* = 0$, $\alpha_{1(i)}^* = 0$, $i = 1,\dots, R$, $\Sigma_j \alpha_{2(j)}^* = 0$, $\delta_{ij}^* = \delta_{ji}^*$, where $\delta_{ij}^* = 0$ if $i = j$. Note that under this set of restrictions, $F_{ijk}^* - F_{jik}^* = \alpha_{2(j)}^* - \alpha_{2(i)}^*$. Sobel et al. (1985) use an analogous parameterization to describe the structure of the two-way intergenerational occupational mobility table. Many other identification rules could have been chosen, and in some contexts, a different set of rules may be preferred.

TABLE 5
Parameter Estimates and Asymptotic Standard Errors Under CQS + $H_{\alpha\beta\delta}$

Parameter	Estimate	Asymptotic Standard Error
μ_2^*	0.086	0.067
β_1^*	2.265	0.080
β_2^*	2.048	0.063
β_3^*	1.473	0.096
β_4^*	2.072	0.095
$\alpha_{2(1)}^*$	-0.047	0.138
$\alpha_{2(2)}^*$	0.467	0.098
$\alpha_{2(3)}^*$	0.078	0.112
$\alpha_{2(4)}^*$	-0.498	0.148
δ_{12}^*	-1.240	0.108
δ_{13}^*	-1.890	0.210
δ_{14}^*	-3.574	0.383
δ_{23}^*	-0.597	0.130
δ_{24}^*	-1.656	0.159
δ_{34}^*	-0.631	0.159

The parameter estimates reveal a relative tendency for the responses to cluster on the diagonal cells of the two bivariate tables, reflecting the relative tendency for husbands and wives to have the same educational status. The association between husband's and wife's education does not vary by the sex of respondent. Furthermore, for fixed i (or fixed j), the relative tendency toward homogamy becomes stronger as the distance $|i-j|$ increases. From (9) and the remarks following (7), we see that the $\hat{\delta}_{ij}$ also suggest that the joint distribution of husband's and wife's education is isotropic (within sex of respondent) and that the stochastic ordering of the row and column variables does not depend upon respondent's sex. However, not all wives and husbands marry partners with the same educational status, because the distribution of husband's education differs from the distribution of wife's education. This is shown by the conditional likelihood ratio test (under CQS + $H_{\alpha\beta}$) for symmetry: $L^2(\text{CS} + H_{\alpha\beta\delta}) - L^2(\text{CQS} + H_{\alpha\beta\delta}) = 28.06$, $df = 3$, $p < 0.001$. The α parameters allow for this, and these parameters account for all marginal heterogeneity. The α^* are normed to sum to 0; thus, $\alpha_{2(j)}^* > 0$ implies that any husband, regardless of his level of education, is more likely to marry a woman from the (j)th educational level than he would be if (under the model) wives had the same distribution of education as husbands. Thus, the estimates of the $\alpha_{2(j)}^*$ suggest an overabundance of wives with 12 years of education and a scarcity of wives with 16 or more years of education. This can also be seen by examining the difference $\hat{\alpha}_{2(2)}^* - \hat{\alpha}_{2(4)}^* = 0.965$, with asymptotic standard error 0.212, which suggests that husbands with 16 or more years of education are $\exp(0.965) = 2.625$ times more likely to be married to wives with 12 years of education than vice versa.

Finally, note that $\hat{\mu}_2^*$ does not differ statistically from 0, suggesting that male and female respondents occur with equal probability. Given that the sample was not stratified by respondent's sex, it would be possible to delete this parameter from the model and obtain a more parsimonious equiprobability model, as described in section 3.1.

The analysis above ignores the fact that educational level is an ordinal variable, although this information is implicitly used to interpret the pattern of association between husband's and wife's education. As indicated previously, a model appropriate for ordinal data could be estimated, and the results could be linked to the models previously considered by expressing the δ_{ij} appropriately. The analysis in section 4.2 will suffice to illustrate the general point.

4. SOME MODELS FOR THE $R \times R \times R$ TABLE

4.1. *The Models*

In this section, I explicitly consider an $R \times R \times R$ table obtained by cross-classifying three discrete variables with a one-to-one correspondence between categories. I assume that $R \geq 3$. For this case, interest centers on both the marginal distributions and the structure of "symmetrical" association in the table. Several of the models considered are identical to various models discussed by Bishop et al. (1975, pp. 299–309), but I show how to parameterize these models in new and informative ways. I assume throughout that a single multinomial distribution has been sampled.

Various generalizations of quasi symmetry have been proposed (see Bishop et al. 1975). The most general model considered here is

$$F_{ijk} = \beta_i \beta_j \beta_k \alpha_{1(i)} \alpha_{2(j)} \alpha_{3(k)} \delta_{ijk}, \tag{18}$$

where $\delta_{ijk} = \delta_{ikj} = \delta_{jik} = \delta_{jki} = \delta_{kij} = \delta_{kji}$; i.e., the δ parameters are "symmetric," which means that these parameters are invariant under permutations of the ordered triple (i, j, k). This model, hereafter called total quasi symmetry (TQS), is equivalent to model 2 in Bishop et al. (1975, p. 303). Darroch (1986) and McCullagh (1982) also consider this model. To identify the model, I impose $R + 2$ restrictions on the α parameters (to be described subsequently) and the restrictions $\delta_{ijk} = 1$ if $i = j = k$. Under this parameterization, $F_{ijk}/F_{kij} = \alpha_{1(i)}\alpha_{2(j)}\alpha_{3(k)}/\alpha_{1(k)}\alpha_{2(i)}\alpha_{3(j)}$, and as in section 2, various ratios of the α parameters, which are invariant with respect to the manner in which these parameters are subsequently identified, quantify the impact of any and all marginal heterogeneity on "asymmetries" (lack of invariance with respect to permutations of the ordered triple (i, j, k)) among the F_{ijk}. Further, such asymmetry is due solely to marginal heterogeneity, as reflected in these ratios. For further details, see the empirical example in section 4.2. Second, under this parameterization, $(\delta_{ijk})^3 = F_{ijk}F_{kij}F_{jki}/F_{iii}F_{jjj}F_{kkk}$, whence the δ parameters measure the "total dependence" in the table, vis-à-vis the "consistent" cells $\{(1,1,1),(2,2,2),\dots,(R, R, R)\}$. For further justification that the δ parameters measure the total dependence in the table, see Altham (1970), from whom this term is borrowed.

The other models considered in the introduction are now easily extended to the situation under consideration, and each of these extensions may be obtained by imposing additional restrictions on the parameters of (18). Thus, the following models are obtained:

$$F_{ijk} = \beta_i\beta_j\beta_k\alpha_{1(i)}\alpha_{2(j)}\alpha_{3(k)}, \qquad i = j = k, \tag{19a}$$

$$F_{ijk} = \beta_i\beta_j\beta_k\alpha_{1(i)}\alpha_{2(j)}\alpha_{3(k)}\delta_i\delta_j\delta_k, \quad \text{otherwise}; \tag{19b}$$

$$F_{ijk} = \beta_i\beta_j\beta_k\alpha_{1(i)}\alpha_{2(j)}\alpha_{3(k)}; \tag{20}$$

$$F_{ijk} = \beta_i\beta_j\beta_k\delta_{ijk}; \tag{21}$$

$$F_{ijk} = \beta_i\beta_j\beta_k, \qquad i = j = k, \tag{22a}$$

$$F_{ijk} = \beta_i\beta_j\beta_k\delta_i\delta_j\delta_k, \quad \text{otherwise}; \tag{22b}$$

$$F_{ijk} = \beta_i\beta_j\beta_k. \tag{23}$$

Equations (19a) and (19b) state that independence holds except when $i = j = k$; thus, the corresponding model is called total quasi independence (TQI). Similarly, the models corresponding to (20), (21),

(22a) and (22b), and (23) are denoted, respectively, TI, TS, TSQI, and TSI. Note that TI is the model of independence for the three-way table and that TS is the model of "complete symmetry" discussed by Madansky (1963), Bishop et al. (1975), and Haberman (1979). Note that TS and the models following it imply homogeneity of the two-dimensional and one-dimensional margins formed by collapsing over any variable and any pair of variables. For related material, see Darroch (1981), Fryer (1971), Kullback (1971), and Mantel and Byar (1978). Degrees of freedom for these models are reported in Table 6. In addition, Table 6 describes each model considered in this section as a pair of hypotheses: The first hypothesis refers to the marginal distribution of the variables (if TQS holds), and the second refers to the structure of dependence among the variables. Subsequently, I will use this description to characterize, in a simple way, the relationships between the models discussed in this section.

When $\delta_{ijk} = \delta_{ij}\delta_{ik}\delta_{jk}$, where, now, $\delta_{ij} = \delta_{ji}$, we obtain various symmetric partial-association models (Clogg 1982a). Thus, by modifying (18) and (21), respectively, we obtain the following models:

$$F_{ijk} = \beta_i\beta_j\beta_k\alpha_{1(i)}\alpha_{2(j)}\alpha_{3(k)}\delta_{ij}\delta_{ik}\delta_{jk}; \tag{24}$$

$$F_{ijk} = \beta_i\beta_j\beta_k\delta_{ij}\delta_{ik}\delta_{jk}. \tag{25}$$

These models are denoted, respectively, TQS + SPA and TS + SPA. Bishop et al. (1975) also consider TS + SPA. Degrees of freedom for these models are reported in Table 6.

Combining the quasi-independence models with the symmetric partial-association models yields the following additional models:

$$F_{ijk} = \beta_i\beta_j\beta_k\alpha_{1(i)}\alpha_{2(j)}\alpha_{3(k)}, \qquad i = j = k, \tag{26a}$$

$$F_{ijk} = \beta_i\beta_j\beta_k\alpha_{1(i)}\alpha_{2(j)}\alpha_{3(k)}\delta_i\delta_j\delta_k\delta_{ij}\delta_{ik}\delta_{jk}, \quad \text{otherwise}; \tag{26b}$$

$$F_{ijk} = \beta_i\beta_j\beta_k, \qquad i = j = k, \tag{27a}$$

$$F_{ijk} = \beta_i\beta_j\beta_k\delta_i\delta_j\delta_k\delta_{ij}\delta_{ik}\delta_{jk}, \quad \text{otherwise}. \tag{27b}$$

Equations (26a) and (26b) state that TQS + SPA holds for all cells (i, j, k) except when $i = j = k$; thus, the model corresponding to these equations is denoted TQS + SPA/CD (total quasi symmetry with symmetric partial association, with consistent cells deleted). Similarly, the model corresponding to (27a) and (27b) is denoted TS + SPA/CD. Degrees of freedom for these models are given in Table 6.

TABLE 6
Descriptions and Degrees of Freedom for the Models in Section 4.1

Model	Description	df
TQS	(NH_{123}, S)	$R^3 - \left((2R-2) + \binom{R+2}{3} \right)$
TQI	(NH_{123}, QI)	$R^3 - ((3R-2) + R)$
TI	(NH_{123}, I)	$R^3 - (3R-2)$
TS	(H_{123}, S)	$R^3 - \binom{R+2}{3}$
TSQI	(H_{123}, QI)	$R^3 - 2R$
TSI	(H_{123}, I)	$R^3 - R$
TQS + SPA	(NH_{123}, SPA)	$R^3 - ((3R-2) + R(R-1)/2)$
TSSPA	(H_{123}, SPA)	$R^3 - (R(R+1)/2)$
TQS + SPA/CD	$(NH_{123}, SPA/CD)$	$R^3 - ((3R-2) + R(R-1)/2 + R)$
TS + SPA/CD	$(H_{123}, SPA/CD)$	$R^3 - (R(R+1)/2 + R))$
TQS + H_{12}	(H_{12}, S)	$R^3 - \left((R-1) + \binom{R+2}{3} \right)$
TQI + H_{12}	(H_{12}, QI)	$R^3 - ((2R-1) + R)$
TI + H_{12}	(H_{12}, I)	$R^3 - (2R-1)$
TQS + H_{12} + SPA	(H_{12}, SPA)	$R^3 - ((2R-1) + R(R-1)/2)$
TQS + H_{12} + SPA/CD	$(H_{12}, SPA/CD)$	$R^3 - ((2R-1) + R(R-1)/2 + R)$
TQS + H_{13}	(H_{13}, S)	$R^3 - \left((R-1) + \binom{R+2}{3} \right)$
TQI + H_{13}	(H_{13}, QI)	$R^3 - ((2R-1) + R)$
TI + H_{13}	(H_{13}, I)	$R^3 - (2R-1)$
TQS + H_{13} + SPA	(H_{13}, SPA)	$R^3 - ((2R-1) + R(R-1)/2)$
TQS + H_{13} + SPA/CD	$(H_{13}, SPA/CD)$	$R^3 - ((2R-1) + R(R-1)/2 + R)$
TQS + H_{23}	(H_{23}, S)	$R^3 - \left((2R-1) + \binom{R+2}{3} \right)$
TQI + H_{23}	(H_{23}, QI)	$R^3 - ((2R-1) + R)$
TI + H_{23}	(H_{23}, I)	$R^3 - (2R-1)$
TQS + H_{23} + SPA	(H_{23}, SPA)	$R^3 - ((2R-1) + R(R-1)/2)$
TQS + H_{23} + SPA/CD	$(H_{23}, SPA/CD)$	$R^3 - ((2R-1) + R(R-1)/2 + R)$

Note: NH_{123} imposes no homogeneity restrictions on the α parameters. H_{12} imposes the homogeneity restrictions $\alpha_{1(i)} = \alpha_{2(i)}$, $i = 1, \ldots, R$. H_{13} imposes the homogeneity restrictions $\alpha_{1(i)} = \alpha_{3(i)}$, $i = 1, \ldots, R$, and H_{23} imposes the homogeneity restrictions $\alpha_{2(j)} = \alpha_{3(j)}$, $j = 1, \ldots, R$. H_{123} imposes the homogeneity restrictions $\alpha_{1(i)} = \alpha_{2(i)} = \alpha_{3(i)}$, $i = 1, \ldots, R$. S is the hypothesis that the dependence is symmetric, and SPA/CD is the hypothesis of symmetrical partial association, excluding the case $i = j = k$. QI is the quasi-independence hypothesis, SPA is the symmetric partial-association hypothesis, and I is the independence hypothesis.

Various other models can be obtained by imposing alternative types of restrictions on the parameters. For example, under the homogeneity restriction $\alpha_{1(i)} = \alpha_{2(i)} = \alpha_i$, $i = 1, \ldots, R$, (18) reduces to

$$F_{ijk} = \beta_i \beta_j \beta_k \alpha_i \alpha_j \alpha_{3(k)} \delta_{ijk}. \tag{28}$$

The model corresponding to (28) is hereafter denoted $TQS + H_{12}$. Under the set of restrictions above, it is apparent that $F_{ijk} = F_{jik}$ and, thus, that $F_{ij.} = \Sigma_k F_{ijk} = \Sigma_k F_{jik} = F_{ji.}$; i.e., symmetry holds in the row-by-column table formed by collapsing over the layer variable. Alternatively, note that the row and column variables are exchangeable. Models in which the row and layer variables and the column and layer variables are exchangeable are constructed in a similar manner. All such models can then be further specialized by imposing restrictions on the structure of dependence in the three-way table. Thus, we obtain models $TQI + H_{12}$, $TI + H_{12}$, $TQS + H_{12} + SPA$, $TQS + H_{12} + SPA/CD$, $TQS + H_{13}, \ldots, TQS + H_{23} + SPA/CD$. Degrees of freedom for the models above are given in Table 6.

To obtain the logical relationships between any subset of the models in this section, it is useful to consider the alternative descriptions in Table 6. These characterize each model in terms of joint restrictions on the α parameters and the dependence parameters. By combining this characterization with the implication graphs in Figure 3, we obtain the logical relationships between any subset of the models in this section. For example, since SPA implies SPA/CD and since H_{12} implies NH_{123}, if the model (H_{12}, SPA) holds, the model $(NH_{123}, SPA/CD)$ holds.

4.2. *Analysis of Table* 2

Maximum likelihood procedures were used to fit the models in section 4.1 to the data in Table 2. The upper panel of Table 7 reports degrees of freedom, the likelihood ratio chi square (L^2), and the goodness-of-fit chi square (χ^2) for each model. The computations were performed using GLIM (Baker and Nelder 1978).

The chi-square approximations reported in Table 7 reveal that only TQS, TQS + SPA, and TQS + SPA/CD fit the data adequately, at the 0.05 level. Further, comparison of TQS and TQS + SPA/CD with TQS + SPA indicates that neither of the former models fits the data better than TQS + SPA at the 0.05 level: L^2(TQS + SPA) −

FIGURE 3.   Implication graphs for the models in section 4.1. (NH_{123} imposes no homogeneity restrictions on the α parameters. H_{12} imposes the homogeneity restrictions $\alpha_1(i) = \alpha_{2(i)}$, $i = 1, \ldots, R$. H_{13} imposes the homogeneity restrictions $\alpha_{1(i)} = \alpha_{3(i)}$, $i = 1, \ldots, R$. H_{23} imposes the homogeneity restrictions $\alpha_{2(j)} = \alpha_{3(j)}$, $j = 1, \ldots, R$. H_{123} imposes the homogeneity restrictions $\alpha_{1(i)} = \alpha_{2(i)} = \alpha_{3(i)}$, $i = 1, \ldots, R$. S is the hypothesis that the dependence is symmetric, while SPA/CD is the hypothesis of symmetric partial association, excluding the case $i = j = k$. QI is the quasi-independence hypothesis, SPA is the symmetric partial association hypothesis, and I is the independence hypothesis.

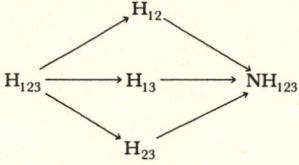

(a) Implications among hypotheses describing the α parameters.

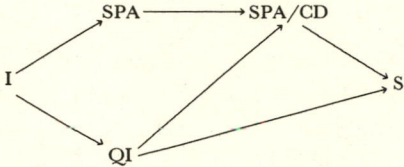

(b) Implications among hypotheses about the structure of dependence.

$L^2(\text{TQS}) = 10.91$, $df = 10$, $p = 0.37$; and $L^2(\text{TQS} + \text{SPA}) - L^2(\text{TQS} + \text{SPA/CD}) = 0.75$, $df = 4$, $p = 0.94$. Thus, TQS + SPA may be preferred for these data.

The additive form of TQS + SPA is

$$F_{ijk}^* = \beta_i^* + \beta_j^* + \beta_k^* + \alpha_{1(i)}^* + \alpha_{2(j)}^* + \alpha_{3(k)}^* + \delta_{ij}^* + \delta_{ik}^* + \delta_{jk}^*,$$

where $F_{ijk}^* = \ln(F_{ijk})$, $\beta_i^* = \ln(\beta_i)$, etc. Table 8 presents estimates for the parameters of this model under the following identification rules: $\delta_{ij}^* = \delta_{ji}^*$, where $\delta_{ij}^* = 0$ if $i = j$, $\alpha_{1(i)}^* + \alpha_{2(i)}^* + \alpha_{3(i)}^* = 0$, $i = 1, \ldots, 4$, $\sum_i \alpha_{1(i)}^* = \sum_j \alpha_{2(j)}^* = \sum_k \alpha_{3(k)}^* = 0$. Many other identification rules could have been chosen, and in some substantive contexts, certain identification rules will appear more useful than others. Note that under the set of constraints above, $\beta_i^* = (1/3)F_{iii}^*$, $i = 1, \ldots, R$.

The parameter estimates reveal a relative tendency for respondents to give consistent responses to the three satisfaction items. To see this, recall that the δ_{ijk} parameters measure the total dependence in the table, relative to the consistent responses $\{(i, i, i), (j, j, j),$

TABLE 7
Analysis of Table 2 Using the Models in Section 4.1

Model	df	L^2	X^2
Panel A			
TQS	38	43.42	44.14
TQI	50	201.88	211.53
TI	54	596.76	967.52
TS	44	281.22	268.26
TSQI	56	407.84	422.30
TSI	60	775.52	1046.61
TQS + SPA	48	54.33	55.85
TS + SPA	54	293.65	285.84
TQS + SPA/CD	44	53.58	54.59
TS + SPA/CD	50	292.71	286.28
TQS + H_{12}	41	83.92	83.51
TQI + H_{12}	53	238.21	256.24
TI + H_{12}	57	630.01	1003.19
TQS + H_{12} + SPA	51	94.55	95.15
TQS + H_{12} + SPA/CD	47	93.91	95.08
TQS + H_{13}	41	259.59	248.69
TQI + H_{13}	53	387.41	389.70
TI + H_{13}	57	757.29	1024.10
TQS + H_{13} + SPA	51	271.99	261.99
TQS + H_{13} + SPA/CD	47	271.04	262.65
TQS + H_{23}	41	149.41	137.68
TQI + H_{23}	53	293.99	298.80
TI + H_{23}	57	674.52	970.55
TQS + H_{23} + SPA	51	162.51	153.74
TQS + H_{23} + SPA/CD	47	161.40	151.70
Panel B			
TUA	53	234.84	271.19
TQUA	49	75.00	76.39
THRC-1	51	206.71	242.36

$(k, k, k)\}$, and recall that if $\delta_{ijk} < 1$, a relative tendency toward consistency is indicated. Next, note that each estimate $\hat{\delta}_{ij}$ is statistically less than 0, at the 0.05 level, and that under TQS + SPA, $\delta_{ijk}^* = \delta_{ij}^* + \delta_{ik}^* + \delta_{jk}^*$. For example, under the model, $\hat{\delta}_{123}^* = (1/3) \ln(\hat{F}_{123}\hat{F}_{312}\hat{F}_{231}/ \hat{F}_{111}\hat{F}_{222}\hat{F}_{333}) = \hat{\delta}_{12}^* + \hat{\delta}_{13}^* + \hat{\delta}_{23}^* = -1.659$, with asymptotic standard error 0.165.

TABLE 8
Parameter Estimates and Asymptotic Standard Errors Under TQS + SPA

Parameter	Estimate	Asymptotic Standard Error
β_1^*	0.917	0.073
β_2^*	0.748	0.082
β_3^*	0.189	0.019
β_4^*	0.163	0.027
$\alpha_{1(1)}^*$	-0.707	0.085
$\alpha_{1(2)}^*$	-0.272	0.064
$\alpha_{1(3)}^*$	0.368	0.045
$\alpha_{1(4)}^*$	0.700	0.053
$\alpha_{2(1)}^*$	0.355	0.066
$\alpha_{2(2)}^*$	0.389	0.053
$\alpha_{2(3)}^*$	-0.274	0.040
$\alpha_{2(4)}^*$	-0.469	0.050
$\alpha_{3(1)}^*$	0.352	0.066
$\alpha_{3(2)}^*$	-0.117	0.056
$\alpha_{3(3)}^*$	-0.094	0.039
$\alpha_{3(4)}^*$	-0.140	0.049
δ_{12}^*	-0.424	0.102
δ_{13}^*	-0.885	0.068
δ_{14}^*	-1.164	0.086
δ_{23}^*	-0.350	0.063
δ_{24}^*	-0.987	0.083
δ_{34}^*	-0.567	0.035

Recall that when TQS holds, the α^* parameters quantify the effect of marginal heterogeneity on asymmetries among the F_{ijk}, and asymmetry is due solely to marginal heterogeneity. Various types of these effects can be considered. Asymmetries between two variables can be studied by considering ratios of the form F_{ijk}/F_{jik}, $i \neq j$ (F_{ijk}/F_{kji}, $i \neq k$, F_{ijk}/F_{ikj}, $j \neq k$). For example, the first of these ratios is the conditional probability that a respondent gives the joint response (ij) to items 1 and 2, respectively, given the response k to item 3, divided by the conditional probability that a respondent gives the joint response (ji) to items 1 and 2, given the response k to item 3. Under any of the models considered in section 4.1, this ratio has the form $(\alpha_{1(i)}/\alpha_{2(i)})/(\alpha_{1(j)}/\alpha_{2(j)})$. From this expression, it is clear that the effect of marginal heterogeneity on asymmetry between the row and column variables is due solely to differences in the marginal distributions of rows and columns. Furthermore, the effect is identical at all levels of the layer variable. If the ratio is unity for all (ij) pairs, the row variable and the column variable are exchangeable. This hypothesis has already been rejected for the data in Table 2. If the ratio has the value c $(c > 0)$, then $F_{ijk} = cF_{jik}$, and thus $F_{ij.} = \Sigma_k F_{ijk} = c\Sigma_k F_{jik} = cF_{ji.}$.

As an application of the material above, let $\hat{F}_{ijk}^*$ be the estimate of F_{ijk}^* under TQS + SPA. Consider the difference $\hat{F}_{12k}^* - \hat{F}_{21k}^* = (\hat{\alpha}_{1(1)}^* - \hat{\alpha}_{2(1)}^*) - (\hat{\alpha}_{1(2)}^* - \hat{\alpha}_{2(2)}^*) = -0.401$, with asymptotic standard error 0.207. A two-tailed test shows that this estimate is statistically different from 0 at the 0.053 level. Thus, the data appear to offer some support to the suggestion that because of different levels of satisfaction with residence and friendships, persons are $\exp(-0.401) \times 100$ percent = 70 percent as likely to be satisfied a fair amount with their residence and less satisfied with their friends than satisfied a fair amount with their friends and less satisfied with their residence, irrespective of their satisfaction with hobbies.

Next, consider a ratio of the form F_{ijk}/F_{kij}. As indicated in section 4.1, this ratio has the form $(\alpha_{1(i)}/\alpha_{2(i)})(\alpha_{2(j)}/\alpha_{3(j)})(\alpha_{3(k)}/\alpha_{1(k)})$. From this expression, it is clear that the ratio reflects the effect of marginal heterogeneity between all sets of any two variables on asymmetry. If all three variables are exchangeable, the model denoted TS holds, and this ratio reduces to 1. If TQS + H_{12} holds (see equation (28)), the row variable and the column variable are exchangeable, and the ratio reduces to $(\alpha_j/\alpha_{3(j)})/(\alpha_k/\alpha_{3(k)})$; under TQS + H_{12}, this reflects the effect of marginal heterogeneity between the third variable and either of the other variables on asymmetry. Note that all exchangeability hypotheses have already been rejected for the data in Table 2.

As an application, consider the ratio F_{123}/F_{312}. Under TQS + SPA, $\hat{F}_{123}^* - \hat{F}_{312}^* = (\hat{\alpha}_{1(1)}^* - \hat{\alpha}_{2(1)}^*) + (\hat{\alpha}_{2(2)}^* - \hat{\alpha}_{3(2)}^*) + (\hat{\alpha}_{3(3)}^* - \hat{\alpha}_{1(3)}^*) = -1.018$, with asymptotic standard error 0.214. Thus, the model predicts that $F_{123} = 0.361 F_{312}$, which represents the effect of marginal heterogeneity on this asymmetry.

To this point, the analysis has ignored the fact that the data are ordinal. To show how the previous results can be combined with models for ordinal data, I consider several special cases of TQS + SPA.

The first model, denoted TUA, is a generalization of the uniform association model (Duncan 1979; Goodman 1979), and the model can be written as

$$F_{ijk} = \beta_i \beta_j \beta_k \alpha_{1(i)} \alpha_{2(j)} \alpha_{3(k)} \delta^{(ij+jk+ik)}.$$

Clogg (1982a) also considers this model. Under this model, parameterized in the manner above,

$$\delta_{ijk} = \delta^{(i(j-i)+j(k-j)+k(i-k))}.$$

The second model, denoted TQUA, is a generalization of the model of quasi-uniform association. The model can be written as

$$F_{ijk} = \beta_i \beta_j \beta_k \alpha_{1(i)} \alpha_{2(j)} \alpha_{3(k)} \delta^{(ij+jk+ik)} \lambda_i^{Z_{ij}} \lambda_j^{Z_{jk}} \lambda_k^{Z_{ik}},$$

where $Z_{ij} = 1$ if $i = j$, 0 otherwise, $Z_{jk} = 1$ if $j = k$, 0 otherwise, and $Z_{ik} = 1$ if $i = k$, 0 otherwise. Under this model, parameterized in the fashion above,

$$\delta_{ijk} = \delta^{(i(j-1)+j(k-j)+k(i-k))} \lambda_i^{(Z_{ij}-1)} \lambda_j^{(Z_{jk}-1)} \lambda_k^{(Z_{ik}-1)}.$$

Note that TQUA is not identical to the model obtained by applying TUA to all but the consistent responses.

TUA and TQUA were applied to the data in Table 2. The results of this analysis are reported in the lower panel of Table 7. It is clear that neither of these models fit the data, at the 0.05 level of significance.

Two other models arise naturally. The model denoted THRC-1 generalizes the homogeneous row-and-column-effects model 1 described by Goodman (1979), and it is a special case of model (2.1) in Agresti and Kezouh (1983). Clogg (1982a) also considered THRC-1. The model can be written as

$$F_{ijk} = \beta_i \beta_j \beta_k \alpha_{1(i)} \alpha_{2(j)} \alpha_{3(k)} \delta^{(ij+jk+ik)} \delta_i^{j+k} \delta_j^{i+k} \delta_k^{i+j}.$$

Under this model, parameterized in the manner above,

$$\delta_{ijk} = \delta^{(i(j-i)+j(k-j)+k(i-k))} \delta_i^{j+k-2i} \delta_j^{i+k-2j} \delta_k^{i+j-2k}.$$

A model called TQHRC-1 also arises, and it is a generalization of the quasi-homogeneous row-and-column-effects model 1 considered by Goodman (1979), appropriate when the association can be described by a symmetric partial-association model. This model can be written as

$$F_{ijk} = \beta_i \beta_j \beta_k \alpha_{1(i)} \alpha_{2(j)} \alpha_{3(k)} \delta^{(ij+jk+ik)} \delta_i^{j+k} \delta_j^{i+k} \delta_k^{i+j} \lambda_i^{Z_{ij}} \lambda_j^{Z_{jk}} \lambda_k^{Z_{ik}}.$$

Under this model,

$$\delta_{ijk} = \delta^{(i(j-i)+j(k-j)+k(i-k))}\delta_i^{\,j+k-2i}\delta_j^{\,i+k-2j}\delta_k^{\,i+j-2k}\lambda_i^{(Z_{ij}-1)}\lambda_j^{(Z_{jk}-1)}\lambda_k^{(Z_{ik}-1)}.$$

Note that TQHRC-1 is not equivalent to the model obtained by applying THRC-1 to all but the consistent responses.

Results obtained by fitting THRC-1 to the data in Table 2 are reported in the lower panel of Table 7. The model does not fit the data, at the 0.05 level of significance. In the $4 \times 4 \times 4$ table, note that if a symmetric partial-association model holds, at most six nonredundant parameters are needed to describe the structure of dependence in the table. Thus, for this case, TQHRC-1 is equivalent to TQS + SPA. Therefore, the conclusions obtained by fitting TQS + SPA and TQHRC-1 are identical. Many other models appropriate for ordered data could also be generated by combining features of the models above with assumptions about exchangeability and alternative assumptions about the structure of dependence. In particular, models could be constructed when the ordering is unknown and when the spacing between the categories of the variables is unknown (Agresti 1984; Goodman 1986).

REFERENCES

Agresti, A. 1983. "Testing Marginal Homogeneity for Ordinal Categorical Variables." *Biometrics* 39:505–10.

—————. 1984. *Analysis of Ordinal Categorical Data*. New York: Wiley.

Agresti, A., and A. Kezouh. 1983. "Association Models for Multi-Dimensional Cross-Classifications of Ordinal Variables." *Communications in Statistics*, ser. A, 12:1261–76.

Altham, P. M. E. 1970. "The Measurement of Association in a Contingency Table: Three Extensions of the Cross-Ratios and Metric Methods." *Journal of the Royal Statistical Society*, ser. B, 32:395–407.

Anderson, J. A. 1984. "Regression and Ordered Categorical Variables." *Journal of the Royal Statistical Society*, ser. B, 46:1–30.

Baker, R. J., and J. Nelder, 1978. *The GLIM System: Release 3*. Oxford: Numerical Algorithms Group.

Bergan, J. 1980. "Measuring Observer Agreement Using the Quasi-Independence Concept." *Journal of Educational Measurement* 17:59–69.

Bhapkar, V. P. 1966. "A Note on the Equivalence of Two Criteria for Hypotheses in Categorical Data." *Journal of the American Statistical Association* 61:228–35.

Bishop, Y. M. M., S. E. Fienberg, and P. W. Holland. 1975. *Discrete Multivariate Analysis*. Cambridge, MA: MIT Press.

Caussinus, H. 1965. "Contribution a l'analyse statistique des tableaux de correlation." *Annales de la Faculte des Sciences de l'Universite de Toulouse* 29:77–182.

Clogg, C. C. 1979. "Some Latent Structure Models for the Analysis of Likert-Type Data." *Social Science Research* 8:287–301.

——————. 1982*a*. "Some Models for the Analysis of Association in Multiway Cross-Classifications Having Ordered Categories." *Journal of the American Statistical Association* 77:803–15.

——————. 1982*b*. "Using Association Models in Sociological Research: Some Examples." *American Journal of Sociology* 88:114–34.

Cohen, J. 1960. "A Coefficient of Agreement for Nominal Scales." *Educational and Psychological Measurement* 20:37–46.

——————. 1968. "Weighted Kappa: Nominal Scale Agreement with Provision for Scaled Disagreement on Partial Credit." *Psychological Bulletin* 70:213–20.

Darroch, J. N. 1981. "The Mantel-Haenszel Test and Tests of Marginal Symmetry: Fixed Effects and Fixed Models for a Categorical Response." *International Statistical Review* 49:285–307.

——————. 1986. "Quasi-Symmetry." Pp. 469–73 in *Encyclopedia of Statistical Sciences*, vol. 7, edited by S. Kotz and N. L. Johnson. New York: Wiley.

Darroch, J. N., and P. I. McCloud. 1986. "Category Distinguishability and Observer Agreement." *Australian Journal of Statistics* 28:371–88.

Davis, J. A. 1980. *Codebook for the 1980 General Social Survey*. Chicago: National Opinion Research Center.

Duncan, O. D. 1979. "How Destination Depends on Origin in the Occupational Mobility Table." *American Journal of Sociology* 84:793–803.

Fryer, J. G. 1971. "On the Homogeneity of the Marginal Distributions of a Multidimensional Contingency Table." *Journal of the Royal Statistical Society*, ser. A, 134:368–71.

Goodman, L. A. 1972. "Some Multiplicative Models for the Analysis of Cross-Classified Data." Pp. 649–96 in *Proceedings of the Sixth Berkeley Symposium on Mathematical Statistics and Probability*, edited by L. Le Cam et al. Berkeley: University of California Press.

——————. 1979. "Simple Models for the Analysis of Association in Cross-Classifications Having Ordered Categories." *Journal of the American Statistical Association* 74:537–52.

——————. 1981. "Association Models and Canonical Correlation in the Analysis of Cross-Classifications Having Ordered Categories." *Journal of the American Statistical Association* 76:320–34.

——————. 1985. "The Analysis of Cross-Classified Data Having Ordered and/or Unordered Categories: Association Models, Correlation Models, and Asymmetry Models for Contingency Tables with or without Missing Entries." *Annals of Statistics* 13:10–69.

—————————. 1986. "Some Useful Extensions of the Usual Correspondence Analysis Approach and the Usual Log-Linear Models Approach in the Analysis of Contingency Tables." *International Statistical Review* 54:243–309.

Haberman, S. J. 1974. *The Analysis of Frequency Data*. Chicago: University of Chicago Press.

—————————. 1978. *Analysis of Qualitative Data*. Vol. 1. New York: Academic Press.

—————————. 1979. *Analysis of Qualitative Data*. Vol. 2. New York: Academic Press.

Hauser, R. M., and M. P. Massagli. 1983. "Some Models of Agreement and Disagreement in Repeated Measurements of Occupation." *Demography* 20:449–60.

Hope, K. 1982. "Vertical and Non-Vertical Mobility in Three Countries." *American Sociological Review* 47:99–113.

Hout, M., O. D. Duncan, and M. E. Sobel. 1987. "Association and Heterogeneity: Structural Models of Similarities and Differences." Pp. 145–84 in *Sociological Methodology 1987*, edited by Clifford C. Clogg. Washington, DC: American Sociological Association.

Ireland, C. T., H. H. Ku, and S. Kullback. 1969. "Symmetry and Marginal Homogeneity of an $R \times R$ Contingency Table." *Journal of the American Statistical Association* 64:1323–41.

Kullback, S. 1971. "Marginal Homogeneity of Multi-Dimensional Contingency Tables." *Annals of Mathematical Statistics* 42:594–606.

Madansky, A. 1963. "Tests of Homogeneity for Correlated Samples." *Journal of the American Statistical Association* 58:97–119.

Mantel, N., and D. P. Byar. 1978. "Marginal Homogeneity, Symmetry, and Independence." *Communications in Statistics*, ser. A, 7:953–76.

McCullagh, P. 1978. "A Class of Parametric Models for the Analysis of Square Contingency Tables with Ordered Categories." *Biometrika* 65:413–18.

—————————. 1982. "Some Applications of Quasi Symmetry." *Biometrika* 69:303–8.

Sobel, M. E. 1983. "Structural Mobility, Circulation Mobility, and the Analysis of Occupational Mobility: A Conceptual Mismatch." *American Sociological Review* 48:721–27.

Sobel, M. E., M. Hout, and O. D. Duncan. 1985. "Exchange, Structure, and Symmetry in Occupational Mobility." *American Journal of Sociology* 91:359–72.

Stuart, A. 1955. "A Test for Homogeneity of the Marginal Distributions in a Two-Way Classification." *Biometrika* 40:105–10.

Tanner, M. A., and M. A. Young. 1985. "Modeling Agreement Among Raters." *Journal of the American Statistical Association* 80:175–80.

$$\mathcal{Z}_{\mathfrak{C}} 7 \mathcal{Z}$$

A Stabilized Newton-Raphson Algorithm for Log-Linear Models for Frequency Tables Derived by Indirect Observation

Shelby J. Haberman*

In a variety of problems involving models from genetics, latent-class analysis, and missing data, I apply a log-linear model to an indirectly observed frequency table. Current algorithms for computation of maximum likelihood estimates for such cases have often been unsatisfactory because they fail to converge at all or they converge at an unacceptable rate. I propose a new algorithm that converges both more quickly and more reliably than currently available alternatives. The algorithm assists in estimation of asymptotic variances of parameter estimates. It may be applied to both grouped and ungrouped data. I illustrate results in two examples from the literature on latent-class analysis.

1. INTRODUCTION

Log-linear models with indirectly observed frequency tables have been used by Haberman (1974a, 1976, 1979) in problems in genetics and in latent-class analysis. Unlike log-linear models for

Research for this paper was partially supported by National Science Foundation grant DMS 8607373 and U.S.-Israel Binational Fund grant 85-00014. This research has greatly benefitted from conversations with Christopher Winship and from extensive testing of the algorithm by James Coverdill. The computer programs used in this paper are available from the author on 5.25-inch floppy disks.

*Northwestern University

directly observed tables, log-linear models for indirectly observed tables do not require the likelihood function to be log-concave. Therefore, computation of maximum likelihood estimates is somewhat more difficult. In this paper, I propose a new algorithm based on the modified Newton-Raphson algorithm in Haberman (1974b, pp. 47–48). This algorithm preserves the stable convergence properties of the iterative scaling algorithm presented in Haberman (1976) and the rapid local convergence properties of the scoring algorithm in Haberman (1979, chap. 10). As in the scoring algorithm, an estimated asymptotic covariance matrix of the parameter estimates is produced as a by-product of computations. This matrix is not provided by the EM algorithm described by Dempster, Laird, and Rubin (1977), which is used for latent-class models by Clogg (1977), Goodman (1974a, 1974b), and Haberman (1977a). I describe the model under study and the conventional Newton-Raphson algorithm in section 2. I also describe conditions under which the estimated asymptotic covariance matrix produced via the proposed algorithm or via the Newton-Raphson algorithm is useful in computation of approximate confidence intervals for parameters. In section 3, I describe the proposed algorithm and demonstrate its properties of stability and rapid convergence. In section 4, I present some examples of its use.

2. THE LOG-LINEAR MODEL

In this section I present a general log-linear model for problems of indirect observation. Unlike the presentation in Haberman (1974a), this presentation emphasizes individual observations rather than tables; however, the model presented does not differ from the models in Haberman (1974a). In section 2.1, I provide the first, second, and third partial derivatives of the logarithm L of the likelihood function. In section 2.2, I summarize the relationship of the gradient vector ∇L and the Hessian matrix $\nabla^2 L$ of L to maximum likelihood estimates. In section 2.3, I show that ∇L and $\nabla^2 L$ may be used to construct the Newton-Raphson algorithm for computation of maximum likelihood estimates and that ∇L, $\nabla^2 L$, and the array $\nabla^3 L$ of third partial derivatives of L may be used to describe convergence properties. In section 2.4, I show that the Hessian $\nabla^2 L$ may be used under very general conditions to provide estimated asymptotic covariances of parameter estimates. In the problems considered in this paper, the

Hessian is easier to use than the Fisher information matrix, because the Hessian can be computed given the sets Z_i without reference to the classes G_i of possible Z_i. In section 2.6, I discuss the stability problem associated with the Newton-Raphson algorithm and justify the stabilized version of the algorithm, which is presented in section 3.

In the problems considered in this paper, a log-linear model is applied to N polytomous random variables Y_i, $1 \le i \le N$, but for each i, it is known only that Y_i has some value in a set Z_i. To increase the generality of results, the set J_i of possible values of Y_i may depend on i. In like manner, Z_i is a member of a collection G_i of disjoint nonempty subsets of J_i, where G_i may depend on i. For example, consider a household survey in which employment status is sought for every adult member of household i. Since the number of adults in the household varies, the set J_i of possible combinations of employment status varies from household to household. If data are complete for household i, then $Z_i = \{Y_i\}$. If the employment status for all household members is not known, then Z_i consists of all possible combinations of employment status consistent with the information provided.

To describe the distribution of the Y_i in terms of log-linear models, let $p_{ij} > 0$ be the probability that $Y_i = j$ for j in J_i. Corresponding to each subject i and each response j in J_i are a scale factor $z_{ij} > 0$ and a vector $\mathbf{x}_{ij}$ of associated fixed variables x_{ijk}, $1 \le k \le r$. Consider the log-linear model which assumes that for some unknown vector β with coordinates β_k, $1 \le k \le r$, and some unknown scalars α_i, $1 \le i \le N$,

$$\log(p_{ij}/z_{ij}) = \alpha_i + \sum_k \beta_k x_{ijk}. \tag{1}$$

To illustrate this class of models, I present two examples from the literature on latent-class analysis.

Example 1. Haberman (1979, p. 589) considers a latent-class model in which an observation Y_i consists of a vector $(U_i, A_i, B_i, C_i, D_i)$, where U_i, A_i, B_i, and C_i are 1 or 2 and D_i is 1, 2, or 3. The variable U_i is a latent variable reflecting the attitude of subject i toward legalized nontherapeutic abortion; A_i, B_i, and C_i are manifest variables that are responses of subject i to three questions concerning conditions under which such abortions should be legal; and D_i is a fixed variable that specifies the year in which subject i was interviewed. Thus, J_i consists of all vectors (u, a, b, c, d) such that u, a, b, and c are 1 or 2 and d is 1, 2, or 3. The set $Z_i = \{(u, A_i, B_i, C_i, D_i): 1 \le z \le 2\}$. It is assumed that given U_i, the variables A_i, B_i, C_i, and D_i are conditionally independent. We can thus write

$$\log p_{iuabcd} = \alpha_d + \lambda_u^U + \lambda_a^A + \lambda_b^B + \lambda_c^C + \lambda_{ua}^{UA} + \lambda_{ub}^{UB} + \lambda_{uc}^{UC} + \lambda_{ud}^{UD},$$

where

$$\sum_u \lambda_u^U = \cdots = \sum \lambda_{ud}^{UD} = \sum_d \lambda_{ud}^{UD} = 0.$$

In (1), we can let $p = 9$, $z_{iuabcd} = 1$, $\beta_1 = \lambda_1^U$, $\beta_2 = \lambda_1^A$, $\beta_3 = \lambda_1^B$, $\beta_4 = \lambda_1^C$, $\beta_5 = \lambda_{11}^{UA}$, $\beta_6 = \lambda_{11}^{UB}$, $\beta_7 = \lambda_{11}^{UC}$, $\beta_8 = \lambda_{11}^{UD}$, $\beta_9 = \lambda_{12}^{UD}$, and let

$$
\begin{aligned}
x_{iuabcd1} &= 1, & u &= 1, \\
&= -1, & u &= 2, \\
x_{iuabcd2} &= 1, & a &= 1, \\
&= -1, & a &= 2, \\
x_{iuabcd3} &= 1, & b &= 1, \\
&= -1, & b &= 2, \\
x_{iuabcd4} &= 1, & c &= 1, \\
&= -1, & c &= 2, \\
x_{iuabcd5} &= 1, & u &= a, \\
&= -1, & u &\ne a, \\
x_{iuabcd6} &= 1, & u &= b, \\
&= -1, & u &\ne b, \\
x_{iuabcd7} &= 1, & u &= c, \\
&= -1, & u &\ne c, \\
\end{aligned}
$$

$x_{iuabcd8} = 1$, $u = d = 1$ or $u = 2$ and $d = 3$,

$\qquad\quad = -1$, $u = 2$ and $d = 1$ or $u = 1$ and $d = 3$,

$\qquad\quad = 0$, $d = 2$,

$x_{iuabcd9} = 1$, $u = 1$ and $d = 2$ or $u = 2$ and $d = 3$,

$\qquad\quad = -1$, $u = 2$ and $d = 2$ or $u = 1$ and $d = 3$,

$\qquad\quad = 0$, $d = 1$.

If n_{abcd} is the number of subjects i with $A_i = a$, $B_i = b$, $C_i = c$, and $D_i = d$, then the values listed in Table 1 are obtained.

Example 2. Goodman (1974a) uses a two-variable latent-class model to analyze Table 2. This table, which is derived from Coleman (1964), cross-classifies self-perceived membership in and attitude toward the

TABLE 1
Responses to Three Questions on Abortion

Response to a[a]	Response to b[a]	Response to c[a]	Year[b]	Count
1	1	1	1	334
1	1	2	1	34
1	2	1	1	12
1	2	2	1	15
2	1	1	1	53
2	1	2	1	63
2	2	1	1	43
2	2	2	1	501
1	1	1	2	428
1	1	2	2	29
1	2	1	2	13
1	2	2	2	17
2	1	1	2	42
2	1	2	2	53
2	2	1	2	31
2	2	2	2	453
1	1	1	3	413
1	1	2	3	29
1	2	1	3	16
1	2	2	3	18
2	1	1	3	60
2	1	2	3	57
2	2	1	3	37
2	2	2	3	430

Source: Haberman 1979, pp. 399, 482.

Note: Respondents were asked whether or not they thought it should be possible for a pregnant woman to obtain a legal abortion (a) if she is married and does not want any more children, (b) if the family has a very low income and cannot afford any more children, (c) if she is not married and does not want to marry the father.

[a] 1 = yes, 2 = no.
[b] 1 = 1972, 2 = 1973, 3 = 1974.

"leading crowd" at two times. The variables under study for subject i are the six 0-1 variables: latent membership U_i, latent attitude V_i, membership A_i at time 1, attitude B_i at time 1, membership C_i at time 2, and attitude D_i at time 2. Thus, $Y_i = (U_i, V_i, A_i, B_i, C_i, D_i)$, and J_i consists of all vectors (u, v, a, b, c, d) with all coordinates equal to 0 or 1. The latent variables U_i and V_i are not observed, so Z_i contains the

TABLE 2
Subjects Classified by Identification with Leading Crowd

| First Interview | | Second Interview | | |
Self-Perceived Membership in Leading Crowd[a] (A)	Attitude Toward Leading Crowd[b] (B)	Self-Perceived Membership in Leading Crowd[a] (C)	Attitude Toward Leading Crowd[b] (D)	Count
1	1	1	1	458
1	1	1	0	140
1	1	0	1	110
1	1	0	0	49
1	0	1	1	171
1	0	1	0	182
1	0	0	1	56
1	0	0	0	87
0	1	1	1	184
0	1	1	0	75
0	1	0	1	531
0	1	0	0	281
0	0	1	1	85
0	0	1	0	97
0	0	0	1	338
0	0	0	0	554

Source: Goodman 1974a, p. 1183.

[a] 1 = membership.

[b] 1 = membership does not require going against one's principles sometimes.

four elements $(u, v, A_i, B_i, C_i, D_i)$, $u = 0$ or 1, $v = 0$ or 1, and G_i consists of the sets $\{(u, v, a, b, c, d): 1 \leq u \leq 2, 1 \leq v \leq 2\}$, where a, b, c, and d may be 0 or 1. Goodman (1974a) considers a model with the standard local independence assumption that given U_i and V_i, the four manifest variables are conditionally independent. The model also assumes that given V_i, U_i and (B_i, D_i) are conditionally independent, and that given U_i, V_i and (A_i, C_i) are conditionally independent. As in Haberman (1979, p. 558), the probability $p_{iuvabcd}$ that $U_i = u$, $V_i = v$, $A_i = a$, $B_i = b$, $C_i = c$, and $D_i = d$ can be written

$$\log p_{iuvabcd} = \lambda + \lambda_U q_u + \lambda_V q_v + \lambda_A q_a + \lambda_B q_b + \lambda_C q_c + \lambda_D q_d$$
$$+ \lambda_{UV} q_u q_v + \lambda_{UA} q_u q_a + \lambda_{UC} q_u q_c + \lambda_{VB} q_v q_b + \lambda_{VD} q_v q_d,$$

so that (1) holds with $\beta_1 = \lambda_U$, $\beta_2 = \lambda_V$, etc.

2.1. *The Likelihood Function*

To use an algorithm based on the Newton-Raphson algorithm, we must consider the log-likelihood function and its derivatives. As in Haberman (1974a), if γ is the vector with coordinates γ_k, $1 \le k \le r$, then the logarithm $L(\gamma)$ of the likelihood function is

$$L(\gamma) = A(\gamma) - B(\gamma),$$

where

$$A(\gamma) = \sum \log Q_i(\gamma),$$

$$B(\gamma) = \sum \log R_i(\gamma),$$

$Q_i(\gamma)$ is the sum of $q_{ij}(\gamma) = \exp(\sum_k \gamma_k x_{ijk})$ over j in Z_i, and $R_i(\gamma)$ is the sum of $q_{ij}(\gamma)$ over j in J_i.

The Newton-Raphson algorithm itself requires the gradient ∇L and Hessian $\nabla^2 L$ of L. Analysis of convergence properties and of large-sample normal approximations requires $\nabla^3 L$, the array of third partial derivatives of L. Let $L_k(\gamma)$ denote the partial derivative of $L(\gamma)$ with respect to γ_k, evaluated at γ, $1 \le k \le r$. Then, the gradient $\nabla L(\gamma)$ is the vector with coordinates $L_k(\gamma)$. Similarly, let $L_{kl}(\gamma)$ be the second partial derivative of $L(\gamma)$ with respect to γ_k and γ_l, evaluated at γ. Then, the Hessian matrix $\nabla^2 L(\gamma)$ is the symmetric $r \times r$ matrix with elements $L_{kl}(\gamma)$, $1 \le k \le r$, $1 \le l \le r$. In like manner, $\nabla^3 L(\gamma)$ is the $r \times r \times r$ symmetric array of third partial derivatives $L_{klm}(\gamma)$ of $L(\gamma)$ with respect to γ_k, γ_l, and γ_m, $1 \le k \le r$, $1 \le l \le r$, $1 \le m \le r$. These derivatives are readily determined given the arguments in Haberman (1974a). To simplify notation, I use the term $\mathbf{a}^2$ to denote the $r \times r$ matrix with elements $a_k a_l$, $1 \le k \le r$, $1 \le l \le r$, and the term $\mathbf{a}^3$ to denote the $r \times r \times r$ array with elements $a_k a_l a_m$, $1 \le k \le r$, $1 \le l \le r$, $1 \le m \le r$.

The gradient $\nabla L(\gamma)$ of L is expressible as the difference for $\beta = \gamma$ between conditional expected values of $\sum \mathbf{X}_i$ given Y_i is in Z_i for $1 \le i \le N$ and the unconditional expected value of $\sum \mathbf{X}_i$, where $\mathbf{X}_i$ is the vector with coordinates x_{ijk}, $1 \le k \le r$, and $j = Y_i$. Thus,

$$\nabla L(\gamma) = \sum \mathbf{F}_i(\gamma) - \sum \mathbf{E}_i(\gamma),$$

where $\mathbf{F}_i(\gamma)$ is the sum of $\mathbf{x}_{ij} q_{ij}(\gamma)/Q_i(\gamma)$ for j in Z_i and $\mathbf{E}_i(\gamma)$ is the sum of $\mathbf{x}_{ij} q_{ij}(\gamma)/R_i(\gamma)$ for j in J_i.

In a similar manner, the Hessian matrix $\nabla^2 L(\gamma)$ of L at γ is the difference for $\gamma = \beta$ between the conditional covariance matrix of $\Sigma \mathbf{X}_i$ given Y_i is in Z_i for $1 \le i \le N$ and the unconditional covariance matrix of $\Sigma \mathbf{X}_i$. Thus,

$$\nabla^2 L(\gamma) = D(\gamma) - C(\gamma) = \sum D_i(\gamma) - \sum C_i(\gamma),$$

where $C(\gamma) = \Sigma C_i(\gamma)$, $C_i(\gamma)$ is the sum over j in Z_i of $[\mathbf{x}_{ij} - \mathbf{E}_i(\gamma)]^2 q_{ij}(\gamma)/Q_i(\gamma)$, $D(\gamma) = \Sigma D_i(\gamma)$, and $D_i(\gamma)$ is the sum over j in J_i of $[\mathbf{x}_{ij} - \mathbf{F}_i(\gamma)]^2 q_{ij}(\gamma)/R_i(\gamma)$.

In the case of $\nabla^3 L(\gamma)$,

$$\nabla^3 L(\gamma) = \sum H_i(\gamma) - \sum G_i(\gamma),$$

where $H_i(\gamma)$ is the sum over j in Z_i of $[\mathbf{x}_{ij} - \mathbf{E}_i(\gamma)]^3 q_{ij}(\gamma)/Q_i(\gamma)$ and $G_i(\gamma)$ is the sum over j in J_i of $[\mathbf{x}_{ij} - \mathbf{F}_i(\gamma)]^3 q_{ij}(\gamma)/R_i(\gamma)$.

In the case of direct observation, Z_i is always the set $\{Y_i\}$,

$$L = -B,$$
$$\nabla L(\gamma) = \sum \mathbf{X}_i - \sum \mathbf{E}_i(\gamma),$$
$$\nabla^2 L(\gamma) = -C(\gamma) = -\sum C_i(\gamma),$$

and

$$\nabla^3 L(\gamma) = -\sum G_i(\gamma).$$

2.2. *Maximum Likelihood Estimates*

In the problems of indirect observation considered in this paper, there may be zero, one, or more than one maximum likelihood estimate $\mathbf{b}$ of β (Haberman 1974a). Nonetheless, if $\mathbf{b}$ is a maximum likelihood estimate, $\nabla L(\mathbf{b}) = 0$ and $\nabla^2(\mathbf{b})$ is nonpositive definite. If $\nabla L(\mathbf{b})$ is $\mathbf{0}$ and $\nabla^2 L(\mathbf{b})$ is negative definite, then $\mathbf{b}$ is at least an isolated local maximum of the log likelihood L. As in Haberman (1977c), the proposed modification of the Newton-Raphson algorithm is designed to reduce the risk of convergence to a solution of the equation $\nabla L(\mathbf{b}) = 0$, which is not a maximum likelihood estimate.

2.3. *The Newton-Raphson Algorithm*

The Newton-Raphson algorithm has a simpler form for the model under study than the scoring algorithm. Let $\mathbf{b}_0$ be an initial approximation to a maximum likelihood estimate $\mathbf{b}$ such that $\nabla^2(\mathbf{b}_0)$ is negative definite. Under the Newton-Raphson algorithm, approximations $\mathbf{b}_t$ of $\mathbf{b}$ are generated by the equation

$$\mathbf{b}_{t+1} = \mathbf{b}_t + \mathbf{s}(\mathbf{b}_t),$$

where

$$\mathbf{s}(\gamma) = -\left[\nabla^2 L(\gamma)\right]^{-1}\nabla L(\gamma).$$

This algorithm involves only the observed sets Z_i rather than all members of G_i. In scoring, the Hessian matrix is replaced by its estimated expected value given that β is $\mathbf{b}_t$. Thus, knowledge of all possible sets G_i is required.

The convergence properties of the Newton-Raphson algorithm are standard. In this paper, it is helpful to note results of Kantorovich and Akilov (1982, pp. 529–33). Let $\|\cdot\|$ be a norm on R^r, so that for any $r \times r$ matrix $\mathbf{M}$, $\|\mathbf{M}\|$ is the supremum of $\|\mathbf{Mc}\|/\|\mathbf{c}\|$ for $\mathbf{c}$ in R^r. For any $r \times r \times r$ array $\mathbf{S}$ with elements S_{ijk}, $1 \le i \le r$, $1 \le j \le r$, $1 \le k \le r$, let $\mathbf{Sc}$ be the $r \times r$ matrix with elements

$$\sum_k S_{ijk} c_k, \qquad 1 \le i \le r, \qquad 1 \le j \le r.$$

Let T be the initial step length $\|\mathbf{s}(\mathbf{b}_0)\|$, let $u > T$, and let V be the supremum of

$$\left\|\left[\nabla^2 L(\mathbf{b}_0)\right]^{-1}\nabla^3 L(\gamma)\mathbf{c}\right\|/\|\mathbf{c}\|$$

for $\mathbf{c}$ in R^r and $\|\gamma - \mathbf{b}_0\| \le u$. Thus, V is a normalized measure of the size of the third partial derivatives of the log likelihood. If $TV < 1/2$,

$$u \ge \left[1 - (1 - 2TV)^{1/2}\right]/V,$$

and

$$u < \left[1 + (1 - 2TV)^{1/2}\right]/V,$$

then $\mathbf{b}_t$ converges to the unique point $\mathbf{b}$ such that $\nabla L(\mathbf{b})$ is $\mathbf{0}$ and $\|\mathbf{b} - \mathbf{b}_0\| \le u$. We have

$$\|\mathbf{b}_t - \mathbf{b}\| \le T(2TV)^{\tau(n)-1}/\tau(n),$$

where $\tau(n) = 2^n$. It easily follows that if $\mathbf{b}$ is a maximum likelihood estimate of β such that $\nabla^2 L(\mathbf{b})$ is negative definite, then for $\mathbf{b}_0$ sufficiently close to $\mathbf{b}$, $\mathbf{b}_t$ converges to $\mathbf{b}$. Since the third partial

derivatives of L are uniformly bounded, it follows from the case $\mathbf{b}_0 = \mathbf{b}$
that if $V^* < \infty$ is the supremum of

$$\left\| \left[\nabla^2 L(\mathbf{b}) \right]^{-1} \nabla^3 L(\gamma) \mathbf{c} \right\| / \|\mathbf{c}\|$$

for $\mathbf{c}$ and γ in R^r, then no $\mathbf{c}$ exists such that $\nabla L(\mathbf{c})$ is $\mathbf{0}$ and
$\|\mathbf{c} - \mathbf{b}\| < 2/V^*$. Thus, the conditions $\nabla L(\mathbf{b}) = \mathbf{0}$ and $\nabla^2 L(\mathbf{b})$ negative
definite ensure that $\mathbf{b}$ is the only local maximum of the likelihood
within an open ball of radius $2/V^*$.

In problems of indirect observation, this algorithm is often quite
satisfactory. Example 1 provides a good example. Consider the crude
starting values $b_{k0} = 0, 1 \leq k \leq 4$, $b_{k0} = 1, 5 \leq k \leq 7$, $b_{k0} = 0, 8 \leq k \leq 9$.
Convergence is rapid enough that no b_{k4} differs from b_{k5} by more than
0.00004. If we use Haberman's (1979, p. 549) starting values for the
scoring algorithm, then no b_{k2} differs from b_{k3} by more than 0.00091, a
result similar to that obtained via the scoring algorithm.

2.4. *Large-Sample Approximations*

A basic advantage of the Newton-Raphson algorithm over the
EM algorithm is in the estimation of asymptotic standard deviations of
parameters. The EM algorithm provides no information on asymptotic
standard deviations. In the Newton-Raphson algorithm, estimates for
asymptotic standard deviations of the maximum likelihood estimates
are obtained as by-products. Let $\mathbf{c}$ be a nonzero constant vector in R^r.
The approximation used states that the normalized difference

$$z = (\mathbf{c}'\mathbf{b} - \mathbf{c}'\beta) \Big/ \left\{ \mathbf{c}' \left[-\nabla^2 L(\mathbf{b}) \right]^{-1} \mathbf{c} \right\}^{1/2}$$

has an approximate standard normal distribution. The estimated
asymptotic standard deviation (EASD) of $\mathbf{c}'\mathbf{b}$ is thus $\{\mathbf{c}'[\nabla^2 L(\mathbf{b})]^{-1}\mathbf{c}\}^{1/2}$.
The estimates and estimated standard deviations of the coefficients b_k
in example 1 are listed in Table 3. These results do not differ
appreciably from those derived from Haberman (1979) via the scoring
algorithm.

To appreciate the significance of the ability to compute estimated asymptotic standard deviations, it is helpful to note that the
normal approximation for z is appropriate under a very wide variety
of conditions. In particular, it is possible to use the normal approximation even when the vectors $\mathbf{x}_{ij}$ vary for each subject i or the dimension
p of the parameter vector β depends on the sample size N.

TABLE 3
Parameter Estimates and Estimated Asymptotic Standard Deviations for Example 1

Parameter	Estimate	EASD
λ_1^U	-0.106	0.087
λ_1^A	-0.316	0.045
λ_1^B	0.327	0.049
λ_1^C	0.012	0.039
λ_{11}^{UA}	1.372	0.045
λ_{11}^{UB}	1.397	0.049
λ_{11}^{UC}	1.293	0.039
λ_{11}^{UD}	-0.105	0.026
λ_{12}^{UD}	0.045	0.026

To study the normal approximation for $\mathbf{b}$, consider the Newton-Raphson algorithm for the starting value $\mathbf{b}_0 = \beta$. Let the norm $\|\mathbf{a}\| = \{\mathbf{a}'[-\nabla^2 L(\beta)]\mathbf{a}\}^{1/2}$, and let $u = 2T$, so that

$$T = \left\{ [\nabla L(\beta)]'[-\nabla^2 L(\beta)]^{-1} \nabla L(\beta) \right\}^{1/2},$$

and V is the supremum of

$$\mathbf{d}'[\nabla^3 L(\gamma)\mathbf{a}]\mathbf{d} / (\|\mathbf{a}\|^{1/2}\|\mathbf{d}\|)$$

for $\mathbf{a}$ and $\mathbf{d}$ in R^r and $\|\gamma - \beta\| \le 2T$. Let the Fisher information $I(\beta)$ be the expected value of $-\nabla^2 L(\beta)$. Let v be the maximum difference

$$\left| \mathbf{a}'[-\nabla^2 L(\beta)]\mathbf{a}/\mathbf{a}'I(\beta)\mathbf{a} - 1 \right|$$

for $\mathbf{a}$ in R^r, and let

$$\kappa = \sum E \left| \mathbf{c}'[I(\beta)]^{-1}[\mathbf{F}_i(\beta) - \mathbf{E}_i(\beta)] \right|^3 \Big/ \left(\mathbf{c}'[I(\beta)]^{-1}\mathbf{c} \right)^{3/2}$$

For $TV < 1/2$, let $\mathbf{b}$ be the limit of $\mathbf{b}_t$. Since Taylor's theorem implies that

$$\mathbf{a}'\nabla^2 L(\mathbf{b})\mathbf{a} = \mathbf{a}'\nabla^2 L(\beta)\mathbf{a} + \mathbf{a}'[\nabla^3 L(\mathbf{d})(\mathbf{b} - \beta)]\mathbf{a}$$

for some $\mathbf{d}$ on the line segment between $\mathbf{b}$ and β, the definition of V and the condition $TV < 1/2$ imply that $\mathbf{b}$ is at least an isolated relative maximum of L, with no other critical point $\mathbf{b}^*$ such that $\|\mathbf{b}^* - \beta\| <$

$2T$. If T^2V converges in probability to 0, v converges in probability to 0, and κ converges to 0, then the distribution function of z converges to the distribution function Φ of the standard normal distribution $N(0, 1)$. The arguments required differ little from those in Haberman (1977b, 1977c) and Friedman (1982).

In the special case of direct observation, results correspond to those in Haberman (1977b, 1977c). In this case, $I(\beta)$ and $-\nabla^2 L(\beta)$ are the same, an isolated local maximum of L is necessarily the maximum likelihood estimate, $\nabla^2 L$ is independent of the observations, and the condition on third absolute moments is redundant.

The conditions described here are trivial in the simple case of $\mathbf{x}_{ij}$, J_i, and G_i independent of i and $I(\beta)$ positive definite. As in Haberman (1977b, 1977c), the distribution of T^2 converges to a central chi square on p degrees of freedom, and V, v, and k are all of order $N^{-1/2}$. This situation applies in Table 1.

As in results of Haberman (1977b, 1977c), there is no need for $\mathbf{x}_{ij}$, J_i, and G_i to be constant over i for the normal approximation to apply. For example, if p is constant, $N[I(\beta)]^{-1}$ is bounded, and the x_{ijk} are uniformly bounded, then the distribution of T^2 still approaches that of a central chi square on p degrees of freedom, and k, V, and v are still of order $N^{-1/2}$, so that all conditions for asymptotic normality are satisfied. For related results for constant p, J_i, and G_i, see Fahrmeir and Kaufmann (1985). Arguments similar to those presented in Haberman (1977b, 1977c) can also be applied when the dimension p increases as the sample size N increases.

The problem of local maxima that are not unique global maxima is quite real, as is evident in the latent-class model for Table 1. We have $L(\mathbf{b}) = L(\mathbf{c})$ if $b_k = -c_k$ for $k = 1, 5, 6, 7, 8$, and 9 and $b_k = c_k$ for $2 \leq k \leq 4$. The asymptotic normality result for $\mathbf{b}$ holds only if we assume that b_4 and β_4 are both positive.

The following variation on the asymptotic normality conditions is occasionally relevant. Instead of $u = 2T$, let $u = WT$ for W a random variable at least 2. Let $\| \cdot \|$ be defined as before, and let the probability approach 1 that $TV < 1/2$. Then the probability approaches 1 that there is only one critical point $\mathbf{b}$ such that $\|\mathbf{b} - \beta\| < 1/V$. In the simple case of $\mathbf{x}_{ij}$, J_i, and G_i independent of i and $I(\beta)$ positive definite, it follows, as in Haberman (1977a), that for some open neighborhood $\mathbf{M}$ of β, the probability approaches 1 that there is exactly one critical point in $\mathbf{M}$. These conditions are met in example 1.

2.5. *Stability Problems*

As is evident from the example, the Newton-Raphson algorithm can work quite well in practice; nonetheless, it is not especially stable, even when $\nabla^2 L(\mathbf{b})$ is negative definite. For instance, in example 2, $\nabla^2 L(\mathbf{b}_0)$ is not negative definite if $b_{k0} = 0$ for $1 \leq k \leq 6$ and $b_{k0} = 1$ for $7 \leq k \leq 11$. This problem can be overcome by better initial values b_{k0}; however, as is evident from Goodman (1974a), good initial estimates cannot be constructed in a trivial fashion.

There are two basic problems that affect stability. The first problem, which is observed in example 2, is that the logarithm of the likelihood function need not be concave. Thus, the Hessian of L need not be negative definite at all points, and for fixed $\mathbf{b}$, $g(\lambda) = L(\mathbf{b} + \lambda \mathbf{s}(\mathbf{b}))$, which has derivative

$$g'(0) = f(\mathbf{b}) = [\nabla L(\mathbf{b})]'[\nabla^2 L(\mathbf{b})]^{-1} \nabla L(\mathbf{b}),$$

may be a decreasing function for $\mathbf{a}$ in the interval $[0, 1]$. This problem can clearly lead to cases in which $L(\mathbf{b}_t)$ exceeds $L(\mathbf{b}_{t+1})$ and no progress is made toward a maximum of the function L. In addition, computation of $\mathbf{s}(\mathbf{b}_t)$ is simpler if the Hessian $\nabla^2 L(\mathbf{b}_t)$ is negative definite. A related difficulty arises: Whenever the Hessian of L is not negative definite at all points, there are also points at which the Hessian is negative definite but nearly singular. This problem can lead to very large vectors $\mathbf{s}(\mathbf{b}_t)$. Instability results because $\mathbf{b}_{t+1}$ is then very far from $\mathbf{b}_t$.

The second problem involves deviation of L from a quadratic approximation. Let $\nabla^2 L(\mathbf{b})$ be negative definite. Were L quadratic, then L would have a unique maximum at $\mathbf{b} + \mathbf{s}(\mathbf{b})$. At this maximum, the value of L would be $L(\mathbf{b}) + (1/2)f(\mathbf{b})$. If the quadratic approximation is poor, then $L(\mathbf{b} + \mathbf{s}(\mathbf{b}))$ may be less than $L(\mathbf{b})$, even though $g'(0)$ is positive and $L(\mathbf{b} + \lambda \mathbf{s}(\mathbf{b}))$ exceeds $L(\mathbf{b})$ for sufficiently small positive λ. In the algorithm considered below, both of these issues are considered.

3. THE ALGORITHM

In the proposed algorithm, a fixed norm $\| \cdot \|$, a fixed α in $(0, 1/2)$, a fixed $\kappa > 0$, and a fixed τ in $(0, 1/2)/(1 - \alpha)$ are selected, and the ordinary Newton-Raphson algorithm is modified whenever either $\nabla^2 L(\mathbf{b}_t)$ is not negative definite, $\|\mathbf{s}(\mathbf{b}_t)\| > k$, or

$$L(\mathbf{b}_t) + \alpha \mathbf{s}(\mathbf{b}_t)' \nabla L(\mathbf{b}_t) > L(\mathbf{b}_t + \mathbf{s}(\mathbf{b}_t)).$$

To describe the algorithm, assume for simplicity that $\mathbf{b}$ is a critical point of L such that $\nabla^2 L(\mathbf{b})$ is negative definite. Since $C(\mathbf{b})$ must be positive definite, it follows that if $\sum_k c_k x_{ijk}$ is constant over j for each i, then each c_k is 0. Therefore, $C(\gamma)$ is positive definite for all γ.

Let $\mathbf{b}_0$ be an initial approximation for $\mathbf{b}$. Recall the definitions of $\nabla L(\gamma)$, $\nabla^2 L(\gamma)$, $C(\gamma)$, and $D(\gamma)$ in section 2.1. Then, a sequence of approximations $\mathbf{b}_t$, $t \geq 0$, is constructed in the following fashion. The sequence satisfies

$$\mathbf{b}_{t+1} = \mathbf{b}_t + \lambda_t \mathbf{u}(\mathbf{b}_t),$$

where

$$\mathbf{u}(\gamma) = [C(\gamma) - m(\gamma)D(\gamma)]^{-1} \nabla L(\gamma),$$

$m(\gamma)$ is 1 if $-\nabla^2 L(\gamma) = C(\gamma) - D(\gamma)$ is positive definite and $\|\mathbf{s}(\gamma)\| \leq \kappa$ and $m(\gamma)$ is 0 otherwise, and λ_t is obtained by the following steps:

1. Let c_{t1} be $\max[1, \kappa/\|\mathbf{u}(\mathbf{b}_t)\|]$, let $k = 1$, and let $e_t = [\mathbf{u}(\mathbf{b}_t)]' \nabla L(\mathbf{b}_t)$.
2. If

$$L(\mathbf{b}_t + c_{tk}\mathbf{u}(\mathbf{b}_t)) \geq L(\mathbf{b}_t) + \alpha c_{tk} e_t,$$

then let $\lambda_t = c_{tk}$. Otherwise, continue on to step 3.
3. Let

$$c_{t(k+1)} = \max\left[\tau c_{tk}, (1/2)c_{tk}e_t / \{ e_t - [L(\mathbf{b}_t + c_{tk}\mathbf{u}(\mathbf{b}_t)) - L(\mathbf{b}_t)]/c_{tk} \} \right],$$

replace k by $k + 1$, and return to step 2.

3.1. *Relationship to the Newton-Raphson Algorithm*

The proposed algorithm is identical to the Newton-Raphson algorithm once $\mathbf{b}_t$ is sufficiently close to $\mathbf{b}$. Thus, the algorithm retains the rapid convergence properties of the Newton-Raphson algorithm. Verification of this identity for $\mathbf{b}_t$ near $\mathbf{b}$ reduces to demonstration that

$$\mathbf{u}(\gamma) = \mathbf{s}(\gamma) \text{ for } \gamma \text{ sufficiently close to } \mathbf{b} \qquad (2)$$

and

$$L(\gamma + \mathbf{s}(\gamma)) \geq L(\gamma) + \alpha \mathbf{s}(\gamma)' \nabla L(\gamma) \text{ for } \gamma \text{ sufficiently close to } \mathbf{b}. \qquad (3)$$

Since $\nabla^2 L(\mathbf{b}) = D(\mathbf{b}) - C(\mathbf{b})$ is negative definite and $\nabla L(\mathbf{b})$ is $\mathbf{0}$, $\mathbf{u}(\gamma) = \mathbf{s}(\gamma)$ for γ sufficiently close to $\mathbf{b}$. Demonstration of (3) depends on standard use of Taylor expansions. Since $\nabla L(\mathbf{b})$ is $\mathbf{0}$ and $\nabla^2 L(\mathbf{b})$ is negative definite, $\mathbf{s}(\gamma) \to \mathbf{0}$ as $\gamma \to \mathbf{0}$. Standard use of Taylor expansions yields the following results:

$$\nabla L(\gamma) = \nabla^2 L(\mathbf{b})\gamma + \mathbf{o}(\gamma),$$

where $\mathbf{o}(\gamma)/\|\gamma - \mathbf{b}\| \to \mathbf{0}$ as $\gamma \to \mathbf{b}$;

$$[\mathbf{s}(\gamma)]'\nabla L(\gamma) = -[\nabla L(\gamma)]'[\nabla^2 L(\gamma)]^{-1}\nabla L(\gamma)$$

$$= -\gamma'\nabla^2 L(\mathbf{b})\gamma + o(\gamma),$$

where $o(\gamma)/\|\gamma - \mathbf{b}\|^2 \to 0$;

$$L(\gamma + \mathbf{s}(\gamma)) = L(\gamma) + [\mathbf{s}(\gamma)]'\nabla L(\gamma) + (1/2)[\mathbf{s}(\gamma)]'\nabla^2 L(\gamma)\mathbf{s}(\gamma) + o_1(\gamma)$$

$$= L(\gamma) - (1/2)\gamma'\nabla^2 L(\mathbf{b})\gamma + o_2(\gamma),$$

where for w equal 1 or 2, $o_w(\gamma)/\|\gamma - \mathbf{b}\|^2 \to 0$ as $\gamma \to \mathbf{b}$;

$$L(\gamma) + \alpha[\mathbf{s}(\gamma)]'\nabla L(\gamma) = L(\gamma) - \alpha\gamma'\nabla^2 L(\mathbf{b})\gamma + o(\gamma).$$

Since α is between 0 and $1/2$, (3) holds.

The modifications of the Newton-Raphson algorithm have several purposes. As shown in section 3.2, the use of $\mathbf{u}(\mathbf{b}_t)$ rather than $\mathbf{s}(\mathbf{b}_t)$ ensures that $w_t(\lambda) = L(\mathbf{b}_t + \lambda\mathbf{u}(\mathbf{b}_t))$ is increasing in λ for small positive λ. To understand the choice of $\mathbf{u}(\mathbf{b}_t)$ for $\nabla^2 L(\mathbf{b}_t)$ not negative definite, consider the following hypothetical situation. Suppose that the EM algorithm were used at step t to define $\mathbf{b}_{t+1}$ and that the Newton-Raphson algorithm with starting value $\mathbf{b}_t$ were applied to the M (maximization) step of the EM algorithm. Then, the first iteration of this Newton-Raphson algorithm would yield $\mathbf{b}_t + \mathbf{u}(\mathbf{b}_t)$.

The scale factor λ_t is intended to approximate the maximum of $w_t(\lambda)$ over λ. The sequence of c_{tk} is normally selected so that $c_{t(k+1)}$ is the location of the maximum of the quadratic function $f_t(\lambda)$ such that at 0, $f_t(\lambda)$ equals $L(\mathbf{b}_t)$ and has derivative e_t, and at c_{tk}, $f_t(\lambda)$ equals $L(\mathbf{b}_t + c_{tk}\mathbf{u}(\mathbf{b}_t))$. However, to prevent unusually small values of c_{tk}, $c_{t(k+1)}$ is constrained to be at least τc_{tk}. To prevent extremely large changes of approximations to $\mathbf{b}$, c_{t1} is restricted to ensure that $\|\mathbf{b}_{t+1} - \mathbf{b}_t\|$ does not exceed κ.

3.2. *Stability Properties*

The algorithm has stability properties that the Newton-Raphson algorithm does not possess. The basic result is that $\mathbf{b}_t$ converges to $\mathbf{b}$ if $W = \{\gamma: L(\gamma) \geq L(\mathbf{b}_0)\}$ is bounded and if $\mathbf{b}$ is the only element γ of W such that $\nabla L(\gamma) = \mathbf{0}$.

Stability is ensured by the condition that $L(\mathbf{b}_t)$ is less than $L(\mathbf{b}_{t+1})$ unless $\nabla L(\mathbf{b}_t) = \mathbf{0}$. To verify this claim, assume that $\nabla L(\mathbf{b}_t) \neq \mathbf{0}$. We must verify that $e_t > 0$ and that λ_t is defined and positive. Since the matrix $C(\mathbf{b}_t) - m(\mathbf{b}_t)D(\mathbf{b}_t)$ is positive definite,

$$e_t = [\mathbf{u}(\mathbf{b}_t)]'\nabla L(\mathbf{b}_t) = [\nabla L(\mathbf{b}_t)]'[C(\mathbf{b}_t) - m(\mathbf{b}_t)D(\mathbf{b}_t)]^{-1}\nabla L(\mathbf{b}_t) > 0.$$

Since $e_t > 0$,

$$L(\mathbf{b}_t + \lambda \mathbf{u}(\mathbf{b}_t)) = L(\mathbf{b}_t) + \lambda e_t + o_3(\lambda),$$

where $o_3(\lambda)/\lambda \to 0$ as $\lambda \to 0$. Thus,

$$L(\mathbf{b}_t + \lambda \mathbf{u}(\mathbf{b}_t)) > L(\mathbf{b}_t) + \alpha\lambda e_t$$

for small enough positive λ. If λ_t is not set equal to c_{tk}, then $c_{t(k+1)}$ must be positive but less than $(1/2)c_{tk}/(1 - \alpha)$. Thus, a k must eventually be encountered such that λ_t can be set equal to $c_{tk} > 0$.

Since the $L(\mathbf{b}_t)$, $t \geq 0$, form a nondecreasing sequence and since each $L(\mathbf{b}_t) \leq L(\mathbf{b})$, $L(\mathbf{b}_{t+1}) - L(\mathbf{b}_t) \to 0$ and $\lambda_t e_t \to 0$. The assumption that $W = \{\mathbf{g}: L(\mathbf{g}) \geq L(\mathbf{b}_0)\}$ is bounded implies that $\{\mathbf{b}_t: t \geq 1\}$ is contained in the closed and bounded set W. Thus e_t, $\|\mathbf{u}(\mathbf{b}_t)\|$, and $\|\lambda_t \mathbf{u}(\mathbf{b}_t)\|$ are bounded above. Since

$$w_t(\lambda) = w_t(0) + \lambda e_t + (1/2)\lambda^2[\mathbf{u}(\mathbf{b}_t)]'\nabla^2 L(\mathbf{d}_t(\lambda))\mathbf{u}(\mathbf{b}_t)$$

for some $\mathbf{d}_t(\lambda) = \mathbf{b}_t + \rho\mathbf{u}(\mathbf{b}_t))$, $0 \leq \rho \leq \lambda$, we can use constants η and ρ to obtain bounds

$$w_t(0) + \lambda e_t + \eta\lambda^2 \leq w_t(\lambda) \leq w_t(0) + \lambda e_t + \rho\lambda^2$$

for $\lambda \leq c_{t1} = \max[1, \kappa/\|\mathbf{u}(\mathbf{b}_t)\|]$. If $\lambda < c_{t1}$, then

$$w_t(\lambda_t/\mu_t) < w_t(0) + \alpha\lambda_t e_t/\mu_t$$

for some μ_t between τ and 1 such that $\lambda_t/\mu_t \leq c_{t1}$. Thus, λ_t is bounded away from 0 and $e_t \to 0$. Since the $C(\mathbf{b}_t) - m(\mathbf{b}_t)D(\mathbf{b}_t)$ form a bounded sequence of matrices if W is bounded, it follows that $\nabla L(\mathbf{b}_t) \to \mathbf{0}$. Since $\mathbf{b}$ is the only element of W such that $\nabla L(\mathbf{b}) = \mathbf{0}$, $\mathbf{b}_t \to \mathbf{b}$.

One modest generalization is important in many problems involving latent-class analysis. Suppose that W contains a finite number of solutions of the equation $\nabla L(\mathbf{b}) = \mathbf{0}$. Then, $\mathbf{b}_t$ converges to one of these solutions.

4. EXAMPLES

The examples presented in this section are designed to illustrate the stability of the modified Newton-Raphson algorithm when quite crude starting values are used. In all examples, α is $1/16$, τ is 0.1, and $\kappa = 10$. The norm

$$\|\mathbf{c}\| = \max_i \max_j \left| \sum_k x_{ijk} c_k \right|.$$

Example 1. Results for the two-variable latent-class model of example 1 with the starting values previously used for the Newton-Raphson algorithm and results for the modified Newton-Raphson algorithm are exactly the same. Thus, the algorithm does not interfere in a case in which convergence is achieved by the conventional algorithm.

Example 2. Consider the starting values tried in the two-variable latent-class model of example 2. In this case, convergence is rapid; i.e., no value of $|b_{k6} - b_{k7}|$ is greater than 0.00048. In this particular example, $\mathbf{u}(\mathbf{b}_0)$ and $\mathbf{u}(\mathbf{b}_1)$ differ from $\mathbf{s}(\mathbf{b}_0)$ and $\mathbf{s}(\mathbf{b}_1)$, respectively. In all subsequent iterations t, $\mathbf{u}(\mathbf{b}_t) = \mathbf{s}(\mathbf{b}_t)$. The step size λ_t is one for all iterations. Final estimates and estimated asymptotic standard deviations are shown in Table 4. The parameters reported in this table can be produced from numbers reported in Goodman (1974*a*); however, the estimated asymptotic standard deviations cannot be obtained from this source.

Further insight into the behavior of the algorithm can be gained through some further experimentation with starting values. We can make the algorithm fail to converge to a maximum likelihood estimate if we let $\mathbf{b}_0$ be 0. In this case, the algorithm converges to the saddle point of L that corresponds to the maximum likelihood estimate of β subject to the independence and equiprobability restrictions that only λ_A, λ_B, λ_C, and λ_D may differ from 0. This problem of saddle points corresponding to very simple initial values can be expected in all latent-class models.

TABLE 4
Parameter Estimates and Asymptotic Standard Deviations for Example 2

Parameter	Estimate	EASD
λ_U	-0.025	0.279
λ_V	-0.087	0.221
λ_A	-0.239	0.082
λ_B	0.102	0.090
λ_C	-0.048	0.186
λ_D	0.191	0.092
λ_{UA}	0.800	0.073
λ_{UC}	1.204	0.163
λ_{UV}	0.304	0.035
λ_{VB}	0.608	0.064
λ_{VD}	0.611	0.066

Nonetheless, even very poor starting values lead to convergence to the maximum likelihood estimate **b** if we avoid accidental assumptions of independence. For example, the algorithm was used with all b_{k0} equal to 0, except for b_{80} and $b_{(11)0}$, which were set to 0.1. Satisfactory convergence to **b** was achieved after 15 iterations. Because of the poor starting values, $s(\mathbf{b}_t)$ was not used until t was 8, and in two subsequent instances, λ_t was not 1. Nonetheless, the algorithm proved quite stable under the circumstances.

REFERENCES

Clogg, C. C. 1977. "Unrestricted and Restricted Maximum Likelihood Latent Structure Analysis: A Manual for Users." Working Paper No. 1977-09. University Park: Penn State University, Population Issues Research Center.

Coleman, J. S. 1964. *Introduction to Mathematical Sociology*. New York: Free Press.

Dempster, A. P., N. M. Laird, and D. B. Rubin. 1977. "Maximum Likelihood from Incomplete Data via the EM Algorithm." *Journal of the Royal Statistical Society*, ser. B, 39:1–39.

Fahrmeir, L., and H. Kaufmann. 1985. "Consistency and Asymptotic Normality of the Maximum Likelihood Estimator in Generalized Linear Models." *Annals of Statistics* 13:342–68.

Friedman, M. 1982. "Piecewise Exponential Models for Survival Data with Covariates." *Annals of Statistics* 10:101–13.

Goodman, L. A. 1974a. "The Analysis of Systems of Qualitative Variables When Some of the Variables are Unobservable. I. A Modified Latent Structure Approach." *American Journal of Sociology* 79:1179–1259.

_____. 1974b. "Exploratory Latent Structure Analysis Using Both Identifiable and Unidentifiable Models." *Biometrika* 61:215–31.

Haberman, S. J. 1974a. "Log-Linear Models for Frequency Tables Derived by Indirect Observation: Maximum Likelihood Equations." *Annals of Statistics* 2:911–24.

_____. 1974b. *The Analysis of Frequency Data.* Chicago: University of Chicago Press.

_____. 1976. "Iterative Scaling Procedures for Log-Linear Models for Frequency Tables Derived by Indirect Observation." Pp. 45–50 in *Proceedings of the Statistical Computing Section, American Statistical Association.* Washington, DC: American Statistical Association.

_____. 1977a. "Product Models for Frequency Tables Involving Indirect Observation." *Annals of Statistics* 5:1124–47.

_____. 1977b. "Log-Linear Models and Frequency Tables with Small Expected Cell Counts." *Annals of Statistics* 5:1148–69.

_____. 1977c. "Maximum Likelihood Estimates in Exponential Response Models." *Annals of Statistics* 5:815–41.

_____. 1979. *Analysis of Qualitative Data.* Vol. 2. New York: Academic Press.

Kantorovich, L. V., and G. P. Akilov. 1982. *Functional Analysis.* 2d ed. Oxford: Pergamon Press.

8

The Analysis of Cross-Classified Categorical Data From Complex Sample Surveys

J. N. K. Rao and D. Roland Thomas*

This paper provides a detailed description of some recent methods for analyzing categorical data from complex surveys involving clustering, stratification, and multistage sampling. The methods are introduced through a discussion of the simple goodness-of-fit problem and are then applied to a variety of other categorical data problems, including tests of homogeneity and independence on two-way tables (with modifications for tables having ordered categories) and the analysis of three-way tables using log-linear models. These analyses are illustrated using data from the Canadian Class Structure Survey and the Canada Health Survey. The primary focus of the paper is on methods that provide first- and second-order corrections to standard multinomial-based chi-square tests by taking account of survey design effects. First-order corrections are particularly useful for secondary analyses from published tables that also include information on design effects or estimated variances for cells and marginal tables. True standard errors of parameter

The authors thank John Myles and the staff of the Canadian Class Structure Project and Susan O'Hara, manager of the Ottawa office of Canadian Facts, for providing additional documentation on the survey design of the CCSS; Monica Boyd and Gail Eno for providing SPSS[X] data definitions; and Georgia Roberts for assistance with the CHS data analysis. We also thank Mark Boudreau for his expert programming and Greg Morrison and Eleanor Thomas for comments on a draft of the paper. We are also grateful to a referee for many constructive comments and suggestions. Microcomputing facilities were provided by the Decision Analysis Laboratory, of which the second author is a member. This work was supported by grants from the Natural Sciences and Engineering Research Council of Canada and from the Ontario Research Leadership Fund.

* Carleton University.

estimates are also given and are compared with those produced by the SPSS^X program LOGLINEAR. Residual analysis to detect model deviations is also considered, again taking account of survey design effects.

1. INTRODUCTION

The need to perform statistical analyses of categorical data in the form of cross-classified tables is frequently encountered in quantitative sociological research. Of the various techniques available, Pearson's chi-square test of association for two-way tables is probably best known, though analysis of three-way and higher-way tables is now common, thanks to the development of log-linear model analysis by Goodman and others. Extensions of these basic methods have also been developed to handle ordered categorical data (see, e.g., Goodman 1984; Agresti 1984) and data in which one or more of the variables can be classified as response variables. In fact, in their variety and modeling flexibility, the techniques presently available for analyzing categorical data now rival those available for analyzing continuous, ratio-scale data. They are described in detail in such texts as Bishop, Fienberg, and Holland (1975), Haberman (1978), and Fienberg (1981).

These methods all rely on the assumption that the data are obtained by simple random sampling (SRS) from one or more large populations. When this assumption is satisfied, the data, in the form of cell counts, follow a multinomial or product-multinomial distribution, and convenient maximum likelihood (ML) methods can be used to estimate model parameters. Flexible computer programs for performing ML estimation for log-linear and related models, together with associated large-sample chi-square tests, have been implemented in such popular statistical packages as SAS, SPSS^X, BMDP, MINITAB, and GLIM and are now widely used by sociologists and other practitioners. However, many of the surveys of interest to sociologists have complex designs involving stratification, clustering, and several stages of selection and therefore yield data that violate the SRS assumptions on which the standard analyses are based.

The effect of these violations can be severe. This is particularly true of clustering. For example, numerous authors have shown that clustering distorts the distribution of Pearson's chi-square statistic, which under SRS tends to a chi-square distribution for large samples. The effect of the distortion is generally to make the test liberal, so that a test that might have a nominal level (i.e., type I error rate) of 5 percent might in fact have an actual level as high as 40 percent (Rao and Scott 1981). Clearly, sociological data from complex surveys should not be routinely analyzed using programs found in the popular statistical packages. Use of the p values printed by these programs, which are predicated on the assumption of SRS, can in some instances lead to highly misleading results.

Though numerous methods have been proposed for analyzing categorical data from complex samples, relatively few have been reported in the sociological literature. The primary purpose of this paper is to describe some of these methods in detail and provide a practical guide to their application. Besides giving a mathematical description of these methods, we present illustrations of their application using data from the Canadian Class Structure Survey (Canadian Facts 1983) and from the Canada Health Survey (1978–79). A brief description of these surveys is given in section 2.

To introduce the technical aspects of complex categorical data analysis, section 3 of the paper focuses exclusively on the simplest of categorical data problems, namely, the goodness-of-fit test of a simple hypothesis. Following a hypothetical example that illustrates the inference problems caused by clustering, several approaches to the goodness-of-fit problem are discussed, leading to a detailed exposition of the methods of Rao and Scott (1979, 1981, 1984, 1987). The remainder of the paper discusses the application of the Rao-Scott approach to a variety of categorical data problems, including

1. goodness-of-fit tests on one-way tables;
2. tests of homogeneity of proportions, and of association, on two-way tables, including modifications for ordinal variables;
3. analysis of three-way and higher-way tables using log-linear models.

All analyses were coded using GAUSS, a matrix-oriented programming language designed for statistical programming (Platt 1986), and were run on an IBM System 2/60 computer.

It should be noted that though this paper deals only with analysis of discrete data (categorical and ordinal), similar inference problems arise when techniques such as regression analysis are applied to ratio-scale data from complex surveys. For a discussion of the effect of clustering on ordinary least squares regression, see Scott and Holt (1982) and the references cited therein.

2. EXAMPLE DATASETS FROM TWO CANADIAN SURVEYS

2.1. *The Canadian Class Structure Survey*

The Canadian Class Structure Survey (CCSS), a national survey of the economically active adult population of Canada, was commissioned by the Department of Sociology and Anthropology at Carleton University and was conducted by Canadian Facts, a commercial survey organization, during the fall and winter of 1982–83. The survey was designed to gather information on the labor process and the social structure in Canada, and it was part of an international project in which similar surveys were carried out in the U.S. in 1980, in Sweden in 1982, and more recently in a number of other European countries. It was funded by the Social Science and Humanities Research Council of Canada.

Usable interviews were obtained from a total of 2,577 respondents; 1,463 of the respondents were employed, 322 were self-employed, and 649 were unemployed. The remaining 143 respondents were engaged in unpaid domestic work. All the examples in this paper are based on the domain of 1,463 employed respondents.

The survey design. The ten Canadian provinces were divided into 35 strata by region (Atlantic, Quebec, Ontario, the Prairies, Alberta, and British Columbia) and by community population size (500,000 or over; 100,000 to 499,999; 30,000 to 99,999; 10,000 to 29,999; 1,000 to 9,999; and rural). Residents of the North West Territories and some remote provincial areas, members of the armed forces, and inmates of institutions were excluded from the surveyed population. Total exclusions amounted to 7 percent of the Canadian population.

Two independent replicates (subsamples) were selected in four stages from each of 34 of the 35 regional/community-size strata. Only one replicate was drawn in one of the strata. In the first stage of sample selection, a sample of communities was selected. In the second stage, a sample of census enumeration areas (EAs) was selected from each selected community. In the third and fourth stages, households were selected from each EA, and one eligible respondent was selected from each listed household. Twelve households were selected per urban EA and nine per rural EA. Interviews were completed in 62 percent of all listed households. Additional details can be found in the CCSS technical documentation (Canadian Facts 1983). The full CCSS dataset, in the form of an SPSS^{X} system file, is available from the Social Science Data Archives, Carleton University. The dataset contains over 600 individual variables, including sample design weights for each dataset case, i.e., for each respondent. These weights incorporate design information based on the selection probabilities at each stage of the sample selection, as well as poststratification (or ratio weight) adjustments designed to match specific sample estimates to external data. The sample weights used in this paper involve two separate poststratification adjustments. The first matches to the 1981 census distribution of household size within geographic region. The second matches to the distribution of age by sex, within region, as determined by the 1983 Labour Force Survey carried out by Statistics Canada.

Variance estimation. The contingency table analysis methods to be described in this paper will require, at a minimum, variance estimates for the proportions of respondents falling into the individual cells of a given table. These proportions will be computed using the survey weights described above, and it will be essential that the variance estimation method take full account of the survey design. The replicated design of the CCSS provides for convenient variance estimation, based on the two independent replicates drawn within strata. The stratum with only one replicate was dropped from the analysis, since at least two replicates are needed for variance estimation.

McCarthy's (1966) method of balanced repeated replication (BRR) was selected for estimating the variances of the cell proportions. In the BRR method, a number of *pseudo half-samples* of the data are constructed by taking for each half-sample only one of the two replicates within each stratum. For the 34 strata of the CCSS, a total of 36 such half-samples are used. For each half-sample, the replicate to be selected from each stratum is indicated by a row of a special matrix of dimension 36×34, whose elements are either 1 or 2. Each column contains an equal number of 1's and 2's. The particular matrix used for this paper is available from the authors. Let the weighted proportion of respondents in a given cell of a contingency table be denoted $\hat{p}$, and for each of the half-samples $h = 1, \ldots, 36$, let the corresponding proportion be denoted $\hat{p}_h$. Here, the hats indicate that these proportions are themselves estimates of a population quantity. Then, a BRR estimate of the variance of $\hat{p}$ is

$$\text{var}(\hat{p}) = \frac{1}{36} \sum_{h=1}^{36} (\hat{p}_h - \hat{p})^2.$$

This approach can easily be extended to give estimates of covariances between different cells of a table, as required by some of the methods to be discussed.

2.2. *The Canada Health Survey*

The Canada Health Survey (CHS) was designed to provide reliable data on the health status of Canadians and on the risk factors to which they were exposed. A major objective was to relate risk factors and health status over time at the provincial and national levels. The survey was conducted for a twelve-month period in 1978–79 but was terminated as a result of government budget cuts.

The CHS used a multi-stage stratified cluster sampling design. The interview component of the survey was tailored to yield an annual sample of 12,000 households from 100 geographical clusters, at the rate of 10 households per month. Questionnaires were administered to all eligible members of each selected household. Additional information on the CHS design together with detailed descriptions of methods for estimating the variances of CHS table proportions are given by Hidiroglou and Rao (1987) and will not be repeated here.

3. BASIC THEORY ILLUSTRATED USING THE GOODNESS-OF-FIT TEST

The work of Kish and Frankel (1974) represents a landmark in the study of the effects of complex survey designs on statistical inference. They examined the effect of stratification and clustering on a number of statistics including subclass (or ratio) means, regression coefficients, and correlation coefficients. They found that the dominant effect on the variances of these statistics was due to the clustering, which, by inducing correlations among sample elements, inflated the variance of each statistic above that which would be found in a simple random sample having the same number of elementary units. In stratified cluster samples, the variance-inflating effect of clustering outweighed the slight variance-deflating effects of stratification. A referee pointed out that substantial variation in the sample weights could also lead to inflated variances, even without clustering. The ratio of the inflated variance of a statistic under a complex sampling scheme to the corresponding SRS variance is called a design effect, or deff (Kish 1965), a concept that will be heavily featured in the remainder of this paper.

The impact of a deff on a simple test can be illustrated by a modification of an example from Sudman (1976). Suppose one wishes to estimate the proportion of black and white households in a neighborhood using a cluster sample of 1,000 households. The design calls for a selection of 50 blocks with 20 households per block. The hypothesis to be tested is $H_0: p_0 = 0.3$, i.e., that the true proportion of black households is 30 percent, and the alternative is $H_a: p_0 \neq 0.3$. Assume that the survey produces an estimate of 340 black households, i.e., an estimated proportion $\hat{p} = 0.34$. If the clustering is ignored and SRS techniques are adopted, H_0 can be tested using the large-sample form of the binomial test, which refers

$$Z_{SRS} = |\hat{p} - p_0| \Big/ \sqrt{\frac{p_0(1 - p_0)}{1000}} \qquad (1)$$

to a standard normal distribution. Here, the denominator of Z_{SRS} is the standard error of $\hat{p}$, i.e., the square root of the variance of $\hat{p}$ under the assumption that H_0 is true. Since

$$Z_{SRS} = 2.76 > z_{0.025} = 1.96,$$

H_0 is rejected at a nominal level of 5 percent, where $z_{0.025}$ is the upper 2.5 percent point of a standard normal distribution. However, suppose the interviewers found that the neighborhood was totally segregated, i.e., that blocks were either totally black or totally white. In this extreme case, only one visit to one household in a block is required to determine all 20 outcomes for that block. Thus, the effective sample size is only 50 rather than the 1,000 assumed earlier, and the appropriate test now becomes, reject if $Z > z_{0.025} = 1.96$, where

$$Z = |\hat{p} - p_0| \Big/ \sqrt{\frac{p_0(1 - p_0)}{50}} = 0.62. \qquad (2)$$

Thus, if we use the correct test in which the standard error of $\hat{p}$ is based on the effective sample size, the hypothesis can no longer be rejected. In this extreme case, the deff is 20, given by the ratio of the squared denominators of the two test statistics, i.e., by the ratio of the correct variance estimate of $\hat{p}$ given the design to the SRS-based variance estimate.

In practice, deffs will be smaller than this. A useful guide to deff size is given by the Hansen, Hurwitz, and Madow (1953) formula for the deff of a sample mean:

$$\text{deff} = 1 + (m - 1)\rho, \qquad (3)$$

where m is the average cluster size and ρ is the intracluster correlation coefficient, a measure of cluster homogeneity. In the above example, $\rho = 1$, so that the deff $= 20$. For a typical cluster size of 10, with $\rho = 0.1$, the deff will be 1.9. It can be shown that ignoring this deff and using the Z_{SRS} test yields an actual level of 15.6 percent, compared with a nominal level of 5 percent. Thus, even a small degree of cluster homogeneity can have serious effects on test significance levels.

As Sudman (1976) notes, deffs also depend on the nature of the character being measured. Were the purpose of the hypothetical survey to study birth patterns, to see if births were more likely to occur in some months than in others, the clustering and racial segregation would have no effect (deff $\doteq 1$), since there is no apparent relationship between birthdate patterns and race; nor would one expect any relationship between birthdates and neighbors. If the number of births in our hypothetical neighborhood were cross-classified by race and by month, the deffs associated with the estimated marginal proportions for *race* could be very different from the deffs associated with the estimated marginal proportions for *months*. Clearly, when we move from inference on binary proportions to inference on multivariate data tables, the deff concept must be generalized, and simple rules of thumb based on the Hansen et al. (1953) formula will no longer suffice. A start can be made by studying the goodness-of-fit test for more than two categories, i.e. $K > 2$ proportions, which provides a suitable framework for an introduction to important recent developments.

3.1. The K-Category Goodness-of-Fit Test

Most treatments of categorical data analysis consider one-way and multi-way tables whose cells sum to the total sample size n that is fixed by design. Because sociologists routinely study subsets of their survey data and rarely include all survey units in any one table, we have chosen throughout the paper to discuss the analysis of tables defined on domains, i.e., subsets of units of the total sample, where the subset size is not fixed in advance. The theoretical results to be described in the paper apply equally to both situations.

Consider a one-way frequency table listing the number of sample units falling in each of K categories of a discrete variable, within some specified domain D. For example, using data from the CHS, Hidiroglou and Rao (1987) examined the six-category age distribution of respondents within the domain of respondents who reported consuming an average of one to six drinks per week. Let n_D, a random variable, represent the number of sample units falling in domain D, and let $n_1, \ldots, n_K$ represent the number of domain units in each of the K categories. Thus, $n_D = \Sigma n_i$. Also, let $p_1, \ldots, p_K$ be the proportions of units in each category within the finite population from which the sample is drawn. The goodness-of-fit problem is then to test the simple hypothesis $H_0: p = p_{0i}$, $i = 1, \ldots, K$, using the data n_i, $i = 1, \ldots, K$, together with knowledge of the survey design. In the Hidiroglou and Rao example, the hypothesized proportions (the p_{0i}'s) were taken to be the projected census age distribution.

If the survey data are treated as a simple random sample, the natural test will be Pearson's statistic, given by

$$X^2_{\text{SRS}} = \sum_{i=1}^{K} (n_i - n_D p_{0i})^2 / (n_D p_{0i})$$

$$= n_D \sum_{i=1}^{K} (\tilde{p}_i - p_{0i})^2 / p_{0i}, \tag{4}$$

where $\tilde{p}_i = n_i/n_D$ is the unweighted proportion of sample units in category i of domain D. Under SRS, X^2_{SRS} will be distributed asymptotically as χ^2_{K-1}, a central chi-square distribution on $K-1$ degrees of freedom, under H_0. The standard test procedure, which gives an approximate α-level test even for moderate sample sizes, is to reject H_0 when

$$X^2_{\text{SRS}} > \chi^2_{K-1}(\alpha), \tag{5}$$

the upper α percent point of χ^2_{K-1}. However, for a general non-SRS design, $\tilde{p}_i$ in (4) is not a consistent estimator of p_i unless the design is self-weighting (i.e., has equal sample weights), which is unlikely in practice. Loosely speaking, an estimator is consistent if its deviation from the parameter it estimates gets progressively smaller in absolute value with increasing sample size. Thus, X^2_{SRS} will not be a useful measure of deviation of the data from H_0, even for large sample sizes, since apparent deviations might simply be a result of inconsistent estimates. For general non-self-weighting designs, it is therefore necessary to replace X^2_{SRS} by a weighted-up form of Pearson's statistic, given by

$$X^2(G) = n_D \sum_{i=1}^{K} (\hat{p}_i - p_{0i})^2 / p_{0i}, \qquad (6)$$

where $\hat{p}_i$ is an estimate of the proportion in category i, based on weighted-up counts, i.e., $\hat{p}_i = \hat{N}_i / \hat{N}_D$. Here, $\hat{N}_D$ is the sum of the sample weights of all units falling in domain D, and $\hat{N}_i$ is the sum of the weights of those units in D that are also in category i. Use of the sample design weights ensures that both $\hat{N}_D$ and $\hat{N}_i$ are consistent estimators of the finite population totals N_D and N_i and that $\hat{p}_i$ is a consistent estimator of p_i, under the sample design. Thus, the version of Pearson's statistic (X^2) given by (6) does provide a meaningful measure of deviations from H_0, for any general survey design.

Among sociologists, a popular method of constructing a Pearson statistic is first to scale the sample weights so that they sum to n_D, the number of sample units in the domain in question, and then to use the scaled weighted-up counts in (4). This procedure is precisely equivalent to the form (6). Note that the scaling is essential; without scaling, use of weighted-up counts in (4) would produce a statistic that is too large by a factor of $\hat{N}_D / n_D$. For weights designed to give estimates of national totals, this factor could be in the hundreds or thousands.

The likelihood ratio statistic G^2 is frequently used in categorical data analysis as an alternative to Pearson's X^2. A form of G^2 that uses weighted-up proportions, and is thus analogous to $X^2(G)$ in (6), is given by

$$G^2(G) = 2n_D \sum_{i=1}^{K} \hat{p}_i \ln(\hat{p}_i / p_{0i}). \qquad (7)$$

Published tables reporting weighted-up counts, $\hat{N}_i$, or the proportions, $\hat{p}_i$, often do not provide the unweighted sample count n_D for analytical domains. For all secondary analyses from such tables, it is necessary to replace n_D, in the formulae for Pearson and likelihood ratio statistics, by an estimate of the expected value of n_D, namely $n\hat{N}_D/\hat{N}$, where $\hat{N}$ is the sum of all n sample weights.

Unfortunately, though $X^2(G)$ and $G^2(G)$ are both natural goodness-of-fit test statistics for complex designs involving clustering, their asymptotic distributions under H_0 will not be the familiar χ^2_{K-1}, even for self-weighting designs (for which $X^2(G) = X^2_{\text{SRS}}$), because of the nonzero intra-cluster correlation. Thus, the rejection rule (5) with X^2_{SRS} replaced by $X^2(G)$ will not provide an α-level test. The asymptotic distributions of $X^2(G)$ and $G^2(G)$ under complex sample designs have been obtained by Rao and Scott (1981) and provide the basis for their approach to the analysis of categorical data from complex surveys. Before the Rao-Scott method is described in detail, it will be instructive to consider some other approaches that have been proposed.

3.2. Alternatives to $X^2(G)$ and $G^2(G)$

Wald tests. Let $\hat{\mathbf{p}} = (\hat{p}_1, \ldots, \hat{p}_{K-1})'$ represent the $(K-1)$ vector of estimated domain proportions with $\hat{p}_K = 1 - (\hat{p}_1 + \cdots + \hat{p}_{K-1})$, and let $\mathbf{p}_0$ represent the corresponding $(K-1)$ vector of hypothesized proportions. Further, let $\mathbf{V}$ represent the $(K-1) \times (K-1)$ covariance matrix of $\hat{\mathbf{p}}$, and denote by $\hat{\mathbf{V}}$ the estimate of $\mathbf{V}$ obtained from the data by some appropriate method that accounts for the survey design. Whenever the full estimate $\hat{\mathbf{V}}$ is available, the Wald statistic,

$$X^2_W(G) = (\hat{\mathbf{p}} - \mathbf{p}_0)'\hat{\mathbf{V}}^{-1}(\hat{\mathbf{p}} - \mathbf{p}_0), \qquad (8)$$

is distributed asymptotically as χ^2_{K-1} under the null hypothesis and therefore provides an asymptotically exact α-level test when referred to $\chi^2_{K-1}(\alpha)$. Used in conjunction with weighted least squares estimation of model parameters, the Wald test provides an asymptotically valid approach to testing a variety of models on complex datasets (Koch, Freeman, and Freeman 1975). Computer programs for implementing this approach have been described by Landis et al. (1976) and Lepkowski (1982). A serious concern with the Wald approach is its sensitivity to the stability of $\hat{\mathbf{V}}^{-1}$, the inverse of the estimated covariance matrix (Fay 1985). For the goodness-of-fit case, Thomas and Rao (1987) showed that the Wald test provides poor control of type I error unless the degrees of freedom, f, for estimating $\hat{\mathbf{V}}$ are much greater than the degrees of freedom for the hypothesis. Since the degrees of freedom for $\hat{V}$ under the survey design are only moderate in most cases (34 for the CCSS dataset), the applicability of the Wald statistic is limited.

An F test that seems to provide better type I error control can, for the goodness-of-fit case, be obtained by referring

$$F_W(G) = \frac{(f - K + 2)}{f(K - 1)} X_W^2(G) \qquad (9)$$

to an F variable on $(K - 1)$ and $(f - K + 2)$ degrees of freedom. However, though $F_W(G)$ is a substantial improvement over $X_W^2(G)$, this modified Wald test is generally inferior to competing procedures in both error control and power. Some examples of these Wald tests will be provided later, for a variety of models.

Fay's jackknifed chi-square tests. An alternative to both the Pearson $X^2(G)$ and Wald $X_W^2(G)$ tests, and to their counterparts for more complex models, is Fay's (1979, 1985) jackknifed chi-square test, which requires survey estimates at the level of primary sampling units (PSUs) or of replicates. Though the jackknifed statistics are not asymptotically exact in general, unlike $X_W^2(G)$, Monte Carlo results for goodness-of-fit tests (Thomas and Rao 1987) show that Fay's method performs well in terms of both control of test level and power and that it is the main competitor to the methods of Rao and Scott. Fay has extended his approach to cover analysis of general log-linear models in the survey context and has implemented his methods in the computer program CPLX (Fay 1982). The jackknifed chi-square approach thus represents an important development in the analysis of categorical survey data, and it provides a viable analysis strategy whenever suitable PSU or replicate data are available. Further research is needed to systematically compare the statistical performance of the Rao-Scott and Fay procedures for general log-linear model analysis. Unfortunately, lack of space precludes any further exploration of Fay's method in this paper.

3.3. *The Rao-Scott Approach*

For the goodness-of-fit problem, Rao and Scott (1979, 1981) showed that $X^2(G)$ (and $G^2(G)$) is distributed asymptotically, under the null hypothesis, as a weighted sum $\delta_1 W_1 + \delta_2 W_2 + \cdots + \delta_{K-1} W_{K-1}$

of $K-1$ independent χ_1^2 random variables, denoted W_i, $i = 1, \ldots,$ $K-1$. The weights δ_i are eigenvalues of a deff matrix given by $\mathbf{P}^{-1}\mathbf{V}$, where $\mathbf{V}$ is as defined in the previous section and $\mathbf{P}$ is the multinomial covariance matrix corresponding to SRS, with H_0 true, i.e., $\mathbf{P} = (n_D^*)^{-1}(\text{diag}(\mathbf{p}_0) - \mathbf{p}_0\mathbf{p}_0')$. Here, n_D^* is the expected value of the number of units in domain D. When estimates are required, n_D^* is replaced by n_D. Note that the hypothetical binomial example given earlier is covered by the Rao-Scott theory, since the square of a large-sample binomial statistic is algebraically equivalent to the corresponding two-category goodness-of-fit X^2 and since the square of a standard normal random variable is a χ_1^2. Thus, the square of Z_{SRS} given in (1) will be distributed approximately as $\delta_1\chi_1^2$, where $\delta_1 = 20$, the simple deff obtained previously. When $K > 2$, the δ_i's, which are always positive, can be thought of as generalized deffs that take account of the multivariate nature of the problem. In fact, for $K > 2$, δ_1, the largest of the δ's, which are numbered in decreasing order, is the largest deff that can be obtained by taking a linear combination of the cell proportions, $\hat{p}_i$, $i = 1, \ldots, K-1$.

For SRS, the standard result is recovered. In this case, the matrix $\mathbf{V}$ will equal $\mathbf{P}$, the multinomial covariance matrix, so that $\mathbf{P}^{-1}\mathbf{V} = \mathbf{I}_{K-1}$, which implies that $\delta_i = 1$, $i = 1, \ldots, K-1$. The asymptotic distribution of $X^2(G)$ (and of $G^2(G)$) will thus be the sum of $K-1$ independent χ_1^2 random variables, which is equivalent to χ_{K-1}^2, a chi square on $K-1$ degrees of freedom. Rao and Scott (1979, 1981) illustrated the nature of the δ_i's for a number of well-known survey designs. For SRS without replacement, when the sampling fraction n/N cannot be ignored, the δ_i's are all equal to $(1 - n/N) < 1$. Thus, the Pearson statistic will be conservative in this case. An asymptotically valid test can be obtained for this sampling plan by referring $X^2(G)/(1 - n/N)$ to χ_{K-1}^2. For stratified random sampling under proportional allocation, $X^2(G)$ is again conservative. In contrast, under various models of two-stage sampling (Brier 1980; Rao and Scott 1979, 1981), Pearson's goodness-of-fit $X^2(G)$ is liberal, as expected.

As noted in the previous section, both the Wald and Fay procedures require detailed survey information from which the covariance matrix $\mathbf{V}$ can be estimated. Such detailed information is often not available. In secondary research from published tables, the best that the researcher can hope for is deffs for cells of the table and perhaps some information on deffs of marginal totals. Thus, an important challenge has been to find methods that can effectively use this limited information and yet provide acceptable tests. The first-order corrections proposed for the goodness-of-fit test and the two-way test of association (Rao and Scott 1979, 1981), and later for multiway tables (Rao and Scott 1982, 1984; Bedrick 1983; Rao and Scott 1987), achieve this. These are described below.

Rao-Scott first-order corrections. These are based on the observation that under the null hypothesis, the expected value of the asymptotic distribution of $X^2(G)$ is $\sum_{i=1}^{K-1} \delta_i$, so that $X^2(G)/\delta.$, where $\delta. = (\sum_{i=1}^{K-1} \delta_i)/(K-1)$, has the same expected value as χ^2_{K-1}, namely $K-1$. An approximate first-order corrected test can thus be obtained by referring $X^2(G)/\delta.$, the corrected Pearson statistic, to $\chi^2_{K-1}(\alpha)$. The individual δ_i's can all be estimated from the data once the full $\hat{V}$ is known. The advantage of the first-order correction, however, is that for the goodness-of-fit test, $\delta.$ can be estimated given only the diagonal elements of $\hat{V}$. In fact,

$$\hat{\delta}. = \frac{n_D}{K-1} \sum_{i=1}^{K} \frac{\hat{v}_{ii}}{p_{0i}} = \frac{1}{K-1} \sum_{i=1}^{K} \frac{\hat{p}_i}{p_{0i}} (1 - \hat{p}_i) \hat{d}_i, \qquad (10)$$

where $\hat{v}_{ii}$ represents the ith diagonal element of $\hat{V}$, and $\hat{d}_i = \hat{v}_{ii}/n_D^{-1}\hat{p}_i(1 - \hat{p}_i)$ is the estimated cell deff for the ith cell, defined independently of H_0. The formula (10) is particularly convenient for secondary data analysis, since estimated cell variances or deffs are often available with published tables. The likelihood ratio statistic can be corrected in the same way. For convenience, the discussion of the Rao-Scott approach will concentrate on corrected versions of $X^2(G)$.

Thomas and Rao (1987) showed that when the degrees of freedom, f, for estimating $\hat{V}$ is not large, the level control performance of the first-order corrected test, $X_c^2(G) = X^2(G)/\hat{\delta}.$, can be improved by treating $FX^2(G) = X_c^2(G)/(K-1)$ as an F variable on $K-1$ and f degrees of freedom. For a sample having two replicates per stratum (e.g., the CCSS), f can be taken as the number of strata. Otherwise, if the first-stage clusters were selected with replacement, or if the sampling fraction of clusters within strata is small, f can be taken as the number of sampled clusters less the number of strata.

It is important to note that the first-order corrected statistics do not involve n_D. They depend only on the weighted estimates $\hat{p}_i$ and their estimated variances $\hat{v}_{ii}$. For example,

$$X_c^2(G) = (K-1)\left(\sum_{i=1}^{K} \hat{v}_{ii}/p_{0i}\right)^{-1}\left(\sum_{i=1}^{K} (\hat{p}_i - p_{0i})^2/p_{0i}\right).$$

Second-order Rao-Scott corrections. When the full estimated covariance matrix $\hat{\mathbf{V}}$ is known, a better approximation to the asymptotic distribution of X^2 can be obtained using the Satterthwaite approximation, which has the same mean and the same variance as the asymptotic distribution of X^2. This second-order correction can be implemented by treating

$$X_S^2(G) = \frac{X^2(G)}{\hat{\delta}.(1 + \hat{a}^2)} = \frac{X_c^2(G)}{(1 + \hat{a}^2)}, \tag{11}$$

under the null hypothesis, as χ_ν^2, a chi-square random variable on $\nu = (K-1)/(1 + \hat{a}^2)$ degrees of freedom, with a corresponding form $G_S^2(G)$ for the likelihood ratio statistic. Here, $\hat{a}$, the coefficient of variation of the estimated δ_i's, is given by

$$\hat{a}^2 = \sum_{i=1}^{K-1} \hat{\delta}_i^2 / \left[(K-1)\hat{\delta}_.^2\right] - 1, \tag{12}$$

where $\hat{\delta}_i$ is the estimate of δ_i. Alternatively, it is possible to calculate $\hat{a}^2$ directly without evaluating the individual eigenvalues, since $\sum \hat{\delta}_i^2$ can be expressed in closed form as

$$\sum_{i=1}^{K-1} \hat{\delta}_i^2 = n_D^2 \sum_{i=1}^{K} \sum_{j=1}^{K} \hat{v}_{ij}^2 / p_{0i} p_{0j}. \tag{13}$$

Note that $X_S^2(G)$ also does not involve n_D. It depends only on the weighted estimates $\hat{p}_i$ and their full estimated covariance matrix $\hat{\mathbf{V}}$, as in the Wald statistic $X_W^2(G)$.

Thomas and Rao (1987) showed that when $\hat{a}$ is small, which implies that the $\hat{\delta}_i$'s and hence the δ_i's are of similar size, the first-order corrections provide good control of the level of the test. In fact, for $a = 0$, when the δ_i's are equal, the first-order corrections are asymptotically exact. However, when the variation among the δ_i's becomes appreciable (e.g., when $a = 0.5$, for $K = 5$), first-order corrections tend to become somewhat liberal. In this case, the second-order corrected tests provide good control of test level, as well as good power characteristics. On the basis of a goodness-of-fit Monte Carlo study,

Thomas and Rao (1987) recommended using the Satterthwaite procedure whenever the full $\hat{V}$ matrix is available. They also compared the performance of X^2 and G^2 versions of both Rao-Scott corrections and found no major differences.

If we assume that the level of the second-order Satterthwaite approximation is approximately equal to the nominal α level, then the actual levels of the X^2 and X_c^2 tests can be approximated by

$$P\left(X^2 \geq \chi^2_{(K-1),\alpha}\right) \doteq P\left(\chi_\nu^2 \geq \chi^2_{(K-1),\alpha}/\left[\hat{\delta}.\left(1 + \hat{a}^2\right)\right]\right) \qquad (14)$$

and

$$P\left(X_c^2 \geq \chi^2_{(K-1),\alpha}\right) \doteq P\left(\chi_\nu^2 \geq \chi^2_{(K-1),\alpha}/\left(1 + \hat{a}^2\right)\right). \qquad (15)$$

Residual analysis. Whenever H_0 is rejected, residual analysis can provide an understanding of the nature of the deviations from H_0. Standardized residuals can be defined as

$$\hat{e}_i = \frac{\hat{p}_i - p_{0i}}{\hat{v}_{ii}^{1/2}} = \frac{e_i}{\hat{d}_i^{1/2}}, \quad i = 1, \ldots, K, \qquad (16)$$

where the e_i's are standardized residuals under the assumption of SRS, i.e.,

$$e_i = \frac{\hat{p}_i - p_{0i}}{\sqrt{\hat{p}_i\left(1 - \hat{p}_i\right)/n_D}}, \qquad (17)$$

and the $\hat{d}_i$'s are the cell deffs, as defined in the text following equation (10). Cells that deviate from H_0 will be indicated by large values of $|\hat{e}_i|$. Clearly, if some of the $\hat{d}_i$'s are large, the use of SRS standardization could lead to erroneous interpretations of the test.

3.4. *Example*: *Goodness-of-Fit Test*

The CCSS dataset contains a variable called employment class, in which each respondent's occupation is categorized by its degree of management control and autonomy. Estimated proportions for this variable, taken from the Canadian, U.S., and Swedish surveys, are reported in Black and Myles (1986, Table 1B) for the domain of salaried employees. Suppose that we wish to test whether the Canadian and U.S. population proportions are the same. As described in section 4, this constitutes a test of homogeneity of proportions. Unfortunately,

TABLE 1

Estimated and Hypothesized Proportions, Deffs, and Residuals for Categories of Employment Class

	Estimated $\hat{p}_i$'s (Canada)	Hypothesized p_{0i}'s (U.S.)	Cell Deffs $(\hat{d}_i$'s)	Residuals $(\hat{e}_i$'s)
Decision-making managers	0.141	0.148	1.10	-0.72
Advisor-managers	0.034	0.052	1.96	-2.80
Supervisors	0.118	0.149	1.31	-3.20
Semi-autonomous workers	0.191	0.110	1.44	6.52
Workers	0.516	0.541	1.87	-1.35
$n_D = 1,463$				

this test could not be implemented, since the required design information on the U.S. survey was not readily available. The best that could be done was treat the U.S. estimates as fixed (i.e., as if they were population data) and perform a goodness-of-fit test. Table 1 presents "hypothesized" category proportions, estimated proportions, cell deffs, and standardized residuals for the five categories of the employment-class variable.

Using equations (6) and (10), we computed $X^2(G)$ and $\hat{\delta}$. to be 106.8 and 1.48 respectively, giving a first-order corrected statistic $X_c^2(G) = 72.3$. Though the correction has reduced $X^2(G)$ considerably, it is clear that when $X_c^2(G)$ is referred to $\chi_4^2(0.05) = 9.45$, the test still provides strong evidence against H_0. From the standardized residuals, it is evident that the proportions of decision-making managers and workers are similar in the two countries but that the number of semi-autonomous workers is higher in Canada than in the U.S. This is balanced by the proportions of advisor-managers and supervisors, both of which are significantly lower in Canada. Had we based the comparisons on the SRS-standardized residuals ($\sqrt{\hat{d}_i}\hat{e}_i$), the standardized value of the difference in the proportions of workers between the U.S. and Canada would have been 1.85, close to the 5 percent point for the standard normal, which might tempt some analysts to treat the difference as substantive. The design-standardized value of 1.35 clearly shows that this difference in the proportions of workers is not significant.

Using the BRR method of variance estimation outlined in section 2, we computed $\hat{V}$ to be

$$\hat{V} = 10^{-5} \begin{pmatrix} 9.063 & 0.557 & -0.375 & -1.230 & -8.015 \\ 0.557 & 4.328 & 1.622 & 0.114 & -6.622 \\ -0.375 & 1.622 & 9.288 & -3.739 & -6.796 \\ -1.230 & 0.114 & -3.739 & 15.163 & -10.308 \\ -8.015 & -6.622 & -6.796 & -10.308 & 31.741 \end{pmatrix},$$

$$(18)$$

giving $\hat{a}^2 = 0.182$ from equations (12) and (13). Thus, $X_S^2(G) = 63.02$ on $\nu = 3.38$ degrees of freedom. By interpolation from standard chi-square tables, we find that $\chi^2_{3.38}(0.05) = 8.45$, so that the second-order corrected test is again highly significant. Under the assumption that the second-order corrected test achieves a level equal to the nominal level of 5 percent, the approximate levels of the uncorrected X^2 and the first-order correction X_c^2 were obtained from (14) and (15) as 18.0 percent and 6.0 percent respectively. The correction is clearly worthwhile.

The Wald statistic (8) becomes $X_W^2(G) = 51.09$, which is smaller than both $X^2(G)$ and $X_c^2(G)$, though much larger than the 5 percent critical point. Thus, for these particular data, the inflation of the Wald statistic due to instabilities in $\hat{V}^{-1}$ is not in evidence. The F-based form of the Wald statistic becomes $F_W(G) = 11.0$, which when referred to $F_{4,144}(0.05) = 2.44$ is again highly significant.

4. TESTS ON TWO-WAY TABLES

Two classes of test for two-way tables will be considered, namely, tests of homogeneity of proportions and tests of association. In the stratified SRS context, a test of homogeneity arises when a table has one set of margins fixed by design, so that table proportions follow a product-multinomial distribution. For the SRS test of association, on the other hand, only the total sample size is fixed, so that the table proportions follow a multinomial distribution. It is well known that the likelihood function for a log-linear model is the same under both distributions (Bishop et al. 1975). Since most of the usual hypotheses of interest can be represented by log-linear models, there is no need to treat homogeneity and independence tests separately under SRS. This is not so for complex designs for which no convenient likelihood function can be specified. Though the Rao-Scott theory can be set up in a general form that includes both homogeneity and independence tests as special cases, these tests will be treated separately in this section. The general theory will be used in later sections to analyze ordinal log-linear models for two-way tables and general log-linear models for multi-way tables. The test of homogeneity will be discussed first because it follows most naturally from the discussion of the goodness-of-fit setup.

4.1. *Tests of Homogeneity of Proportions*

The comparison of proportions of some categorical variable realized in independent samples is termed a test of homogeneity of proportions. In complex sample surveys, tests of homogeneity can arise in several ways. For example, the comparison of proportions across regional strata within a single national survey and the comparison of proportions obtained in two or more different national surveys both constitute tests of homogeneity.

We will consider a test of the homogeneity of proportions of a K-category variable across R regions. The null hypothesis is given as

$$H_0: \mathbf{p}_1 = \mathbf{p}_2 = \cdots = \mathbf{p}_R, \tag{19}$$

where $\mathbf{p}_r$, $r = 1, \ldots, R$, denotes the $(K-1)$ vector of proportions in region r, having elements p_{ri}, $i = 1, \ldots, K-1$. A natural Pearson statistic for testing H_0 is given by

$$X^2(H) = n_D \sum_{r=1}^{R} \alpha_r \sum_{i=1}^{K} (\hat{p}_{ri} - \hat{p}_{+i})^2 / \hat{p}_{+i}, \tag{20}$$

where $\alpha_r = n_D(r)/n_D$, $n_D(r)$ is the number of domain units in region r, n_D is the total domain size given by $\sum_{r=1}^{R} n_D(r)$, $\hat{p}_{ri}$ is the estimate of p_{ri} based on weighted-up counts, and $\hat{p}_{+i} = \sum_{r=1}^{R} \alpha_i \hat{p}_{ri}$. If $n_D(r)$ is unknown, it is replaced by an estimate of its expected value given by $n(r)\hat{N}_D(r)/\hat{N}(r)$, where $\hat{N}(r)$ and $\hat{N}_D(r)$ are the sums of sample weights, in region r, of all units and of those units falling in domain D, respectively.

Scott and Rao (1981) showed that the asymptotic distribution of $X^2(H)$, under the null hypothesis, is of the form $\delta_1 W_1 + \cdots + \delta_{(R-1)(K-1)} W_{(R-1)(K-1)}$, where the W's are again independent chi-square random variables, each on one degree of freedom. For the case of two regions, the δ's will be estimated by $\hat{\delta}_i$, $i = 1, \ldots, (K-1)$, the eigenvalues of an estimated *generalized deff matrix* given by

$$\hat{\mathbf{D}}_H = n_D \big(\alpha_1 (1 - \alpha_1) \hat{\mathbf{P}}_+^{-1} \big) \big(\hat{\mathbf{V}}_1 + \hat{\mathbf{V}}_2 \big), \tag{21}$$

where $\hat{\mathbf{P}}_+ = \mathrm{diag}(\hat{\mathbf{p}}_+) - \hat{\mathbf{p}}_+ \hat{\mathbf{p}}'_+$, and $\hat{\mathbf{V}}_1, \hat{\mathbf{V}}_2$ are the estimated covariance matrices of $\hat{\mathbf{p}}_1$ and $\hat{\mathbf{p}}_2$ respectively. For the general case, the form of $\hat{\mathbf{D}}_H$ is more cumbersome, namely,

$$\hat{\mathbf{D}}_H = n_D \big(\mathbf{A} \otimes \hat{\mathbf{P}}_+^{-1} \big) \hat{\mathbf{\Delta}}_H, \tag{22}$$

where $\mathbf{A} = \mathrm{diag}(\boldsymbol{\alpha}) - \boldsymbol{\alpha}\boldsymbol{\alpha}'$, $\boldsymbol{\alpha} = (\alpha_1, \ldots, \alpha_{R-1})'$, and

$$\hat{\mathbf{\Delta}}_H = \bigoplus_{r=1}^{R-1} \hat{\mathbf{V}}_r + \hat{\mathbf{V}}_R \otimes \mathbf{J}_{R-1}. \tag{23}$$

Here, $\hat{\mathbf{V}}_r$, $r = 1, \ldots, R$, are estimated covariance matrices for each independent region, and $\mathbf{J}_{R-1}$ is an $(R-1) \times (R-1)$ matrix of ones. The symbol $\oplus_{r=1}^{R-1}$ denotes the direct sum of $R-1$ matrices, which results in a block diagonal matrix, with blocks $\hat{\mathbf{V}}_i$, $i = 1, \ldots, R-1$. The symbol $\otimes$ denotes the direct, or Kronecker, product, which for an $m \times m$ matrix $\mathbf{M}$, having elements m_{ij}, and a $q \times q$ matrix $\mathbf{Q}$, having elements q_{ij}, results in a block matrix of dimension $mq \times mq$, where the ijth block, $i = 1, \ldots, m$, $j = 1, \ldots, m$, is given by $m_{ij}\mathbf{Q}$.

Rao-Scott corrections. We can construct first-order corrections to $X^2(H)$ that require only a knowledge of the cell deffs within regions. For the general case of R regions, the mean of the estimated eigenvalues, $\hat{\delta}_.$, is given by

$$\hat{\delta}_. = \frac{1}{(K-1)(R-1)} \sum_{r=1}^{R} (1 - \alpha_r) \sum_{i=1}^{K} \frac{\hat{p}_{ri}}{\hat{p}_{+i}} (1 - \hat{p}_{ri}) \hat{d}_{r(i)}, \tag{24}$$

where $\hat{d}_{r(i)} = n_D \hat{v}_{r(ii)} / \hat{p}_{ri}(1 - \hat{p}_{ri})$ are the cell deffs for the ith region, $\hat{v}_{r(ii)}$ being the ith diagonal element of $\hat{\mathbf{V}}_r$. The first-order corrected test is then obtained by referring $X_c^2(H) = X^2(H)/\hat{\delta}_.$ to $\chi^2_{(R-1)(K-1)}(\alpha)$. As for the goodness-of-fit case, a second-order correction $X_S^2(H) = X_c^2(H)/(1 + \hat{a}^2)$ can be obtained, where $\hat{a}^2$ is again given by (12), with $\hat{\delta}_.$ replaced by (24), $\Sigma \hat{\delta}_i^2$ replaced by the trace $\hat{\mathbf{D}}_H^2$ (i.e., by the sum of the diagonal elements of $\hat{\mathbf{D}}_H^2$), and $(K-1)$ replaced by $(R-1)(K-1)$. It may be noted that $\hat{\delta}_.$ can be computed alternatively from $(R-1)(K-1)\hat{\delta}_. = \mathrm{tr}\,\hat{\mathbf{D}}_H$. Corresponding modifications to G^2 can be similarly defined.

Note that both $X_c^2(H)$ and $X_S^2(H)$ do not involve the domain sample sizes $n_D(r)$ but only the weighted estimates $\hat{p}_{ri}$ and their estimated variances $\hat{v}_{r(ii)}$ in the case of $X_c^2(H)$ and the estimated covariance matrix $\hat{\mathbf{V}}_r$ in the case of $X_S^2(H)$.

A Wald test. An asymptotically exact Wald test of the homogeneity hypothesis is obtained by referring $X_W^2(H)$ to $\chi^2_{(R-1)(K-1)}(\alpha)$, where

$$X_W^2(H) = \hat{\mathbf{q}}' \hat{\boldsymbol{\Delta}}_H^{-1} \hat{\mathbf{q}} \tag{25}$$

with $\hat{\mathbf{q}}' = ((\hat{\mathbf{p}}_1 - \hat{\mathbf{p}}_R)', (\hat{\mathbf{p}}_2 - \hat{\mathbf{p}}_R)', (\hat{\mathbf{p}}_{(R-1)} - \hat{\mathbf{p}}_R)')$. This Wald test is prone to the same stability problems as the goodness-of-fit Wald test, though detailed Monte Carlo evidence is not available. An F-based version can be constructed by referring

$$F_W(H) = \left(\frac{f - (R-1)(K-1) + 1}{f(R-1)(K-1)} \right) X_W^2(H)$$

to an F distribution on $(R-1)(K-1)$ and $(f - (R-1)(K-1) + 1)$ degrees of freedom. No empirical study of the performance of this modified test has been carried out.

Standardized residuals. Standardized deviations of each element of $\hat{\mathbf{p}}_r$ from $\hat{\mathbf{p}}_+$, the estimated overall proportion under H_0, can again be defined as adjuncts to a rejection of H_0. These standardized residuals, which have an approximate standard normal distribution under H_0, are given by

$$\hat{e}_{ri} = (\hat{p}_{ri} - \hat{p}_{+i})/\sqrt{\operatorname{var}(\hat{p}_{ri} - \hat{p}_{+i})}, \qquad r = 1, \ldots, R, \qquad i = 1, \ldots, K, \tag{26}$$

where

$$\operatorname{var}(\hat{p}_{ri} - \hat{p}_{+i}) = \frac{1}{n_D^2} (\hat{p}_{+i}(1 - \hat{p}_{+i}))$$

$$\times \left\{ \frac{n_D(n_D - 2n_D(r))}{n_D(r)} \hat{d}_{r(i)} + \sum_{l=1}^{R} n_D(l) \hat{d}_{l(i)} \right\}. \tag{27}$$

Example: Test of homogeneity, $R = 2$. Consider the hypothesis that there is no difference in the distributions of employment class between Eastern and Western Canada. Eastern Canada is defined as the three survey regions consisting of the Atlantic provinces, Quebec, and

TABLE 2

Estimated Proportions, Deffs, and Residuals for Employment Class Within Region

	Proportions $\hat{p}_r$, $r = 1, 2$		Regional Deffs $\hat{d}_{(r)}$, $r = 1, 2$		Std. Residuals $\hat{e}_r$, $r = 1, 2$	
	East	West	East	West	East	West
Decision-making managers	0.134	0.160	0.84	1.77	−1.01	1.01
Advisor-managers	0.033	0.035	2.37	0.91	−0.21	0.21
Supervisors	0.111	0.138	1.11	1.66	−1.18	1.18
Semi-autonomous workers	0.194	0.180	1.17	2.26	0.46	−0.46
Workers	0.528	0.487	1.38	3.34	0.83	−0.83
$n_D(1) = 1,054$						
$n_D(2) = 409$						

Ontario, and Western Canada consists of the three Western survey regions, namely the Prairie provinces, Alberta, and British Columbia. Since design strata in the CCSS are subsets of the above six regions, and since poststratification is carried out separately within these six regions, the East/West split constitutes two independent samples. Separate BRR variance estimations were performed for East and West, using 17 design strata in each. Table 2 lists the estimated proportions, the cell deffs, and the standardized residuals for both East and West.

$X^2(H)$ and $\hat{\delta}_.$ were computed as 4.47 and 1.76 from equations (20) and (24) respectively, giving a first-order corrected statistic $X_c^2(H) = 2.54$. Compared with a nominal 5 percent critical value $\chi_4^2(0.05) = 9.45$, $X^2(H)$ and hence $X_c^2(H)$ are not significant. Thus, there is no reason to doubt the East/West equality of employment-class proportions. The squared coefficient of variation, $\hat{a}^2$, of the eigenvalues of the deff matrix (21) was computed as 0.267, giving a second-order corrected test statistic $X_S^2(H) = 2.00$. This must be referred to a chi-square distribution on $\nu = 3.16$ degrees of freedom, for which the interpolated 5 percent critical value is 8.08. Thus, $X_S^2(H)$ also is not significant. From equations (14) and (15), with $K - 1$ changed to $(R - 1)(K - 1)$, the actual levels of $X^2(H)$ and $X_c^2(H)$, corresponding to a nominal 5 percent test, are approximately 25.6 percent and 6.5 percent respectively. Clearly, corrected tests are required for these data, and it can be seen that the first-order correction results in an actual level that is close to the nominal test level. In this specific example, of course, since the $X^2(H)$ test is not significant, the analysis could have been immediately terminated. The Wald statistic was computed to be $X_W^2(H) = 3.51$, which is smaller than $X^2(H)$. Once again, the Wald statistic shows no evidence of instability for these data.

Cell residuals are not normally of interest when the null hypothesis is not rejected. Those listed in Table 2 merely confirm that the data show no large deviations from H_0.

4.2. Tests of Independence

Consider a two-way cross-classification of variables A and B, having I and J categories respectively, in some domain D containing n_D sample units. Let $p_{ij} = N_D(ij)/N_D$ be the population proportions in the ijth cell of domain D, estimated by $\hat{p}_{ij} = \hat{N}_D(ij)/\hat{N}_D$, where the hats denote estimates of domain totals based on weighted-up counts. Also, let $\hat{p}_{i+} = \Sigma_{j=1}^J \hat{p}_{ij}$, $i = 1, \ldots, I$, and $\hat{p}_{+j} = \Sigma_{i=1}^I \hat{p}_{ij}$, $j = 1, \ldots, J$, be estimates of the row and column marginal proportions, p_{i+} and p_{+j}, respectively. The hypothesis of independence can be stated as

$$H_0: \; p_{ij} = p_{i+} p_{+j}, \qquad i = 1, \ldots, I, \qquad j = 1, \ldots, J. \tag{28}$$

The appropriate Pearson X^2 statistic for testing H_0, using estimated proportions, is given by

$$X^2(I) = n_D \sum_{i=1}^I \sum_{j=1}^J \frac{\left(\hat{p}_{ij} - \hat{p}_{i+}\hat{p}_{+j}\right)^2}{\hat{p}_{i+}\hat{p}_{+j}}. \tag{29}$$

An alternative matrix expression for $X^2(I)$ can be given, in terms of

$$\hat{h}_{ij} = \hat{p}_{ij} - \hat{p}_{i+}\hat{p}_{+j}, \qquad i = 1, \ldots, I, \qquad j = 1, \ldots, J,$$

i.e., the residual differences between the observed proportions and their estimated expected values under H_0;

$$\hat{\mathbf{h}} = \left(\hat{h}_{11}, \ldots, \hat{h}_{1,(J-1)}, \ldots, \hat{h}_{(I-1),1}, \ldots, \hat{h}_{(I-1),(J-1)} \right)',$$

i.e., a vector of residuals of length $(I-1)(J-1)$;

$$\hat{\mathbf{p}}_{I+} = \left(\hat{p}_{1+}, \ldots, \hat{p}_{(I-1)+} \right)',$$

$$\hat{\mathbf{p}}_{+J} = \left(\hat{p}_{+1}, \ldots, \hat{p}_{+(J-1)} \right)',$$

i.e., both vectors of marginal proportions, of length $(I-1)$ and $(J-1)$

respectively; and

$$\hat{\mathbf{P}}_I = \text{diag}(\hat{\mathbf{p}}_{I+}) - \hat{\mathbf{p}}_{I+}\hat{\mathbf{p}}'_{I+},$$

$$\hat{\mathbf{P}}_J = \text{diag}(\hat{\mathbf{p}}_{+J}) - \hat{\mathbf{p}}_{+J}\hat{\mathbf{p}}'_{+J}.$$

Then

$$X^2(I) = n_D\hat{\mathbf{h}}'\big(\hat{\mathbf{P}}_I^{-1} \otimes \hat{\mathbf{P}}_J^{-1}\big)\hat{\mathbf{h}}, \qquad (30)$$

where $\otimes$ again denotes the direct product. With the Pearson statistic expressed in this form, it has been shown (see Rao and Scott 1979, 1981) that $X^2(I)$ will be distributed asymptotically, under the null hypothesis, as a weighted sum $\delta_1 W_1 + \cdots + \delta_{(I-1)(J-1)} W_{(I-1)(J-1)}$, where the δ's are estimated by the eigenvalues of the estimated deff matrix

$$\hat{\mathbf{D}}_I = \big(\hat{\mathbf{P}}_I^{-1} \otimes \hat{\mathbf{P}}_J^{-1}\big)\hat{\mathbf{V}}_h. \qquad (31)$$

Here, $\hat{\mathbf{V}}_h$ is the estimated covariance matrix of $\hat{\mathbf{h}}$, the vector of residuals. For the CCSS, $\hat{\mathbf{V}}_h$ was obtained directly using the BRR method of variance estimation, which involves evaluating $\hat{\mathbf{h}}$ on each of 36 pseudo half-samples. For the CHS, $\hat{\mathbf{V}}_h$ was estimated by approximating the design as sampling with probability proportional to size (PPS) with replacement, within strata, and applying Taylor series linearization to take account of both the poststratification and the nonlinear relationship between $\hat{\mathbf{h}}$ and the $\hat{p}_{ij}$'s. Details are given by Hidiroglou and Rao (1987).

Rao-Scott corrections to $X^2(I)$. A first-order correction to the Pearson statistic can again be obtained by dividing $X^2(I)$ by $\hat{\delta}_.$, the mean of the eigenvalues of the generalized deff matrix (31). For the independence test described above, the deff matrix is defined in terms of $\hat{\mathbf{V}}_h$, the estimated covariance matrix of $\hat{\mathbf{h}}$, unlike the goodness-of-fit and homogeneity tests, in which the generalized deffs are functions of $\hat{\mathbf{V}}$, the estimated covariance matrix of the $\hat{p}$'s themselves. Information on $\hat{\mathbf{V}}_h$ is never available with published tables. As noted earlier, some information on $\hat{\mathbf{V}}$ may be available in the form of deffs for cells, and possibly for the marginals, of the table in question. Estimates of $\hat{\delta}_.$, the mean of the eigenvalues of $\hat{\mathbf{D}}(I)$, which depend only on this partial information on $\hat{\mathbf{V}}$, have been given by Rao and Scott (1982, 1984), Bedrick (1983), and Gross (1984). The Rao-Scott and Bedrick results also cover estimation of $\delta.$ for multi-way tables and will be discussed in more detail in the next section. For the independence test on a two-way table,

$$\hat{\delta}. = \frac{1}{(I-1)(J-1)} \sum_{i=1}^{I} \sum_{j=1}^{J} \frac{\hat{p}_{ij}(1-\hat{p}_{ij})}{\hat{p}_{i+}\hat{p}_{+j}} \hat{d}_{ij} - \sum_{i=1}^{I} (1-\hat{p}_{i+})\hat{d}_{A(i)}$$

$$- \sum_{j=1}^{J} (1-\hat{p}_{+j})\hat{d}_{B(j)}, \qquad (32)$$

where

$$\hat{d}_{ij} = \text{estvar}(\hat{p}_{ij})/\left(n_D^{-1}\hat{p}_{ij}(1-\hat{p}_{ij})\right) \qquad (33)$$

is the (i, j)th cell deff, and

$$\hat{d}_{A(i)} = \text{estvar}(\hat{p}_{i+})/\left(n_D^{-1}\hat{p}_{i+}(1-\hat{p}_{i+})\right)$$

$$\hat{d}_{B(j)} = \text{estvar}(\hat{p}_{+j})/\left(n_D^{-1}\hat{p}_{+j}(1-\hat{p}_{+j})\right) \qquad (34)$$

are the deffs of the ith row and jth column margin, respectively. The first-order corrected test now consists of referring $X_c^2(I) = X^2(I)/\hat{\delta}.$ to $\chi_{(I-1)(J-1)}^2(\alpha)$.

When the full estimated covariance matrix of the $\hat{p}_{ij}$'s is known, the covariance matrix of $\hat{\mathbf{h}}$ can be estimated via the Taylor series approach as $\hat{\mathbf{H}}'\hat{\mathbf{V}}\hat{\mathbf{H}}$, where $\hat{\mathbf{H}}$ is the matrix of partial derivatives of $\mathbf{h}$ with respect to p_{ij}, $i = 1,\ldots,(I-1)$, $j = 1,\ldots,(J-1)$, evaluated at $p_{ij} = \hat{p}_{ij}$. Alternatively, if sample estimates are available at the primary cluster level or at the replicate level, $\hat{\mathbf{V}}_h$ can be estimated directly via the BRR or some other sample re-use method, such as the jackknife. A second-order Rao-Scott statistic, given by $X_S^2(I) = X_c^2/(1 + \hat{a})$, can then be obtained, where $\hat{a}^2$ is given by (12), with $\hat{\delta}.$ replaced by (32), $\Sigma\hat{\delta}_i^2$ replaced by

$$\sum_{l=1}^{(I-1)(J-1)} \hat{\delta}_l^2 = \sum_{i,i'}^{I-1} \sum_{j,j'}^{J-1} \hat{v}_{h,ij,i'j'}^2 / (\hat{p}_{i+}\hat{p}_{+j})(\hat{p}_{i'+}\hat{p}_{+j'}), \qquad (35)$$

and $(K-1)$ replaced by $(I-1)(J-1)$, where $\hat{v}_{h,ij,i'j'}$ is the element of $\hat{\mathbf{V}}_h$ corresponding to the covariance of $\hat{p}_{ij}$ and $\hat{p}_{i'j'}$. The second-order test procedure refers $X_S^2(I)$ to $\chi_\nu^2(\alpha)$, where $\nu = (I-1)(J-1)/(1+\hat{a}^2)$.

Note that $X_c^2(I)$ does not involve n_D and depends only on the weighted estimates $\hat{p}_{ij}$, $\hat{p}_{i+}$, and $\hat{p}_{+j}$, as well as their variances.

Similarly, $X_S^2(I)$ does not depend on n_D, though in addition to the above-mentioned weighted estimates and variances, it requires full knowledge of the relevant estimated covariances. Similar properties hold for the Rao-Scott tests on multi-way tables, which will be described in section 5.

A Wald test. A convenient Wald test procedure consists of referring

$$X_W^2(I) = n_D \hat{\mathbf{h}}' \hat{\mathbf{V}}_h^{-1} \hat{\mathbf{h}} \tag{36}$$

to $\chi^2_{(I-1)(J-1)}(\alpha)$. An F-based version of this test, analogous to (9), refers

$$F_W(I) = \left(\frac{f - (I-1)(J-1) + 1}{f(I-1)(J-1)} \right) X_W^2(I) \tag{37}$$

to an F distribution on $(I-1)(J-1)$ and $(f - (I-1)(J-1) + 1)$ degrees of freedom. No empirical results are available on the type I error control and power of this modified test, though it is expected to be more stable than $X_W^2(I)$.

Standardized residuals. Standardized residuals that have approximate standard normal distributions when H_0 is true are given by

$$\hat{e}_{ij} = e_{ij} / \left\{ \hat{d}_{h,ij} \right\}^{1/2}, \tag{38}$$

where the

$$e_{ij} = \hat{h}_{ij} / \left\{ \hat{p}_{i+} \hat{p}_{+j} (1 - \hat{p}_{i+})(1 - \hat{p}_{+j}) \right\}^{1/2} \tag{39}$$

are the standardized residuals defined under an assumption of SRS and

$$\hat{d}_{h,ij} = \hat{v}_{h,ij,ij} / \left\{ n_D^{-1} \hat{p}_{i+} \hat{p}_{+j} (1 - \hat{p}_{i+})(1 - \hat{p}_{+j}) \right\}^{1/2} \tag{40}$$

are the estimated deffs of the residuals, $\hat{h}_{ij}$, under H_0.

Example: Test of independence, 5×2 table. Consider the null hypothesis of no association between employment class and sex for the domain of salaried employees. Table 3 presents estimated cell proportions and their deffs for the relevant 5×2 table.

For the employment-class variable, the marginal proportions $\hat{p}_{i+}$ and corresponding deffs $\hat{d}_{A(i)}$ are the same as those reported for the goodness-of-fit example, namely (0.141, 0.034, 0.118, 0.190, 0.516) and (1.09, 1.95, 1.30, 1.44, 1.86) respectively. Estimated marginal proportions $\hat{p}_{+j}$ and corresponding deffs $\hat{d}_{B(j)}$ for the sex variable are (0.540, 0.460) and (1.29, 1.29) respectively. The marginal deff for sex, equal to

TABLE 3
Estimated Proportions and Deffs for Employment Class by Sex

	Estimated Proportions ($\hat{p}_{ij}$'s)		Deffs of $\hat{p}_{ij}$'s ($\hat{d}_{ij}$'s)	
	Males	Females	Males	Females
Decision-making managers	0.103	0.038	1.20	1.31
Advisor-managers	0.018	0.016	0.74	1.95
Supervisors	0.075	0.043	1.81	0.92
Semi-autonomous workers	0.105	0.085	0.71	1.85
Workers	0.239	0.278	1.42	1.15
$n_D = 1,463$				

1.29, is smaller than the average of the marginal deffs for employment class, equal to 1.53, probably because of the variance-reducing effect of the age/sex poststratification. From (29), the unadjusted Pearson statistic was computed to be $X^2(I) = 54.8$, clearly significant at the traditional 5 percent level ($\chi_4^2(0.05) = 9.49$). From (32) and the data of Table 3, the average of the eigenvalues of the generalized deff matrix $\hat{\mathbf{D}}_I$ was computed as $\hat{\delta}_. = 1.11$, giving a first-order corrected statistic $X_c^2(I) = 50.0$, again significant. The effect of the clustering in this case is moderate; from (14), with $(K-1)$ replaced by $(I-1)(J-1)$, the estimated level of the unadjusted X^2 is 8.8 percent, not a serious inflation. The level for the first-order X_c^2 statistic is 6.6 percent.

Holt, Scott, and Ewings (1980), in their analysis of the British Household Survey, noted that the inflation due to clustering is often less for tests of independence than for tests of goodness of fit or for tests of homogeneity. This observation appears to apply to the CCSS examples studied so far, though in the above case, a contributory factor may be the inclusion of the poststratifying sex variable.

The values of the second-order adjusted test and the Wald test were calculated as $X_S^2(I) = 38.4$, on $\nu = 3.07$ degrees of freedom, and $X_W^2(I) = 35.6$, respectively, both significant at the 5 percent level.

Though the effect of violation of the SRS assumption on the 5 percent critical point of $X^2(I)$ is not serious in this case, the asymptotic distribution of $X^2(I)$ still differs markedly from the χ_4^2 form it would have under SRS. The actual eigenvalues of the generalized deff matrix

TABLE 4

Residuals and Deffs for Employment Class by Sex

	Residuals ($\hat{h}_{ij}$'s)		Deffs ($\hat{d}_{h,ij}$'s)		Std. Residuals ($\hat{e}_{ij}$'s)	
	Males	Females	Males	Females	Males	Females
Decision-making managers	0.0268	−0.0268	1.14	1.14	5.53	−5.53
Advisor-managers	−0.0001	−0.0001	0.71	0.71	−0.05	0.05
Supervisors	0.0113	−0.0113	1.35	1.35	2.30	−2.30
Semi-autonomous workers	0.0021	−0.0021	0.84	0.84	0.45	−0.45
Workers	−0.0401	0.0401	1.69	1.69	−4.74	4.74
$n_D = 1,463$						

(31) are, in decreasing order, 2.06, 1.06, 0.85, and 0.42, giving a coefficient of variation $\hat{a} = 0.55$. One effect of this large variation in the eigenvalues, which would all equal one under SRS, is that the relative inflation of the true level of $X^2(I)$ becomes progressively greater as the α level of the test is decreased. For example, for a 1 percent test, the estimated true level of $X^2(I)$ corresponding to $\hat{\delta}. = 1.11$ is 2.7 percent, nearly three times the nominal value. For the first-order corrected test, the estimated level is 1.8 percent, still an appreciable inflation in relative terms.

Results pertaining to the residual analysis are shown in Table 4. The residuals and their deffs are given, together with standardized residuals that take account of the design. Note that the residuals, standardized and unstandardized, sum to zero across sex and that the deffs are the same for both sexes. The residual analysis clearly shows that the statistically significant sex difference in employment-class proportions is most marked in the decision management and worker categories and that the direction of the difference favors the males in the former case and the females in the latter. There are also proportionately more male than female supervisors, though this difference is not so striking. Use of unstandardized residuals in this example would have led to some distortions, but no incorrect inferences, since the workers category, which has the largest deff, also has a very large residual.

5. LOG-LINEAR ANALYSIS OF TWO-WAY AND MULTI-WAY TABLES

Log-linear models provide a versatile method of analyzing nominal and ordinal data tables. This section of the paper will describe how to apply the general log-linear model to data from complex surveys. The methodology will be illustrated on two problems: (a) the analysis of a two-way table in which one of the variables is ordinal, and (b) the testing of specific hypotheses on three-way tables.

So far in this paper, we have discussed all hypotheses in terms of the finite population proportions, $\mathbf{p}$, with inferences based on the randomization induced by the survey design. This is the design-based approach to inference in sample surveys, advocated for example by Kish and Frankel (1974). As described by Nathan (1981), some authors prefer to consider hypotheses relating to the parameters of a hypothetical *superpopulation* model and to regard the finite population of interest as a sample from this infinite superpopulation. This model-based view of the hypothesis-testing framework is particularly appealing in the context of general log-linear models, given their superficial similarity to classical linear models. Fortunately, these two views of hypothesis testing are not in conflict, since as noted by Pfefferman and Nathan (1985), the design-based inferences applied in this paper also constitute inference on the parameters of the infinite superpopulation, provided that the finite population is large, in which case the finite population proportions, $\mathbf{p}$, will be close to their superpopulation analogues, $\boldsymbol{\pi}$. Thus, in our discussion of the log-linear model, we will consider a parameter vector, $\boldsymbol{\pi}$, which can represent either a vector of finite population cell proportions or a vector of superpopulation cell probabilities. This duality also applies to the tests of goodness of fit, homogeneity of proportions, and independence described earlier.

5.1. *The General Log-Linear Model*

We consider a multi-way cross-classification of nominal and/or ordinal variables, defined on some domain D containing n_D survey units. To simplify notation, the cells in the general multi-way table will be numbered in lexicographic order, as $t = 1, \ldots, T$, where T is the total number of cells. For example, in a $2 \times 2 \times 2$ table, where each variable takes on levels 1 and 2, the ordering of the cells corresponding to the lexicographic order, $t = 1, \ldots, 8$, will be 111, 112, 121, 122, 211, 212, 221, 222, with an obvious extension to higher-order tables having two or more levels per variable.

The $T \times 1$ vector π, representing cell proportions or probabilities, can be represented as a general log-linear model of the form

$$\ln(\pi) = \tilde{u}(\theta)1 + X\theta, \tag{41}$$

where $\ln(\pi)$ denotes a $T \times 1$ vector of log probabilities with elements $\ln(\pi_t)$, $t = 1, \ldots, T$; 1 denotes a $T \times 1$ vector of ones; X denotes a $T \times r$ matrix of full column rank ($r \leq T - 1$), with $X'1 = 0$; and θ is an $r \times 1$ vector of parameters. The term $\tilde{u}(\theta)$ is a normalizing constant which ensures that $\sum \pi_t = 1$. It can be written explicitly as $\tilde{u}(\theta) = \ln\{1/1'\exp(X\theta)\}$, where $\exp(X\theta)$ denotes a $T \times 1$ vector having elements $\exp(x_t'\theta)$, and x_t' is the tth row of the design matrix X.

As an example of a log-linear model, consider a 3×2 contingency table with cell proportions (or probabilities) π_{ij}, $i = 1, 2, 3$, $j = 1, 2$. For this simple example, the traditional cell-indexing notation will be used. In the notation of Bishop et al. (1975), the log-linear model for these proportions can be written as

$$\ln(\pi_{ij}) = \tilde{u} + u_{1(i)} + u_{2(j)} + u_{12(ij)}, \qquad i = 1, 2, 3, \qquad j = 1, 2, \tag{42}$$

where the u parameters satisfy the side constraints

$$\sum_i u_{1(i)} = \sum_j u_{2(j)} = \sum_i u_{12(ij)} = \sum_j u_{12(ij)} = 0. \tag{43}$$

There is no unique way of expressing θ in terms of the u's. A standard choice is

$$\theta = \left(u_{1(1)}, u_{1(2)}, u_{2(1)}, u_{12(11)}, u_{12(21)} \right)'. \tag{44}$$

The omitted parameters $u_{1(3)}$, $u_{2(2)}$, $u_{12(12)}$, $u_{12(22)}$, $u_{12(31)}$, and $u_{12(32)}$ can be expressed in terms of the elements of θ using the side conditions (43). In this case, the model (42) can be written in the general form (41), with

$$X = \begin{pmatrix} 1 & 0 & 1 & 1 & 0 \\ 1 & 0 & -1 & -1 & 0 \\ 0 & 1 & 1 & 0 & 1 \\ 0 & 1 & -1 & 0 & -1 \\ -1 & -1 & 1 & -1 & -1 \\ -1 & -1 & -1 & 1 & 1 \end{pmatrix}. \tag{45}$$

A systematic method of generating $\mathbf{X}$ matrices of this type is described in the appendix. This particular matrix has maximum rank $r = T - 1 = 5$ and corresponds to the so-called saturated model, which is not strictly a model but merely a re-expression of the data. A variety of models can, however, be obtained from (45) simply by dropping appropriate columns. If the last two columns are dropped, the resulting log-linear model corresponds to the classical hypothesis of independence of row and column proportions, with $\theta = (u_{1(1)}, u_{1(2)}, u_{2(1)})'$. Further details can be found in Bishop et al. (1975).

5.2. Estimation and Testing Under Complex Designs

Pseudo ML estimators. Under an SRS design, the parameter vector, θ, for a general log-linear model can be estimated by solving the ML equations corresponding to the multinomial distribution, given in matrix terms by

$$\mathbf{X}'\hat{\boldsymbol{\pi}}_{\text{SRS}} = \mathbf{X}'\tilde{\mathbf{p}}, \tag{46}$$

where $\tilde{\mathbf{p}}$ is the vector of unweighted proportions of sample units in each of the $t = 1, \ldots, T$ cells of the table, and $\hat{\boldsymbol{\pi}}_{\text{SRS}}$ is the vector of maximum likelihood estimates (MLEs) of π. Since π satisfies the log-linear model (41), the smoothed estimate $\hat{\boldsymbol{\pi}}_{\text{SRS}}$ will be a function of $\hat{\theta}_{\text{SRS}}$, the MLE of the model parameter vector θ. Iterative solution of these equations via the Newton-Raphson algorithm is now standard in most computer packages. This method of solution converges faster than the alternative method of iterative proportional fitting (IPF) and has the additional advantage over IPF of directly yielding the estimated parameter vector, $\hat{\theta}_{\text{SRS}}$, along with its covariance matrix (Haberman 1978).

As noted earlier, ML methods are not feasible when the data come from complex surveys because of the lack of a convenient likelihood function. For the analyses discussed to date, test statistics were based on weighted-up proportions and then suitably adjusted to account for the design. For the general log-linear model, the analogous approach is to replace $\tilde{\mathbf{p}}$ in (46) by $\hat{\mathbf{p}}$, the vector of weighted-up cell proportions, to create a set of *pseudo* ML equations,

$$\mathbf{X}'\hat{\boldsymbol{\pi}} = \mathbf{X}'\hat{\mathbf{p}}, \tag{47}$$

where $\hat{\boldsymbol{\pi}}$ is the vector of pseudo MLEs of the cell proportions, or probabilities, π. Because $\hat{p}$ is a consistent estimator of π under the survey design, the smoothed estimate $\hat{\pi} = \hat{\pi}(\hat{\theta})$, obtained by solving (47), will also be a consistent estimator of π, assuming the model (41) is true. The approach outlined above is analogous to using ordinary least squares when the errors are not independent, a situation that is explored in detail for survey data by Scott and Holt (1982).

Test statistics for model fit. No log-linear model technique is complete without a test of the goodness of fit of the model. A suitable test for a model specified by a design matrix $\mathbf{X}$, having rank $r < T$, is given by a Pearson-type statistic defined in terms of the pseudo MLEs, $\hat{\pi}$, and the weighted-up proportions, $\hat{p}$, as

$$X^2(L) = n_D \sum_{t=1}^{T} (\hat{p}_t - \hat{\pi}_t)^2 / \hat{\pi}_t. \tag{48}$$

A statistic analogous to the multinomial likelihood ratio, G^2, can be defined as

$$G^2(L) = 2 n_D \sum_{t=1}^{T} \hat{\pi}_t \ln(\hat{p}_t / \hat{\pi}_t). \tag{49}$$

Rao-Scott theory. Rao and Scott (1984) showed that both $X^2(L)$ and $G^2(L)$ are distributed asymptotically, under the specified log-linear model, as weighted sums of $T - r - 1$ independent χ_1^2 random variables; i.e.,

$$X^2(L) \text{ and } G^2(L) \sim \sum_{t=1}^{T-r-1} \delta_t W_t, \tag{50}$$

where the χ_1^2 random variables are denoted W_t, and the weights, δ_t, are eigenvalues of a generalized deff matrix, a distributional result that is similar to those obtained previously for goodness of fit, homogeneity, and independence. The generalized deff matrix corresponding to the log-linear model (41) is given by

$$\hat{\mathbf{D}}_L = (\tilde{\mathbf{Z}}'\hat{\mathbf{P}}\tilde{\mathbf{Z}})^{-1}(\tilde{\mathbf{Z}}'\hat{\mathbf{V}}\tilde{\mathbf{Z}}), \tag{51}$$

where $\hat{\mathbf{P}} = n_D^{-1} (\text{diag}(\hat{\pi}) - \hat{\pi}\hat{\pi}')$ is the multinomial covariance matrix corresponding to the pseudo MLE, $\hat{\pi}$, for the model (41). Here, $\hat{\mathbf{V}}$ is the estimated covariance matrix of $\hat{p}$, under the complex design, and

$$\tilde{\mathbf{Z}} = \left(\mathbf{I} - \mathbf{X}(\mathbf{X}'\hat{\mathbf{P}}\mathbf{X})^{-1}\mathbf{X}'\hat{\mathbf{P}} \right)\mathbf{Z}, \tag{52}$$

where $\mathbf{Z}$ is a matrix of dimension $T \times (T - r - 1)$ such that $(\mathbf{1}, \mathbf{X}, \mathbf{Z})$ is nonsingular, and $1'Z = 0$; i.e., the columns of Z are contrasts. Z is often referred to as the completion of X, since adjoining it to X results in a saturated model. For the 3×2 independence example given above, Z could be taken as the last two omitted columns. With this choice, it is easy to verify that $Z'X = 0$, in which case an alternative form of $\hat{D}_L$ can be used, which does not require the transformation (52). It is given by

$$\hat{D}_L(A) = \left(Z'D_{\hat{\pi}}^{-1}Z\right)^{-1}\left(Z'D_{\hat{\pi}}^{-1}\hat{V}D_{\hat{\pi}}^{-1}Z\right), \tag{53}$$

where $D_{\hat{\pi}}$ is the diagonal matrix having diagonal elements $\hat{\pi}_t$, $t = 1, \ldots, T$.

Provided that an estimate of the covariance matrix, V, of the weighted-up counts, $\hat{p}$, is available, both first- and second-order corrections for $X^2(L)$ and $G^2(L)$ can be obtained by calculating the required adjustment parameters, $\hat{\delta}$. and $\hat{a}^2$, from the eigenvalues of $\hat{D}_L$. In practice, whenever $\hat{V}$ is known, one will always choose the second-order correction. Rao and Scott (1982, 1984) and Bedrick (1983) showed that closed-form expressions for $\hat{\delta}$., which do not require full knowledge of $\hat{V}$, can be obtained for all log-linear models that possess direct estimates, i.e., those models for which the solutions of the pseudo ML equations (47) can be written as explicit functions of the data $\hat{p}$. This method of obtaining first-order corrected statistics (denoted $X_c^2(L)$ and $G_c^2(L)$) will be described in section 5.4. It should also be noted that $\hat{a}^2$ can be obtained as before from equation (12), with (13) replaced by the trace of $\hat{D}_L^2$, and $(K - 1)$ replaced by $T - r - 1$. This approach avoids direct computation of the eigenvalues of $\hat{D}_L$, though the computational advantage of this on a modern computer system is slight. Whichever method is used, the computation of $\hat{a}^2$ requires that the full $\hat{V}$ matrix be known.

A Wald test of model fit. Whenever an estimate, $\hat{V}$, of the covariance matrix of $\hat{p}$ is available, a goodness-of-fit Wald statistic can be constructed that is asymptotically $\chi^2_{(T-r-1)}$ under the model (41). Consider the saturated model corresponding to (41), written in the form

$$\ln(\pi) = \tilde{u}(\theta)1 + X\theta + Z\theta_Z, \tag{54}$$

where θ_Z is a $(T - r - 1) \times 1$ vector of parameters. The test of goodness of fit of model (41) is thus equivalent to

$$H_{01}: \theta_Z = 0.$$

Further, if Z satisfies $Z'1 = 0$, and $Z'X = 0$, then H_{01} is equivalent to

$$H_{02}: Z'\ln(\pi) = \phi = 0,$$

where ϕ is a vector of dimension $(T - r - 1) \times 1$. A Wald statistic for testing H_{02} is then obtained by referring

$$X_W^2(L) = \hat{\phi}'(\hat{D}(\hat{\phi}))^{-1}\hat{\phi} \tag{55}$$

to $\chi_{(T-r-1)}^2$, where $\hat{\phi}$, the estimate of ϕ under the saturated model, is given by $Z'\ln(\hat{p})$, and $\hat{D}(\hat{\phi})$ is the estimated covariance matrix of $\hat{\phi}$, given by

$$\hat{D}(\hat{\phi}) = Z'D_{\hat{p}}^{-1}\hat{V}D_{\hat{p}}^{-1}Z. \tag{56}$$

Here, $D_{\hat{p}}$ is the diagonal matrix having elements $\hat{p}_t$, $t = 1, \ldots, T$, on the diagonal. Clearly, the Wald test (55) requires that all weighted-up cell proportions, $\hat{p}_t$, $t = 1, \ldots, T$, must be nonzero.

If the number of degrees of freedom, f, for estimating V is not large relative to $T - r - 1$, an improved test statistic can be obtained by referring

$$F_W(L) = \left(\frac{f - T + r + 2}{f(T - r - 1)}\right) X_W^2(L) \tag{57}$$

to an F distribution on $T - r - 1$ and $f - T + r + 2$ degrees of freedom respectively.

Standard errors of model parameters. As shown by Rao and Scott (1984), the asymptotic covariance matrix of the pseudo MLE, $\hat{\theta}$, of the model parameter vector, θ, can be readily obtained from earlier results given by Bishop et al. (1975). The estimate of this asymptotic covariance matrix becomes

$$\hat{D}(\hat{\theta}) = (n_D^{-2})(X'\hat{P}X)^{-1}(X'\hat{V}X)(X'\hat{P}X)^{-1}, \tag{58}$$

where $\hat{P}$ is the multinomial covariance matrix based on the pseudo MLEs, $\hat{\pi}$, of the cell proportions, as defined above. Standard errors of the individual parameter estimates $\hat{\theta}_i$, $i = 1, \ldots, r$, are then given by the square roots of the corresponding diagonal elements of $\hat{D}(\hat{\theta})$. The log-linear analysis programs found in the popular statistical packages routinely print out the parameter estimates $\hat{\theta}$ together with "standard errors" based on the assumption of SRS. These are obtained as above from the diagonal elements of the matrix

$$\hat{D}(\hat{\theta})_{SRS} = (n_D^{-2})(X'\hat{P}X)^{-1}, \tag{59}$$

which is identical to (58) only when $\hat{V} = \hat{P}$. For complex survey data with $\hat{V} \neq \hat{P}$, these are clearly inappropriate. A comparison of the true estimated standard errors obtained from (58) with those produced by the SPSS^X program LOGLINEAR is given in section 5.4.

Standardized residuals. Rao and Scott (1984) also showed that the covariance matrix of $\hat{p} - \hat{\pi}$, namely, the residual difference between the vector of weighted-up proportions and the vector of pseudo MLEs, can be estimated as

$$\hat{V}_{Res} = Q'\hat{V}Q, \tag{60}$$

where $Q = (I - X(X'\hat{P}X)^{-1}X'\hat{P})$, and $\hat{V}$ is the estimated covariance matrix of $\hat{p}$. Standardized residuals can then be defined as

$$e_t = (\hat{p}_t - \hat{\pi}_t)/\sqrt{\hat{v}_{tt,Res}}, \qquad t = 1, \ldots, T, \tag{61}$$

where $\hat{v}_{tt,Res}$ is the tth diagonal element of $\hat{V}_{Res}$.

5.3. *Estimation and Testing of Nested Log-Linear Models*

The testing of nested log-linear models arises whenever a step-down approach is taken to model building. Consider the model (41) written in partitioned form as

$$\ln(\pi) = \tilde{u}(\theta)1 + X_1\theta_1 + X_2\theta_2, \tag{62}$$

where $X = (X_1, X_2)$, $\theta = (\theta_1', \theta_2')'$, and θ_1, θ_2 are of dimension $s \times 1$ and $(r - s) \times 1$ respectively. Under the hypothesis H_N: $\theta_2 = 0$, we get the reduced model

$$\ln(\pi) = \tilde{u}(\theta_1)1 + X_1\theta_1. \tag{63}$$

Model (63) is nested within model (62), which is equivalent to model (41), and conditional on the fit of (41), a test of H_N will generally provide a more powerful test of the adequacy of the reduced model (63) than would the tests of model fit described in section 5.2 (Agresti 1984, p. 88).

The Rao-Scott approach to testing. Let $\hat{\theta}_1$ represent the pseudo MLE of the parameter vector θ_1 under the reduced model (63), and let $\hat{\theta}_1$ and $\hat{\theta}_2$ denote the partitions of the pseudo MLE, $\hat{\theta}$, corresponding to the full model ([41] or [62]). Further, let $\hat{\hat{\pi}} = \pi(\hat{\theta}_1)$ represent the estimated cell proportions corresponding to the reduced model, with $\hat{\pi}$ as before representing cell estimates under the full model. Then, a

Pearson-type statistic for testing the nested hypothesis H_N: $\theta_2 = 0$ is given by

$$X^2(N) = n_D \sum_{t=1}^{T} \left(\hat{\pi}_t - \hat{\hat{\pi}}_t \right)^2 / \hat{\hat{\pi}}_t, \qquad (64)$$

with an analogous form for the likelihood ratio statistic $G^2(N)$. Rao and Scott (1984) showed that the asymptotic distributions of $X^2(N)$ and $G^2(N)$, under H_N, are again weighted sums of independent chi squares, with a generalized deff matrix given by

$$\hat{\mathbf{D}}_N = \left(\tilde{\mathbf{X}}_2' \hat{\hat{\mathbf{P}}} \tilde{\mathbf{X}}_2 \right)^{-1} \left(\tilde{\mathbf{X}}_2' \hat{\mathbf{V}} \tilde{\mathbf{X}}_2 \right). \qquad (65)$$

Here, $\tilde{\mathbf{X}}_2$ is given by equation (52) with $\mathbf{X}$ replaced by $\mathbf{X}_1$, $\hat{\mathbf{P}}$ by $\hat{\hat{\mathbf{P}}}$, and $\mathbf{Z}$ by $\mathbf{X}_2$. $\hat{\hat{\mathbf{P}}}$ is simply the multinomial form of the covariance matrix based on $\hat{\hat{\pi}}$. First- and second-order Rao-Scott tests can thus be obtained as described in section 5.2.

A Wald test. For the full model (41), the estimated covariance matrix, $\hat{\mathbf{D}}(\hat{\theta})$, of the pseudo MLE of the parameter vector θ is given by equation (58). Any linear hypothesis on these model parameters of the form $\mathbf{H}\theta = \mathbf{h}$ can be tested using the Wald statistic

$$X_W^2(\mathbf{H}\theta) = (\mathbf{H}\hat{\theta} - \mathbf{h})' \left(\mathbf{H}'\hat{\mathbf{D}}(\hat{\theta})\mathbf{H} \right)^{-1} (\mathbf{H}\hat{\theta} - \mathbf{h}), \qquad (66)$$

where $\mathbf{H}$ and $\mathbf{h}$ are of dimension $q \times r$ and $q \times 1$ respectively. When $\mathbf{h} = \mathbf{0}$ and $\mathbf{H} = (\mathbf{0}, \mathbf{I})$ with $\mathbf{H}$ of dimension $(r - s) \times r$ and I the identity matrix of order $r - s$, the Wald statistic (66) provides an alternative test of the nested hypothesis H_N: $\theta_2 = \mathbf{0}$.

5.4. *Example: Two-Way Table With One Ordinal Variable*

Hidiroglou and Rao (1987) illustrated the methods of section 4.2 using a two-way table constructed from CHS data showing the number of different drugs consumed $(0, 1, 2, 3 +)$ by the sex of the respondent. They calculated the unadjusted Pearson chi-square statistic as $X^2(L) = 774$ and the estimated mean for the generalized deffs as $\hat{\delta}. = 1.77$. Thus, the first-order Rao-Scott corrected statistic became $X_c^2 = 437$ on 3 degrees of freedom, which provides strong evidence against the null hypothesis of no association between drugs and sex $(\chi_3^2(0.05) = 7.81)$.

The drug-use variable in this example is ordinal, and as noted by Hidiroglou and Rao, it may be possible to find a more complex but still unsaturated model that provides an adequate fit to the data (see Goodman 1984; Agresti 1984). This question will be explored using the general log-linear methods outlined above.

A *log-linear column-effects model.* Agresti (1984, p. 84) describes a model for an ordinal-by-nominal table that includes all *main effects* (i.e., terms representing separate row and column effects) but includes only those interaction terms corresponding to the linear contrast on the ordinal variable. With equally spaced scores $v_i = 2i$, $i = 1,\ldots,4$, assumed for the levels of the drug-use variable, this model corresponds to Goodman's (1979) *log-linear column-effects* model and can be written as

$$\ln \pi_{ij} = \tilde{u} + u_{1(i)} + u_{2(j)} + \rho_j (v_i - \bar{v}), \qquad (67)$$

subject to the side constraints $\sum_i u_{1(i)} = \sum_j u_{2(j)} = \sum_j \rho_j = 0$. When the parameter vector is chosen as $\theta = (u_{1(1)}, u_{1(2)}, u_{1(3)}, u_{2(1)}, \rho_1)'$, the log-linear column-effects model (67) is of the general form (41), with an **X** matrix given by

$$\mathbf{X} = \begin{pmatrix} 1 & 0 & 0 & 1 & -3 \\ 1 & 0 & 0 & -1 & 3 \\ 0 & 1 & 0 & 1 & -1 \\ 0 & 1 & 0 & -1 & 1 \\ 0 & 0 & 1 & 1 & 1 \\ 0 & 0 & 1 & -1 & -1 \\ -1 & -1 & -1 & 1 & 3 \\ -1 & -1 & -1 & -1 & -3 \end{pmatrix}$$

(see the appendix). From a Newton-Raphson solution of the pseudo ML equations (47), using weighted-up proportions calculated from the CHS data as

$$\hat{\mathbf{p}} = (0.293, 0.228, 0.134, 0.159, 0.048, 0.072, 0.021, 0.045)',$$

the pseudo MLEs of the cell proportions, or probabilities, become

$$\hat{\pi} = (0.291, 0.230, 0.138, 0.155, 0.047, 0.074, 0.020, 0.045)'.$$

Here, the vector elements are labeled in lexicographic order. Estimates of the model parameters θ together with their standard errors are presented and discussed later. A comparison of the above values of $\hat{\mathbf{p}}$ and $\hat{\pi}$ shows that the model (67) fits well. With a total domain size of 31,668, the unadjusted Pearson test of model (67) yields $X^2(L) = 11.3$ on 2 degrees of freedom, a dramatic reduction from the value $X^2(L) =$

774 obtained for the independence model. However, the value of the unadjusted Pearson chi-square statistic is still considerably larger than the 5 percent critical value of 5.99, so that Rao-Scott corrected statistics should be examined to obtain an assessment of model fit that takes into account the effects of the survey design.

Rao-Scott tests. The Rao-Scott corrected tests will depend on the generalized deff matrix (51), which requires that we specify the (8×2) matrix $\mathbf{Z}$ defined in the text following equation (52). Using the methods described in the appendix, we can obtain $\mathbf{Z}$ as the direct product of two matrices of contrasts, $\mathbf{D}_{42}$ and $\mathbf{S}_{21}$, representing the drug and sex variables respectively. Let $\mathbf{D}_{42} = (\mathbf{l}_2, \mathbf{l}_3)$, where $\mathbf{l}_2 = (1, -1, -1, 1)'$ and $\mathbf{l}_3 = (-1, 3, -3, 1)'$ are quadratic and cubic orthogonal polynomial contrasts, respectively, and let $\mathbf{S}_{21} = (1, -1)'$ represent the single contrast on the sex variable. Then, $\mathbf{Z} = \mathbf{D}_{42} \otimes \mathbf{S}_{21}$ and

$$\mathbf{Z}' = \begin{pmatrix} 1 & -1 & -1 & 1 & -1 & 1 & 1 & -1 \\ -1 & 1 & 3 & -3 & -3 & 3 & 1 & -1 \end{pmatrix}.$$

Using a $\hat{\mathbf{V}}$ matrix calculated from CHS data (see Hidiroglou and Rao 1987), we computed the estimated deff matrix (51) as

$$\mathbf{D}_L = \begin{pmatrix} 1.207 & 1.775 \\ 0.071 & 2.287 \end{pmatrix},$$

with eigenvalues $\hat{\boldsymbol{\delta}} = (1.100, 2.393)'$. Since the matrix $\mathbf{Z}$ was constructed using orthogonal polynomials, it follows that $\mathbf{Z}'\mathbf{X} = \mathbf{0}$, so that the alternative form $\hat{\mathbf{D}}_L(A)$ could be used in this case. This computes as

$$\hat{\mathbf{D}}_L(A) = \begin{pmatrix} 1.207 & 0.358 \\ 0.355 & 2.287 \end{pmatrix},$$

which has identical eigenvalues to $\mathbf{D}_L$.

The first-order Rao-Scott corrected statistic, based on the mean of the above eigenvalues ($\hat{\delta}_. = 1.75$), becomes $X_c^2 = 6.5$. Of course, given that $\hat{\mathbf{V}}$ is available, one should choose to use the second-order correction, which in this case is $X_S^2(L) = 5.7$, on $\nu = 1.8$ degrees of freedom. The interpolated critical value for this test becomes 5.56, so that the goodness-of-fit test of the model is just significant at the 5 percent level. For comparison, the value of the Wald test of model fit (55) here yields $X_W^2 = 8.56$. The second-order Rao-Scott test does not indicate serious lack of fit in this case, since with a domain size of 31,668, the test of model fit at the 5 percent level has power close to one and is thus capable of detecting very small deviations from the data. If desired, the fit can be further improved by including in the model the term corresponding to the interaction of sex and the quadratic contrast on the drug variable, i.e., by including in $\mathbf{X}$ the first of the two columns of $\mathbf{Z}$. In this case, $X_c^2(L) = X_S^2(L) = 2.1$ on 1 degree of freedom, which is not significant at 5 percent.

We can illustrate the nested model methods of section 5.3 by specifically testing whether or not this quadratic interaction term makes a statistically significant contribution to the model, i.e., by testing the hypothesis H_N: $\theta_6 = 0$. The relevant Rao-Scott statistics become $X^2(N) = 6.45$ with $\hat{\delta}. = 1.12$, so that $X_c^2(N) = X_S^2(N) = 5.76$ on 1 degree of freedom, which is clearly significant at the 5 percent level. Since the nested hypothesis has only one degree of freedom, the first- and second-order corrected tests are identical in this case. The corresponding Wald test yields $X_W^2(N) = 5.84$, very close to the Rao-Scott corrected tests.

Approximate first-order corrections for testing fit. The log-linear column-effects model, called model M for convenience, does not admit a closed-form solution for the pseudo MLEs, so there is no exact formula for the mean of the generalized deffs, $\hat{\delta}.$, that depends only on cell and marginal deffs. However, Rao and Scott (1987) have recently shown that a *nearly conservative* correction, requiring only cell and marginal deffs, can be obtained in terms of a model M^*, having a $T \times r^*$ design matrix $\mathbf{X}^*$, which is closest to M in the sense that $r - r^*$ is as small as possible. For the drugs-by-sex example, M^* will be the independence model, so that $r - r^* = 1$. Using only cell and marginal deffs, Hidiroglou and Rao (1987) estimated $\delta.^*$ to be 1.77. The *nearly conservative* correction proposed by Rao and Scott (1987) is then given by

$$\tilde{\delta}. = \left(\frac{T - r^* - 1}{T - r - 1} \right) \delta.^* = 3\delta.^*/2 = 2.67. \tag{68}$$

The resulting first-order corrected statistic becomes $\tilde{X}_c^2(L) = 4.2$, on 2 degrees of freedom, which is not significant at the 5 percent level.

Standard errors of model parameters. An appropriately weighted set of "counts" for the drugs-by-sex table can be obtained (see section 3.1) by multiplying the CHS proportions, $\hat{\mathbf{p}}$, by $n_D = 31,668$, the number of CHS respondents in the table domain. Analysis of these "counts" under the log-linear column-effects model, using the SPSS^X program

LOGLINEAR, yields model parameter estimates

$$\hat{\theta} = \left(u_{1(1)}, u_{1(2)}, u_{1(3)}, u_{2(1)}, \rho_1 \right)'$$
$$= (1.051, 0.380, -0.435, -0.144, -0.087)',$$

with corresponding "standard errors" given by

$$SE(\hat{\theta})_{SPSS} = 10^{-2}(0.96, 1.07, 1.37, 0.76, 0.32)'.$$

The above parameter estimates are identical to those obtained by a direct Newton-Raphson solution of equation (47), as expected. However, as noted in section 5.2, the SPSS[X] "standard errors" differ from those given by the square roots of the diagonal elements of equation (58). The latter are the valid parameter standard errors, which account for the variance inflation induced by the survey design. For the column-effects model, they become

$$SE(\hat{\theta}) = 10^{-2}(1.87, 2.21, 1.80, 0.56, 0.39)'.$$

With one exception, the SPSS[X] "standard errors" are too small, so that corresponding "z scores," also produced by SPSS[X], will be too large when treated as normal z scores. The exception is the sex parameter, $u_{2(1)}$, whose true estimated standard error is smaller than that given by SPSS[X]; i.e., the deff for this parameter is less than one. This may be due to the variance-reducing effect of the age/sex poststratification adjustments that are incorporated in the final CHS survey weights.

5.5. *Explicit Estimates of $\hat{\delta}$. for Multi-Way Tables*

Rao and Scott (1982, 1984) and Bedrick (1983) showed that estimates of the mean of the generalized deffs, $\hat{\delta}_.$, can be obtained using only information on cell and marginal deffs whenever the model admits direct estimates, i.e., whenever the pseudo MLE, $\hat{\pi}$, can be written as an explicit function of the data, $\hat{p}$. For large tables, this is an important finding, because first-order corrected tests, X_c^2, based on cell and marginal deffs require far less data than second-order test procedures based on a full estimate of the covariance matrix, $\mathbf{V}$.

When they exist, direct estimates take the form of a ratio of products of marginal cell proportions, which, in the notation of Bishop et al. (1975), can be expressed as

$$\hat{\pi}_\theta = \prod_l \hat{p}_{\theta_l} \Big/ \prod_m \hat{p}_{\phi_m}, \tag{69}$$

where θ indexes a cell of the full table and θ_l and ϕ_m refer to sets of indices that define the cells of marginal tables. For example, in a three-way table, the model of conditional independence of variables A and B given C (defined below and illustrated in the following example) has direct estimates of the form

$$\hat{\pi}_{ijk} = (\hat{p}_{i+k}\hat{p}_{+jk})/\hat{p}_{++k}, \tag{70}$$

where " $+$ " refers to marginal summation across an index. In this section, when we refer to models of tables having a specific number of dimensions, we will use the traditional cell-indexing notation in place of the lexicographic scheme described earlier for the general case. The form of $\hat{\delta}$ for a model admitting direct estimates and having $T - r - 1$ degrees of freedom is

$$(T - r - 1)\hat{\delta} = \sum_{\theta} \frac{\hat{p}_{\theta}}{\hat{\pi}_{\theta}}(1 - \hat{p}_{\theta})\hat{d}_{\theta} - \sum_{l}\sum_{\theta_{l}}(1 - \hat{p}_{\theta_{l}})\hat{d}_{\theta_{l}}$$
$$+ \sum_{m}\sum_{\phi_{m}}(1 - \hat{p}_{\phi_{m}})\hat{d}_{\phi_{m}}. \tag{71}$$

Summation over θ_{l} and ϕ_{m} here refers to summation over each cell of the corresponding marginal table. The deff $\hat{d}_{\theta}$ in (71) is equal to $\text{estvar}(\hat{p}_{\theta})/(n_{D}^{-1}\hat{p}_{\theta}(1 - \hat{p}_{\theta}))$, with corresponding forms for the deffs $\hat{d}_{\theta_{l}}$ and $\hat{d}_{\phi_{m}}$. All deffs are defined with respect to the multinomial variances based on observed cell proportions (the $\hat{p}$'s) rather than on the pseudo MLEs (the $\hat{\pi}$'s) and are therefore independent of the model being tested.

Application to a three-way table. The saturated log-linear model for a three-way table takes the form

$$\ln(\pi_{ijk}) = \tilde{u} + u_{1(i)} + u_{2(j)} + u_{3(k)} + u_{12(ij)}$$
$$+ u_{13(ik)} + u_{23(jk)} + u_{123(ijk)}, \tag{72}$$

where the sum of any u term over its subscripts is zero. Bishop et al. (1975) and Fienberg (1981) discuss the four basic hierarchical models of interest that can be defined by selectively setting terms of (72) to zero (see also Hidiroglou and Rao 1987).

The model of complete independence of the three variables A, B, and C (denoted $A * B * C$) corresponds to the hypothesis

$$H_{0}(1): u_{12(ij)} = u_{13(ik)} = u_{23(jk)} = u_{123(ijk)} = 0, \quad \text{for all } i, j, k. \tag{73}$$

The model corresponding to $H_{0}(1)$ admits direct estimates given by $\hat{\pi}_{ijk} = \hat{p}_{i++}\hat{p}_{+j+}\hat{p}_{++k}$.

The model of independence of A with variables B and C taken jointly (denoted $A * BC$) corresponds to

$$H_0(2): u_{12(ij)} = u_{13(ik)} = u_{123(ijk)} = 0, \quad \text{for all } i, j, k, \quad (74)$$

with analogous forms for the hypotheses $B * AC$ and $C * AB$. The model corresponding to $H_0(2)$ admits direct estimates given by $\hat{\pi}_{ijk} = \hat{p}_{i++}\hat{p}_{+jk}$.

The model of conditional independence of A and B given C (denoted $A * B|C$) corresponds to

$$H_0(3): u_{12(ij)} = u_{123(ijk)} = 0, \quad \text{for all } i, j, k, \quad (75)$$

with analogous forms for the hypotheses $A * C|B$ and $B * C|A$. The model corresponding to $H_0(3)$ admits direct estimates of the form $\hat{\pi}_{ijk} = (\hat{p}_{i+k}\hat{p}_{+jk})/\hat{p}_{++k}$.

Finally, the model of no three-factor interaction corresponds to

$$H_0(4): u_{123(ijk)} = 0, \quad \text{for all } i, j, k. \quad (76)$$

This model does not admit closed-form estimates.

As an example of the application of equation (71), we give below the expression for $\hat{\delta}$. for the conditional independence hypothesis $H_0(3)$ for a three-way table having dimensions $I \times J \times K$.

$$
\begin{aligned}
(I-1)(J-1)K\hat{\delta}. = & \sum_{i=1}^{I} \sum_{j=1}^{J} \sum_{k=1}^{K} \frac{\hat{p}_{ijk}(1 - \hat{p}_{ijk})}{(\hat{p}_{i+k}\hat{p}_{+jk}/\hat{p}_{++k})} \hat{d}_{ijk} \\
& - \sum_{i=1}^{I} \sum_{k=1}^{K} (1 - \hat{p}_{i+k})\hat{d}_{ik} - \sum_{j=1}^{J} \sum_{k=1}^{K} (1 - \hat{p}_{+jk})\hat{d}_{jk} \\
& + \sum_{k=1}^{K} (1 - \hat{p}_{++k})\hat{d}_{k}. \quad (77)
\end{aligned}
$$

The second and third terms in this expression are summations over the cells of the marginal tables indexed in the numerator of the direct estimate (70), i.e., the index sets θ_1 and θ_2. Similarly, the last term is a summation over the marginal table indexed in the denominator of (70), i.e., the index set ϕ_1. The term $\hat{d}_{ijk} = \text{estvar}(\hat{p}_{ijk})/(n_D^{-1}\hat{p}_{ijk}(1 - \hat{p}_{ijk}))$ is the estimated deff of $\hat{p}_{ijk}$, $\hat{d}_{ik} = \text{estvar}(\hat{p}_{i+k})/(n_D^{-1}\hat{p}_{i+k}(1 - \hat{p}_{i+k}))$ is the estimated deff of the two-way marginal $\hat{p}_{i+k}$, and $\hat{d}_{k} = \text{estvar}(\hat{p}_{++k})/(n_D^{-1}\hat{p}_k(1 - \hat{p}_k))$ is the estimated deff of $\hat{p}_k$, etc. The term $\text{estvar}(\hat{p}_{ijk})$ will equal $\hat{v}_{tt}$, the tth diagonal element of $\mathbf{V}$, where t is the lexicographic index corresponding to the three-way cell index ijk. Estimated variances of marginal $\hat{p}$'s will be obtained in a similar way from their covariance matrices, which will be matrix quadratic forms based on $\hat{\mathbf{V}}$. As an example, consider the covariance matrix $\hat{\mathbf{V}}_{I+K}$ of the vector of marginal proportions $\hat{\mathbf{p}}_{I+K}$, having elements $\hat{p}_{i+k}$, $i = 1, \ldots, I$, $k = 1, \ldots, K$. It can be written as

$$\hat{\mathbf{V}}_{I+K} = \mathbf{M}\hat{\mathbf{V}}\mathbf{M}', \tag{78}$$

where $\mathbf{M} = \mathbf{I}_I \otimes \mathbf{1}'_J \otimes \mathbf{I}_K$, $\mathbf{I}_I$ and $\mathbf{I}_K$ are identity matrices of dimension $I \times I$ and $K \times K$ respectively, and $\mathbf{1}_J$ is a $J \times 1$ vector of ones. Other marginal covariance matrices can be obtained by an appropriate placement of $\mathbf{I}$'s and $\mathbf{1}''$s in the definition of $\mathbf{M}$. The generalization to higher-way tables is straightforward.

5.6. *Example 1: Conditional Independence in a Three-Way Table*

For the CCSS dataset, the independence of employment class and sex was tested and rejected in section 4.2. A similar analysis shows that income and sex are also related. Eno (1985) considered the proposition that this relationship between income and sex would disappear when employment class was held constant, i.e., that for each separate class, males and females would have similar incomes. Using regression analysis methods, she tested and rejected this hypothesis. With income represented as a categorical variable, this proposition is equivalent to the three-way log-linear model hypothesis of conditional independence of income and sex, given employment class. The corresponding log-linear analysis is described below, taking into account the effect of the survey design.

The domain of the analysis and the definition of employment class are the same as for the earlier independence example. Income is defined as a four-category variable: \$0 to \$9,999; \$10,000 to \$19,999; \$20,000 to \$34,999; and over \$35,000. Proportions in each of the 40 cells of the resulting three-way table, based on weighted-up counts, are given in Table 5, with cell deffs in parentheses. From equation (77), it can be seen that estimation of δ for the conditional independence hypothesis requires deff information on two marginal two-way tables (namely, income by class and sex by class) and on one one-way marginal (namely, class). Deffs for these marginal tables are given in Table 6. Marginal proportions can be easily obtained from Table 5.

TABLE 5
Weighted-Up Proportions ($\times 10^2$) and Deffs (in parentheses) for Income $\times$ Sex $\times$ Employment Class

	Employment Class				
	Decision-Making Manager	Advisor-Manager	Super-visor	Semi-Autonomous Worker	Worker
Income $0 to $9,999					
Male	0.26	0.12	0.22	0.94	2.79
	(0.51)	(0.24)	(0.28)	(0.74)	(1.18)
Female	0.30	0.30	0.92	1.64	7.63
	(1.77)	(0.71)	(2.11)	(3.08)	(2.06)
Income $10,000 to $19,999					
Male	0.61	0.49	3.06	2.21	10.21
	(0.48)	(0.89)	(1.85)	(1.06)	(1.34)
Female	1.53	0.39	2.17	2.77	12.93
	(1.58)	(1.31)	(0.40)	(0.81)	(1.16)
Income $20,000 to $34,999					
Male	5.71	1.15	4.04	5.10	10.73
	(1.41)	(0.72)	(1.16)	(1.48)	(2.05)
Female	1.32	0.55	1.16	4.40	3.31
	(1.59)	(0.45)	(0.78)	(1.76)	(1.42)
Income over $35,000					
Male	4.78	0.33	1.46	2.37	0.81
	(0.55)	(0.91)	(1.77)	(1.20)	(1.87)
Female	0.62	0.11	0.23	0.00	0.33
	(0.63)	(0.32)	(0.55)	—	(1.02)
$n_D = 1,463$					

Table 5 and the cell deffs of Table 6 represent the minimum amount of information required to test the specific hypothesis of interest. If our intent was to search for a suitable model from among all possible three-way models, then deffs would be required for the three two-way marginal tables and the three one-way marginal tables.

The uncorrected Pearson statistic was calculated as $X^2(L) = 169.5$. Using the data of Tables 5 and 6, we calculated $\hat{\delta}.$ from equation (77) as $\hat{\delta}. = 1.1$, giving a first-order Rao-Scott corrected chi-square statistic $X_c^2(L) = 153.6$ on 15 degrees of freedom. The

TABLE 6
Design Effects for Marginal Tables

	Employment Class				
	Decision-Making Manager	Advisor-Manager	Supervisor	Semi-Autonomous Worker	Worker
Income					
$0 to $9,999	1.24	0.75	0.95	1.88	1.04
$10,000 to $19,999	1.02	1.17	1.47	1.22	1.28
$20,000 to $35,000	1.62	0.54	0.95	2.62	2.55
over $35,000	0.44	0.92	1.34	0.68	1.59
Sex					
Male	1.17	0.90	1.52	0.62	1.39
Female	1.48	0.59	0.86	1.63	1.26
One-Way	1.19	1.14	1.12	1.39	2.10
$n_D = 1,463$					

corresponding 5 percent critical value is 25.0, so that $X_c^2(L)$ provides strong evidence against the conditional independence hypothesis, confirming Eno's (1985) conclusion.

Since we do have access to the full covariance matrix, $\hat{V}$, in this example, the second-order Rao-Scott statistic $X_S^2(L)$ can also be computed. To evaluate the deff matrix $\hat{D}_L(A)$ of equation (53), we constructed the design matrix, X, and its completion, Z, using the method described in the appendix. The squared coefficient of variation of the eigenvalues of $\hat{D}_L(A)$ was calculated as $\hat{a}^2 = 1.20$, yielding a second-order corrected statistic $X_S^2(L) = 69.7$, on 6.6 degrees of freedom. Compared with an interpolated 5 percent critical point of 15.7, $X_S^2(L)$ also provides strong evidence against the proposed model. Under the assumption that the second-order corrected statistic achieves a significance level that is reasonably close to the nominal level of 5 percent, the actual levels of $X^2(L)$ and $X_c^2(L)$ were estimated from (14) and (15) as 16.0 percent and 11.4 percent respectively. The uncorrected statistic is clearly too liberal, and though the first-order correction is an improvement, its error rate is still somewhat high.

The Wald statistic (15) cannot be evaluated for this example, since one of the elements of $D_{\hat{p}}$ in equation (56) is zero (see Table 5).

TABLE 7

Weighted Proportions ($\times 10^2$) for the CHS Drugs $\times$ Age $\times$ Sex Table

	Ages 15–44		Ages 45–64		Ages 65 +	
	Males	Females	Males	Females	Males	Females
Drugs						
0	21.53	15.74	6.39	4.31	1.70	1.47
1	7.30	9.69	3.66	4.29	1.63	1.92
2	2.08	4.21	1.56	2.44	1.07	1.46
3 +	0.66	1.79	0.82	1.99	0.66	1.62
$n_D = 23{,}791$						

Since the income variable is ordinal, it may be possible to find a more complex but still unsaturated model that provides an adequate fit to the data, as in the two-way example of section 5.4. For simplicity, we have not investigated this possibility here.

5.7. *Example 2*: *Analysis of a Three-Way Table from the CHS*

When analyzing a two-way table taken from a survey dataset, one should always bear in mind the possibility of extraneous association caused by collapsing over other related variables. The two-way table from the CHS analyzed in section 5.4 is a case in point. Though an acceptable model was found by exploiting the ordinal nature of one of the variables, a more informative model can be found by including the respondent's age and analyzing the resulting three-way table. The weighted-up proportions for the three-way table are shown in Table 7.

Conditional independence models. Results of tests of the three possible hypotheses of conditional independence on the three variables, drugs, age, and sex, are shown in Table 8. Drugs and sex are defined as in the example of section 5.2. Age is defined in terms of three categories: 15 to 44, 45 to 64, and over 65. For the three-way table, children under age 15 were excluded, reducing the size of the domain to 23,791.

From the adjusted statistics given in Table 8, it can be seen that not one of the three conditional independence models fits the data well. Of these three hypotheses, the one that comes closest to a fit is the

TABLE 8

Conditional Independence for Drugs (D), Age (A), and Sex (S)

Statistic	Conditional Hypotheses		
	$D*A\|S$	$D*S\|A$	$A*S\|D$
$X^2(L)$	1,849	934	35
$df = T - r - 1$	12	9	8
$\hat{\delta}.$	2.12	1.66	1.22
$X_c^2(L)$	871	561	28.5
$\hat{a}^2$	0.71	0.54	0.85
$X_S^2(L)$	508	365	15.4
$v = df/(1 + \hat{a}^2)$	7.0	5.9	4.3
$X_W^2(L)$	3,075	730	196
Level (X^2)	56.5%	34.0%	16.9%
Level (X_c^2)	9.2%	8.2%	9.5%
$n_D = 23,791$			

hypothesis of conditional independence of age and sex, given the drugs category. For this hypothesis, the second-order Rao-Scott statistic is $X_S^2(L) = 15.4$, on 4.3 degrees of freedom, which must be compared with an interpolated 5 percent critical value of 10.0. An alternative model is clearly required. This hypothesis, moreover, is not likely to be of interest.

Table 8 provides a striking example of the potential seriousness of ignoring the survey design when testing hypotheses. For the hypothesis of conditional independence of drugs and age, given sex, the mean and the squared coefficient of variation of the generalized deffs (the $\hat{\delta}$'s) are $\hat{\delta}. = 2.12$ and $\hat{a}^2 = 0.71$, respectively. These values are indicative of strong clustering effects and result in an estimated level of 56.5 percent for the unadjusted $X^2(L)$ test, which was based on a nominal level of 5 percent. In comparison, the estimated level for $X_c^2(L)$, the first-order Rao-Scott statistic, is 9.2 percent.

As noted in section 3, first-order corrected tests will be asymptotically exact provided the generalized deffs are all equal, in which case $a^2 = 0$. For the CHS data of Table 7, $\hat{a}^2$ ranges from 0.54 to 0.85, indicating large variations among the $\hat{\delta}_i$'s and hence large variations among the δ_i's. The effect on the first-order statistics is to render them somewhat liberal, the lowest actual level being 8.2 percent for the hypothesis $D * S|A$. For the hypothesis $A * S|D$, which has the largest value of $\hat{a}^2$ (equal to 0.85), the estimated level is the highest of the three at 9.5 percent, despite its having the least inflated $X^2(L)$ statistic (an estimated level of 16.5 percent).

Another interesting aspect of Table 8 is its illustration of the instability of the Wald statistic. For all three hypotheses, the value of $X_W^2(L)$ exceeds that of $X_c^2(L)$, which is referred to the same critical value. In particular, for the hypothesis of conditional independence of age and sex, given drugs, the value of $X_W^2(L)$ is 196, compared with an $X_c^2(L)$ of 28.5 and an $X^2(L)$ of 35.0.

A model of no three-factor interaction. For the drugs-by-age-by-sex data, the only candidate that might provide an adequate fit to the data, from among the models listed in section 5.5, is the model of no three-factor interaction. All other models are nested within one of the conditional independence models; i.e., they can all be defined by setting to zero one or more of the u terms of a particular conditional independence model. They cannot therefore be expected to provide a better fit than their parent model. Since the model of no three-factor interaction does not admit direct estimates, we will follow the general approach to estimation and testing described in section 5.2, using weighted-up proportions, $\hat{p}$, and a corresponding covariance matrix, $\hat{V}$, supplied by Statistics Canada. We will also exhibit the approximate methods of Rao and Scott (1987), which do not require access to the full estimated covariance matrix (see also section 5.4).

To obtain pseudo MLEs and the generalized deff matrix (53), the design matrix, X, and its completion, Z, must be specified. Both can be constructed using the methods described in the appendix. For the sex variable, the contrast matrix is unique (to a multiplicative constant) and is given by $S_{21} = (1, -1)'$, where the suffix relates to the dimension of the contrast matrix. For the ordinal variables drugs and age, suitable contrast matrices are not unique. An orthogonal polynomial contrast matrix, D_{43}, of dimension 4×3 was constructed for the drug variable, based on the equispaced category scores defined in section 5.4. It is given by

$$D_{43}' = \begin{pmatrix} -3 & -1 & 1 & 3 \\ 1 & -1 & -1 & 1 \\ -1 & 3 & -3 & 1 \end{pmatrix}.$$

An orthogonal polynomial contrast matrix, A_{32}, of order 3×2 was also constructed for the age variable, based on the unequally spaced category scores, a_i, $i = 1, 2, 3$, equal to 30, 55, and 75 years respectively. The first two scores are range midpoints, and the third represents the open 65 + category. The two columns of $\mathbf{A}_{32}$ consist of orthogonal linear and quadratic contrasts respectively, defined on the above scores. It is given by

$$\mathbf{A}_{32} = \begin{pmatrix} -14 & 17.8197 \\ 1 & -39.8443 \\ 13 & 22.0246 \end{pmatrix},$$

where the coefficients of the linear contrast, $\mathbf{q}_1$, are given by $q_{1i} = (3/5)(a_i - \bar{a}_i)$, $i = 1, 2, 3$, and the coefficients of the orthogonalized quadratic contrast, $\mathbf{q}_2$, are given by $q_{2i} = (3/25)(a_i^2 - \bar{a}_i^2) - (2543/122)q_{1i}$, $i = 1, 2, 3$.

When the methods of the appendix are applied to the no-three-factor-interaction model defined by (72) and (76), the columns of the design matrix, $\mathbf{X}$, can be assembled term by term, giving

$$\mathbf{X} = (\mathbf{D}_{43} \otimes \mathbf{1}_3 \otimes \mathbf{1}_2, \mathbf{1}_4 \otimes \mathbf{A}_{32} \otimes \mathbf{1}_2, \mathbf{1}_4 \otimes \mathbf{1}_3 \otimes \mathbf{S}_{21},$$

$$\mathbf{D}_{43} \otimes \mathbf{A}_{32} \otimes \mathbf{1}_2, \mathbf{D}_{43} \otimes \mathbf{1}_3 \otimes \mathbf{S}_{21}, \mathbf{1}_4 \otimes \mathbf{A}_{32} \otimes \mathbf{S}_{21}). \qquad (79)$$

The matrix $\mathbf{Z}$ then corresponds to the omitted third-order interaction, i.e.,

$$\mathbf{Z} = (\mathbf{D}_{43} \otimes \mathbf{A}_{32} \otimes \mathbf{S}_{21}). \qquad (80)$$

Note that in the appendix, the superscript P is used to distinguish orthogonal polynomial contrast matrices from contrast matrices for nominal variables. This superscript has been omitted from equations (79) and (80) to avoid unnecessarily cumbersome notation.

Identical pseudo MLEs, $\hat{\pi}$, and identical test statistics would be obtained for the model of no three-factor interaction, irrespective of the form of the contrast matrices selected to represent the drugs and age variables. This follows because the $\mathbf{X}$ matrix (79) is based only on contrast matrices of maximum column rank for each variable. This situation differs from that of the *log-linear column-effects* model of section 5.4, where only one column of the 4×3 contrast matrix for the drug variable was included in $\mathbf{X}$. The remaining two columns were incorporated into $\mathbf{Z}$. Thus, the nominal contrasts of the appendix could have been used in (79) for both drug and age variables. The above choice of polynomial contrasts, based on meaningful category scores, is convenient in that it allows for easy extensions of the no-three-factor-interaction model, along the lines of the *log-linear column-effects* model, in case an adequate fit to the data is not obtained. For $\mathbf{X}$ and $\mathbf{Z}$ as defined in (79) and (80), respectively, it can be shown that $\mathbf{Z}'\mathbf{X} = \mathbf{0}$, so that the generalized deff matrix (53) can be used. For the CHS data, the mean and squared coefficient of variation of the eigenvalues of this matrix become $\hat{\delta}_. = 1.60$ and $\hat{a}^2 = 0.42$, respectively. From a solution of the ML equations (47), based on the above $\mathbf{X}$ matrix, the unadjusted Pearson chi-square statistic (48) becomes $X^2(L) = 21.4$ on 6 degrees of freedom (the number of columns in $\mathbf{Z}$). When the above values of $\hat{\delta}_.$ and $\hat{a}^2$ are used, the second-order Rao-Scott statistic becomes $X_S^2(L) = 9.4$ on 4.2 degrees of freedom. The interpolated 5 percent critical point is 9.80, so there is no strong evidence in favor of rejecting the hypothesis of no three-factor interaction. An examination of standardized residuals, given by equation (61), does indicate some lack of fit that is not clearly identified by the above test. This can be removed by the addition of two columns of $\mathbf{Z}$, corresponding to the interaction of linear and quadratic drugs contrasts with the linear age and sex contrasts. Details are omitted for lack of space.

As demonstrated in section 5.4, Rao and Scott's (1987) approximation to the first-order corrected statistic provides a test procedure that does not require the full covariance matrix, $\hat{\mathbf{V}}$, even for models that do not admit direct estimates. The *nearest* model to that of no three-factor interaction that admits direct estimates is the model of conditional independence of age and sex, given drugs, which has degrees of freedom $T - r^* - 1 = 8$, and $\delta_.^* = 1.22$ (see Table 7). Rao and Scott's *nearly conservative* correction then becomes

$$\tilde{\delta}_. = \left(\frac{T - r^* - 1}{T - r - 1} \right) \delta_.^* = (4/3) \times 1.22 = 1.62,$$

which is very close to the true estimated value, $\hat{\delta}_. = 1.60$. In this case, the approximate first-order corrected test becomes $\tilde{X}_c^2 = 13.2$, which slightly exceeds the 5 percent critical value of 12.6. The estimated level of this approximate first-order test is 7.4 percent, again slightly liberal.

6. SOFTWARE

The computer software used to produce the examples in this paper was written using the matrix algebra language GAUSS (see

Platt 1986). Prior data processing was handled by SPSS^X in the CCSS and by SAS in the CHS. GAUSS is particularly convenient for programming the methods described in this paper because it also provides an extensive library of mathematical and statistical procedures, including routines for solving systems of nonlinear equations. For those prepared to program their own analyses, the SAS matrix language offers similar advantages.

Several options are now available to sociologists and others who are not prepared to write their own analysis software. Fay's (1982) CPLX program, which implements his jackknifed chi-square statistics, was briefly discussed in section 3. This program offers a comprehensive analysis option whenever estimates are available at the individual replicate level. Fay has recently produced another program called RSPLX, designed along the lines of CPLX; it implements the second-order corrections of Rao and Scott for the full range of hierarchical log-linear models covered by CPLX. RSPLX can directly read in estimated cell proportions and the corresponding covariance matrix. Versions of both programs, called PC-CPLX and PC-RSPLX, are now available for IBM XT, AT, and compatible microcomputers. All are in the public domain.

First- and second-order Rao-Scott corrections for testing independence in two-way tables are available through another microbased program called PC CARP, which runs on IBM XT, AT, and compatible computers. Developed by Fuller et al. (1987), PC CARP produces variance estimates and deffs for a variety of statistics under two-stage cluster sampling designs. For example, it can furnish estimates of deffs for the marginals of a multi-way contingency table. Thus, in addition to its preprogrammed analysis for two-way tables, it can provide the basic information required for computing first-order Rao-Scott corrections for log-linear models of multi-way tables, provided these models admit closed-form estimates (see section 5.5). By extension, it can furnish the basic information for testing any log-linear model whenever the analyst is satisfied with approximations to the first-order corrections, as described in sections 5.4 and 5.7.

7. SUMMARY AND CONCLUDING REMARKS

The primary purpose of this expository paper has been to present a detailed description of some recent methods (Rao and Scott

1979, 1981, 1984, 1987; Scott and Rao 1981) for dealing with data from complex surveys involving clustering, stratification, and multistage sampling. Illustrations of their application using data from the CCSS and from the CHS (1978–79) are also given. These methods essentially provide first-order and second-order corrections to standard multinomial-based chi-square tests by taking account of the survey deffs. The first-order corrections are useful for secondary analyses from published tables that provide deffs or estimated variances for cells of the table and of marginal totals, in addition to weighted-up counts or cell proportions. On the other hand, the more accurate second-order corrections require knowledge of the full estimated covariance matrix of cell estimates, seldom available in published tables. The methods are applied to a variety of categorical data problems, including (a) simple goodness of fit; (b) tests of homogeneity and of association on two-way tables, including modifications for tables having ordered categories; and (c) analysis of three-way tables using log-linear models.

Because of space limitations, we have not been able to treat several other problems, including logistic regression (or logit) models using binary or polytomous response variables (Rao and Scott 1987; Roberts, Rao, and Kumar 1987; Roberts 1986). We are currently trying to extend these methods to the association (or log-multiplicative) models of Goodman (1979), Clogg (1982), and others and to generalized linear models (McCullagh and Nelder 1983) for cross-classified categorical data.

In addition to the methods of Rao and Scott, we have outlined the corresponding Wald test procedures and have cautioned that these procedures often yield inflated test statistics because of instabilities in the estimated inverse of the covariance matrix of cell proportions. Striking examples of this instability are given in section 5.7 in connection with tests of conditional independence on a three-way table. For lack of space, we have not dealt in any detail with the jackknifed chi-square tests of Fay (1979, 1985). Current evidence indicates that these tests compare well with the second-order corrections of Rao and Scott, and as noted earlier, they provide a viable analysis strategy whenever survey estimates are available at the replicate level.

APPENDIX

This appendix describes a method of routinely generating model design matrices, X, given a u-term specification as in (72) together with particular model specifications such as hypotheses (73) through (76). The method will be defined using models for two- and three-way tables to avoid unnecessarily cumbersome notation. The generalization to tables of higher dimension will be immediately apparent. We first present the algorithm for the nominal case and then treat the ordinal case.

Consider first a three-way table of categorical variables A, B, and C having levels I, J, and K, respectively. Let $\mathbf{1}_I$, $\mathbf{1}_J$, and $\mathbf{1}_K$ be column vectors of ones of length I, J, and K, respectively. Also, let $\mathbf{A}_{I(I-1)}$, $\mathbf{B}_{J(J-1)}$, and $\mathbf{C}_{K(K-1)}$ be contrast matrices of dimension $I \times (I - 1)$, $J \times (J - 1)$, and $K \times (K - 1)$, respectively, such that $\mathbf{1}_I' \mathbf{A}_{I(I-1)} = \mathbf{1}_J' \mathbf{B}_{J(J-1)} = \mathbf{1}_K' \mathbf{C}_{K(K-1)} = \mathbf{0}'$; i.e., their columns sum to zero. A convenient form of contrast matrix for nominal variables is

$$\mathbf{A}_{I(I-1)} = \begin{pmatrix} \mathbf{I}_{I-1} \\ -\mathbf{1}_{I-1}' \end{pmatrix}, \tag{A-1}$$

where $\mathbf{I}_{I-1}$ is an identity matrix of dimension $(I - 1) \times (I - 1)$. The contrast matrices $\mathbf{B}_{J(J-1)}$ and $\mathbf{C}_{K(K-1)}$ are defined analogously.

The columns of the $\mathbf{X}$ matrix corresponding to the u terms in the saturated model (72) can be defined in terms of these contrast matrices as follows:

1. $\mathbf{A}_{I(I-1)} \otimes \mathbf{1}_J \otimes \mathbf{1}_K, \mathbf{1}_I \otimes \mathbf{B}_{J(J-1)} \otimes \mathbf{1}_K, \mathbf{1}_I \otimes \mathbf{1}_J \otimes \mathbf{C}_{K(K-1)}$ for the main effects $u_{1(i)}$, $u_{2(j)}$, and $u_{3(k)}$, respectively;
2. $\mathbf{A}_{I(I-1)} \otimes \mathbf{B}_{J(J-1)} \otimes \mathbf{1}_K, \mathbf{A}_{I(I-1)} \otimes \mathbf{1}_J \otimes \mathbf{C}_{K(K-1)}, \mathbf{1}_I \otimes \mathbf{B}_{J(J-1)} \otimes \mathbf{C}_{K(K-1)}$ for the second-order interactions $u_{12(ij)}$, $u_{13(ik)}$, and $u_{23(jk)}$, respectively;
3. $\mathbf{A}_{I(I-1)} \otimes \mathbf{B}_{J(J-1)} \otimes \mathbf{C}_{K(K-1)}$ for the single third-order interaction $u_{123(ijk)}$.

The number of columns in the design matrix $\mathbf{X}$ corresponding to any of these terms is easily determined from the multiplication rules for direct products. For example, the columns representing the u terms $u_{23(jk)}$, $j = 1, \ldots, J$, $k = 1, \ldots, K$, are given by the direct product of three matrices having dimensions $I \times 1$, $J \times (J - 1)$, and $K \times (K - 1)$, respectively (see the last term in [2] above). This product yields a matrix of dimension $IJK \times (1)(J - 1)(K - 1)$, i.e., a total of $(J - 1)(K - 1)$ columns.

A specific nonsaturated model—for example, the conditional independence model specified by the hypothesis (75)—can be obtained simply by dropping from the saturated X matrix those columns corresponding to u terms set to zero in the hypothesis. This approach can clearly be extended to tables of any dimension. All that is required are contrast matrices of appropriate dimension and a u-term specification of the model.

The contrast matrices defined in (A-1) are convenient for nominal variables but are not unique. For ordinal variables, contrast matrices having columns of orthogonal polynomial contrasts can be used instead. If the natural scores for the ordinal variables are evenly spaced, the tables given by Kirk (1968, p. 538) are a convenient source of such contrasts. Different nominal and ordinal contrast matrices can be used together as convenient, and specific columns of the contrast matrix can be dropped for one or more variables to construct specialized models. For example, the log-linear column-effects model of section 5.4, which features one nominal and one ordinal variable, uses nominal contrasts to define the main effects of the drugs variable and one linear polynomial contrast on the drugs variable to construct the linear drugs-by-sex interaction. Using nominal contrast matrices D_{43} and S_{21}, of type (A-1), to represent main effects of drugs and sex, the design matrix for the column effects model (67) can be expressed as

$$X = (D_{43} \otimes 1_2, 1_4 \otimes S_{21}, \ell_1 \otimes S_{21}), \qquad (A-2)$$

where $\ell_1 = (-3, -1, 1, 3)'$, the linear contrast for drugs. An equivalent model, which results in identical cell estimates (but different parameter estimates), can be constructed using the polynomial contrast matrix $D_{43}^{(P)} = (\ell_1, \ell_2, \ell_3)'$ for the drugs variable, where ℓ_1, ℓ_2, and ℓ_3 are linear, quadratic, and cubic orthogonal polynomial contrasts, respectively. The linear contrast ℓ_1 is defined above, and $\ell_2 = (1, -1, -1, 1)'$, $\ell_3 = (-1, 3, -3, 1)'$. The alternative version of the design matrix is then given by (A-2) with D_{43} replaced by $D_{43}^{(P)}$. The latter strategy was used to construct the design matrix for the model of no three-factor interaction in section 5.7.

REFERENCES

Agresti, A. 1984. *Analysis of Ordinal Categorical Data*. New York: Wiley.

Bedrick, E. J. 1983. "Adjusted Goodness-of-Fit Test for Survey Data." *Biometrika* 70:591–95.

Bishop, Y. M. M., S. E. Fienberg, and P. W. Holland. 1975. *Discrete Multivariate Analysis: Theory and Practice*. Cambridge, MA: MIT Press.

Black, D., and J. Myles. 1986. "Dependent Industrialization and the Canadian Class Structure: A Comparative Analysis of Canada, the United States, and Sweden." *Canadian Review of Sociology and Anthropology* 23:157–81.

Brier, S. S. 1980. "Analysis of Contingency Tables Under Cluster Sampling." *Biometrika* 67:591–96.

Canadian Facts. 1983. *National Survey of Class Structure and the Labour Process in Canada*. Technical Report. Ottawa: Canadian Facts.

Clogg, C. C. 1982. "Some Models for the Analysis of Association in Multi-Way Cross-Classifications Having Ordered Categories." *Journal of the American Statistical Association* 77:803–15.

Eno, G. M. 1985. "Class Position and Gender: Differences in Income Returns to Education in Canada." M.A. thesis, Carleton University.

Fay, R. E. 1979. "On Adjusting the Pearson Chi-Square Statistic for Cluster Sampling." Pp. 402–405 in *Proceedings of the Social Statistics Section, American Statistical Association*. Washington, DC: American Statistical Association.

——————. 1982. "Contingency Table Analysis for Complex Sample Designs: CPLX." Pp. 44–52 in *Proceedings of the Survey Research Methods Section, American Statistical Association*. Washington, DC: American Statistical Association.

——————. 1985. "A Jackknifed Chi-Squared Test for Complex Samples." *Journal of the American Statistical Association* 80:148–57.

Fienberg, S. E. 1981. *The Analysis of Cross-Classified Categorical Data*. 2d ed. Cambridge, MA: MIT Press.

Fuller, W. A., D. Schnell, G. Sullivan, and W. J. Kennedy. 1987. "Survey Variance Computations on the Personal Computer." Invited paper, 46th Session of the International Statistical Institute, Tokyo.

Goodman, L. A. 1979. "Simple Models for the Analysis of Cross-Classifications Having Ordered Categories." *Journal of the American Statistical Association* 74:537–52.

——————. 1984. *The Analysis of Cross-Classified Data Having Ordered Categories*. Cambridge, MA: Harvard University Press.

Gross, W. F. 1984. "A Note on 'Chi-Squared Tests with Survey Data'." *Journal of the Royal Statistical Society*, ser. B, 46:270–72.

Haberman, S. J. 1978. *Analysis of Qualitative Data*. 2 vols. New York: Academic Press.

Hansen, M. H., W. N. Hurwitz, and W. G. Madow. 1953. *Sample Survey Methods and Theory*. Vol. 2. New York: Wiley.

Hidiroglou, M. A., and J. N. K. Rao. 1987. "Chi-Squared Tests with Categorical Data from Complex Surveys: Parts I and II." *Journal of Official Statistics* 3:117–32, 133–40.

Holt, D., A. J. Scott, and P. O. Ewing. 1980. "Chi-Squared Tests with Survey Data." *Journal of the Royal Statistical Society*, ser. A, 143:302–20.

Kirk, R. E. 1968. *Experimental Design: Procedures for the Behavioral Sciences*. Belmont, CA: Brooks/Cole.

Kish, L. 1965. *Survey Sampling*. New York: Wiley.

Kish, L., and M. R. Frankel. 1974. "Inference from Complex Samples" (with discussion). *Journal of the Royal Statistical Society*, ser. B, 36:1–37.

Koch, G. G., D. H. Freeman, and J. L. Freeman. 1975. "Strategies in the Multivariate Analysis of Data from Complex Surveys." *International Statistical Review* 93:59–78.

Landis, J. R., J. L. Freeman, W. M. Stanish, G. G. Koch, and A. L. Lewis. 1976. "GENCAT: A Computer Program for the Generalized Chi-Square Analysis of Categorical Data Using Weighted Least Squares." *Computer Programs in Biomedicine* 6:196–231.

Lepkowski, J. M. 1982. "The Use of OSIRIS II to Analyze Complex Sample Survey Data." Pp. 38–43 in *Proceedings of the Survey Methods Section, American Statistical Association*. Washington, DC: American Statistical Association.

McCarthy, P. J. 1966. "Replication: An Approach to the Analysis of Data From Complex Surveys." *Vital and Health Statistics*, ser. 14, 2. Washington, DC: National Center for Health Statistics.

McCullagh, P., and J. A. Nelder. 1983. *Generalized Linear Models*. London: Chapman and Hall.

Nathan, G. 1981. "Notes on Inference Based on Data from Complex Sample Designs." *Survey Methodology* 7:109–29.

Pffefferman, D., and G. Nathan. 1985. "Problems in Model Identification Based on Data from Complex Sample Surveys." *Bulletin of the International Statistical Institute* 51:topic 12.

Platt, W. G. 1986. "GAUSS." *American Statistician* 40:164–69.

Rao, J. N. K., and A. J. Scott. 1979. "Chi-Squared Tests for Analysis of Categorical Data from Complex Surveys." Pp. 58–66 in *Proceedings of the Survey Research Methods Section, American Statistical Association*. Washington, DC: American Statistical Association.

―――――――――. 1981. "The Analysis of Categorical Data from Complex Sample Surveys: Chi-Squared Tests for Goodness of Fit and Independence in Two-Way Tables." *Journal of the American Statistical Association* 76:221–30.

―――――――――. 1982. "On Chi-Squared Tests for Multi-Way Tables with Cell Proportions Estimated from Survey Data." Paper presented at the Israeli Statistical Association International Meetings on Analysis of Sample Survey Data and on Sequential Analysis, Jerusalem, June 14–18.

―――――――――. 1984. "On Chi-Squared Tests for Multi-Way Tables with Cell Proportions Estimated from Survey Data." *Annals of Statistics* 12:46–60.

―――――――――. 1987. "On Simple Adjustments to Chi-Square Tests with Sample Survey Data." *Annals of Statistics* 15:385–97.

Roberts, G. 1986. "Generalized Response Models for Survey Data." Pp. 31–36 in

Proceedings of the Survey Research Methods Section, American Statistical Association. Washington, DC: American Statistical Association.

Roberts, G., J. N. K. Rao, and S. Kumar. 1987. "Logistic Regression Analysis of Sample Survey Data." *Biometrika* 74:1–12.

Scott, A. J., and D. Holt. 1982. "The Effect of Two-Stage Sampling on Ordinary Least Squares Methods." *Journal of the American Statistical Association* 77:848–54.

Scott, A. J., and J. N. K. Rao. 1981. "Chi-Squared Tests for Contingency Tables with Proportions Estimated from Survey Data." Pp. 247–66 in *Current Topics in Survey Sampling*, edited by D. Krewski, R. Platek and J. N. K. Rao. New York: Academic Press.

Sudman, S. 1976. *Applied Sampling*. New York: Academic Press.

Thomas, D. R., and J. N. K. Rao. 1987. "Small-Sample Comparisons of Level and Power for Simple Goodness-of-Fit Statistics Under Cluster Sampling." *Journal of the American Statistical Association* 82:630–36.

9

An Application of Item Response Theory to the Measurement of Depression

Nora Cate Schaeffer*

Studies of group differences in a subjective phenomenon are generally concerned with differences in the degree of the trait. To determine differences in degree, however, it is first necessary to determine that the items used to measure the trait in the groups do not differ in kind. In other words, the items must be unbiased. Evaluating differences in kind and in degree requires the ability to scale questions and respondents. Item response theory (IRT) models offer a method for scaling questions and respondents with respect to a subjective phenomenon. These models state that the probability of a correct response depends on the level of the trait the person has and on the characteristics of the item being answered. This paper presents an application of the two-parameter logistic IRT model to the measurement of depression.

I am grateful to Robert J. Mislevy for his patient advice throughout this analysis, for his test of group differences, and for his comments on an earlier draft of this paper. The comments of Robert D. Mare, Gerald Marwell, Sara S. McLanahan, Joy P. Newmann, and Elizabeth Thomson and discussions with Ross L. Matsueda were very helpful. The careful and challenging suggestions of the anonymous reviewers of this paper resulted in many improvements. I do not point out where specific suggestions have been incorporated, but I hope that the reviewers will recognize the results of their labors here. I also thank Robert J. Mislevy and R. Darrell Bock for permission to use BILOG, Leonard I. Pearlin for permission to analyze these data, and Systat, Inc., for the use of a pre-release version of its graphics software. Any errors are my own. This research was partially supported by grants from the Illinois Department of Mental Health and Developmental Disability and from the Research Committee of the Graduate School of the University of Wisconsin–Madison.
*University of Wisconsin–Madison.

Results are presented for items and respondents. The data were collected from 1,710 whites in Chicago in 1972. The set of 11 items is based on the Hopkins Symptom Checklist.

1. INTRODUCTION

The study of group differences requires close attention to what discussions of measurement refer to as scaling objects and scaling subjects (Duncan 1984a). The scaling of objects (items or stimuli) estimates the levels of a trait indicated by answers to different items. It establishes the range of the trait about which a set of items provides information and shows whether or not the scale characteristics of the items are the same for all subjects. The scaling of respondents enables the researcher to compare the distribution of the trait across groups. These two goals are recognized in different ways by Thurstone scaling and Guttman scaling and more recently by item response theory (IRT) models.

Both kinds of scaling are needed for a comparison of the degree or level of some trait across groups.[1] Such a comparison presupposes that the items used to measure a trait are understood and answered in the same way in the groups being compared, that is, that the difference between the groups with respect to the items is not one of kind (Andrich 1985). This is another way of saying that studying the origins or causes of group differences in some trait requires that measures of the trait be unbiased. Ruling out biased measurement that would render any observed group difference artifactual is logically prior to the search for other explanations. If the scale values of items appear to be similar in the groups being compared, conclusions about differences of degree depend on comparisons of individual scores or scale values.

The distinction between the two goals of scaling can be illustrated by considering Thurstone scaling, in which a set of survey items designed to measure some trait is scaled by a set of judges. The

---

[1] To be consistent with the measurement literature, which discusses the measurement of latent traits, I use the word *trait* to refer to the subjective phenomenon being measured. *Trait* thus refers to an individual-level subjective construct. This usage is not meant to imply that the subjective phenomenon measured is a personality trait or permanent characteristic of a person.

scale values of the items are then used to derive scale values for respondents when they are presented with the scaled items. Methods such as Thurstone scaling use different data to scale objects and subjects. In contrast, Guttman scaling and IRT models order both objects and subjects from the same set of answers. One IRT model, the Rasch model, is closely related to Guttman's model (Wright and Panchapakesan 1969; Andrich 1985). Unlike scaling techniques, which require that scale values capture properties of distance and order in the trait being measured, traditional true-score psychometric methods select items and develop scores that discriminate among respondents without ordering or scaling items (see, e.g., Lord and Novick 1968).

The IRT models state that the probability of a given response is a function of the respondent's level of the trait and one, two, or three item parameters; both respondent and item parameters can be estimated from the same data (Hulin, Drasgow, and Parsons 1983; Lord 1980). The IRT models provide a method for comparing the characteristics of items across groups and for estimating the trait levels of respondents, the distributions of which can then be compared. This paper applies the two-parameter binary logistic IRT model to the study of sex differences in depression.

Sex differences in symptoms of depression and related forms of distress have been observed frequently (see, e.g., Dohrenwend and Dohrenwend 1969; Gove and Tudor 1973; Weissman and Klerman 1977; Kessler 1979; Bebbington et al. 1981; Eaton and Kessler 1981; Frerichs, Aneshensel, and Clark 1981; and Mirowsky and Ross 1986). The differences persist even when a wide range of background characteristics is controlled (Eaton and Kessler 1981).[2] A recurring question in the study of psychological distress is whether or not measurement inaccuracies contribute to observed group differences in distress (Dohrenwend 1966; Phillips and Clancy 1970; Gove et al. 1976; Klassen, Hornstra, and Anderson 1975; Gove and Geerken 1977; Carr and Krause 1978; Ross and Mirowsky 1984c). This paper begins by reviewing traditional approaches to studying bias in the measurement

---

[2] This pattern appears in these data as well. For example, when the number of depression symptoms is regressed on age, education, marital status, income, and housewife status, the regression coefficient for the dummy variable indicating that the respondent is female remains substantial and significant (1.19, SE = 0.16). Radloff (1975) discusses similar relationships with depression scores.

of psychological distress. The IRT model used in the analysis is described briefly as an alternative approach. The first part of the analysis focuses on the items used to measure depression or depressive distress and examines whether or not differences in kind by sex exist; item parameters are estimated under different assumptions and the results are compared. The second part of the analysis examines whether or not differences in degree exist; the results obtained using various respondent scores are compared. The concluding discussion briefly reviews some implications of the analysis of item parameters for measuring depression. Although this discussion focuses on the study of depression, the approach is applicable to the study of other subjective phenomena.

2. STUDYING BIAS IN THE MEASUREMENT OF DISTRESS

An item in a scale designed to measure a trait or characteristic may be considered unbiased with respect to a group variable if all respondents with a given level of the trait give the same response to the item regardless of their group membership. By extension, a scale composed entirely of such unbiased items will be unbiased. When an item is biased, persons who have the same level of a trait but who belong to different groups may give different answers to the item. In such a case, the set of items will be unidimensional in a sample that is homogeneous on the group variable. When bias is present, the dimensionality of the set of items used to measure the trait depends on whether or not the group being measured is heterogeneous with respect to the group variable.

There are at least two ways to study bias when it is defined in this way. First, one can identify, measure, and control the trait believed to be contaminating responses to the items; this is the trait that destroys the unidimensionality of the set of items and varies with the group variable. For example, an item may contain information about both depression and expressiveness, and expressiveness may vary by sex. In this case, estimates of sex differences in depression will be contaminated by sex differences in expressiveness. Second, one can focus directly on the properties of the items rather than attempt to identify a trait that contaminates responses. This approach is applicable even when, using a set of items considered unidimensional, the level of the trait that an

item indicates varies with group membership because of causes associated with that specific item. For example, because of differences in
socialization, the degree of depression that triggers suicidal thoughts in
women and men may differ: Women may have suicidal thoughts when
moderately depressed, but men may have such thoughts only when
very depressed. If this is true, estimates of sex differences will be
inaccurate when the item about suicidal thoughts is scored in the same
way for men and women. The approach used to analyze or detect bias
in a scale depends on the way bias is defined.

Traits that cause bias. Much of the sociological literature on the
measurement of psychological distress in general populations approaches the question of bias by first hypothesizing a characteristic of
the respondent that might interact with the form or content of the
items in a scale and thereby bias responses to the items. For example,
expressiveness might be a source of sex bias in reports of depression if it
is related to reports of symptoms of depression and if it varies by sex
(Phillips and Segal 1969; Cooperstock 1971). A series of studies has
identified three respondent characteristics suspected of causing bias in
responses about psychiatric symptoms or similar topics: (a) acquiescence (or such variations as yeasaying/naysaying), (b) a need for
approval, and (c) perceived trait desirability, also called the social
desirability of the trait (Phillips and Clancy 1972; Clancy and Gove
1974; Gove et al. 1976; Gove and Geerken 1977; Allen et al. 1979;
Ross and Mirowsky 1984c). All the studies (except Allen et al.'s) show
that controlling for possible sources of bias sometimes alters an estimated sex difference but does not eliminate it.

When the biasing variables are located, the relationship between
the source of bias and the trait being measured can be analyzed and
interpreted. However, the conceptualization of the source of bias may
be ambiguous, and its measurement may also be biased (DeMaio 1984;
Schuman and Presser 1981; Stocking 1979). Furthermore, this approach does not allow one to locate specific problems in a scale, assess
their impact, and correct them; nor does it allow one to draw general
conclusions about the adequacy of the scale items.

Bias in scale and item properties: Factor analysis. Rather than ask
whether a specific respondent trait other than that being measured
generates the answers of one sex and not those of the other, we could
ask whether men's and women's responses to the scale items measure
the trait in a similar way. Factor analysis can be used to examine

whether or not a set of items exhibits factorial invariance with respect
to groups defined by a group variable such as race or sex. An index of
invariance can then be used to estimate whether the factor structure or
dimensionality of the items is similar across groups. For example, in a
study of dimensionality bias in the Langer Index of Mental Illness,
which contains some questions on symptoms of depression, Johnson
and Meile (1981, pp. 422–26) found no sex bias in factor loadings, in
contributions of index components to total index score, or in the
covariance of index components. There was evidence of slight sex bias
in the path analysis of the true scores for the index. A comparison of
the factor structures of the Center for Epidemiological Studies' depression scale (CES-D) for men and women found that they were essentially the same except that the crying symptom was associated with a
depressed affect factor for women but constituted a separate factor for
men (Radloff 1977; Ross and Mirowsky 1984a).

Factor analytic approaches present problems for items that
measure such traits as psychiatric symptoms, some of which are rare
even in the clinical populations on which the scales were developed and
tested. Maxwell (1972) has argued that item distributions in which zero
scores predominate (e.g., distributions of a rare trait) yield inflated
correlation estimates; the magnitudes of the factor loadings are also
inflated and cannot be accepted at face value. The effects on group
comparisons are probably variable and depend on the configuration of
responses in a particular sample, since factor structures are sample-
specific.

Confirmatory factor analytic techniques for continuous variables, which provide a means of testing the equality of covariance and
factor structures in subgroups, are a variation of this approach to the
study of group differences. These techniques are not suitable for the
present analysis because they require the strong assumption that
the distributions of both the manifest and the latent variables are
multivariate normal (Long 1976). Most techniques currently available
for estimating and comparing factor loadings assume normal distributions of the manifest variables within groups and thus are not suitable
for dichotomous data; observed differences in factor structure between
groups may be due to failure of the assumption of normality rather
than to bias. Even when items distributed like those in the depression
scale analyzed here are not dichotomized, their variance is not independent of their mean; that is, the variance will increase with the mean

because of the large number of zero scores. Because the amount of variability limits the degree of covariance or covariation, differences in covariation can be confounded with differences in levels of the trait.[3]

Bias in scale and item properties: Traditional psychometric approaches. In addition to factor analytic techniques to study item bias, there is what Lord (1980, pp. 213–17) labels the conventional approach, in which traditional item difficulties and item discriminations in each group are compared. The definition of item difficulty used in this approach—the proportion answering an item correctly—may be adequate for estimating relative levels of the trait within a group, but it is inadequate for making comparisons between groups because it confounds item bias and true group differences.[4] There are similar problems with the traditional indicator of item discrimination, i.e., the item-total correlation. These correlations are sensitive to the marginal distributions of the items; therefore, they depend on the distribution of the trait in the group being studied.

Bias in scale and item properties: Item response theory. One limitation shared by all these approaches to examining the measurement properties of a set of items is their inability to estimate characteristics of items and scales—or, by extension, to evaluate bias—independently of the distribution of the trait in the group responding to the items. In factor analytic methods, the structures that appear depend on the clustering of symptoms in a particular clinical or general population sample. However, there is no reason to believe that the clustering of symptoms in one kind of sample is inherently superior to clustering in another or less a function of factors other than the trait being measured. In traditional psychometric statistics, one cannot determine whether group differences are due to differences in the trait or to bias.

---

[3] Using tetrachoric or polychoric correlations can mitigate some of the problems associated with the factor analysis of discrete variables; for example, spurious relationships between mean levels and relationships are eliminated (Muthén 1978). Normality assumptions are still required, but they apply to hypothetical process variables underlying the observable variables. Both LISREL 6 (Jöreskog and Sörbom 1985) and LISCOMP (Muthén 1987) provide this capability. The analysis presented here specifies the normal distribution for the latent variable and is essentially equivalent to Muthén's factor analysis with the number of factors set equal to one.

[4] An extended illustrated discussion of this distinction is provided by Thissen, Steinberg, and Gerrard (1986), who also show how to examine items for bias.

One family of IRT models describes a response to an item as a function of the person's level of the trait (θ) and up to three item parameters. Detailed discussions of item response theory can be found in Birnbaum (1968), Lord (1980), and Hulin et al. (1983). The model used in the analysis presented here describes the probability that a person whose level of the trait is θ_i will answer item j (that is, P_{ij}) as a two-parameter logistic function:

$$P_{ij} = \frac{e^{z_{ij}}}{1 + e^{z_{ij}}},\qquad(1)$$

where $z_{ij} = 1.7a_j(\theta_i - b_j)$, e is the base of the natural logarithm, and 1.7 is a scaling constant.[5]

The item parameters in this model are slope, or discrimination, and threshold, or difficulty (Lord 1980). *Slope, or discrimination*, is the degree to which the item is related to the underlying trait. The item slope is directly related to the reliability with which an item measures a trait (Bock and Mislevy 1981*b*, p. 24); items with higher slopes are more reliable. When the underlying trait is normally distributed, the slope is a monotonic increasing function of the biserial correlation between the test items and the trait. *Threshold, or difficulty*, is the point of inflection of the item response curve. In the one-parameter and two-parameter models, this point indicates the level of the trait at which the individual has an even chance of answering the item correctly or giving the answer that indicates the higher level of the trait.

Figure 1 presents two hypothetical item response curves and illustrates the meaning of the item response parameters. The curves illustrate the effects of varying the item parameters. The curve for item X is *more discriminating* than the curve for item Y (the slope of curve X is steeper than that of curve Y) and *less difficult* (the point of inflection

---

[5] The three-parameter logistic response model includes a parameter c that indicates the probability that a person at the lowest level of ability will answer the item correctly:

$$P_{ij} = c_j + \left(1 - c_j\right)\frac{e^{z_{ij}}}{1 + e^{z_{ij}}}.\qquad(2)$$

Under the two-parameter model there is no guessing. Under the one-parameter model, or Rasch model, the item discriminations are the same for all items and there is no guessing. If the one-parameter model holds, then estimating the two-parameter model amounts to using a different estimation procedure; if the one-parameter model does not hold, estimating that model is inappropriate (Lord 1980).

FIGURE 1. Examples of item characteristic curves.

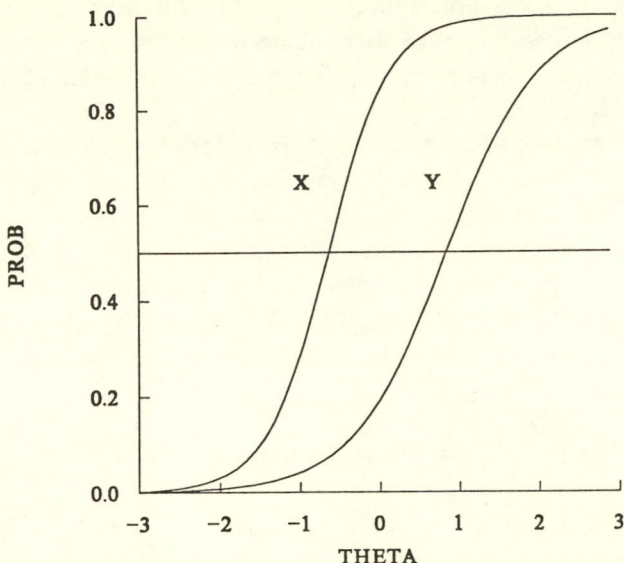

of curve X is lower than that of curve Y). The choice of unit and origin for the θ scale is arbitrary; the scale is usually established so that the estimated mean of the sample of subjects used to calibrate the items is zero and their estimated variance is one. The indeterminacy can also be resolved through the item parameters, in this case by centering the thresholds at zero and the slopes at one. This method facilitates comparison of estimates across samples of subjects, as this analysis requires. The item thresholds use the same scale as the levels of the trait; therefore, levels of the trait can be interpreted by referring to item content. Furthermore, θ values can be expressed, through equation (1), as the probability of a correct response, yielding an interpretable metric. Unlike the proportion-correct item statistic described above, these item parameters do not depend on the distribution of the trait in the group tested. The item response function can be viewed as the regression of item score on ability; since the regression is invariant with respect to changes in the frequency distribution of the predictors, the slope and threshold will be the same regardless of the group tested (Lord 1980, p. 34). For this reason, these models are particularly suitable for studying bias.

Most discussions of item response theory use the language of ability testing. Some of this language requires modification when the trait being measured is a report of a symptom, attitude, or behavior (Reiser 1981). In this application, the level of "ability" corresponds to the level of depression, and answering an item "correctly" corresponds to reporting that a symptom is present. The interpretation of the slope does not change.[6]

Variation in item thresholds between groups corresponds to the definition of bias given earlier; that is, the item indicates different levels of the trait in different groups. Variation between groups in slopes suggests that the extent to which the item is related to the underlying trait varies by group, or alternatively, that the reliability of the item varies by group. Though this kind of bias may be important, the present analysis focuses on the comparison of item thresholds across groups.[7]

3. METHODS

The sample. The data were collected in 1972 by Pearlin in the Urbanized Area of Chicago, which includes some Chicago suburbs and sections of northwestern Indiana. Clusters of four households were

---

[6] Interpretation is more difficult for the lower asymptote that is included in the three-parameter model. The lower asymptote indicates the probability that someone at the lowest ability level will agree with an item. In ability testing it is usually assumed that except in rare cases, persons will not be motivated to mask their level of ability but will attempt (e.g., by guessing) to display more ability than they have. When self-reports of attitudes, experiences, and behaviors are solicited, the meaning of this parameter changes. A process of inflation similar to guessing could be assumed to influence reports of desirable behaviors or attitudes. However, when information about painful or embarrassing behaviors and experiences is solicited, it can be safely assumed that most persons without the trait will not be motivated to pretend they have the trait by guessing. In this case, persons may be motivated to conceal their true trait level by claiming not to have symptoms. (If this behavior were systematically elicited from one group and not from the other, we would find a departure from unidimensionality.) In the present case, the lower asymptote might be interpreted as a level of systematic error, such as yea-saying.

[7] In the present research, agreement between groups of the slopes is less important than agreement of the thresholds because the slopes are estimated less accurately than the thresholds (Hulin, Drasgow, and Parsons 1983, p. 100), particularly when the number of items is very small, as it is here, and when some of the item distributions are very skewed. Furthermore, for items with moderate slopes (as most of these have), it is the individual's trait level and the item threshold that most affect the probability of a given response (Reiser 1980, pp. 15–16). Because of the problems in estimating slopes, the present discussion is limited to bias in item thresholds. The interaction between bias in the slopes and bias in the thresholds is discussed by Hulin et al. (1983).

selected in each sampled block, and the sex of the person interviewed within each household was predesignated. Approximately 70 percent of the sampled households responded. (See Pearlin and Johnson [1977] for details.) The analyses presented here use data from the 1,710 white respondents. Blacks and other races were omitted because the hypothesis of bias by race should be tested before the groups are combined (Bachman and O'Malley 1984; Klassen et al. 1975), and the power of such a test would be limited by the relatively small number of blacks in the sample.

The depression scale items. Respondents were presented with 11 symptoms of depression. They were asked how often during the past week they

1. lacked enthusiasm for doing anything
2. had a poor appetite
3. felt lonely
4. felt bored or had little interest in doing things
5. lost sexual interest or pleasure
6. had trouble getting to sleep or staying asleep
7. cried easily or felt like crying
8. felt downhearted or blue
9. lacked energy
10. felt hopeless about the future
11. had any thoughts of possibly ending their life

Four response categories were offered: never, once in a while, fairly often, and very often. Ten of the eleven depression items (all, that is, except the item about enthusiasm) were taken directly from the Hopkins Symptom Checklist (HSCL) developed by Derogatis et al. (1974) or were adapted from HSCL items.[8] On the basis of a factor analysis of

[8] This set of items has been largely superseded in practice by such recently developed instruments as the CES-D (Radloff 1977) or the Psychiatric Evaluation Research Interview Depression (PERI) Scale (Dohrenwend et al. 1980). However, sets of items similar to these were commonly used to measure depression in general population surveys, and the newer scales include items similar to those analyzed here. Of the symptoms included in this study, only loneliness and crying are not highly similar to symptoms mentioned as criteria for diagnosing a major depressive episode. Crying is, however, mentioned as an associated feature. The set of items omits three dimensions that may be considered in diagnosing depression: psychomotor agitation or retardation, cognitive disturbance, and feelings of worthlessness, self-reproach, or guilt (American Psychiatric Association 1980, pp. 210–17).

data from a large sample of patients, the original investigators assigned eight of these items to depression as the primary factor.

The invariance of the factors originally identified in the HSCL has been investigated for doctors' ratings as compared with patients' ratings and for patients of different social classes (Derogatis et al. 1971). The investigators concluded that the items exhibited factorial invariance across raters and across patient class, with the exception of the lowest social class. When anxious and depressed neurotics were compared, the invariance of the depression dimension of the HSCL was considerably lower than that of other HSCL factors (Derogatis et al. 1972, p. 663). This finding serves as a reminder that broad psychiatric categories such as depression are still quite heterogeneous and that factor analytic results may be highly sample-specific. In any case, items that are biased can still exhibit factorial invariance. Under appropriate assumptions, factorial invariance corresponds to invariant slopes. An analysis of factorial invariance will not, however, reveal variation between groups in the item thresholds.

The response distributions for the symptom items reflect the rarity of some of the symptoms. The item standard deviations generally increase with the mean of the item, because the proportion of respondents claiming never to have had a symptom ranges from 0.42 to 0.99. Thus, the item scores all bunch at the asymptomatic end. The mean level of symptom frequency, the proportion indicating presence of the symptoms, and the item standard deviation are all higher for women than for men. This is true for each item, although in some cases the sex difference is trivial. The item distributions also reveal that not all the response categories were well used. Of the four categories offered, "fairly often" and "very often" together were never used by more than 11 percent of the sample on any one item. Over all eleven items, an average of 6 percent of the sample used the two categories indicating greatest frequency. Thus, all the items except the item about enthusiasm were used like dichotomies, and all are dichotomized to indicate whether the symptom occurred at all for the item analysis.[9] (Appendix A presents descriptive statistics for the symptom items.)

---

[9] In this particular case, little information is lost by dichotomizing the items. In addition, the dichotomization increases the interpretability of the items; the way in which "vague quantifiers" are used depends on the respondent's feelings about the reported events and on the actual frequency of the event (Bradburn and Miles 1979). Such relative frequency categories must be considered different from categories that record the number of times an event occurred.

Analysis plan. The analysis proceeds in two parts: The first is concerned with the scaling of objects (in this case, symptoms), and the second is concerned with the scaling of subjects. In the first part, the depression items are analyzed; that is, item parameters are estimated. This item calibration, as it is sometimes called, is performed separately for males and females and then for the pooled sample. As a result of examining these three initial models, a fourth and final model is estimated. The item analysis has two goals: (a) to examine the characteristics of the set of items, for example, the range of the item difficulties, and (b) to determine whether or not the items are unbiased, that is, whether there are differences in kind by sex that would complicate the search for differences of degree. Conclusions about the existence of a difference of degree are usually based on comparisons of subject scores. Thus, the second part of the analysis compares the results obtained using several different individual depression scores, some of which take the results of the item analysis into account.

4. DIFFERENCES IN KIND AND SCALING OBJECTS: THE ITEM ANALYSIS

Dimensionality of the depression scale items. Though multidimensional models are possible, the estimation procedure used here assumes that the set of items is unidimensional; that is, at a given trait level, item responses are assumed to be uncorrelated. The argument that a set of items measures a single trait is supported, although not rigorously demonstrated, if the set is unidimensional for a tested group. In practice, however, a set of items may appear unidimensional even though one or more items in the set are sensitive to an additional dimension. For example, there may be aspects unique to an item that elicit some trait other than that being measured. Furthermore, analysis may find only a single dimension in a set of items designed to measure a multidimensional trait if the items do not adequately represent all dimensions of the trait or if there are idiosyncracies in the distribution of the trait in the group to which the items were administered.[10]

Lord has suggested a practical procedure to examine the dimensionality of a set of items based on the latent roots of a matrix of

[10] Compare, for example, the results of this analysis with the dimensionality of the CES-D (Radloff 1977; Ross and Mirowsky 1984a) or the PERI depression scale (Newmann 1984).

tetrachoric correlations with estimated communalities on the diagonal. If the first root is larger than the second and the second is not much larger than the remaining roots, then the items are approximately unidimensional (Lord 1980, p. 21). That the tetrachoric correlations have one common factor is a sufficient, but not necessary, condition for unidimensionality (Lord and Novick 1968, p. 382). Tetrachoric correlations are based on the assumption that the underlying relationship between each pair of items is bivariate normal. Although this assumption is probably not met by these symptom reports, and conclusions based on this approach may not be conservative (Bock and Lieberman 1970, p. 191), Lord (1980) suggests that the procedure is a useful approximation.[11]

This test for unidimensionality was performed separately for males and females. Maximum likelihood procedures were used to extract initial factors from a matrix of tetrachoric correlations with estimated communalities on the diagonal. The matrix included all items except the one about suicidal thoughts, which was very highly skewed. The plots of the eigenvalues from this analysis meet Lord's criteria and suggest that the items may be considered unidimensional for men and women. (See Schaeffer [1984, pp. 73–75] for details of this analysis.) Given that the items are unidimensional in each group, significant variation in thresholds indicates that an item is biased by sex, probably for idiosyncratic reasons.

Estimating item parameters and model fit. Each of the models referred to below estimated item parameters for a two-parameter logistic response model.[12] The strategy followed in the analysis of the symptom

---

[11] Later developments are presented in Mislevy (1986), Rosenbaum (1984), Bock and Aitkin (1981), and Muthén (1978).

[12] Computations were performed using the BILOG computer program (Bock and Mislevy 1981a). Details of the estimation procedures can be found in Bock and Aitkin (1981), Mislevy and Bock (1982), and Bock and Mislevy (1981a). With a single exception—the question about interest in sex—the number of missing responses was negligible. Missing responses were coded to indicate that the symptom was absent so that the respondent could be retained in the analysis that yielded the exact G^2 tests. The larger number of unrecorded responses for the question about interest in sex was probably caused by interviewers' omission of the question. One step of the analysis was repeated, omitting cases for which the response to any item was missing; parameter estimates differed only slightly from those obtained when missing responses were scored as absence of the symptom. Thus, it appears that the treatment of missing responses adopted in this analysis did not distort the results.

items was to estimate separate models for males (model 1) and females (model 2) and to compare these with a pooled model (model 3). The final model (model 4) incorporates the results of that comparison. Item parameters for all the models reported here were estimated by the method of marginal maximum likelihood using the EM algorithm (see Bock and Aitkin 1981). The calculations require the assumption that the respondents are a random sample from the population of interest and an initial assumption about the distribution of the trait in the population. The information the sample provides about the distribution of the underlying trait is ambiguous, because very few respondents have any symptoms and because the relationship between the symptoms that were measured in the scale and all symptoms that could have been measured is unknown. For estimation to proceed, the small amount of distributional information in the sample must be supplemented by an assumption about the distribution of the latent variable. The unit normal distribution was assumed because it represents maximal uncertainty in a distribution with finite mean and variance (Bock and Aitkin 1981, p. 450). The item parameters, however, are relatively insensitive to the shape of the prior distribution that is assumed (Bock and Aitkin 1981, p. 449). Along with item parameter estimates, prior distributional assumptions and individual item responses are used to calculate a posterior distribution of the trait.

Three initial models reflecting different assumptions were estimated: Model 1 was estimated for males only, model 2 was estimated for females only, and model 3 was estimated for males and females. Model 3 thus assumes that the parameters for each item are the same for males and females; models 1 and 2 make no such assumptions. The models represent the extremes of restrictiveness and nonrestrictiveness with respect to sex bias. The item parameters for these models are presented in Tables 1 and 2. The parameters are rescaled so that the arithmetic mean of the thresholds equals zero and the geometric mean of the slopes equals one. This rescaling allows comparisons between men and women and among the different item response models. Because the level of depression indicated by suicidal thoughts is higher than that indicated by other items, most of the item thresholds have negative values.

A first step in selecting a final model is to examine the absolute and relative fit of these models. The likelihood ratio chi-square approximation (G^2) is used as a test of goodness of fit. In the present case,

TABLE 1
Depression Scale Item Parameters for IRT Models Estimated Within Sex

Scale Item	Slope	SE	Threshold	SE
A. Model 1: Males				
($n = 746$)				
Lack of enthusiasm	0.833	0.067	-2.515	0.161
Poor appetite	0.760	0.060	0.359	0.305
Loneliness	1.263	0.072	-0.603	0.244
Boredom	1.261	0.080	-1.276	0.210
Low interest in sex	1.021	0.066	-0.316	0.252
Sleeping problems	0.616	0.056	0.069	0.294
Crying	0.845	0.074	2.298	0.550
Feeling blue	1.295	0.073	-0.638	0.243
Low energy	1.170	0.075	-1.141	0.212
Feeling hopeless	1.002	0.065	0.842	0.347
Suicidal thoughts	1.228	0.104	2.922	0.820
B. Model 2: Females				
($n = 961$)				
Lack of enthusiasm	0.808	0.054	-2.421	0.169
Poor appetite	0.721	0.049	0.986	0.239
Loneliness	0.881	0.057	-0.276	0.176
Boredom	0.967	0.061	-0.497	0.172
Low interest in sex	0.543	0.045	0.223	0.200
Sleeping problems	0.679	0.049	-0.164	0.176
Crying	1.161	0.064	-0.056	0.194
Feeling blue	1.609	0.091	-0.693	0.194
Low energy	0.860	0.059	-1.163	0.154
Feeling hopeless	1.177	0.057	1.091	0.250
Suicidal thoughts	2.882	0.098	2.971	0.793

the statistic for testing the number expected in each response pattern under the model against the number observed assuming a general multinomial alternative is

$$G^2 = 2\left(\sum_l^s r_l \log_e \frac{r_l}{NP_l} \right), \tag{3}$$

where l subscripts the response patterns, r_l is the number of subjects responding in pattern l, N is the total sample size, and P_l is the estimated probability of the response pattern under the fitted model (Bock and Aitkin 1981). Patterns with small expected frequencies are

TABLE 2
Depression Scale Item Parameters for Pooled IRT Models

Scale Item	Slope	SE	Threshold	SE
A. Model 3: Pooled				
($N = 1,707$)				
Lack of enthusiasm	0.845	0.043	− 2.372	0.116
Poor appetite	0.740	0.038	0.770	0.188
Loneliness	1.059	0.045	− 0.362	0.144
Boredom	1.052	0.047	− 0.745	0.133
Low interest in sex	0.734	0.038	0.039	0.154
Sleeping problems	0.693	0.037	− 0.115	0.148
Crying	1.070	0.042	0.433	0.172
Feeling blue	1.503	0.057	− 0.657	0.150
Low energy	1.017	0.048	− 1.072	0.125
Feeling hopeless	1.126	0.042	0.977	0.199
Suicidal thoughts	1.531	0.066	3.105	0.509
B. Model 4: All items				
pooled except crying				
($N = 1,707$)				
Lack of enthusiasm	0.850	0.044	− 2.315	0.115
Poor appetite	0.747	0.038	0.803	0.186
Loneliness	1.065	0.046	− 0.318	0.143
Boredom	1.077	0.048	− 0.709	0.133
Low interest in sex	0.736	0.038	0.086	0.154
Sleeping problems	0.693	0.037	− 0.067	0.148
Feeling blue	1.504	0.058	− 0.609	0.148
Low energy	1.019	0.048	− 1.023	0.124
Feeling hopeless	1.131	0.042	1.016	0.199
Suicidal thoughts	1.553	0.066	3.137	0.509
Crying (females)	1.168	0.056	− 0.126	0.190
Crying (males)	0.842	0.082	2.638	0.566

collapsed with those of neighboring estimated ability until the expected frequency is greater than five. The degrees of freedom are the number of patterns after pooling minus the number of item parameters.[13]

[13] Calculating G^2 requires the specification of a prior distribution. For model 1 (males only) and model 2 (females only), the posterior distribution from the respective item calibration step was used as the prior distribution to incorporate information from the sample about the distribution of depression among men and women. Obtaining appropriate prior distributions to use in the calculations for the pooled models (model 3 and model 4) required an additional step. This step

Evaluating absolute fit when the effects of sample design cannot be summarized simply is ambiguous. Close fit is indicated by a low G^2, but G^2 increases with the degrees of freedom and sample size; the ratio of the G^2 to the degrees of freedom is sometimes used to provide standardization in comparisons. Furthermore, the nonindependence of the elements in a clustered sample can be expected to reduce the effective sample size; therefore, the test of fit computed in the sample will be inflated relative to the test of fit computed using the "true" sample size. The goodness-of-fit statistics for these models are presented in Table 3.[14]

The fit of two hierarchical models can be compared by subtracting the G^2. The degrees of freedom for the significance test of the difference equal the difference in the number of parameters estimated between the models being compared. The G^2 test for the equality of the item parameters for males and females compares the sum of the G^2 for the models calculated for males and females separately with the sum of the G^2 for the male and female models that used pooled item parameters. This G^2, presented in Table 3, is then

$$G^2_{\text{equality}} = \left(G^2_{f,p} + G^2_{m,p} \right) - \left(G^2_{f,f} + G^2_{m,m} \right), \qquad (4)$$

where the first subscript indicates the sample used to compute the prior

---

allowed the mean and variance of the trait distribution to vary by sex even though the item parameters were estimated on the pooled sample: The posterior distribution from calibrating and rescaling the pooled item parameters was used as the prior distribution in calculating individual scores and an estimated marginal latent distribution. It is this marginal latent distribution (along with the pooled item parameters) that was used to obtain the separate G^2 for males and females under the pooled model. The marginal latent distribution so calculated is on the same scale for men and women but does not assume that the distribution of the trait is the same for men and women. In the case of the pooled models (3 and 4), G^2 statistics were calculated separately for males and females so that the pooled models could be compared with models 1 and 2.

[14] The extent of the expected "inflation" can be summarized in an average sample design effect. The information needed to compute a design effect is not available in these data. A recent analysis of a subsample of these data that used confirmatory factor analysis to model scale responses, however, selected final models for seven scales with ratios of G^2 to the degrees of freedom that ranged from 2.17 to 4.35 (Mullan 1981), thus assuming a sample design effect in the range of 2 to 4. In addition, the fit of the unrestricted model here provides a kind of limit; no restricted model can fit better.

TABLE 3

Goodness-of-Fit Statistics and Comparisons for Four IRT Models

Model	Group for Whom Parameters Were Estimated	G^2	df	G^2/df
Model 1 (males)	Males	95.5	70	1.36
Model 2 (females)	Females	277.1	137	2.03
Model 3 (males)	Pooled	150.5	76	1.98
Model 3 (females)	Pooled	265.1	132	2.01
Model 4 (males)	Pooled except crying	107.3	70	1.53
Model 4 (females)	Pooled except crying	263.4	133	1.98

A. Comparison between model 3 and models 1 and 2:

$$G^2 = (958.49 + 675.21) - (903.83 + 554.86) = 175.01$$
$$df = (282 + 159 + 22) - (282 + 159) = 22$$
$$G^2/df = 7.96$$

B. Comparison between model 3 and model 4:

$$G^2 = (958.49 + 675.21) - (926.67 + 590.89) = 116.14$$
$$df = (282 + 159 + 22) - (282 + 159 + 20) = 2$$
$$G^2/df = 58.07$$

C. Comparison between model 4 and models 1 and 2:

$$G^2 = (926.67 + 590.89) - (903.83 + 554.86) = 58.87$$
$$df = (282 + 159 + 20) - (282 + 159) = 20$$
$$G^2/df = 2.94$$

Note: In calculating the G^2 for the tests of absolute fit, BILOG collapses cells so that the minimum expected value in each cell is 5. Thus, the degrees of freedom vary slightly from model to model and the models are not perfectly nested. A G^2 calculated without collapsing is used for the hierarchical tests in panels A through C.

distribution used in the calculation of the G^2, and the second subscript indicates the sample used to estimate the item parameters (Mislevy 1982, pers. comm.).

For example, the first G^2 term in panel A of Table 3 describes the fit of the model calculated using the posterior marginal latent distribution calculated for females as the prior distribution and the pooled model 3 item parameters. The degrees of freedom for the test are calculated in a parallel fashion.[15] Panel A indicates that the difference in fit between the pooled model, model 3, and models 1 and 2 is significant at the 0.01 level; the fit of models 1 and 2 is better.

If depression is substantially the same thing for men and women, however, it does not seem reasonable to accept a model in which the item parameters differ for men and women for all items. Furthermore, models 1 and 2 capitalize on chance differences between males and females. A strategy that does not seek to minimize group differences in the item parameters might be justifiable when two groups with different psychiatric diagnoses—primary and secondary depression, for example—are being compared. In the present analysis, however, there are compelling theoretical reasons to attempt first to obtain a model that allows the parameters of as few items as possible to differ for men and women. The conceptual complexity introduced by allowing parameters of several items to vary would be considerable.

A review of the clinical literature on measuring depression provides a clear hypothesis about sex bias in item parameters. Beck (1967, p. 20) reports that women cry at much lower levels of depression than men. Furthermore, at a given level of sadness, men are less likely to cry, and this pattern can be interpreted by referring to male and female roles (Ross and Mirowsky 1984b). These observations can be translated directly into a hypothesis that the item threshold for crying will be higher for men than for women; the evidence for this hypothesis can be examined by comparing the thresholds estimated for males and females separately.

The relationship between the separate parameter estimates for males and females provided by models 1 and 2 can be most easily examined in graphic form. Figure 2 plots the item thresholds for males against those for females. If the parameter estimates were the same for both groups, the points would fall along the diagonal. Fit to this line is thus a rough indicator of agreement in threshold estimates between the two groups.

---

[15] However, since only 22 degrees of freedom are lost in calculating the pooled item parameters and 2 degrees of freedom have been subtracted for each of the 11 items in the calculation of each of the G^2 statistics, 22 degrees of freedom must be added for model 3.

FIGURE 2. Plot of rescaled item thresholds, models 1 and 2.

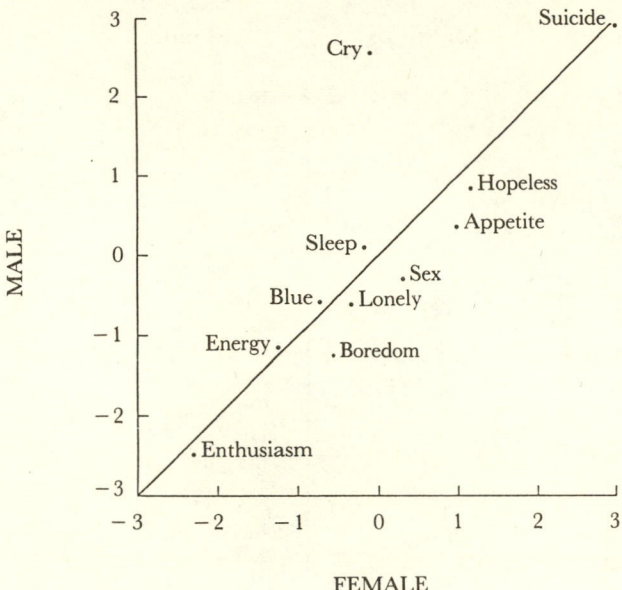

Using the rough criterion that parameter differences less than approximately two average standard errors indicate a reasonable fit, we can conclude that the fit is moderately good for the items about boredom, interest in sex, and appetite, and good for the other items except the item about crying. The difference between men's and women's thresholds for the crying item is quite large (2.35 scale units) and in the expected direction; that is, women cry at much lower levels of depression than men. For men, the only item with a higher threshold than crying is the item about suicidal thoughts.

Figure 3 shows the ranking of the item thresholds as well as the distances between them. If there were no sex bias in the scale, the order of the item thresholds would be the same in both groups. Several general points can be made about the presentation in this graph. First, the items are split into two groups; no items cross from the five most negative coefficients to the upper six. The similarity in the rankings is captured by the Spearman rank-order correlation coefficient of 0.90. The item that has the greatest effect in lowering the coefficient is that about crying.

FIGURE 3.   Ranking of rescaled item thresholds, models 1 and 2.

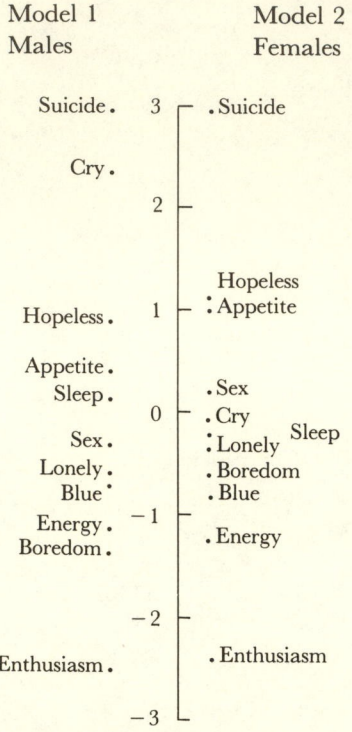

A comparison of the thresholds of models 1 and 2 suggests that an acceptable common fit might be expected for the thresholds for all items except that about crying. Thus, in model 4, all item parameters except those for the crying item were constrained to be identical for men and women. This procedure is equivalent to specifying that there are two crying items, one answered by men and one answered by women. With this difference, the steps in the estimation process are the same as those described earlier for model 3. Model 4 represents an attempt to obtain a parsimonious final model that fits reasonably well and provides a test of the hypothesis that the crying item is biased. The item parameters for this model were rescaled in the manner already described, except that the crying item was not included. The item parameters are presented in panel B of Table 2. There are only minor differences between models 3 and 4 in the parameters that the two models share.

Panel B of Table 3 compares the two pooled models, models 3 and 4. Model 4 has an appreciably better fit than model 3. The fit obtained for women is almost identical under the two models; the improvement in fit is due almost entirely to improved fit in the parameters for men.[16] Finally, the G^2 for the comparison between model 4 and models 1 and 2 is presented in panel C of Table 3. The combination of models 1 and 2 provides a somewhat better fit than model 4, but the improvement in fit obtained from the separate models is much less than that in panel A of Table 3. Furthermore, the parsimony of model 4 is compelling, particularly if depression and closely related constructs are conceptualized as the same for men and women. Model 4 appears to be an appropriate choice, although a conservative one, even though those items for which slopes in Table 1 appear to differ by sex have been estimated with common slopes.

Comment. As mentioned earlier, two important goals in the scaling of items are to examine the range of the trait represented by the items and to determine whether or not there is bias. This analysis suggests that except for the item about crying, there is little threshold bias in these items. Because the model calibrates the symptoms as reported, it is irrelevant whether or not men cry more often than they report; if at each level of depression the variables that might affect propensity to report crying are constant, the item threshold refers to the level of depression at which men report crying. Because the crying item must be treated differently for men and women, for some purposes the item might be dropped from the set of items used to measure depression.

[16] When item parameters are calculated on the pooled sample, the estimates for the item slopes are also pooled. This is equivalent to assuming that the items for which the slopes are so estimated are equally discriminating for men and women. One consequence is that items with pooled slope estimates will be given the same weights for men and women in score calculations. Using the rough criterion described earlier, we see that the slopes in Table 1 fall into three groups: those for which agreement between males and females is good (lack of enthusiasm, poor appetite, sleeping problems, and feeling hopeless), moderately poor (loneliness, boredom, crying, feeling blue, low energy), and poor (low interest in sex and suicidal thoughts). The Spearman rank-order correlation between the two sets of slopes is 0.52. There is no obvious explanation for or pattern to these differences. Note that more variation is to be expected among slopes, since the data offer much less information about slopes than about thresholds.

The analysis makes clear, however, that the items cover only a highly restricted range of the trait depression. For both males and females, the great majority of these 11 items range from -1.25 to 1.0 on the θ scale; the range of all items is approximately -2.5 to 3.0. If the assumption that depression is continuous is appropriate, then items that indicate a greater range of levels of depression, particularly the moderately high range of 2 to 3, should be identified.

5. DIFFERENCES IN DEGREE AND SCALING SUBJECTS: DISTRIBUTIONAL RESULTS

The technique described here provides two methods for examining differences in degree: (a) estimating subjects' latent values and (b) estimating the parameters of the distribution of the trait (the mean and standard deviation of the marginal latent distribution).[17] Decisions about group differences in subjective traits, as well as analyses at the individual level, are usually based on individual scores. These scores are typically either raw symptom scores (corresponding to number-right scoring in ability testing) or scores that use ad hoc weights for response categories or factor weights for items. Assumptions about the relationship between the distribution of the scores and the distribution of the trait are rarely explicit. This section examines how the choice of scoring procedure affects the conclusions about the distribution of a trait. Estimates of individual latent values under several IRT models are compared with raw symptom scores, and both are compared with parameters estimated for the marginal latent distribution.

Individual latent values. Individual latent values or trait scores were estimated using the Bayes (expected a priori, or EAP) estimator. (See Bock and Aitkin [1981, p. 453] for a description.) This estimator is the expected trait value given the individual's response pattern; its calculation requires prior specification of a trait distribution.[18] The item slopes can be thought of as weights in the calculation of these individual distributions.

[17] This discussion is concerned only with zero-order differences between men and women. Including other variables could alter the conclusions given here.

[18] The prior distribution was the same as that used for calculating G^2, described in note 13. Scores were calculated separately for males and females under the pooled models.

During EAP score estimation, an updated estimate of the marginal latent distribution of the trait in the population can also be obtained. This distribution is calculated by summing the probabilities (densities from the posterior distribution of each subject calculated during scoring) at each of the points of the distribution. That is, the individual subjects' posterior distributions, of which their individual scores are the mean, are averaged to obtain an updated estimate of the marginal latent distribution. Thus, this final estimated distribution has been updated with information on the distribution of the trait in the sample obtained during score estimation. These final scores and resulting updated marginal latent distributions are on the same scale for men and women, because all have been calculated with respect to the common scale defined by the item parameters.

Trait distribution. Panel A of Table 4 presents the raw symptom scores by sex, and panel B presents the scores obtained under models 1–4. In addition to the standard deviations of the trait scores, panel B presents the standard deviations of the marginal latent distribution estimated during score calculation. The estimated variance of the latent distribution may differ from the variance of the individual scores for several reasons. Individual scores incorporate an error term, which tends to inflate the variance of the scores compared with the variance of the respondents' true abilities. The variance of the latent distribution may be deflated by a floor effect when zero scores predominate, as they do in these data; scores pile up at one end of the distribution because there is not enough information to discriminate abilities for this group.

Although the scoring systems differ, they lead to substantially the same conclusion about sex differences in depression, that is, that women have higher levels of depression than men. The size of the difference varies somewhat, however, depending on the scores used. The group means provided by the IRT models can be interpreted by referring to the item thresholds presented earlier. For example, according to models 1 and 2, the direct estimate of the mean for men is -2.51, suggesting that the average level of depression among the males is a little lower than the level indicated by lack of enthusiasm; for women, the mean level of depression is -1.43, somewhat lower than the level indicated by low energy.

It is difficult to compare these scales; the assumptions of each are different. However, the differences between the conclusions that would be drawn using the different scores can be summarized by

TABLE 4

Comparison of Five Depression Score Distributions, by Sex

	Mean	SD of Scores	Sex Difference	t	SD of Marginal Latent Distribution
A. Estimates from raw score distribution					
Raw score (males)	2.19	2.36	−1.32	−10.55	
Raw score (females)	3.52	2.82			
B. Estimates from latent distribution					
Model 1 (males)	−2.51	1.56	−1.27	−13.40	1.81
Model 2 (females)	−1.44	1.73			1.92
Model 3 (males)	−2.40	1.54	−0.97	−12.40	1.79
Model 3 (females)	−1.43	1.69			1.88
Model 4 (males)	−2.28	1.59	−0.86	−10.81	1.84
Model 4 (females)	−1.43	1.68			1.84
C. Direct improved estimates					
Model 1 (males)	−2.15	1.34	−0.91	−12.63	
Model 2 (females)	−1.24	1.64			
Model 4 (males)	−2.02	1.41	−0.76	−10.52	
Model 4 (females)	−1.26	1.56			

Note: Only the t value for model 4 assumes equal variances.

comparing the t values, which incorporate information on group differences in both means and variances. From the t values it can be seen that compared with the other trait scores, the scores from model 4 minimize the difference between men and women because they treat crying differently for men and women. At any given level of depression (as defined by the other items), women are expected to cry more often than men; therefore, women's crying does not inflate their depression scores. Both the raw symptom scores and the model 3 scores consider the reported difference in crying as a difference in the level of depression. The results obtained using the raw symptom scores are comparable to those obtained using model 4.

In addition to affecting means, the choice of score clearly also affects the variances. Equalizing variances is frequently a goal of data transformations, and the differences among the scores in this respect are striking. Only the variances calculated using the model 4 scores pass the test for equality of variances by sex. These scores overcome one of the problems discussed earlier in that the scale variance does not depend on the scale mean. Such scores are inherently more suitable for many analytic techniques because group differences in trait variability are less likely to be confounded with group differences in trait levels.

An alternative to using the distributional information available in the individual scores is to estimate the distribution directly from individual responses under each of the item response models using the method described by Mislevy (1984). The marginal latent distribution was estimated for two of the models using a normal distribution as the prior distribution. These results are presented in panel C of Table 4. Both the means and the variances in panel C are considerably lower than those for the corresponding model in panel B. The difference between men and women in depression scores appears to be less in panel C than in panel B, but because the estimated variance also changes, the conclusions suggested by the estimates in panel B, as indicated by the t values, are not substantially different from those suggested in panel C. In the present case, the conclusion about group differences appears to be the same regardless of the approach used, but such consistency depends on both the distribution of the trait in the group and the range of the item thresholds.

Score distribution. Although the direct estimates of the parameters of the marginal latent distribution are preferable to estimates based on individual scores, most analyses of differences of degree must rely on such scores. Furthermore, such analyses generally assume that the distribution of scores preserves important characteristics of the distribution of the trait. To illustrate the impact of taking the item analysis into account, histograms for model 4 scores and the raw symptom scores are presented for women in Figure 4. The large number of women with no symptoms provides no information about the distribution of depression; the trait scores use the assumptions of underlying normality and symmetry and the distributional information for that portion of the sample with symptoms to infer the shape of the distribution. The effect of these assumptions is clear.

Assuming that the distribution of scores is interpretable, a close examination of the model 4 scores suggests that the difference between males and females may be smallest at the very highest level of depressive distress. Thirty percent of the men report no symptoms,

FIGURE 4. Histograms of two depression scores, females.

A. Raw Depression Scores for Females

	Cumulative		One Symbol Equals Approximately
Count	Percentage	Value	4.00 Occurrences
164	17.1	0	***
116	29.1	1	*****************************
140	43.3	2	***********************************
110	55.2	3	***************************
99	45.5	4	*************************
95	75.3	5	************************
68	82.4	6	*****************
62	88.9	7	****************
43	93.3	8	***********
41	97.6	9	**********
19	99.6	10	*****
4	100.0	11	*

```
        I\.............I....... .....I.... .... ....I............I Number
        0           40          80          120         160
```

B. Model 4 Depression Scores for Females

	Cumulative		One Symbol Equals Approximately
Count	Percentage	Midpoint	6.74 Occurrences
166	17.1	−4.0	************************
0	17.1	−3.6	
0	17.1	−3.2	
96	27.1	−2.8	**************
25	29.7	−2.4	****
109	41.0	−2.0	****************
77	49.0	−1.6	***********
106	60.0	−1.2	****************
78	68.2	−.8	***********
87	77.2	−.4	************
58	83.2	.0	*********
50	88.4	.4	*******
39	92.5	.8	******
24	95.0	1.2	****
23	97.4	1.6	***
16	99.1	2.0	**
5	99.6	2.4	*
4	100.0	2.8	*
0		3.2	

```
        I.............I.............I..................I Percent
        0           7           14          21
```

compared with 17.1 percent of the women; 62.0 percent of the men and 34.0 percent of the women have scores of -2.0 units or less (data for computing these percentages are not shown). The percentage difference between males and females is considerable at the level of depression that is approximately indicated by lack of enthusiasm. The percentage difference in the distributions declines as the level of depression increases: 3.8 percent of the men and 7.4 percent of the women have scores of 1.0 units or more; 2.4 percent of the men and 4.3 percent of the women have scores of 1.5 units or more. The ratio of the proportion male to the proportion female varies between 1.7 and 1.9 throughout this range. At the highest level of distress, 1.0 percent of the men and 1.0 percent of the women have scores of 2.0 or more. By comparison, the raw symptom scores show that 0.8 percent of the men and 2.4 percent of the women report 10 or more symptoms. There is some suggestion that the sex difference at the highest level of distress appears smaller when the latent values are used than when raw symptom scores are used. However, the symptom that indicates the highest level of depression (suicidal thoughts) is rare, and the difference is subject to considerable sampling variability.

The sex difference is concentrated at and below the level of depression indicated by lack of enthusiasm. The estimated proportions of males and females with high levels of depression appear somewhat more similar when the trait scores are used than when the raw symptom scores are used. Although this finding must be regarded as tentative, the pattern is compatible with the suggestion that some of the difference between males and females in average depression scores can be attributed to a difference in prevalence rather than to severity of symptoms (Craig and Van Natta 1979) or to a difference in transient mood rather than to depression (Newmann 1984).

Comment. The various estimates of the parameters of the distribution of depression all suggest that women have higher levels of depression than men. An advantage of using the scores estimated under the IRT models is that the group averages can be roughly characterized by referring to the item parameters.[19] The trait scores obtained under the final model equalize the variances for men and women, and the group variances of the latent trait scores are not

---

[19] This characterization is only approximate in the two-parameter model in which the scores contain information about slopes and thresholds.

dependent on the group means—additional advantages of these scores
for many analytic techniques. The individual trait levels are estimated
relatively imprecisely, but the scores are compared with the raw score
statistic because person-level analysis must rely on such scores. It is
substantively important in the study of depression to determine whether
or not, as the model 4 scores suggest, the sex difference is concentrated
at low levels of depression and diminishes at high levels of depression,
that is, at levels that are more likely to be associated with psychiatric
disorder. This concentration of the sex difference at lower levels of
depression may suggest the need to further refine the conceptualization
of depression used in the study of general population samples
(Newmann 1984). This is particularly true if the causes of the symptoms asked about differ for those who would and those who would not
be classified as having major depressive disorders or dysthymia.

6. CONCLUSION

This analysis strengthens the evidence that there is a sex difference in depression because the difference persists when bias in item
thresholds is taken into account. Furthermore, the sex difference appears to be concentrated at relatively low levels of distress. The analysis
of the item parameters also has broader implications for the study of
depression among individuals. The heaping of scores at the lowest
depression score may be a function of the sample of items or of the
distribution of depression, but these respondents provide no information about depression and represent a kind of limit on what is known
about depression in general populations. If depression can be usefully
thought of as a continuum, then it should be possible to obtain
information about the low levels of depression experienced by most
people. This is another way of saying that the analysis indicates the
need to expand the range of item thresholds. At least three courses of
action can be taken. First, we can identify "symptoms" of the low
levels of depression experienced by members of the general population
(as well as symptoms of the moderately high levels of depression, i.e.,
the range 1 to 3 on this theta scale). Second, we can study the response
dimensions and categories of such items. Previous work suggests that
response dimensions for depression items should permit a distinction
between prevalence and persistence (Craig and Van Natta 1979).
Models for polytomous variables can be used to make such compari-

sons (Andrich 1985). It may be possible to design response categories in such a way that they make better distinctions among respondents who now receive the lowest score. Third, we can extend the conceptualization of depression to distinguish among those with very low scores. For example, the dimensionality of depression might be extended to include such positive dimensions as mastery and self-esteem (Beck 1967; Brown and Harris 1978).[20] If we cannot find desirable ways of distinguishing among those with low scores but still conceptualize depression as continuous, then we must make adjustments during analysis (Tobin 1958).

This paper has focused on item thresholds, but the implications of the item slopes should also be considered. There is currently discussion about the relative merits of IRT models with one or two item parameters (Lord 1980; Andrich 1985). Partly at issue are the desirable criteria for measurement. The two-parameter model estimated here permits items to have different slopes, that is, to have different degrees of relationship to the underlying construct; the model can fit even when item slopes differ. In contrast, the one-parameter model for dichotomous items, the Rasch model, holds only when item discriminations are identical across items. When this model fits, several strong criteria for measurement obtain (Andrich 1985; Duncan 1984b; Duncan 1984c, pp. 215–18; Perline, Wright, and Wainer 1979). Under the Rasch model, the raw score is a sufficient statistic for estimating individual ability; that is, the raw score contains all the information about ability that the data can supply. Furthermore, the raw score preserves ordering on the trait continuum; the Rasch model is consistent with number-right scoring. This ordering, and its interval translation on the θ scale, makes comparisons based on person scores more accurate and interpretable. When item discriminations vary across items, individual scores may no longer be monotonically related to trait level; as a result, respondents may be misclassified.

The two-parameter IRT model offers flexibility in modeling the characteristics of a set of items and in studying their behavior. This is particularly useful in the study of depression, because the range of symptoms identified in the literature is relatively limited and because, importantly, most symptoms of depression also have other causes.

---

[20] This is not to say that scores on depression and self-esteem items should simply be added together.

Heterogeneity in causes is one source of variability in the discriminations of the symptom items, and this variation can also be studied usefully using the two-parameter model. Obviously, it is in the final selection of items used to score individuals—that is, in the measurements of a construct in a group of individuals—that the heterogeneity of the item slopes becomes important. This paper has examined individual scores based on items with heterogeneous slopes, but the items could be studied further to identify a set that would meet the Rasch criteria of homogeneous slopes.[21] The best selection of such items, however, would be made from a set with a broader range of thresholds than that found among these items.

APPENDIX A: DESCRIPTIVE STATISTICS FOR DEPRESSION SCALE ITEMS

Scale Item	Males			Females			
	Mean	SD	%	Mean	SD	%	t
Lack of enthusiasm	1.61	0.71	50	1.81	0.75	.64	−5.73
Poor appetite	1.21	0.53	16	1.31	0.68	.22	−2.77
Loneliness	1.25	0.56	20	1.44	0.72	.34	−6.44
Boredom	1.35	0.60	29	1.45	0.68	.37	−3.09
Low interest in sex	1.25	0.58	19	1.51	0.82	.35	−7.05
Sleeping problems	1.27	0.58	22	1.48	0.78	.35	−5.82
Crying	1.06	0.30	5	1.40	0.74	.29	−13.66
Feeling blue	1.24	0.52	20	1.49	0.74	.38	−7.82
Low energy	1.32	0.56	28	1.62	0.79	.47	−8.03
Feeling hopeless	1.12	0.44	9	1.21	0.57	.15	−3.53
Suicidal thoughts	1.01	0.15	1	1.02	0.16	2	−0.46

Note: The number of cases ranges from 726 to 746 for males and from 894 to 961 for females. Total numbers are 747 males and 963 females. Original items have four response categories: never (low value), once in a while, fairly often, and very often (high value). The percentages indicate the proportions of those who experienced symptoms at all in the previous week. The *t* values indicate the sex differences in the percentages.

[21] To facilitate such study by those so inclined, Appendix B provides the joint frequency distribution by sex of a set of items that seem likely to meet the criteria of the Rasch model: i.e., lack of enthusiasm, low energy, sleeping problems, feeling hopeless, and poor appetite.

APPENDIX B: JOINT FREQUENCIES FOR FIVE DEPRESSION SCALE ITEMS, BY SEX

Lack of Enthusiasm	Low Energy	Sleeping Problems	Feeling Hopeless	Poor Appetite	Number of Males	Number of Females	Total
0	0	0	0	0	272	228	500
0	0	0	0	1	11	13	24
0	0	0	1	0	12	3	15
0	0	1	0	0	31	32	63
0	0	1	0	1	7	2	9
0	0	1	1	0	2	4	6
0	1	0	0	0	20	29	49
0	1	0	0	1	5	1	6
0	1	0	1	0	1	7	8
0	1	0	1	1	1	1	2
0	1	1	0	0	7	21	28
0	1	1	0	1	1	2	3
0	1	1	1	0	1	4	5
0	1	1	1	1	2	2	4
1	0	0	0	0	135	133	268
1	0	0	0	1	20	22	42
1	0	0	1	0	4	9	13
1	0	0	1	1	2	3	5
1	0	1	0	0	31	43	74
1	0	1	0	1	10	17	27
1	0	1	1	0	1	3	4
1	0	1	1	1	1	4	5
1	1	0	0	0	62	117	179
1	1	0	0	1	23	31	54
1	1	0	1	0	12	16	28
1	1	0	1	1	5	18	23
1	1	1	0	0	27	82	109
1	1	1	0	1	15	45	60
1	1	1	1	0	8	25	33
1	1	1	1	1	18	46	64
					747	963	1,710

Note: Data are for white respondents from the "Problems of Everyday Life" study conducted in 1972 by Pearlin (Pearlin and Johnson 1977). Those who reported that they had the symptom in the previous week were coded 1. Those who reported that they did not have the symptom or who did not answer the item were coded 0.

REFERENCES

Allen, Richard H., Maxine L. Weinman, Ronald Lorimor, James L. Claghorn, George McBee, and Blair Justice. 1979. "The Effects of Response Bias on Sex Differences in a Psychiatric Population." *The Journal of Nervous and Mental Disease* 167:437–41.

American Psychiatric Association, Committee on Nomenclature and Statistics. 1980. *Diagnostic and Statistical Manual of Mental Disorders*. 3d ed. Washington, DC: American Psychiatric Association.

Andrich, David. 1985. "An Elaboration of Guttman Scaling with Rasch Models." Pp. 33–79 in *Sociological Methodology* 1985, edited by Nancy Brandon Tuma. San Francisco: Jossey-Bass.

Bachman, Jerald G., and Patrick M. O'Malley. 1984. "Yea-Saying, Nay-Saying, and Going to Extremes: Black-White Differences in Response Styles." *Public Opinion Quarterly* 48:491–509.

Bebbington, Paul, Jane Hurry, Christopher Tennant, Elizabeth Sturt, and J. K. Wing. 1981. "Epidemiology of Mental Disorders in Camberwell." *Psychological Medicine* 11:561–79.

Beck, Aaron T. 1967. *Depression: Clinical, Experimental, and Theoretical Aspects*. New York: Harper and Row.

Birnbaum, Allan. 1968. "Some Latent Trait Models and Their Use in Inferring an Examinee's Ability." Pp. 397–479 in *Statistical Theories of Mental Test Scores*, edited by Frederic Lord and Melvin Novick. Reading, MA: Addison-Wesley.

Bock, R. Darrell, and Murray Aitkin. 1981. "Marginal Maximum Likelihood Estimation of Item Parameters: An Application of the EM Algorithm." *Psychometrika* 46:443–59.

Bock, R. Darrell, and Marcus Lieberman. 1970. "Fitting a Response Model for *n* Dichotomously Scored Items." *Psychometrika* 35:179–97.

Bock, R. Darrell, and Robert J. Mislevy. 1981*a*. *BILOG: Maximum Likelihood Item Analysis and Test Scoring with Logistic Ogive Models*. Chicago: International Educational Services.

———. 1981*b*. *The Profile of American Youth*. Chicago: National Opinion Research Center.

Bradburn, Norman M., and Carrie Miles. 1979. "Vague Quantifiers." *Public Opinion Quarterly* 43:92–101.

Brown, George W., and Tirril Harris. 1978. *Social Origins of Depression*. New York: Free Press.

Carr, Leslie G., and Neal Krause. 1978. "Social Status, Psychiatric Symptomatology, and Response Bias." *Journal of Health and Social Behavior* 19:86–91.

Clancy, Kevin, and Walter Gove. 1974. "Sex Differences in Respondents' Reports of Psychiatric Symptoms: An Analysis of Response Bias." *American Journal of Sociology* 80:205–16.

Cooperstock, Ruth. 1971. "Sex Differences in the Use of Mood-Modifying Drugs: An Explanatory Model." *Journal of Health and Social Behavior* 12:238–44.

Craig, Thomas J., and Pearl A. Van Natta. 1979. "Influences of Demographic Characteristics on Two Measures of Depressive Symptoms." *Archives of General Psychiatry* 36:149–54.

DeMaio, Theresa J. 1984. "Social Desirability and Survey Measurement: A Review." Pp. 257–82 in *Surveying Subjective Phenomena*, vol. 2, edited by Charles F. Turner and Elizabeth Martin. New York: Russell Sage.

Derogatis, Leonard R., Ronald S. Lipman, Lino Covi, and Karl Rickels. 1971. "Neurotic Symptom Dimensions as Perceived by Psychiatrists and Patients of Various Social Classes." *Archives of General Psychiatry* 24:454–64.

——————. 1972. "Factorial Invariance of Symptom Dimensions in Anxious and Depressive Neurosis." *Archives of General Psychiatry* 27:659–65.

Derogatis, Leonard R., Ronald S. Lipman, Karl Rickels, E. H. Uhlenhuth, and Lino Covi. 1974. "The Hopkins Symptom Checklist: A Self-Report Symptom Inventory." *Behavioral Science* 19:1–15.

Dohrenwend, Bruce P. 1966. "Social Status and Psychological Disorder: An Issue of Substance and an Issue of Method." *American Sociological Review* 31:14–43.

Dohrenwend, Bruce P., and Barbara S. Dohrenwend. 1969. *Social Status and Psychological Disorder*. New York: Wiley.

Dohrenwend, Bruce P., Patrick E. Shrout, Gladys Egri, and Frederick S. Mendelsohn. 1980. "Measures of Nonspecific Psychological Distress and Other Dimensions of Psychopathology in the General Population." *Archives of General Psychiatry* 37:1229–36.

Duncan, Otis Dudley. 1984a. "Measurement and Structure: Strategies for the Design and Analysis of Subjective Survey Data." Pp. 179–230 in *Surveying Subjective Phenomena*, vol. 1, edited by Charles F. Turner and Elizabeth Martin. New York: Russell Sage.

——————. 1984b. "Rasch Measurement in Survey Research: Further Examples and Discussion." Pp. 367–404 in *Surveying Subjective Phenomena*, vol. 2, edited by Charles F. Turner and Elizabeth Martin. New York: Russell Sage.

——————. 1984c. *Notes on Social Measurement, Historical and Critical*. New York: Russell Sage.

Eaton, William E., and Larry G. Kessler. 1981. "Rates of Symptoms of Depression in a National Sample." *American Journal of Epidemiology* 114:528–38.

Frerichs, Ralph R., Carol S. Aneshensel, and Virginia A. Clark. 1981. "Prevalence of Depression in Los Angeles County." *American Journal of Epidemiology* 113:691–99.

Gove, Walter R., and Michael R. Geerken. 1977. "Response Bias in Surveys of Mental Health: An Empirical Investigation." *American Journal of Sociology* 82:1289–1317.

Gove, Walter R., James McCorkel, Terry Fain, and Michael D. Hughes. 1976. "Response Bias in Community Surveys of Mental Health: Systematic Bias or Random Noise." *Social Science and Medicine* 10:497–502.

Gove, Walter R., and Jeannette F. Tudor. 1973. "Adult Sex Roles and Mental Illness." *American Journal of Sociology* 78:812–35.

Hulin, Charles L., Fritz Drasgow, and Charles K. Parsons. 1983. *Item Response Theory: Application to Psychological Measurement*. Homewood, IL: Dow Jones-Irwin.

Johnson, David R., and Richard L. Meile. 1981. "Does Dimensionality Bias in Langer's 22-Item Index Affect the Validity of Social Status Comparisons? An Empirical Investigation." *Journal of Health and Social Behavior* 22:415–32.

Jöreskog, Karl G., and Dag Sörbom. 1985. *LISREL VI* [Computer program]. Mooresville, IN: Scientific Software, Inc.

Kessler, Ronald C. 1979. "Stress, Social Status, and Psychological Distress." *Journal of Health and Social Behavior* 20:259–72.

Klassen, Diedre, Robijn K. Hornstra, and Peter B. Anderson. 1975. "Influence of Social Desirability on Symptom and Mood Reporting in a Community Survey." *Journal of Consulting and Clinical Psychology* 43:448–52.

Long, J. Scott. 1976. "Estimation and Hypothesis Testing in Linear Models Containing Measurement Error." *Sociological Methods and Research* 5:157–206.

Lord, Frederic M. 1980. *Applications of Item Response Theory to Practical Testing Problems*. Hillsdale, NJ: L. Erlbaum Assoc.

Lord, Frederic M., and Melvin R. Novick. 1968. *Statistical Theories of Mental Test Scores*. Reading, MA: Addison-Wesley.

Maxwell, A. E. 1972. "Difficulties in a Dimensional Description of Symptomatology." *British Journal of Psychiatry* 121:19–26.

Mirowsky, John, and Catherine E. Ross. 1986. "Social Patterns of Distress." *Annual Review of Sociology* 12:23–45.

Mislevy, Robert J. 1984. "Estimating Latent Distributions." *Psychometrika* 49:359–82.

———. 1986. "Recent Developments in the Factor Analysis of Categorical Variables." *Journal of Educational Statistics* 11:3–31.

Mislevy, Robert J., and R. Darrell Bock. 1982. "The Implementation of the EM Algorithm in the Estimation of Item Parameters: The BILOG Computer Program." Paper presented at the IRT/CAT Invitational Conference at the University of Minnesota.

Mullan, Joseph T. 1981. "Parental Distress and the Transition to the Empty Nest." Ph.D. diss., Department of Behavioral Sciences, University of Chicago.

Muthén, Bengt. 1978. "Contributions to Factor Analysis of Dichotomous Variables." *Psychometrika* 43:551–61.

———. 1987. *LISCOMP* [Computer program]. Mooresville, IN: Scientific Software, Inc.

Newmann, Joy P. 1984. "Sex Differences in Symptoms of Depression." *Journal of Health and Social Behavior* 25:136–59.

Pearlin, Leonard I., and Joyce S. Johnson. 1977. "Marital Status, Life-Strains, and Depression." *American Sociological Review* 42:104–15.

Perline, Richard, Benjamin D. Wright, and Howard Wainer. 1979. "The Rasch Model as Additive Conjoint Measurement." *Applied Psychological Measurement* 3:237–55.

Phillips, Derek, and Kevin Clancy. 1970. "Response Biases in Field Studies of Mental Illness." *American Sociological Review* 35:503–15.

—————. 1972. "Some Effects of 'Social Desirability' in Survey Studies." *American Journal of Sociology* 77:921–40.

Phillips, Derek, and Bernard Segal. 1969. "Sexual Status and Psychiatric Symptoms." *American Sociological Review* 34:58–72.

Radloff, Lenore. 1975. "Sex Differences in Depression: The Effects of Occupation and Marital Status." *Sex Roles* 1:245–65.

—————. 1977. "The CES-D Scale: A Self-Report Depression Scale for Research in the General Population." *Applied Psychological Measurement* 1:385–401.

Reiser, Mark R. 1980. "A Latent Trait Model for Group Effects." Ph.D diss., Department of Behavioral Sciences, University of Chicago.

—————. 1981. "Latent Trait Modeling of Attitude Items." Pp. 117–44 in *Social Measurement: Current Issues*, edited by George W. Bohrnstedt and Edgar Borgatta. Beverly Hills: Sage.

Rosenbaum, Paul R. 1984. "Testing the Conditional Independence and Monotonicity Assumptions of Item Response Theory." *Psychometrika* 49:425–35.

Ross, Catherine E., and John Mirowsky. 1984a. "Components of Depressed Mood in Married Men and Women." *American Journal of Epidemiology* 119:997–1004.

—————. 1984b. "Men Who Cry." *Social Psychology Quarterly* 47:138–45.

—————. 1984c. "Socially Desirable Response and Acquiescence in a Cross-Cultural Survey." *Journal of Health and Social Behavior* 25:189–97.

Schaeffer, Nora Cate. 1984. "Distress in Major Adult Roles and Depression among White Men and Women." Ph.D. diss., Department of Sociology, University of Chicago.

Schuman, Howard, and Stanley Presser. 1981. "The Acquiescence Quagmire." Pp. 203–30 in *Questions and Answers in Attitude Surveys*. Orlando: Academic Press.

Stocking, Carol. 1979. "Reinterpreting the Marlowe-Crowne Scale." Pp. 85–106 in *Improving Interview Method and Questionnaire Design*, edited by Norman Bradburn and Seymour Sudman and Associates. San Francisco: Jossey-Bass.

Thissen, David, Lynne Steinberg, and Meg Gerrard. 1986. "Beyond Group-Mean Differences: The Concept of Item Bias." *Psychological Bulletin* 99:118–28.

Tobin, James. 1958. "Estimation of Relationships for Limited Dependent Variables." *Econometrica* 26:24–36.

Weissman, Myrna M., and Gerald L. Klerman. 1977. "Sex Differences in the Epidemiology of Depression." *Archives of General Psychiatry* 34:91–111.

Wright, Benjamin, and Nargis Panchapakesan. 1969. "A Procedure for Sample-Free Item Analysis." *Educational and Psychological Measurement* 29:23–48.

10

Evaluating a Multiple-Imputation Method for Recalibrating 1970 U.S. Census Detailed Industry Codes to the 1980 Standard

Donald J. Treiman, William T. Bielby[†]
and Man-tsun Cheng[‡]*

In this paper, we evaluate a multiple-imputation procedure for converting data coded into the 1970 U.S. census detailed classification of industries to the categories of the 1980 classification. For a sample of 127,125 persons in the labor force drawn from responses to the U.S. census of 1970, we compare 1980 codes directly assigned by coders working from the narrative descriptions in the census questionnaires with 1980 codes imputed via a logistic regression procedure from the 1970 codes and other information about

Preparation of this paper was supported by National Science Foundation grant SES 83-11483. An earlier version of the paper was presented at the 1987 meetings of the American Sociological Association, Chicago, and the final version was prepared while Treiman was an ASA/NSF/Census Fellow. Clifford Clogg, Robert Johnson, Ann Miller, Charles Nam, John Priebe, Patricia Roos, Donald Rubin, Nathaniel Schenker, Tom Scopp, Paul Siegel, Lynn Weidman, and three anonymous referees provided helpful comments on an earlier version. We are grateful to the staff of the UCLA Social Sciences Computing Facility for support in data processing.

* University of California at Los Angeles.
[†] University of California at Santa Barbara.
[‡] University of California at Los Angeles.

respondents. By replicating the imputation several times—in this case, five —and appropriately combining the multiple imputations, we can estimate the additional uncertainty introduced by the imputation procedure. We show that the additional error due to imputation tends to be small relative to sampling error and that using imputed data in large (2 percent) Public-Use Microdata Samples is preferable to using directly assigned data from the smaller 127,125 case sample. We offer various cautions regarding the appropriate use of imputed data.

1. INTRODUCTION

Students of social change are perennially plagued by problems of data noncomparability. The very changes that are the object of study ordinarily engender changes in the way the data necessary to analyze change are collected. Industrial and occupational data are prime examples. Each decade the U.S. Census Bureau collects relatively detailed data on the industrial and occupational composition of the U.S. labor force.[1] But for each census, the detailed industry and occupation classifications are changed to reflect salient variations among industries and occupations at the time of data collection. Thus, new industries and occupations are added and declining industries and occupations are deleted. Moreover, categories are sometimes recombined in complex ways.

For example, the 1960 census contained no specific occupation category for computer programmers, including the 8,700 or so programmers in the labor force at that time in the residual category, "professional, technical, and kindred workers, n.e.c." (Priebe, Heinkel, and Greene 1972, p. 191). By 1970 there were 263,000 computer specialists, divided into three categories in the 1970 census classification: "computer programmers," "computer systems analysts," and "computer specialists, n.e.c." (U.S. Bureau of the Census 1973, p. 1). In 1980 the classification was changed still again, this time reducing the number of categories to two: "computer systems analysts and

---

[1] *Occupation* refers to the characteristics of a job—the function fulfilled and the tasks performed to accomplish it. Examples of occupations include carpenter, secretary, and physician. *Industry* refers to the goods or services produced by the enterprise within which the job is performed. Examples of industries are automobile manufacturing, construction, and educational services.

scientists" (a subcategory of "mathematical and computer scientists") and "computer programmers" (a subcategory of "technicians, except health, engineering, and science") (U.S. Bureau of the Census 1981, pp. xi, xiii). The 1970 category "computer programmers" was split between the two 1980 categories, but the two other 1970 categories mapped only into the 1980 category "computer systems analysts and scientists" (Vines and Priebe 1988, Table 1).

Many other recombinations were even more complex, and fewer than one third of the occupation categories in the 1970 detailed occupation classification mapped into a single category in the 1980 detailed occupation classification (Vines and Priebe 1988, Table 1). Moreover, the categories least likely to change tended to be those involving small numbers of workers, so that less than 15 percent of the labor force in 1970 was in a category that mapped into a single 1980 category (computed from Vines and Priebe 1988, Table 1).

Over the past several censuses, changes in the classification of detailed industries have not been as extensive as changes in the detailed occupation classification (because of the adoption of the *Standard Industrial Classification* prior to the 1940 census), but they are still substantial. About 24 percent of the 1970 industry categories mapped into more than one 1980 category classification, and the non-matching categories included about 36 percent of the 1970 labor force (Vines and Priebe 1988, Table 3).

While the decadal changes in the detailed classification schemes for industry and occupation have little practical consequence for cross-sectional analysis, they pose severe difficulty for many kinds of cross-temporal analysis. For example, it is currently impossible to assess adequately from census data the effect of a decade of affirmative action, since it is impossible to answer accurately such questions as, "Has the proportion of women in management changed between 1970 and 1980?" The difficulty is that there is no way of knowing whether a given job would be counted as a managerial occupation in one scheme but not in the other. Indeed, a person who had the same job in 1970 and 1980 might have moved into or out of a detailed occupational category that we would be willing to count as a managerial occupation simply because of a change in the occupational coding scheme. Similar problems plague attempts to assess changes in the industrial distribution of the labor force. For example, assessment of the claim that jobs in secondary industries are increasingly occupied by women, minorities, and immigrants depends on consistent classification of industries over time.

The Census Bureau has been concerned with the problem of cross-temporal comparability of industry and occupation classifications for a very long time. The census of 1900, for example, includes a comparison of occupation data from 1820 to 1900, although these comparisons were somewhat limited (U.S. Bureau of the Census 1904). In the early 1940s, Alba Edwards undertook a major monographic study on occupational comparability since 1870 (Edwards 1943). In addition to data for 1940, Edwards's monograph provided detailed occupational data for 1930, reclassified into the 1940 classification, and comparable data for 1870 through 1930, classified according to the 1930 classification. This was followed by a similar effort by Kaplan and Casey (1958), which provided detailed occupational distributions for males and females for 1900 through 1950, classified according to the 1950 classification. The Edwards and Kaplan and Casey monographs each provided extremely useful data because they permitted estimates of historical change in the occupational structure that were uncontaminated by changes in the classification scheme. But, of course, they permitted no detailed analysis of change in the occupational composition of the labor force with respect to characteristics other than sex.

Subsequent to these efforts, census technical papers were published analyzing change in the industry and occupation classification systems between 1950 and 1960 (Priebe 1968), between 1960 and 1970 (Priebe et al. 1972), and between 1970 and 1980 (Vines and Priebe 1988). In each case, a subsample of census returns was "double coded." That is, they were coded with the industry and occupation classification for the subsequent census in addition to the one used initially. This provided two kinds of information: the distribution of the labor force for two successive census years coded into the same classification, and a map relating the categories in one classification to the categories in the other. Like the earlier exercises, however, these were very limited. The estimates of industrial and occupational change were at the national level, broken down only by sex. And the mapping between classifications was at an aggregate level, showing for one year the distribution of the categories for the other year that mapped into it. These distributions can tell us nothing about the fate of any particular job. What the mapping does tell us, for example, is that of those classified as working in "health services, n.e.c." in 1970, 11 percent would have been classified as working in "offices of health practitioners, n.e.c.," 61 percent as working in "health services, n.e.c.," 5 percent as working in "job training and vocational rehabilitation services," and 23 percent as working in "administration of human resources programs," according to the 1980 detailed classification of industries. But the map does not tell us how to assign each 1970 worker in "health services, n.e.c." to a particular 1980 category, which would be necessary, for example, to compare Public-Use Microdata Sample (PUMS) data on individuals from the two censuses.

The inherent difficulty of comparing industry and occupation distributions based on different classification schemes has not deterred analysts from attempting to do so. In the absence of a principled way of converting data from one classification scheme to another, however, analysts have had no choice but to resort to a variety of *ad hoc* matching schemes (e.g., Treiman and Terrell 1975; Williams 1976; Pampel, Land, and Felson 1977; Synder, Hayward, and Hudis 1978; Blau and Hendricks 1979; Rumberger 1981).

A major difficulty with the *ad hoc* schemes commonly employed, apart from their lack of standardization, is that they treat the recalibration process as error free. Thus, inferences about changes over time in industry or occupation characteristics will generally appear stronger than warranted. Moreover, the amount of error is likely to vary substantially, and in unknowable ways, in different parts of the classification scheme. The result is that the analyst of social change is ordinarily hard pressed to know the extent to which observed differences in industrial and occupational data reflect true changes in social structure and the extent to which they represent classification error.

There are only two ways out of this dilemma. One is to return to the original data and recode them with the new classification scheme. In the case of PUMSs from the U.S. census, this is prohibitively expensive. The other is to develop a statistically principled way of converting data from one classification scheme to another, a method that (a) will be relatively accurate and (b) will permit an assessment of the degree of error entailed in the conversion process. In this paper, we evaluate such an effort.

The research reported here is part of an ongoing project evaluating the efficacy of procedures for imputing 1980 codes for detailed industry and occupation into data from the 1970 U.S. census.

The project, which is a cooperative effort involving statisticians, sociologists, and Census Bureau personnel,[2] is the outgrowth of recommendations by the joint Census Bureau/Social Science Research Council Subcommittee on Comparability of Occupation Measurement (1983). The present report is a first evaluation of the accuracy with which industry codes assigned to 1970 data can be recalibrated from the 1970 classification to the 1980 classification. Subsequent reports will present a parallel evaluation of the accuracy with which occupation codes can be converted and will present a number of "worked examples" of procedures for using the recalibrated, or "imputed," data.

The basic approach derives from work on the theory of *multiple imputation*, proposed by Rubin (1978) to handle problems of missing data in surveys and developed in a number of subsequent publications (see, in particular, Rubin 1987, and Rubin and Schenker 1986). The general strategy is to predict, or "impute," the missing values from the relationships existing among variables in those cases without missing data. However, instead of obtaining a single imputation, or point estimate, of the missing values, we repeat the imputation a number of times and create a range of estimates corresponding to the distribution of responses in the complete data. This distribution of estimates—that is, these *multiple imputations*—can then be combined to (a) produce an overall best estimate and (b) compute standard error statistics that reflect both the usual variability inherent in samples and the additional variability due to the imputation process.

In the present case, the complete data are from the 127,125 case Double-Coded Sample (DCS) of 1970 respondents used by the Census Bureau to create the 1980 detailed industry and occupation classifica-

[2] The project is funded by parallel grants from the National Science Foundation to Donald J. Treiman, Department of Sociology, UCLA (SES 83-11483), and Donald B. Rubin, Department of Statistics, Harvard University (SES 83-11428). Clifford Clogg, Departments of Sociology and Statistics, Pennsylvania State University, and William Bielby, Department of Sociology, University of California at Santa Barbara, are consultants to the project. Census Bureau personnel involved in the project include Tom Scopp, Chief, Labor Force Branch, Population Division; John Priebe, Labor Force Branch; Lynn Weidman, Principal Researcher, Statistical Research Division; and Nathaniel Schenker, Undercount Research Staff, Statistical Research Division.

tions. This is a probability sample of labor force cases drawn from responses to the long-form questionnaire administered in 1970 (both the 5 percent and 15 percent versions). The narrative responses to the questions on industry and occupation were assigned codes in the 1980 classification in a special coding operation. Thus, this data set constitutes a sample of the 1970 labor force and includes all the information available in the 1970 PUMS data that was common to the two versions of the long-form questionnaire plus industry and occupation codes in the 1980 classification assigned by trained coders (hereafter referred to as coder-assigned data). (See Priebe [1985] for additional details on the construction of the data set.)

This data set was used to impute, or estimate, five sets of 1980 codes for industry from the respondents' 1970 industry codes and other personal characteristics.[3] (At the time of writing, a similar imputation of 1980 *occupation* codes was not yet completed.) Each 1970 industry category was treated separately. For each 1970 industry, i, a polytomous logistic model was used to represent the probability, p_{ij}, that a person classified in the industry in the 1970 classification scheme would be classified in industry j in the 1980 classification scheme. For estimation purposes we factored this model into a series of conditional dichotomous logistic models that are linear functions of demographic and other personal characteristics of respondents. The characteristics used as predictors were age, race, sex, class of worker, residence in a Standard Metropolitan Statistical Area, education, hours worked per week, weeks worked per year, and region of residence. For each model, the maximum likelihood estimates of the parameters and their covariance matrix were calculated using the appropriate records from the DCS and a specified prior. The posterior distribution of these estimated parameters is multivariate normal. For each imputation, a set of parameters was drawn from these posterior distributions of the conditional models, the probabilities of the 1980 codes were calculated for each record, and an imputed 1980 code was drawn at random according to these probabilities. From a Bayesian perspective, the imputations

---

[3] The choice of five as the number of imputations is, of course, arbitrary. But it can be shown that the improvement in the accuracy of the imputed data is large for each additional imputation up to about five but then decreases rapidly as the number of imputations increases above five.

are selected from the posterior distribution of the p_{ij}'s. Thus, the set of imputed industry codes for each respondent (in this case, five) corresponds to the distribution of predicted 1980 industry codes for respondents with a given 1970 industry code and a specific set of additional characteristics, i.e., sex, race, age, etc.

Consider (for the sake of simplicity) a hypothetical example. Suppose a 1970 industry, "rice or wheat producers," were subdivided into two categories in 1980: "rice producers" and "wheat producers." Suppose further that rice is grown mainly in Louisiana and Texas and that wheat is grown mainly in the plains states but that there is also substantial wheat production in Texas. Suppose, finally, that in Texas, "rice producers" tend to be black and "wheat producers" tend to be white or Hispanic. Then, a logistic regression equation predicting the odds of being coded in the 1980 classification as a "rice producer" rather than as a "wheat producer" given that one was coded as a "rice or wheat producer" in the 1970 classification would do a good job of distinguishing the two groups, with large parameters for the race and region variables.[4] A 1980 code would then be imputed to each individual by drawing values for the coefficients of each variable from the multivariate normal distributions of the parameters implied by the equation, using these to estimate the conditional odds that the individual would fall into each of the candidate 1980 categories, converting the odds to probabilities, and using the probabilities to assign a 1980 code at random but with probability proportionate to the conditional probabilities. This process would be repeated five times to get five 1980 imputed codes for each individual.

This sort of procedure was applied to each code in the 1970 detailed classification of industries that mapped into more than one

---

[4] To estimate the actual imputation equations, we dichotomized the race variable ("black" vs. "other") and trichotomized the region variable ("North," consisting of census regions "New England," "Middle Atlantic," and "East North Central"; "South," consisting of census regions "South Atlantic," "East South Central," and "West South Central"; and "West," consisting of census regions "West North Central," "Mountain," and "Pacific"). Residence in the "West" would predict "wheat growing" over "rice growing," and residence in the "South" would predict "rice growing" over "wheat growing." The distinction between "wheat growing" and "rice growing" among Texans (which is in the "South" region) would be represented by the race variable; "black" would predict "rice growing" over "wheat growing."

code in the 1980 classification.[5] The outcome is a set of six 1980 detailed industry codes for each respondent in the DCS: the coder-assigned 1980 code and five imputed codes.[6] These six codes constitute the data for the evaluation exercise in the remainder of this paper.

Two major questions are addressed. First, how well do the imputed codes approximate the coder-assigned ("actual") codes? For these purposes, we treat the coder-assigned codes as "true scores," since they represent the data that would be available if the narrative

---

[5] Although only 52 of the 213 detailed industry codes for 1970 (excluding "allocation" codes and code 999, "industry not reported") have valid matches with more than one 1980 code (Vines and Priebe 1988, Table 3), we estimated imputation equations for 180 categories because we based our analysis on *uncorrected* 1970 data. The 1970 industry codes we used were those assigned during standard processing of the 1970 census. The 1980 codes were assigned by specially trained coders in the Labor Force Branch of the Census Bureau. In the course of assigning 1980 codes, these coders corrected errors in the 1970 codes whenever they encountered them. The *corrected* 1970 codes were used by Vines and Priebe to create a valid mapping of 1970 codes into 1980 codes. However, since the PUMSs to which we plan to apply the imputations contain *uncorrected* 1970 codes, it seemed to us appropriate to model the relationship between the uncorrected 1970 codes and the 1980 codes in the DCS. The result is, of course, that in some cases we will impute invalid 1980 codes to the 1970 data. However, the alternative would also have led to invalid imputations, but of a much more insidious kind, since the use of the *corrected* 1970 codes in the modeling process would have created imputation equations that implicitly treat erroneous 1970 codes in the PUMS as if they are correct.

To include a 1980 code in the set of codes to which a 1970 code could be mapped, we required that for a given 1970 code, at least two cases exist in the DCS with a common 1980 code. The 1970–1980 matches represented by a single case were not modeled because including them would have introduced excessive noise into the imputed data when imputations were made to the large PUMSs.

In five cases, individuals were assigned 1980 code 990 ("industry not reported") because in these cases, 1970 codes had been erroneously assigned when there was insufficient information to assign a code. Because two of these cases had the same uncorrected 1970 code (609, "department and mail order establishments —retail trade"), 1980 code 990 was regarded as a legitimate code for imputation for this category. As it happens, in nine cases (out of 2,494), at least one of the five imputations assigned code 990. (For imputations 1–3, one case was assigned imputed code 990; for imputation 4, two cases were so assigned; and for imputation 5, three cases were so assigned.) For this reason, the frequencies shown in Table 3 for each of the imputations and the coder-assigned data differ slightly among one another.

[6] For 1970 industries mapping into a single 1980 industry, no imputation equation was estimated. In these cases, each of the "imputed" codes is just the 1980 code into which the 1970 code maps.

descriptions from one or more 1970 PUMSs were directly coded with the 1980 classification. Second, is it worthwhile to use the logistic regression imputation equations to impute 1980 industry codes to two of the 1 percent PUMSs for 1970 (as is currently planned), or would we be better off ignoring the imputations altogether and simply using the DCS with the coder-assigned 1980 scores as the 1970 data set for purposes of comparisons between 1970 and 1980? That is, does the loss in precision from imperfect prediction of 1980 codes more than offset the reduction in sampling variability in the large PUMSs? To anticipate our results, (a) the imputations closely approximate the coder-assigned codes, and (b) it clearly is preferable to impute codes to PUMSs rather than rely on the smaller DCS.

Before beginning our evaluation exercise, we summarize those aspects of the theory of multiple imputation that pertain to our analysis.

2. MULTIPLE-IMPUTATION THEORY

The basic idea underlying the multiple-imputation approach is to partition the uncertainty in statistics based on imputed data—measured by the standard error of these statistics—into two components: a portion associated with variance within each imputation, which is equivalent to the uncertainty associated with sampling variability in the absence of imputation, and a portion associated with the added uncertainty due to imputation. These components are estimated by treating each of the imputations as a variable in a *completed* data set (together with the remaining variables in the data set) and estimating the appropriate complete-data statistics as many times as there are imputations. For example, if we had five imputations (as we do here), we would estimate the statistics of interest five times, using standard complete-data procedures, as if we had five separate data sets. We would then combine these statistics as indicated below, following Rubin (1987, pp. 75–77) and Rubin and Schenker (1986, pp. 366–67), to estimate the components and evaluate them to test hypotheses and establish confidence intervals.

Suppose Q is a statistic to be estimated for which, for complete data, the sampling distribution is approximately normal with mean 0 and variance U. That is, suppose $Q - \hat{Q} \sim N(0, U)$, where $\hat{Q}$ and $\hat{U}$ are estimates of Q and the variance of $Q - \hat{Q}$, respectively. Now, suppose that $\hat{Q}$ is computed from imputed data and there are m imputations. Each of the data sets containing imputed data is known as a *completed* data set. Let $\hat{Q}_{*i}$ and $\hat{U}_{*i}$ ($i = 1 \ldots m$) be the estimates of Q and $\hat{U}$ derived from each of the completed data sets. Then it can be shown that the appropriate estimate of Q is

$$\hat{Q}_{*.} = \sum_{i=1}^{m} \hat{Q}_{*i}/m \tag{1}$$

and that the appropriate estimate of the variance of $Q - \hat{Q}_{*.}$ is T_*, given by

$$T_* = \hat{W} + ((m+1)/m)\hat{B}, \tag{2}$$

where

$$\hat{W} = \sum_{i=1}^{m} \hat{U}_{*i}/m \tag{3}$$

is the average within-imputation variance of $(Q - \hat{Q}_{*.})$ and

$$\hat{B} = \sum_{i=1}^{m} (\hat{Q}_{*i} - \hat{Q}_{*.})^2/(m-1) \tag{4}$$

is the between-imputation variance of $(Q - \hat{Q}_{*.})$. Inferences about Q can be made by considering the ratio $\hat{Q}_{*.}/T^{1/2}$, which is distributed as t with ν degrees of freedom, where ν is given by

$$\nu = \left[1 + \left(\frac{m}{m+1} \right) \frac{\hat{W}}{\hat{B}} \right]^2 (m-1). \tag{5}$$

These results can be used both to assess how much extra uncertainty is introduced into an analysis by using imputed data rather than complete data and to arrive at correct estimates of uncertainty for an analysis based on imputed data. Specifically, the component $((m+1)/m)\hat{B}$ in equation (2) is a measure of the extra uncertainty introduced by the use of imputed data. Ideally, this component will be small relative to $\hat{W}$, which measures the amount of uncertainty due to sampling variability. Certainly, the larger the added uncertainty due to imputation, the less desirable it is to rely upon imputed data and the greater the need to consider additional data collection or, in the case of the census data, a large-scale recoding effort. The relative size of the two components of equation (2) is, however, an empirical question, which must be considered separately for each specific data set. In the present case, our interest is in whether recalibration of the 1970 census detailed classification of industries via a multiple-imputation procedure provides sufficiently accurate data to warrant the use of the imputed data for 1970–1980 comparisons. We now turn to an assessment of this question.

3. EVALUATION

Our basic strategy is to compute various statistics of the sort researchers interested in industrial differences in labor force character-istics might compute. We compute parallel statistics using the imputed data and the coder-assigned data and compare them. We report these results as answers to a set of questions a researcher might put to these data. We also consider their implications for the properties of imputed data in a 2 percent PUMS.

How similar are the imputed distributions of industry codes to each other and to the actual 1980 codes? To answer this, we compute an index of dissimilarity, Δ, between each pair of imputations of detailed (three-digit) industry codes and between each set of imputed codes and the actual codes. The index of dissimilarity is defined as

$$\Delta = \frac{\sum |p_i - q_i|}{2}, \tag{6}$$

where p_i is the percentage of cases in category i of one distribution, q_i is the percentage of cases in category i of the other distribution, and the summation is over all categories. We interpret Δ in the conven-tional way, as the percentage of cases in one distribution that would have to be shifted to another category to make the two distributions identical.

Table 1 shows the Δ's for pairs of imputations and for each imputation and the coder-assigned (actual) 1980 industry codes. Thus, in this table, Δ indicates the percentage of cases that would have to be shifted to different categories to make the distributions based on two imputations (or on an imputation and the coder-assigned codes) identi-cal. All the Δ's are very small. The net error in classification resulting from each of the imputations is less than one percent; the average Δ is 0.86. The error in a distribution formed by pooling the five imputa-tions (by averaging over the five percentage distributions) would, of course, be even smaller. (We refer to *net* error of classification, since Δ

TABLE 1

Indexes of Dissimilarity (Δ) Between Five Imputations of 213 1980 Detailed (Three-Digit) Industry Codes and Actual (Coder-Assigned) Detailed Industry Codes, for the Double-Coded Sample

	Imputation				
	2	3	4	5	Actual Codes
Imputation 1	1.04	0.88	0.99	1.01	0.88
Imputation 2		1.03	0.99	0.94	0.87
Imputation 3			1.07	1.10	0.86
Imputation 4				0.92	0.80
Imputation 5					0.89
Mean of Δ's (actual vs. imputed)					0.86

measures the proportion of cases that would have to be shifted among categories to make two distributions identical; Δ does not measure offsetting classification errors, in which person A, who is in category i in the coder-assigned classification, is imputed to category j and person B, who is in category j in the coder-assigned classification, is imputed to category i.)

How accurate are estimates of the dissimilarity in the distribution of population groups across industries based on the imputed data? Table 2 shows Δ's measuring the dissimilarity in the distribution of men and women across detailed industry groups and the dissimilarity in the distribution of blacks and nonblacks, computed separately from each set of imputed codes and also from the coder-assigned codes. Again, the estimates based on the imputed data are very close to those derived from the coder-assigned data. In each case, the Δ's based on the imputed codes are within about one-half percentage point of the Δ computed from the coder-assigned codes.

Note that the Δ's computed from the imputed data tend to be fractionally smaller than the Δ's computed from the coder-assigned data. There is no obvious reason for this, since both sex and race were used as imputation variables. Because the magnitude of the difference is so small, it is of little practical import.

These statistics are quite gross. They tell us that imputation error is not likely to be important when making comparisons across

TABLE 2

Indexes of Dissimilarity (Δ) Between Population Subgroups Across 213 1980
Detailed Industry Codes

Statistics based on	Men vs. Women	Blacks vs. Nonblacks
Imputation 1	44.92	24.74
Imputation 2	45.06	24.69
Imputation 3	45.18	24.57
Imputation 4	44.88	24.20
Imputation 5	45.09	24.38
Mean of Δ's	45.03	24.52
Actual codes	45.48	24.81

industry categories for the entire labor force. This is hardly surprising, since in overall comparisons, between-group differences are likely to be large relative to within-group differences. *Often, however, researchers wish to analyze smaller and more narrowly defined subsamples. What is the magnitude of error in such cases?* To answer this, we assess the error in various statistics computed for each of thirteen major industry groups and for each of eight selected detailed industry categories. The statistics we compute are the mean number of years of school completed by workers in each industry category, the slope coefficient (b) from the regression of annual income on years of school completed, the percentage female, and the percentage black. We also present results for a simple log-linear model relating sex, employment status, and income for two of the thirteen major industry groups.

Since the size of each of the categories is itself determined by the imputation procedure, it is of some interest to know the extent to which the category sizes vary across imputations. Table 3 shows the frequency of each major industry group, based on the coder-assigned codes and each of the imputed codes, and Table 4 shows the corresponding frequencies for the eight detailed industry categories utilized in the subsequent analysis. As expected, the counts vary to some degree, but the variability is very small relative to the size of the categories. Among the thirteen major groups, no imputation yields a count that deviates from that based on the coder-assigned codes by more than 3 percent; and among the eight detailed groups, the largest deviation is

TABLE 3

Frequency Distribution of 1980 Major Industry Groups Based on Coder-Assigned (Actual) Codes and Five Imputations

Major Industry Group	Imputation					Actual Codes
	1	2	3	4	5	
Agriculture, etc.	4,346	4,334	4,344	4,342	4,330	4,337
Mining	1,006	994	1,014	1,015	1,005	990
Construction	7,846	7,833	7,804	7,877	7,840	7,825
Manufacturing	33,427	33,468	33,479	33,360	33,423	33,492
Transport, etc.	9,584	9,612	9,621	9,590	9,577	9,593
Wholesale trade	5,346	5,348	5,389	5,316	5,389	5,357
Retail trade	19,397	19,337	19,323	19,400	19,347	19,327
Finance, etc.	6,051	6,022	6,039	6,039	6,034	6,007
Business service, etc.	3,955	3,941	3,979	4,029	3,928	3,949
Personal service	5,358	5,402	5,378	5,364	5,390	5,398
Entertainment, etc.	1,055	1,053	1,030	1,038	1,036	1,047
Professional service	20,774	20,765	20,799	20,707	20,800	20,777
Public administration	5,453	5,489	5,399	5,520	5,496	5,495
Total[a]	123,598	123,598	123,598	123,597	123,595	123,594

Note: There are 127,125 cases in the full DCS. But 599 cases assigned "allocation" codes in 1970 were excluded, as were 2,987 cases missing data on one or more of the predictor variables included in the imputation equations. These exclusions yield 123,599 cases for which 1980 industry codes were imputed.

[a] The N's differ from 123,599 because in a few cases that were erroneously coded in the 1970 classification, coders assigned code 990 ("industry not reported") in the 1980 classification. Hence, in a few instances, code 990 was imputed. See note 5 for additional details.

17 percent and the second largest is 11 percent. Both of these deviations are for the smallest industry analyzed here: industry 150 ("miscellaneous textile products"), for which the count based on coder-assigned codes is 101. Thus, it appears that the imputation process produces more or less consistent counts of industries and that the only non-negligible variability in the counts occurs among very small industries, as we expected.

How valid are estimates of the mean years of school completed by workers in each major industry group based on the imputed data? To assess this, consider Tables 5 and 6. Table 5 shows the mean years of school completed by workers in each major industry group estimated from each of the five imputations, the mean of these five estimates, the mean

TABLE 4

Frequency Distribution of Selected 1980 Detailed Industry Groups Based on Coder-Assigned (Actual) Codes and Five Imputations

Major Industry Group	Imputation					Actual Codes
	1	2	3	4	5	
030 Forestry	109	109	116	112	111	107
150 Miscellaneous textile products	103	84	99	90	94	101
331 Machinery, except electrical	1,545	1,570	1,515	1,540	1,566	1,529
470 Water and irrigation	237	234	241	234	233	232
601 Grocery stores	2,734	2,705	2,671	2,691	2,692	2,685
712 Real estate	1,213	1,199	1,198	1,229	1,214	1,189
741 Detective services	140	135	143	138	142	136
860 Education services	194	171	167	199	193	183

years of school completed estimated from the coder-assigned data, and the difference between the estimates based on the coder-assigned data and the imputed data. When we compare the mean of the estimates based on the imputed data and the estimate based on the coder-assigned data, we see that they are very close: The largest discrepancy is four points in the second decimal place. If these estimates were based on independent samples, we would conclude that the samples were drawn from the same population, because when the standard t test of the significance of the difference between two means is applied, none of the t ratios exceeds unity. Moreover, the estimates based on the coder-assigned data are neither systematically larger nor smaller than the mean of the estimates based on the imputed data: Six are larger, five are smaller, and two are identical to two decimal places. Once again, substantive conclusions would not be affected by use of the mean of the imputed estimates rather than estimates based on the coder-assigned data.

What is the effect of the imputation procedure on the reliability of the estimates of mean years of school completed by workers in each industry? That is, what is the magnitude of the standard errors of means computed from the imputed data relative to the standard errors of means computed from the coder-assigned data? This information is presented in Table

TABLE 5

Mean Years of School Completed by Workers in Thirteen Major Industry Groups, Estimated from Five Imputed Distributions and Actual Distribution of 1980 Detailed Industry Codes

Major Industry Group	Imputation					Mean	Actual Data	Difference: (7)–(6)
	1 (1)	2 (2)	3 (3)	4 (4)	5 (5)	(6)	(7)	(8)
Agriculture, etc.	9.76	9.76	9.78	9.77	9.78	9.77	9.74	−0.03
Mining	10.93	10.93	10.91	10.91	10.94	10.92	10.96	0.04
Construction	10.37	10.36	10.37	10.37	10.37	10.37	10.34	−0.03
Manufacturing	10.99	10.99	10.99	10.99	10.99	10.99	10.98	−0.01
Transport, etc.	11.33	11.34	11.34	11.33	11.33	11.33	11.33	0.00
Wholesale trade	11.53	11.57	11.55	11.56	11.57	11.56	11.58	0.02
Retail trade	11.13	11.13	11.14	11.13	11.13	11.13	11.13	0.00
Finance, etc.	12.58	12.58	12.58	12.58	12.59	12.58	12.60	0.02
Business service, etc.	11.72	11.67	11.69	11.72	11.69	11.70	11.67	−0.03
Personal service	10.01	10.03	10.04	10.02	10.03	10.03	9.99	−0.04
Entertainment, etc.	11.74	11.64	11.64	11.64	11.64	11.66	11.67	0.01
Professional service	13.67	13.67	13.66	13.68	13.66	13.67	13.69	0.02
Public administration	12.43	12.47	12.44	12.43	12.44	12.44	12.47	0.03

6. Columns 1 and 2 show the standard errors of the means computed from the imputed data (following equations [2]–[4]) and the means computed from the coder-assigned, or actual, data, and column 10 shows their ratio. When we inspect the ratios, we see that for most major industry groups, the increase in the standard error due to imputation is negligible.

For four major industry groups ("wholesale trade," "business and repair services," "entertainment and recreation services," and "public administration"), however, the increase in the standard errors is large enough to take seriously, ranging from 12 to 16 percent. It is instructive to consider the sources of this increase. As we noted above, the standard error of a statistic based on the imputed data has two sources: within-imputation sampling variance and between-imputation variance (equations [3] and [4]). Column 4 shows the within-imputa-

TABLE 6

Estimates of Standard Error of Mean Years of School Completed for Thirteen Major Industry Groups, Actual and Imputed Data

Major Industry Group	SE of Actual Data (1)	SE of Imputed Data (2)	Variance of Imputed Data (3)	Within-Imputation Sampling Variance (4)	Adjusted Between-Imputation Variance[a] (5)	Expected SE for PUMS[b] (6)	SE for PUMS Without Imputation[b] (7)	Ratio: (1)/(6) (8)	Ratio: (6)/(7) (9)	Ratio: (2)/(1) (10)
Agriculture, etc.	0.04905	0.05009	0.00251	0.00239	0.00012	0.01779	0.01401	2.76	1.27	1.02
Mining	0.10075	0.10129	0.01026	0.01004	0.00022	0.03227	0.02873	3.12	1.12	1.01
Construction	0.03233	0.03260	0.00106	0.00104	0.00002	0.01046	0.00924	3.09	1.13	1.01
Manufacturing	0.01557	0.01563	0.00024	0.00024	0.00000	0.00448	0.00448	3.48	1.00	1.00
Transport, etc.	0.02542	0.02620	0.00069	0.00065	0.00004	0.00946	0.00731	2.69	1.29	1.03
Wholesale trade	0.03662	0.04149	0.00172	0.00139	0.00034	0.02121	0.01067	1.73	1.99	1.13
Retail trade	0.01712	0.01786	0.00032	0.00030	0.00002	0.00695	0.00492	2.46	1.41	1.04
Finance, etc.	0.03122	0.03150	0.00099	0.00097	0.00002	0.01018	0.00892	3.07	1.14	1.01
Business service, etc.	0.04535	0.05085	0.00259	0.00202	0.00056	0.02702	0.01289	1.68	2.10	1.12
Personal service	0.03852	0.04079	0.00166	0.00151	0.00016	0.01673	0.01113	2.30	1.50	1.06
Entertainment, etc.	0.08437	0.09789	0.00958	0.00718	0.00240	0.05468	0.02430	1.54	2.25	1.16
Professional service	0.02234	0.02420	0.00059	0.00050	0.00008	0.01119	0.00642	2.00	1.74	1.08
Public administration	0.03534	0.04002	0.00160	0.00128	0.00032	0.02071	0.01025	1.71	2.02	1.13

[a]Adjusted by ratio $((m + 1)/m)$. See equation (2).
[b]See text for explanation.

tion variance and column 5 shows the adjusted between-imputation variance; column 3 shows their sum (equation [2]). Column 2 is, of course, just the square root of column 3. For all thirteen major industry groups, the within-imputation variance is large relative to the adjusted between-imputation variance,[7] but the smallest ratios are those for the four industries with non-negligible imputation error. Columns 4 and 5 show that this is due to the relatively large size of the between-imputation variance and not to anything systematic about the within-imputation variance. For whatever reasons, the imputation procedure assigned detailed 1980 industry codes in such a way as to produce in these groups a substantial amount of variability from one imputation to another in mean years of schooling. This, of course, is just another way of saying that education is not a very good predictor of whether a particular individual will be included in each of these four 1980 major industry groups, conditional on inclusion in particular 1970 industry categories.

From a practical standpoint, the important question is not the size of the standard errors in the imputed data for the DCS, but rather the size of the standard errors we can expect in the 2 percent PUMS into which 1980 industry codes will be imputed. Put simply, *the issue is whether a researcher would be better off using the coder-assigned data for the DCS or the imputed data in the 2 percent PUMS*. The data necessary to answer this question are shown in columns 6 and 8 of Table 6. Column 6 shows estimates of the standard errors we expect in the PUMS, given that the PUMS is simply a larger sample drawn from the same population as the DCS. (Actually, this is not strictly correct, since the DCS is clustered by enumeration districts [Priebe 1985] and hence is not as efficient as a random sample. For this reason, our estimates of the improvement in the standard errors in the PUMS relative to the DCS are conservative. Unfortunately, estimates of the size of the design effect in the DCS are not available, so we cannot derive more precise estimates of the extent of improvement.)

The estimates in column 6 were derived by assuming that the between-imputation variance in the PUMS will be the same as in the

[7] The between-imputation variance is adjusted by $(m + 1)/m = 6/5$ to take account of the fact that the number of imputations is finite, as per equation (2).

DCS but that the within-imputation variance will be reduced by a factor of 12.168, which is the ratio of the size of 2 percent of the labor force in 1970 (U.S. Bureau of the Census 1973, Table 1) to the number of cases for which industry was imputed in the DCS.[8] This is, in fact, a very conservative assumption, since, in general, the between-imputation variance should also decrease as sample size increases.[9]

Column 8 shows that the expected standard errors in the PUMS are always substantially smaller than the standard errors estimated from coder-assigned data in the DCS. Thus, insofar as these results hold for other variables and population subgroups, we can conclude

[8] The size of the labor force in 1970 was 80,071,130 (U.S. Bureau of the Census 1973, Table 1). However, 103,340 persons were unemployed and had not worked since 1959; no information on industry was available for these persons. For the remainder of the labor force, those not providing sufficient information to permit the coding of industry were allocated to industry major groups and were assigned special "allocation" codes in the 1970 industry classification. Although these categories will be imputed in the PUMS, they were not used in the exercise reported here. Hence, the 4,771,640 persons in the 1970 labor force with allocation codes for industry were excluded from the base used to calculate the denominator of the ratio of the size of the card-deck sample to the size of the 2 percent PUMS. The resulting base is 75,196,150 (= 80,071,130 − 103,340 − 4,771,640), of which 2 percent is 1,503,923. Similarly, we excluded from the DCS 539 allocation cases and 2,987 cases missing data on the independent variables used in the logistic regression models, leaving an effective sample of 123,599. (Note that there are no missing data in the PUMSs, since all missing values are imputed as part of the editing process; see U.S. Bureau of the Census [1976, pp. 15–65, 15–66] for a discussion of the procedures utilized.) The ratio 1,503,923/123,599 = 12.168.

[9] Our computations rely on comparisons of actual data from the DCS with imputations to the same data set. Multiple imputation of the PUMS would, of course, apply logistic results from the DCS to new data. However, in both instances, logistic coefficients for each of the five imputations are sampled from a multivariate normal distribution with a covariance matrix estimated from the logistic regression. Thus, sampling variability in the logistic coefficients is represented in the imputation procedure, even when it is applied to the data that generated the coefficients. Consequently, the coefficients do not "overfit" the DCS, and the between-imputation variance should be the same in both data sets except insofar as it is affected by sample size. According to Rubin (pers. comm. 1987), the ratio of between-imputation variance to total (within- plus between-imputation) variance should not be affected by sample size, which suggests that the between-imputation variance as well as the within-imputation variance would be reduced by a factor of 12.168 in the 2 percent PUMS. We have, however, chosen to make an extremely conservative assumption regarding the between-imputation variance to avoid any chance of overstating the advantage accruing from use of the imputed data.

that there is a real gain in precision when we use imputed data in the PUMS rather than coder-assigned data in the smaller DCS.

It is also important to assess the magnitude of the increase in error resulting from the use of imputed data in the PUMS relative to the error we would expect in PUMS data from sampling variability alone. Column 7 shows the hypothetical standard errors that we would expect if we had double-coded the PUMS. They are, in fact, the same as the estimates in column 6 except that the between-imputation variance is assumed to be zero. Column 9 shows the ratio of the two PUMS estimates and thus gives us a hypothetical estimate of the cost of imputation in samples as large as the 2 percent PUMS. When we inspect the coefficients in column 9, we see that for one industry, "manufacturing," there is no error associated with imputation (to the level of precision associated with two decimal places) but that for many industries, the increase in the standard errors is substantial. Moreover, as before, the effect of imputation on the standard errors varies substantially across industries, increasing the standard error by a factor of 2.25 for the most strongly affected industry, "entertainment and recreation services." From these results, we conclude that a researcher could err seriously by using the imputed data as if they were double-coded data and neglecting to compute the correct standard errors. Not only would this lead to the conclusion that the data are more precise than they actually are, but the relative precision of different statistics would change in unknown ways.

So far, we have focused on comparisons of major industry groups and thus have dealt with samples of about 1,000 cases or larger. We now study the same statistic, mean years of school completed, for eight selected detailed industry categories. These subsamples are, of course, much smaller; there are only 101 cases in the smallest, "miscellaneous textile products." Tables 7 and 8 show data corresponding to the data in Tables 5 and 6. Generally, the conclusions we reach are similar to those we discussed above. The means based on the imputed data are similar to those based on the coder-assigned data, and the largest discrepancy is 0.06 (again, no t ratio for the significance of the difference between two means exceeds unity); there are both positive and negative deviations of the imputed means from the means based on the coder-assigned data; the expected reductions in the standard errors in the PUMS relative to the standard errors for the coder-assigned data in the DCS are on the whole large; and the increases in the

TABLE 7

Mean Years of School Completed by Workers in Eight Detailed (Three-Digit) Industry Categories, Estimated from Five Imputed Distributions and Actual Distribution of 1980 Detailed Industry Codes

Detailed Industry Category	Imputation					Mean	Actual Data	Difference: (7)–(6)
	1 (1)	2 (2)	3 (3)	4 (4)	5 (5)	(6)	(7)	(8)
030 Forestry	12.33	12.39	12.40	12.38	12.50	12.40	12.46	0.06
150 Miscellaneous textile products	10.11	9.94	10.21	10.44	10.48	10.24	10.19	−0.05
331 Machinery, except electrical	11.16	11.21	11.21	11.21	11.20	11.20	11.19	−0.01
470 Water and irrigation	10.76	10.85	10.78	10.76	10.84	10.80	10.78	−0.02
601 Grocery stores	10.94	10.93	10.94	10.94	10.92	10.93	10.93	0.00
712 Real estate	11.68	11.73	11.73	11.75	11.77	11.73	11.75	0.02
741 Detective services	10.86	10.93	10.91	10.90	10.93	10.91	10.96	0.05
860 Educational services	13.68	13.67	13.40	13.68	13.51	13.59	13.63	0.04

TABLE 8
Estimates of Standard Error of Mean Years of School Completed for Eight Detailed (Three-Digit) Industry Categories, Actual and Imputed Data

Detailed Industry Category	SE of Actual Data (1)	SE of Imputed Data (2)	Variance of Imputed Data (3)	Within-Imputation Sampling Variance (4)	Adjusted Between-Imputation Variance (5)	Expected SE for PUMS (6)	SE for PUMS Without Imputation (7)	Ratio: (1)/(6) (8)	Ratio: (6)/(7) (9)	Ratio: (2)/(1) (10)
030 Forestry	0.32869	0.31708	0.10054	0.09592	0.00462	0.11182	0.08879	2.94	1.26	0.96
150 Miscellaneous textile products	0.34826	0.45226	0.20454	0.14295	0.06160	0.27082	0.10839	1.29	2.50	1.30
331 Machinery, except electrical	0.06624	0.07110	0.00506	0.00449	0.00056	0.03055	0.01921	2.17	1.59	1.07
470 Water and irrigation	0.17923	0.18946	0.03590	0.03359	0.00230	0.07117	0.05254	2.52	1.35	1.06
601 Grocery stores	0.04188	0.04328	0.00187	0.00178	0.00010	0.01556	0.01209	2.69	1.29	1.03
712 Real estate	0.09193	0.09661	0.00933	0.00807	0.00126	0.04386	0.02576	2.10	1.70	1.05
741 Detective services	0.21952	0.22676	0.05142	0.05042	0.00100	0.07169	0.06437	3.06	1.11	1.03
860 Educational services	0.17815	0.24921	0.06210	0.04258	0.01952	0.15173	0.05916	1.17	2.57	1.40

standard errors in the PUMS relative to the size of the standard errors we would expect if the 1980 industry codes in the PUMS were based on coder-assigned rather than imputed data are also non-negligible.

One figure in Table 8 requires special comment. For workers in "forestry," the standard error based on the imputed data is *smaller* than the standard error based on the coder-assigned data. This can arise when the within-imputation sampling variance is smaller than the sampling variance of the mean computed from the coder-assigned data, as it is in the current case. In turn, this implies that the average standard deviation of education is smaller in the imputed data than in the coder-assigned data, since the frequencies in the imputed and coder-assigned data are about the same size (3.27 for the imputed data and 3.40 for the coder-assigned data). Were this to arise frequently or systematically, it would imply that our imputation procedure was overdetermining the relationship between respondents' 1970 characteristics and their 1980 industry codes. However, of the 45 comparisons in Tables 6, 8, 10, 12, and 14, only four show smaller standard errors for statistics computed from the imputed data than for statistics computed from the coder-assigned data, and for the most part they are only trivially smaller.

Tables 9 through 14 replicate the analysis presented above for three additional variables: the slope coefficient from the regression of annual income on years of school completed, the percentage female, and the percentage black. In each case, comparisons are made for the eight detailed industry categories. Because the results have been so consistent, we felt it unnecessary to report the corresponding data for the thirteen major industry groups, which all involve much larger sample sizes. We have made the computations and inspected them. They contain no surprises and hence we do not include them here.

There is little news in Tables 9 through 14. Again, a detailed analysis of these tables would yield the same conclusions that we have already drawn. But two additional points may be noted. First, the relative size of the statistics based on the actual and imputed data in each of the industries is not consistent across statistics. Thus, the value of one statistic based on the coder-assigned data may be larger than that of the corresponding statistic based on the imputed data, while the relative sizes of a different statistic computed for the coder-assigned and imputed data may be reversed. Similarly, not only does the relative importance of sampling error and imputation error as compo-

TABLE 9

Slope Coefficients (b's) from Regressions of Annual Income on Years of School Completed by Workers in Eight Detailed (Three-Digit) Industry Categories, Estimated from Five Imputed Distributions and Actual Distribution of 1980 Detailed Industry Codes

Detailed Industry Category	Imputation					Mean	Actual Data	Difference: (7)–(6)
	1 (1)	2 (2)	3 (3)	4 (4)	5 (5)	(6)	(7)	(8)
030 Forestry	691	746	679	685	824	725	755	30
150 Miscellaneous textile products	697	515	652	634	738	647	631	−16
331 Machinery, except electrical	634	615	624	644	637	631	527	−104
470 Water and irrigation	500	381	403	393	499	435	348	−87
601 Grocery stores	326	309	321	309	294	312	297	−15
712 Real estate	714	705	700	738	702	712	681	−31
741 Detective services	100	122	136	120	126	121	143	22
860 Educational services	311	202	27	321	263	225	36	−189

TABLE 10

Estimates of Standard Error of b (Slope Coefficient for Regression of Annual Income on Years of School Completed) for Eight Detailed (Three-Digit) Industry Categories, Actual and Imputed Data

Detailed Industry Category	SE of Actual Data (1)	SE of Imputed Data (2)	Variance of Imputed Data (3)	Within-Imputation Sampling Variance (4)	Adjusted Between-Imputation Variance (5)	Expected SE for PUMS (6)	SE for PUMS Without Imputation (7)	Ratio: (1)/(6) (8)	Ratio: (6)/(7) (9)	Ratio: (2)/(1) (10)
030 Forestry	136	154	23,583	19,049	4,534	78	40	1.74	1.97	1.13
150 Miscellaneous textile products	132	167	27,949	19,430	8,520	101	40	1.31	2.52	1.27
331 Machinery, except electrical	57	60	3,616	3,460	156	21	17	2.72	1.24	1.05
470 Water and irrigation	91	120	14,369	10,162	4,207	71	29	1.28	2.46	1.32
601 Grocery stores	41	43	1,834	1,649	186	18	12	2.29	1.54	1.04
712 Real estate	70	72	5,220	4,928	292	26	20	2.65	1.31	1.03
741 Detective services	119	117	13,773	13,565	208	36	33	3.27	1.09	0.99
860 Educational services	138	183	33,400	16,064	17,337	136	36	1.01	3.76	1.32

TABLE 11

Percentage Female Among Workers in Eight Detailed (Three-Digit) Industry Categories, Estimated from Five Imputed Distributions and Actual Distribution of 1980 Detailed Industry Codes

| Detailed Industry Category | Imputation | | | | | Mean | Actual Data | Difference: (7)–(6) |
	1 (1)	2 (2)	3 (3)	4 (4)	5 (5)	(6)	(7)	(8)
030 Forestry	9.2	11.0	10.3	14.3	12.6	11.5	10.3	−1.2
150 Miscellaneous textile products	35.0	35.7	32.3	33.3	33.0	33.9	33.7	−0.2
331 Machinery, except electrical	17.2	16.8	18.5	18.0	18.5	17.8	17.5	−0.3
470 Water and irrigation	14.8	14.5	14.9	14.5	16.3	15.0	15.1	0.1
601 Grocery stores	38.3	38.7	38.5	37.9	37.8	38.2	38.1	−0.1
712 Real estate	38.9	39.8	38.5	38.9	38.7	39.0	38.4	−0.6
741 Detective services	12.1	12.6	13.3	11.6	12.7	12.5	13.2	0.7
860 Educational services	67.0	70.8	72.5	71.9	64.2	69.3	68.9	−0.4

nents of the total standard error vary across industries for each statistic, but the pattern of industry variability varies from statistic to statistic. These results are encouraging because they suggest that the imputation procedure has introduced no systematic distortion pertaining to identifiable subsamples—at least for the limited number of comparisons we have made here. The results also underscore the importance of explicitly computing the impact of imputation unreliability on statistical precision for *all* statistics, since the ratio of sampling to imputation error varies across statistics.

Second, for one industry, "educational services, n.e.c.," the standard error expected from the 2 percent PUMS is *larger* than the standard error computed from the coder-assigned data in the DCS for two of the four statistics studied. This serves to remind us that imputation is not without cost. When the imputation is very uncertain, as it apparently is in the assignment of cases to "educational services, n.e.c.," there is a net loss in precision when the imputed codes in the

TABLE 12

Estimates of Standard Error of Percentage Female Among Workers in Eight Detailed (Three-Digit) Industry Categories, Actual and Imputed Data

Detailed Industry Category	SE of Actual Data (1)	SE of Imputed Data (2)	Variance of Imputed Data (3)	Within-Imputation Sampling Variance (4)	Adjusted Between-Imputation Variance (5)	Expected SE for PUMS (6)	SE for PUMS Without Imputation (7)	Ratio: (1)/(6) (8)	Ratio: (6)/(7) (9)	Ratio: (2)/(1) (10)
030 Forestry	2.94	3.73	13.90	9.09	4.81	2.36	0.86	1.25	2.73	1.27
150 Miscellaneous textile products	4.70	5.14	26.39	23.94	2.45	2.10	1.40	2.24	1.50	1.09
331 Machinery, except electrical	0.97	1.29	1.66	0.95	0.71	0.89	0.28	1.09	3.19	1.33
470 Water and irrigation	2.35	2.47	6.08	5.41	0.67	1.06	0.67	2.22	1.59	1.05
601 Grocery stores	0.94	1.03	1.05	0.88	0.18	0.50	0.27	1.88	1.86	1.09
712 Real estate	1.41	1.50	2.26	1.96	0.30	0.68	0.40	2.08	1.69	1.07
741 Detective services	2.90	2.88	8.31	7.81	0.50	1.07	0.80	2.72	1.33	0.99
860 Educational services	3.42	5.16	26.66	11.50	15.16	4.01	0.97	0.85	4.13	1.51

TABLE 13

Percentage Black Among Workers in Eight Detailed (Three-Digit) Industry Categories, Estimated from Five Imputed Distributions and Actual Distribution of 1980 Detailed Industry Codes

Detailed Industry Category	Imputation					Mean	Actual Data	Difference: (7)–(6)
	1 (1)	2 (2)	3 (3)	4 (4)	5 (5)	(6)	(7)	(8)
030 Forestry	6.4	4.6	4.3	4.5	4.5	4.9	5.6	0.7
150 Miscellaneous textile products	10.7	15.5	12.1	15.6	16.0	14.0	13.9	−0.1
331 Machinery, except electrical	4.6	3.9	4.6	4.7	4.6	4.5	4.3	−0.2
470 Water and irrigation	8.0	8.1	7.9	9.0	7.7	8.1	7.8	−0.3
601 Grocery stores	5.6	5.4	5.4	5.7	5.8	5.6	5.6	0
712 Real estate	6.9	8.0	7.0	7.1	6.9	7.2	7.3	0.1
741 Detective services	5.0	5.2	4.9	5.1	4.9	5.0	5.9	0.9
860 Educational services	4.1	5.8	8.4	4.5	5.7	5.7	4.4	−1.3

large PUMS are used rather than the coder-assigned codes in the DCS. Fortunately, however, this is likely to occur only infrequently, because in only 2 of the 45 comparisons made here are the expected standard errors for the large PUMS larger than those based on the actual data in the DCS. Hence, we think that in most situations, analysts would be better served by the large PUMS than by the smaller DCS.

How valid are inferences about log-linear models made from imputed data? Thus far we have dealt with scalar variables—means, proportions, and regression coefficients. But many problems require the analysis of categorical data, for example, via log-linear modeling procedures. Hence, it is useful to assess the adequacy of imputed data for these sorts of problems as well. Typically, log-linear analysis involves first finding the best fitting model from among a set of hierarchical models and then estimating and analyzing the effect parameters associated with that model. The effect parameters constitute no special problem. We simply treat them the same way we treat any other scalar statistic, that is, the same way we dealt with the means, proportions, and regression coefficients above. Finding the best fitting model is, however, a bit more cumbersome. To do this, we need to generate for each

TABLE 14

Estimates of Standard Error of Percentage Black Among Workers in Eight Detailed (Three-Digit) Industry Categories, Actual and Imputed Data

Detailed Industry Category	SE of Actual Data (1)	SE of Imputed Data (2)	Variance of Imputed Data (3)	Within-Imputation Sampling Variance (4)	Adjusted Between-Imputation Variance (5)	Expected SE for PUMS (6)	SE for PUMS Without Imputation (7)	Ratio: (1)/(6) (8)	Ratio: (6)/(7) (9)	Ratio: (2)/(1) (10)
030 Forestry	2.22	2.25	5.06	4.16	0.90	1.12	0.58	1.99	1.91	1.01
150 Miscellaneous textile products	3.44	4.46	19.90	12.91	6.99	2.84	1.03	1.21	2.76	1.30
331 Machinery, except electrical	0.52	0.64	0.41	0.28	0.13	0.39	0.15	1.33	2.58	1.23
470 Water and irrigation	1.76	1.86	3.47	3.17	0.30	0.75	0.51	2.34	1.47	1.06
601 Grocery stores	0.44	0.48	0.23	0.20	0.04	0.23	0.13	1.90	1.84	1.09
712 Real estate	0.75	0.90	0.81	0.55	0.26	0.55	0.21	1.36	2.60	1.19
741 Detective services	2.02	1.85	3.44	3.42	0.02	0.55	0.53	3.68	1.04	0.92
860 Educational services	1.52	2.52	6.34	2.95	3.39	1.91	0.49	0.80	3.87	1.66

candidate model an adjusted likelihood ratio χ^2 statistic (hereafter, L^2) that reflects the additional uncertainty due to imputation. As before, we begin with the *complete-data* L^2's estimated for each of the completed (imputed) data sets and combine them to obtain the adjusted L^2. Specifically (following Rubin 1987, pp. 99–102), we compute for a given model

$$\hat{D}_m = \frac{\dfrac{\bar{d}_m}{k} - \dfrac{m-1}{m+1}\hat{r}_m}{1 + \hat{r}_m}, \tag{7}$$

where $\bar{d}_m$ is the mean of the L^2 values estimated from each of the five sets of imputed data; $m = 5$, the number of imputations; k is the number of degrees of freedom associated with a given hypothesis, that is, a given L^2; and $\hat{r}_m$ is given by

$$\hat{r}_m = \frac{(1 + 1/m)s_d^2}{2\bar{d}_m + \left[4\bar{d}_m^2 - 2ks_d^2\right]_+^{1/2}}, \tag{8}$$

where s_d^2, the variance in the L^2's, is

$$s_d^2 = \sum_{i=1}^{m} (d_i - \bar{d}_m)^2 / (m - 1), \tag{9}$$

and the "+" associated with the bracketed quantity in equation (8) indicates that the quantity must be non-negative. Therefore, computed negative values (which sometimes occur) are set to zero.

The statistic $\hat{D}_m$ is distributed as F with k and $(1 + 1/k)\hat{v}/2$ degrees of freedom, where $\hat{v}$ is estimated by

$$\hat{v} = (m - 1)(1 + 1/\hat{r}_m)^2. \tag{10}$$

The statistic $\hat{D}_m$ has a one-to-one correspondence to L^2 with k degrees of freedom; the correspondence is defined by the values of $\hat{D}_m$ and L^2 associated with a given probability level on the F and χ^2 distributions, respectively. Thus, to find the L^2 value corresponding to a $\hat{D}_m$ value, we determine the p value associated with the value of $\hat{D}_m$, from an F table, and then, in a χ^2 table, find the L^2 value corresponding to that p value.[10] We convert $\hat{D}_m$ to L^2 rather than make inferences directly

---

[10] In practice, this is best done by using an algorithm for converting F values to χ^2 values (an inverse χ^2 function), since tables of F values give too crude an approximation. We are indebted to T. E. Raghunathan, Department of Statistics, Harvard University, and to Nathaniel Schenker, U.S. Bureau of the Census, for their assistance in effecting the conversions reported here.

TABLE 15

Likelihood Ratio χ^2 (L^2) Statistics for Log-Linear Models of the Relationship between Sex (S), Employment Status (E), and Earnings (I) for Two Major Industry Groups ("Construction" and "Entertainment and Recreation Services"), Estimated from Actual and Imputed Data

Model	df	Imputation 1	2	3	4	5	Based on Imputed Data	Based on Actual Data	Probability (p) Imputed Data	Probability (p) Actual Data
Entertainment										
(1) $[S][E][I]$	12	122.21	129.73	127.37	131.32	129.74	54.50	123.96	$p < 0.0000005$	[b]
(2) $[SE][I]$	8	109.06	113.82	106.50	117.43	115.22	[a]	109.24	[b]	[b]
(3) $[SI][E]$	10	22.32	23.89	29.12	23.09	27.08	21.64	23.73	$0.02 > p > 0.01$	$0.01 > p > 0.005$
(4) $[EI][S]$	10	116.51	120.75	124.13	122.73	119.16	49.86	117.76	$p < 0.0000005$	[b]
(5) $[SE][SI]$	6	9.16	7.98	8.25	9.20	12.56	8.03	9.01	$0.25 > p > 0.10$	$0.25 > p > 0.10$
(6) $[SE][EI]$	6	103.36	104.84	103.26	108.85	104.65	[a]	103.04	[b]	[b]
(7) $[SI][EI]$	8	16.62	14.90	25.88	14.50	16.51	10.30	17.53	$0.25 > p > 0.10$	$0.05 > p > 0.02$
(8) $[SE][SI][EI]$	4	3.16	0.58	5.85	1.81	2.05	0.17	3.67	$p > 0.995$	$0.5 > p > 0.25$
(5)–(8)	2	6.00	7.40	2.13	7.39	10.51	4.17	5.43	$0.25 > p > 0.10$	$0.1 > p > 0.05$
(7)–(8)	4	13.46	14.32	20.03	12.69	14.46	11.88	15.41	$0.02 > p > 0.01$	$0.005 > p > 0.001$
N		793	784	775	783	780	—	781	—	—

Construction										
(1) $[S][E][I]$	12	419.51	426.93	410.58	412.02	394.40	a	380.23	b	b
(2) $[SE][I]$	8	290.74	284.82	283.16	281.33	274.40	a	259.71	b	b
(3) $[SI][E]$	10	146.56	159.33	146.74	147.28	137.87	a	137.23	b	b
(4) $[EI][S]$	10	400.44	406.01	388.87	391.69	374.43	a	362.07	b	b
(5) $[SE][SI]$	6	17.79	17.22	19.32	16.59	17.88	17.36	16.71	$0.01 > p > 0.005$	$0.02 > p > 0.01$
(6) $[SE][EI]$	6	271.67	263.91	261.44	260.99	254.43	a	241.55	b	b
(7) $[SI][EI]$	8	127.49	138.41	125.03	126.95	117.91	a	119.07	b	b
(8) $[SE][SI][EI]$	4	1.78	1.42	1.53	0.72	1.65	1.28	1.87	$0.9 > p > 0.75$	$0.9 > p > 0.75$
(5)–(8)	2	16.01	15.80	17.79	15.87	16.23	16.67	14.84	$p < 0.0005$	$p < 0.001$
(7)–(8)	4	125.71	136.99	123.50	126.23	116.26	a	117.20	b	b
N		7,413	7,384	7,362	7,436	7,393	—	7,387	—	—

[a] χ^2 is very large. χ^2 cannot be computed by the available inverse χ^2 function.
[b] $p < 0.00000005$.

from the values of $\hat{D}_m$ because F statistics are not additive when comparing nested models; χ^2 statistics are.[11]

To assess the adequacy of imputed data for fitting log-linear models, we estimate for two major industry groups ("entertainment and recreation services" and "construction") a simple log-linear model relating income (three categories), class of worker (self-employed, salaried, and government worker), and sex. Table 15 shows the results. Several points may be noted. First, and most important, on the whole, the L^2 values computed from the imputed data lead to the same inferences as the L^2 values computed from the coder-assigned (actual) data. For example, using the conventional 0.05 significance level, we find only one instance in the table in which the actual and imputed data would lead to a different inference: the contrast of models 7 and 8 for "entertainment and recreation services." Using a 0.01 level of significance would lead to a different inference in three cases, but not all in the same direction: The imputed data (but not the actual data) would lead us to conclude that model 5 does not fit the data for "construction"; and the actual data (but not the imputed data) would lead us to conclude that model 5 does not fit the data for "entertainment and recreation services" and that the fit of model 8 is significantly better than the fit of model 7 (also for "entertainment and recreation services"). Second, the L^2's computed from the imputed data are neither uniformly larger nor uniformly smaller than the L^2's computed from the actual data. For "entertainment and recreation services," the L^2's estimated from the combined imputed data (using the inverse χ^2 function) are all smaller than those estimated from the actual data, but this is not true for "construction." Nor is there a consistent difference between the actual and imputed L^2's for contrasts between models. In sum, these results reinforce our earlier conclusions based on scalar data: Imputed data yield results generally similar to those obtained from coder-assigned data, but it is necessary in each instance to carry out the computations required to get correct adjusted L^2 values from the imputed data.

Inferences about differences between two statistics. Using imputed data to make inferences about differences between two statistics, such as means, proportions, or effect parameters for log-linear models, is a

---

[11] Rubin (1987) also presents other methods for obtaining p values that are more accurate but require more effort.

straightforward application of the procedures discussed above. The statistic in question—e.g., the difference between two means—is computed for each of the completed data sets, and the five estimates are averaged, as per equation (1). The standard error of the statistic is also computed for each of the completed data sets and the five estimates are combined as per equations (2)–(4). The ratio of the statistic estimated by equation (1) to its standard error (the square root of the quantity estimated by equation [2]) is then computed and evaluated with reference to a t distribution, for degrees of freedom estimated as per equation (5).

CONCLUSION

Although the theory of multiple imputation is well developed, there have been few applications of multiple-imputation procedures to large-scale practical problems. Indeed, we believe that the Census project is the first such application. Not only is the problem of recalibrating the industry (and occupation) codes assigned to 1970 data to the 1980 classification of great practical importance to students of social change, but it also constitutes an important test of the efficacy of multiple imputation as a practical solution to recalibration problems of this sort. The complexity of the application, involving hundreds of logistic regression equations and the imputation of a large number of distinct industry codes, meant that the adequacy of the imputations could not be assessed analytically but had to be evaluated by an empirical exercise—specifically, by comparing the results obtained from imputed data with those obtained from the coder-assigned data that the imputations were intended to approximate.

The conclusion of this first exercise, involving only the industry imputations, is that multiple imputation is a viable approach to the recalibration of detailed census classifications. It yields results closely approximating those obtainable from data that have been directly recoded from the narrative reports of respondents, and it provides a way of recalibrating full PUMSs at a small fraction of the cost required for direct recoding.

However, these results also suggest that the appropriate use of imputed data for analysis will require somewhat more complex and extensive statistical manipulations than analysts are used to. Specifically, it will always be necessary to take account of the fact that one is using data subject to error due to imputation by computing the correct estimates of statistics and the correct standard errors of these statistics using the equations we have presented above. Tempting shortcuts, such as arbitrarily picking one of the five imputed values, treating it as actual data, and incrementing the resulting standard errors by some percentage, are not legitimate; as we have seen, the extent of the error due to imputation varies across subsamples and across statistics.

This is but the first of a number of papers reporting on the Census multiple-imputation project. A companion paper evaluating the occupation imputation that is currently underway will be our next effort. It is fairly likely that the error due to imputation will be relatively larger for the occupation imputations than for the industry imputations because of the greater complexity of the occupational classification. But whether the reduction in precision will be substantial enough to seriously undercut the value of the imputed occupation data remains to be seen. As an aid to users of the imputed data, we also expect to produce a monograph that includes a number of "worked examples" in conjunction with release of a PUMS tape for 1970 containing imputed industry and occupation codes in the 1980 classification.

REFERENCES

Blau, Francine D., and Wallace E. Hendricks. 1979. "Occupational Segregation by Sex: Trends and Prospects." *Journal of Human Resources* 14:197–210.

Edwards, A. M. 1943. *Sixteenth Census of the United States: 1940. Population. Comparative Occupational Statistics for the United States, 1887 to 1940: A Comparison of the 1930 and 1940 Census Occupation and Industry Classifications and Statistics; a Comparable Series of Occupation Statistics, 1887 to 1930; and a Socio-Economic Grouping of the Labor Force, 1910 to 1940.* Washington, DC: U.S. Government Printing Office.

Kaplan, D. L., and M. C. Casey. 1958. *Occupational Trends in the United States 1900 to 1950.* Working Paper No. 5. Washington, DC: U.S. Bureau of the Census.

Pampel, Fred C., Kenneth C. Land, and Marcus Felson. 1977. "A Social Indicator Model of Changes in the Occupational Structure of the United States, 1947–1974." *American Sociological Review* 42:951–64.

Priebe, J. A. 1968. *Changes between the 1950 and 1960 Occupation and Industry Classifications—with Detailed Adjustments of 1950 Data to the 1960 Classifications.* Bureau of the Census Technical Paper No. 18. Washington, DC: U.S. Government Printing Office.

————————. 1985. "1970 Census Sample with Industry and Occupation Descriptions." Unpublished manuscript, U.S. Bureau of the Census.

Priebe, J. A., J. Heinkel, and S. Greene. 1972. *1970 Occupation and Industry Classification Systems in Terms of their 1960 Occupation and Industry Elements.* Washington, DC: U.S. Government Printing Office.

Rubin, Donald B. 1978. "Multiple Imputations in Sample Surveys—A Phenomenological Bayesian Approach to Nonresponse. Pp. 20–34 in *Proceedings of the Survey Research Methods Section, American Statistical Association.* Washington, DC: American Statistical Association.

——————. 1987. *Multiple Imputation for Survey Nonresponse.* New York: Wiley.

Rubin, Donald B., and Nathaniel Schenker. 1986. "Multiple Imputation for Interval Estimation from Simple Random Samples with Ignorable Nonresponse." *Journal of the American Statistical Association* 81:366–74.

Rumberger, Russell. 1981. "Changing Skill Requirements of Jobs in the U.S. Economy." *Industrial and Labor Relations Review* 34:578–90.

Synder, David, Mark D. Hayward, and Paula M. Hudis. 1978. "The Location of Change in the Sexual Structure of Occupations, 1950–1970: Insights from Labor Market Segmentation Theory." *American Journal of Sociology* 84:706–17.

Subcommittee on Comparability of Occupation Measurement. 1983. *Alternative Methods for Effecting the Comparability of Occupation Measurement over Time: Report to the SSRC Advisory and Planning Committee on Social Indicators and the U.S. Bureau of the Census.* Washington, DC: Social Science Research Council.

Treiman, D. J., and K. Terrell. 1975. "Women, Work, and Wages—Trends in the Female Occupational Structure Since 1940." Pp. 157–99 in *Social Indicator Models,* edited by K. C. Land and S. Spilerman. New York: Russell Sage.

U.S. Bureau of the Census. 1904. *Twelfth Census of the United States 1900. Special Reports. Occupations at the Twelfth Census.* Washington, DC: U.S. Government Printing Office.

——————. 1973. *Census of the Population: 1970. Subject Reports. Final Report PC(2)-7A. Occupational Characteristics.* Washington, DC: U.S. Government Printing Office.

——————. 1976. *1970 Census of Population and Housing: Procedural History. Report PHC(R)1.* Washington, DC: U.S. Government Printing Office.

——————. 1981. *Census of Population Alphabetical Index of Industries and Occupations.* 2d ed. Washington, DC: U.S. Government Printing Office.

Vines, Paula, and John A. Priebe. 1988. *The Relationship between the 1970 and 1980 Industry and Occupation Classification Systems.* Washington, DC: U.S. Government Printing Office.

Williams, Gregory. 1979. "Trends in Occupational Differentiation by Sex." *Demography* 16:73–88.

11

Causality in the Social Sciences

Margaret Mooney Marini* and Burton Singer[†]

1. INTRODUCTION

The words *cause* and *causal* are often used by social scientists. In using these words, most social scientists seek to distinguish causation from association, recognizing that causes are responsible for producing effects, whereas noncausal associations are not. Although causal terminology has been imprecise and has waxed and waned in popularity (Bunge 1979; Bernert 1983), the ideas of agency and productivity which it conveys have continued to be viewed as distinctive and important in social science. Thus, when the word *cause* fell into disfavor in the early part of the twentieth century, sociologists used such synonyms as *forces*, *controls*, and *energies* to capture the meaning of what had been referred to formerly as causes (Bernert 1983).

In all branches of social science, the identification of genuine causes is accorded a high priority because it is viewed as the basis for understanding social phenomena and building an explanatory science. Causal judgments are made to *explain* the occurrence of events, to understand *why* particular events occur. With causal knowledge it is

This paper was written while M. M. Marini was supported by National Institute on Aging grants K04-AG00296 and R01-AG05715 and while B. Singer was supported by NICHD grant R01-HD19226. We are indebted to Richard A. Berk, James J. Heckman, Paul W. Holland, Clark Glymour, and an anonymous reviewer for helpful comments on an earlier draft.

* University of Minnesota.
[†] Yale University.

often possible to predict events in the future or new observations and to exercise some measure of control over events. It is knowledge of causes that makes intervention for the production of desired effects possible.

Despite the recognized importance of identifying causes, relatively little attention has been devoted by social scientists to considering what causality actually means and how knowledge of causes is acquired. Thinking is usually guided by a natural, or intuitive, idea of causality, leading to attempts to consider directional relationships that are not spuriously determined. However, the "causal" effects estimated in the social sciences often do not provide much causal understanding, not only because the methodology is faulty but also because some of the effects hypothesized fit our natural view of causality better than others.

The purpose of this paper is to consider both ontological and epistemological aspects of the problem of causality in the social sciences. We begin by examining philosophical thinking on the ontological problem, which focuses on the question, What *is* causality: What are causal relationships; are such relationships real; what is the nature of causal laws; what can be a cause? We examine ideas on the meaning of causality to arrive at a more precise understanding that can inform attempts at operationalization. Recently, several statisticians (see Holland [1986] and Holland's paper in this volume for discussion and references) have suggested that methodological issues surrounding the measurement of causal effects should dictate what we think of as a cause. This position, which establishes precise guidelines for valid causal inference in narrowly circumscribed studies and argues that talk of causality outside that framework is misguided, is antithetical to our own. In our view, an understanding of the meaning of causality gives rise to a diversified and flexible research approach, in which subject-matter considerations dictate the kind of evidence that should be sought to establish a basis for causal inference. Often the evidence is observational rather than experimental and is accumulated across multiple studies in multiple settings. Regardless of the research approach taken, the degree of belief in a causal hypothesis depends on the strength of the evidence available to support it.

Consideration of the meaning of causality draws attention to several specific aspects of the concept that have largely unrecognized implications for research practice. First, causal relationships are always identified against the background of some causal field, and specification of the field is critical to interpretation of an observed relationship.

Second, causes are often disjunctions of conjunctions, and failure to consider the conjunctive properties of relationships may lead to failure to detect a causal relationship. Third, causes are of different types, involving, for example, extrinsic determination, intrinsic determination, self-determination, and teleological determination, and different types of causes require different approaches to empirical analysis. Fourth, because much human behavior is purposive, the temporal ordering of behavior or even of behavioral intentions may not be a valid indication of causal direction.

After examining the meaning of causality, we turn to the epistemological, or methodological, problem of causality by considering how we acquire causal knowledge: How do we learn about causal relationships; how do we test causal claims and hypotheses? This problem has been a major concern in all branches of social science, although, as indicated by Cook and Campbell (1979, p. 10), "the epistemology of causation, and of the scientific method more generally, is at present in a productive state of near chaos." We consider this problem by examining the process of causal inference in detail. We discuss the criteria upon which causal inferences are based and operational strategies for building a body of evidence to support such inferences.

We argue that initial ideas of causal relationships are usually triggered by empirical cues and inductive reasoning. We discuss the detection and interpretation of empirical cues, including covariation of various types, temporal plausibility, and contiguity. Because our discussion of the meaning of causality suggests that causes are often conjunctions, after general consideration of covariation we describe a couple of new approaches to detecting conjunctions. The role played by the existing body of relevant knowledge in forming causal hypotheses, including knowledge of the world gained through previous experience with similar empirical relations, is also discussed.

After examining the use of empirical cues and inductive reasoning in the formation of causal hypotheses, we consider the process by which cumulation of a body of evidence leads to the confirmation of causal hypotheses. This process involves demonstrating that an association is consistently observed, that the association cannot be attributed to an alternative explanation, and that there is an identifiable mechanism by which the cause produces the effect. We discuss the general process of induction by which evidence leads to acceptance of a causal claim and the methodological issues that arise in gathering evidence to support an inductive inference. An important implication of our analysis is that subject-matter considerations play a critical role in identifying the evidence needed to support a causal inference and, therefore, must play a critical role in designing research to obtain that evidence. Although statistical tools also play a critical role in the gathering of evidence, there is no context-free statistical method or set of methods that defines causality. The process of causal inference usually involves multiple studies, which successively increase the degree of belief attached to a causal hypothesis.

To illustrate key aspects of the process of causal inference, we present an example at the end of the paper which focuses on attempts to identify an effective treatment for the rehabilitation of heroin addicts. It illustrates the importance of specifying the causal field and considering the possibility that a cause may be a disjunction of conjunctions. It also illustrates the way in which evidence from multiple studies, most of which are observational, can be combined to provide a basis for choosing between competing theories.

2. WHAT IS CAUSALITY?

2.1. *Causal Criteria*

Because philosophers have debated the meaning of causality for centuries and continue to do so, there is no universally accepted definition of causality. At one time, attempts to define causality focused on the idea of logical necessity, and causes were seen as logically entailing their effects (Ducasse 1966). An effect was considered to be "necessitated" by a preceding cause in accordance with the laws of logic and mathematics that establish relations among ideas rather than empirical entities. By the logical relation of implication, the truth of a conclusion is necessitated by the truth of given premises, and there is a contradiction if the premises are true and the conclusion is false.

In one of the most important contributions to our understanding of causality, Hume ([1739] 1896, [1740] 1938, [1748] 1900) set out to show that causes do not logically entail their effects and that the "idea" of causation arises from the *empirical* relations of contiguity, temporal succession, and constant conjunction—i.e., when empirical objects are contiguous in time and space, when one follows the other, and when they always appear together. Influenced by a general empiricist thesis, Hume argued that a relation of necessity is not something that is perceived empirically but that exists only in the mind. The constant conjunction of empirical entities establishes a mental association between them, leading to a feeling of inevitability when one moves in thought from a cause to its effect. It is this subjective feeling projected upon the empirical world that constitutes the "necessary connection" that Hume considered an essential criterion of causation. Although few later philosophers would defend Hume's argument exactly as he proposed it, the idea that causation involves regularity in relations between empirical entities is widely accepted. Those who accept this criterion as a *sine qua non* are often referred to as "regularity" theorists (Beauchamp 1974).

One problem with Hume's argument is that a causal relation cannot be recognized without a backlog of relevant experience. Since *individual* causal relatedness cannot be perceived, a causal relation cannot be detected in a single case.[1] This problem was addressed by later regularity theorists who claimed that singular causal statements were derivable from causal regularities, or laws, of which they were instances (Beauchamp 1974). Thus, even in the analysis of historical events, which in their full particulars are unique, or unrepeatable, it was argued that a degree of causal understanding was accomplished by reference to general laws (Hempel 1942). An individual sequence was regarded as causal if it could be considered an instance of a general law, which might be known or unknown. As Popper ([1959] 1972, app. X) speculated, "One might suppose that it is this logically necessary dependence upon true statements of higher universality, conjectured to exist, which suggested in the first instance the idea of 'necessary connection' between cause and effect." Because of the logical connection required between individual and general causal statements, regularity theorists emphasized the proper analysis of causal laws. Laws were seen as true, contingent, and universal generalizations. Talk of "necessity" arose because natural laws were used as premises

---

[1] Surprisingly, Hume ([1739] 1896, p. 104) admits that "not only in philosophy, but even in common life, we may attain the knowledge of a particular cause merely by one experiment, provided it be made with judgement, and after a careful removal of all foreign and superfluous circumstances." The relationship of this statement to his argument that constant conjunction is an essential criterion for causation is unclear.

for inference. Although these laws implied necessary connections between antecedent and consequent events, such connections were seen as gratuitous (Beauchamp 1974). Other theorists have rejected the view that individual causal statements are derivable from causal laws. Mackie (1974), for example, argues that singular causal statements are *prior to* general ones and are supported by the assumption that a singular causal sequence is an instance of some perhaps as yet unknown or unsuspected regularity.

Another criticism of regularity analyses of causation is that not all regularities of sequence express causal relations. The following of night by day and of day by night, the regular motions of the planets, the occurrence of hair growth on babies before the growth of teeth are examples of noncausal regularities. To distinguish these regularities from those expressing causal relations, arguments have been advanced to permit a distinction between factual statements expressing constant conjunctions, or "accidental universals," and nomological generalizations, or universal laws, which express empirically necessary connections (Kneale 1950, 1961; Popper [1959] 1972; Beauchamp 1974). The principle approach to capturing this idea of "natural necessity" has been the requirement that causal laws sustain counterfactual conditional statements (Kneale 1950, 1961). Because this requirement "connects the notion of natural law with that of the validity of states of affairs other than the actual" (Kneale 1961, p. 99), it is seen as distinguishing causal laws from accidental generalizations. However, reduction of the distinction to purely syntactical considerations relating to the form of lawlike statements has been widely criticized (Ayer 1956; Nagel 1961; Mackie 1966, 1974). Mackie (1966, 1974) further explicated the meaning and use of counterfactuals by arguing that counterfactuals must not be construed as statements with truth values or as statements that follow logically from other statements. Rather, they reflect imagined situations and have the form of condensed arguments that are only entertained and not argued. One is justified in advancing them only if the beliefs that support them are justified—i.e., if there is relevant *empirical evidence*. In the case of law-governed counterfactuals, the problem then becomes that of deciding when there is evidence to support an inductive generalization—the general problem of induction.

When causal relations are characterized as counterfactual relations, "X caused Y" means that "X occurred and Y occurred and in the circumstances Y would not have occurred if X had not" (Lewis 1973; Mackie 1974). This concept of causation has been prominent in the singular judgements of causation required in criminal law. For example, in the case of a crime defined in terms of harmful results, the prosecution must show that the defendant's act was the "cause in fact" of the harm, and for an act to be a "cause in fact" of the result, it must be the "but for" antecedent of the result. This means that "if the result *would have happened anyway*, even had the act not occurred, the act is *not a cause in fact* of that result" (Emanuel 1979, p. 41). Consider the following example:

> D shoots at V, but only grazes him, leaving V with a slightly bleeding flesh wound. X then comes along and shoots V through the heart, killing him instantly. D's act is clearly not a "cause in fact" of V's death, since V would have died, and in just the manner he did, even if D had not shot him. (Emanuel 1979, p. 41)[2]

When causal relations are characterized as counterfactual relations, a cause is something that is both necessary and sufficient in the circumstances for the production of its effect (Bunge 1979; Beauchamp 1974; Mackie 1974). A cause is sufficient for the production of its effect when "sufficient in the circumstances" is taken to mean "given the circumstances, if X occurs then Y will." However, this sufficiency criterion is met by any sequence in which X and Y actually occurred and therefore does not distinguish causal sequences. Mackie (1974) has argued that it is only if "sufficient in the circumstances" is taken in the strong counterfactual sense to mean that "if Y had not been going to occur, X would not have occurred" that causal sequences can be distinguished from noncausal sequences. A cause is usually, although not always, sufficient for its effect in this strong counterfactual sense, whereas this relation does not hold for noncausal sequences.

In defining causal relations, the phrase "in the circumstances" is used to indicate that causal statements are usually made in some

---

[2] Attention has also been given to considering the assignment of responsibility in more complex cases involving alternative over-determination, or "fail-safe" causes (see, e.g., Hart and Honore 1984; Mackie 1974, p. 44–46).

context. As Mackie (1974, p. 34) states, causal statements are made

> against a background of some *causal field*.... Both cause and effect are seen as differences within a field; anything that is part of the assumed (but commonly unstated) description of the field itself will, then, be automatically ruled out as a candidate for the role of cause.

Thus, although there may be a set of factors that are jointly sufficient and severally necessary to produce a result, we are more willing to say that an event, particularly one that is seen as intrusive, caused the effect than that either a standing condition or an event that occurs within some going concern did. For example, we are more likely to say that a spark rather than the presence of flammable material caused a fire, that the severing of an artery rather than the pumping of the heart caused a loss of blood, or that divorce rather than the division of labor within marriage caused a woman to be poor. These preferences are sometimes related to conceptions of what is normal, right, and proper, since what is viewed as abnormal or wrong is more likely to arouse causal interest. Such preferences do not reflect the meaning of causal statements but the uses to which causal statements are put. Because judgments of causal relevance reflect the degree to which a variable is a "difference in a background" (Einhorn and Hogarth 1986), the determination of causal relevance depends critically on context. For example, if we are told that a watch face has been hit by a hammer and the glass breaks, we tend to assume that the hammer caused the glass to break. However, if we are told that the same event occurred during a testing procedure in a watch factory, we tend to view a defect in the glass as the cause of the breakage. The breadth of the causal field determines whether specific alternatives are ruled in or out and thereby affects the number and salience of alternative explanations. In a recent article on statistics and causal inference, Holland (1986) shows awareness of the important role of a causal field or background when he argues that the effect of a cause, X, is always measured relative to other causes, including not X, or $\overline{X}$.

A single cause rarely, if ever, produces an effect. Usually a plurality of causes is involved in two ways. As described by Bunge (1979), *conjunctive plurality of causes* occurs when various factors, symbolized by A, B, C, etc., must be there jointly to produce an effect, Y. Thus, in field Z, Y occurs whenever some conjunction of A and B and C, symbolized as ABC, occurs, but Y does not occur when only the conjunction of A and B, symbolized as AB, occurs. *Disjunctive plurality of causes*, which is often identified as genuine "multiple causation," occurs when the effect is produced by each of several factors alone, and the joint occurrence of two or more factors does not alter the effect (Bunge 1979; Mackie 1965, 1974; Skyrms 1980). Thus, if it is not only the case that, in field Z, the conjunction ABC is followed by Y but also that DEF is followed by Y and that GHI is followed by Y, we have a disjunction of conjunctions: "In Z, (ABC or DEF or GHI) is followed by Y " (Mackie 1974). In Z, (ABC or DEF or GHI) is a condition that is both necessary and sufficient for Y, whereas each conjunction alone is sufficient but not necessary for Y. Using the notation of Einhorn and Hogarth (1986), if we label the conjunction ABC in Z as α, that is, $\alpha = (A \cap B \cap C|Z)$, α is a minimally sufficient condition for Y if

$$p(Y|\alpha) = 1, \quad \text{but } p(\alpha|Y) \neq 0,1.$$

In other words, given α, Y always follows, but given Y, α may or may not occur—it is neither certain nor impossible. However, α would no longer be sufficient if any of its conjuncts, A or B or C, were not present. Thus, a single factor, such as A, is necessary but not sufficient for α:

$$p(A|\alpha) = 1, \quad \text{but } p(\alpha|A) \neq 0,1.$$

Since α is itself sufficient but not necessary for Y, A is neither necessary nor sufficient for Y but is what Mackie (1974, p. 62) has labeled an *inus* condition: "an *insufficient* but *nonredundant* part of an *unnecessary* but *sufficient* condition" (the term *inus* being derived from the first letters of the italicized words).

Since most effects result from multiple causation, what we typically refer to as a cause is an inus condition. For example, if experts investigating the cause of a house fire conclude that an electrical short circuit (X) caused the fire (Y), they are not saying that X was a necessary or sufficient condition for Y. They know that smoking in bed, the overturning of a lighted oil stove, or any one of a number of other events, if it had occurred, might have set the house on fire. They also know that it was the short circuit conjoined with a particular set of conditions (e.g., flammable material near the short circuit, no sprinkler system, etc.) that actually led to the fire.[3] Thus, when we say that X caused Y, we rarely mean that X is either necessary or sufficient for Y. What we mean is that X, when conjoined with other factors, leads to Y. Specifically, we mean that "(a) X is an inus [condition] for Y; (b) X occurred; (c) the other conjuncts occurred; and (d) all minimally sufficient conditions for Y not having X in them were absent on the occasion in question" (Einhorn and Hogarth 1986, p. 7). For X to be a necessary cause of Y, it would have to be in all minimally sufficient conjunctions that produce Y. For X to be a sufficient cause of Y, it would always have to conjoin with its conjuncts. Because the traditional notions of necessity and sufficiency in causation pertain to complex scenarios, often involving a disjunction of conjunctions that we rarely, if ever, know fully, our elliptical understanding of these scenarios results in the observation of probabilistic regularities between identifiable "causes" and their effects.

In the social sciences our interest focuses on scientific theories pertaining to classes of events or things. We are therefore usually interested in the identification of what we might call a causal structure, as reflected in the disjunctive plurality of causes that may produce an effect. In discussing evolutionary theory, Sober (1984) suggests that these disjunctive properties be referred to as explanations rather than causes, since they are not themselves causally efficacious. Disjunctions identify a plurality of causes, any one of which may produce the effect, but do not pinpoint the actual cause that produced the effect in a particular case. Sometimes a concept representing a disjunctive plurality of causes plays an important role in formulating general patterns of explanation. For example, Sober (1984) argues that the concept of the overall fitness of an organism, which summarizes the chances of mortality due to all possible causes, including ones that will not actually be the cause of death, plays an explanatory but not a causal role in evolutionary theory.[4] The concept of overall fitness resembles the concept of life expectancy familiar to social scientists and epidemiologists. If an individual is identified as having high susceptibility to

---

[3] A version of this example was first cited by Mackie (1965), and other versions have been used widely since then.

[4] By comparison, the concept of selection for properties of organisms plays a causal role, since "selection for a given property means that having that property *causes* success in survival and reproduction" (Sober 1984, p. 100).

several causes of death and dies shortly thereafter, this information offers some explanation of why the individual died but does not single out the actual cause of death. It may be irrelevant to know which of several possible causes produces an effect if one is interested only in calculating the effects of the present state of an organism or system on its future.

Because complex regularities are seldom, if ever, fully known, we are usually in a position to formulate only incomplete propositions reflecting them, from which inferences can be made *with probability* about the relation between a cause, which is actually an inus condition, and its effect. Although such causes are not sufficient for their effects, the causing itself is not necessarily probabilistic. The statistical regularity we perceive may indicate that A is likely to be, in some particular case, necessary in the circumstances for Y, rather than that A is likely to necessitate Y (Mackie 1974). Thus, an incomplete causal generalization can sustain the counterfactual conditionals involved in a singular causal judgement. The generalization may be probabilistic when the relation in any particular case that fulfills it is one of necessity, and perhaps sufficiency, in the circumstances. Although even complex regularities involving disjunction of conjunctions may be necessary for Y and therefore deterministic rather than probabilistic, it is unknown whether strict determinism ever holds, since all laws have statistical features when framed in operational terms because of measurement error. One problem with *theories* of probabilistic causality is that although only statistical regularities are observed, causation on the ontic level may not be probabilistic (Salmon 1980).

Since the introduction of quantum mechanics in physics at the beginning of the twentieth century, the idea that at least some aspects of nature are, in fact, irreducibly probabilistic has gained wide acceptance (Sober 1984; Crutchfield et al. 1986; Kolata 1986). Causal laws are probabilistic or statistical if there are sequences of events that fulfill them and if the proportionality of the outcome—e.g., that A's produce Y's in x percent of cases—is observed repeatedly when the causal conditions occur. A statistical law involves the assignment of a measured probability or chance to each individual that falls under it—i.e., to each instance of the relevant assemblage of conditions. It is of the form, "Every A has an x percent chance of becoming (or producing) Y" (Mackie 1974). Statistical laws reflect constancies in nature, but what is constant is the proportionality of the outcome.

Regardless of whether causal laws on the ontic level are deterministic or probabilistic, we observe probabilistic regularities, involving covariation but not necessary connection between X and Y. Rather than indicating that if X occurs, Y must occur, empirical regularities indicate that if X occurs, the probability of Y occurring increases (or changes). As noted above, this fact has led to the formulation of probabilistic theories of causality, which actually define causal relations probabilistically. Thus far, these formal theories have been found to have serious flaws when applied to some empirical situations (Reichenbach 1956; Good 1961, 1962; Suppes 1970; Skyrms 1980; Salmon 1980).

According to philosophers, necessity in the circumstances, as reflected in empirically supported counterfactuals, is not the only distinguishing feature of a cause. Because causal relations are commonly recognized to reflect some genetic connection through a process, they are also asymmetrical, or directional (Bunge 1979; Mackie 1974). According to Mackie (1974, p. 180), this idea of *causal priority* is best captured by the notion of fixity: "An effect cannot be fixed at a time when its cause is not fixed." Or, as Bunge (1979, p. 63) states, "The causal principle requires that the cause be there if the effect is to occur." The notion of fixity bears a strong relationship to temporal succession, which Hume ([1739] 1896, [1740] 1938, [1748] 1900) regarded as an essential criterion for causation. However, causal priority is something more than temporal priority and can be variously directed with respect to time. Modern philosophers tend to agree that temporal priority is not required for causation, although it is usually consistent with a cause's being there before its effect occurs (Bunge 1979; Mackie 1974).

One reason temporal priority is not required for causation is that causation has been conceived to involve contemporaneous links; i.e., causes can occur simultaneously with their effects. For example, Kant considered the case of a leaden ball resting on a cushion and causing a hollow. This example shows how causal priority is established between simultaneous cause and effect when these are continuations of events between which there is a temporal sequence. Another example of simultaneous causes and effects is a Newtonian gravitational set-up in which the acceleration of a body at a point in time causally depends on the masses and distances of other bodies at the same point in time

(Mackie 1974). An example of simultaneously occurring cause and effect in the social sciences is the occurrence of poor mental functioning as a result of depression. Being in a state of depression at a point in time causes poor mental functioning at the same point in time. Backward causation, in which the effect precedes its cause in time, has also been proposed and has become a subject of extensive debate among philosophers (Brier 1974; Mackie 1974, p. 162). An example of backward causation is direct precognition. A literal foreseeing of future events would mean that the future event was affecting the precognizer. Although contemporaneous and backward causation are rare, if they exist at all, the concept of causal priority, or fixity, allows for these possibilities, whereas temporal priority does not. As a practical matter, causal priority usually involves forward causation, or temporal succession.

Skyrms (1980) observes that with the exception of some elementary particle interactions, none of the basic theories in the physical sciences is time-asymmetric. The familiar time asymmetries of physical macrophenomena are represented by the repeated operation of the basic theories of electrodynamics and statistical mechanics, which produce changing states in an ongoing process. For example, if one throws a pebble into a still pond, waves of water radiate coherently out to shore. The temporal inverse of this process is permitted by theory but is never observed. A similar situation may pertain in many social science settings in which basic theories (e.g., decision theories) are time-symmetric, but asymmetries in conditions produced by ongoing processes result in time-asymmetric behavior patterns. For example, after one enters the labor market, wages increase rather than decrease over the life course. The inverse of this process is permitted by basic theories that are time-symmetric, but age-related asymmetries in the actual conditions affecting the decisions of workers and employers make such an inverse unlikely.

In general, the language of causation is more likely to be used when causal laws are molar, or stated in terms of large or complex objects. These laws usually involve delayed causation, mediated via causal chains that operate through time. Molar causal laws are particularly likely to involve disjunctions of conjunctions of the type described above. As a result, the observation of molar relationships tends to be contingent upon many conditions. Until these conditions are more fully known, molar causal laws will be highly fallible and, hence, probabilistic.

> It is probably the case that the more molar the causal
> assertion and the longer and more unspecified the
> assumed micromediational causal chain, the more fallible the causal law and the more probabilistic its
> supporting evidence. (Cook and Campbell 1979, p. 33)

In the social sciences causal generalizations are difficult to make and, when made, are highly probabilistic because most attempts at causal explanation have been of this molar type.

By comparison, ahistorical, more microlevel field theories that directly mediate delayed effects have been dominant in the physical sciences. These "micromediational" laws specify causal connections at a smaller level of particles and on a finer time scale that is often instantaneous. The focus in these theories is on variables in the present. Although delayed causes may exert effects through these immediate influences, the historical forces that impinge on the present are neglected. The mediational processes that operate through time are made explicit by focusing on influences at a given point in time that impinge directly on the persons or objects under study. As noted above, social science examples of this type of ahistorical, instantaneous, micromediational theory can be found in theories of purposive action, or decision making.

The idea of causal priority has also been argued to be captured by the notion of manipulability. A causal relation is seen as one in which Y is produced by the manipulation of X (Collingwood 1940; Gasking 1955; von Wright 1971). Agents bring about certain ends by manipulating means to those ends, or by creating circumstances that are conditions productive of effects. Thus, a causal relation depends on the concept of action; a causal connection can be distinguished from a noncausal regularity only if manipulation of one factor can bring about another. However, because there are some circumstances in which nothing can be manipulated, it is argued that it is enough that we *assume* that if we *could* manipulate X, we could bring about Y (von Wright 1971). Thus, thought experiments in which we manipulate putative causes that cannot be manipulated at will, if at all, play an important role in the social sciences. In writing about economics, Haavelmo (1944, p. 6) states,

> When we set up a system of theoretical relationships and use economic names for the otherwise purely theoretical variables involved we have *in mind* [emphasis added] some actual *experiment*, or some *design of an experiment*, which we could at least imagine arranging, in order to measure those quantities in real economic life that we think might obey the laws imposed on their theoretical namesakes.

Pratt and Schlaifer (1984) have also noted that meteorologists subject even the Rocky Mountains to "conceptual manipulation" when they assert that there would be more snow in Denver if the Rocky Mountains were lower.

In addition to necessity in the circumstances, which may be reflected in complex regularities that, in their elliptical form, constitute part of what we know as causation in the empirical world, and causal priority, which is reflected in the ideas of fixity and manipulability, the existence of an underlying causal mechanism, or continuity of process, may distinguish causal sequences. A number of philosophers have argued that because basic laws are, in part, forms of persistence, causal sequences governed by laws are processes that have some qualitative or structural continuity (Russell 1948, 1959; Kneale 1949; Mackie 1965, 1974; Salmon 1984). Thus, it is suggested that to provide the *connection* between cause and effect which Hume called "the cement of the universe," we must analyze causal relations not only in terms of an event that constitutes the cause and an event that constitutes the effect but also in terms of a causal process that connects the two events and explains their relationship.

In describing what he termed a "causal line," Russell (1948, 1959) focused attention on the importance of space-time structure, "which often remains constant, or approximately constant, throughout a series of causally connected events" (1959, p. 198). He regarded a causal line as the persistence of something:

> Throughout a given causal line, there may be constancy of quality, constancy of structure, or a gradual

> change of either, but not sudden changes of any
> considerable magnitude. (Russell 1948, p. 459)

A causal line may describe the persistence of objects and self-maintaining processes that do not involve qualitative change, or it may describe the persistence of structure throughout changes in quality. Russell identified examples of causes and effects with similar structure that differed in intrinsic quality; for example, he noted that there are qualitative differences but structural similarities among what is printed in a book, the noises made by someone reading aloud from the book, the noises heard by someone else listening to the reader, and the words written down as dictation by the listener. Kneale (1949) argued that even processes that on the face of it exhibit no structural similarity can be assumed to involve some continuity and persistence in structure that cannot be observed but that are expressible in the language of mathematics. At the perceptual level, a cause may be followed by an utterly different effect, such as when a match is struck and a flame appears. But if this macroscopic picture were replaced by a detailed picture of molecular and atomic movements linked by an adequate physicochemical theory to the perceived process, it is argued that more continuity and persistence would be found (Mackie 1974).

Salmon (1984, p. 179) proposes that we take processes rather than events as the basic entities, viewing causal processes as "the means by which structure and order are *propagated* or transmitted from one space-time region of the universe to other times and places." This concept of spatio-temporal continuity is related to Hume's ([1739] 1896, [1740] 1938, [1748] 1900) claim that contiguity in space and time is a criterion of causation,[5] since contiguity makes qualitative or structural continuity possible. What distinguishes causal processes from other processes is that causal processes are capable of transmitting their own structure and, therefore, certain modifications in that structure (Salmon 1984). Because causal processes are self-determined and independent of what goes on elsewhere, they transmit uniformities of

---

[5] Hume, like modern philosophers, did not require that every cause be contiguous with its effect but that when this was not the case, cause and effect would be viewed as joined by a chain of intermediate factors, where each item was the effect of a prior item and the cause of a succeeding item and was contiguous with both (Mackie 1974). However, Hume hesitated to include even this broad view of contiguity as a criterion of causation.

structural and qualitative features. By transmitting their structure, they are "capable of propagating a causal influence from one space-time locale to another" (Salmon 1984, p. 155). An intervention at a particular point in the process transforms it in a way that persists from that point on. Evidence supporting laws that reflect this partial persistence justifies the use of the counterfactuals that seem to sustain them.

2.2. *Types of Causes*

Elaborating on scattered ideas of Plato, Aristotle provided the first codification of the word *cause* in his *Physics* (Book 2, chap. 3, 194b). He identified four causes that were responsible for the production of an effect: formal, material, efficient, and final. A formal cause contributed the essence or quality of a thing and could be thought of as that *into which* a thing was made. A material cause was the matter or substrate *out of which* the thing was made. An efficient cause was the motive force *which made* the thing, and a final cause was the purpose or goal *for which* the thing was made. This view of causes predominated until the Renaissance, when the birth of modern science focused attention exclusively on Aristotle's efficient cause (Bunge 1979; Kuhn 1977). Formal and final causes were abandoned because they were outside the bounds of experiment, and material causes were taken for granted in all natural phenomena. The concept of cause in science therefore came to be equated with *efficient cause*. Accordingly, in his analysis of causality in modern science, Bunge (1979) defines causation as "determination of the effect by the efficient (external) cause" (p. 17) and restricts the meaning of cause to "extrinsic motive agent, or external influence producing change" (p. 33). When the concept is used in this narrow sense, activity and productivity are inherent in causation. However, causal determination in this narrow sense is only one of a number of types of determination that figure prominently in science, and it is the broader principle of determinacy, or lawful production, that now occupies the place once held by the principle of efficient cause (Bunge 1979). In considering the concept of cause in physics, Kuhn (1977) describes how the concept of efficient cause predominated during the seventeenth and eighteenth centuries but gave way to a broader concept in the nineteenth and twentieth centuries. Now, use of the concept of cause focuses generally on explanation: "To describe the cause or causes of an event is to explain why it occurred" (Kuhn

1977, p. 23). However, despite this broadening of the concept, the narrow concept of efficient (external) cause is sometimes taken as fundamental or regarded as distinct. Thus, in his recent article on statistics and causal inference, Holland (1986) uses the term *cause* to refer only to extrinsic determination.

Recognition of the importance of intrinsic, or internal, determination and its causal role in the production of effects is evident in discussions of interaction between external influences and internal processes. When the concept of cause is restricted to external causes, extrinsic agents tend to be seen as molding a passive lump of clay. Now, it is more common to view extrinsic agents as interacting with inner processes, which reflect the influence of predispositions, preconditions, and immanence or heritability (Bunge 1979; Rothman 1976; Koopman 1977; Cox 1986). Thus, a synthesis of intrinsic and extrinsic determination has provided a more adequate picture of causal relations.

Although the concept of cause has been broadened to include internal as well as external causes, philosophers and scientists alike maintain that the concept has limited usefulness when applied to some types of internal processes. A failure to understand these limits has proved to be a serious problem in social science. One type of relation to which application of the concept of cause is usually not helpful is the relation between an earlier and a later state of a *continuous self-maintaining process*. In such a process there is an unfolding of states that differ from one another only in quantitative respects that can be characterized as self-determination. Although it is possible to argue that in the absence of any constraint or external force, the earlier state is necessary and sufficient for the later state, and is therefore a "cause" of the later state, we are unlikely to view the earlier state as anything more than an intermediate cause. When there is an ongoing process, it is of primary interest to look for an initiating or sustaining cause of the *process*. When additional determiners, such as constraints and external forces, are present, interest focuses primarily on these as causes of a change in the process, and the earlier state of the process is relegated to the "causal field." The earlier state of an ongoing process is not a satisfactory cause of the later state because such states (qualities, dispositions) have no productive capacity relative to one another. Although one state in the process can be an antecedent of another, it cannot act upon another state.[6] A state in an ongoing process can only be an *outcome* of inner processes or external influences or both. Thus, an earlier state is more appropriately viewed as a boundary condition than as a cause of a later state. As Mackie (1974, p. 156) states,

> It is especially where we are inclined to ask why-questions that we will be ready to accept because-statements as answers to them, and we are particularly ready to call causes those items that can be described by clauses introduced by "because."

If we ask a why-question about the state of a process at t_1, we are unlikely to accept a description of the state of the process at t_0 as a satisfactory answer. For the same reason, we are also unlikely to accept the mere passage of time as a satisfactory answer.

Another type of determination that can be argued to fit within a broad conception of the meaning of *cause* but is unlikely to provide satisfactory answers to why-questions is *teleological determination*. Teleological determination, or what Aristotle would have called a final cause, is determination of the means by the ends, or goals. Since much human behavior is directed to the satisfaction of goals, intentions, or motives, conscious purposive human action falls into this category. Teleological determination therefore plays an important role in social science. An actor believes that an action, X, will bring about a result, Y, and this belief coupled with the actor's wanting or intending to bring about Y causes the actor to do X. As Mackie (1974) argues, teleological determination has the distinguishing features of a causal relation but is additionally characterized by a subjective or relative point of view. A goal or an intention or a motive may be considered an intermediate cause of behavior, but, again, we are unlikely to accept such a cause as a satisfactory answer to why the behavior occurred.

[6] Our statement that a state in an ongoing process is not a satisfactory cause differs from Holland's (1986) far more sweeping claim that "attributes," such as sex and race, cannot be causes. Like most of those commenting on Holland's article (Glymour 1986; Granger 1986; Rubin 1986), we see no reason to exclude attributes as causes.

3. BASES OF CAUSAL INFERENCE

Having considered the meaning of causality in general and as reflected in different types of causes, we now turn to the epistemological question of how we acquire causal knowledge. Since Hume ([1739] 1896, [1740] 1938, [1748] 1900) first argued that causation is an "idea" inferred from observed relations between empirical objects, it has been recognized that empirical evidence constitutes the basis on which inductive inferences of causation are made. The process of induction involves the use of empirical cues in the initial conception of causal hypotheses, laws, and theories and the cumulation of a body of evidence to confirm them, or justify their acceptance. Induction is an inferential process that expands knowledge in the face of uncertainty, involving reasoning from a part to a whole, from the particular to the general, or from the individual to the universal (Holland et al. 1986).

3.1. *Empirical Cues*

The first idea of a causal relation is derived from empirical cues. Observational criteria that follow from the meaning of causality lead us to consider the possibility that a causal relation exists. Empirical cues suggest that a causal inference may be justified, although none constitutes indisputable evidence for or against the causal hypothesis, and none is a *sine qua non*. A subjective element in judging the evidence from empirical cues is an unavoidable aspect of causality assessments.

In *A Treatise on Probability* (1921), Keynes considered the possibility of characterizing induction within a mathematical theory of probability, where probability was interpreted as "degree of belief." He was concerned with the question of when observed instances warrant acceptance of a generalization. One of his conclusions was that before examining the evidence for or against a suggested generalization, a nonzero probability (degree of belief) must be attached to the generalization on the basis of prior knowledge. As discussed by Russell (1959), this prior knowledge comes from empirical cues, which lead to inferences that are not logically demonstrative. "Nondemonstrative inference" differs from inference based on deductive logic in at least two ways. First, when the premises are true and the reasoning correct, the conclusion is only probable. Second, the premises are often uncertain. Thus, empirical indications of causality lead to the formation of causal hypotheses, to which varying degrees of "credibility" or "doubtfulness" can be attached. In the social sciences, these empirical cues include covariation of various types, temporal plausibility, and spatiotemporal contiguity.

Covariation

Our natural conception of causality derives from a program in the brain that "allows the forecast that sequences of events that have been repeatedly connected in the past will (probably) be connected in the future" (Young 1978, p. 234). Such a conception of causality is derived relative to the degree of detailed knowledge available about the empirical phenomena under investigation and can be established with varying degrees of probability. The existence of covariation between X and Y is consistent with Hume's concept of causality and with several early methods of experimental inquiry identified by Mill (1843) for the study of causation. Covariation is also viewed as an important cue to causality by modern statisticians (Suppes 1970; Mosteller and Tukey 1977; Holland 1986), social scientists (e.g., Granger 1969, 1980; Gibbs 1982; Davis 1985), and epidemiologists (Evans 1976, 1978). Although covariation is not sufficient for causation, where covariation exists and it is possible to imagine a mechanism whereby X could cause Y, a causal hypothesis is likely to be entertained.

Covariation may be exhibited either cross-sectionally or longitudinally. For example, it may be observed that if any two members of a population differ in their values of Y, they also tend to differ in their values of X. Or it may be observed that if the value of Y has changed for any member of the population, the value of X for that same individual will tend to have changed. These two associations are not the same, and one can be true when the other is false. However, since not all X's can change, it may be impossible to observe the association of a change in X with a change in Y. For example, except in rare and special cases, attributes such as sex and race cannot change. For attributes of this type, change can be observed only at the population level. A change in the proportion of women in management positions, for example, may be associated with a change in the nature of interaction in the workplace. In general, because the concept of causality reflects ideas of agency and productivity, covariation between *changes* in the values of X and Y provides the most convincing evidence of causality.

Coherence. One can also look for coherence in the relationships among variables with which X and Y are associated. If X and Y covary, the relationships of these variables to other variables should be consistent with that covariation. For example, if labor force participation encourages an instrumental rather than expressive orientation toward interpersonal relationships, and if males spend more time in the labor force than females, males should be more instrumentally oriented in their relationships than females. Evidence of associations of this type may be particularly valuable if X and Y are difficult to measure directly or if direct measures are not available in the population under study.

Strength. Not only the existence of covariation but its *strength* has been argued to be an important cue to causality. For example, in evaluating the relationship between smoking and lung cancer, the U.S. Surgeon General's Advisory Committee identified a *high degree* of association as one of five criteria to be used in epidemiologic decisions about causality, and these criteria have now been widely accepted in that field (Feinstein 1986). It is viewed as particularly instructive when the hypothesized cause bears a higher degree of association to the effect than do other factors that can be viewed as alternative causes (Hill 1965).

Since a high degree of association between X and Y is suggestive of a causal link, its observation usually leads to efforts to rule out alternatives to the causal hypothesis. A low degree of association, or even the absence of an association, however, may not be a valid indication of a lack of causal connection. As described above, X is likely to be an inus condition of Y, i.e., one of several factors that conjoin to constitute a minimally sufficient condition for Y. The degree of association between X and Y is therefore affected not only by the boundaries of the reference population, which reflect the selection of a field against which the degree of association is assessed, but by the distribution of other variables in the population, including especially the joint distribution of X and its conjuncts for the production of Y and the joint distribution of factors constituting other minimally sufficient conditions for Y (i.e., alternative causes). As described by Einhorn and Hogarth (1986), if we think of a 2×2 table in which the occurrence or nonoccurrence of X (x and $\bar{x}$, respectively) is crossed with the occurrence or nonoccurrence of Y (y and $\bar{y}$, respectively), x and y will occur jointly only when x and all its conjuncts are present. If x is present but one or more of its conjuncts is absent, x will not produce y, thereby causing x and $\bar{y}$ to occur jointly. This could result from either the absence of an enabling condition or the presence of a counteracting condition. The more x must conjoin with other factors to produce y and the more likely counteracting factors are to offset x, the weaker will be the association between X and Y. Similarly, if there are alternative causes of y in which x is not a factor, the conjunction of conditions that constitute these alternative causes will produce y in the absence of x. Thus, if the minimally sufficient condition for y of which x is a part is only one of a larger number of minimally sufficient conditions for y (i.e., if there are multiple causes of y), $\bar{x}$ and y will occur jointly. The strength of association between X and Y is therefore affected by the distributions of other causally relevant variables in the population. These other variables may act not only as dichotomous threshold triggers that condition the action of other variables but as more finely graded effect modifiers producing complex synergistic effects. There are a large number of possible ways in which variables may interact to affect the association of X and Y (Koopman 1977).

Congruity. In addition to the presence of covariation, one may observe congruity in an association. Congruity refers to some form of similarity between cause and effect. The type of congruity used most often as a cue to causality is similarity of the strength or duration of cause and effect. If an effect is large, one is inclined to expect the cause(s) of the effect to be of comparable size; strong causes produce strong effects, and weak causes produce weak effects. A good example of this type of congruity, or concomitant variation, is the "dose-response curve," in which a disease rate increases with the *amount* of exposure to the purported cause. In considering whether smoking is a cause of lung cancer, the fact that the death rate from lung cancer increases linearly with the number of cigarettes smoked per day is considered important evidence beyond that contained in the observation that cigarette smokers have a higher death rate than nonsmokers (Hill 1965). Of course, congruity between the strength or duration of cause and effect may not occur. When it does not, some sort of amplifying or dampening process must be postulated to connect cause and effect (Einhorn and Hogarth 1986). When small causes are hypothesized to have big effects, a linkage process involving amplification must be postulated. When big causes are hypothesized to have small effects, a linkage process involving dampening must be postulated. A recent example of this type of incongruity, where small causes were hypothesized to have big effects via an amplifying process, is available in the work of Cole and Singer (1987) on gender differences in the productivity of scientists. An example outside the social sciences is Darwin's ([1859] 1964) formulation of evolution.

Another type of congruity that is sometimes used to make causal inferences is qualitative or structural resemblance between cause and effect. For example, physical similarity between offspring and adults helps to identify particular adults as causal agents of those offspring. A cause and effect may also be similar in space-time structure but different in intrinsic quality. For example, in broadcasting, where electromagnetic waves cause the sensations of hearers, there is a resemblence in structure between cause and effect. All visual and auditory perceptions involve the transmission of structure but not intrinsic quality. Similarly, the power and prestige hierarchy of a group produces a patterning in the interactions of group members, but the resemblance between cause and effect is in structure only. Complex structures can therefore be transmitted causally throughout changes of intrinsic quality.

Responsiveness. In situations in which it is possible to intervene and manipulate X, it is possible to obtain direct evidence of the responsiveness of Y to changes in X. Such responsiveness may be observed in either a natural or a controlled experimental setting, since one can introduce a treatment or withdraw a treatment and observe the response in either setting. Even taking preventative action with respect to X may provide an opportunity to observe the responsiveness of Y in a natural setting (Evans 1978; Cook and Campbell 1979). For example, one can observe whether those who stop smoking have lower rates of lung cancer than those who do not. Although randomization of treatment assignment or withdrawal is not a feature of all controlled experiments, in a controlled randomized experiment it is possible, at least in principle, to eliminate all alternative sources of influence and thereby increase the strength of the evidence that X causes Y. However, for studying many aspects of human behavior, controlled experimentation is either impossible or unwise. It is often impossible to undertake experimentation for practical and ethical reasons, and because the naturally occurring relationships of X to other variables are frequently ignored in an experiment, experimentation introduces the real possibility of obtaining results that have no applicability in a natural setting (Fienberg, Singer, and Tanur 1985; Heckman and Hotz 1987).

Conjunctions

As noted above, what we typically refer to as a cause is what Mackie (1974) called an inus condition. X is usually one of a number of factors that, when conjoined, constitute one of a number of minimally sufficient conditions for Y. Because the conjuncts of X for the production of Y are often unknown, the strength and consistency of the relationship between X and Y may appear considerably weaker than would be the case if the relationship of X to its conjuncts were known and taken into consideration.

Although it is recognized that causation usually involves disjunctive plurality of causes, consideration of conjunctive plurality is rare in the social sciences. It seems likely that such consideration has been impaired by the popularity of statistical techniques for the estimation of linear, additive models and the relative inaccessibility of effective tools for identifying interactions. During the past 15 years, several new exploratory data-analytic methods have been put forth to deal directly with the problem of detecting conjunctions without imposing strong a priori linearity and normality assumptions. As might be anticipated, these methods are very computer intensive and still in need of further theoretical and practical development before they can be regarded as broadly applicable, "well-understood" techniques. We briefly discuss two such methods because of the insight they have already provided in a diversity of scientific problems in which the detection of relationships—conjunctions—among variables in a high-dimensional state space was of central importance. Much further methodological research and testing of these and analogous strategies in a broad array of social science problems will be necessary if a good technology for efficient detection of conjunctions as candidate causes is to be widely available.

Projection pursuit. The fundamental problem that any method for detecting conjunctions with many variables must confront is the fact that high-dimensional space is mostly empty. Projection pursuit techniques deal with this problem by selecting low-dimensional projections of high-dimensional point clouds, which an investigator then examines visually and attempts to interpret substantively.

The selection of projections has been carried out via the PRIM-9 program at Stanford Linear Accelerator Center, where the user may select any three variables at a time and have them displayed as a two-dimensional image of the projection of the points along any direction. By continuously moving the direction, the three-dimensional configuration of the points is revealed. To the best of our knowledge, the PRIM-9 system has not been used to detect relationships among variables in a social science setting; however, it has been used very effectively in medical contexts. (See, especially, Reaven and Miller [1979] for an application of PRIM-9 to a study of the etiology of diabetes.)

Automated machine selection of potentially interesting projections of a high-dimensional point cloud is carried out by numerical maximization of a "projection index," which, in its original version (Friedman and Tukey 1974), was the product of a robust measure of scale (trimmed standard deviation) and a measure of clumpiness (weighted count of the number of "close pairs" of data points). This kind of criterion is motivated by some limited experience gained watching scientists examine projections and attempt to characterize, in a general way, those projections that they regard as "interesting." Although *interesting* cannot be given a completely context-free definition, the common denominator of the judgments is that *non*normal projections tended to be interesting. This immediately suggests that maximizing some measure of clumpiness is important for any algorithm that is looking for interesting projections by searching a high-dimensional space. Further support for basing projection indices on clumpiness arises from a general mathematical result of Diaconis and Freedman (1984), who show that for *most* high-dimensional point clouds, *most* low-dimensional projections are approximately normal. Thus, the interesting and unusual projections should tend to be *non*normal.

Projection pursuit may, of course, be carried out on aggregations of variables (e.g., on linear or selected nonlinear combinations of them), thereby increasing the possible complexity of conjunctions that might be exposed when an investigator visually explores many projections. The reader interested in learning more about this technology and its scope and limitations as seen to date should consult Friedman and Tukey (1974), Friedman and Stuetzle (1982), and Huber (1985).

Grade-of-membership representations. The activity of exploring high-dimensional data for interpretable conjunctions may often be viewed as an attempt to classify heterogeneous populations on the basis of a large number of characteristics, each of which is important for distinguishing some subgroup, however small, of the full population. Attempts at developing a small number of categories (conjunctions), defined in terms of the original large list of characteristics, such that each member of the population can defensibly be classified as a member of just one category frequently fail for a very fundamental reason. Many individuals are represented by multiple interrelated characteristics, no combination of which occurs with high frequency in the full population. Thus, we have a high-dimensional state space, most portions of which are either occupied by a few individuals or simply empty. Such data do not readily lend themselves to aggregation into a small number of *interpretable* categories, into only one of which any given individual should be classified.

Rather than strive for crisp classification with high-dimensional sparse data structures, we seek a *representation* of individual response vectors in terms of similarity, or grade-of-membership (GOM), scores relative to interpretable profiles (conjunctions) of conditions. If, for example, we construct—compatible with the data, in a sense to be made precise below—four "meaningful" sets of levels or categories extracted from an original long list of potentially important variables and for each individual assign GOM scores g_1, g_2, g_3, and g_4 such that $g_k \geq 0$ and $\sum_{k=1}^{4} g_k = 1$, then we identify an individual as having degree of similarity score g_1 relative to profile 1, degree of similarity score g_2 relative to profile 2, etc. If $g_k = 1$ for some profile k, then the individual is viewed as expressing only the characteristics of the kth profile. If $g_{k*} = 0$ for some profile k^*, then the individual is interpreted as having no resemblance to profile k^*. The basic point is that for very heterogeneous populations in which individuals are initially described by high-dimensional vectors and in which no combination of responses occurs with very high frequency, it is often useful to *represent* individuals by GOM scores relative to a set of ideal (or pure-type) profiles.

To clarify the structure of GOM representations, let $\mathbf{X} = (X_1, \ldots, X_J)$ be a vector whose components are discrete variables, each of which can only assume a finite number of possible values. Thus, any continuous variables will be assumed to have been approximated by an ordinal categorical variable having a similar distribution. The distribution of $\mathbf{X}$ will be denoted by $\text{Prob}(\mathbf{X} = \mathbf{l})$, where $\mathbf{l} = (l_1, \ldots, l_J)$ is a vector whose coordinates are possible levels of the variables $X_1, \ldots, X_J$. The basic idea of a GOM representation for $\text{Prob}(\mathbf{X} = \mathbf{l})$ is the

transferring of the stochastic dependence among the original variables
into GOM scores for individuals and then, conditional on these scores,
assuming that the original variables are independent.

More formally, we associate with each individual a set of scores
$\mathbf{g} = (g_1, \ldots, g_K)$ such that $g_k \geq 0$ and $\sum_{k=1}^{K} g_k = 1$. Then we label an
individual's response vector as $\mathbf{X}^{(\mathbf{g})} = (X_1^{(\mathbf{g})}, \ldots, X_J^{(\mathbf{g})})$, and the distribution of $\mathbf{X}$ will, henceforth, be denoted by $\mathrm{Prob}(\mathbf{X}^{(\mathbf{g})} = \mathbf{l})$. Now we
assume that conditional on the values of $\mathbf{g}$, the original variables are
independent. This leads immediately to the representation

$$\mathrm{Prob}(\mathbf{X}^{(\mathbf{g})} = \mathbf{l}) = \int_{S_K} \mathrm{Prob}(\mathbf{X}^{(\mathbf{g})} = \mathbf{l} | \mathbf{g} = \boldsymbol{\gamma}) \, d\mu(\boldsymbol{\gamma})$$

$$= \int_{S_K} \prod_{j=1}^{J} \mathrm{Prob}(X_j^{(\mathbf{g})} = l_j | \mathbf{g} = \boldsymbol{\gamma}) \, d\mu(\boldsymbol{\gamma}), \qquad (1)$$

where $\mu(\boldsymbol{\gamma})$ is the distribution of GOM scores and $S_K = \{\boldsymbol{\gamma} = (\gamma_1, \ldots, \gamma_K): \gamma_k \geq 0, \sum_{k=1}^{K} \gamma_k = 1\}$ is the unit simplex with K
vertices. We further *assume* that the conditional probabilities in (1) are
given by

$$\mathrm{Prob}(X_j^{(\mathbf{g})} = l_j | \mathbf{g} = \boldsymbol{\gamma}) = \sum_{k=1}^{K} \gamma_k \lambda_{k, j, l_j}, \qquad (2)$$

where

$$\sum_{l_j \in L_j} \lambda_{k, j, l_j} = 1 \quad \text{for } 1 \leq k \leq K, \qquad 1 \leq j \leq J$$

and $L_j =$ the set of possible levels of variable X_j.

The probability distributions $\{\lambda_{k, j, l_j}\}_{l_j \in L_j}, 1 \leq j \leq J, 1 \leq k \leq K$,
have the interpretation $\lambda_{k, j, l_j} =$ (probability in profile [pure-type] k of
observing level l_j on variable X_j). They are the basis for defining the
ideal, or pure-type, profiles. To this end, we introduce the following
definition.

Definition 1. A family of probability distributions $\{\lambda_{k, j, l_j}\}_{l_j \in L_j}, 1 \leq j \leq$
$J, 1 \leq k \leq K$, will be said to define a set of K *extreme admissible profiles* if
the following are true:

a. There is at most one profile, call it k_0, such that $\lambda_{k_0, j, l_j} = 0$ for
$1 \leq j \leq J$ and all "distinguished" levels $l_j \in L_j$.

Remark. One or more levels of each variable will be called *distinguished* if they represent a priori designated characteristics that

should be the basis for designating membership in a pure-type profile.

Thus, k_0 is identified as a profile in which no distinguished characteristic occurs.

b. For all profiles other than k_0, there is at least one variable for which $\lambda_{k, j, d_j} = 1$, where $d_j =$ the set of distinguished levels on variable j. For all variables not satisfying this condition, $\lambda_{k, j, d_j} = 0$.

c. For each pair of profiles (k, k') not including k_0, there is at least one variable for which $\lambda_{k, j, d_j} = 1$ and $\lambda_{k', j, d_j} = 0$. This means that there is at least one condition that distinguishes each profile from all of the others.

Conditions (a)–(c) imply that the *joint* probability of occurrence of "distinguished" conditions associated with each profile, except k_0, is one. Thus, an individual for whom $g_k = 1$ is characterized as someone who must have *all* the distinguishing characteristics associated with profile k. The important interpretive feature of extreme admissible profiles is that they are described by logical AND statements (i.e., a conjunction) involving distinguished levels of subsets of the original variables $X_1, \ldots, X_J$. The sense in which (1) and (2) with $\{\lambda_{k, j, l_j}\}_{l_j \in L_j}$, $1 \le j \le J$, $1 \le k \le K$, satisfying (a)–(c) define a new *representation* of a data set $\mathbf{X}^{(1)}, \ldots, \mathbf{X}^{(N)}$, where $N =$ number of individuals, is the fact that we define a point mapping from J-coordinate space $X_1 \otimes \cdots \otimes X_J$ (defined by the variables $X_1, \ldots, X_J$) to the simplex S_K whose vertices are identified with extreme admissible profiles. Each individual's GOM score $\mathbf{g}^{(m)} = (g_1^{(m)}, \ldots, g_K^{(m)})$, $1 \le m \le N$, defines a location for that individual in S_K.

For some applications, criteria (a)–(c) prove to be excessively stringent. Thus, it is important to have a somewhat more general definition of *admissible profile* whose logical interpretation is slightly more intricate than that of *extreme admissible profile*. To this end, we introduce the following definition.

Definition 2. A family of probability distributions $\{\lambda_{k, j, l_j}\}_{l_j \in L_j}$, $1 \le j \le J$, $1 \le k \le K$, will be said to define a set of K *admissible profiles* if the following are true:

a′. There is at most one profile, call it k_0, such that $\lambda_{k_0, j, d_j} < 2 \operatorname{Prob}(X_j \in d_j)$ for $1 \le j \le J$ and d_j are the distinguished levels for variable X_j.

b'. For all profiles other than k_0 there is at least one variable for which $\lambda_{k,j,d_j} > c \operatorname{Prob}(X_j \in d_j)$, where c is chosen by the investigator subject to the constraint, $c \geq 2$.

c'. For each pair of profiles (k, k') not including k_0, there is at least one variable for which

$$\lambda_{k,j,d_j} > c \operatorname{Prob}(X_j \in d_j)$$

and

$$\lambda_{k',j,d_j} < c \operatorname{Prob}(X_j \in d_j).$$

A verbal interpretation of (a')–(c') is given by the following:

1. The *joint* probability—within profile k—of occurrence of distinguished levels is much greater than the joint frequency of these levels in the population as a whole.

2. The probability within each profile other than k_0 of the occurrence of at least one distinguished level is much greater than the frequency of occurrence of the same level(s) in the population as a whole.

The above specifications are restricted to static representations of heterogeneous populations. An extension of these ideas to vector stochastic processes is of great importance and is presented in Manton et al. (1987), where estimation strategies and computational issues are also discussed. For an insightful application of grade-of-membership representations in detecting conjunctions in psychiatry, see Swartz et al. (1986).

Our purpose in presenting these brief summaries of projection pursuit and grade-of-membership representations is to indicate by explicit example that there are flexible strategies currently available and under development which should facilitate the search for conjunctions.

Temporal Plausibility

Temporal succession is widely regarded as an important cue to causality because it is strongly tied to the criterion of asymmetry, or causal priority, reflected in the requirement that a cause must be there if its effect is to occur. Causes usually occur prior to their effects. Contemporaneous and backward causation are possible, as noted above, but genuine instances of them are rare, and it is a matter of debate whether they even exist. This is not to say that measurements are always, or even often, refined enough to identify temporal succession but that temporal succession characterizes almost all causal relations in the empirical world. Thus, the requirement that a cause precede or be contemporaneous with its effect (i.e., that Y not occur before X) plays an important role in operational attempts to identify causal relations in all branches of social science (Granger 1969; Davis 1985; Einhorn and Hogarth 1986) and epidemiology (Hill 1965; Evans 1978; Feinstein 1986). In general, longitudinal data are required to assess temporal plausibility. Even when a cause is believed to be contemporaneous with its effect, tests of causal priority usually require that variations in the postulated cause be related to later variations in the postulated effect. Thus, one seeks to observe that changes in the cause have temporal precedence over changes in the effect prior to reaching a state of contemporaneous causation (Cook and Campbell 1979).

A major problem with use of the criterion of temporal plausibility in social science is that the temporal order in which behavior occurs, or in which events resulting from behavior occur, is often not a good indication of causal priority. Because human beings can anticipate and plan for the future, much human behavior follows from goals, intentions, and motives; i.e., it is teleologically determined. As a result, causal priority is established in the mind in a way that is not reflected in the temporal sequence of behavior or even in the temporal sequence of the formation of behavioral intentions.

For example, consider the relationship between women's educational attainment and the timing of entry into marriage, where the temporal sequencing of exit from school and entry into marriage does not provide an appropriate basis for distinguishing a hypothesized causal effect of educational attainment on the timing of marriage from a hypothesized causal effect of the timing of marriage on educational attainment. Among women who leave full-time schooling *prior to* entry into marriage, there are some who will leave school and then decide to get married and others who will decide to get married and then leave school in anticipation of the impending marriage. For example, among women who terminate their schooling with the completion of college and then marry are women who will finish college, find a desirable mate, and then marry and women who will find a desirable mate while in college, abandon plans for graduate school in anticipation of an impending marriage, and then marry. Both groups of women experience exit from school and entry into marriage in the same temporal sequence, but the causal mechanisms at work are different. For the former group, educational attainment is causally prior to the timing of entry into marriage; for the latter group, the timing of entry into marriage is causally prior to educational attainment. That is, for the latter group the intention to marry causes women to truncate their schooling earlier than they would otherwise, lowering their educational attainment. Since the anticipation of entry into marriage may affect educational attainment prior to entry into marriage, whether education occurs before or after entry into marriage does not distinguish the effect of educational attainment on the timing of marriage from the effect of the timing of marriage on educational attainment. Moreover, this problem is not necessarily solved by considering the temporal sequence of the formation of behavioral intentions. In a situation such as this, in which there is perceived incompatibility between future activities, a single decision may jointly (i.e., simultaneously) produce a related set of behavioral intentions. To identify causal priority, therefore, one must search for evidence that is not reflected in the *temporal* sequence of behavior or even of thought. This evidence may be obtainable only by asking people about the causal processes at work. Although such information can be affected by distortions in perception, memory, and reporting, it is sometimes the only evidence with which to establish causal priority in the social sciences.

Contiguity

Evidence that events are contiguous in time and space is another empirical indication of causality. As noted by Hume ([1739] 1896, [1740] 1938, [1748] 1900), when contiguity is high—i.e., when there is little time or distance between the occurrence of X and Y—one is more likely to suspect a connection between X and Y and to postulate a causal mechanism by which X and Y are related. By comparison, when contiguity is low, one is less likely to suspect a causal connection, and it is only the identification of a causal mechanism linking the events that justifies the inference that causality is involved. For example, some knowledge of human biology and chemistry is needed to bridge the temporal gap between intercourse and birth in maintaining that there is a causal relation between these events (Einhorn and Hogarth 1986). It is impossible to establish specific, universally applicable time and space boundaries within which both X and Y must fall to satisfy a contiguity criterion of causation. High contiguity is an aid to causal inference, but it need not be present if a mechanism linking X and Y can be identified. Contiguity facilitates the identification of relationships and thereby leads to speculation about causal mechanisms that may produce them.

3.2. *Theoretical Development*

Causal inference occurs not only through the "bottom-up" process of forming hypotheses on the basis of empirical observation but also through the "top-down" process of relating what is observed empirically to an existing body of relevant knowledge, including knowledge of the world gained through previous experience with similar empirical relations. In drawing on knowledge of similar empirical relations, use of analogies plays an important role. If X and Y are similar to other variables for which there is already a body of knowledge to suggest the existence of a cause-effect relationship, the similarity among the separate causes and among their separate effects will be suggestive of a cause-effect relationship between X and Y. For example, if there is reason to believe that gender stereotypes unconsciously affect assessments of the performance of women and men, it is reasonable to expect, by analogy, that racial stereotypes unconsciously affect assessments of the performance of blacks and whites.

A causal inference is strengthened if there is a carefully reasoned explanation (theory) that provides details of a mechanism by which the cause is related, often step by step, to the effect. As noted by Simon, the postulating of a causal mechanism occurs by a process of induction:

> Mechanisms and laws are theoretical constructs that are derived *inductively* from empirical evidence but are not derivable *deductively* from that evidence. We can never show that a particular mechanism did, in fact, cause certain phenomena; we can only show that a particular mechanism *could* have produced the phenomena—that, if the mechanism had been at work, the phenomena would have appeared. (Simon 1979, p. 71)

Because the possible causal mechanisms that are likely to be imagined are derived from the empirical indications of causality discussed above and knowledge of the world gained through experience with similar empirical relations, they should be consistent with empirical evidence and the existing body of relevant knowledge. (See Simon [1986] for a discussion of the problems arising in economics from insufficient attention to empirical evidence in the development of theory.) In linking statements that X causes Y to a postulated causal mechanism reflecting a subject-matter theory, subjectivity and beliefs in the plausibility (or lack thereof) of particular theories will enter into causality assessments. The controversial nature of claims of substantive coherence (i.e., strong arguments on behalf of a particular theory about how X drives Y) is an integral part of the process of assembling evidence to support the claim that X causes Y.

As noted by Einhorn and Hogarth (1986), it has been suggested that attributions of physical causation involve the perception that causes and effects are linked by a "generative" force. This implies a mechanistic view in which there is a physical transfer of causal "energy" from X to Y. Events are seen as linked via a causal chain so that the force can be transmitted from one link to the next. This view makes it clear that if one cannot construct a causal chain to link X and Y, there is no basis on which to claim that X causes Y. Thus, the causal chain connecting X and Y is only as strong as its weakest link; if one link in the chain cannot be made, the explanation is incomplete.

In scientific contexts, we seek to make generalizations that denote lawful regularities. These are distinguished from "accidental" regularities by direct inductive confirmation and by their relationship to other laws. Although a strict separation between what is observable and what is not may be impossible, observational laws, which deal with observable things and processes, can be contrasted with theoretical laws, which postulate unobservables. The development and use of theories take on particular significance because theories explain and unify broad classes of facts, demonstrating that phenomena thought to be disparate are similar.[7] Theories differ from sets of laws in several respects (Holland et al. 1986). First, an observational law gives an account of a set of observations, whereas a theory often explains sets of laws. For example, a theory of power-dependence relations may explain why both increases in female earnings and improvement in household technology increase the probability of divorce. Second, theories are intended to unify phenomena in different domains. Thus, a

---

[7] This characteristic of a theory was termed consilience by Whewell (1967).

theory of power-dependence relations may explain changes in the relative position of a disadvantaged group as well as changes in the probability of divorce. Third, it is by postulating unobservable entities, such as power and dependence, that theories usually achieve their unifications.

3.3. *Confirmation*

After empirical observation and inductive reasoning have led to the formation of a causal hypothesis, which is often linked to a postulated causal mechanism, a body of evidence must be assembled to support the claim that X causes Y. There are no hard-and-fast rules of evidence that *must* be obeyed before a causal inference is justified. Causal inferences can never be made with absolute certainty but are made with varying degrees of confidence depending upon the evidence available. As noted by Russell (1959, p. 102), "'Knowledge' is not a precise conception, but merges into 'probable opinion'." Confirming the hypothesis that X causes Y involves demonstrating consistency in the association of X and Y, demonstrating that the association between X and Y is not attributable to alternative explanations, and identifying the mechanism by which X causes Y. This process of confirmation is usually accomplished by accumulating a body of evidence from multiple studies.

Consistency

Consistency refers to the need to replicate an association, i.e., to demonstrate that it is consistently observed. This is, of course, a well-recognized general criterion for increasing the evidence relevant to any hypothesis in all branches of science. In accumulating evidence to support a generalization in the social sciences, it is usually desirable to replicate the association in different localities and by different methods to establish that it exists under varying conditions. As noted by Keynes (1921),

> No one supposes that a good induction can be arrived at merely by counting cases. The business of strengthening the argument chiefly consists in determining whether the alleged association is stable, when the accompanying conditions are varied.

For hundreds of years, philosophers have attempted to characterize the process of induction whereby inferences lead from knowledge of particular observations to acceptance of a generalization. In the last several decades, this activity has focused largely on the question of when a general hypothesis can be considered confirmed by its instances. Because of the advances made by the use of formal logic in the study of deduction, in which the truth of an inference is guaranteed by the truth of the premises on which it is based, most recent work on induction has been governed by syntactic approaches. Beginning with Keynes (1921) and followed up by Nicod (1930), Hempel (1945), Carnap (1950), Carnap and Jeffrey (1971), and Salmon (1967), to name only some of the principals, we have a series of increasingly refined attempts to build rigorous, purely logical theories of induction and confirmation of evidence that would, in effect, do for induction what Frege ([1884] 1961) and Russell (1908) did for deduction. These theories use the formalism of logic and probability theory, most recently employing Bayesian probability theory and decision theory. However, this primarily formal and syntactic approach to inductive reasoning has been shown to give rise to numerous paradoxes; see, especially, Hempel (1945) and Goodman (1965).

Holland et al. (1986) have initiated a thorough and very different rethinking of induction at the interface of cognitive psychology, artificial intelligence, and philosophy. In their view, purely syntactic accounts are insufficient because they do not consider the kinds of things about which inferences are being made and the goals the inferences serve. Some time ago, Mill (1919, p. 206) noted that the number of instances required to warrant acceptance of a generalization is not constant. He asked, "Why is a single instance, in some cases, sufficient for a complete induction, while in others myriads of concurring instances, without a single exception known or presumed, go such a very little way towards establishing a universal proposition?" Holland et al. (1986) have argued that the number of instances is only one of two major components in evaluating the acceptability of a generalization. The other consists of knowledge of the statistical properties of the populations about which one wishes to generalize, including the distributions of events and the role of chance in producing them. If the events of interest are known to be the kinds of things that are highly invariant and not much subject to random fluctuation, generalization from a few instances will be considered legitimate.

However, if such things are highly variant or highly subject to randomness, generalization will require many confirming instances.

When people are able to code the uncertainty of events, their reasoning is affected because they invoke abstract inferential rules, or "pragmatic reasoning schemas," that embody statistical reasoning. As a result of differences across different content domains in the variability of events and the role of chance, the inferential rules used in different domains differ. In the social sciences, where variability is high and chance plays an important role, inductive reasoning is guided by inferential rules that embody statistical principles. The inferential rules employed are not domain-specific empirical rules tied to particular types of events but abstract inferential rules describing relations over general classes of objects, relationships between events, and problem goals. Thus, inductive reasoning involves knowledge structures at an intermediate level of abstraction. Pragmatic reasoning schemas potentially apply across a wide range of content domains but are constrained by certain broad types of goals and event relationships in a way that content-free logical rules are not. This revised perspective on induction, which is rooted in an understanding of the cognitive processes by which humans acquire, develop, and accept (as plausible) new knowledge, suggests that the body of evidence required to support the claim that X causes Y will be affected by the distributions of X and Y and the degree to which X and Y are subject to both random fluctuation and measurement error. Knowledge of this type helps to establish the "finite antecedent probability" described by Keynes (1921) as necessary to validate inductions based on a number of observed instances. To a degree, awareness of such probabilities is embedded in the norms that emerge within scientific specialties regarding the strength of evidence required to support the claim that X causes Y. Such norms arise from the nature of the phenomena under study, the goals (end uses) of causality assessments, the measurement technology in the substantive area of inquiry, and the richness of the proposed explanatory theories being investigated.

Because the association between X and Y is affected by the joint distribution of factors constituting various minimally sufficient conditions for Y, the association between X and Y is likely to vary across populations, even being absent in some. As noted by Gibbs (1982, p. 97), "It would be unrealistic for sociology and perhaps all observational sciences to require that each finding support a causal assertion."

Similarly, when Sober (1984) discusses population-level causation in the context of evolution, he suggests that a positive causal factor must raise the probability of the effect in *at least one* background context without lowering it in any. Although we believe it is impossible to establish a specific, universally applicable level of consistency that must be met to satisfy an associational criterion of causation, the greater the degree of consistency with which a high level of association is observed and the greater the ability to explain situations in which an association is not observed, the stronger the basis for causal inference.

In the social sciences two types of consistency are particularly important for establishing the validity of a causal assertion. Consistency across methods establishes "construct validity," and consistency across localities establishes what Cook and Campbell (1979) have called "external validity." Construct validity is established by demonstrating *convergence* across different measures of the same thing and *divergence* between measures of related but conceptually distinct things. External validity is established by demonstrating that a causal relationship is generalizable to and across populations of persons, settings, and times. Thus, one is interested in demonstrating that a relationship is limited to neither a particular idiosyncratic sample nor to a particular population but holds in different populations, across settings and times. It is often through attempts to assess the consistency of an association across settings and times that knowledge of the factors that constitute various minimally sufficient conditions for the production of an effect is acquired. Ultimately, variation in the association between X and Y across populations should be attributable to variation in these contingent conditions.

In attempting to assess the consistency of an association, one faces the problem of knowledge synthesis, namely, the need for defensible strategies for combining the evidence from multiple studies to support or refute claims that there is an association (response) relating X and Y. This problem has a long history, the rigorous development of which is traceable to the work of Fisher (1946), Pearson (1933), and Tippett (1931). Fisher's work, in particular, has had a major influence on subsequent developments. It focuses primarily on combining evidence from independent studies that purport to measure the same quantity and where measured effects in any single study are just at the borderline of being declared significant (i.e., weak association in a single study), while the "combined" evidence from all studies indicates a very significant (in the sense of statistical significance) association. The difficulties involved in combining estimates of effects from multiple studies in which a similar, but *not the same*, quantity is being measured were treated in early papers of Cochran (1937) and Yates and Cochran (1938) and have received intermittent attention since then, as reviewed, for example, in Hedges and Olkin (1985). Two recent papers on this topic which deserve close reading are Mosteller and Tukey (1982, 1983). A fundamental issue in all of this literature, which requires further development, is the provision of a good rationale for the inevitably subjective weights that are used to combine (pool) the comparisons from studies of varying size and quality and involving the measurement of similar, but *not the same*, quantities.

The early literature we refer to on combining evidence usually involves consideration of evidence from controlled experiments or at least from studies of the same type; i.e., they are all controlled randomized experiments or all observational studies involving the same or very similar data-collection plans. In many settings, such as the evaluation of educational interventions (teaching materials, kinds of homework, classroom organization, discipline, etc.), the evidence about potential causal relationships comes from both experimental and observational studies. The assessment of effect sizes in the contemporary meta-analysis literature (Hedges and Olkin 1985; Wolf 1986) represents one approach for dealing with the knowledge-synthesis problem in this kind of heterogeneous setting. However, more in-depth, quantitative syntheses in a variety of substantive contexts are needed to develop broadly applicable strategies for supporting claims about the consistency of an association.

Ruling Out Alternatives to the Causal Hypothesis

The existence of empirical cues such as covariation, temporal plausibility, and contiguity raises the question of whether there is a causal relation. However, to justify acceptance of the causal hypothesis, it is necessary to establish that the relationship between X and Y is one of agency and productivity, i.e., that it is not attributable to common causes of X and Y or to a causal effect of Y on X. In ruling out the possibility that the X, Y relation is spurious, the task is not to rule out the existence of other causes of Y, since the possibility of multiple causation is fully acknowledged, but to rule out the possibility that one or more of these causes accounts for the relationship between X and Y.

Einhorn and Hogarth (1986) draw a distinction between the "gross strength" of the evidence that X causes Y, which is determined by the causal field and empirical indications of a causal relation between X and Y, and the "net strength" of the evidence that X causes Y, which is the gross strength of the X, Y relation discounted by the gross strengths of alternative explanations or causes. The net strength of a causal explanation increases as its gross strength increases but decreases as the gross strengths of its alternatives increase. Thus, the strength of the evidence in support of a causal claim is greatest when there are no plausible alternative explanations and is lower when there are such alternatives.

Consideration of alternative explanations has been an important emphasis in the work of Campbell and his colleagues on threats to "internal validity" (Campbell and Stanley 1963; Cook and Campbell 1979). In assessing internal validity, one asks what factors other than X could have produced Y. Consideration of *specific* alternatives is important because one can consider empirical indications of their plausibility and replace the current explanation with an alternative when the plausibility of the current explanation is reduced. To rule out alternative explanations, it is necessary to show

> that either there are no plausible common causes of X and Y or that the quantitative relationships between the plausible common causes and X and Y are inadequate to explain an observed clear and consistent association. (Mosteller and Tukey 1977, p. 261)

It is also desirable to show that Y cannot cause X.

Ruling out alternative explanations and thereby demonstrating that the X, Y relation is causal requires, in effect, a demonstration that the outcome with respect to Y would have been different in the absence of X. The usual approach to accomplishing this is to examine the relationship between X and Y under conditions in which alternative explanations are rendered inoperative. If X and Y covary under these conditions, there is greater reason to believe that X causes Y.

An experiment is sometimes the preferred method for gathering evidence to support the claim that X causes Y. Experimental control permits manipulation of the values of X, making it possible to observe the responsiveness of Y to changes in X rather than merely the association of differing values of X and Y across population units or even the association of changes in the values of X and Y for individual population units. When experimental control involves randomization to treatments, a further attempt is made to make the distribution of X independent of the distributions of other variables that may affect Y, rendering alternative explanations of the association between X and Y inoperative. As noted above, experiments—including both controlled laboratory experiments and randomized experiments in field settings—are often not possible in social science and, even when possible, are not always the preferred method. Thus, although experiments can play an important role in some areas of research, most causal inferences will, of necessity, be based on other kinds of evidence. For more detailed discussion of the advantages and limitations of experiments, see Campbell and Stanley (1963), Cochran (1965), Cook and Campbell (1979), Rubin (1974), Fienberg et al. (1985), Singer (1986), Holland (1986), Heckman (1987), Heckman and Hotz (1987), and Berk (1988).

Quasi experiments, which have treatments, outcome measures, and experimental units but do not involve randomization to treatment, are another means of gathering evidence to support causal inferences in field settings. In quasi experiments comparisons to determine the effect of a treatment are based on nonequivalent groups, and the task in interpreting the results is to separate the effects of the treatment from those due to the initial noncomparability of treatment groups. Quasi-experimental designs are of two principle types: (a) nonequivalent group designs, in which responses of a treatment group and a comparison group are measured before and after a treatment, and (b) interrupted time-series designs, in which the effects of a treatment are examined by comparing measures taken at many time intervals before the treatment with measures taken at many time intervals after the treatment (Cook and Campbell 1979). These designs combine experimental manipulation with different data collection plans to provide a stronger basis for causal inference than would be possible without manipulation.

In nonexperimental, or "observational," research the role played by alternative causes must be examined without experimental manipulation. In some cases it is possible to collect data on what are, in effect, "natural experiments," in which X is distributed more independently of the hypothesized alternative causes of Y than is usually the case, and the X, Y relation can be observed more apart from these influences. For example, in seeking to understand the effects of heredity and environment on behavior, scientists have sought to identify naturally occurring situations in which one of these influences is relatively constant while the other varies, such as when identical twins are separated at birth and reared in different environments. The modes of analysis used in quasi experiments can sometimes be employed when the "treatment" is a natural occurrence, such as a natural disaster, rather than a planned intervention. Analytic approaches appropriate for interrupted time-series designs can be used when the event being examined is abrupt and precisely dated and when it does not result from prior change in the level of the indicator. Analytic approaches appropriate for nonequivalent group designs can be used even when the "treatment" is a permanent institution. As in quasi experiments, the availability of measures of Y taken before and after a "treatment" can provide a sounder basis for causal inference.

When it is impossible to obtain observational data that approximate a natural experiment, statistical analysis alone is used to "partial out" alternative causes that covary with X under the assumption that the X, Y relation that remains after partialling is likely to be causal. In the past several decades it has become common practice to represent (model) hypothesized causal relations by systems of equations. Since the development of path analysis by Wright (1921, 1934, 1954), there has been extensive development and application of linear models, referred to variously as structural equation models, factor analytic models, path analysis models, or even regression models (see, e.g., Simon 1953, 1957, 1979; Blalock 1964, 1971; Fisher 1966; Goldberger and Duncan 1973; Aigner and Goldberger 1977; Bielby and Hauser 1977). In these models a set of causal relationships among variables is represented by a set of equations relating the variables of the model and a set of stochastic assumptions about the probability distributions of those variables, jointly and individually. The models usually assume linearity in both variables and parameters and an underlying multivariate normal distribution. (See Freedman's [1987] critique on the use of structural equation models and other related articles in the *Journal of Educational Statistics*, volume 12, number 2.) The use of stochastic process models to represent evolving processes has also occurred but has been less common (see, e.g., Bush and Mosteller 1955; Cootner 1965; White 1970; Bartholomew 1982; Malliaris and Brock 1982).

Although the technology for causal analysis has at times been subject to mindless application, it properly involves the formal representation of hypothesized causal relations. It is not a way of deducing causation but of quantifying already hypothesized relationships. As noted by Fisher (1946, p. 191), causality cannot be identified by statistical operations alone:

> If...we choose a group of social phenomena with no antecedent knowledge of the causation or absence of causation among them, then the calculation of correlation coefficients, total or partial, will not advance us a step toward evaluating the importance of the causes at work.

All attempts to define causality within the context of a formal model require some imposed structure. Using available knowledge, including existing theory and the kinds of empirical indications of causality discussed above, a scheme of causal relations is postulated and then quantified. A priori assumptions reflecting postulated causal mechanisms make estimation of the coefficients of the model possible.

Because the coefficients estimated are conditioned on an assumed causal structure, knowing that they are statistically significant and can generate good predictions of the data does not prove the existence of causal relations. It indicates only that the data are consistent with the proposed causal hypothesis. Of course, if a causal hypothesis is first suggested by observed correlations or partial correlations in the data analyzed, estimation of a causal model using the same data cannot provide *independent* confirmation of the hypothesis.

To develop causal models that more accurately reflect empirical causal relations, the meaning of causality, as discussed above, needs to be kept in mind when models are formulated. One factor rarely considered now in the formulation of causal models is the likelihood that the "causes" identified are not additive. The "causes" studied are likely to be inus conditions, which conjoin with other "causes" to produce effects. Attention needs to be paid, therefore, to understanding the relationships among candidate causes. Absent from most "partialling" exercises is any awareness that a conjunction of factors may constitute a minimally sufficient cause of Y, that several such conjunctions may be multiple causes of Y, and that a single factor may operate in one or several of these conjunctions. Partialling out other "causes" of an outcome in an effort to estimate the effect of a single cause, as is commonly done, may not be appropriate. With well-formulated models of the interrelationships among the independent variables in an equation, the basis for making causal inferences from observational data could be strengthened considerably beyond what it has been thus far.

A second factor requiring more attention when models are formulated is the use of temporal succession as an indication of causal priority. Temporal order has been used heavily as a guide in model formulation because causes do not follow their effects in time. However, as noted above, the order in which behaviorial events or behavioral intentions occur is not always indicative of causal priority when purposive human action is involved. Moreover, in the process of operationalizing cause-effect relationships, the reference point used in establishing temporal, and therefore causal, order is often the time at which a measurement is taken rather than the time at which an influence occurs, particularly if the measurement refers to an ongoing process rather than to a discrete event. Because the number of measurements taken is finite and because they may be spaced at wide intervals, ordering variables primarily on the basis of the time at which they are measured can grossly misrepresent the influence process. This problem is particularly serious when measures of mental states or attitudes are involved, since these reflect ongoing processes that are difficult to measure repeatedly.

A third factor warranting more attention in model formulation is the distinction among types of causes, particularly those involving extrinsic determination, self-determination, and teleological determination. In some branches of social science, it is quite common to treat the earlier state of an ongoing process as a "cause" of a later state in the same manner that causes extrinsic to the process are treated. As noted above, self-determination of this type does not have the same causal status as extrinsic determination. Similarly, measures of intentions are often treated in the same way as other causes. Although inclusion of these measures reflects an awareness of teleological determination, the distinct role played by teleological determination requires more attention than it has received thus far. (See Frydman and Phelps [1983] for an example of an attempt to deal with this issue in economics.)

Although causal models were developed to represent hypothesized causal relations, many models have not been well tuned to the phenomena under investigation and the theories driving them. The absence of explicit subject-matter considerations, including theory, for example, has been a major criticism of the Wiener-Granger tests of causality applied in the analysis of economic time-series (Geweke 1984; Zellner 1979). Stochastic variables and temporal succession are central to the Wiener-Granger framework, and within that framework, a "cause" is identified on the basis of its ability to *predict* an effect. Thus, if time series $\{X_t, t \geq 0\}$ and time series $\{Y_t, t \geq 0\}$ are conditionally independent given time series $\{Z_t, t \geq 0\}, \{X_t, t \geq 0\}$ is not a cause of $\{Y_t, t \geq 0\}$. Rather than rely on purely statistical criteria of this type, we take it as essential that (a) a link be provided between the context-free class of models usually employed in Wiener-Granger causality analyses (e.g., ARIMA models) and a focused theory, (b) an assessment via multiple goodness-of-fit tests of empirical data to the autoregressive models be carried out, and (c) a clear statement be presented defending the time periods over which stationary processes are a reasonable approximation of the phenomena under observation.

The importance of explicit subject-matter considerations is emphasized in a recent paper by Basmann (1988), which considers the problem of observational equivalence in interdependent, or nontriangular, systems of equations. Previous discussion of the causal interpretation of parameters in simultaneous equations by econometricians, such as Strotz and Wold (1960), has tended to view the problem in terms of algebraic operations. Since a given probability distribution determines a unique reduced form, coefficients in triangular recursive systems have been considered to have a "causal interpretability." The role of nonstatistical subject-matter information has been minimized or eliminated in these earlier treatments, and causality has been viewed as testable by methods of statistical inference alone. However, in nontriangular systems a given probability distribution determines an infinite class of observationally equivalent simultaneous equations representations. These representations, each of which corresponds to a set of identifying restrictions, assert different and contradictory hypotheses about causal relations but have the same significance probability and power when tested on the data.

In such a situation, in which statistical tests cannot support one choice against the others, information external to the model is needed to warrant the use of one specific representation as truly "structural." The information must come from the existing body of knowledge relevant to the domain under consideration. If this information is insufficient to rule out all but one of the observationally equivalent structural representations, a unique causal relation cannot be singled out. The problem of observational equivalence is not addressed by solving the problem of identifiability, since alternative observationally equivalent representations are identified under different identifying restrictions (Koopmans and Reiersol 1950).

In some instances models are not devoid of subject-matter considerations, but the importance of their being able to predict an empirical reality external to the model is not recognized. For example, Simon (1953, 1957) viewed causality as a deductive logical property of models and was not concerned with the ability of the model to predict empirically observable outcomes. As Simon stated in the first chapter of *Models of Man* (1957, p. 12),

> The aim of this chapter is to provide a clear and rigorous basis for determining when a causal ordering can be said to hold between two variables or groups of variables in a model.... The concepts to be defined all refer to a model—a system of equations—and not to the "real" world the model purports to describe.

Simon's notion of causal order can be viewed as part of a larger program of establishing causality provided (a) the models are a formalization of mechanistic theories of the manner in which X could have produced Y, and (b) the models have been tested against data, where context-specific multiple goodness-of-fit criteria are set up as a standard of performance.

The relevance of causal models to empirical phenomena is often open to question because assumptions made for the purpose of model identification are arbitrary or patently false. The models take on an importance of their own, and convenience or elegance in the model building overrides faithfulness to the phenomena. Whether assumptions made in order to estimate a model impair the usefulness of the model for confirming or disconfirming causal hypotheses is a question warranting more attention. Important aids in addressing this question can be additional research to test the plausibility of the assumptions and the estimation of alternative models to examine the sensitivity of estimates to differing assumptions (Leamer 1978).

When comparisons are made between what happens under the action of a candidate cause and what would have happened without it, statements of the magnitude of a comparison that will be regarded as "strong" (or "large") are both subjective and context-dependent. An important set of unresolved statistical research problems are associated with the comparison activity, particularly in the context of stochastic processes. The issue is one of delineating what empirical regularities, or what details of an evolving process, a model will be required to reproduce with some fidelity before it is regarded as an adequate descriptive model of the underlying phenomena. Examples of the kinds of features we have in mind are

1. differences in rates of change of an outcome variable in a population exposed to a candidate cause vs. the corresponding quantity in an unexposed population,
2. the ratio of the number of occurrences of a given event in an exposed (to the candidate cause) population to the same count for an unexposed population,
3. the difference between the "delay" in response to a secondary stimulus (not the candidate cause) in an exposed (to the candidate cause) population relative to the response delay in an unexposed population.

Multiple criteria such as (1)–(3) lead to vector optimality criteria (Tukey 1987) for fitting models to data and *multiple* goodness-of-fit tests for assessing the descriptive adequacy of models. An informal assessment (comparison) of multiple models subject to multiple criteria is a routine part of much empirical analysis (see, e.g., Bush and Mosteller [1959] for a comparative study of eight stochastic learning models subject to multiple goodness-of-fit criteria), but a deep understanding of the properties of such tests lies in the future. Comparative analysis and multiple tests to assess "large" differences ("strong" associations) are presented in a linear models context in Glymour et al. (1987), in a log-linear context in Goodman (1973), and in a counting process context in Heckman and Walker (1987). Much remains to be done in this direction to put the comparative analysis component of causality assessments on a firm foundation.

Identifying the Causal Mechanism

In addition to seeking evidence that X causes Y by attempting to rule out the possibilities that the X, Y association is spurious and that Y causes X, one is interested, at least ultimately, in understanding *why* X causes Y. In other words, one seeks to identify the mechanism by which X causes Y. To date, most empirical work in the social sciences has sought to identify causal relationships at a molar level, providing evidence of empirical regularities, or observational laws. Attempts to "explain" a causal relation usually involve the identification of other observed variables measured at the same level that are part of a causal chain linking X and Y. This approach to elaborating a causal chain has produced an increasingly detailed picture of empirical relationships, often varying across time and place. Although knowledge of such relationships is essential for the development of theories that are tuned to the phenomena, there has as yet been little attempt to use these observations as a basis for the development of theories aimed at unifying broad classes of facts by postulating unobservables. In economics considerable theoretical work has been carried out, but theory development is largely a deductive exercise, often done with little attention to its relationship to empirical phenomena. In other fields, such as sociology, the importance of theory in developing a cumulative body of knowledge has gone largely unrecognized, and the documentation of empirical regularities is an end goal in itself. Once theories have been developed to account for what appears, on the basis of prior observation and research, to be a causal relation between X and Y, research designed to test these theories will be needed. A confirmed theory identifying the mechanism by which X causes Y greatly strengthens the basis for causal inference.

Cumulating a Body of Evidence

Few would question that the use of "causal" models has improved our knowledge of causes and is likely to do so increasingly as the models are refined and become more attuned to the phenomena under investigation. However, causal models have limitations that call for the use of other operational approaches in building a body of evidence to support causal inferences. One limitation noted by Cordray (1986, p. 17) is that causal models are "mechanistic and inflexible" because "the logic of testing rival explanations is buried in the statistical machinery." Since there are limits to the kinds of alternative models that can be considered and compared within the framework of a single study, evidence from multiple studies that examine a variety of consequences of a causal explanation and test the effectiveness of the operationalization can greatly increase the confidence with which causal inferences are made. Because it is usually possible to imagine different consequences of the truth of a causal hypothesis, multiple studies can be used to determine whether each of these consequences holds. Often, if-then conjectures about the nature of the influence process and its observable results require the specification of conditional relationships: If this influence process occurs, we expect that outcome; or, if that result occurs, it could have been produced this way or that way (Cordray 1986). When there are two (or more) rival explanations, conjectures of this type can identify situations in which the explanations would lead to different consequences, thereby permitting a "critical test" of their relative effectiveness. In short, reasoning about the implications of causal explanations can be accompanied by reasoning about appropriate methodological strategies. Since there are numerous ways to gather evidence, multiple research designs, as well as multiple measures and multiple analyses, provide a means of broadening the evidential base.

4. EXAMPLE: REHABILITATION OF HEROIN ADDICTS

To illustrate some key aspects of the process of causal inference, we finally consider an example that focuses on attempts to identify an effective treatment for the rehabilitation of heroin addicts. This example illustrates the importance of considering the causal field and the possibility that a cause may be a disjunction of conjunctions. The process by which evidence can be cumulated from multiple studies, most of which are observational, is also illustrated. In this case the evidence is used to test competing theories of addiction that call for different modes of treatment.

4.1. *Statement of the Problem*

Heroin abuse occurs in widely disparate environments and in varying degrees. The incidence of heroin abuse fluctuates dramatically with geographical location and macrolevel historical events, such as the end of World War II, major recessions, and the Vietnam War protest movement. In urban ghetto neighborhoods, it is frequently associated with grossly inadequate parental support in early childhood, unemployment in the teen and young adult years, and strong peer influence supporting heroin usage. The natural history of heroin addiction seems to be invariant no matter what the geographical setting. Once heroin abuse has begun, most users go through periods of temporary abstinence but, after six to eight years of heroin use, tend to persist as chronic, daily drug-seeking users. With increasing age, the death rate among chronic users rises rapidly and is substantially higher than the age-specific mortality rates for heroin nonusers (Vaillant 1966b).

Individual addiction histories, free of any formal treatment program, involve transitions back and forth between periods of active addiction and temporary abstinence. Persons who start abusing heroin between ages 16 and 22 and who abuse for less than one or at most two years tend to revert to permanent abstinence with no treatment, even if they have been daily users for spells of several months or even one year. Persons who continue with sustained, essentially daily heroin use for more than two years (chronic users) rarely revert voluntarily to even temporary abstinence. In a 25-year follow-up study of 50 heroin addicts from New York City who had used heroin for an *average* of 3 1/2 years at the start of the study, roughly 40 percent achieved stable abstinence by age 42 (Vaillant 1966a, b, c, d, 1973). Of addicts who became permanently abstinent, as measured by abstinence for at least three years and without known subsequent relapse, two thirds found stable employment, supported themselves and a family, did not engage in serious alcohol, barbiturate, or tranquilizer abuse, and refrained from the criminal activity that was necessary to support heroin addiction. In the course of an addiction "career," the average addict in the study spent only six years actively addicted. Roughly five more years were spent in jail and one year in a hospital. The average addict was known to have been withdrawn from drugs either in jail or in a hospital a total of nine times and, thus, relapsed a minimum of eight times. From the vantage point of social disability, the average addict was neither in jail nor actually addicted for 13 years out of the 25-year period of the follow-up study. Nevertheless, he was abstinent and fully employed for less than four years out of 25. This characterization of the natural history of heroin addiction forms the baseline against which treatment programs are to be evaluated.

We focus attention here on Methadone Maintenance Treatment (MMT) programs whose aim is *rehabilitation*, defined as termination of and sustained abstinence from heroin use, stable employment, and stable family life (Dole and Nyswander 1965; Dole, Nyswander, and Kreek 1966). We seek to determine whether there is a basis for inferring a causal relationship between X and Y, where $X = MMT$ and $Y =$ rehabilitation. MMT programs vary with respect to at least five identifiable components:

$A_1 =$ proper drug (methadone) dosage,

$A_2 =$ compliance in schedule of administration (daily),

$A_3 =$ presence in the program of sensitive psychological counseling personnel,

$A_4 =$ availability in the program of supportive personnel to assist in job search,

$A_5 =$ supportive home base or peers.

Which of these five components constitutes the true cause of Y has been a source of disagreement. Proponents of a metabolic theory of addiction claim that prolonged daily injections of heroin trigger a metabolic disorder so that no matter how hard an addict may try to stop the use of heroin, the addict is simply overwhelmed by an inner drug-seeking drive and persists in the addiction. MMT is argued to be necessary for rehabilitation, and a high-quality MMT program is believed to be one that combines drug therapy with social and psychological support. The cause, X, of Y is therefore seen as a disjunction of conjunctions, where $X = [A_1 \cap A_2 \cap A_5 \cap (A_3 \cup A_4)]$ and each of the components A_i, $1 \leq i \leq 5$, can be interpreted as an inus condition. Proponents of a psychologically based theory of addiction oppose MMT programs. They point to the effects of peer influence, unstable home life during early childhood, and a social environment accepting of drug use on initiation of heroin abuse and claim that willpower and desire by a motivated addict can generate Y in the absence of drug therapy. Thus, they argue that $X' = [(A_3 \cap A_5) \cup (A_3 \cap A_5 \cap A_4)]$ causes Y and that the amendment of $(A_1 \cap A_2)$, while possibly helpful, is not necessary to achieve Y. A psychologically based theory leading to X' has provided the rationale for both drug-free therapeutic communities and government resistance in many countries to the proliferation of MMT programs. (See Dole and Nyswander [1968] for a lucid statement of both metabolic and psychological theories of addiction.)

4.2. *The Body of Evidence*

The following associational evidence suggesting that X causes Y has been obtained from a diversity of studies in the U.S., Canada, several West European countries, and Hong Kong:

1. Prior to the discovery of methadone as a narcotic blockade, chronic daily users of heroin had a progressively degenerating life, very frequently leading to early death. Except for exceedingly rare isolated cases, Y virtually never occurred in the population of chronic users who persisted in daily use for more than two years.
2. In early MMT programs in New York and later in Sweden, Y occurred with very high frequency when X was operative. $(A_1 \cap A_2)$ alone was only rarely associated with Y. A_1 alone or A_2 alone was never associated with Y in any program anywhere.
3. In Hong Kong, $(A_1 \cap A_2 \cap A_4 \cap A_5)$ was strongly associated with Y.
4. In Hong Kong and Sweden, when methadone was withdrawn or withheld from a control group selected by randomization, $[A_5 \cap (A_3 \cup A_4)]$ alone was not associated with Y.
5. In Vietnam veterans who experienced at most one year of daily use of heroin in Vietnam and returned immediately to the U.S., A_5 and Y were strongly associated (Robins, Helzer, and Davis 1975). At first glance, this study appears to lend strong support to X'. However, careful examination of the entry criteria for MMT programs reveals that no one in the Vietnam veterans study would qualify for MMT. Two years of daily use of heroin was a minimal admission requirement for MMT clinics everywhere. An important feature of this study is that together with (1)–(4), it suggests that two different causal claims are warranted, depending on the causal background. "X' causes Y" is supported for the population of heroin users with at most 1–$1\,1/4$ years of daily use, whereas "X causes Y" is supported for the population of heroin users with two or more years of daily use.

Nearly all associations in (1)–(5) were determined from observational studies. The only controlled, randomized experimentation was in studies of $(A_1 \cap A_2)$ vs. placebo in Hong Kong (Newman and Whitehill 1979) and vs. no treatment in Sweden (Gunne and Gronbladh 1981) to ascertain whether $(A_1 \cap A_2)$ was related to retention in the MMT program of addicts who had already self-selected into the program and met the admission criteria. The setting for assessing whether X caused Y in the context of MMT is prototypical for the evaluation of a wide range of complex programs in which (a) voluntary self-selection into a treatment program is a condition of entry; (b) it is unknown whether the decision criteria for entry used by volunteers are the same or different from those used by nonvolunteers; (c) the program has a multiplicity of components constituting the treatment; and (d) a control group from the target population cannot be assembled. Conditions (a)–(d) are also present in evaluating rehabilitation programs for chronic alcoholics, family planning programs in developing countries, and manpower training programs, to name only a few instances.

In the context of MMT programs, the effect of $(A_1 \cap A_2)$ is recognizable almost immediately. At a daily dose (usually from 50 to 100 mg), the concentration of methadone in the addict's blood is kept at all times above the threshold for withdrawal symptoms and well below the threshold for narcotic effects (Dole 1980). When the MMT patient is thus stabilized, he/she is functionally normal, protected from narcotic effects by pharmacological tolerance of the drug *and* from withdrawal symptoms by the constant presence of methadone in the blood stream. Thus, there is no question about contiguity of $(A_1 \cap A_2)$ and the initial signs that Y might occur. Since, operationally, rehabilitation means abstinence from heroin use for at least $1\,1/2$–2 years *and* stable employment and family life, contiguity of X and Y requires that this time period be judged to be adequate for seeing the influence of A_3, A_4, and A_5. In fact, contiguity can clearly be claimed, since prior to MMT, most daily users of heroin are unemployed, heavily engaged in street crime, and have no stable family life.

Although the associational evidence accumulated to date supports the metabolic theory of addiction, several types of additional evidence would enhance the support for this theory. First, it would be desirable to demonstrate that treatment programs designed to provide only social and psychological support for chronic addicts are ineffective in accomplishing their rehabilitation goal. Unfortunately, long-term follow-up data comparable to that collected on MMT programs are not available for drug-free therapeutic communities, which detoxify addicts and assist them in developing the inner resources to adopt alternative, more effective life-styles. Although the withdrawal of methadone from control groups in Hong Kong after initial stabilization in an MMT program indicated that the social and psychological support available to program participants was insufficient for rehabilitation in the absence of methadone treatment, it would be desirable to demonstrate that a treatment program designed specifically to provide only social and psychological support was ineffective in rehabilitating chronic addicts. Second, it would be desirable to have an analogue of the Vietnam veterans study for two-or-more-years daily users of heroin. That study forms the only natural experiment of a psychological theory of addiction to date, and it supports the psychological theory for up-to-one-year daily users of heroin. If there had been a population of two-or-more-years daily users of heroin in Vietnam who achieved Y upon returning to the U.S. without $(A_1 \cap A_2)$, the metabolic theory would be in serious doubt. An experiment analogous to the Vietnam veterans experiment for two-or-more-years daily users of heroin would involve the physical transfer of a population of persons who satisfy MMT admission criteria to a new environment where $[A_5 \cup A_5 \cap (A_3 \cup A_4)]$ is available. For example, it would be interesting to know how chronic heroin addicts in New York City who meet the MMT program admission criteria would behave if they were simply transferred to a highly favorable environment several thousand miles away. If Y did not occur under such circumstances, there would be further evidence to rule out X' as a spurious cause of Y for persons eligible for admission to MMT programs. Unfortunately, establishing such an experiment is highly impractical. Third, it would be desirable to identify a biological mechanism triggering a clearly defined metabolic disorder in persons with two or more years of daily heroin use. To date, no biological mechanism that can be claimed to generate a metabolic disorder has been identified.

5. CONCLUSIONS

We have tried to present a global picture of causality in the social sciences, starting from basic philosophical and conceptual issues and proceeding through questions of operational strategies for confirming or refuting claims that X causes Y. A broad unifying discussion in a paper of limited size carries with it the price of lack of thoroughness, which would arise in a sustained in-depth analysis of a particular problem. This, of necessity, must be the focus of another paper. Our aim here has been to isolate the central features of the concept of causality *and* their relationship to operational strategies for cumulating a body of evidence, an integration that seems to be lacking in the extant literature and is critical for any assessment of causality.

Our basic position with regard to the nature of causes in most social science settings—which stands in sharp distinction to the way most analyses that purport to be causal are currently carried out—is that the plausible candidates for causes are usually disjunctions of conjunctions. This has major implications for the formal modeling and rigorous testing of explanatory theories in that coupled nonlinear dynamical systems will, of necessity, be the natural mathematical language within which to describe conjunctions and their evolution. The variables currently incorporated in the wide-spread applications of path analysis are usually best thought of as inus conditions and thus represent only individual components of causes.

The causes operating in social science settings also represent different types of determination, including extrinsic determination, intrinsic determination, self-determination, and teleological determination. In our view, restricting the concept of cause to extrinsic determination, as recommended by Holland (1986), is artificial and disfunctional, since external influences often interact with internal processes in producing effects. Moreover, mental processes are a major focus of study in the social sciences because they mediate most human action. What requires far more attention is the special nature of self-determination and teleological determination. In many instances the concept of cause has limited usefulness when applied to these types of determination. For example, it is usually not helpful to refer to the relation between an earlier and a later state of a continuous self-maintaining process as causal, since the earlier state has no productive capacity relative to the later state, and it is of primary interest to look for an initiating or sustaining cause of the *process*. Similarly, it is usually not helpful to treat goals, intentions, and motives in the same way that other causes are treated, since they play a distinct role in social science theories.

One implication of the importance of teleological determination in the social sciences is that the temporal ordering of behavior or even of the formation of behavioral intentions is often not a valid indication of causal priority. In the absence of other information, there has been a tendency to make unwarranted causal inferences on the basis of the temporal sequencing of behavioral measures. To make valid causal inferences about the actions of individuals will require far more direct questioning of individuals and the mounting of longitudinal studies with successive waves of data collection spaced at short intervals.

Criteria for making causal inferences do not seem to us to be specifiable across the full range of scientific inquiry, or even the full range of inquiry in the social sciences. Criteria employed in a diversity of problems are dependent on the nature of the phenomena under study, the end uses of the causality assessments, ever-evolving measurement technology, and the degree of fine-grained detail in proposed explanatory theories. These points are clearly illustrated by Evans's (1976) historical discussion of the evolution of causality criteria in epidemiology, starting in 1890 with the Henle-Koch postulates and changing, of necessity, with the development of new measurement technology and the discovery of new phenomena (e.g., slow viruses), which were associated with different explanatory theories. The criteria put forth by Evans are focused primarily on a setting where scientific explanation is the end use of the causality assessment. These criteria stand in contrast to the modified causality criteria, also in epidemiology, which were put forth by the U.S. Surgeon General's Advisory Committee on smoking and lung cancer, where regulation (at least of cigarette advertising) in a policy setting was the end use of the causality assessment.

In this paper we have outlined the kinds of empirical cues and inductive reasoning that lead to the formation of causal hypotheses and the kinds of evidence needed to confirm them. The stronger the demonstrated consistency of an association under conditions that rule out alternative hypotheses and the stronger the evidence regarding a mechanism that can explain the observed association, the more likely we are to accept the causal hypothesis. Usually the evidence required to confirm a causal hypothesis is cumulated across multiple studies, many of which are, of necessity, observational. Although a wide variety of research designs and analytic techniques are available to assist in gathering evidence to support a causal inference, they are helpful only to the extent that their use is guided and constrained by appropriate subject-matter considerations. No method or set of methods defines causality.

The integrated philosophical and operational framework we have presented represents a set of flexible guideposts that now require systematic incorporation in a diversity of social science investigations.

It is our opinion that this will lead to a systematic evolution of confirmations of causality and a more organized cumulative development of new knowledge in the social sciences.

REFERENCES

Aigner, D. J., and Arthur S. Goldberger, eds. 1977. *Latent Variables in Socio-Economic Models*. Amsterdam: North-Holland.

Aristotle. 1930. *Physics*. In *The Works of Aristotle*, vol. 2, edited by W. D. Ross. Oxford: Clarendon Press.

Ayer, A. J. 1956. "What is a Law of Nature?" *Revue Internationale de Philosophie* 10:144–65.

Bartholomew, D. J. 1982. *Stochastic Models for Social Processes*. 3d ed. London: Wiley.

Basmann, R. L. 1988. "Causality Tests and Observationally Equivalent Representations of Econometric Models." *Journal of Econometrics*, in press.

Beauchamp, Tom L., ed. 1974. *Philosophical Problems of Causation*. Encino, CA: Dickenson.

Berk, Richard A. 1988. "Causal Inference for Sociological Data." In *Handbook of Sociology*, edited by N. Smelser. Beverly Hills: Sage.

Bernert, Christopher. 1983. "The Career of Causal Analysis in American Sociology." *British Journal of Sociology* 34:230–54.

Bielby, William T., and Robert M. Hauser. 1977. "Structural Equation Models." Pp. 137–61 in *Annual Review of Sociology*, vol. 3, edited by A. Inkeles, J. Coleman, and N. Smelser. Palo Alto: Annual Reviews.

Blalock, Hubert M., Jr. 1964. *Causal Inferences in Nonexperimental Research*. Chapel Hill: University of North Carolina Press.

——————, ed. 1971. *Causal Models in the Social Sciences*. New York: Aldine/Atherton.

Brier, Robert. 1974. *Precognition and the Philosophy of Science: An Essay on Backward Causation*. New York: Humanities Press.

Bunge, Mario. 1979. *Causality and Modern Science*. 3d rev. ed. New York: Dover.

Bush, Robert R., and Frederick Mosteller. 1955. *Stochastic Models for Learning*. New York: Wiley.

——————. 1959. "A Comparison of Eight Models." Pp. 293–307 in *Studies in Mathematical Learning Theory*, edited by R. R. Bush and W. K. Estes. Stanford: Stanford University Press.

Campbell, Donald T., and Julian C. Stanley. 1963. *Experimental and Quasi-Experimental Designs for Research*. Chicago: Rand McNally.

Carnap, Rudolf. 1950. *Logical Foundations of Probability*. Chicago: University of Chicago Press.

Carnap, Rudolf, and Richard C. Jeffrey, eds. 1971. *Studies in Inductive Logic and Probability*. Berkeley: University of California Press.

Cochran, William G. 1937. "Problems Arising in the Analysis of a Series of Similar Experiments." *Journal of the Royal Statistical Society*, suppl., 4:102–118.

——————. 1965. "The Planning of Observational Studies of Human Populations." *Journal of the Royal Statistical Society*, ser. A, 182:234–55.

Cole, Jonathan, and Burton Singer. 1987. "A Theory of Limited Differences: Explaining the Productivity Puzzle in Science." Technical Report. New York: Columbia University, Center for the Social Sciences.

Collingwood, R. G. 1940. *An Essay on Metaphysics*. Oxford: Clarendon Press.

Cook, Thomas D., and Donald T. Campbell. 1979. *Quasi-Experimentation: Design and Analysis Issues for Field Settings*. Chicago: Rand McNally.

Cootner, Paul, ed. 1965. *The Random Character of Stock Market Prices*. Cambridge, MA: MIT Press.

Cordray, David S. 1986. "Quasi-Experimental Analysis: A Mixture of Methods and Judgement." Pp. 9–27 in *Advances in Quasi-Experimental Design and Analysis*, edited by W. M. K. Trochim. New Directions for Program Evaluation, No. 31. San Francisco: Jossey-Bass.

Cox, D. R. 1986. "Comment on 'Statistics and Causal Inference'." *Journal of the American Statistical Association* 81:963.

Crutchfield, James P., J. Doyne Farmer, Norman H. Packard, and Robert S. Shaw. 1986. "Chaos." *Scientific American* 254:46–57.

Darwin, Charles. (1859) 1964. *On the Origin of Species*. Cambridge, MA: Harvard University Press.

Davis, James A. 1985. *The Logic of Causal Order*. Beverly Hills: Sage.

Diaconis, Persi, and David Freedman. 1984. "Asymptotics of Graphical Projection Pursuit." *Annals of Statistics* 12:793–815.

Dole, Vincent P. 1980. "Addictive Behavior." *Scientific American* 243:138–54.

Dole, Vincent P., and Marie E. Nyswander. 1965. "A Medical Treatment for Diacetylmorphine (Heroin) Addiction." *Journal of the American Medical Association* 193:646–50.

——————. 1968. "Methadone Maintenance and Its Implications for Theories of Heroin Addiction." Pp. 359–66 in *The Addictive States*. Association for Research in Nervous and Mental Disease, Volume 66.

Dole, Vincent P., Marie E. Nyswander, and Mary-Jeanne Kreek. 1966. "Narcotic Blockade." *Archives of Internal Medicine* 118:304–9.

Ducasse, C. J. 1966. "Critique of Hume's Conception of Causality." *The Journal of Philosophy* 63:141–48.

Einhorn, Hillel J., and Robin M. Hogarth. 1986. "Judging Probable Cause." *Psychological Bulletin* 99:3–19.

Emanuel, Steven. 1979. *Criminal Law*. New Rochelle: Emanuel Law Outlines.

Evans, Alfred S. 1976. "Causation and Disease: The Henle-Koch Postulates Revisited." *Yale Journal of Biology and Medicine* 49:175–95.

Evans, Alfred S. 1978. "Causation and Disease: A Chronological Journey." *American Journal of Epidemiology* 108:249–58.

Feinstein, Alvan. 1986. "Decisions About Causality." Lecture notes in Quantitative Clinical Epidemiology, Yale University.

Fienberg, Stephen E., Burton Singer, and Judith M. Tanur. 1985. "Large-Scale Social Experimentation in the United States." Pp. 287–326 in *A Celebration of Statistics*, edited by A. C. Atkinson and S. E. Fienberg. New York: Springer-Verlag.

Fisher, Franklin M. 1966. *The Identification Problem in Econometrics*. New York: McGraw-Hill.

Fisher, Ronald A. 1946. *Statistical Methods for Research Workers*. 10th ed. Edinburgh: Oliver and Boyd.

Freedman, David A. 1987. "As Others See Us: A Case Study in Path Analysis." *Journal of Educational Statistics* 12:101–28.

Frege, Gotlob. (1884) 1961. *Die Grundlagen der Arithmetic Eine logischmathematische Untersuchung über de begriff der Zahl*. Breslau: Hildesheim, G. Olms Verlag.

Friedman, J. H., and W. H. Stuetzle. 1982. "Projection Pursuit Methods for Data Analysis." In *Modern Data Analysis*, edited by R. Launer and A. F. Siegel. New York: Academic Press.

Friedman, J. H., and J. W. Tukey. 1974. "A Projection Pursuit Algorithm for Exploratory Data Analysis." *IEEE Transactions on Computers* C-23:881–89.

Frydman, Roman, and Edmund S. Phelps. 1983. *Individual Forecasting and Aggregate Outcomes*. New York: Cambridge University Press.

Gasking, Douglas. 1955. "Causation and Recipes." *Mind* 64:479–87.

Geweke, John. 1984. "Inference and Causality in Economic Time Series Models." Pp. 1101–44 in *Handbook of Econometrics*, vol. 2, edited by Z. Griliches and M. D. Intriligator. New York: Elsevier.

Gibbs, Jack P. 1982. "Evidence of Causation." Pp. 93–127 in *Current Perspectives in Social Theory*, vol. 3. Greenwich, CT: JAI Press.

Glymour, Clark. 1986. "Comment: Statistics and Metaphysics." *Journal of the American Statistical Association* 81:964–66.

Glymour, Clark, Richard Scheines, Peter Spirtes, and Kevin Kelly. 1987. *Discovering Causal Structure: Artificial Intelligence, Philosophy of Science and Statistical Modelling*. New York: Academic Press.

Goldberger, Arthur S., and Otis Dudley Duncan, eds. 1973. *Structural Equation Models in the Social Sciences*. New York: Seminar Press.

Good, I. J. 1961. "A Causal Calculus I." *British Journal of the Philosophy of Science* 11:305–18.

_____. 1962. "A Causal Calculus II." *British Journal of the Philosophy of Science* 12:43–51.

Goodman, Leo A. 1973. "Guided and Unguided Methods for the Selection of Models for a Set of *T* Multidimensional Contingency Tables." *Journal of the American Statistical Association* 68:165–75.

Goodman, Nelson. 1965. *Fact, Fiction, and Forecast*. 2d ed. Indianapolis: Bobbs-Merrill.

Granger, Clive W. J. 1969. "Investigating Causal Relations by Econometric Models and Cross-Spectral Methods." *Econometrica* 37:424–38.

——————. 1980. "Testing for Causality: A Personal Viewpoint." *Journal of Economic Dynamics and Control* 2:329–52.

——————. 1986. "Comment on 'Statistics and Causal Inference'." *Journal of the American Statistical Association* 81:967–68.

Gunne, Lars-M., and Leif Gronbladh. 1981. "A Swedish Methadone Maintenance Program: A Controlled Study." *Drug and Alcohol Dependence* 7:249–56.

Haavelmo, Trygve. 1944. "The Probability Approach in Econometrics." *Econometrica* 12:S1–118.

Hart, H. L. A., and A. M. Honoré. 1984. *Causation in the Law.* 2d ed. Oxford: Oxford University Press.

Heckman, James J. 1987. "Selection Bias and Self Selection." Pp. 287–97 in *The New Palgrave*, vol. 4, edited by J. Eatwell, M. Milgate, and P. Newman. New York: Stockton.

Heckman, James J., and V. Joseph Hotz. 1987. "Do We Need Experimental Data To Evaluate the Impact of Training on Earnings." *Evaluation Review*, in press.

Heckman, James J., and James R. Walker. 1987. "Using Goodness of Fit and Other Criteria to Choose Among Competing Duration Models: A Case Study of Hutterite Data." Pp. 247–307 in *Sociological Methodology* 1987, edited by C. C. Clogg. Washington, DC: American Sociological Association.

Hedges, Larry V., and Ingram Olkin. 1985. *Statistical Methods for Meta-Analysis.* Orlando: Academic Press.

Hempel, Carl G. 1942. "The Function of General Laws in History." *Journal of Philosophy* 39:35–48.

——————. 1945. "Studies in the Logic of Confirmation." *Mind* 54:1–26, 97–121.

Hill, Austin Bradford. 1965. "The Environment and Disease: Association or Causation?" *Proceedings of the Royal Society of Medicine* 58:295–300.

Holland, John H., Keith J. Holyoak, Richard E. Nisbett, and Paul R. Thagard. 1986. *Induction.* Cambridge, MA: MIT Press.

Holland, Paul. 1986. "Statistics and Causal Inference." *Journal of the American Statistical Association* 81:945–60.

Huber, Peter. 1985. "Projection Pursuit." *Annals of Statistics* 13:435–525.

Hume, David. (1739) 1896. *A Treatise of Human Nature.* Oxford: Clarendon Press.

——————. (1740) 1938. *An Abstract of a Treatise of Human Nature.* Cambridge: Cambridge University Press.

Hume, David (1748) 1900. *An Enquiry Concerning Human Understanding.* Chicago: Open Court.

Keynes, John Maynard. 1921. *A Treatise on Probability.* London: Macmillan.

Kneale, William C. 1949. *Probability and Induction.* Oxford: Oxford University Press.

_____. 1950. "Natural Laws and Contrary-to-Fact Conditionals." *Analysis* 10:121–25.

_____. 1961. "Universality and Necessity." *British Journal for the Philosophy of Science* 12:89–102.

Kolata, Gina. 1986. "What Does It Mean to be Random?" *Science* 231:1068–70.

Koopman, James S. 1977. "Causal Models and Sources of Interaction." *American Journal of Epidemiology* 106:439–44.

Koopmans, Tjalling C., and O. Reiersol. 1950. "The Identification of Structural Characteristics." *Annals of Mathematical Statistics* 21:165–81.

Kuhn, Thomas S. 1977. *The Essential Tension.* Chicago: University of Chicago Press.

Leamer, Edward. 1978. *Specification Searches.* New York: Wiley.

Lewis, David. 1973. "Causation." *Journal of Philosophy* 70:556–72.

Mackie, J. L. 1965. "Causes and Conditions." *American Philosophical Quarterly* 2:245–64.

_____. 1966. "Counterfactuals and Causal Laws." Pp. 65–80 in *Analytical Philosophy: First Series,* edited by R. J. Butler. Oxford: Basil Blackwell.

_____. 1974. *The Cement of the Universe: A Study of Causation.* Oxford: Oxford University Press.

Malliaris, A. G., and William A. Brock. 1982. *Stochastic Methods in Economics and Finance.* Amsterdam: North-Holland.

Manton, Kenneth G., Eric Stallard, Max A. Woodbury, H. Dennis Tolley, and Anatoli I. Yashin. 1987. "Grade-of-Membership Techniques for Studying Complex Event History Processes with Unobserved Covariates." Pp. 309–46 in *Sociological Methodology* 1987, edited by C. C. Clogg. Washington, DC: American Sociological Association.

Mill, John Stuart. 1919. *A System of Logic Ratiocinactive and Inductive.* 8th ed. London: Longmans, Green, Reader and Dyer.

Mosteller, Frederick, and John W. Tukey. 1977. *Data Analysis and Regression.* Reading, MA: Addison-Wesley.

_____. 1982. "Combination of Results of Stated Precision: I. The Optimistic Case." *Utilities Mathematica* 21A:155–78.

_____. 1983. "Combination of Results of Stated Precision: II. A More Realistic Case." Unpublished manuscript, Bell Laboratories.

Nagel, Ernest. 1961. *The Structure of Science.* New York: Harcourt Brace Jovanovich.

Newman, R. G., and W. B. Whitehill. 1979. "Double-Blind Comparison of Methadone and Placebo Maintenance Treatments of Narcotics Addicts in Hong Kong." *Lancet* 2:485–88.

Nicod, Jean. 1930. *Foundations of Geometry and Induction.* New York: Harcourt, Brace.

Pearson, Karl. 1933. "On a Method of Determining Whether a Sample of Given Size *N* Supposed to Have Been Drawn From a Parent Population Having a Known Probability Integral Has Probably Been Drawn at Random." *Biometrika* 25:379–410.

Popper, Karl. (1959) 1972. *The Logic of Scientific Discovery*. London: Hutchinson.

Pratt, J. W., and R. Schlaifer. 1984. "On the Nature and Discovery of Structure." *Journal of the American Statistical Association* 79:9–21.

Reaven, G. M., and R. G. Miller. 1979. "An Attempt to Define the Nature of Chemical Diabetes Using a Multidimensional Analysis." *Diabetologia* 16:17–24.

Reichenbach, Hans. 1956. *The Direction of Time*. Berkeley: University of California Press.

Robins, L. N., J. E. Helzer, and D. H. Davis. 1975. "Narcotic Use in Southeast Asia and Afterward." *Archives of General Psychiatry* 32:955–61.

Rothman, Kenneth J. 1976. "Causes." *American Journal of Epidemiology* 104:587–92.

Rubin, Donald B. 1974. "Estimating Causal Effects of Treatments in Randomized and Nonrandomized Studies." *Journal of Educational Psychology* 66:688–701.

——————. 1986. "Comment: Which Ifs Have Causal Answers?" *Journal of the American Statistical Association* 81:961–62.

Russell, Bertrand. 1908. "Mathematical Logic As Based on the Theory of Types." *American Journal of Mathematics* 30:222–62.

——————. 1948. *Human Knowledge: Its Scope and Limits*. New York: Simon and Schuster.

——————. 1959. *My Philosophical Development*. New York: Simon and Schuster.

Salmon, Wesley C. 1967. *The Foundations of Scientific Inference*. Pittsburgh: University of Pittsburgh Press.

——————. 1980. "Probabilistic Causality." *Pacific Philosophical Quarterly* 61:50–74.

——————. 1984. *Scientific Explanation and the Causal Structure of the World*. Princeton: Princeton University Press.

Simon, Herbert A. 1953. "Causal Ordering and Identifiability." Pp. 49–74 in *Studies in Econometric Method*, edited by W. C. Hood and T. C. Koopmans. New Haven: Yale University Press.

——————. 1957. *Models of Man: Social and Rational*. New York: Wiley.

——————. 1979. "The Meaning of Causal Ordering." Pp. 65–81 in *Qualitative and Quantitative Social Research*, edited by R. K. Merton, J. S. Coleman, and P. H. Rossi. New York: Free Press.

——————. 1986. "The Failure of Armchair Economics." *Challenge* (November–December):18–25.

Singer, Burton. 1986. "Self-Selection and Performance-Based Ratings: A Case Study in Program Evaluation." In *Drawing Inferences from Self-Selected Populations*, edited by H. Wainer. New York: Springer-Verlag.

Skyrms, Brian. 1980. *Causal Necessity*. New Haven: Yale University Press.

Sober, Elliot. 1984. *The Nature of Selection: Evolutionary Theory in Philosophical Focus*. Cambridge, MA: MIT Press.

Strotz, Robert H., and H. O. A. Wold. 1960. "Recursive vs. Nonrecursive Systems: An Attempt at Synthesis." *Econometrica* 28:417–27.

Suppes, Patrick. 1970. *A Probabilistic Theory of Causality.* Amsterdam: North-Holland.

Swartz, Marvin, Dan Blazer, Max Woodbury, Linda George, and Richard Landermare. 1986. "Somatization Disorder in a U.S. Southern Community: Use of a New Procedure for Analysis of Medical Classification." *Psychological Medicine* 16:595–609.

Tippett, L. H. C. 1931. *The Method of Statistics.* London: Williams and Norgate.

Tukey, John. 1987. "Configural Polysampling." *SIAM Review* 29:1–20.

Vaillant, George E. 1966a. "A 12-Year Follow-up of New York Narcotic Addicts: I. The Relation of Treatment to Outcome." *American Journal of Psychiatry* 122:727–37.

————. 1966b. "A 12-Year Follow-up of New York Narcotic Addicts: II. The Natural History of a Chronic Disease." *New England Journal of Medicine* 275:1282–88.

————. 1966c. "A 12-Year Follow-up of New York Narcotic Addicts: III. Some Social and Psychiatric Characteristics." *Archives of General Psychiatry* 15:599–609.

————. 1966d. "A 12-Year Follow-up of New York Narcotic Addicts: IV. Some Determinants and Characteristics of Abstinence." *American Journal of Psychiatry* 123:573–84.

————. 1973. "A 20-Year Follow-up of New York Narcotic Addicts." *Archives of General Psychiatry* 29:237–41.

von Wright, Georg Henrik. 1971. *Explanation and Understanding.* Ithaca: Cornell University Press.

Whewell, William. 1967. *The Philosophy of the Inductive Sciences.* 2d ed. London: Frank Cass.

White, Harrison C. 1970. *Chains of Opportunity.* Cambridge, MA: Harvard University Press.

Wolf, F. M. 1986. *Meta-Analysis: Quantitative Methods for Research Synthesis.* Beverly Hills: Sage.

Wright, Sewall. 1921. "Correlation and Causation." *Journal of Agricultural Research* 20:557–85.

————. 1934. "The Method of Path Coefficients." *Annals of Mathematical Statistics* 5:161–215.

————. 1954. "The Interpretation of Multivariate Systems." Pp. 11–33 in *Statistics and Mathematics in Biology*, edited by O. Kempthorne, T. A. Bancroft, J. W. Gowen, and J. L. Lush. Ames, IA: Iowa State College Press.

Yates, F., and W. G. Cochran. 1938. "The Analysis of Groups of Experiments." *Journal of Agricultural Science* 28:556–80.

Young, J. Z. 1978. *Programs of the Brain.* Oxford: Oxford University Press.

Zellner, Arnold. 1979. "Causality and Econometrics." Pp. 9–54 in *Three Aspects of Policy and Policymaking*, edited by K. Brunner and A. H. Meltzer. Amsterdam: North-Holland.

𝔵12𝔵

Exploring Causal Structure with the TETRAD Program

Clark Glymour, Richard Scheines and Peter Spirtes*

1. INTRODUCTION

This paper describes some aspects of a new approach to the search for adequate causal explanations of nonexperimental and quasi-experimental data. The ideas are embodied in a computer program, TETRAD, and are described in much more detail in a recent book, *Discovering Causal Structure: Artificial Intelligence, Philosophy of Science and Statistical Modeling* (Glymour et al. 1987). In addition, some new results about our methods are reported in what follows.

For quantitative sociologists and psychometricians, the methods should have a familiar heritage. They are computerized extensions of ideas that were proposed in the early days of correlation analysis by followers of Charles Spearman. In more recent decades, Herbert Simon, Hubert Blalock, Herbert Costner, O. D. Duncan, and many others have worked on model specification through the analysis of constraints on covariances; Simon not only contributed to some of the central ideas connecting multivariate analysis with causal explanation, he is also the most articulate exponent of the role of *heuristic search* in scientific discovery. The TETRAD program uses new mathematical results to combine these lines of work into a computer package to aid in model specification. In what follows, we briefly describe the kind of

* Carnegie Mellon University.

problem to which the program is addressed, the mathematical results that make it possible, and the search strategy used, and we give a number of illustrations of the application of the procedures.

2. MODEL SPECIFICATION PROBLEMS

Social science research papers that use causal modeling techniques usually contain an explicit *specification problem*: Something about causal relations among measured or unmeasured variables is unknown and is to be discovered. Examples abound:

1. Maruyama and McGarvey (1980) are concerned with whether variation in a latent variable interpreted as student peer popularity causes variation in a latent variable interpreted as disposition for academic achievement, or whether the causal relation is in the other direction, or whether the variables have no direct effects on one another.
2. Miller, Slomczynski, and Schoenberg (1981) and Schoenberg and Richtand (1984) are concerned with whether correlations among responses to a survey questionnaire can be accounted for by a single latent variable, or whether further causal dependencies are needed to explain the data, and if so, what dependencies.
3. McPherson, Welch, and Clark (1977) are concerned with whether correlations among responses to a questionnaire administered to the same cohort at two different times can be explained as the result of a single latent factor acting at each time, or whether further causal dependencies are present.

In each of these examples, and in many other modeling problems, a partial model is specified, and the researchers are interested in how, if at all, it should be extended. Sometimes the number of a priori possible extensions is very large, even in cases such as these. Costner and Schoenberg (1973) discuss a model of industrial and political development to which they recommend adding two additional causal connections (see Figure 1). Two directed edges or correlated errors can be added to their initial model in more than 9,900 different ways.

There is often no well-confirmed justification even for the initial, partial model, which means that a serious scientific case requires the consideration of alternative initial models. A recent study by

FIGURE 1.   Costner and Schoenberg's initial model.

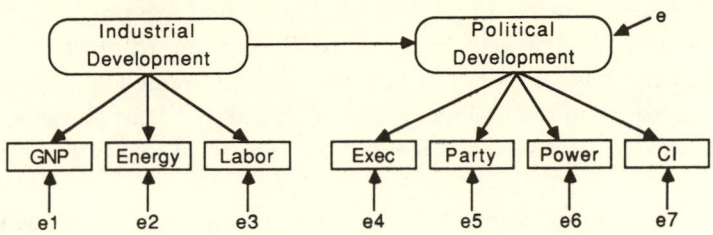

Timberlake and Williams (1984), for example, treats data for four variables concerning foreign investment and economic and political development in "peripheral" nations. Parameter estimates from a particular regression model are used to support their causal conclusions, even though there are 262,144 alternative specifications of the connections among four variables (including models with correlated errors, but not counting latent variable models), which include several plausible models that explain patterns in the Timberlake and Williams data, that are testable, that show excellent fit, and that support causal hypotheses contrary to the ones Timberlake and Williams favor. The number of alternatives grows exponentially with the number of measured variables. Jay Magidson (1977, p. 413) put the problem this way:

> The problem we face is that there is an infinite number of ways to formulate a causal model, and it is not a straightforward matter to determine how to go about doing it, particularly when the causes are unknown and/or unobserved. It is important for researchers to formulate not one but many models so that they can determine whether their conclusions may differ if they accept a different set of assumptions. It is also important to follow some general guidelines in building (formulating) models when the researcher has limited information about the causal process.

Similar concerns have been voiced by many other authors. Clearly, in many cases there are a lot of alternative causal models, even granted the assumption of linearity and the usual statistical assumptions made in structural equation modeling. Any real scientific effort, therefore, has to make a case for the causal hypotheses that are proposed, and it looks as though that may be a very difficult thing to do. Exactly for this reason, several critics claim that causal modeling in practice amounts to a kind of pseudoscience. There are at least three ways in which a case could be made for the causal assumptions of a model:

1. Prior knowledge or *well-justified* theory could imply a unique set of causal assumptions, or at least reduce the alternatives that need to be considered to a very small number. That is not usually the case in social scientific work. It is certainly not enough to appeal to "theory" when the theory to which appeal is made has not been subjected to severe tests and is not well confirmed.
2. Experimental controls could be systematically introduced to isolate causal effects. That is rarely feasible in social scientific work and has limited feasibility even in medical science, epidemiology, and other areas.
3. Using whatever prior knowledge may be available, one could conduct a systematic search for alternative models, showing that the proposed explanation provides, or is likely to provide, the best available explanation of the data.

A considerable body of work in social science methodology has focused on the third of these alternatives. Although a variety of approaches to model specification have been sketched, two approaches have dominated investigations in sociology and related subjects. One of them, associated with Jöreskog and Sörbom (1984) and the LISREL program, uses maximum likelihood estimation and any of several associated fitting statistics; the other, illustrated in the work of Blalock, Costner, Duncan, Simon, and others, compares the *constraints* implied by models with constraints satisfied by the data.

2.1. *Maximum Likelihood Methods*

Maximum likelihood specification techniques focus on elaborations of an initial model. Several techniques have been employed, all of which share a dependency on properties of maximum likelihood estimates of the parameters in an initial model or in elaborations of the initial model. Jöreskog and Sörbom use a general procedure in the more recent editions of the LISREL program. Essentially, the method is to consider partial derivatives of the LISREL fitting statistic taken with respect to each of the fixed parameters of the model. Provided the difference in chi-square values is significant, the method recommends freeing that fixed (usually at zero) parameter with the largest partial derivative (and the right sign for the second derivative). McPherson et al. (1977), who are concerned with whether or not a certain measurement model is stable over time, examine the *size* of the coefficients connecting a latent variable at two different times with the respective measures of an observed variable at two different times. Many authors compare correlations computed from an estimated model with the empirical correlations. Maruyama and McGarvey (1980), interested in the direction of a hypothetical causal relation between latent variables, modify their initial model in two ways, once by adding the hypothetical causal relation in one direction and estimating the coefficient with LISREL, and a second time by adding instead a hypothetical causal relation in the other direction and estimating the coefficient with LISREL. They then infer that the numerically larger coefficient is associated with the real direction of causation.

2.2. *Analyzing Constraints on Correlations*

Blalock's (1961) method analyzed the constraints on partial correlations that are implied by path models. Two models such as those in Figure 2 can in principle be discriminated empirically because they *robustly imply* different constraints on the population covariances. Model I robustly implies that $\rho_{23.1} = 0$, but model II does not. A model robustly implies a constraint if it implies that the constraint is satisfied no matter what the values of the free linear coefficients of the model

FIGURE 2.

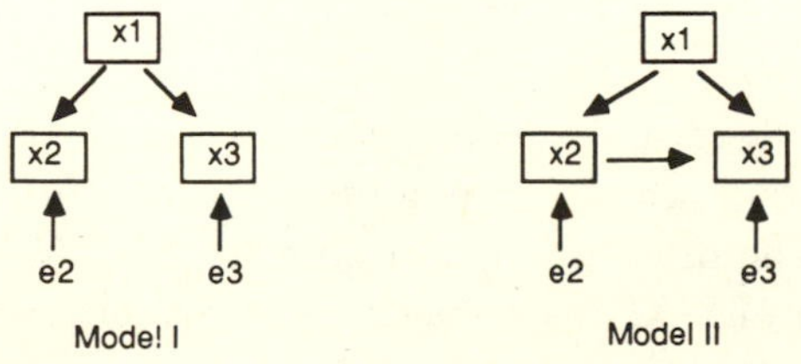

Model I   Model II

FIGURE 3.

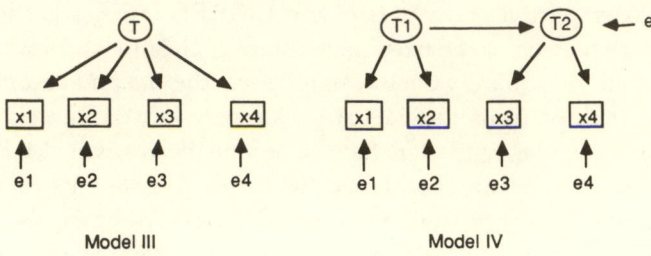

Model III   Model IV

may be. Blalock called such constraints *prediction equations* and emphasized that they may be used to test a model. The Spearman school,
which originated the analysis of covariance constraints, emphasized
that models that robustly imply empirically correct constraints are to
be preferred to models that are merely consistent with the constraints
for particular values of their linear coefficients. Similar methodological
ideas were developed for latent variable models by Costner, Duncan,
and others. Multiple indicator latent variable models do not robustly
imply vanishing partial correlations for their measured variables, but
they can in principle be discriminated by the *vanishing tetrad differences*
they imply. Thus, in Figure 3, model III implies the constraints

$$\rho_{12}\rho_{34} = \rho_{13}\rho_{24} = \rho_{14}\rho_{23},$$

while model IV implies only that $\rho_{13}\rho_{24} = \rho_{14}\rho_{23}$. Costner and
Schoenberg (1973) proposed a kind of mixture of the LISREL and the
constraint analysis approaches. Given a multiple indicator model, their
method for model revision proposed to examine those submodels like
IV and to test them by maximum likelihood chi-square procedures. If
a submodel failed the test, the larger model was to be modified by
correlating an indicator of one of the latent variables in the submodel
with an indicator of the other latent variable in the submodel.

2.3. *Comparisons of Maximum Likelihood and Constraint Analysis Methods*

Each of these approaches has advantages and disadvantages,
and the limitations also affect combined methods such as Costner and
Schoenberg's. The disadvantages of Jöreskog and Sörbom's modification procedure in LISREL are that it leads to a narrow "beam" search

through the space of possible elaborations of a model, it may stop too soon, and the derivatives of the fitting statistic may miss plausible modifications. The considerable advantage is that it is computerized and fast and can therefore be carried out without considerable theoretical effort or excessive computational demands. Choosing elaborations on the basis of correlation residuals is known in many cases to be unreliable (see Herting and Costner 1985). The other methods described lack any convincing theoretical justification, although they sometimes work in the sense that they improve model fit. None of the methods offers any guidance in constructing an initial model.

The advantage of the analysis of correlation constraints is that it appeals to intuitions about scientific explanation that go back to the very beginnings of covariance analysis and that have played a major role in the historical successes of the natural sciences (see Glymour et al. [1987] for a discussion of the historical background). The intuition is that, other things equal, those models that explain patterns in the data without having to specify particular nonzero values for various parameters are best. Kepler used the same intuition to argue for Copernican theory, and Eddington used it to argue for general relativity. Cannizarro used the same principle to argue for his system of atomic weights, and it was the fundamental idea behind all the statistical work done by the Spearman school in the 1920s.

The strategy of searching for models by analyses of constraints on correlations promises to *localize* errors in model specification in a principled way, since particular submodels of a given model may be responsible for the implication of false constraints. And in principle, the approach promises guidance in initial model specification. Yet the disadvantages of the approach may seem overwhelming:

1. No statistical test for vanishing tetrad differences is reported or used in the sociological literature.
2. Blalock, Costner, and the many other researchers who followed their lead published no general algorithm for determining the constraints robustly implied by an arbitrary model. There are scores of papers, and some books, showing how to use constraints on covariances or correlations to distinguish between particular sets of alternative models, but there is no statement of a general algorithm, let alone a computer implementation. Nothing in the literature, for example, shows whether or not the property of robustly implying a vanishing

partial correlation or a vanishing tetrad difference depends on the distribution assumptions of the model. Heise (1975) gives the basis for an algorithmic procedure for computing implied constraints from the graphs of acyclic standardized models, but it is left open how to calculate the implications when the model is not acyclic, a problem that we have only partially solved.

3. Save for Costner and Schoenberg's (1973) mixed and partly informal procedure, no scheme has been developed for organizing the search for the elaborations of an arbitrary initial model that will best explain the constraints satisfied empirically.

3. THE TETRAD PROJECT

In the last several years we have attempted to answer the technical questions just raised concerning the foundations of the constraint analysis strategy and to apply the answers we have obtained to form a computerized aid for model specification. Our procedures rest on strong methodological sensibilities, but they are free of many of the metaphysical concerns that are the focus of other papers in this volume.

3.1. *Causality*

We assume only two things about causal relations. Suppose A and B are quantities that can take any of a continuum of values in a population, and assume that the population is unbounded in size. We assume, first, that if A causes B, then B is a function of A and perhaps of other variables. Our specific methods apply when the function is linear. Second, if A does not cause B and B does not cause A and there are no common causes of A and B, then A and B are statistically independent in the population.

This minimal understanding of causality gives a reading to the graphs that often accompany or are implicit in linear models: The graphs encode not only the linear structural equations of the model but also the *independence assumptions* of the model.

We do not take any more detailed stand on the nature of causality because our methods do not depend on these issues.[1]

---

[1] For comments on Holland's views about causality, see Glymour (1985).

Because our methods make only these assumptions, they apply to cases that some would insist do not involve causal relations at all. Thus, some factor analysis procedures distinguish "measurement models" from "causal models" or "theoretical models," and some hold, for reasons we do not pretend to understand, that relations between a latent variable and its measured indicators, or relations between different measured indicators, are not causal relations. From our perspective, this is a purely verbal dispute: As long as a model is associated with a directed graph that represents functional dependencies and statistical independence assumptions, our methods apply.

Neither do we have any objection to causal models with "latent" variables.[2] Since data sets throughout the social and behavioral sciences usually measure only a fragment of the variables that might be relevant to one another, unmeasured variables should be expected in plausible causal explanations of many data sets in sociology, economics, social psychology, and other areas. Even models that contain latent variables that are not associated with some factor known to be directly measurable—e.g., psychometric models—are preferable to models that do not contain them, provided the latent variable models have better explanatory power. In Glymour and Spirtes (forthcoming), we have described one statistically determinable respect in which in some cases latent variables can have superior explanatory power.

3.2. *Mathematical Results*

The constraint analysis strategy could be carried out generally and automatically provided that some mathematical results can be established.

First, does whether a model implies a vanishing tetrad difference or a vanishing first-order partial correlation for all values of its linear coefficients depend on the *variances* of the independent variables and of the error terms? If not, then the constraints of these two kinds implied by a linear model are determined *entirely by the directed graph associated*

---

[2] We do, however, have various objections to the interpretations often given to such variables (cf. Blalock 1982).

with the model. The following theorem has been proved:

Theorem 1. For all linear models, the implied tetrad and first-order partial correlation constraints are independent of the variances of the independent variables and error terms.

In view of theorem 1, it is proper to speak of the constraints implied *by a graph*, since all models that share the same graph of causal relations will imply the same vanishing tetrad differences and vanishing partial correlations.

Second, given that the constraints implied by a model are determined by its associated graph of causal relations, what local graph theoretic properties determine whether or not any particular constraint is implied? If such properties could be found, then they might be used in a general algorithm for computing the constraints implied by a model.

The answers we have found to the second question are a little complicated, and we give only the simplest case.

Define a *trek* between vertices $v1$ and $v2$ in a directed graph G to be a pair of acyclic paths, one terminating in $v1$ and one terminating in $v2$, having the same origin, called the *source* of the trek, and intersecting nowhere save at the origin. We allow one of the paths to be empty, so that a single path between $v1$ and $v2$ also counts as a trek between $v1$ and $v2$.

Then we have the following local graph theoretic characterization of necessary and sufficient conditions for any graph, whether cyclic or acyclic, to imply a vanishing first-order partial correlation:

Theorem 2. For any directed graph G and any three distinct variables x, y, and z that are vertices of G, the following two conditions are equivalent:

1. G implies that $\rho_{xz} - \rho_{xy}\rho_{yz} = 0$.
2. Every trek between x and z contains y, and either every trek between y and z is an acyclic path from y to z or every trek between x and y is an acyclic path from y to x.

A comparably geometric but more complicated necessary and sufficient condition for the implication of a vanishing tetrad difference has recently been proved (see Spirtes 1988).

One can take advantage of these results to construct an algorithm that will compute the vanishing first-order partial correlations implied by an arbitrary graph and the vanishing tetrad differences implied by an arbitrary acyclic graph.

Theorem 3. There is an algorithm for computing the vanishing first-order partial correlations implied by any directed graph and the vanishing tetrad differences implied by any acyclic graph such that the number of steps required by the computation increases by no more than the cube of the number of vertices of the graph.

An easy but important result is that adding additional causal relations or correlated errors to a graph of causal relations *never results in the implication of additional constraints not implied by the initial graph*.

Theorem 4. If graph G is a subgraph of graph G' and if G' implies a vanishing tetrad difference or vanishing first-order partial correlation among variables occurring in G, then G also implies that vanishing tetrad difference or vanishing first-order partial correlation.[3]

3.3. *Statistics and Computation*

In the 1920s, Spearman's followers pursued a model specification strategy that started, in every case, with a single latent common cause of every measured variable, compared the implied tetrad constraints with the constraints satisfied empirically, and then added additional latent factors until the modified model implied all and only the constraints found to be satisfied in the data. The results of the previous subsection, together with the well-known fact that a one-factor model implies every possible tetrad equation among the measured variables, explain why the strategy worked, insofar as it did. In practice, Spearman's strategy was limited by the substantive assumptions associated with his own psychological theory and by computational difficulties. Guilford (1936) gave the difficulty of computing the implied tetrad equations as the chief argument for abandoning constraint analysis in favor of factor analysis.

---

[3] Because of a typographical error, this result is misstated in one place in Glymour et al. (1987), but the result stated here is proved there.

The work of the Spearman school prompted John Wishart (1929) to investigate the variance of the sampling distribution of tetrad differences under the assumption that the variables are jointly multinormally distributed. Wishart's results enable us to construct an asymptotic test of the hypothesis that any particular tetrad difference vanishes. Tests of hypotheses about vanishing first-order partial correlations can of course be based on the sampling distribution of the correlation coefficient (see Anderson 1984). For a given data set, a test of this kind can be automatically conducted separately for each possible constraint, and the TETRAD program carries out such a procedure either automatically at a series of significance levels or at a user-specified significance level. Since in general the tests are not independent, the procedure is not ideal, but it avoids a vast series of complicated simultaneous testing problems (see Miller 1981). We regard it as an example of Simon's recommendation to "satisfice" in those cases in which the ideal solution is infeasible.

3.4. *Automatic Search Strategy*

The mathematical results make feasible an automatic search strategy that shares some features of the strategy of the Spearman school.

1. Start with a simple model but not necessarily with a one-factor model.
2. Add directed edges and correlated errors to the graph of the model until, insofar as possible, you obtain a modified graph (or graphs) that imply all and only the empirically correct constraints implied by the initial model.

The strategy is illustrated in Figure 4. TETRAD contains an automatic procedure that carries out a version of this strategy. To make the program run in tolerable time on personal computers widely available in 1987, the automatic search is restricted to latent variable multiple indicator models. New hardware developments and algorithm improvements should permit us to relax this restriction in subsequent versions of the program.

FIGURE 4.

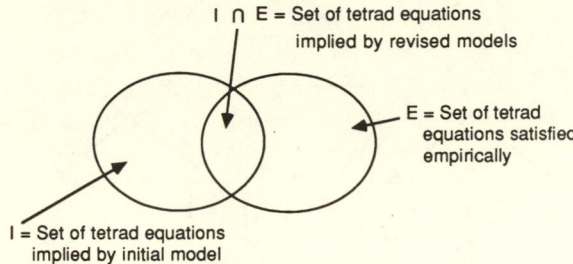

I ∩ E = Set of tetrad equations
implied by revised models

E = Set of tetrad
equations satisfied
empirically

I = Set of tetrad equations
implied by initial model

3.5. *Power*

The strategy makes sense only if the constraints considered are sufficient in many cases to distinguish between alternative models. That question can be investigated systematically using the TETRAD program itself and a little mathematics to generalize the results. We report here only the simplest relevant results that we have obtained.

Say that a model is *skeletal* if every measured variable depends on one and only one latent variable, if no measured variable has a direct effect or correlated error with any other measured variable, and if the model is acyclic.

Theorem 5. Consider any set of models consisting of a skeletal model and all models that can be obtained by adding at most one directed edge or correlated error to the skeletal model. Assume further that each latent variable has at least three measured indicators and that there are at least five measured variables.

Then, all models in such a set imply distinct collections of vanishing tetrad differences save that

1. if A and B are measured indicators of the same latent variable, then the models formed by adding to the skeleton exactly one of "A causes B," "B causes A," and "A and B have a correlated error" are indistinguishable from each other;
2. if A is a latent variable and B is a measured indicator of a different latent variable, then the models formed by adding to the skeleton

FIGURE 5.   Generating skeleton.

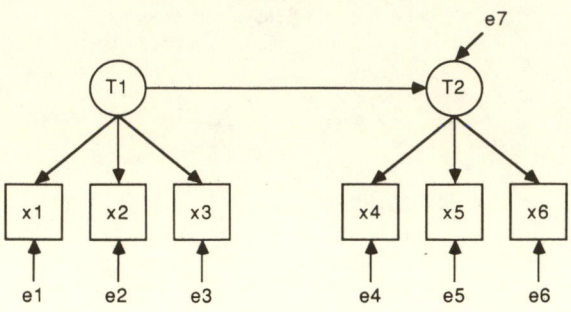

exactly one of "*A* causes *B*," "*B* causes *A*," and "*A* and *B* have a new common cause" are indistinguishable from each other.

Similar but more complicated results have been obtained for two edge additions to skeletal models. The power of the result stated here can be illustrated by a simulation study. Consider the skeletal model in Figure 5. Models with this sort of structure are typical in studies that repeat measurements for the same cohort at different times. Such simple skeletal models are often incorrect, and the effect of the common cause may be confounded with direct effects of earlier measures on later measures, or with other common causes that produce correlated errors.

    Each indicator of the first latent variable can be connected with each indicator of the second latent variable in three different ways. We illustrate the possibilities in Figure 6. Each of these elaborations of the initial model implies a distinct set of tetrad constraints. The inequivalence of these models is shown in Table 1. Every possible tetrad equation among the six measured variables is listed in a row. A row contains a y in a column just in case the model corresponding to that column implies the equation listed in that row.[4]

    It should, therefore, be possible to distinguish data sets generated by the three models in Figure 6. In fact, the point is much more general. Rather than focus on the three different ways of connecting $x3$

---

[4] The tetrad equation $\rho_{x1, x2}\rho_{x3, x4} = \rho_{x1, x3}\rho_{x2, x4}$ is abbreviated $x1\,x2,\ x3\,x4 = x1\,x3,\ x2\,x4$.

FIGURE 6. Three elaborations of the generating skeleton.

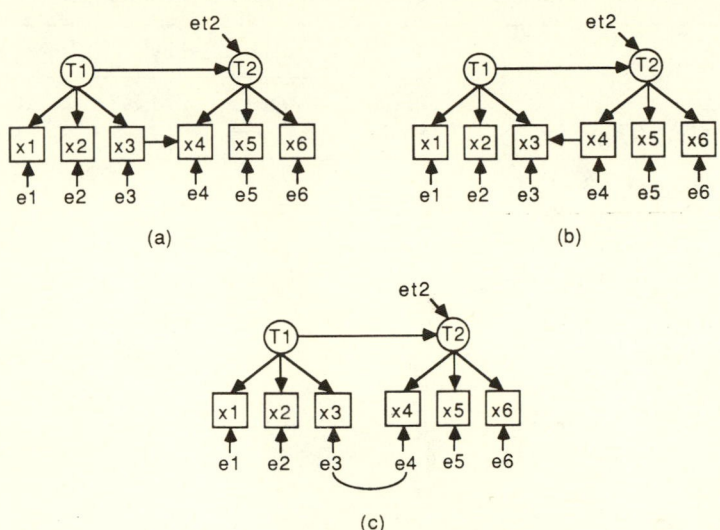

(a)   (b)

(c)

and $x4$, consider the 27 different ways of connecting one indicator of $T1$ and one indicator of $T2$, and consider as well the skeletal model of Figure 5: *Each of these models implies a distinct set of tetrad constraints.* Thus, in principle it should be possible to distinguish each of these models from the others based on the set of tetrad constraints satisfied by the data.

We generated data sets from models of these kinds using SYS-TAT BASIC. We produced data for the exogenous variables with a pseudorandom number generator distributed normally with mean 0 and variance 1. All other variables are linear combinations of their respective immediate ancestors in the directed graph of the model. The linear coefficients were also chosen at random, although their values for each particular model are nonstochastic constants. $T1$ and $T2$ are to be interpreted as unmeasured latent variables, and $e1-e7$ as unmeasured error terms. $T1$ and $e1-e7$ are exogenous, and $x1-x6$ are our measured variables. The sample size is 2,000. Choosing at random 5 of the 27 elaborations of the initial model, we generated five data sets, each of which, along with the skeletal model shown in Figure 5, was given to a TETRAD user. The user did not know which of the 27

TABLE 1
TETRAD Implications of Initial Model and its Modifications

	Implied by			
Tetrad Equation	Initial Model	Model a $x3 \to x4$	Model b $x4 \to x3$	Model c $x3 \to x4$
$x1\,x2,\ x3\,x4 = x1\,x3,\ x2\,x4$	y			
$x1\,x2,\ x4\,x3 = x1\,x4,\ x2\,x3$	y			
$x1\,x3,\ x4\,x2 = x1\,x4,\ x3\,x2$	y	y	y	y
$x1\,x2,\ x3\,x5 = x1\,x3,\ x2\,x5$	y	y		y
$x1\,x2,\ x5\,x3 = x1\,x5,\ x2\,x3$	y	y		y
$x1\,x3,\ x5\,x2 = x1\,x5,\ x3\,x2$	y	y	y	y
$x1\,x2,\ x3\,x6 = x1\,x3,\ x2\,x6$	y	y		y
$x1\,x2,\ x6\,x3 = x1\,x6,\ x2\,x3$	y	y		y
$x1\,x3,\ x6\,x2 = x1\,x6,\ x3\,x2$	y	y	y	y
$x1\,x3,\ x4\,x5 = x1\,x4,\ x3\,x5$				
$x1\,x3,\ x5\,x4 = x1\,x5,\ x3\,x4$				
$x1\,x4,\ x5\,x3 = x1\,x5,\ x4\,x3$	y			
$x1\,x3,\ x4\,x6 = x1\,x4,\ x3\,x6$				
$x1\,x3,\ x6\,x4 = x1\,x6,\ x3\,x4$				
$x1\,x4,\ x6\,x3 = x1\,x6,\ x4\,x3$	y			
$x1\,x4,\ x5\,x6 = x1\,x5,\ x4\,x6$	y		y	y
$x1\,x4,\ x6\,x5 = x1\,x6,\ x4\,x5$	y		y	y
$x1\,x5,\ x6\,x4 = x1\,x6,\ x5\,x4$	y	y	y	y
$x2\,x3,\ x4\,x5 = x2\,x4,\ x3\,x5$				
$x2\,x3,\ x5\,x4 = x2\,x5,\ x3\,x4$				
$x2\,x4,\ x5\,x3 = x2\,x5,\ x4\,x3$	y			
$x2\,x3,\ x4\,x6 = x2\,x4,\ x3\,x6$				
$x2\,x3,\ x6\,x4 = x2\,x6,\ x3\,x4$				
$x2\,x4,\ x6\,x3 = x2\,x6,\ x4\,x3$	y			
$x2\,x4,\ x5\,x6 = x2\,x5,\ x4\,x6$	y		y	y
$x2\,x4,\ x6\,x5 = x2x6,\ x4\,x5$	y		y	y
$x2\,x5,\ x6\,x4 = x2\,x6,\ x5\,x4$	y	y	y	y
$x3\,x4,\ x5\,x6 = x3\,x5,\ x4\,x6$	y			
$x3\,x4,\ x6\,x5 = x3\,x6,\ x4\,x5$	y			
$x3\,x5,\ x6\,x4 = x3\,x6,\ x5\,x4$	y	y	y	y

models had generated which data set. His task was to identify the model from the data. The chance of randomly choosing the correct sequence of models is less than 1 in 14 million. In five minutes a TETRAD user identified the sequence perfectly.

It should be noted that the inferences TETRAD makes with such simulated data are much more demanding than the application to longitudinal measurement models requires. In such applications, one knows that the measurements taken at the later time cannot cause the measurements made at an earlier time, and thus one can rule out a priori models in which, say, $x4$ has a direct effect on $x3$. Under appropriate conditions, TETRAD can discriminate among such models even without the information provided by time ordering. This means that in empirical cases in which there are additional direct effects between measurements made at different times, TETRAD can be used to infer the time order from the correlations. Such inferences may sometimes provide a useful nonstatistical test of a model.

3.6. *The TETRAD Program*

The TETRAD program lets the user specify an initial model by means of a *graph of proposed causal relations*. No equations or distribution assumptions need to be described. The error terms do not have to be explicitly entered (the program infers that they are present). An alternative initial model can be specified simply by adding or deleting edges from whatever graph the program is previously given. Thus, a model that would require a page of specifications in an easily used maximum likelihood estimation package, such as EQS, can be described in TETRAD simply by giving a list of the variables between which there are direct causal connections.

The simplification of input and operation is possible because of the purpose of the TETRAD program and because of some mathematical facts. The purpose of the program is not to estimate values of free parameters in a model, since there are already plenty of programs that do that. The purpose of the TETRAD program is instead to explore causal specifications and to discover those causal models that have mathematical properties that are important in explaining the data.

428   CLARK GLYMOUR, RICHARD SCHEINES AND PETER SPIRTES

TETRAD helps the user search in the following way:

1. The user provides covariance data and an initial model.
2. TETRAD determines all the vanishing partial correlations and all the vanishing tetrad differences that pass a statistical test at a significance level specified by the user.
3. TETRAD determines all the vanishing partial correlations and all the vanishing tetrad differences implied by the initial model.
4. TETRAD compares the implied constraints with the constraints that hold empirically.
5. TETRAD provides the user with a similar comparison for every elaboration of the initial model that adds one causal connection or correlated error to the initial model.
6. If the initial model is a multiple indicator model, the automatic TETRAD search strategy will find the elaborations of the initial model that imply the same empirically correct constraints as the initial model while implying as few empirically incorrect constraints as possible. This information is given in the form of suggested trek additions to the initial model, and the user must judge how best (if at all) to realize the suggested trek additions by directed edges or correlated errors.

In addition, the information the program provides can be used to search for other models not suggested by the automatic search procedure. In what follows, we describe such searches as *TETRAD-aided*.

We imagine TETRAD to be used in the following way:

1. The researcher uses prior knowledge (e.g., about what the variables mean, how they were measured, how they cluster, etc.) to formulate a class of alternative initial models. The TETRAD program may help in this process by locating constraints satisfied in the data that perhaps ought to be explained.
2. The initial models are elaborated with TETRAD, either using the automatic search component or step by step using the information the program gives at each stage about the properties of one-step additions to a model and using substantive knowledge.
3. The investigator applies whatever is known about the domain to rule out models suggested by TETRAD that contradict established principles or are nonsensical.

4. The remaining models are subjected to statistical test, or if possible to nonstatistical testing.

4. EXAMPLES

In what follows, we present a series of studies of empirical data using the TETRAD program. Most, but not all, of these cases are described in more detail in Glymour et al. (1987), where a variety of other cases are considered in detail. Here, we will simply state the task and the TETRAD results. The examples are chosen because they illustrate a variety of ways in which the program may be used, but they do not begin to exhaust the wealth of kinds of applications for the TETRAD procedures.

In few of these cases do we mean to endorse the substantive claims of the particular models we consider. The point of the exercise is to illustrate the power of the program and its heuristics in finding alternative elaborations of real models for real data, alternatives that are at least as plausible as published models, that provide comparable or better fit, and that explain constraints found to be satisfied by the data. Details of the models, their interpretation, and the procedures by which the data were obtained can be found in the references given in each case.

4.1. *Finding Omitted Correlated Errors*

A study by Wheaton et al. (1977) on the stability of alienation has become a standard example in manuals for computer programs that perform statistical analyses of structural equation models. Jöreskog and Sörbom (1984) discuss the example in the LISREL manuals, and Bentler discusses the example in the EQS manual. The initial causal model considered by these authors is shown in Figure 7. Alienation is a latent construct measured by anomie and powerlessness at two different times, 1967 and 1971. SES is the latent construct interpreted as socioeconomic status and measured by Duncan's index (SEI) and by an index of educational achievement . The probability of this model's chi-square statistic (with 6 degrees of freedom) is less than 0.01.

Using the LISREL technique for model revision, Jöreskog and Sörbom revise the initial model by freeing two parameters that corre-

FIGURE 7. Alienation: Original model.

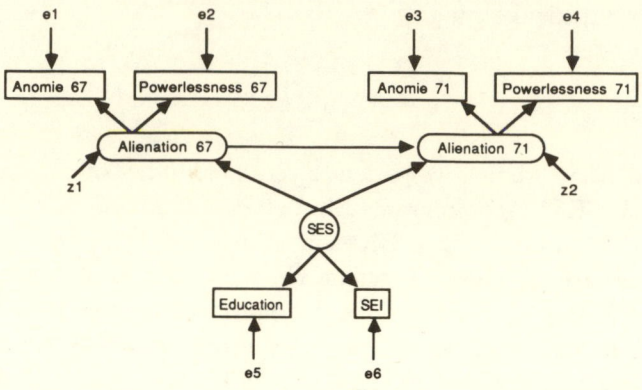

spond to correlations for error terms for the same indicator measured at different times. The revised model, shown in Figure 8, has 4 degrees of freedom and $p = 0.335$. The revised model is plausible enough and has acceptable fit, by the usual standards. But are there other models, based on the same initial causal hypotheses, that are substantively plausible and have comparable or better fit?

The automatic portion of the TETRAD program finds one such model, illustrated in Figure 9. The model has one less degree of freedom than the previous revision, but the p value of its chi-square statistic is 0.91. One other model with comparable fit ($p = 0.8$, same degrees of freedom) can be located by a TETRAD-aided search.

4.2. *Alternatives to Regression Models*

Timberlake and Williams (1984) claim that foreign investment in Third World or "peripheral" nations causes the exclusion of various groups from the political process within a peripheral country. Put more simply, foreign investment promotes dictatorships and oligarchies. They also claim that "foreign investment penetration increases government repression in noncore countries" (p. 144). It is clear that such theses, if true, have important policy implications. Timberlake and Williams try to support their first claim by means of a simple regression model.

FIGURE 8. Alienation: Amended model.

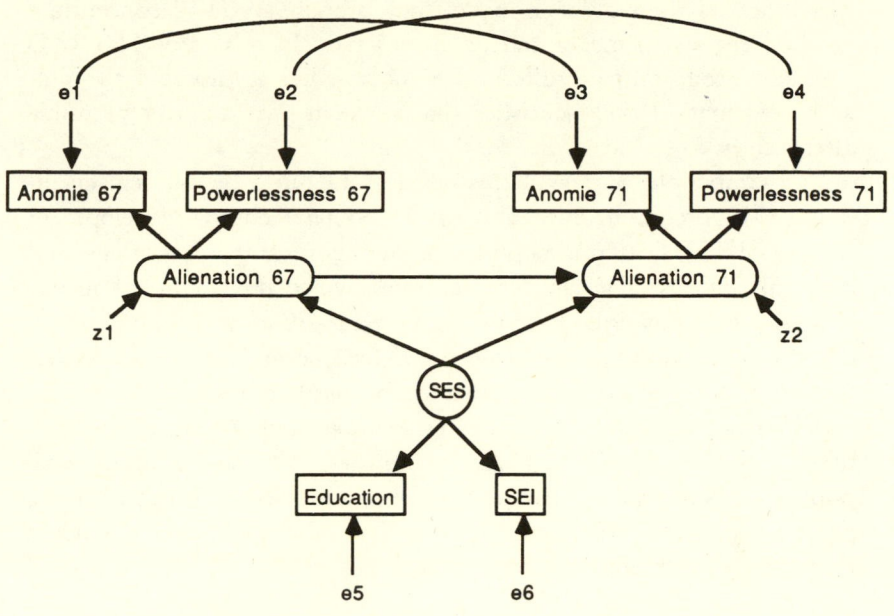

FIGURE 9. TETRAD revision.

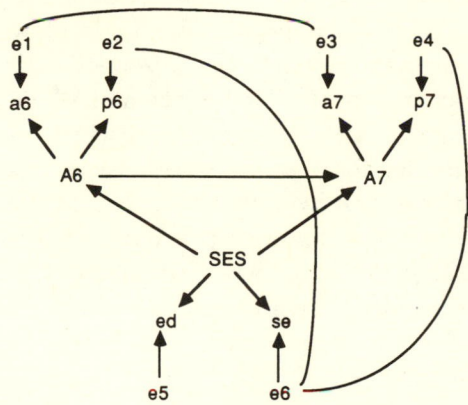

Their more complicated argument for the second thesis depends on the correctness of the regression model they propose. We will concentrate on their regression model and its alternatives. In this case, TETRAD does not itself construct alternative models, but it provides the user with information and heuristics that make it easy to find plausible alternatives.

Timberlake and Williams develop measures of political exclusion (po), foreign investment penetration (fi), energy development (en), civil liberties (cv), population, and government sanctions and political protests. The last two variables, which do not figure in our analysis, were measured over two time spans (1968–72 and 1973–77), but the other variables were measured for one and the same period; therefore, time of occurrence cannot be used to restrict the causal relations among those variables. Timberlake and Williams correlate these measures for 72 "noncore" countries. All the variables, save population, have substantial positive or negative correlations with one another; absolute values range from 0.123 to 0.864. It should be noted that their investment data concern a period preceding the increase in petrodollars loaned to Third World countries following the dramatic OPEC increases in oil prices.

A straightforward embarrassment to the theory is the finding that political exclusion is *negatively* correlated with foreign investment penetration and that foreign investment penetration is *positively* correlated with civil liberties and negatively correlated with government sanctions. Everything appears to be just the opposite of what the theory requires. The gravamen of the Timberlake and Williams argument is that these correlations are misleading, and when other appropriate variables are controlled for, the effects are reversed.

To sustain their first hypothesis, they regress the political exclusion variable on foreign investment penetration together with energy development and civil liberties (measured on a scale whose increasing values measure decreases in civil liberties) (see Figure 10). They find a statistically significant positive regression coefficient for foreign investment penetration and conclude that their first hypothesis is supported.

Timberlake and Williams thus claim to have found evidence that foreign investment in Third World nations causes governments to be unrepresentative and undemocratic. Their conclusion suggests that the development of democracy and human rights would have been furthered in the early 1970s if international corporations, private

FIGURE 10.   Timberlake and Williams's first hypothesis.

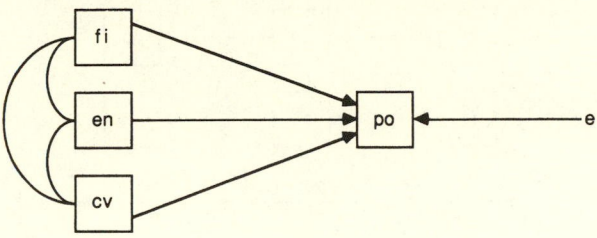

banks, and other organizations based in industrial countries had not invested in Third World nations.

There are some puzzling features of the data, which we might expect a good theory to explain. For example, there are in the data some relations among the correlations that hold much more exactly than we expect by chance. Using TETRAD, we find that the following relations hold almost exactly in the sample data:

$$\rho_{po,\,fi} - \rho_{po,\,en}\rho_{en,\,fi} = 0, \tag{1}$$

$$\rho_{en,\,cv} - \rho_{en,\,po}\rho_{po,\,cv} = 0. \tag{2}$$

These equations are interesting exactly because *they are the kind of relationship among correlations that can be explained by causal structure.* Equation (1) can be explained by supposing that the only effects of political exclusion on foreign investment, or of foreign investment on political exclusion, or of any third factor on both political exclusion and foreign investment, are mediated by per-capita energy consumption; one variable affects another only through its effect on energy consumption. More visually, equation (1) will be explained provided the causal connections between political exclusion and foreign investment are as illustrated in Figure 11.

In the same way, equation (2) can be explained by supposing that any correlations between energy consumption and absence of civil liberties are due to the effects of political exclusion; e.g., if increases in per-capita energy consumption cause an increase in civil liberties, they do so because of their direct effect on totalitarianism.

Timberlake and Williams's model does not provide any causal explanation of relations (1) and (2), but it is easy to find assumptions that do explain these patterns, and explain them rather neatly. We

FIGURE 11.　Causal explanations of equation (1).

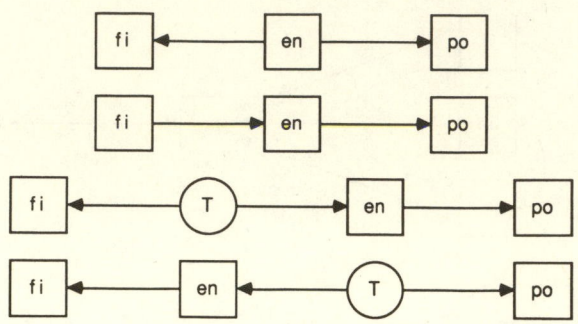

exhibit some alternative explanations in Figure 12. T signifies a latent common cause. The causal hypotheses in all alternatives, under the assumption of linearity, imply that both (1) and (2) hold in the population, *no matter what the values of the linear coefficients may be*.

Model I, for example, gives a chi-square statistic for 2 degrees of freedom with $p = 0.94$. If we accept model I, then we conclude that foreign investment in peripheral nations neither promotes nor inhibits the development of democracy and civil liberties but that raising the energy consumption per capita promotes both foreign investment and more representative government and, through representative government, increases respect for civil liberties. On this data, and given the alternatives, we would not argue that model I should be accepted. We do claim that it, and very likely the alternatives suggested here, are preferable to Timberlake and Williams's regression model.

4.3. *The Stability of Measurement Models*

McPherson et al. (1977) consider a model of responses to a four-item scale assumed to measure indicators of political efficacy or, more clearly, the respondents' judgments of their political influence. Measures of the same four items were obtained from a chart of 978 persons in 1956 and in 1960. Their initial model is shown in Figure 13.

After considerable discussion, the authors conclude that there is a factor acting on $v6$ and $v0$ and some other factor acting on $c6$ and $c0$. The conclusion is based on the fact that the linear coefficients

FIGURE 12.   Alternatives to the regression model.

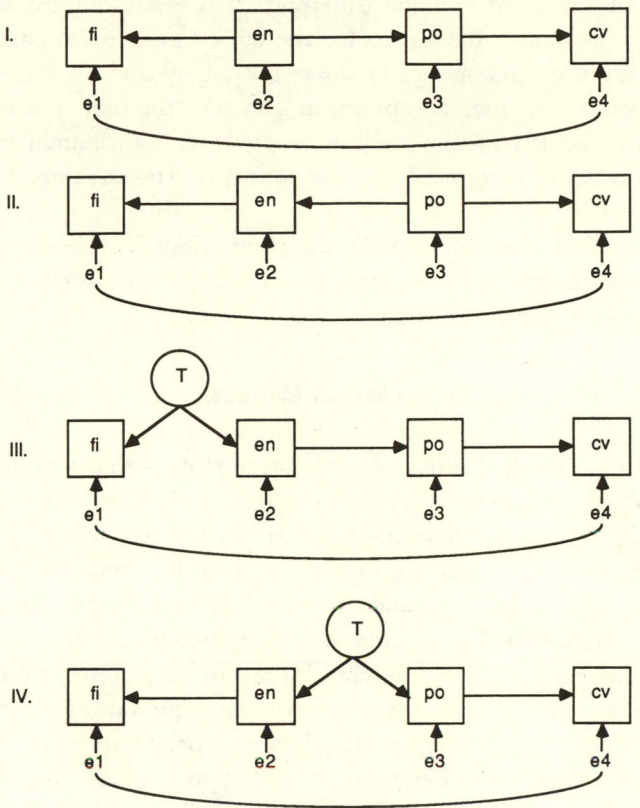

FIGURE 13.   McPherson, Welch and Clark's initial model.

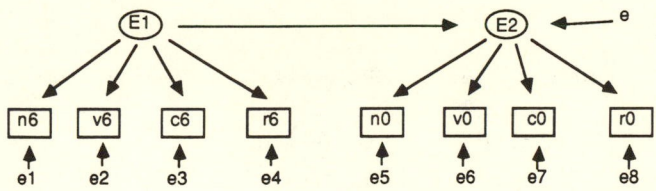

connecting these variables with their parent latent variables are the smallest of the eight and the difference between estimated and empirical correlations is the largest for the $v6-v0$ and $c6-c0$ pairs.

TETRAD automatically suggests that $v6$ and $v0$ must have a further common cause. The program also tells the user that a further common cause of $c6$ and $c0$ will improve fit with a minimal reduction in the number of empirically correct tetrad constraints implied by the model.

The basis for TETRAD's discriminations in this case has already been partly demonstrated in the study with simulated data described in a previous section.

4.4. *Determining Causal Order from Correlations in One-Factor Models*

Kohn (1969) describes several large studies that investigate the relationships among social class, attitudes, and personality structure. For data from five questions intended to measure an authoritarian-conservative personality trait, Kohn suggests a simple factor model, shown in Figure 14. Schoenberg and Richtand (1984) suggest the revision shown in Figure 15. The sample size is larger than 3,000.

One reason for residual correlations in measurement models for survey data may be that responses to earlier questions set a mood or create a desire for consistency and thus, independently of the value of the latent variable the items are intended to measure, influence the responses given to later items (see Campbell et al. 1966). On this assumption, we gave the data and Kohn's initial model to TETRAD and considered only revisions that postulate direct effects between

FIGURE 14. Initial authoritarian-conservatism measurement model.

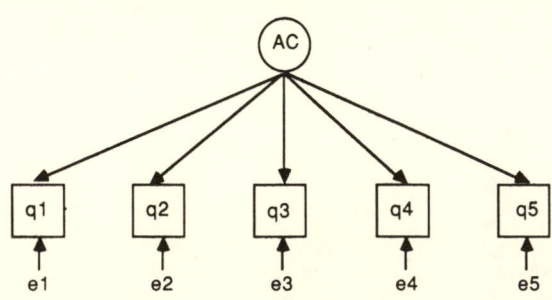

FIGURE 15. Schoenberg and Richtand's revised model.

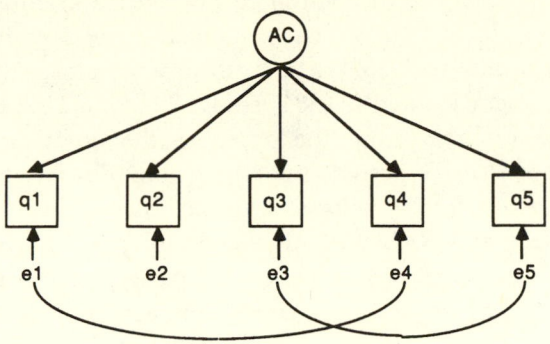

measured variables. For reasons to be explained shortly, we did so in ignorance of the order in which the five questions had been asked. We found two "best" revisions of the initial model under these assumptions, namely, models that add to the model in Figure 14 either the edges

$$q1 \rightarrow q3, q2 \rightarrow q5, q5 \rightarrow q3$$

or the edges

$$q1 \rightarrow q3, q5 \rightarrow q2, q5 \rightarrow q3.$$

Each of these models gives a chi-square statistic with $p = 0.994$. The hypothesis that the data was generated by one or the other of these models implies restrictions on the order in which four of the five questions were asked. There are 24 possible orderings of four questions, and only eight of them are consistent with the hypothesis, namely,

$$1\text{-}5\text{-}3\text{-}2$$
$$5\text{-}1\text{-}3\text{-}2$$
$$1\text{-}5\text{-}2\text{-}3$$
$$5\text{-}1\text{-}2\text{-}3$$
$$5\text{-}2\text{-}1\text{-}3$$
$$1\text{-}2\text{-}5\text{-}3$$
$$2\text{-}1\text{-}5\text{-}3$$
$$2\text{-}5\text{-}1\text{-}3.$$

The actual order of the five questions on Kohn's survey is 2-1-4-5-3, which is consistent with the seventh ordering in the list permitted by our hypotheses.

The case provides an unintended illustration of the power of TETRAD's methods to distinguish causal order and illustrates a kind of *nonstatistical* prediction that can sometimes be derived from a model or small set of alternative models. In this case, we took the data from Schoenberg and Richtand's (1984) study. They number the questions in an order different from the order of the questions on Kohn's questionnaire. We discovered, initially to our dismay, that the best TETRAD models were *inconsistent* with the order of the questions given by Schoenberg and Richtand. After consulting Kohn's book, we discovered that the program and the substantive hypothesis about anchoring had led us unwittingly to a correct prediction of the order of the questions.

5. OBJECTIONS AND QUESTIONS

The very idea of using heuristic search in applied statistics creates a variety of misgivings. Many of the objections are mutually inconsistent: No methodology could satisfy all of them. Others are misplaced and suppose that heuristic search procedures impose some condition they do not. Often the misgivings depend on the strictest application of principles that are unscientific in a straightforward sense: If the principles were used in the natural sciences, modern physical science would never have emerged.[5] Since the objections we consider are never given as full, clear arguments, we are forced to reconstruct what we take to be the implicit arguments behind brief remarks, and we therefore avoid attributions. The most frequent objections have no explicit argument at all and amount to simple name calling: Heuristic computerized search is "data dredging" or "ransacking." In so far as any argument lies behind these epithets, we hope one or another of the following considerations may capture it.

5.1. *Data Separation*

Many people believe that a theory or model should always be tested on samples that are distinct from the sample used to generate the model, and they may even hold that the data used to generate the

---

[5] Most of the objections are considered in more detail in Glymour et al. (1987).

model provides no support for it. While we think the *general* principle erroneous, it is in any case irrelevant to the appropriateness of the TETRAD program. TETRAD automatically separates the data in one respect, since model generation is based on only an *aspect* of the data—the covariance constraints—which contain less information than the full set of covariances. But those who insist on complete sample separation can use the TETRAD program with equanimity simply by searching on one sample and testing the models that result on another sample. We have done exactly that in our studies of the Head Start program.

5.2. *Sample-Dependent Generation*

Some writers hold that any procedure in which the model or models generated depends on the sample obtained, and will vary with different samples from the same population, is unacceptable. The prejudice seems to be founded on two very different arguments, which we will treat separately.

Argument 1. No model-generation procedure should be sample-dependent, because in the worst case, sample-dependent procedures will with high probability find spurious dependencies. For example, if one searches the data for correlations, there are cases (with appropriate sample sizes and numbers of independent variables) in which a random sample of values of independent variables will with high probability exhibit a significant correlation for *some* pair of variables. A sample-dependent procedure would therefore with high probability incorrectly conclude that the variables are correlated even though in reality they are independent. Therefore, such procedures should not be used.

For several reasons, the conclusion of this argument does not follow from the case that is imagined:

1. The difficulty can be avoided simply by refusing to make inferences when the sample size is inappropriately small for the number of variables considered. The generation procedure can still be sample-dependent.
2. The difficulty can be avoided by testing any generated model on an independent sample.
3. The worst-case argument against a general procedure fails to consider the *expected* case.

FIGURE 16. Procedure 1.

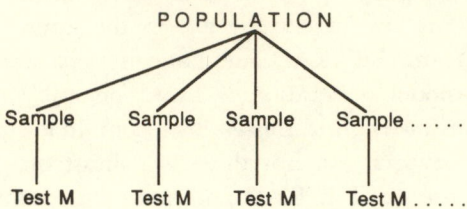

4. The argument considers only the risk of drawing a false conclusion; it fails to consider the risk of failing to draw a correct conclusion. No argument of such a form for a methodological restriction can be valid.

Argument 2. Model-generation procedures should always be sample-independent; otherwise, test statistics are "meaningless." That is, if model generation is sample-dependent, then the p values of test statistics such as chi square cannot be given a long-run frequency interpretation. The usual long-run frequency interpretation of the p value of a statistic is the frequency with which a value more extreme than the computed value of the statistic would be obtained in a long sequence of tests on samples of the same size drawn at random from a population truly described by the model tested (see Figure 16). The objection is that if probabilities are long-run (or limits of) frequencies, the chi-square statistic for a model obtained for a sample is not the long-run frequency of the following sequence of sampling, model generation, and statistical testing procedures (see Figure 17).

     The last point is correct, but the argument contains a logical blunder. The claim of the argument is that no long-run frequency interpretation can be found for the p value of a test statistic of a model obtained by a sample-dependent generation procedure. But the argument shows only that the sequence in Figure 17 does not provide such an interpretation. That is well short of showing that no frequency interpretation can be given. One can. There is a frequency interpretation for the chi-square probability obtained when a model generated by a sample-dependent procedure is tested, and it is the interpretation associated with the sequence shown in Figure 18.

FIGURE 17. Procedure 2.

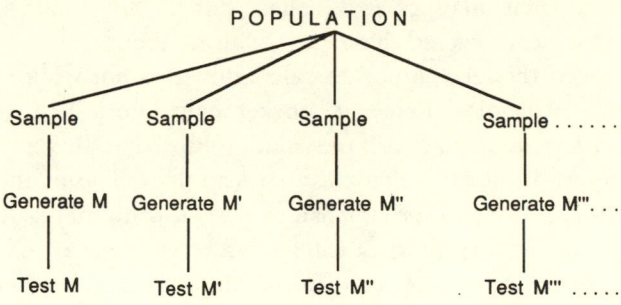

FIGURE 18. Procedure 3.

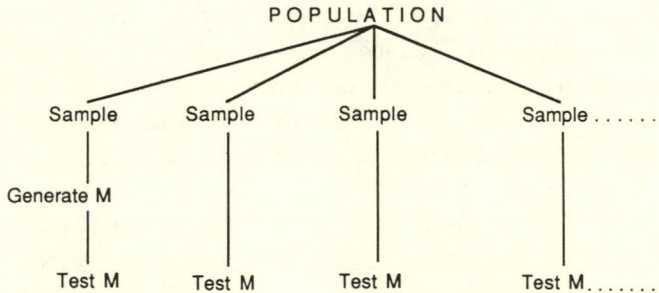

This sequence gives the correct probability interpretation in the only relevant sense; namely, the long-run frequency corresponds to the p value. Any continued argument that this interpretation is not the "right" frequency interpretation is bootless or tacitly changes the argument completely. The argument, recall, was that there is no frequency interpretation that can be given to test statistics for models obtained with a sample-dependent procedure. But there is such an interpretation, and there is no relevant objection to be made to it that does not apply to frequency interpretations generally.

5.3. *Is TETRAD Fit for Bayesians?*

One question is whether TETRAD is consistent with the philosophical viewpoint of Bayesian statisticians and econometricians. TETRAD does not do explicitly Bayesian calculations; it does not assign prior probabilities and change them by conditioning on the evidence, and that may give Bayesian statisticians qualms. Yet a Bayesian statistician would have no qualms about using a pocket calculator, even though the pocket calculator does not work explicitly on Bayesian principles. Like the pocket calculator, TETRAD determines *mathematical* relationships, relationships that humans cannot conveniently and reliably calculate for themselves. The mathematical relationships are, moreover, relationships that *ought* to matter to Bayesians. A Bayesian statistician may entertain a set of alternative hypotheses to account for a body of data, but if he or she is wise, some prior probability is usually reserved for the catch-all hypothesis that none of the explicitly considered hypotheses is correct. Since the mathematical structure and properties of whatever theories may be contained in the catch-all hypothesis are generally unknown, the Bayesian cannot determine much about the likelihood such hypotheses give to the data or to features of the data. One way of viewing the TETRAD program is that it searches the vast space of alternatives encompassed by the catch-all hypothesis; in its search, TETRAD looks for models that give a high likelihood to constraints on population covariances that are suggested by the data. What it reports are mathematical facts about the existence and properties of such models. In that respect, it is no different from the pocket calculator. The user, whether a self-conscious Bayesian or not, is free to use these mathematical facts in many ways in the light of prior belief, but one would be unwise to ignore them altogether.

5.4. *Hypothesis Testing Only*

Some people seem to think that the only meaningful comparisons of alternative models are those that test one model against the other in Neyman-Pearson fashion. They have no use for comparisons of p values of test statistics of different models on the same data, for comparisons of explanatory power, or for simplicity. But comparisons of the p values of alternative models are perfectly meaningful; they are comparisons of likelihoods. And if the only methodological comparisons permitted were hypothesis tests, most of the history of science would have to be dismissed, along with a great deal of contemporary natural science.

5.5. *Should We Use Theories Suggested by a Computer?*

Someone might take the view that we need to consider only the hypotheses explicitly proposed *by people*: Any hypotheses discovered by computer search can be ignored and thus in effect given zero prior probability. This prejudice may derive from the conviction that, after all, people know a lot more than computers do. They know about how things were measured and what they mean; they know about social practices, about time order, and about prior theorizing. All of that is true, but not really relevant. The special knowledge humans have can interact with the special computational powers computers have in at least two ways. First, humans can use their knowledge to restrict the range of search the computer conducts and to edit and choose from among the results of the computer search. Second, humans can explicitly represent their knowledge within the computer program and let the computer automatically apply that knowledge in conducting a search. The TETRAD program relies on the first procedure rather than the second, but the second procedure is perfectly feasible in searching for causal models.

Sometimes, *part* of discovering a theory can be reduced to combinatorial analysis, and when it can, why shouldn't we have a computer do it? Nothing guarantees us (or even makes it likely) that the truth about some subject matter must be contained in one of the theories entertained by some human at some particular time. There is a world of mathematical possibilities, and we humans cannot very well search through that world unaided; if computers can aid us in the search, why shouldn't we use them? In using the computer to help us search for models with special mathematical properties or special relationships to the data, we are simply using a computational device to help us do the sort of thing that has been fundamental to theory development in the natural sciences. Newton, for example, did not just posit the inverse square gravitational force law without searching for alternatives. A major theorem in Newton's *Principia* characterizes features of the orbits of a body about a central source for *every* inverse power law for the attractive force. For decades, physicists have carried out the same kind of systematic search for alternatives to the general theory of relativity. If, in the course of such a search, a computer were needed to provide numerical approximations to solutions of differential equations, no one would hesitate to use it. In applied statistics, the space of possible linear models is usually so large that humans cannot search it for models that have interesting mathematical relationships to the data. If a computer can help in that search, and TETRAD shows that it can, it would be unscientific not to make use of it.

5.6. *Varieties of Conservatism*

A related doubt about using computer aids for search rests on a kind of conservatism. Someone might think that we should not search for alternative theories unless the most popular current theory has run into trouble. Such a view defies the practice throughout the natural sciences, in which, for example, research programs have for many years attempted systematically to search for alternative theories to quantum mechanics and to general relativity.

Some people think that a body of evidence should never be used to search for more than a single theory. We may be very glad that our scientific ancestors did not think the same way. If they had, we would not have had Copernican astronomy, or Kepler's laws, or modern tables of atomic weights, or indeed most of physical science.

5.7. *Will Computerized Search Make Modeling Practice Better or Worse?*

Any technical innovation can be used badly. If the possibility for misuse were grounds for dismissing a technical innovation, then we should have to do without the telescope, the micrometer, the photographic plate, the cyclotron, indeed virtually every scientific instrument. All have at times been poorly used to produce erroneous conclusions. The same is true of statistical innovations and computational aids. The general principle that says that a technical innovation ought not to be used if it can be used badly is a policy for ending science, not furthering it.

All considered, programs such as TETRAD should produce better, not worse, scientific practice. Perhaps the most striking defect of causal modeling is the difficulty researchers have in considering alternative explanations for their data. That is the chief point in criticisms of causal modeling that point out that investigators often fail to make any reasoned, persuasive case for the structural equations they assume. The difficulty people have in constructing alternatives has two unfortunate consequences. First, we sometimes rush to embrace a causal explanation when other, better explanations exist. Second, the case for a particular causal explanation may sometimes be weaker than it need be, because even when a researcher has found the very best explanation, he or she cannot provide an argument that there are not better alternatives that have been overlooked. TETRAD makes a small contribution toward removing both difficulties. Scientific papers routinely end with a call for further research, but what further research is relevant depends in large part on what alternative explanations need to be distinguished empirically. That kind of question is likely to become more focused if systematic search procedures find wide use.

5.8. *Reliability*

There is no bound to the number and variety of bad arguments and red herrings that can be contrived, and no matter how many are addressed, others will spring up in their place. It is better to focus on the central issue about the TETRAD procedures and about any other discovery procedure, automated or not. The central issue is always this: Where can the procedure be relied upon, and exactly what can it be relied upon to do? That question cannot be answered by methodological dogmas. It can be addressed through systematic proofs about the classes of models whose members are asymptotically distinguishable by constraints of various kinds. It can be addressed by detailed studies of the behavior of the search strategy on simulated data samples of varying sizes, generated from known structures with a variety of probability distributions. And it can be addressed by comparative studies of alternative search procedures, including search procedures that employ no computational aids. Some of the results of such studies have been reported here, and we are conducting further studies of the same kind.

6. FUTURE DEVELOPMENTS

Consider a system that could do all of the following:

1. The user specifies whatever is known about a domain, including the knowledge that specific variables are or are not causally connected, or do or do not have common causes; that connections between

specific variables must be of a specific sign, positive or negative; that specific variables are lags of one another; that specific variables may have a common cause; that specific variables must have symmetric relationships to other variables; that no cycles occur, etc. The information might be as detailed as a specific initial model, or it might be much less definite.

2. The program finds a variety of initial models consistent with the user's specifications and lets the user add to them or eliminate any number of them.

3. The program finds the elaborations of the initial models that best explain patterns in the data, that are simple, and that fit the covariances.

4. The program compares the elaborations of different initial models, eliminating those that are redundant or inferior.

5. The program gives maximum likelihood estimates and chi-square tests for every remaining model, using whatever data set the user specifies.

A program of this kind would make it genuinely feasible for researchers to explore a large space of alternative models. It would leave people free to focus on the aspects of theory construction that good researchers are really good at—finding restrictions on models based on prior knowledge, providing substantive constraints on model specification, assigning a plausible interpretation to latent variables, wondering about measurement procedures, putting a causal story in a more general framework, making policy inferences from a causal explanation—and it would leave to the computer what the computer is really good at—computing mathematical relationships. A program of this kind would be elementary to use, and while it might require considerable computer time to operate, it would require very little of the *user's* time.

TETRAD is not a program of this sort. It is very restrictive in the kind of prior information it uses, and it gives output that is hard to interpret without considerable practice. Nonetheless, we believe the TETRAD program provides the core of a system of the kind just outlined, and we are in the process of carrying out its development and implementation. Thus far, we have done the following:

1. We have written an extension of TETRAD that automatically writes an input file to EQS for any model the user wishes to have

evaluated; the model is given simply by a list of causal edges or correlated errors. The input files for EQS are collected in a batch file. To run EQS on any number of models, the user need only construct the graphs of the models in TETRAD, tell TETRAD it wishes EQS files, and type "run." The result is EQS data on all the models considered. A similar extension can be written for LISREL.

2. We have written a program to implement an algorithm that considers additional constraints besides tetrad equations and vanishing partial correlations. Whether a model implies that a tetrad difference is positive or negative, or that a partial correlation is positive or negative, depends only on the graph of the model and on the *signs* of the linear coefficients. Peter Spirtes has implemented an algorithm that computes these features for a wide class of models, given the graph and the signs. This feature will permit us to modify TETRAD to do a more discriminating search than hitherto possible.

We expect that over the next two years, these pieces can be expanded to a fully automatic system of the kind described and that the system will run successfully on relatively inexpensive personal workstations.

REFERENCES

Anderson, T. 1984. *An Introduction to Multivariate Statistical Analysis*. New York: Wiley.

Blalock, H. M. 1961. *Causal Inferences in Nonexperimental Research*. Chapel Hill: University of North Carolina Press.

——————. 1982. *Conceptualization and Measurement in the Social Sciences*. Beverly Hills: Sage.

Campbell, D., R. Schwartz, L. Sechrest, and E. Webb. 1966. *Unobtrusive Measures: Nonreactive Research in the Social Sciences*. Chicago: Rand McNally.

Costner, H., and R. Schoenberg. 1973. "Diagnosing Indicator Ills in Multiple Indicator Models." Pp. 168–99 in *Structural Equation Models in the Social Sciences*, edited by A. S. Goldberger and O. D. Duncan. New York: Seminar.

Glymour, C. 1985. "Statistics and Metaphysics." Educational Testing Service Technical Report 85–63. Princeton: Educational Testing Service.

Glymour, C., R. Scheines, P. Spirtes, and K. Kelly. 1987. *Discovering Causal Structure*. San Diego: Academic Press.

Guilford, J. 1936. *Psychometric Methods*. New York: McGraw Hill.

Heise, D. 1975. *Causal Analysis*. New York: Wiley.

Herting, J., and H. Costner. 1985. "Respecification in Multiple Indicator Models." Pp. 321–93 in *Causal Models in the Social Sciences*. 2d ed., edited by H. M. Blalock, Jr. New York: Aldine.

Jöreskog, K., and D. Sörbom. 1984. *LISREL VI User's Guide*. 3d ed. Mooresville, IN: Scientific Software.

Kohn, M. *Class and Conformity*. Homewood, IL: Dorsey.

Magidson, J. 1977. "Toward a Causal Model Approach for Adjusting for Preexisting Differences in the Nonequivalent Control Group Situation." *Evaluation Quarterly* 1:399–420.

Maruyama, G., and B. McGarvey. 1980. "Evaluating Causal Models: An Application of Maximum Likelihood Analysis of Structural Equations." *Psychological Bulletin* 87:502–12.

McPherson, J. M., S. Welch, and C. Clark. 1977. "The Stability and Reliability of Political Efficacy: Using Path Analysis to Test Alternative Models." *American Political Science Review* 71:509–21.

Miller, J., K. Slomczynski, and R. Schoenberg. 1981. "Assessing Comparability of Measurement in Cross-National Research: Authoritarian-Conservatism in Different Sociocultural Settings." *Social Psychology Quarterly* 44:178–91.

Miller, R. 1981. *Simultaneous Statistical Inference*. New York: Springer.

Schoenberg, R., and C. Richtand. 1984. "Application of the EM Method." *Sociological Methods and Research* 13:127–50.

Spirtes, P. 1988. "Fast Geometrical Calculations of Overidentifying Constraints." Unpublished manuscript, Department of Philosophy, Carnegie Mellon University.

Spirtes, P., and C. Glymour. Forthcoming. "Latent Variables, Causal Models and Overidentifying Constraints." *Journal of Econometrics*.

Timberlake, M., and K. R. Williams. 1984. "Dependence, Political Exclusion, and Government Repression: Some Cross-National Evidence." *American Sociological Review* 49:141–46.

Wheaton, B., B. Muthén, D. Alwin, and G. Summers. 1977. "Assessing Reliability and Stability in Panel Models." Pp. 84–136 in *Sociological Methodology 1977*, edited by D. Heise. San Francisco: Jossey-Bass.

Wishart, J. 1928. "Sampling Errors in the Theory of Two Factors." *British Journal of Psychology* 19:180–87.

✼13✼

Causal Inference, Path Analysis, and Recursive Structural Equations Models

*Paul W. Holland**

Rubin's model for causal inference in experiments and observational studies is enlarged to analyze the problem of "causes causing causes" and is compared to path analysis and recursive structural equations models. A special quasi-experimental design, the encouragement design, is used to give concreteness to the discussion by focusing on the simplest problem that involves both direct and indirect causation. It is shown that Rubin's model extends easily to this situation and specifies conditions under which the parameters of path analysis and recursive structural equations models have causal interpretations.

1. INTRODUCTION

The perspective on causal inference developed extensively by Rubin (1974, 1977, 1978, 1980, 1986) provides a solid basis for considering issues of causal inference in complex cases, and it is the only one that is grounded where causal inferences are relatively uncontroversial—in experimental science. In Holland (1986*a, b*), I described this perspective and dubbed it *Rubin's model*, as I will refer to it here, too, even though a more general term, such as *the experimental model*,

I thank David Freedman, Clark Glymour, Edward Leamer, Margaret Marini, James Robins, David Rogosa, Donald Rubin, Burton Singer, and Howard Wainer for their many helpful comments on an earlier draft of this paper.
*Educational Testing Service.

may be more appropriate. Robins (1984, 1985, 1986) gives a closely related model in the context of epidemiological studies. One goal of this paper is to extend Rubin's model to accommodate a class of quasi-experimental procedures that are called encouragement designs by Powers and Swinton (1984). These designs involve both randomization and self-selection as well as both direct and indirect causation. Encouragement designs provide a simple yet useful "laboratory" in which the issues of direct and indirect causal relationships can be carefully examined. I hope to clarify the relationship between the systematic structure of Rubin's model and the less formal approaches of path analysis and structural equations modeling. My own experience has been that *any* discussion of causation is enriched by an analysis using Rubin's model (e.g., Holland and Rubin 1987; Rosenbaum 1987; Holland 1988).

Before proceeding, I want to make a few general comments about causation to set the stage for the subsequent discussion.

In most discussions of causation, all too little attention is given to distinguishing between the *cause* of a given effect and the *effect* of a given cause. Since the time of Aristotle, philosophers have tried to define what it means for A to be a cause of B. This activity still continues (Lewis 1986; Marini and Singer, this volume). Yet, the attribution of causation has been known to be fraught with difficulty since, at least, Hume's analysis in the mid 1700s. A statement like "A is a cause of B" is usually false because it is, at best, a tentative summary or theory of our current knowledge of the cause (or causes) of B. For example, do bacteria cause disease? Well, yes ...until we dig deeper and find that it is the toxins the bacteria produce that really cause the disease. Yet this is not quite correct either: Certain chemical reactions are the real causes, and so on, *ad infinitum*. Experiments, on the other hand, do not identify causes. Rather, experiments measure the *effects* of given causes (i.e., the effects of the experimental manipulations). The results of an experiment can be summarized by a statement of the form "An effect of A is B," but not by one of the form "A is a cause of B," unless we mean by the latter no more than the former. I would be surprised if most modern scientists were willing to equate theoretical statements like "A is a cause of B" with empirical regularities like "The effect of A is B." Theories may come and go, but old, replicable experiments never die; they are just reinterpreted.

The strength of Rubin's model is that it builds on the success of experimentation and focuses on the measurement of the effects of causes rather than on attempting to identify the causes of effects. Statistics has made major contributions to issues of causal inference when it has addressed the problem of measuring the effects of causes. It does less useful things when its methodology claims to identify the causes of effects. Rubin's model focuses our attention on what can be done well rather than on what we might like to do, however poorly.

I do not mean to imply that the search for the causes of a phenomenon is a useless endeavor. Indeed, it is a driving force that motivates much of science. Rather, I mean that a logical analysis of the search for causes follows from an analysis of the measurement of causal effects, and it is not logically prior to this more basic activity. Defensible inferences about the *causes* of an effect are always made against a background of measured causal effects and relevant theories.

I have tried to follow several goals in writing this paper. First, I discuss population quantities rather than sample estimates of population quantities. Thus, it is best to think of the populations that occur here as large or infinite. I do not apologize for this, since such a view is implicit in most discussions of path analysis. My aim is to define causal parameters rather than to discuss ways of estimating them. Second, I may, on occasion, appear overly notational, and I apologize for that. My defense is that I wish to be very clear about what I mean, and since causation is a subtle idea, an adequate notation is essential to understanding it. Unfortunately, my notation is not identical to that usually used in path analysis or structural equations models, but it is only intended to be more explicit than these other schemes. Finally, my goal is to put the, to me, complex and intuitive models used in path analysis into a framework that I find helpful in complex problems. I hope others find it useful too.

In section 2, I define and give an example of an encouragement design that is used in the rest of this paper to focus the discussion. These designs are interesting in their own right, because they attempt to measure the effects of self-selected treatments. In section 3, I review three related topics that concern path analysis: deterministic linear systems, path analysis, and recursive structural equations models. In section 4, I extend Rubin's model to the case of encouragement designs to allow for both direct and indirect causation. I conclude the paper

with a short discussion. I also include an appendix, in which I apply
Rubin's model to experiments and observational studies to make the
paper reasonably self-contained.

2. ENCOURAGEMENT DESIGNS

While it is common to discuss path analysis and causal models
in terms of abstract systems of variables, I find it easier to discuss issues
of causal inference in the context of specific examples or classes of
examples. For this reason I will use a fairly concrete quasi-experimental design, the encouragement design, as the basis of my discussion of
causal theories that involve direct and indirect causation. The encouragement design is a simple and relatively clear-cut type of study in
which many of the issues of direct and indirect causation arise.

I will introduce encouragement designs by giving an example
that is used throughout the paper. Suppose we are interested in the
effects of various amounts of study on the performance of students on a
test. I will suppose that there are two experimental treatments: one
that encourages a student to study for the test ($t =$ treatment) and one
that does not ($c =$ control). After exposure to one of these treatments, a
student will then study for the test for some amount of time, R.
Subsequently, the student is tested and gets a test score, Y. An example
of an encouragement design, similar to the one just described, is given
in Powers and Swinton (1984). My first exposure to a formal analysis
of encouragement designs was in Swinton (1975).

The only experimental manipulation in an encouragement design is exposure to the "encouragement conditions," which are just t or
c here but could involve more than two levels, of course. Hence, using
standard methods, we can measure the effect of encouragement on the
amount of study, i.e. R, and on test performance, i.e. Y. However, we
may also be interested in the effect of *studying* on test performance.
Thus, random assignment of encouragement conditions might be possible, but the students will then self-select their own exposure levels to
the amount they study, R. This self-selection is a critical feature of
encouragement designs, and it is why I refer to them as a type of
quasi-experimental design, after Campbell and Stanley (1963). The
other critical feature of encouragement designs is the analyst's interest
in measuring the causal effect of the amount of study, R, on test
performance. I have chosen this example specifically because from an

individual student's point of view, the amount one studies is a self-imposed treatment that can be measured and over which one can exercise control. However, from the analyst's point of view, the amount a student studies is a response to the encouragement condition, as is the student's test performance. In this very special type of situation, "amount of study" plays both the role of a response and the role of a self-imposed treatment; i.e., it is both an effect and a cause.

Encouragement designs can arise in *any* study of human subjects in which the treatments or causes of interest must be voluntarily applied by the subjects to themselves. Other potential examples are medical studies that encourage voluntary healthful activities among patients or economic studies that attempt to alter people's spending behavior by various inducements. The analysis of surgical trials may involve randomization of the "intention to treat" patients, but because of clinical intervention, the actual treatment patients get may not be the one to which they were randomly assigned. This is similar to an encouragement design, but the models discussed in this paper may not be appropriate to that case, since I treat "amount of study" as a continuous variable. The general ideas are the same, however.

I suspect that encouragement designs are quite widespread but may not always be recognized. On the other hand, the special nature of these designs cannot be overemphasized. While it is plausible that "amount of study" is both an effect and a cause, this dual role is not always a plausible assumption, and ignoring this fact can lead to some rather curious causal statements. It is critical, in the analysis developed here, that those things that play the role of causes or treatments have levels that are, in principle, alterable. The statement "I could have studied but I didn't" has this flavor, but "I might have scored higher on the test but I didn't" does not. See Holland (1986*b*, sect. 7; 1988) for more emphasis on this very important point.

The basic elements of an encouragement design are, thus, (a) an experimental manipulation of "degrees" of encouragement (here, just t and c) to perform some activity, (b) measurement of the subsequent amount of the encouraged activity, (c) measurement of a final outcome or response variable, and (d) an interest in measuring the causal effect of the encouraged activity on the response variable. Encouragement designs are more often applied to human populations than to other types of experimental units because of the self-selected or voluntary nature of much of human activity.

3. DETERMINISTIC LINEAR SYSTEMS, PATH ANALYSIS, AND RECURSIVE STRUCTURAL EQUATIONS MODELS

In this section I review three related topics: deterministic linear systems, path analysis, and structural equations models. All three will arise in my discussion of encouragement designs in section 4. I frame this review in terms of the structure of encouragement designs.

Extended discussions of path analysis and structural equations models are numerous (e.g., Blalock 1964, 1971; Duncan 1966, 1975; Freedman 1987; Goldberger 1964; Goldberger and Duncan 1973; Heise 1975; Kenny 1979; Saris and Stronkhorst 1984; Tukey 1954; and Wright 1934). I follow Tukey (1954) in *not* standardizing the variables to have zero mean and unit standard deviation and in emphasizing regression coefficients rather than standardized regression coefficients.

3.1. *Deterministic Linear Systems*

Suppose there are two linear functions, f and g, of two variables, s and r, of the form

$$f(s) = as + d, \tag{1}$$

and

$$g(s, r) = bs + cr + d', \tag{2}$$

where a, b, and c are the important slope parameters, and d and d' are constants that play no essential role in this theory. We introduce a third variable, y, into this system via the definition

$$y = g(s, r), \tag{3}$$

and we assume that r and s are related by the functional relationship

$$r = f(s). \tag{4}$$

Such a system captures the idea that r is functionally dependent on s and y is functionally dependent on s and r. Since f and g are linear, *changes* in y and r are determined by the slope parameters, a, b, and c. This system may be represented by the "path" diagram in Figure 1. The coefficients a, b, and c are the "path" coefficients, or the "direct effects"; i.e., a is the direct effect of s on r, c is the direct effect of r on y, and b is the direct effect of s on y.

FIGURE 1.

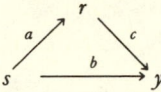

The "total effect" of s on y is found by substituting the equation for r into that for y. This yields

$$y = g(s, f(s)) = bs + c(as + d) + d',$$
$$= (b + ca)s + (cd + d'),$$

so that

$$y = (b + ac)s + d''. \tag{5}$$

Hence, the total effect of s on y is $b + ac$, which may also be calculated as the sum of the products of all the direct effects along all the paths connecting s and y in the path diagram in Figure 1; i.e., s to y yields b, and s to r to y yields ac, so the sum is $b + ac$.

I use the phrase *deterministic linear system* to refer to a path diagram that arises from a set of nonstochastic linear equations like the ones just described.

Viewed simply as a visual representation of a deterministic linear system, path diagrams are easy to understand and can help keep track of the bookkeeping that is associated with the total effects of one variable on another. The real appeal of path diagrams arises in systems that involve more than three variables, but the basic ideas are already present in systems with three.

The path diagram in Figure 1 is not the only one we could draw using three variables, but it is relevant to encouragement design in the following way. If $s = 1$ or 0 as there is encouragement or not and if r denotes the resulting amount of study and y denotes the subsequent test score, then the parameters a, b, and c have the following interpretation. The change in amount of study due to encouragement to study is a, and $b + ac$ is the change in test scores due to encouragement to study. The change in test scores due to a unit change in the amount of study within each level of the encouragement condition, s, is c.

When one of the coefficients a, b, or c is zero, it is customary to delete the corresponding arrow from the path diagram. For example, if $b = 0$, we have the diagram in Figure 2.

FIGURE 2.

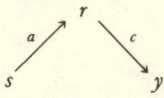

In the encouragement-design example, the path diagram in Figure 2 would be interpreted as displaying no effect of encouragement on test scores except through its effect on studying. We will return to this idea later in section 4.

Deterministic linear systems not only motivate the nondeterministic linear models of path analysis and structural equations models but also play a role in what I call the ALICE "causal model" in section 4.2.

3.2. *Path Analysis*

Deterministic linear systems do not really describe data, except in certain special circumstances, usually in the physical sciences. Suppose instead that there is a population U of "units" and that for each unit u in U we can obtain measurements on three numerical variables, $S(u)$, $R(u)$, and $Y(u)$. In our application, the units are students; $S(u) = 1$ if u is encouraged to study, and $S(u) = 0$ if otherwise; $R(u)$ is the amount that u studies; and $Y(u)$ is u's test score.

As u varies over U, $(S(u), R(u), Y(u))$ forms a trivariate distribution. This distribution can be used to define quantities such as the conditional expectation of R given S, $E(R|S=s)$. This conditional expectation is the average value of R for those units in U for which $S(u) = s$. The conditional expectation, $E(Y|R=r, S=s)$, has a similar definition in terms of averages over U. The expected value $E(Y|R=r, S=s)$ is the "true" regression function of Y on R and S in the sense that it is what one is trying to estimate by a least squares regression fit of Y regressed on R and S. However, in general, $E(Y|R=r, S=s)$ need not be linear in r and s.

In the example of an encouragement design, there is a natural "causal order" to the variables S, R, and Y: S comes first, then R, and then Y. A path analysis uses a causal ordering to focus on certain regression functions; in the encouragement design, they are the two described above: $E(R|S=s)$ and $E(Y|S=s, R=r)$. Suppose, for sim-

FIGURE 3.

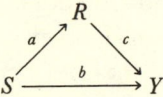

plicity, that they are both linear, i.e., that

$$E(R|S=s) = f(s) = as + d \tag{6}$$

and

$$E(Y|S=s, R=r) = g(s,r) = bs + cr + d'. \tag{7}$$

This defines a deterministic linear system, as described above, when we identify y with $g(s,r)$ and equate r and $f(s)$. We may associate the path diagram in Figure 1 with this system, but because we are dealing with the measurements S, R, and Y rather than the abstract variable s, r, and y, we relabel the nodes of the graph with S, R, and Y, as in Figure 3. The path coefficients in Figure 3 are just the (population) linear regression coefficients that may be estimated by a (linear) regression of R on S, and of Y on S and R. The same terminology is used as before for the direct effects: The regression coefficients are the direct effects. The "total effect" of S on Y, i.e. $b + ac$, can be interpreted as the coefficient of S in the regression of Y on S alone:

$$\begin{aligned}
E(Y|S) &= E(E(Y|S,R)|S) \\
&= E(bS + cR + d'|S) \\
&= bS + cE(R|S) + d' \\
&= bS + c(aS + d) + d' \\
&= (b + ac)S + dc + d'.
\end{aligned} \tag{8}$$

I will use the phrase *empirical path diagram* to refer to any path diagram constructed from a causal ordering and the implied set of linear regression functions. An empirical path diagram is, therefore, simply the result of computing certain regression coefficients and arranging them in the appropriate places in the diagram.

In path analysis, the causal order is given, often rather vaguely, by some sort of theory. One nice feature of encouragement designs is that the causal order of "S before R before Y" is consistent with the way the data might be collected and with our intuition about study and test performance. Once given, the causal order tells us which (linear) regression functions to estimate from the data. In the estimated regression functions, the coefficient of each independent variable is interpreted as the "effect" of that independent variable on the dependent variable. Thus, in (7), c is the "effect" of studying on test performance. This usage is typical of the casual causal talk (lamented by Rogosa [1987]) that often accompanies regression analyses. In section 4, I will show how causal effects can be precisely defined within Rubin's model and how specific assumptions are needed to conclude that regression coefficients are equal to causal effects.

A causal ordering is not sufficient to justify interpreting a regression coefficient as a causal effect. A causal ordering only tells the analyst which regression functions to estimate.

3.3. *Structural Equations Models*

In some areas of applied statistics—notably econometrics, but also parts of sociology, psychometrics, and even political science—it has become standard practice to use a framework that is, in a sense, more general than the conditional expectations and regression functions of path analysis, just described. These are called both structural equations models and simultaneous equations models. Instead of formulating a causal ordering or causal model for the encouragement design in terms of the regression functions, $E(R|S = s)$ and $E(Y|S = s, R = r)$, a structural equations model for such a design would be expressed as the following system of two equations:

$$R(u) = d + aS(u) + \varepsilon_1(u), \tag{9}$$

and

$$Y(u) = d' + bS(u) + cR(u) + \varepsilon_2(u). \tag{10}$$

In (9) and (10), S, R, and Y are as before, but $\varepsilon_1(u)$ and $\varepsilon_2(u)$ are new variables defined for all u's in U, so that equations (9) and (10) hold exactly for each u. The ε_1 and ε_2 are called error or disturbance terms; they take up the slack in the empirical relationship between R and S and between Y and R and S. The system (9) and (10) is "recursive," in the language of structural equations, because $Y(u)$ does not occur on the right-hand side of equation (9) (Goldberger 1964). The disturbance terms differ from the variables Y, R, and S in that they are unobservable. The three-variable system $(S(u),\ R(u),\ Y(u))$ is thus enlarged to a five-variable system $(S(u),\ R(u),\ Y(u),\ \varepsilon_1(u),\ \varepsilon_2(u))$, which defines a five-dimensional, multivariate distribution as u varies over U. This is what is meant by saying that S, R, Y, ε_1, and ε_2 are random variables. The causal interpretation of structural equations models, such as (9) and (10), is based on the following extension of the notion of "effect" in regression discussed earlier. For example, in equation (9), a is the "effect" of S on R, and ε_1 is that part of R that is determined by.all other relevant causes that are not measured (see Goldberger [1964] for an explicit statement along these lines). Thus, the equation $R = d + aS + \varepsilon_1$ is a tidy totaling of the effects of all causes, both measured (i.e. S) and unmeasured (i.e. ε_1), on R. The point of view that underlies such an interpretation of equation (9) is that the value of $R(u)$ is "caused," in some sense, by numerous factors including $S(u)$. This sense of causation is quite unclear because it makes vague references to the "causes" of the value of a variable, i.e. of $R(u)$, rather than to measuring the effect of the experimental manipulation described by $S(u)$. In section 4.4, I show how Rubin's model can be used to give causal interpretation of the parameters of models like (9) and (10) in some situations.

It is easy to show that without further assumptions on the joint distribution of the disturbance terms, ε_1 and ε_2, with R and S, equations (9) and (10) cannot necessarily be interpreted as conditional expectations. This is often discussed in econometrics as the conditions under which ordinary least squares estimates give unbiased estimates of structural parameters (e.g., Goldberger 1964). For example, if we assume equation (9) and compute $E(R|S = s)$, we get

$$E(R|S = s) = E(d + aS + \varepsilon_1 | S = s)$$
$$= d + as + E(\varepsilon_1 | S = s).$$

Thus, for $E(R|S = s) = as + d$, we need the joint distribution of ε_1 and S over U to satisfy

$$E(\varepsilon_1 | S = s) = 0, \quad \text{for } s = 0, 1. \tag{11}$$

A sufficient condition for this is the independence of ε_1 and S and the usual zero-expected-value condition, $E(\varepsilon_1) = 0$, for ε_1. Similarly, for

$$E(Y|S = s, R = r) = d' + bs + cr, \tag{12}$$

we need to satisfy the following condition:

$$E(\varepsilon_1 | S = s, R = r) = 0, \text{ for all } s \text{ and } r.$$

Structural equations models like (9) and (10) may be regarded as more general than the regression functions (6) and (7) precisely because we may impose assumptions on the distribution of the disturbance terms, ε_1 and ε_2, that *do not* necessarily result in a correspondence between the equations (9) and (10) and the regression functions (6) and (7). Unfortunately, since ε_1 and ε_2 are unobservable, it is not always evident how to verify assumptions made about them. For example, why should ε_1 be independent of S over U when by definition $\varepsilon_1 = R - aS - d$, i.e., when the very definition of ε_1 involves S? Such assumptions must be justified by considerations that go beyond the empirical data.

Structural equations models do little more to justify the causal interpretation of their coefficients than the causal orderings of path analysis. In both approaches, such causal interpretations are established by fiat rather than by deduction from more basic assumptions. Rubin's model, as I will show in the next section, allows one to formally state assumptions about unit-level causal effects that imply causal interpretations of regression coefficients and structural parameters.

4. A CAUSAL MODEL FOR ENCOURAGEMENT DESIGNS

The appendix gives an overview of Rubin's model as applied to randomized experiments and observational studies. In this section, I will extend that model to accommodate the added complexity of encouragement designs, with two levels of encouragement, t and c. I have tried to write this extension of Rubin's model so that the reader does not need to refer to the appendix to understand it, except for amplification of a few points.

4.1. *The General Model*

The key property of encouragement designs is that there is one cause—i.e. encouragement (indicated, as before, by $S(u) = 1$ or 0 as u is either exposed to t or c)—that affects another cause—i.e. amount of study (indicated by R)—and that these two causes, in turn, can affect the response of interest—i.e. test performance (indicated by Y). However, the mathematical structure of R and Y is really quite different from that used in section 3, where R and Y were both simply regarded as functions of u alone, $R(u)$ and $Y(u)$.

To begin, the amount that u studies depends, potentially, on u and on the encouragement condition to which u is exposed, so that R is really a function of u and s, where $s = t$ or c, i.e. $R(u, s)$. Thus,

$$R(u, t) = \text{amount } u \text{ studies if encouraged to study},$$
$$R(u, c) = \text{amount } u \text{ studies if not encouraged to study}. \tag{13}$$

Let $K = \{t, c\}$; then K is the set of encouragement conditions and R is a real-valued function on $U \times K$.

What about Y? The test performance of u depends, potentially, on u, on whether u is encouraged to study or not (s), and on the amount of time u studies (r). Hence, Y is a function of u, s, and r ($Y(u, s, r)$). Thus,

$$Y(u, t, r) = \text{test score for } u \text{ if } u \text{ is encouraged to study}$$
$$\text{and } u \text{ studies for } r \text{ hours},$$
$$Y(u, c, r) = \text{test score for } u \text{ if } u \text{ is } not \text{ encouraged to study}$$
$$\text{and } u \text{ studies for } r \text{ hours}. \tag{14}$$

The variable $S(u)$ depends only on u, as it did in section 3, since $S(u)$ indicates whether u is exposed to t or to c. I will engage in a slight abuse of notation and use $S(u) = t$ or c to index the encouragement condition to which u is exposed and $S(u) = 1$ or 0 to indicate the same thing when I need $S(u)$ to be a treatment indicator or dummy variable in a regression function, as in section 3.

In summary, the model for an encouragement design is a quintuple (U, K, S, R, Y), where U and K are sets, S maps U to K, R is a real-valued function of (u, s), and Y is a real-valued function of (u, s, r).

A subscript notation is useful, and we let

$$R_s(u) = R(u, s), \tag{15}$$

and

$$Y_{sr}(u) = Y(u, s, r). \tag{16}$$

Some people find such an explicit notation—i.e. $R(u, s)$ and $Y(u, s, r)$—loathsome, but I do not see how one can precisely define the elusive concepts that underlie causal inference without them. $R(u, s)$ and $Y(u, s, r)$ are not directly observable for all combinations of u, s, and r. This is the main reason why causal inference is difficult and involves something more than merely the study of associations. In section 3, I used $R(u)$ and $Y(u)$ to denote the values of R and Y that are observed for unit u. This standard notation is actually misleading because it does not reveal the causal structure of the problem. In terms of $S(u)$, $R(u, s)$, and $Y(u, s, r)$, the *observed values* of R and Y are properly defined as follows:

$$R_S(u) = R(u, S(u)) = \text{the observed } R\text{-response},\qquad (17)$$

and

$$Y_{SR_S}(u) = Y(u, S(u), R(u, S(u))) = \text{the observed } Y\text{-response.}\quad (18)$$

The use of "multiple versions" of the dependent variable— e.g. R_t and R_c, Y_{tr} and Y_{cr}—goes back to Neyman (1935) in the experimental design literature and is often implicit in the early work of Fisher (1926). See Holland (1986*b*, sect. 6) for more on the history of this notation.

The dependence of $R(u, s)$ and $Y(u, s, r)$ on the unit, u, is the way that Rubin's model accommodates individual variation in response to causes. This individual variation is just another way of conceptualizing the idea that the value of a response, say Y, depends both on causes that are measured, like s and r, and on other factors that affect u's responses in various ways.

The data obtained from any unit u in an encouragement design is the triple

$$\big(S(u), R_S(u), Y_{SR_S}(u)\big).\qquad (19)$$

In an encouragement design, the values of $S(u)$ are under experimental control, so that the value of $S(u)$ for each u can be determined by randomization. When U is infinite, randomization implies that $S(u)$ is statistically independent of $R_s(u)$ and $Y_{sr}(u)$ over U for any choices of s and r. When U is finite and large, randomization implies that the independence of S and R_s and of S and Y_{sr} over U holds approximately. This is discussed in more detail in the appendix. An important difference between the variables R_s and R_S and between Y_{sr} and Y_{SR_S} is that, except in very special circumstances, randomization does not imply that the observed variables R_S or Y_{SR_S} are statistically independent of S over U even though R_s and Y_{sr} are. For example,

$$P(R_S = r \mid S = t) = P(R_t = r \mid S = t) = P(R_t = r),$$

and unless $P(R_t = r) = P(R_c = r)$, it follows that $P(R_S = r|S = t) \neq P(R_S = r)$. (The "probabilities," $P(R_S = r|S = t)$, $P(R_t = r)$, etc., are to be interpreted simply as proportions of unit in U [see the appendix].) Thus, randomization may be used to justify the assumption that S and $\{R_s, Y_{sr}, \text{ for all } s, r\}$ are independent but not that S and the *observed values*, R_S and Y_{SR_S}, are independent.

There are four types of unit-level causal effects in this system: three different effects of encouragement (t) and one effect of studying (R). Thus, t can affect both R and Y, and two of the t effects are defined as follows:

$$R_t(u) - R_c(u) = \text{the causal effect of } t \text{ on } R, \qquad (20)$$

$$Y_{tR_t(u)}(u) - Y_{cR_c(u)}(u) = \text{the causal effect of } t \text{ on } Y. \qquad (21)$$

The definition in (20) is interpreted as the increment in the amount that unit u would study if encouraged to study over how much u would study if not encouraged. The definition in (21) is similar in that it is the increment in the test score u would receive if u were encouraged to study (and studied for $R_t(u)$ hours) over the test score u would receive if u were not encouraged to study (and studied for $R_c(u)$ hours).

In addition to (20) and (21), to specify the ALICE model in the next section, we need to define the effect of t on Y for fixed r, i.e., the effect of t on $Y(\cdot, \cdot, r)$. This is

$$Y_{tr}(u) - Y_{cr}(u) = \text{the causal effect of } t \text{ on } Y(\cdot, \cdot, r). \qquad (22)$$

Definition (22) is the "pure" effect of encouragement on test scores because it is the increment in u's test score when u studies r hours and is encouraged to study, compared with u's test score when u studies r hours but is not encouraged to study. Definition (22) is an explicit statement of the idea that the amount u studies is a self-selected treatment that can differ from what actually occurs, i.e., from the particular values $R_t(u)$ and $R_c(u)$ that appear in definition (21). The idea behind (22) is quite subtle and central to the notion of indirect causation. In the studying example used throughout this paper, it may be plausible to suppose that causal effects defined in (22) are all zero, but I will not make that assumption at this stage of the development so that I can apply the model to other cases in which these causal effects might not be zero.

The amount of study, R, can affect only Y, and the effect of R is defined as follows:

$$Y_{sr}(u) - Y_{sr'}(u) = \text{the effect of } R = r \text{ relative to } R = r' \text{ on } Y(\cdot, s, \cdot).$$
$$(23)$$

Definition (23) is also an explicit statement of the idea that amount of study is a self-selected treatment and can differ from the amount the student did study; i.e., r could have taken on values other than $R_t(u)$ and $R_c(u)$. In (23), the encouragement condition is fixed, s, and the causal effect of R is the change in test score that results when u studies r versus r' hours.

These four types of causal effects, i.e.,

$$R_t(u) - R_c(u), Y_{tR_t(u)}(u) - Y_{cR_c(u)}(u), Y_{tr}(u) - Y_{cr}(u)$$

$$\text{and } Y_{sr}(u) - Y_{sr'}(u),$$

are all defined on each unit and express the effect of encouragement and of studying on the behavior of individual students.

The key feature of Rubin's model is its use of unit-level causal effects as the basic building blocks for defining all other causal parameters. (Rogosa [1987] also emphasizes the importance of models that start at the level of individual units and build up.) Unit-level causal effects are never directly observable because of what I call the fundamental problem of causal inference (see the appendix), but they may be used to define causal parameters that can be estimated or measured with data.

Averaging each of the four types of unit-level causal effects over U results in the important causal parameters called *average causal effects*, or ACEs. The four ACEs are

$$\text{ACE}_{tc}(R) = E(R_t - R_c), \qquad (24)$$

$$\text{ACE}_{tc}(Y) = E(Y_{tR_t} - Y_{cR_c}), \qquad (25)$$

$$\text{ACE}_{tc}(Y(\cdot, \cdot, r)) = E(Y_{tr} - Y_{cr}), \qquad (26)$$

and

$$\text{ACE}_{rr'}(Y(\cdot, s, \cdot)) = E(Y_{sr} - Y_{sr'}). \qquad (27)$$

In (24)–(27) and below, we use $E(\ )$ to denote expectation or average over U. The ACEs are typically the only causal parameters that can be estimated with data. Under some conditions, such as those defined by the ALICE model discussed in section 4.2, an ACE may be interpreted as a unit-level causal effect, but in general it is not.

The ACEs must be distinguished from the *prima facie average causal effects*, or FACEs, which are defined in terms of the observables $S(u)$, $R_S(u)$, and $Y_{SR_S}(u)$. The four FACEs are the following differences in regression functions:

$$\text{FACE}_{tc}(R) = E(R_S|S=t) - E(R_S|S=c), \qquad (28)$$

$$\text{FACE}_{tc}(Y) = E(Y_{SR_S}|S=t) - E(Y_{SR_S}|S=c), \qquad (29)$$

$$\text{FACE}_{tc}(Y(\cdot,\cdot,r)) = E(Y_{SR_S}|S=t, R_S=r)$$
$$- E(Y_{SR_S}|S=c, R_S=r), \qquad (30)$$

$$\text{FACE}_{rr'}(Y(\cdot,s,\cdot)) = E(Y_{SR_S}|S=s, R_S=r)$$
$$- E(Y_{SR_S}|S=s, R_S=r'). \qquad (31)$$

Because they are based on the observables, the FACEs are associational parameters rather than causal parameters. They are *prima facie* ACEs rather than ACEs because they may or may not equal their corresponding ACEs, depending on whether certain assumptions are met. Causal inference in Rubin's model means inference about causal parameters, such as the ACEs. Such inferences must be made from observable data and hence the FACEs play an important role. For example, consider $\text{FACE}_{tc}(R)$. Since S is independent of R_t and R_c by assumption (a consequence of the random assignment of the encouragement conditions), we have

$$\begin{aligned}
\text{FACE}_{tc}(R) &= E(R_S|S=t) - E(R_S|S=c) \\
&= E(R_t|S=t) - E(R_c|S=c) \\
&= E(R_t) - E(R_c) \\
&= \text{ACE}_{tc}(R).
\end{aligned} \qquad (32)$$

Thus, because of random assignment, the causal parameter, $\text{ACE}_{tc}(R)$, and the associational parameters, $\text{FACE}_{tc}(R)$, are equal. Similarly, one may show that

$$\text{FACE}_{tc}(Y) = \text{ACE}_{tc}(Y), \qquad (33)$$

also because of the random assignment of encouragement.

The other two FACEs involve R_S, whose distribution is not under experimental control. First consider $\mathrm{FACE}_{tc}(Y(\cdot,\cdot,r))$

$$= E\big(Y_{SR_S}|S=t,R_S=r\big) - E\big(Y_{SR_S}|S=c,R_S=r\big)$$

$$= E(Y_{tr}|S=t,R_t=r) - E(Y_{cr}|S=c,R_c=r) \tag{34}$$

$$= E(Y_{tr}|R_t=r) - E(Y_{cr}|R_c=r).$$

In general, this does not equal $E(Y_{tr}) - E(Y_{cr})$. Therefore, we cannot use $\mathrm{FACE}_{tc}(Y(\cdot,\cdot,r))$ for $\mathrm{ACE}_{tc}(Y(\cdot,\cdot,r))$ without additional assumptions.

Next consider $\mathrm{FACE}_{rr'}(Y(\cdot,s,\cdot))$

$$= E\big(Y_{SR_S}|S=s,R_S=r\big) - E\big(Y_{SR_S}|S=s,R_S=r'\big)$$

$$= E(Y_{sr}|S=s,R_s=r) - E(Y_{sr'}|S=s,R_s=r') \tag{35}$$

$$= E(Y_{sr}|R_s=r) - E(Y_{sr'}|R_s=r').$$

Again, in general this does not equal the corresponding ACE, i.e. $E(Y_{sr}) - E(Y_{sr'})$, which is the average causal effect of studying on test performance that interests us in an encouragement design.

What can we conclude so far? First, assuming random assignment of the encouragement conditions to units, the FACEs based on the conditional expectations of R_S and of Y_{SR_S} given S are equal to their corresponding ACEs and thus have causal interpretations as ACEs. These FACEs would be estimated, in practice, by treatment-control mean differences for R_S and Y_{SR_S}, respectively. This result is not surprising, and related material is discussed in the appendix. The other two FACEs, those based on the conditional expectation of Y_{SR_S} given both S and R_S, do not equal their corresponding ACEs, in general; and in particular, without further assumptions it is not true that the "effect of studying" on test performance that one would obtain from a regression analysis of Y_{SR_S} on S and R_S can be interpreted as an average causal effect over U.

4.2. *The ALICE Model*

In Rubin's model, a causal theory specifies, or partially specifies, values for $R(u,s)$ and $Y(u,s,r)$. An important causal theory that I find helpful in understanding the relationship between this extension of Rubin's model and path analysis and structural equations models is what I call the *a*dditive, *li*near, *c*onstant *e*ffect, or ALICE, model. It is given by three equations that involve unit-level causal effects:

$$R_t(u) - R_c(u) = \rho, \tag{36}$$

$$Y_{tr}(u) - Y_{cr}(u) = \tau, \tag{37}$$

$$Y_{sr}(u) - Y_{sr'}(u) = \beta(r - r'). \tag{38}$$

In this model, the effects of t and r on Y for a given unit, u, are *additive*, the effect of values of r on Y enters *linearly*, and the causal effects of t on R and Y and of r on Y are constant, not depending on the unit; i.e., this is a causal theory with *constant effects* (see the appendix for more on constant effects). Equations (36)–(38) involve three of the four unit-level causal effects in (20)–(23). The fourth one, i.e. (21), can be expressed in terms of the other three:

$$Y_{t_{R_t}}(u) - Y_{c_{R_c}}(u) = \tau + \rho\beta. \tag{39}$$

In (36), ρ is the (constant) number of hours that encouragement increases each student's amount of study. In (39), $\tau + \rho\beta$ is the (constant) improvement in test scores due to encouragement to study. In (37), τ is the (constant) amount that encouragement increases the test scores of a student who always studies r. In (38), β is the (constant) amount that studying one hour more increases a student's test scores.

The ALICE model in (36)–(38) is equivalent to these two functional relations of the variables s and r for each fixed unit, u:

$$R_s(u) = R_c(u) + \rho s, \tag{40}$$

$$Y_{sr}(u) = Y_{c0}(u) + \tau s + \beta r. \tag{41}$$

On the right-hand sides of (40) and (41), s is a 0/1 variable, $Y_{c0}(u)$ is the test performance of u if u is not encouraged to study and doesn't study, and $R_c(u)$ is the amount u studies if not encouraged to study. The values of $Y_{c0}(u)$ and $R_c(u)$ will vary from student to student and are the vehicle for introducing unit heterogeneity into this model (see the appendix on unit homogeneity).

For a fixed unit, (40) and (41) are a deterministic linear system involving the functions $Y_{sr}(u)$ and $R_s(u)$ of the variables s and r. If we equate r and $R_s(u)$, then we have a deterministic linear system, and as in section 3, we may associate the path diagram of Figure 4 with it. I have left off the subscripts for R and Y in Figure 4 to emphasize that it does not describe empirical relationships in data; i.e., it is not an

FIGURE 4.

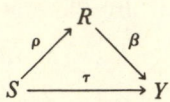

empirical path diagram. Rather, it is a theory about the values of $Y(u, s, r)$ and $R(u, s)$; i.e., it is a causal model or a causal theory.

The ALICE model may appear to be an extremely strong model, yet we shall see presently that it is not strong enough to ensure that the regression coefficients of path analysis have the desired causal interpretations.

The parameters of the ALICE model (ρ, β, and τ) may be used to express the four ACEs of the model. These are

$$\text{ACE}_{tc}(R) = \rho, \tag{42}$$

$$\text{ACE}_{tc}(Y) = \tau + \beta\rho, \tag{43}$$

$$\text{ACE}_{tc}(Y(\cdot, \cdot, r)) = \tau, \tag{44}$$

$$\text{ACE}_{rr'}(Y(\cdot, s, \cdot)) = \beta(r - r'). \tag{45}$$

The ALICE causal model is an example of a "constant effect" model (see the appendix). Consequently, in the ALICE model, the ACEs are interpretable as unit-level causal effects. This is seen by comparing (42)–(45) with (36)–(39).

We see that the "total effect" of S on Y in Figure 4 (i.e. $\tau + \beta\rho$) is an ACE. In addition, for the ALICE model, ρ, τ, and β can all be interpreted as ACEs. What about the FACEs? From the results of the previous subsection, we know that because of randomization,

$$\text{FACE}_{tc}(R) = \text{ACE}_{tc}(R) = \rho \tag{46}$$

and

$$\text{FACE}_{tc}(Y) = \text{ACE}_{tc}(Y) = \tau + \beta\rho. \tag{47}$$

The other two FACEs are more complicated. They may be shown to be given by the following formulas:

$$\text{FACE}_{tc}(Y(\cdot, \cdot, r)) = \tau + \mu_c(r - \rho) - \mu_c(r), \tag{48}$$

and

$$\text{FACE}_{tc}(Y(\cdot, s, \cdot)) = \beta(r - r') + \mu_s(r) - \mu_s(r'), \tag{49}$$

where

$$\mu_s(r) = E(Y_{c0}|R_s = r) \text{ for } s = t, c. \tag{50}$$

Thus, the two remaining FACEs both equal their corresponding ACEs plus biases that involve the regression of Y_{c0} on R_s, i.e. $\mu_s(r)$.

The value of $\mu_c(r)$ is the average value of test scores for students when they are not encouraged to study *and* they do not study, for all those students who would study an amount r when they are not encouraged to study. Thus, $\mu_c(r)$ is a "counterfactual" regression because Y_{c0} and R_s can *never* be simultaneously observed except when $R_s = 0$. Hence, $\mu_c(r)$ is inherently unobservable, and assumptions made about it have no empirical consequences that can be directly tested. The function $\mu_c(r)$ is a complicated quantity and one that is not easily thought about. Suppose, for simplicity, that it is linear, i.e., that

$$\mu_c(r) = \gamma + \delta r. \tag{51}$$

A positive δ means that the more a student would study when not encouraged, the *higher* he or she would score on the test without studying and without encouragement. A negative δ means that the more a student would study when not encouraged, the *lower* he or she would score without studying and without encouragement.

The quantities computed in path analysis are the conditional expectations

$$E(R_S|S) = E(R_c) + \rho S \tag{52}$$

and

$$E(Y_{SR_S}|S, R_S) = \mu_c(R_S - \rho S) + \tau S + \beta R_S, \tag{53}$$

in which S is a $1/0$ indicator variable. If we make the untestable assumption that $\mu_c(r)$ is linear, e.g. (51), then (53) becomes

$$E(Y_{SR_S}|S, R_S) = \gamma + (\tau - \delta\rho)S + (\beta + \delta)R_S. \tag{54}$$

Equations (52) and (54) are both linear and may be combined into the empirical path diagram in Figure 5.

Comparing Figures 5 and 4, we see that even if the ALICE model holds and $\mu_c(r)$ is linear, the estimated path coefficients are

FIGURE 5.

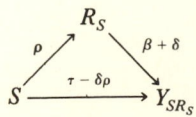

biased estimates of the causal effects τ and β unless $\mu_c(r)$ does not depend on r (i.e. $\delta = 0$). Furthermore, these problems stem from the inhomogeneity of the units with respect to the values of $R_c(u)$ and $Y_{c0}(u)$. This inhomogeneity is, I believe, the proper way to view the "disturbance terms" of the structural equations model (9) and (10) in section 3 (see section 4.4). One nice thing is that while the *direct effects* are not the same in Figures 5 and 4, the total effects are: Both equal $\tau + \rho\beta$.

4.3. *Two Different Ways to Estimate the Causal Effect of the Encouraged Activity*

The message of the previous subsection is that the effect of study on test performance cannot be estimated by the usual regression methods of path analysis without making untestable assumptions about the counterfactual regression function, $\mu_c(r)$. If we assume that $\mu_c(r)$ is constant, then the biases shown in Figure 5 vanish and the usual path coefficients may be interpreted as causal effects, i.e. as ACEs. However, because $\mu_c(r)$ is so difficult to think about, there is little reason to believe that it is constant. Nor can δ be easily assessed as either positive or negative, since, in this example, there are reasons why it might be either: If students who study a lot tend to be those who do well even when they don't study, then δ is positive; but if those who study a lot are those who need to study, then δ is negative.

An alternative approach is to suppose that encouragement, of and by itself, has no effect on Y. In the studying example, this might be a plausible assumption. This corresponds to the restriction that

$$\tau = 0. \tag{55}$$

Now the empirical path diagram becomes that in Figure 6, and the path diagram for the causal theory becomes that in Figure 7. The total effect of S on Y_{SR_S} is now $\rho\beta$, whereas the total effect of S on R_S is ρ.

FIGURE 6.

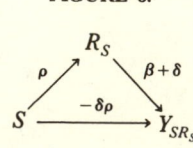

FIGURE 7.

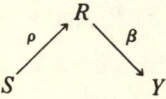

Hence,

$$\beta = \frac{\rho\beta}{\rho} = \frac{\text{total effect of } S \text{ on } Y_{SR_S}}{\text{total effect of } S \text{ on } R_S}. \tag{56}$$

This is also easily seen from the definitions of the ACEs and the FACEs. Under the assumption that $\tau = 0$,

$$\text{ACE}_{tc}(Y) = \text{FACE}_{tc}(Y) = \beta\rho, \tag{57}$$

regardless of whether or not $\mu_c(r)$ is linear, and hence

$$\beta = \frac{\text{ACE}_{tc}(Y)}{\text{ACE}_{tc}(R)} = \frac{\text{FACE}_{tc}(Y)}{\text{FACE}_{tc}(R)}. \tag{58}$$

The two FACEs in (58) may be estimated simply by the treatment-control mean difference in Y_{SR_S} and R_S, as mentioned earlier, so that (58) provides an alternative way to estimate β that does not assume that $\mu_c(r)$ is constant. In Powers and Swinton (1984), (58) was used to estimate β.

4.4. Deriving a Structural Equations Model

The ALICE model may be used to derive the structural equations model given in (9) and (10). If we substitute $S(u)$ for s in (40) and $S(u)$ for s and $R_S(u)$ for r in (41), we get the following pair of equations that involve the observables, S, R_S, Y_{SR_S}:

$$R_S(u) = R_c(u) + \rho S(u) \tag{59}$$

and

$$Y_{SR_S}(u) = Y_{c0}(u) + \tau S(u) + \beta R_S(u). \tag{60}$$

Now let

$$\eta_1(u) = R_c(u) - E(R_c)$$

and

$$\eta_2(u) = Y_{c0}(u) - E(Y_{c0}),$$

and then define

$$\alpha = E(R_c), \alpha' = E(Y_{c0}).$$

The following equations, which parallel the structural equations model of (9) and (10), follow immediately:

$$R_S(u) = \alpha + \rho S(u) + \eta_1(u), \tag{61}$$

$$Y_{SR_S}(u) = \alpha' + \tau S(u) + \beta R_S(u) + \eta_2(u). \tag{62}$$

It is easy to see from the definition of η_1 and η_2 that by the independence assumption (justified by randomization), S is independent of η_1 and η_2 over U. But R_S is not independent of η_2 in general. In fact, the condition that equation (62) be interpretable as a conditional expectation is exactly that $\mu_c(r)$ be constant. It follows from the standard theory of structural equations models that ordinary least squares estimates of β are biased in general, so that a simple regression analysis of (62) would not lead to an estimate of the causal effect of studying on test scores. Substituting (61) for R_S in (62) yields

$$\begin{aligned} Y_{SR_S}(u) &= \alpha' + \beta\alpha + (\tau + \rho\beta)S(u) + \beta\eta_1(u) + \eta_2(u) \\ &= a'' + (\tau + \rho\beta)S(u) + \eta_3(u). \end{aligned} \tag{63}$$

Equations (61) and (63) constitute the so-called reduced form of the system (61) and (62). Since S is independent of η_1 and η_2, S is also independent of $\eta_3 = \beta\eta_1 + \eta_2$ in (63). Thus, (61) and (63) can be interpreted as regression functions; therefore, in the language of structural equations models, (61) can be used to estimate ρ and (62) can be used to estimate $\tau + \rho\beta$. Assuming $\tau = 0$ now leads to the second estimate of β discussed in section 4.3.

In closing this section, I point out that the ALICE model leads to the structural equations system (61) and (62); but the ALICE model could be wrong, in various, often testable, ways. Freedman (1987) has argued that models like (61) and (62) should be tested before they are used. Rubin's model gives us a framework for doing that testing. But an assumption like $\tau = 0$ is not testable with the data in hand and must be justified on other grounds.

5. DISCUSSION

One purpose of this paper is to show that path analysis and its generalization, structural equations models, do not justify causal interpretations of regression coefficients. Instead, these models simply define certain regression coefficients as causal effects by fiat, using the loose causal terminology of regression analysis. Rubin's model, on the other hand, precisely defines unit-level causal effects, and these, in turn, may be used to deduce causal interpretations of *some* regression coefficients under *some* assumptions. By explicitly separating the causal theory, $R(u, s)$ and $Y(u, s, r)$, from the observed data, ($S(u)$, $R_S(u)$, and $Y_{SR_S}(u)$), Rubin's model provides analysts with a set of tools that engender careful thought about causal theories and their relationship to data.

One example of such "careful thought" is the care that must be exercised in identifying variables in complex path models that can truly play the role of both effect and cause. Such variables must measure the amount of exposure of units to a cause and be themselves influenced by another cause. I used the encouragement design to focus my analysis precisely because it is a clearly interpretable example of indirect causation in this sense. Many causal models in the literature are not careful about this point; at best, they merely measure the association between variables rather than produce estimates of causal effects.

I am a little reluctant to place as much emphasis as I have on the ALICE model of section 4, because I do not wish to appear to endorse it as the only way to analyze data from encouragement designs. (For example, it would be inappropriate if "studying" were measured simply as a studied/didn't study dichotomy.) I simply put the ALICE model forward as a basic case from which deductions are easily made and which has interesting consequences for path analysis models. It is a model that captures some of the complexity of encouragement designs and self-selected treatments. Heterogeneity, nonlinearity, and nonadditivity can be added to the ALICE model in various ways to add complexity when that is necessary for proper analyses.

The two alternative ways to estimate the effect of studying on test scores given in section 4.3 were discussed simply to illustrate how the causal model must be used to produce estimates of causal effects. In the studying example, at least, the untestable assumption that $\tau = 0$ is more believable (and understandable) than the untestable assumption that leads to the usual path analytic estimate of the causal effect, i.e. $\delta = 0$. Furthermore, though the structural equations model of (61) and (62) can be used to obtain the ratio estimate of β in section 4.3, there is no way to justify these equations except through the ALICE model, or its generalizations.

FIGURE 8.

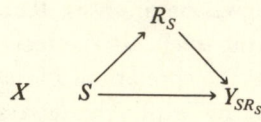

The assumption of random assignment of the encouragement condition is an important starting place, but there may be applications in which this is impossible or implausible, and we need to consider the corresponding observational study in which S is not independent of $\{R_s\}$ and $\{Y_{sr}\}$. An interesting generalization is to replace randomization by a strong ignorability type of condition given a covariate, $X(u)$ (see the appendix). For example, suppose that there is a covariate X such that given X, S is conditionally independent of $\{R_s\}$ and $\{Y_{sr}\}$. Now, all the equations of section 4 will hold conditionally given X, and the calculation of the FACEs is replaced by the corresponding *covariate-adjusted* FACEs, i.e. the C-FACEs (see the appendix). How might we wish to represent such a system in terms of path diagrams? In Holland (1986b), I suggested that an arrow connect two variables only if one indicated a cause (like S or R_S) and the other measured a response (like R_S or Y_{SR_S}). A covariate does not have the status of a causal indicator or of a response, so it ought not be involved with the arrows, according to such a view. Hence, the four-variable system of $(X(u), S(u), R_S(u), Y_{SR_S}(u))$ could be represented as in Figure 8, in which X precedes S and R, to indicate that it is not affected by either causal variable. However, it might be useful to indicate the conditional independence of S and all the variables $\{R_s\}$ and $\{Y_{sr}\}$ given X. This should be done, not in an empirical path diagram like Figure 8, but in a path diagram for a causal theory, like Figure 4. Conditional independence also plays an important role in structural equations models with latent variables, but that is a subject worthy of another paper. The importance of conditional independence suggests the use of two types of arrows in path diagrams: e.g., solid arrows to indicate causal relations and something like dashed arrows to indicate conditional independence. In the complex causal models of the current literature, such distinctions are not made and all arrows indicate causality. This is a mistake and leads to careless and casual causal talk. I hope that my illustration of how Rubin's model can be used to give precision to causal modeling will stimulate similar analyses of more complex causal models.

APPENDIX: A BRIEF REVIEW OF RUBIN'S MODEL
FOR EXPERIMENTS AND OBSERVATIONAL STUDIES

Discussions of Rubin's model similar to the one here may be found in Holland (1986*a*, *b*). Uses of the model in a variety of significant applications appear in Rubin (1974, 1977, 1978), Holland and Rubin (1983, 1987), Rosenbaum and Rubin (1983*a*, *b*; 1984*a*, *b*; 1985*a*, *b*), Rosenbaum (1984*a*, *b*, *c*; 1987), and Holland (1988). In the simplest case, the logical elements of Rubin's model form a quadruple (U, K, S, Y) where U is a population of units, K is a set of causes or treatments to which each one of the units in U may be exposed, $S(u) = s$ if s is the cause in K to which u is actually exposed, and $Y(u, s) = $ the value of the response that would be observed if unit $u \in U$ were exposed to cause $s \in K$.

The meaning of $Y(u, s)$ needs some explanation. The response variable, Y, depends both on the unit *and* on the cause or treatment to which the unit is exposed. The idea is that if u were exposed to $t \in K$, then we would observe the response value $Y(u, t)$; but if u were exposed to $c \in K$, then we would observe the response value $Y(u, c)$. The requirement that Y be a function on *pairs* (u, s) means that $Y(u, s)$ represents the measurement of some property of u after u is exposed to cause $s \in K$. This has the important consequence of forcing the things that are called causes in K to be *potentially exposable* to any unit in U. This restriction on the notion of cause is of fundamental importance because it prevents us from interpreting a variety of associations as causal: e.g., associations between sex and income or between race and crime. This is discussed more extensively in Holland (1986*b*, sect. 7) and in Holland (1988). The function Y is called the *response function*. In the references cited at the beginning of this section, a subscript notation is used for $Y(u, s)$; i.e.,

$$Y_s(u) = Y(u, s).$$

The subscript notation is convenient, and I will use it when appropriate.

The mapping, S, is the *causal indicator* or assignment rule because it indicates the cause to which each unit is exposed.

The elements of the quadruple (U, K, S, Y) are the *primitives* of Rubin's model, and they serve as the undefined terms. All other concepts are defined in terms of these primitives.

The most basic quantity in need of definition is the *observed response* on each unit $u \in U$. This is given by

$$Y_S(u) = Y(u, S(u)).$$

The value $Y_S(u)$ is the value of Y that is actually observed for unit u. The observed data for unit u, in the simplest case, is the pair

$$(S(u), Y_S(u)),$$

where $S(u)$ is the cause or treatment in K to which u is actually exposed and $Y_S(u)$ is the observed value of the response, Y. It is important to distinguish $Y_S(u)$ from $Y(u, s)$: $Y_S(u)$ is the response that is actually observed on unit u, and $Y(u, s)$ is a potentially observed value that is actually observed only if $S(u) = s$.

Note that in the subscript notation, the observed response, $Y_S(u)$, is $Y_{S(u)}(u)$, so that in the usual probabilistic sense, Y_s has a "fixed" subscript and Y_S has a "random" subscript.

In Rubin's model, *causes* are taken as *undefined* elements of the theory, and *effects* are *defined* in terms of the elements of the model.

Definition. The unit-level causal effect of cause $t \in K$ relative to cause $c \in K$ (as measured by Y) is the difference

$$Y(u, t) - Y(u, c) = T_{tc}(u).$$

Hence, the *causal effect*, $T_{tc}(u)$, is the *increase* in the value of $Y(u, t)$, which is what would be observed if u were exposed to t, over that of $Y(u, c)$, which is what would be observed if u were exposed to c. Glymour (1986) points out that in Rubin's model, effects are defined *counterfactually*; i.e., their definitions include sentences of the form "If A were the case then B would be the case," in which A could be false. It should also be noted that $T_{tc}(u)$ is defined *relatively* (i.e., the effect of one cause or treatment is *always* relative to another cause) and at the level of individual units.

The fundamental problem of causal inference. The most vexing problem in causal inference is that it is impossible to simultaneously observe both $Y(u, t)$ and $Y(u, c)$ for two distinct causes t and c; therefore, the causal effect, $T_{tc}(u)$, is *never* directly observable. Rubin's model makes this explicit by separating the *observed data* (S, Y_S) from the function Y. A *causal model* or a *causal theory* is a specification or partial specification of the values of the function Y. Causal inference consists of combining

(a) a causal theory, (b) assumptions about data collection, and (c) the observed data to draw conclusions about causal parameters. Many techniques of experimental science are aimed at overcoming the fundamental problem of causal inference by assuming plausible causal theories and then combining them appropriately with data. Some examples of such causal theories are given in the next several paragraphs.

Unit homogeneity. In a scientific laboratory, care is exercised to prepare homogeneous samples of material for study. Such care is often taken to make the following partial specification of Y plausible:

$$Y(u, s) = Y(v, s) \quad \text{for all } u, v \in U \text{ and all } s \in K.$$

This means that the responses of *all* units to cause s are the same, i.e., that units respond homogeneously to each cause. In Holland (1986a), I called this the assumption of *unit homogeneity.* It is a partial specification of Y because it restricts the values that Y can take on but it does not specify them completely. If one assumes unit homogeneity, then the causal effect, $T_{tc}(u)$, is easily seen to be given by

$$T_{tc}(u) = Y_t(u) - Y_c(v),$$

for any two distinct units u and v in U. In this case, the effect of t (relative to c) is constant and does not depend on the unit under consideration—a case I call constant effect (see below). Unit homogeneity solves the fundamental problem of causal inference by letting us use the data from two units to measure the causal effect on any single unit.

Fisher's null hypothesis. An assumption about Y that has a long history in statistics and that is formally similar to unit homogeneity is Fisher's null hypothesis:

$$Y(u, s) = Y(u, s') \quad \text{for all } u \in U \text{ and all } s, s'.$$

This means that the response of each unit is unaffected by the cause or treatment to which it is exposed. This is also a partial specification of Y and is a causal theory. Fisher's null hypothesis addresses the fundamental problem of causal inference by assuming that once we observe the value of Y for the pair (u, s), we know the value of Y for the pair (u, s') for any other value of $s' \in K$. Under Fisher's null hypothesis,

$$T_{tc}(u) = 0 \quad \text{for all } u \in U \text{ and all } t, c \in K.$$

So far, I have not given any examples in which assumptions about the data collection process matter. At the population level, "data collection" is contained in the causal indicator variable, S, since S describes the cause to which each unit in U is exposed. Suppose we now consider the joint distribution of S with $\{Y_s : s \in K\}$ as u varies over all of U. By using the term *joint distribution*, I do not mean to imply that S or the $\{Y_s\}$ are stochastic. However, we can use the language of probability to describe this joint distribution. For example, $P(S = s)$ is the proportion of units for which $S(u) = s$, and $E(Y_S | S = t)$ is the average value of Y_S for all those units for which $S(u) = t$. This use of probability notation allows us to discuss other, more statistical, approaches to solving the fundamental problem of causal inference in a convenient manner.

The average causal effect (ACE). We may define an important causal parameter, the ACE, as the average value of $T_{tc}(u)$ over U, or

$$\mathrm{ACE}_{tc} = E(T_{tc}).$$

In this notation, $E(T_{tc})$ denotes the average value of $T_{tc}(u)$, over all $u \in U$. But by definition of $T_{tc}(u)$, this is equivalent to the difference

$$\mathrm{ACE}_{tc}(Y) = E(Y_t) - E(Y_c).$$

The ACE is a useful summary of the unit-level causal effects, $T_{tc}(u)$, when $T_{tc}(u)$ varies little as u ranges over U. In some cases, we are interested in average behavior over the population of units, and in such a case, the ACE is useful regardless of how much $T_{tc}(u)$ varies with u.

When we look at data, we can only observe $S(u)$ and $Y_S(u)$ over U; hence, we can observe data only from the joint distribution of S and Y_S (as opposed to S and $\{Y_s : s \in K\}$). For example, the average value of the observed response Y_S among all those units exposed to cause t is

$$E(Y_S | S = t) = E(Y_t | S = t),$$

and the average value of the observed response among all those units exposed to cause c is

$$E(Y_S | S = c) = E(Y_c | S = c).$$

The difference in average responses between those units exposed to t and those units exposed to c is the *prima facie average causal effect* (FACE) and is given by

$$\mathrm{FACE}_{tc}(Y) = E(Y_S | S = t) - E(Y_S | S = c)$$
$$= E(Y_t | S = t) - E(Y_c | S = c).$$

I use FACE and ACE to draw attention to the fact that we can always compute the FACE from data but that it does not necessarily equal the quantity about which we wish to make an inference, i.e. the ACE. The difference between the FACE and the ACE resides in the difference between

$$E(Y_t) \text{ and } E(Y_t|S = t)$$

and between

$$E(Y_c) \text{ and } E(Y_c|S = c).$$

$E(Y_t)$ is the average of Y_t over all of U, whereas $E(Y_t|S = t)$ is the average of Y_t over only those units that are actually exposed to t. The same is true for $E(Y_c)$ and $E(Y_c|S = c)$.

Independence. It is now time to show the effect of randomization on Rubin's model. Suppose S is independent of $\{Y_s: s \in K\}$. When independence holds we have

$$E(Y_t|S = t) = E(Y_t)$$

and

$$E(Y_c|S = c) = E(Y_c).$$

Hence, if S is independent of $\{Y_s: s \in K\}$, the FACE and the ACE are equal; i.e.,

$$\begin{aligned}
\text{FACE}_{tc}(Y) &= E(Y_t|S = t) - E(Y_c|S = c) \\
&= E(Y_t) - E(Y_c) \\
&= \text{ACE}_{tc}(Y).
\end{aligned}$$

Thus, independence is important because it relates a causal parameter, i.e. the ACE, to an associational parameter, i.e. the FACE, that can be computed or estimated from the observed data, S and Y_S.

Randomization is related to independence in the following way. Independence is an assumption about the data collection process, i.e., about the relationship between S and Y over the population U. Randomization is a physical process that gives *plausibility* to the independence assumption in some important cases. For example, if U were infinite, then the strong law of large numbers coupled with randomization implies that almost every realization of S would be independent of $\{Y_s\}$. Randomization does not *always* make independence plausible; the best example of this is the case of a small population of units. If U contains only two units, then the physical act of randomization does not make the independence assumption plausible, even though it may still be useful in forming the basis of a test of Fisher's null hypothesis.

Constant effect. An important causal theory is the *constant effect* assumption. Constant effect holds when $T_{tc}(u)$ does not depend on u, i.e., when $T_{tc}(u) = \tau_{tc}$ for all u. This is equivalent to

$$Y_t(u) = Y_c(u) + \tau_{tc}.$$

Thus, *constant effect* is the same as *additivity* in the ANOVA sense. I prefer *constant effect*, since it is more descriptive of the causal theory being assumed.

When constant effect holds, it is easy to see that τ_{tc} equals the $\mathrm{ACE}_{tc}(Y)$:

$$\mathrm{ACE}_{tc}(Y) = E(T_{tc}) = \tau_{tc}.$$

What about the FACE?

$$\begin{aligned}
\mathrm{FACE}_{tc}(Y) &= E(Y_t|S=t) - E(Y_c|S=c) \\
&= E(Y_c + \tau_{tc}|S=t) - E(Y_c|S=c) \\
&= \tau_{tc} + \{ E(Y_c|S=t) - E(Y_c|S=c) \}.
\end{aligned}$$

Hence, under the constant effect assumption,

$$\mathrm{FACE}_{tc}(Y) = \mathrm{ACE}_{tc}(Y) + \mathrm{BIAS},$$

where $\mathrm{BIAS} = E(Y_c|S=t) - E(Y_c|S=c)$. The term BIAS involves the "counterfactual conditional expectation," $E(Y_c|S=t)$, which cannot be computed from data because it is the average value of Y_c among all those units that were exposed to t (and for which only the value of Y_t is known). Under independence, $\mathrm{BIAS} = 0$, and as before, the FACE and the ACE are equal.

Introducing other variables into Rubin's model. So far, I have discussed the simplest form of Rubin's model, in which there is only one variable measured on the units—aside from the causal indicator, S. Now suppose there is a second variable, X. In Rubin's model, X is introduced as a second real-valued function on $U \times K$, $X(u, s)$. The fact that X is real-valued is not important; it could be vector-valued. What is important is that we allow for the fact that, in general, X could depend on both u and s. A special class of variables are the *covariates*.

Definition. X is a covariate if $X(u, s)$ does not depend on s for any $u \in U$.

In Holland (1986a), I used the term *attributes* to refer to *covariates*, but the latter term is preferable because it corresponds to normal experimental usage. Variables measured on units prior to their exposure to treatments are always covariates. Rosenbaum (1984c) discusses post-treatment concomitants and their use in statistical adjustments. A post-treatment concomitant is a variable measured *after* the exposure of a unit to the causes in K. For a post-treatment concomitant, the possibility that $X(u, s)$ *does* depend on s cannot be ignored and must be decided. If $X(u, s)$ does depend on s, then X is *not* a covariate in the sense used here.

Observational studies. When the active experimenter is replaced by a passive observer who cannot arrange the values of $S(u)$ to achieve independence, we enter the realm of observational studies. In such studies we are also interested in measuring causal effects; i.e., Rubin's model still applies, but now S is not automatically independent of $\{Y_s\}$. In an observational study, we typically have a covariate, X, and we may check the distribution of X in each exposure group by comparing the values of

$$P(X = x | S = s)$$

across the values of $s \in K$. If there is evidence that $P(X = x | S = s)$ depends on s, then, depending on the nature of X and Y, we may not believe that the independence assumption holds in an observational study. However, we might be willing to entertain a weaker *conditional independence* assumption of the form, given the covariate, X, the variables S, and $\{Y_s : s \in K\}$ are conditionally independent. Combined with the assumption that $P(S = s | X = x) > 0$, the conditional independence assumption is called *strong ignorability* (Rosenbaum and Rubin 1983a).

Strong ignorability is the basis for all covariate-adjusted causal effects in observational studies. Covariate adjustments are based on the conditional expectations or regression functions $E(Y_S | S = s, X = x)$, which are used to form the *covariate-adjusted* FACE, i.e., the C-FACE, given by

$$\text{C-FACE}_{tc}(Y) = E\{E(Y_S | S = t, X) - E(Y_S | S = c, X)\}.$$

The C-FACE is like the FACE in that it is generally *not* equal to the

ACE, but under conditional independence it is:

$$\text{C-FACE}_{tc}(Y) = E\{E(Y_t|S=t, X) - E(Y_c|S=c, X)\}$$

$$= E\{E(Y_t|X) - E(Y_c|X)\}$$

$$= E(Y_t) - E(Y_c)$$

$$= \text{ACE}_{tc}(Y).$$

Rubin's model was really developed to address the problem of causal inference in observational studies, and thorough discussions of its application to these types of studies can be found in Rubin (1974, 1977), Holland and Rubin (1983), Rosenbaum and Rubin (1983a, b; 1984b; 1985a, b), and Rosenbaum (1984a, b, c; 1987).

REFERENCES

Blalock, H. M. 1964. *Causal Inferences in Nonexperimental Research*. Chapel Hill: University of North Carolina Press.

——————. 1971. *Causal Models in the Social Sciences*. Chicago: Aldine.

Campbell, D. T., and J. C. Stanley. 1963. *Experimental and Quasi-Experimental Designs for Research*. Chicago: Rand-McNally.

Duncan, O. D. 1966. "Path Analysis: Sociological Examples." *American Journal of Sociology* 72:1–16.

——————. 1975. *Introduction to Structural Equation Models*. New York: Academic Press.

Fisher, R. A. 1926. "The Arrangement of Field Experiments." *Journal of Ministry of Agriculture* 33:503–13.

Freedman, D. A. 1987. "As Others See Us: A Case Study in Path Analysis." *Journal of Educational Statistics* 12:101–28.

Glymour, C. 1986. "Statistics and Metaphysics." Discussion of "Statistics and Causal Inference" by P. W. Holland. *Journal of the American Statistical Association* 81:964–66.

Goldberger, A. S. 1964. *Econometric Theory*. New York: Wiley.

Goldberger, A. S., and O. D. Duncan. 1973. *Structural Equations Models in the Social Sciences*. New York: Seminar Press.

Heise, D. R. 1975. *Causal Analysis*. New York: Wiley.

Holland, P. W. 1986a. "Which Comes First, Cause or Effect?" *New York Statistician* 38:1–6.

——————. 1986b. "Statistics and Causal Inference." *Journal of the American Statistical Association* 81:945–70.

_____. 1988. "Causal Mechanism or Causal Effect: Which is Best for Statistical Sciences?" Discussion of "Employment Discrimination and Statistical Science" by A. P. Dempster. *Statistical Science* (in press).

Holland, P. W., and D. B. Rubin. 1983. "On Lord's Paradox." Pp. 3–25 in *Principals of Modern Psychological Measurement*, edited by H. Wainer and S. Messick. Hillsdale, NJ: Lawrence Erlbaum.

_____. 1987. "Causal Inference in Retrospective Studies." Technical Report No. 87-73. Princeton: Educational Testing Service Program Statistics Research.

Kenny, D. A. 1979. *Correlation and Causality*. New York: Wiley.

Lewis, D. 1986. *Philosophical Papers*. Vol. 2. Oxford: Oxford University Press.

Neyman, J. 1935. (With K. Iwaszkiewicz and S. Kolodziejczyk) "Statistical Problems in Agricultural Experimentation" (with discussion). *Journal of the Royal Statistical Society*, Suppl., 2:107–80.

Powers, D. E., and S. S. Swinton. 1984. "Effects of Self-Study for Coachable Test Item Types." *Journal of Educational Measurement* 76:266–78.

Robins, J. M. 1984. "A Statistical Method to Control for the Healthy Worker Effect in Intracohort Comparisons." *American Journal of Epidemiology* 120:465.

_____. 1985. "A New Theory of Causality in Observational Survival Studies—Application to the Healthy Worker Effect." *Biometrics* 41:311.

_____. 1986. "A New Approach to Causal Inference in Mortality Studies with a Sustained Exposure Period—Application to the Control of the Healthy Worker Survivor Effect." *Mathematical Modelling* 7:1393–1512.

Rogosa, D. 1987. "Casual Models Do Not Support Scientific Conclusion: A Comment in Support of Freedman." *Journal of Educational Statistics* 12:185–95.

Rosenbaum, P. R. 1984a. "From Association to Causation in Observational Studies: The Role of Tests of Strongly Ignorable Treatment Assignment." *Journal of the American Statistical Association* 79:41–48.

_____. 1984b. "The Consequences of Adjustment for a Concomitant Variable that has been Affected by the Treatment." *Journal of the Royal Statistical Society*, ser. A, 147:656–66.

_____. 1984c. "Conditional Permutation Tests and the Propensity Score in Observational Studies." *Journal of the American Statistical Association* 79:565–74.

_____. 1987. "The Role of a Second Control Group in an Observational Study" (with discussion). *Statistical Science* 2:292–316.

Rosenbaum, P. R., and D. B. Rubin. 1983a. "The Central Role of the Propensity Score in Observational Studies for Causal Effects." *Biometrika* 70:41–55.

_____. 1983b. "Assessing Sensitivity to an Unobserved Binary Covariate in an Observational Study with Binary Outcome." *Journal of the Royal Statistical Society*, ser. B, 45:212–18.

_____. 1984*a*. Discussion of "On the Nature and Discovery of Structure" by J. W. Pratt and R. Schlaifer. *Journal of the American Statistical Association* 79:26–28.

_____. 1984*b*. "Reducing Bias in Observational Studies using Subclassification on the Propensity Score." *Journal of the American Statistical Association* 79:516–24.

_____. 1985*a*. "Constructing a Control Group using Multivariate Matched Sampling Methods that Incorporate the Propensity Score." *American Statistician* 39:33–38.

_____. 1985*b*. "The Bias Due to Incomplete Matching." *Biometrics* 41:103–16.

Rubin, D. B. 1974. "Estimating Causal Effects of Treatments in Randomized and Nonrandomized Studies." *Journal of Educational Psychology* 66:688–701.

_____. 1977. "Assignment of Treatment Group on the Basis of a Covariate." *Journal of Educational Statistics* 2:1–26.

_____. 1978. "Bayesian Inference for Causal Effects: The Role of Randomization." *Annals of Statistics* 6:34–58.

_____. 1980. Discussion of "Randomization Analysis of Experimental Data: The Fisher Randomization Test" by D. Basu. *Journal of the American Statistical Association* 75:591–93.

_____. 1986. "Which Ifs Have Causal Answers?" Discussion of "Statistics and Causal Inference" by P. W. Holland. *Journal of the American Statistical Association* 81:961–62.

Saris, W. E., and L. H. Stronkhorst. 1984. *Causal Modeling in Nonexperimental Research*. Amsterdam: Sociometric Research Foundation.

Swinton, S. 1975. "An Encouraging Note." Unpublished manuscript.

Tukey, J. W. 1954. "Causation, Regression, and Path Analysis." Pp. 35–66 in *Statistics and Mathematics in Biology*, edited by O. Kempthorne. Ames, IA: Iowa State College Press.

Wright, S. 1934. "The Method of Path Coefficients." *Annals of Mathematical Statistics* 5:161–215.

𝕏14𝕏

Discussion

*Edward E. Leamer**

What's the news?

Let's take a blue-collar attitude toward these discussions of causality. Doesn't the typical person have a pretty fair understanding of what is meant by the statement "X is a cause of Y"? And isn't it also pretty clear what is evidence of a causal connection and what is not? Certainly courts of law proceed as if this were the case. Few court cases get involved with the philosophical complexities of defining the concept of causation. But that doesn't mean that us working folks have nothing to learn about causation. It only means that the burden of proof is on those who claim otherwise.

I confess to being primarily a theoretical econometrician. But I do some data analyses aimed at drawing causal inferences. And I read lots of papers that attempt to draw causal conclusions from observations of social science phenomena. We social scientists need to be told when we are making mistakes. We need to read methodological papers that improve our methods. We don't need to read papers that only offer a new language to express things that our current language handles adequately, unless the new language is so much improved that the gains in efficiency of communication more than offset the costs of learning. Do these papers convince me that they might improve the methods of drawing inferences from social science data sets? Or are these only new languages to express old ideas, and if so, is it worth the effort to learn these languages?

*The University of California at Los Angeles

More specifically, I read these three papers on causality with three hypotheses in mind:

1. Everything that needs to be said about causation can be expressed in the traditional econometric language, which includes vocabulary for discussing simultaneity, heterogeneity, and self-selection.
2. A simple-minded understanding of the word *cause* is quite adequate. (*Simple-minded* is defined to be equivalent to *my*.) Another way of expressing this hypothesis is to say that social scientists have not been making major mistakes in drawing inferences because they do not have a deep understanding of this word. (*Deep* is anything that I don't understand.)
3. Mechanical estimation methods, like stepwise regression, are inappropriate for estimating models and for studying subtle questions about causation.

The paper by Paul Holland is implicitly suggested as evidence against my first hypothesis that the econometric tradition is adequate for discussing causality issues. This paper contains much of interest on the issue of causality, but does Holland offer convincing evidence against my hypothesis? Or is he only expressing in a new language ideas that I already understand?

Holland's paper includes a discussion of ACE (the average causal effect), FACE (the prima facie average causal effect), "independence," and "BIAS." This discussion consumes several pages in his manuscript, and discussions like it consume many more elsewhere. Here is my alternative: If it were possible to observe precisely the same subject both with and without a treatment, it would be a matter of simple arithmetic to compute both the effect of the treatment on this subject and the average effect over all subjects (Holland calls this ACE). But it is logically impossible to observe *precisely* the same subject both with and without the treatment. We can compute the difference in the average responses of treated and untreated subjects. (Holland calls this FACE.) The question facing the statistician is, Under what conditions is FACE a useful estimate of ACE? The traditional answer seems right to me: If the choice of subjects for treatment is randomized, then we can write FACE = ACE + NOISE. Is Holland saying something more? I am really not sure, since my familiarity with his language is not that great.

Here is my attempt at a translation: What I have called NOISE he calls BIAS, which seems to me to be unfortunate given my investment in the usage of the word. He identifies a condition, independence, under which (in my language) ACE = FACE. Again, the language (*independence*) is unfortunate for me. I would prefer to say that before the treatments are selected we can expect the treatments and the effects to be independent, but in almost all realized samples they will not be. Thus, the variance of NOISE is not zero. Holland's language, which does not distinguish *ex post* from *ex ante* probabilities, also leads him to distinguish the case of many subjects from the case of few (two in particular). "If U contains only two units, then the physical act of randomization does not make the independence assumption plausible." But isn't this just a simple question of sample size, three being better than two, and four better still? Thus, I challenge Holland to explain how inference from a few observations (even two) should proceed differently from inference from many. If the answer is not at all, let's not use our scarce time learning this aspect of this new language.

Another section of Holland's paper deals with an "encouragement design." This section allows me to continue to test my hypothesis that I already know all that I need to know. Here is a simple version of the model in my language:

$$Y_u = \alpha_u + \beta_u R_u,$$

$$R_u = \theta_u + \delta_u S_u,$$

where u indexes the subjects, Y is the test score, R is the amount of studying, and S is a zero-one variable indicating whether a subject was encouraged to study. (Note that to simplify the discussion I have assumed that encouragement does not have a direct effect on the test score.) Items of interest might be β_u, the effect of "studying" on the test score of subject u, or $\beta_u \delta_u$, the effect of encouragement on the test score of subject u. More likely, we would be interested in features of the distributions of these parameters, like their means or variances across a randomly selected group of subjects.

A set of assumptions that allows the estimation of the mean effect of studying on test scores from a regression of the test scores on studying is $E([\alpha_u, \beta_u]|R_u) = [\alpha, \beta]$. But this is not a very appealing assumption. It seems likely that subjects would have at least some knowledge of the effect of studying on their personal test scores; and it is also likely that there is some relationship between the amount of studying and its effect. Possibly, the greatest amount of studying would occur for students for whom the effect is moderate. If the studying effect is large, only a little studying would be necessary to achieve a high test score; if the studying effect is small, studying might not seem worth the effort.

Economists attack this kind of problem by building models. These models are not taken literally; they are only ways of organizing one's thoughts. Suppose that students maximize $\log(Y) - p_s R$, where p_s is the "price" of studying, and where encouragement is equivalent to a payment that lowers this cost. Then the level of studying that maximizes this function is $R_u = -(\alpha_u/\beta_u) + 1/p_s$. This level of studying is negatively related to its price and to the "natural ability," α_u, and is positively related to the effectiveness of studying, β_u. Writing the inverse price as $1/p_s = \theta + \delta S_u$, where θ and δ are treated as uncertain parameters, we have $R_u = -(\alpha_u/\beta_u) + \theta + \delta S_u$. Finally, again to simplify the argument, assume that the effect of studying is the same for all subjects, $\beta_u = \beta$. Now the model becomes

$$Y_u = \alpha_u + \beta R_u,$$
$$R_u = -(\alpha_u/\beta) + \theta + \delta S_u.$$

From these equations it is clear that the relationship between α_u and R_u will prevent the regression of Y on R from yielding a consistent estimate of β. The conditional mean of Y given R is actually a nonlinear function, depending on the distribution of α. To establish what can be estimated, we can solve for the reduced form

$$Y_u = \alpha_u + \beta\left[-(\alpha_u/\beta) + \theta + \delta S_u\right] = \beta\left[\theta + \delta S_u\right],$$
$$R_u = -(\alpha_u/\beta) + \theta + \delta S_u.$$

This model implies an estimate of β that is the ratio of the estimate for $\beta\delta$ divided by the estimate of δ. Remembering that S_u is a zero-one variable that separates encouraged from untreated subjects, we can estimate β as the difference in the mean test scores of the two groups, divided by the difference in the means of their studying rates.

I don't suggest that this is a general solution to the problem. I have gone through this lengthy but specialized exercise only to illustrate an alternative way of thinking about complicated settings of causal inference. This is the approach that is common among economists. I think that the approach is adequate to address all the issues. For me, anyway, it seems superior to Holland's.

Though I still don't think there is much for the average econometrician to learn from a study of the "deep" issues of causation, there is one point that has great practical significance, since it is both important for drawing causal inferences and since it is often overlooked: The word *cause* carries with it an implicit intervention or counterfactual that is often better made explicit. For example, when I say that weathermen do not cause rain, both you and I have in mind an intervention that affects what the weatherman predicts but does not also alter the atmospheric conditions. An intervention that is allowed is holding a gun to the weatherman's head. An intervention that is disallowed is seeding clouds. We understand that seeding the clouds could alter the weatherman's forecast and also induce rain, but we don't then say that the weatherman causes rain.

The encouragement example of Holland suffers from not being clear about the form of the intervention that is being considered. Holland claims that "it is the effect of *studying* on test performance that is of concern." What is the intervention that is implicit here? One thing that I might like to know is, if I encourage my children to study harder, will they attain higher scores? But that is the encouragement effect, not the studying effect. Or maybe what I want to know is, if I study harder, will I do better? But this too is an encouragement effect, since I would be personally encouraged by reviewing the data to study harder. There is no compelling reason to expect the estimated effect of studying to be the same when the form of the encouragement differs.

The real question of interest seems to me not to be the effect of studying, but rather the effect of different *kinds* of encouragement, since only encouragement interventions are possible. If you found that vastly different kinds of encouragement that led to the same amount of studying all had the same effect on test scores, then it would be convenient to talk about the effect of studying, standing implicitly for a family of encouragements. But this could not be the same literally for all interventions, since, for example, studying at gun point is unlikely to have the same effect as being paid to study.

The paper by Margaret Marini and Burton Singer is implicitly offered as evidence against my second hypothesis: Social scientists are not suffering from their lack of familiarity with the philosophical literature on causation. This paper has what seems to me a very lucid survey of the philosophical literature. I don't really feel competent to comment on this aspect of the paper except to express a feeling of appreciation and admiration. My question here, however, concerns not the literary/philosophical merit of the paper, but rather the specific advice it offers to data analysts. Here is the advice that I found in the section titled "Operational Approaches":

1. Causal inferences will be model-dependent, and you'd better be prepared to show that minor changes in your assumptions don't reverse your inferences about causality.
2. Context-free inferences such as studies of Granger causation need to be combined with a focused theory.
3. There ought to be goodness-of-fit tests that aim at examining the plausibility of the assumptions that underlie any causal inference.
4. Nonadditive models should be considered.
5. Care must be exercised when temporal succession is used as a guide to causal priority.
6. Multiple and diverse studies ought to be done.

These seem to be standard concerns that require no direct knowledge of the philosophical literature. A more direct connection to the philosophical literature is also offered:

> A factor warranting more attention in model formulation is the distinction among types of causes, particularly those involving extrinsic determination, self-determination, and teleological determination.

My blue-collar self finds this rather heavy going. It would be helpful to have a concrete example in the text.

TETRAD, by Glymour, Scheines, and Spirtes, is proposed as an automated system for "discovering" causal relationships from data. This contrasts with the traditional task of "estimating" the structure of a model. By claiming that TETRAD is a tool for "discovery," the authors free themselves from the discipline of statistical theory, which would require them either to make clear the sampling properties of their method or to give the method a Bayesian justification with a clear prior distribution. But as far as I can tell, TETRAD is a method of estimation, not a method of hypothesis discovery. As such, it needs to be evaluated in the traditional manner. It is not enough merely to sniff the "pudding" they present, since my nose is insufficiently sensitive to tell from a whiff or two whether pudding is good or not.

To expand this point, I need to make the following comments about the foundations of statistical theory. A data analysis consists of three phases: (a) *planning* of responses to hypothetical data sets, (b) *criticizing* the initial plans given an actual data set, and (c) selecting a *response*. If the criticism is unsuccessful, then the planned response is carried out. If the criticism is successful, the planned response is revised. The difference between a planned response and a revision is a matter of predictability. A planned response is programmable and therefore completely predictable. A revision is not.

Classical inference presumes the existence of plans that are complete and fully committed, since in order to compute sampling properties it is necessary to establish in advance what will be the response to every conceivable data set. Bayesian theory is not greatly different, since the prior distribution and the loss function imply the response to every conceivable data set. If data are not allowed to change the prior distribution or the loss function, then a Bayesian also has an implicit set of complete plans.

Statistical theory is a theory of planning. Classically, plans are evaluated by studying sampling properties. From the Bayesian perspective, admissible plans are evaluated in terms of the prior distributions and loss functions that they embody. But there is no well-developed theory of criticism; nor is there any guidance on choosing revisions or adjusting planned responses to allow for the fact that the plans are not fully committed. (An exception is Leamer 1978.)

The question that I now propose is the following: Is TETRAD a method of estimation or a tool for criticism and revision? If TETRAD is a method of estimation, then it needs to be subjected to the same kind of scrutiny to which we subject other methods of estimation. If on the other hand it is a tool for criticism and revision, then I really don't know how I can evaluate it. But I believe that TETRAD is only a method of estimation. It seems to me possible to write down the complete class of models that can be "discovered" by TETRAD. It seems further possible before the data are observed to indicate what estimates TETRAD will produce for every possible data set. Thus, TETRAD is a method of estimation, not a method of hypothesis discovery.

All the TETRAD models take the form $\beta y_i = \alpha + \gamma \chi_i + \varepsilon_i$, $i = 1, \ldots, N$, where y_i is a $p \times 1$ observable vector, α is a $p \times 1$ unobservable (parameter?) vector, χ_i is a $p \times 1$ unobservable (latent variable) vector, ε_i is a $p \times 1$ unobservable (residual?) vector, and β and γ are $p \times p$ unobservable (parameter?) matrices. It is further assumed that the vector χ comes from a multivariate normal distribution with mean vector zero and covariance matrix Ω and that ε comes from a multivariate normal distribution with mean vector zero and covariance matrix Λ, a diagonal matrix. Normality implies that all the information in the data is contained in the first two moments. The information in the data means is exhausted in estimating α. What remains is the sample covariance matrix, say S. Method-of-moments estimation would set the sample covariance matrix equal to the theoretical moment matrix, $S = \beta^{-1}(\gamma \Omega \gamma' + \Lambda)\beta'^{-1}$. Clearly these equations cannot be solved uniquely for the uncertain parameters, β, γ, Ω, and Λ; in other words, the model is underidentified. There are untold ways in which to impose further restrictions on these parameters and to attain an identified model. Usually, further restrictions would be imposed and the model would be overidentified, in which case the moment equations cannot be satisfied exactly. The discrepancy between sample and theoretical moments can then be measured in one of several ways, the method of maximum likelihood using a particularly appealing measure.

Whatever method is used to limit the dimension of the model and to form estimates, one thing is sure: The method will work well for some structures $(\beta, \gamma, \Omega, \Lambda)$ and poorly for others. It is then essential to identify as clearly as possible the structures that are "favored." What structures does TETRAD favor? I am not altogether sure. But TETRAD does produce an estimated model in the class that I have indicated. It works well for some structures but poorly for others. Actually, I am not sure that it works well for any structures, since TETRAD is not justified in terms of sampling properties or conformance with Bayes rules. It may well be the case that viewed as a method of estimation, TETRAD is inadmissible: There is another estimation method that is better regardless of the structure that generated the data.

Thus, I have the impression that a causal inference requires the equivalent of a family of alternative statistical models and a prior distribution over the parameter that indexes the family. The prior serves to identify the structures that are favored in the analysis. Any computer program for detecting causal linkages must embody both of these. But,

1. Usually the family of models in these programs is much too large to estimate with a diffuse prior distribution.
2. The implicit nondiffuse prior that is employed is context-free and of doubtful relevance for inference in real contexts.
3. The implicit prior distribution is usually very difficult to articulate clearly, so you don't really know what you are assuming.
4. The method of estimation is usually inappropriate in the sense that it does not combine optimally the information in the data and the prior information that is implicitly employed.
5. No meaningful measures of uncertainty can be attached to the estimates that are computed.
6. The methods masquerade as "exploratory" when really they are only methods of estimation. The programs are only one method of estimating the parameters of this very high-dimensional parameter space. A danger is that these methods, which appear to be exploratory, can discourage real exploratory analyses and can limit the genuine discoveries that might be made from a data set.

One more thing: I really dislike the word pair *observational data*. Isn't it equivalent to *observational observations*?

REFERENCES

Leamer, Edward E. 1978. *Specification Searches*. New York: Wiley.

NAME INDEX

SUBJECT INDEX

purpose: exploration not estimation, 427

TETRAD project, 418–429

and TETRAD-aided search, 428–429, 430

Theory

of a "spiral of silence," 72

of addiction (metabolic vs. psychological), 395, 397, 400

of backward recurrence time (in renewal processes), 105, 106

Bayesian (probability), 315, 382

as central scientific task, 2

and consilience, 380n

construction, 29, 446

of criticism, 491

decision, 359, 382

development (in natural science), 443

electrodynamics and statistical mechanics, 359

evolutionary, 356, 370, 384

focused, 490

of intragenerational status attainment, 158

micromediational (ahistorical instantaneous, as in physical science), 360

ML (maximum likelihood), 147

physicochemical, 362

of power-dependence relations, 380–381

of probabilistic causality, 357–358

psychological (of Spearman), 421

and quantum mechanics (in physics), 357

renewal, 106, 129

of social processes, 2

of structural equations model, 472

See also Item response theory (IRT) model; Multiple-imputation theory; Statistical theory

Third World, 430, 432–433

Threshold, 73–74, 82–83, 85, 87–89, 95–96, 99, 278–279, 280, 282, 284, 285–287, 290–292, 293, 295, 299n, 301

bias, 293

and decision reversal, 86–87

definition of, 73, 278

as difficulty, 278–279

distribution of, 74

diversity-type, 74

and lag behavior, 99

lower (segregation), 87–89, 93–96, 100

measurement of, 99–103

point of curve inflection of item response curve, 278

range of item, 297, 300, 302

upper (integration), 87–89, 93–96, 99, 100

See also Residential tipping; Tolerance ratio

Threshold model

change in distribution of sensitivity, 73

sensitivity to opinion distribution, 73

Tolerance ratio, 77n, 78–79, 86

See also Threshold

Trait

defined, 272n

degree (level) of, 271, 272, 277–280, 294–300

distribution of, 272–273, 277, 285, 288n, 294–300

distribution of underlying, 278, 285

distribution vs. score distribution, 294, 297

range of (level of), 272–273, 293–300

Trait score (individual latent values), 294–300

See also Score (scale value of items)

Transition probability, 150

Transition rate, 138, 139, 141, 144, 148, 149–150, 151, 153, 155–157

destination-specific, 138, 139, 141, 149–150, 153

instantaneous, 144, 146

overall, 139, 141, 148, 149–150, 151, 153, 154, 155–157

Transition rate decomposition

destination-specific, 149–150, 151, 152–153

overall, 150

Turnout. *See* Voter turnout

Turnout rate (as odds on voting), 15, 20–23

age-specific, 4

logit, 15

Type I error. *See* Hypothesis test: Type I error (rate)